Kenya

Africa: Policies for Prosperity

Series Editors

Christopher S. Adam and Paul Collier

For the first time in more than a generation, sustained economic growth has been achieved across the continent—despite the downturn in global economic fortunes since 2008—and in many countries these gains have been realized through policy reforms driven by the decisive leadership of a new generation of economic policymakers. The process of reform is continuous, however, and the challenge currently facing this new generation is how to harness these favourable gains in macroeconomic stability and turn them into a coherent strategy for sustainable growth and poverty reduction over the coming decades. These challenges are substantial and encompass the broad remit of economic policy. Each volume in this series brings leading scholars into the policy arena to examine these challenges and to lay out, in a rigorous but accessible manner, key challenges and policy options facing policymakers on the continent.

BOOKS PUBLISHED IN THIS SERIES

Kenya: Policies for Prosperity
Edited by Christopher S. Adam, Paul Collier, and Njuguna Ndung'u

Kenya

Policies for Prosperity

Edited by
Christopher S. Adam, Paul Collier, and Njuguna Ndung'u

OXFORD
UNIVERSITY PRESS

OXFORD
UNIVERSITY PRESS

Great Clarendon Street, Oxford OX2 6DP

Oxford University Press is a department of the University of Oxford.
It furthers the University's objective of excellence in research, scholarship, and education by publishing worldwide in

Oxford New York

Auckland Cape Town Dar es Salaam Hong Kong Karachi
Kuala Lumpur Madrid Melbourne Mexico City Nairobi
New Delhi Shanghai Taipei Toronto
With offices in
Argentina Austria Brazil Chile Czech Republic France Greece
Guatemala Hungary Italy Japan South Korea Poland Portugal
Singapore Switzerland Thailand Turkey Ukraine Vietnam

Published in the United States by Oxford University Press Inc., New York

Reprinted 2012

ISBN 978-0-19-960237-7

Printed in the United Kingdom by
Lightning Source UK Ltd., Milton Keynes

Series Preface

Policies for Prosperity

This is the first volume in a new series of books on contemporary economic policy issues in Africa. Since the mid-1990s the economic prospects for Africa have been transformed. The change has been uneven: some countries remain mired in conflict and economic stagnation. But for many countries macroeconomic stability has been achieved – even through the recent global economic crisis – and far-reaching policy reforms have been put in place. For these countries, growth prospects in the early twenty-first century are much brighter than at any time during the final quarter of the last century. But converting good prospects into sustained growth and decisive poverty reduction requires a degree of good luck, good policy formulation, resources, and a lot of good economic management. For policy improvements to be sustained they must be underpinned by more fundamental shifts in political power; sectional interests ruling through patronage must be defeated by the public interest, and for the shift in power to be decisive, the achievements of individual reformers must be locked in through the development of institutions. The challenges are, thus, formidable: they range beyond the conventional agenda of macroeconomic management, infrastructure provision, and the improvement of the investment climate. For example, land policy, which has usually been left dormant, will need to be rethought in the face of high population growth rates and growing urbanization. Trade and industrial policies will need to be rethought so as to engage more effectively with changing global opportunities and the continent will need to develop adaptive policies in the face of rapid climate change.

Often, the successes of the last decade have been wrought by the progressive leadership of a new generation of policy-makers. To build on these successes, this same generation needs both the support of, and restraint by, an informed and engaged society. This is the fundamental philosophy of this series: informed societies are strong societies. If citizens are to hold governments to account they require information, debate, and dispassionate analysis on the challenges and choices confronting countries and their people. This is especially relevant in the realm of economic policy where path-dependency is powerful and the consequences of choices are far-reaching and long-lasting.

In many industrialized economies there is a long tradition of informed debate and analysis sustained in large measure by high-quality financial journalism. In Africa, by contrast, while a dynamic and often fearless free press is now quite widely established, it still lacks a tradition of solid, durable, and independent writing on economic policy. As a result, local debate is too often ill-informed or is perceived to be driven by the agendas, and chequebooks, of sectional interests and international organizations.

There is now considerable academic research on the issues that matter for Africa and it could potentially inform Africa's debates. But to date it has been disconnected from them. Increasingly, academics write only for other academics rather than to inform the public. With this series of books we seek to build bridges between the evidence from solid research and contemporary policy debates. Each book aims to bring together the best international and domestic scholars with policy-makers working on economic policy issues across the continent. Throughout, our contributors are required to write with clarity, avoiding academic jargon, but equally avoiding advocacy. Focusing on the key issues that matter for a society, each chapter aims to leave readers better able to draw their own conclusions about important choices.

Christopher S. Adam
Paul Collier
Series Editors
Oxford, September 2010

Acknowledgements

Support for this project has been received from a number of quarters. In particular, we thank the Nairobi offices of the UK Department for International Development, the African Development Bank and the International Development Research Centre for financial support. The Central Bank of Kenya anchored the project in Kenya, generously hosting the authors' preliminary workshop in January 2009 and providing the environment for Central Bank staff to actively participate in the project. The Central Bank of Kenya acknowledges the support of the World Bank provided through its Institutional Reform and Capacity Building Project. Finally, we owe a huge debt of thanks to Rose Page, our 'fourth editor', without whose dedicated and professional support this book would not have been completed. Rose managed the project at every stage, negotiating contracts, chasing authors (and editors) for draft papers, turning messy text into a crisp and clear manuscript and helping turn a good idea into what we hope is an interesting and thought-provoking book.

Christopher S. Adam
Paul Collier
Njuguna S. Ndung'u

Contents

Illustrations

Tables

Tables

Contributors

Editors

Christopher S. Adam is Reader in Development Economics and Research Associate at the Centre for the Study of African Economies, University of Oxford

Paul Collier is the Director of the Centre for the Study of African Economies, University of Oxford

Njuguna S. Ndung'u is the Governor of the Central Bank of Kenya and an Associate Professor of Economics at the University of Nairobi (on leave of absence)

Contributors

Daniel Amanja is Assistant Director in the Research Department at the Central Bank of Kenya

Rosemary Atieno is a Senior Research Fellow in Development Economics at the Institute for Development Studies, University of Nairobi

Dulacha Barako is a Principal Researcher, Financial Sector at the Central Bank of Kenya

Thorsten Beck is Professor of Economics and Chair, European Banking Center, Tilburg University

Arne Bigsten is Professor of Development Economics at University of Gothenburg and Director of the Gothenburg Centre for Globalization and Development

Crispin Bokea is a Researcher at the Central Bank of Kenya

Tessa Bold is Assistant Professor in Economics at the Institute for International Economic Studies, Stockholm University and Research Associate at the Centre for the Study of African Economies, University of Oxford

Robert Cull is Lead Economist in the Development Economics Research Group of the World Bank

Michael Fuchs is Adviser, Finance and Private Sector Development, Africa Region, the World Bank

Leonardo Garrido is a Research Consultant for the World Bank on the areas of Growth, Poverty and Inequality; and a Member of the Executive Committee at the Global Earthquake Model

Peter Gatere is Manager, Bank Supervision, Central Bank of Kenya

Jared Getenga is Manager, Bank Supervision, Central Bank of Kenya and Project Manager, Kenya Credit Information Sharing Initiative

Roxana Gutiérrez-Romero is a Research Officer at the Department of International Development, University of Oxford

Peter S. Heller is a Senior Adjunct Professor of International Economics at the Paul H. Nitze School of Advanced International Studies of the Johns Hopkins University

Patricia Kameri-Mbote is Professor of Law, Strathmore University

Joseph Karugia is the Coordinator of the Regional Strategic Analysis and Knowledge Support System for Eastern and Central Africa (ReSAKSS-ECA) based at the International Livestock Research Institute in Nairobi, Kenya

Joseph Kieyah is a Senior Policy Analyst and Head of Private Sector Development Division at the Kenya Institute for Public Policy Research and Analysis (KIPPRA)

Mwangi S. Kimenyi is a Senior Fellow and Director, Africa Growth Initiative, Global Economy and Development, Brookings Institution and the Department of Economics, University of Connecticut

Peter Kimuyu is Chairman of the Privatization Commission of Kenya and Professor of Economics in the University of Nairobi

Jane Kiringai is an Economist with the World Bank

Praveen Kumar is a Lead Economist with the World Bank

Isaya Maana is Manager of the Monetary Policy Committee Secretariat at the Central Bank of Kenya

Benjamin O. Maturu is a Senior Economist at the Central Bank of Kenya. He is currently on secondment to the IMF Resident Representative's Office in Nairobi, Kenya

Chris Milner is Professor of International Economics and Head of the School of Economics at the University of Nottingham. He is also a Research Fellow at GEP and CREDIT at the University of Nottingham

Germano Mwabu is Professor of Economics, School of Economics, University of Nairobi

Francis M. Mwega is currently Director and Associate Professor, School of Economics, University of Nairobi

Lydia Ndirangu is Head of the Social Sector Division at the Kenya Institute of Public Policy Research and Analysis (KIPPRA)

Rose W. Ngugi is a Senior Lecturer at the University of Nairobi, Kenya, and a member of the Central Bank of Kenya Monetary Policy Committee

Hezron Nyangito is the Deputy Governor of the Central Bank of Kenya and a Senior Lecturer at the University of Nairobi, Department of Agricultural Economics (on leave of absence)

Stephen A. O'Connell is Eugene M. Lang Research Professor of Economics at Swarthmore College and Research Associate at the Centre for the Study of African Economies, University of Oxford

R. Owino Otieno is Director of the Debt Management Programme at Macroeconomic and Financial Management Institute of Eastern and Southern Africa (MEFMI)

John Randa is the Advisor to the Governor of the Central Bank of Kenya. He is currently on leave from the World Bank, where he works as an Economist

Justin Sandefur is a Research Officer at the Centre for the Study of African Economies, University of Oxford

Moses Sichei is a Researcher at the Research Department of the Central Bank of Kenya

Måns Söderbom is an Associate Professor at the University of Gothenburg and Research Associate at the Centre for the Study of African Economies, University of Oxford

Tavneet Suri is the Mitsubishi Career Development Assistant Professor of Applied Economics at the MIT Sloan School of Management

Kamau Thugge is a Deputy Division Chief in the African Department of the International Monetary Fund

Mircea Trandafir is Assistant Professor in the Department of Economics, Université de Sherbrooke

Anthony Wambugu is a Lecturer at the School of Economics, University of Nairobi

Maureen Were is a Researcher in the Research Department of the Central Bank of Kenya

1

Introduction

Christopher S. Adam, Paul Collier, and Njuguna S. Ndung'u

In June 2008, President Mwai Kibaki officially launched *Kenya Vision 2030,* proclaiming it as a roadmap for 'accelerating [the] transformation of our country into a rapidly industrializing middle-income nation by the year 2030'.[1] *Vision 2030* is partly a planning document, but it is also a statement of a soaring political ambition, setting out a programme for the profound transformation of Kenyan society and its economy within the space of a single generation. As Chapter 3 describes, *Vision 2030* foresees an economy in which prosperity emerges from the successful exploitation of its strategic location both as a prime tourist destination and as a major exporter of high-value agricultural and manufactured goods to Europe, the Middle East, and Asia. This vision is underpinned by a programme of strategic investment in public capital, skills, and education, supported by a responsive and accountable political system.

In reality, the explosion of ethnic violence that followed the presidential and parliamentary elections in December 2007, combined with the adverse effects of the global economic crisis in 2008 and 2009 and a sequence of very poor harvests, has already put paid to the early-year targets laid out in the *Vision*: there is now very little chance that these intermediate milestones will be met. The post-election violence, which was rooted in deep-seated and historical ethnic tensions within Kenyan society, many of which surfaced only with the emergence of competitive politics in the early 1990s, did severe damage to the economy, and not just in the short run. The immediate effect was a collapse in tourism earnings and escalating fears about personal security, which weakened domestic markets and interrupted the regular planting and harvesting cycle in traditional agriculture. Foreign direct investment (FDI) and other short-term capital inflows also dried up as the country's international risk premium soared, bringing to a halt the rising trend in investment that had spurred growth in the previous decade (see Chapter 8). Although the economy is starting to slowly recover (see World Bank, 2009), the legacy of the events of 2007 and 2008 persists: the erosion of trust in society, combined with concerns that the underlying causes of conflict have not been addressed, continue to keep investment risks high, while the costs of maintaining the political co-habitation that emerged from the 2008 peace settlement add a significant burden to an otherwise prudent fiscal stance. Most damaging of all, the horizon for political debate in Kenya has been foreshortened as policy-makers have been increasingly drawn into a zero-sum game between political interest groups concerned more with seeking short-term political advantage within an uneasy political coalition than with engaging substantively with the strategic questions of economic performance and growth.

It may be tempting, therefore, to dismiss *Vision 2030* as woefully over-optimistic and to regard the huge and widening gaps between the *Vision*'s targets and reality as a measure of the folly of such exercises. But more than ever, Kenya needs a vision of common prosperity to counter disputes over the distribution of current poverty. By mid-2007, Kenya could point to a recent economic performance, which, while disappointing from the perspective of potential, had broken free from the stagnation of the two previous decades.[2] It could also point to an economic regime that was instinctively more liberal and more responsive to changing circumstances and ultimately more successful than in most African countries. For example, the lessons from Kenya's macroeconomic management of the coffee price boom of the mid-1970s still have a powerful influence on the behaviour of policy-makers across the continent in dealing with highly variable commodity prices. More recently, Kenyan policy-makers could also point to the unprecedented period of economic prosperity in the early years of the twenty-first century that was, to a large extent, the outcome of decisive economic reform measures put in place in the mid-1990s. From the early 2000s, Kenya enjoyed a period of macroeconomic stability, steadily increasing growth – peaking at 7 per cent per annum in 2007 – and significant gains in poverty reduction.[3] Importantly, this growth derived from increased market penetration of Kenyan goods in export markets, both internationally and regionally, rather than simply from the favourable movement in the terms of trade, which so dramatically improved the fortunes of many resource-dependent African economies at the time. Even some of the 'challenges of affluence' were becoming visible: pressures on power generation and urban traffic congestion began to feature large, while lifestyle illnesses – obesity and coronary disease in particular – were becoming more apparent in the urban population. For good and ill, as *Vision 2030* was being finalized in late 2007, Kenyan society was beginning to get a sense of what sustained rapid growth and prosperity might really mean.

The second reason not to dismiss *Vision 2030* is that the events of recent years reinforce rather than detract from the importance of remaining focused on the goal of high growth: Kenyan society only managed to pull back from the brink of violent conflict because a critical mass of people recognized that an achievable future prosperity would be imperilled. Viewed in this light, *Vision 2030* can be re-read as an exercise in 'reverse engineering': it starts from the simple premise – what defines the middle-income nation status to which Kenya appropriately aspires? – and then works backwards to derive the path required to reach that status by 2030. The result is a sobering analysis of the enormous challenges facing Kenya, an analysis which, incidentally, finds echo in a range of very similar long-term planning exercises being carried out by other African countries at the present time. The bottom line is stark: to reach middle-income status, the Kenyan economy needs to achieve an annual average growth rate of around 10 per cent per annum over the next quarter of a century (more given the growth interruptions of 2008 and 2009), compared with a long-run average growth over the quarter century preceding 2007 of 3.4 per cent (which is barely positive in per capita terms).[4] And to generate this growth requires a tremendous increase in the level and productivity of investment, from what may be termed a historical 'African average' of around 15–20 per cent of gross domestic product (GDP) to levels in excess of 30 per cent of GDP, matching or exceeding those achieved by the East Asian tiger economies from the 1960s until the Asian financial crisis in the late 1990s.

Sustained growth rates of the scale envisaged by *Vision 2030* are certainly at the very top end of the range of experience, but they are not unheard of, and the evidence from countries that have achieved these sorts of growth rates is highly instructive. In 2006, the *Commission on Growth and Development*, chaired by Nobel Laureate, Michael Spence, studied those countries around the world that had sustained such growth rates.[5] The Commission identified four key proximate factors around which country-specific growth strategies may be designed. In many respects, these factors are wholly conventional, and all appear in some guise in the Kenyan growth strategy. The first was a fundamental commitment to market-based resource allocation combined with openness to trade, both in goods and in technological know-how. The second was a policy framework that delivered a high degree of predictability in macroeconomic policy-making and a stable macroeconomic environment over the medium term; and the third a strong 'future orientation', in other words an environment that supports high domestic savings to fund high levels of public and private investment. The Commission argued that, at least in the early stages of development, the greatest constraint to growth is a low rate of investment which, in turn, reflects too low a saving rate. Although foreign savings can play an important role in supporting this future orientation – especially in the early stages of a growth take-off – sustained growth ultimately requires high *domestic* savings: foreign capital inflows, either in the form of FDI or concessional aid in the case of low-income counties, are imperfect substitutes for domestic savings, liable to be associated with a range of adverse effects, from capital account volatility to problems of 'sudden stops'. The final critical ingredient identified by the Commission was a 'capable, credible and committed government', by which it meant a system of governance and leadership that has the flexibility to adjust policy and to shape institutional structures to changing circumstances and opportunities, but to do so in a manner that is credible and commands broad public support. This final requirement is essential: all the successful countries examined by the Growth Commission succeeded in making growth tolerably inclusive, although, as the list of high-growth countries suggests, this does not necessarily require a system of democratic politics.

These basic *Growth Commission* principles must necessarily underpin any growth strategy for Kenya – and for other African economies – over the coming years. But the challenge is not simply to generate more investment or more productive investment in order to raise the growth rate of output along the current growth path, although this is surely part of what is required. Rather, the economy must at the same time undergo a much more profound transformation. Although the overall population growth rate has declined from 3.8 per cent per annum in the early 1980s to around 2.6 per cent per annum today, the demographic transition in Kenya is far from complete: this is still one of the highest population growth rates in the world. Consequently, Kenya remains a very young country with more than 40 per cent of the population aged less than 14 years.[6] This alone has profound implications for investment if the economy is to achieve the levels of capital-per-worker typical of middle-income countries. But with usable land in limited supply, population pressures imply that Kenya must also accelerate the movement of (principally young) people away from traditional economic activities that are firmly based in agriculture into labour-intensive non-agricultural employment, in the manufacturing and services sectors, which have a much more marked outward orientation and are better placed to reap the gains from being a 'coastal' economy (see Ndulu *et al.*, 2008). This transition is, of course, wholly consistent with *rising* output per worker in agriculture and, indeed, it is one of the hallmarks of all successful economic transitions. In such circumstances, as the economy grows, the share of agriculture in GDP declines relative to manufacturing, whereas the share of employment in agriculture declines even faster as agricultural productivity rises. It is this process that allows the non-agricultural economy to grow while ensuring that those remaining in agriculture also enjoy rising incomes.

This process is already under way to some extent and, in particular, the pace of urbanization is already rapid. The urban population in Kenya has more than trebled since 1980, from around 2.5 million to 7.6 million today, with the population of Nairobi rising from around 800,000 in 1980 to 3.5 million today, a large fraction of whom are living in overcrowded informal settlement. Supporting the movement of people out of agriculture, while at the same time ensuring this does not simply result in a large, substantially underemployed peri-urban population places heavy demands on public policy. An effective prosperity-generating transition requires the provision of education and training to equip the population with the skills to compete in the expanding sectors. It requires trade and industrial policies to be configured appropriately, and it requires investment in public infrastructure to accommodate an increasingly urbanized population.

The chapters in this volume seek to address these challenges. They cover four main areas: strategies for growth; the macroeconomic environment; the private sector environment; and the political economy of factor markets. The collection opens with a set of three chapters concerned with the overarching question of the medium-term growth strategy: what are the principal opportunities and what are the major constraints to realizing them? Chapter 2 by Collier and Ndung'u reviews recent thinking on growth and growth strategies in low-income countries and uses this to outline the key choices facing Kenya in the coming decades. Their analysis draws on the influential work by Ndulu *et al.* (2008) on *The Political Economy of Growth in Africa* and in particular on the options facing a 'coastal economy' such as Kenya where key growth opportunities reside in the exploitation of proximity to world markets for labour-intensive exports. Strategies built around this endowment focus on exploiting the potential economies of scale associated with producing for world markets and emphasize the role of policies aimed at driving down real unit labour costs. This need not imply that real wages should be reduced, but rather that labour productivity should be increased, both directly through investment in education and skills and indirectly through the provision of other complementary inputs including backbone infrastructure investments and effective regulatory systems. Complementing higher productivity, key 'wage goods', notably food, need to be as cheap as possible, implying an end to agricultural protectionism. Chapter 3 by Ndung'u and Otieno, summarizing the key elements of *Vision 2030*, builds a bridge between the preceding conceptual discussion on growth strategies and specific policy initiatives and debates that are discussed later in the volume. Garrido, Kumar, Ndung'u, and Randa further extend this discussion to identify the key inhibitors to growth in Kenya. Their chapter is an application of the widely used 'binding constraint' method proposed by Hausmann *et al.* (2005), which seeks to distinguish between those constraints on growth that reflect weaknesses in the mobilization of savings (either domestic or foreign) and those that reflect low returns to investment. The latter may, in turn, derive from a paucity of complementary inputs, infrastructure, skills, market-appropriate regulations, and so forth, or from an excessively predatory political economy, which can result in high and distortionary taxation, ill-defined and insecure property rights, weak contract enforcement, high corruption and crime, and weak or narrow interest-driven macroeconomic policy formulation. Consistent with Collier and Ndung'u, and with themes that emerge later in the book, the authors conclude that the biggest challenges facing a substantial investment take-off in Kenya are not problems of savings mobilization but rather a combination of weaknesses in key complementary inputs, in infrastructure and human capital, and the 'appropriability risks' associated with political instability and pervasive corruption in public life.

The remaining sections of the book systematically address the principal themes that emerge from these diagnostic and overview papers. Part II focuses on the policy questions that will shape the macroeconomic environment for growth. A recurring theme in these papers is that the challenges in this arena are no longer simply those of achieving basic macroeconomic stability and of eliminating gross policy distortions. Instead, the emphasis is on the continued development and adaptation of what is already a broadly effective macroeconomic framework so as to support the deeper structural changes needed for the future. In the areas of monetary and exchange rate policy, the chapters by Adam, Maturu, Ndung'u, and O'Connell and by O'Connell, Maturu, Mwega, Ndung'u, and Ngugi discuss how policy frameworks that have been relatively successful in supporting macroeconomic stabilization and growth during the 1990s and early 2000s can be adapted to the dual task of anchoring a credible commitment to low and stable domestic inflation and supporting the inflow of foreign capital. Capital inflows will be required to meet the levels of investment anticipated under *Vision 2030*, but they should be managed so that they neither undermine external competitiveness nor expose the economy to excessive balance of payments risks. As Reinhart and Rogoff (2010) have shown in their recent history of financial crises, managing the 'Trojan horse' risks associated with large private capital flows demands a much greater flexibility in macroeconomic policy-making, and much greater attention paid to systemic risk than policy-makers have hitherto typically done. This task is particularly challenging in economies such as Kenya where the underlying country risk premium is relatively high.

The link between macroeconomic policy and the 'real side' constraints to growth in small open economies – issues of complementary inputs and appropriability risks – come through the configuration of fiscal and trade policy. Whereas the challenges in monetary and exchange rate policy are in large measure technical, those discussed by Thugge, Heller, and Kiringai on fiscal policy and Were, Sichei, and Milner on trade are more overtly political. In trade policy, there are two interrelated challenges. One is how to position Kenya within the web of regional and international preferential trade arrangements to which it is a signatory in a manner that best supports the economy's dynamic comparative advantage. The other is how to ensure that tariff structures and the supporting architecture of trade policy are consistent with a manufacturing strategy that must increasingly address new forms of global production, the trend commonly referred to as 'trade in tasks', contrasting with the former pattern of 'trade in goods'. On the fiscal side, Thugge and colleagues consider the changing demands for public spending arising from a rapidly growing and urbanizing population. They suggest that the combination of a reasonable track record on fiscal policy and the fiscal 'gain' from the demographic transition as the ratio of taxpayers to dependants increases can create the scope to finance key complementary inputs. However, the authorities will need to learn from global best practice in the use of public–private partnership (PPP) arrangements that leverage private resources into the provision of public infrastructure and services.

In the second half of the book, the emphasis shifts from the narrow confines of conventional macroeconomic and trade policy to a consideration of the markets on which private sector activity depends and of the political economy that shapes policy choices. The natural starting point for this discussion is in the agricultural and manufacturing sectors whose interrelationship is central to the structural transformation of the economy. Throughout history and across the world, the growth and prosperity of nations has come about as people have moved out of traditional, smallholder agriculture and into higher paying and less volatile wage employment in the industrial and service sectors, including in agro-processing. This movement is typically associated with falling population growth and rising savings, which together allow for 'capital deepening' to occur, the process of equipping labour with more and more capital – both physical and human – which further increases labour productivity and with it real wages. This is what powers the transformation of the economy, and one major challenge for Kenyan policy-makers is how public policy can help to accelerate this process. To craft policy appropriately, we need to focus on both the 'push side' of agriculture and the 'pull side' of manufacturing and services.

As Karugia, Ndirangu, Nyangito, and Suri argue, the key issue in agriculture is how to raise the persistently low levels of labour productivity, for two reasons. First, improved productivity is essential to tackle currently high chronic poverty, which, in Kenya as elsewhere in Africa, is overwhelmingly a rural phenomenon. Agricultural policy should therefore be directly concerned with improving livelihoods within the agricultural sector itself. This means improving farming practice, diversifying production into less risky and higher value activities, improved input use, and better functioning output markets so that productivity gains can be realized. But increased productivity in agriculture has a second and, arguably, more durable effect: it is the mechanism through which labour is released to the manufacturing sector and through which food prices are kept low. In other words, it is part of the mechanism that keeps unit labour costs globally competitive in the emerging modern sectors of the economy. Bigsten, Kimuyu, and Söderbom focus on the 'pull side' of the structural transformation process. Although the textbook model envisages the labour that moves off the land being absorbed in a 'modern' sector characterized by economies of scale and agglomeration with high and rising productivity, the authors' review of the evidence from Kenya paints a rather different and depressing picture. Output and employment in the formal manufacturing sector has actually grown very slowly over the last decade, whereas the informal sector has continued to grow rapidly. The combined effect is that average labour productivity in manufacturing has grown by a mere 5 per cent in total during the high growth years between 2000 and 2007. Bigsten and colleagues examine why this is so and what role policy has in reversing the low level of productivity growth. Drawing on firm-level survey data, they describe a very segmented manufacturing sector in which investment, technology upgrading, and hence labour demand is concentrated in small clusters of large and well-established firms that tend to export and/or participate in global production networks. The challenge, they argue, is how to expand this pool so as to better exploit potential economies of scale and agglomeration. This means tackling issues in trade policy (the tariff structure in Kenya currently acts as a disincentive to Kenyan firms participating in the global production chain, for example); lowering transaction costs – in terms of both access to finance and the cost and reliability of utility services; tackling the spread of corruption; promoting capabilities in the area of outsourcing; reducing inefficiencies in the supply system, particularly those arising from slow and inefficient goods clearance at airports and the Mombasa port; and encouraging the formation of modern industrial clusters, including through the rejuvenation of export processing zones.

But many of the deep challenges facing policy-makers in both agriculture and manufacturing, as well as in other sectors of the economy, are not problems of the output markets themselves, but can be traced back to constraints to the effective functioning of factor markets for land, labour, and capital. Chapters 11 to 16 therefore focus on the factor market constraints to growth and policy options to address these constraints. Bigsten and Wambugu return to the problem of why formal sector employment has grown so slowly in Kenya over the last five decades and why the rapid growth in labour supply has been overwhelmingly absorbed in the informal economy. They argue that the problem is not the conventional one of labour market imperfections such as minimum wage legislation, excessive employment regulation, powerful trade unions, and so forth, which might drive up the fixed costs of employment in the formal sector. A far greater drag on formal sector, high-wage employment has been the slow pace of capital accumulation, which has failed to keep pace with the growth in the labour supply since the early 1980s. As a result, rather than being absorbed by rising labour demand from (large-scale) capital-intensive firms in manufacturing and modern agriculture, labour has been moving out of smallholder agriculture as pressure on the land increased and into the low-skill, labour-intensive, informal wage economy and into low capital self-employment sectors. With a rapidly growing labour supply, this has led to falling real market-clearing wages in the informal sector.

The key message from Bigsten and Wambugu is simple: without capital accumulation, the powerful 'pull factors' that can contribute to a rapid and strongly poverty-reducing increase in labour demand will be stifled. This applies equally to the accumulation of human capital, and raises the question of whether the workforce in Kenya is being equipped with the education and skills suitable for growth, what *Vision 2030* refers to as '...a globally competitive and adaptive human resource base to meet the requirements of a rapidly industrialising economy'. Seeking to respond to this need, the Kenyan government has been drawn into a wide range of interventions at all levels of the educational process, from primary and secondary schooling to vocational training and higher education. Setting aside the public finance implications of a major expansion in education and training, addressed earlier by Heller and colleagues, this raises a deeper question of how far and how effectively the state can simultaneously increase access – which may also be driven by concerns other than supporting rapid growth, for example equity concerns or the well-documented impacts on teenage pregnancy and the general welfare of girls – and at the same time improve on the relatively poor quality levels in public education and training. This tension has already emerged with the introduction in 2003 of nationwide free primary education (FPE). In the short run, there have been immediate gains in enrolment especially in poorer districts. But as Bold, Sandefur, Kimenyi, and Mwabu argue, concerns about quality have quickly surfaced. Using frontier evaluation techniques, the authors examine the impact of FPE on standardized measures of school performance. Although theirs is a relatively small-scale study, the implications are important: scaling up the inputs to education may be necessary but will only deliver improvements in outcome if systems of accountability and monitoring keep pace. They place particular importance on the risk that large-scale, centralized provision of FPE dilutes the incentives for local-level monitoring of quality and that, as quality falls, parents who can, move their children to the private sector, further undermining the disciplining effect of local community-level monitoring and quality control in government schools. The implications of this vicious circle are profound and will apply with equivalent force as and when similar initiatives are considered at the secondary level: without attention being paid to maintaining quality and accountability, widespread provision of publically provided education risks substantially raising the pressures on public finances without delivering the transformative improvements in the quality of education and skills required to appropriately equip the Kenyan labour force.

Similar concerns about the institutional foundations to factor markets cut through the question of land reform. As population pressures increase and the economy becomes more urbanized, the status of property rights becomes more important to the efficient functioning of a market-based economy, but they can also become increasingly contested. As the work of the Peruvian economist Hernando de Soto argues, security of property rights, especially for the poor, plays a critical role in development. Most fundamentally, security of rights and the enforceability of contracts allow property to be collateralized for investment purposes and for more efficient allocation of wealth within and across generations. But formalization, particularly in peri-urban areas, may also have additional benefits, such as allowing households to allocate less time to protecting their property through informal enforcement of rights, thereby releasing resources for more directly productive activities. Kieyah and Kameri-Mbote draw on this security-of-rights framework to review the history of land rights in Kenya and to consider the implications of alternative institutional approaches to protecting rights. They argue that informal approaches, relying on existing local-level, traditionally based institutions appear to be cheaper and, perhaps, more trusted, but typically the security offered is less robust and the domain of informal protection is (spatially) bounded, limiting the marketability of asset claims. In contrast, formal land titling offers much greater prospects for exploiting the capital value of land. But to date, formal titling – which has remained voluntary – has not progressed far. Registration is still complicated and protracted so that land claims remain harder than they ought to be to collateralize, and the transformative gains from the formalization of land rights have yet to be seen.

The final three chapters in this cluster examine the performance of the financial sector and the market for the third factor, capital. Beck, Cull, Fuchs, Getenga, Gatere, Randa, and Trandafir provide a wide-ranging assessment of the structure and performance of the financial sector in Kenya, focusing on issues of access and the tension between improving (low-cost) access to financial services and the need to ensure that expansion does not significantly increase systemic risks (which are likely to increase as the economy seeks to integrate further with global capital markets). Their analysis shows that the financial sector in Kenya is comparatively well developed and, following crises in the 1980s and 1990s, reasonably stable and efficient. Looking forward, much of their discussion turns on the question of market structure and the implications for regulation – how to exploit economies of scale in finance without handing excess monopoly profits to financial firms. These themes are picked up by Ngugi, Amanja, and Maana, who concentrate on the role of the formal capital market in mobilizing finance for investment. A similar picture emerges of a market that is, by regional standards, reasonably well developed, but where the capacity to mobilize substantial domestic savings remains limited. With the exception of a small number of very important high-profile listings – most notably the initial public offering by the mobile telecommunications firm, Safaricom, in 2007 – both the equity and the bond markets in Kenya are relatively inactive. The authors focus on a range of reforms that are required to energize this market. Finally, Atieno, Barako, and Bokea write about the potentially transformative introduction of mobile banking in Kenya, the so-called *M-Pesa*. The application of mobile phone technology to the perennial problem of improving access to finance, in which mobile phone companies rather than banking firms have become the key providers of financial services, has had an enormous impact on people's livelihoods, particularly in remote areas, and has, almost at a stroke, transformed the way in which the financial sector operates. This pace of change is likely to accelerate, not just as the take-up and coverage of *M-Pesa* expands, but as providers extend the scope of their activities. At present, mobile banking concentrates almost entirely on providing cash transfer and account settlement activities. The next big development is likely to be into savings and credit services, the traditional domain of the finance and, especially, microfinance institutions.

The final chapter in the book, by Collier, Gutiérrez-Romero, and Kimenyi, turns its attention to the political pillar of *Vision 2030* by examining what the ethnic violence of 2007 and early 2008 might mean for the design of political structures in Kenya. Can institutions be designed that can accommodate or overcome the deep ethnic divisions that exist within Kenyan society, but do so in a manner that is conducive to what the Growth Commission referred to as 'capable, credible and committed government'? Using detailed data collected at the time of the elections on voter attitudes, intentions, and outcomes, they identify a fundamental tension between a widespread belief (or desire) that multiparty coalition democracy can thrive in Kenya and a patent lack of interethnic trust. This tension needs to be addressed from both sides, by tackling at source the low levels of trust and by developing models of political representation that both accommodate and are robust to deep ethnic cleavages. In this latter respect, the authors argue that Kenyan society needs to confront the choice between a cohabitation model of peaceful if not necessarily friendly political co-existence – a model that has functioned adequately in countries such as Switzerland and Canada – and a model that places the emphasis on prioritizing a sense of national over regional or ethnic identity. Here, the model may be closer to home: in Tanzania and Zambia – under the umbrella of 'African socialism' – the nation-building project was firmly rooted in notions of common interest. In many respects, although the *economic* policy choices of Tanzania (and Zambia) in the early post-Independence years were disastrous, in *political* terms, Nyerere (and Kaunda) got things right. To many, this is the fundamental challenge facing Kenya today, one that casts a shadow over all other endeavours.

To be sure, Kenya faces huge political and economic challenges. But at the same time, it is one of only a few African countries with the chance of soon becoming a genuine emerging market economy. Whether it can make this transition will be determined by political will and sound judgement in the economic policy sphere. A range of critical, and often tough, economic policy measures must be put in place, and they must be co-ordinated and maintained. This, in turn, depends upon their purpose being understood by a critical mass of citizens. This book, and indeed this series, is designed to help build that critical mass.

Notes

1 Although completed in late 2007, the official launch of *Vision 2030* was delayed by six months due to the political crisis that swept Kenya from December 2007. The quotation from President Kibaki dates from the version of the *Vision* that was finalized in October 2007, prior to the elections.
2 See, for example, the discussion by Mwega and Ndung'u (2008) of the disappointing growth record of the 1980s and 1990s relative to the booming years of the 1970s.
3 Headcount poverty relative to the national poverty line fell from around 56 per cent in 1997 to 46 per cent in 2006 (World Bank, *World Development Indicators* 2010, online edition).
4 *Ibid.* Annual percentage growth rate of GDP computed at constant local currency market prices.
5 The Commission took as its sample all those countries that had averaged 7 per cent per annum growth for a quarter of a century or more since 1950, a rate being consistent with a doubling in size every decade. Fourteen countries satisfied this condition: Botswana, Brazil, China, Hong Kong, Indonesia, Japan, South Korea, Malaysia, Malta, Oman, Singapore, Taiwan, China, and Thailand. India and Vietnam were the closest 'runners up', with their growth rates falling just short of the target.
6 World Development Indicators, *op cit.*

References

Commission on Growth and Development, 2008, *The Growth Report: Strategies for Sustained Growth and Inclusive Development.* Washington, DC: World Bank.

Hausmann, R., D. Rodrik and A. Velasco, 2005, 'Growth Diagnostics'. Mimeo. Harvard University, John F. Kennedy School of Government. March 2005.

Mwega, F. M. and N. S. Ndung'u, 2008, 'Explaining African Economic Growth Performance: the Case of Kenya', in Ndulu *et al.* (eds) *The Political Economy of Growth in Africa: 1960–2000*, Vol. 2. Cambridge, UK: Cambridge University Press.

Ndulu, B. J. *et al.*, 2008, *The Political Economy of Growth in Africa: 1960–2000.* Cambridge, UK: Cambridge University Press.

Reinhart, C. and K. Rogoff, 2010, *This Time Is Different: Eight Centuries of Financial Folly.* Princeton, NJ: Princeton University Press.

World Bank, 2009, 'Still Standing: Kenya's Slow Recovery from a Quadruple Shock', *Kenya Economic Update* No. 1, December 2009. World Bank, PREM Unit, Africa Region.

I

Strategic Choices

2

Strategies for Growth

Paul Collier and Njuguna S. Ndung'u

2.1 Introduction

Kenya needs rapid economic growth. It is poor even by African standards, with per capita income some 30 per cent below the average for the region. Its natural endowments are limited: it lacks high-value natural resources and has only half as much land per person as the African average. Yet its population is growing rapidly: 43 per cent of its people are under the age of 15.[1] Despite a long record of social stability, in early 2008, Kenyan society came dangerously close to breakdown following nationwide political unrest. Political instability and social instability are intertwined. Political instability creates social duress and civil conflict, during which households may need to disinvest in physical and human capital in order to cope with disruptions in market and productive activities. In an economy with already low savings and wealth, such disruptions are very damaging to long-run development and the restoration of peace and security. Thus, rapid growth is not merely desirable, but it may well be a necessity for social peace. Further, it has to be spatially equitable, opening opportunities for each of Kenya's major areas. The development strategy since the 1960s seems to have failed, or rather did not produce the desired results. This has called for a rethinking not only for a new development strategy but also to deal with institutional constraints that inhibit the desired results. This chapter focuses on the feasible strategies for growth and sets the tone for this volume and a menu of policies and actions that should be taken.

Sustained rapid economic growth is something that Kenya has never had. Following two decades of stagnation at the end of the twentieth century, the economy did indeed start to grow. But by international standards, the pace was modest: during 2000–06, per capita gross domestic product (GDP) increased by 1.5 per cent per year, much slower than the average for Africa, at 2.4 per cent, let alone that for low- and middle-income countries as a group, which was 4.4 per cent. The best performing period 2003–07 (see Table 2.1) in Kenya's history raised the average per capita growth to just 2.0 per cent, still below the African average. But during this time, key policy reforms were initiated, and some of the basic foundations for longer term growth were laid down. This continues in the current decade with the imminent promulgation of a new constitution in Kenya, which, it is hoped, may help Kenya to build on the gains made in the first decade of the new millennium and achieve the growth target outlined in *Vision 2030*. That might seem a Herculean task, but it is possible. This chapter scans the landscape for the strategic choices for growth, comparing Kenya and the region as well as other successful emerging economies.

In Section 2.2, we give a brief overview of Kenya's recent growth and policy reforms. Although growth began to accelerate during the decade, even before the global crisis, it had proved to be fragile. Section 2.3 argues that this fragility is best addressed by building stronger institutional foundations for social peace and economic policies. In subsequent sections, we progressively pan down from global experience, through the generic insights provided by economic geography, to specifically Kenyan constraints. Section 2.4 reviews the global generic characteristics of successful growth strategies and assesses Kenyan performance on each of them. The conclusion is that the key weakness in Kenya's approach to date has been its radically inadequate rate of investment. In Section 2.5, we get more specific, focusing on the opportunities implied by Kenya's fundamental economic geography. We suggest that the coastal region, led by Mombasa, has credible opportunities for the expansion of garment exports. The central region, led by Nairobi, has credible opportunities both for agricultural exports that are air-freighted and for the export of regional services. The western region, led by Kisumu, could potentially harness its advantage in low-wage labour for e-services. Each of these would require targeted supporting policies, some of which are already in progress. In Section 2.6, we discuss some specifically Kenyan concerns, such as the acute infrastructure

Table 2.1 Percentage growth rates (%), 2002–10

	2002	2003	2004	2005	2006	2007	2008	2009	2010
Real GDP	0.5	2.9	5.1	5.8	6.4	7.0	1.6	2.6	4.5
Population	2.6	2.6	2.6	2.6	2.6	2.6	2.6	2.6	2.6
Per capita GDP	–2.1	0.3	2.5	3.2	3.8	4.4	–1.2	–0.2	0.9

Source: Kenya National Bureau of Statistics (KNBS)/World Bank (2009).

constraints consequent on many years of underinvestment, and the need to reduce perceived inequalities.

2.2 Recent growth experience and policy regime change

Kenya ushered in the twenty-first century at a time when political uncertainty was causing uncertainty about the economic outlook. Investor confidence was low and the government's relations with donors were at an impasse. Attempts to maintain a tight monetary policy, implemented in the face of limited fiscal control and reduced aid flows, drove real interest rates sharply upwards as the government borrowed heavily in domestic debt markets, putting the economy into prolonged recession (see Buffie, 2003). The peaceful change in political leadership in December 2002, which saw the presidency change hands from Daniel Arap Moi to Mwai Kibaki as the National Rainbow Coalition (NARC),[2] brought to an end almost forty years of Kenya African National Union (KANU) dominance of parliament, producing a large economic dividend.

Starting in 2003/04, there was a perceptible change for the better in Kenya's economic outcomes (World Bank, 2008). Fiscal control was enhanced, interest rates declined, external assistance started to recover, investor confidence improved, and growth prospects improved. Growth increased to 2.9 per cent in 2003, reaching a peak of 7.0 per cent in 2007 (Table 2.1). This recovery was attributed to the peaceful political transition, and an 'orthodox' economic reform agenda known as the Economic Recovery Strategy (ERS) for employment and wealth generation. The ERS reform agenda was anchored on redefining the role of the government as that of providing an enabling environment for private sector growth and investment, and emphasized three key themes: strong economic growth supported by a stable macroeconomic environment; enhanced equity and poverty reduction; and improved governance geared towards enhancing efficiency and effectiveness in the economy.

During the period 2003–07, several aspects of economic performance improved. Crucially, the public sector deficit was contained, which helped to bring interest rates down without threatening inflation, which was converging on its target (see Chapter 7). This was supported by a broadly stable exchange rate, reflecting a strong balance of payments position, which was occasioned by large inflows of remittances, high receipts from tourism, and improved foreign direct investment (FDI).

The balance of payments position was also strengthened in the late 1990s as the reserves of foreign exchange were rebuilt. This gave confidence to overseas private investors that remittances of dividends and loans service would not be jeopardized. These reserves also enabled an acceleration of the flow of imports to support investments.

The ERS also implemented key structural reforms, and particularly regulatory reforms in the telecommunications, railway, and energy sectors; and trade openness improved with the re-formation of the East African Community (EAC) (World Bank, 2008). The World Bank notes that one of the most significant achievements in this period was to reduce the ratio of debt to GDP from 60 per cent to 40 per cent. This created fiscal space to fund public investment: an ambitious stimulus package without compromising macroeconomic stability. But the crisis of 2008–09 has raised this ratio to 44 per cent, a small increase compared with the impact of the crisis (World Bank, 2010).

Economic growth has had perceptible effects upon the lives of ordinary citizens. The incidence of poverty declined from 52 per cent in 1997 to 47 per cent in 2005/06. In addition to the decline in poverty, basic public services were extended. Most notably, the policy of universal free primary education (FPE) was implemented. Additionally, funds were allocated for a programme that decentralized public spending targeted on youth and women through the Constituency Development Fund (CDF). The CDF was designed to finance community-based projects that have long-term effects on people's economic well-being. Similarly, a Youth Enterprise Development Fund (YEDF) was launched in 2006 targeted at youth unemployment. Apart from the FPE, which has been rated as relatively successful (see Chapter 12 in this volume for an assessment), proper assessment of the effectiveness of the other initiatives has not been documented in the literature.

In addition to pursuing macroeconomic stability, the government implemented comprehensive structural reforms and changed the composition of its spending. Results-based management was introduced into the public sector. There was also an attempt to reduce unnecessary regulation: 315 licences were eliminated, and the state divested itself of various state-owned enterprises through privatization. By 2009, when the first ratings for Africa from the World Bank's *Doing Business* assessment were undertaken, Kenya was one of the top-rated African business environments, coming eighty-fourth in the global rankings, ahead of Ghana and the other East African countries.

2.3 Sustainable growth for the medium and long term

The slowdown in economic growth following the post-election violence has led to questions as to whether Kenya can resume growth even to pre-crisis levels. The World Bank (2008) argues that the two underlying causes behind the recent growth have been weakened. First, macroeconomic policy credibility has been under strain in view of the fiscal pressures of crisis-related expenditure and the demands of a coalition government. Additional structures of government proposed in the draft new constitution will add more fiscal pressures unless new sources of revenue are identified. In addition, estimates of political risk are likely to have been revised upwards and are likely to remain elevated until the implementation of the new constitution and possibly until the general election of 2012, with inevitable adverse effects on investment, particularly foreign investment. Second, the five-year growth spurt had temporary components – both domestic and external in origin – that cannot be assumed in the future. The domestic component was the improvement in capacity utilization after prolonged stagnation, and the external component was the favourable environment such as low international interest rates and high growth rates in partner countries. But what was also clear was that the ERS was a success and that a conscious policy with achievable targets can succeed in Kenya.

Hence, given the post-election experience in early 2008, recently achieved growth rates cannot be safely assumed. The agenda for policy must therefore not only address the new concerns raised by the crisis of 2008, but also seek to restore and eventually exceed pre-crisis growth rates. The new concerns are essentially about macroeconomic and political risk, poverty, and inequality, whereas pressing forward on unfinished business will entail resolving infrastructural bottlenecks, strengthening institutions at the microeconomic level (such as those dealing with trading across borders and providing security) and at the macro level (public service reform, judiciary, and parliament), and finally, the difficult task of raising the efficiency of public services.

Growth in Kenya is very sensitive to perceptions of political and macroeconomic risks. If political risk is high, businesses will make fewer new investments. In a study of the impact of ethnic violence in Kenya prior to the 2007 outbreak, Kimenyi and Ndung'u (2005) show that the political cycle damages growth and significantly increases the perceptions of country risk. Being in government allowed politicians to control national resources. Ethnic violence distorted the voting pattern, encouraging ethnic voting and thereby enabling politicians who based their appeal on ethnic identity to remain in control of national resources and institutional capture in general. The way we look at it is that, once in power and institutional capture, existing laws and new laws can be implemented to protect the flow of economic rents and entrench power. In addition to political fractures, macroeconomic instability is an important source of uncertainty. In turn, uncertainty undermines private investment, and thereby growth. But one big lesson learnt from the period 2003–07 is that sustained attention to policy reform can produce results that improve the well-being of ordinary citizens.

The post-election crisis in 2008 demonstrated the fragility of Kenya's political stability. It raised questions about the strength of institutions in ensuring peaceful political transition; it dispelled the widespread perception that political risk had declined; and it brought to the top of the agenda the deeper determinants of political instability. The crisis demonstrated that Kenya's economic growth is contingent on latent social conflict factors: any growth strategy for

Kenya must be sufficiently inclusive to ensure that the growth process reduces rather than exacerbates the deep-rooted ethnic and social tensions, which, as 2007 and 2008 have shown, can so quickly eliminate the accumulated gains of the previous half decade.

2.4 Generic aspects of growth strategies

Growth strategies have some generic features and some that are applicable to particular typologies of country characteristics. We consider these in turn. A useful guide to the generic features is the *Commission on Growth and Development* (2006), led by Nobel laureate Michael Spence. Having compared all countries that had sustained growth rates in excess of 7 per cent, the Commission identified five common characteristics. Kenya can be assessed on each of these.

2.4.1 Leadership and governance

During the long presidency of Daniel Arap Moi, 1978–2002, the Kenyan economy had very slow growth: the economy was evidently not the president's main priority. During this period, Kenya was also poorly rated on various indicators of governance. By the last years of his rule, Kenya was in the bottom quartile on five of the six governance indicators used by the World Bank.

The leadership during the NARC government showed strong commitment to enhanced governance by setting up institutions to fight corruption and by undertaking legislative reforms geared towards enhanced transparency and increased efficiency in the public sector. As in many cases of reform from an initial position of pervasive corruption, there have been mixed signals. There have been numerous institution-building initiatives, all of which point to an intention to phase out corruption. However, alongside these institutional efforts, individual incidents of corruption have continued to reveal an ingrained pattern of dysfunctional behaviour.

The governance reforms were initiated based on the NARC government policy of zero tolerance to corruption. Some of these reforms include:

(i) The Anti-Corruption and Economic Crimes Act, 2003, which set up the Kenya Anti-Corruption Commission (KACC) as Kenya's premier anti-corruption institution. Although this institution has been rated as weak and ineffective by various circles in Kenya, it should be noted that, since its inception, some achievements have been made in the number of corruption-related cases investigated and recommendations for prosecution made to the Attorney General. For instance, between September 2004 and June 2007, of the total 19,310 complaints of suspected corruption received from Kenyans, 3,145 cases were fully investigated and presented to the Attorney General for further action. Similarly, by August 2007, 332 complete investigation files were forwarded to the Attorney General with 75 per cent of these cases recommending prosecution (KACC, 2007).

(ii) The Public Procurement and Disposal Act, 2005, established an autonomous Public Procurement Oversight Authority (PPOA) responsible for ensuring that the regulations and procedures of procurement as stipulated in the Act are followed in the public sector with the objective of enhancing transparency, integrity, fairness, public confidence, and efficiency. The need for this reform measure arose in order to standardize and streamline procurement processes, which were previously open to abuse from government officials.

(iii) The Privatization Act, 2005, established a privatization commission charged with responsibility for ensuring transparency in the privatization of state-owned enterprises, thereby strengthening accountability, reducing rent-seeking behaviour, and improving the efficiency of resource use. Furthermore, the accelerated privatization, which led to the witnessing of unprecedented levels of investor appetite during initial public offerings (IPOs), was a deliberate move to increase corporate governance and efficiency at the firm level. However, current assessment of the success of this reform is complicated by external factors, particularly the global financial crisis, which has made assets sales more difficult.

Other related governance initiatives include the development of the National Anti-Corruption Plan implemented through the Governance Action Plan (GAP) July 2006–December 2007. The initiatives under the GAP focused on prevention, investigation, and recovery of corruptly acquired assets and strengthening of prosecutorial capacity as provided for in the Public Officer Ethics Act, 2003. Other initiatives are the formation of the Kenya National Audit Office as an independent office away from the Ministry of Finance, the creation of the Office of the Ombudsman, and the creation of ministerial and departmental audit committees. Administrative reforms such as abolition of the Harambee system[3] in the public sector, overhaul of business licensing regime, and tax administration reforms, among others, reduced the opportunities for corruption and enhanced efficiency during this regime.

Consequently, tax revenues have increased as a result of enhanced compliance. Further reflecting the progress in governance, Kenya won the United Nations Public Service Award in the category 'Improving Transparency, Accountability and Responsiveness in the Public Service' in 2007. In addition, the 2008 World Bank *Doing Business* report ranked Kenya among the top ten global reformers in terms of ease of doing business in 2007.

The current coalition government policy agenda covers all aspects of public policy including governance policy. Constitutional change, strengthening anti-corruption institutions, particularly the judiciary, and the establishment of a Truth and Restitution Commission are among the governance reforms being discussed by the coalition government. These initiatives clearly indicate positive intent towards enhancing governance. Building consensus on policy issues and particularly governance issues requires making compromises on the part of the coalition partners. Potentially, the new constitution could mark a turning point.

2.4.2 Openness: imports of knowledge and exports to the world market

To date, relative to other low-income countries, Kenya has been well integrated into global knowledge. Much of its professional class is trained abroad, and it serves as the regional headquarters for many international firms. However, limited access of ordinary citizens to broadband may now be widening the knowledge gap with developed societies.

In respect of trade, the position has been less satisfactory. A useful summary measure of trade barriers is the relevant component of the *Doing Business* survey of the World Bank. Kenya is badly rated relative to most other countries on the ease of cross-border trade, ranking 148th in the world, but has been ranked quite high for its fast reforms in the last few years (Table 2.2).

In addition, the World Bank's Logistic Performance Index, which measures the performance of trade logistics as a package by taking into account customs procedures, logistics costs, ability to track and trace shipments, timeliness in reaching the destination, and the efficiency of domestic logistics, ranked Kenya at 76 out of 150 countries. In comparison, South Africa ranked at 24, China at 30, and India at 39. Kenya's rankings on the competence of public and private logistics service providers, domestic logistics costs, and transport infrastructure are particularly low and highlight the need for priority attention to these areas.

2.4.3 Market allocation

At the time of independence, when the philosophy of African socialism was being discussed by the continent's intellectuals, Nkrumah in Ghana moved

Table 2.2 Doing Business indicators

Indicator	Kenya	SSA region	OECD
Documents for exports (number)	9	7.8	4.5
Time for exports (days)	29	34.7	10.7
Costs to export (US$ per container)	2,055	1,879	1,069
Documents for imports (number)	8	8.8	5.1
Time for imports (days)	26	41.1	11.4
Costs to import (US$ per container)	2,190	2,279	1,133

SSA, sub-Saharan Africa; OECD, Organization for Economic Co-operation and Development.

towards scientific socialism, whereas Nyerere in Tanzania moved towards an indigenous *Ujamaa*. Sessional Paper No. 10 of 1966, although espousing the language of African socialism, in fact ensured a continuation of the colonial-style market economy. This market orientation ensured that Kenya was based on capitalist rather than Marxist economics. It did not ensure that the markets were efficient, but rather perpetuated the economic rents of the colonial era. In the course of the first twenty years of independence, the market orientation of Kenya was further distorted by the limited number of indigenous entrepreneurs; hence, many parastatals came into being with the assumption that resources were being held in trust until the education system produced the required managers and entrepreneurs. This aspect of economic sovereignty was widespread on the continent. Price controls were introduced, effectively nullifying the efficiency of the market. These price controls ranged over goods prices, interest rates, rents, and wages, and affected profit remittances through exchange control regulations, giving rise to adverse gearing ratios in industry.

Nevertheless, from the mid-1980s to the mid-1990s, the economy was largely deregulated so that markets could fulfil their conventional roles, but competition leading to efficiency was largely lacking on account of protection. The *Doing Business* survey rated Kenya's labour and credit market as adequate, and its regulatory quality is the best governance indicator, being around the global median. Legislation introduced in the 1980s and 1990s to curtail restrictive practices has been largely ineffective, whereas legislation to create the Capital Markets Authority (CMA) to enable divestiture of parastatals to occur efficiently has had to be revisited on various occasions and has had limited success in getting new listings on the Nairobi Stock Exchange.

2.4.4 Macro stability, including sustainable public finances

Kenya has a long record of reasonably prudent macroeconomic management, certainly by African standards. Since 2000, the rate of consumer price inflation has averaged around 8 per cent, and that of the implicit GDP deflator only around 4 per cent. The debt levels are relatively modest by African standards. By 2005, public and publicly guaranteed external debt was only around 28 per cent of GDP. In addition, as noted before, the fiscal space created between 2003 and 2009 reduced total debt from 60 per cent of GDP to the current 44 per cent of GDP without the Highly Indebted Poor Countries (HIPC) support.

2.4.5 Future orientation

By 'future orientation', Mohamed and Spence (2006) mean an effective commitment on the part of government to the long-term development of the economy. Although there are a range of policies that determine long-term development, the single most important one is the rate of investment. Here, Kenya's performance has been both poor and deteriorating. Its investment rates have been low even by the standards of the region, and have declined sharply from their already low level in the 1990s. Debt relief, which provided the government with an opportunity to increase other expenditures, was not used to increase public investment, and private investment has also been low. Kenya took a policy decision that, if it does not default on external debt, would build its credibility. Specifically, the share of gross fixed capital formation in GDP has declined from 24 per cent in 1990 to only 17 per cent by 2005. The average for Africa is 19 per cent, but even this is manifestly too low when benchmarked against other developing regions. The investment rate in South Asia is 31 per cent, and that in East Asia is 38 per cent. Further, Kenya still has one of the highest rates of population growth in the world, and this implies that its investment rate should be higher than in Asia, where population growth rates are considerably lower.

2.4.6 A summing up of generic growth strategies

On the above generic criteria for a growth strategy, it is evident that Kenya's major problem is the shortfall in investment. The scale of the shortfall is not marginal: to sustain rapid growth, Kenya would need to raise its investment rate by at least 10 percentage points of GDP. To have credible hopes of converging with those developing economies that are already succeeding, it would probably need a further increase of around 5 percentage points; this would require the investment to GDP ratio to stand at 32 per cent. The main question is how to achieve this target and the strategies required, given that there is still an ambiguous political stance with respect to the ownership of domestic assets, particularly land, by foreigners. This political problem must be addressed if foreign savings are to be transferred to the country in significant amounts. These are necessary as the magnitude of domestic savings, even if the savings rate is very high, would be insufficient to generate either the required growth or jobs.

None of the prospects for financing an increase in investment of this scale is promising. In an economy in which per capita income is only rising slowly, it is hard to finance extra investment out of increased savings. Recall that, during 2000–06, per capita GDP was increasing at only 1.5 per cent per year. At this modest rate of growth in income, even if all the growth were used to increase savings, with per capita consumption held constant, it would take a decade for domestic savings to rise by 15 percentage points of GDP. However, for the extra investment to be externally financed would require large increases in either aid or FDI. For aid to finance the increment would need not only a major donor re-rating of the government, but also an acceptance by donors that the priority should be investment rather than social spending.

The prospects for a large increase in FDI have evidently deteriorated following the socio-political disturbances of 2008, and have also been hit by the global economic crisis.

We suggest possible solutions to these difficult choices.

One approach is to adopt policies that temporarily raise the growth rate without the need for a large increase in investment. The extra growth would then be used to raise investment rather than consumption. For example, if the growth of per capita GDP could be increased to 5 per cent and held there for four years, then per capita consumption could continue increasing at 1.5 per cent while investment increased to around 31 per cent of GDP. A phase of faster growth without higher investment should be possible in Kenya because there is still substantial misallocation of resources as a result of inherited policy errors. Reforms to address these misallocations would raise output.

A second approach is to temporarily sustain the gradual increase in the consumption level of ordinary citizens by redistributing income from richer households. Given that income inequality in Kenya is among the highest in the world, there may well be scope for such redistribution. During this tempoary phase of increasing equity, economic growth could then be used to augment investment. The Constituency Development Fund, the Local Authority Transfer Fund, and the 2009/10 economic stimulus programmes meet these criteria for redistribution. Although redistribution could provide room to finance extra investment, it does not of itself induce that investment. Hence, as with the other financing policies, it would need to be complemented by policies that raise the return on investment.

Conditional upon additional savings being forthcoming through one or other of the above strategies, they would need to finance increases in both public and private investment. The government has already locked into increased public investment through the issue of infrastructure bonds, which would tap into the increased savings. The proceeds of these bonds would have dedicated uses and so would not be diverted into public consumption.

A phase of around four years during which growth rates were raised by policy reforms that did not depend upon investment, and the consumption of ordinary citizens was moderately increased by redistribution, would provide the macroeconomic space for a transformative increase in investment. Of course, this raises the question of 'investment in what?' To address this question, we must turn to the specific opportunities available to Kenya given its basic geographic characteristics.

2.5 Growth strategies appropriate for resource-scarce, coastal economies

Although the above features of a growth strategy are generic to all developing countries, others apply only to the opportunity groups defined by fundamental features of geography. Following Ndulu *et al.* (2008), we distinguish opportunities according to whether a country is coastal or landlocked, and resource rich or resource scarce. Clearly, on this classification, Kenya is coastal and resource scarce. As a coastal economy, it does not face the natural barriers to participation in the global economy that constrain many others, including its neighbours such as Uganda. Not only is it coastal, but also it is well located in respect of key markets, with the Middle East on its doorstep, and one of the shortest sea routes to Europe, around half that of China. As a resource-scarce economy, it avoids the economic and political difficulties that have beset many resource-rich societies such as Nigeria.

The 'internal' geography of Kenya also matters. The country is large and faces acute socio-geographic sensitivities. It is politically imperative that the opportunities for growth be broadly spread geographically. Thus, a growth strategy needs to be sufficiently multifaceted so that areas with quite different geographic characteristics all have viable prospects. We distinguish between the opportunities facing Mombasa, Nairobi, and Kisumu. Mombasa is the country's main port, Nairobi is the country's main city, and Kisumu is the regional capital for what is now a particularly low-income area.

The key growth strategy for those coastal, resource-scarce developing countries that have grown rapidly has been to find a niche for exporting something, the production of which can be expanded without encountering a natural constraint. We consider the potential of the various sectors of the economy for finding such a niche and scaling up.

2.5.1 Agriculture

Although agricultural products have the advantage that they build upon the traditional skill base of the Kenyan labour force, to an extent, they have the disadvantage of being subject to the limitations of land availability. The least subject to these limitations are those that are not very land intensive, such as high-value horticulture. However, for these products, Kenya's coastal location confers relatively little advantage as, although inputs are often imported by sea, the export of produce is by air. Hence, to harness these opportunities, a country needs a major international airport and a good road network that links agricultural areas to both the airport for exporting goods and the port for importing inputs. Fortunately, Kenya has the regional air hub at Nairobi and so the agricultural areas around Nairobi are well placed for such exports. But an effective and efficient road network would open up larger areas for this economic activity.

2.5.2 Services

Two export services are of potential pertinence for Kenya: tourism and e-services. Although Kenya has already succeeded in tourism, the sector has three disadvantages. It is fairly capital intensive, it is sensitive to fluctuations in Kenya's international image, and its expansion encounters natural limits in the endowment of tourist attractions such as beaches and game. It is therefore necessary to seek possibilities for tourism diversification through attracting the motion picture industry to Kenya's climatic and scenic advantages.

In contrast, e-services are much more labour intensive, are not sensitive to consumer image, and are not constrained by natural endowments. However, as they do not depend upon coastal access for either inputs or outputs, being a coastal economy confers no advantage. There is nevertheless a need for stable and secure power sources and increased bandwidth. This may, however, be pertinent for Kenya's inland areas. For example, Kisumu is a long way from Mombasa and so is at a disadvantage in activities that are intensive in sea transport, and also quite distant from Nairobi and so at a disadvantage in activities that are intensive in air transport. Its comparative advantage is thus in e-services. The key inputs into e-services are education and international telecommunications. Kenya has a large pool of workers with education levels sufficient for employment in e-services, but its international telecommunications have been among the most expensive in the world. For many years, Kenyan international telecommunications were a monopoly of the national post office, and services were kept expensive in order to generate a large profit with which to cross-subsidize postal employment. Hence, opportunities for e-services in Kisumu were precluded by this strategy. Although additional jobs were created in the postal service in the short term, in the longer term, many more jobs may have been lost because, unlike the postal service, e-services for export have the potential to scale up without limit: if one firm is profitable, others are profitable.

The government has highlighted a number of proposals for the e-services sector in the Medium-Term Plan, 2008–12 in line with the *Vision 2030*. Business process offshoring/outsourcing (BPO) aims to expand exports of services through the internet to companies and organizations in the developed world. In 2006, the government launched a national information and communications technology (ICT) policy with an objective of making Kenya an ICT hub and a premier location for BPO in Africa. In an effort to promote the BPO sector further, the government plans to establish a BPO park and digital villages with the facilitation of a fibre optic cable, which was launched in 2009. As of 2010, there were already around sixty companies in the sector. The BPO sector is expected to create 20,000 jobs and make a contribution of Ksh 10 billion to GDP in five years (Medium-Term Plan, 2008–12; Government of Kenya, 2008).

2.5.3 Manufacturing

The sector that most lends itself to unlimited expansion for a coastal, resource-scarce economy is labour-intensive manufacturing. Production requires little land and capital, and is characterized by scale economies. Hence, far from unit costs rising as expansion encounters bottlenecks, unit costs tend to decline. The nature of the scale economies in manufacturing is distinctive. Geographers and urban economists have long been aware that manufacturing and service industries tend to cluster in concentrated geographical areas, most often cities. However, the relevance of that phenomenon for trade and industrial development has only recently been rediscovered as part of the new economic geography (Krugman, 1991; Fujita *et al.*, 1999). Manufacturing benefits from agglomeration economies that are external to the firm but internal to a group of firms concentrated in a specific geographical location. Marshall (1920) argued that the proximity of firms in similar or related activities can lead to a number of localized external economies. Among the advantages he identified were access to a pool of specialized workers, quick access to supplies of inputs, and access to knowledge relevant for the firm. The newer literature on agglomeration emphasizes knowledge and pecuniary externalities arising from the concentration of industrial activity in a specific location. Agglomeration effects generally fall into three categories:

- Externalities that arise from the presence of a large number of firms *in the same industry* in a specific location.
- Externalities that arise from the presence of a large number of *closely related industries* – including suppliers and purchasers – in a specific location.
- Externalities that arise from the presence of a large number of firms *in unrelated industries* in the same location.

To a great extent, the first two types of agglomerations conform to the popular view of an industrial cluster. The third type is more closely related to urbanization. All three forms of agglomeration offer advantages to firms located near each other, but they may act on production costs and productivity in different ways.

Clustering among firms in the same industry is driven by common needs for inputs and access to markets, industry-specific knowledge flows, and the need for specialized skills. One potential advantage of clustering is information spillovers, such as the sharing of technological or marketing knowledge. Another type of knowledge that may spread more easily within an agglomeration of similar firms is knowledge of improved management techniques. Learning effects may be easier to achieve when firms are located close together. When firms in the same industry are located near one another, it is easier to monitor what neighbours do and to learn from their successes and mistakes, and competitive pressures may lead to innovation and increase productivity. Clusters may also attract traders and reduce the costs for firms to market their goods.

Proximity to input suppliers and customers may allow them to realize economies of scale and resolve co-ordination problems. As market scale increases, firms tend to outsource service functions to local suppliers. For some activities, the proximity of suppliers to their customers lowers transportation and transaction costs significantly. Close proximity between suppliers and purchasers may also help to ensure timely delivery, lower inventory costs, and enhance quality. Co-location may facilitate sharing of indivisible goods and facilities, such as infrastructure, and joint actions by producers, including lobbying government officials, may also be facilitated if they are located near each other.

Proximity of closely related industries can also generate pecuniary externalities such as a thick labour market. Workers with skills specialized in a sector will be attracted to areas where employment in the sector is large relative to the total labour force. The density of employment reduces search costs and provides a measure of insurance against unemployment. Similarly, firms will be attracted to areas in which there are a large number of workers (or managers) with skills relevant to their industry. Location in a large labour market makes it easier to find specialized labour, such as designers, engineers, and consultants.

Externalities from the spatial concentration of unrelated industries – urbanization externalities – are thought to arise from common skills and services (accounting, law) and from knowledge spillovers that are not specific to individual production technologies. For example, there are likely to be important cross-sector effects in urban areas, with industrial diversity raising productivity via the exchange of information and pecuniary externalities. There may also be better information within an urban area about which entrepreneurs can be trusted, thus facilitating informal contract enforcement and co-operation.

Most of the evidence on the economic impact of agglomeration has been drawn from advanced industrial economies and a few middle-income countries, but it provides persuasive evidence of the existence of agglomeration economies. Several studies have found that agglomeration effects strongly encourage firm entry and employment growth, due to productivity, price, or cost changes (UNIDO, 2009).

Agglomeration economies in manufacturing have two extremely important implications for Kenya. One is that it is very difficult for a new producer to break into markets in competition with established low-income exporters. The established producers, such as China, have already built up agglomerations and so will have lower unit costs than a new entrant. The other implication is that, if only this entry hurdle can be surmounted, expansion can proceed virtually without limit: as the agglomeration grows, unit costs fall and so exporting becomes more competitive. In effect, there is an entry threshold that constitutes a hurdle to be surmounted. (There are spectacular Kenyan case studies of monopolistic competition in price-cutting wars to retain privilege, e.g. Rothmans v BAT; Castle Beer v EABL.)

In turn, this implies that, although labour-intensive manufacturing could potentially generate enormous numbers of jobs, Kenya will be unable to break into it except where it has some offsetting advantage relative to existing low-income producers. Kenya has one such advantage, namely its privileged access to the US market under the Africa Growth and Opportunity Act (AGOA). East Asia does not benefit from a similar arrangement, and so the privileged market access confers an advantage on those products where the USA levies a significant tariff, which AGOA exports do not incur. The product that still has significant tariff protection is garments, and so this is the key product for Kenya to scale up. As with all trade policy, the devil is in the detail: duty-free, quota-free access is not enough unless it is combined with generous rules of origin. Fortunately, AGOA has such rules for garments. Collier and Venables (2007) show how it has enabled Africa to expand its garments exports sevenfold since 2001, whereas the European scheme, Everything-but-Arms, which did not have generous rules of origin, has been ineffective. The European scheme is now being replaced by Economic Partnership Agreements, the negotiation of which provide an important opportunity for Kenya to gain equivalent access to the European market.

However, although AGOA confers an advantage on Kenyan exports of garments, the margin of advantage is modest. Hence, it is important to reduce other costs that can be influenced by government policy. The benchmark is to make garment production globally competitive despite the initial disadvantage that clusters are smaller than those of competitors. At best, the advantage conferred by AGOA may offset the higher initial costs of small cluster size, so that in aggregate, all other costs cannot exceed the costs faced by competitors. The major costs for garment producers are wages, electricity and transport. Hence, each of these costs needs to be benchmarked on China.

Currently, despite the fact that Kenyan per capita income is now much lower than that in China, wages in Kenyan manufacturing are higher than those in China. One reason is that the cost of the main wage good, food, is above world levels. Tackling this issue is primarily a matter of trade policy: Kenyan food prices need be no higher than those in China if prices are allowed to be set by the world market. For example, the interventions of the National Cereals and Produce Board (NCPB) in the buying and selling of maize have led to additional price increases, which are detrimental to the large majority of Kenyans. The price of Kenyan maize in 2009 was double the international price, and higher than in Uganda or Tanzania. Another reason is that wage levels in large firms tend to be considerably above wage levels elsewhere in the economy. In turn, this may reflect the fact that, for many years, most of Kenya's large firms have been privileged monopolies producing for the domestic market, and in such circumstances, the monopoly rents tend to be shared with the workforce, in part to bolster the political lobby for continued monopoly. There may be scope here for encouraging differentiation between wages in export clusters and elsewhere in the economy: the Kenyan workforce clearly has a strong interest in the expansion of job opportunities. (The workforce is interested in the expansion of job opportunities but NOT at the cost of higher salaries and by those currently in jobs.)

Potentially, electricity could be cheaper in Kenya than in China. Much of Kenya's electricity is already generated from hydropower, and there is scope for vast, low-cost expansion once the River Congo is properly exploited by the Democratic Republic of Congo (DRC) and power transmitted to its neighbours. This need not require direct transmission from the DRC to Kenya: for example, Uganda currently uses hydropower that could be sold to Kenya once Uganda has met its needs from neighbouring DRC. This emphasizes the importance of regional solutions to power problems.

If clusters are properly located near a major port, the only significant transport cost that firms face is the port itself. In Kenya, there are currently two reasons why transport costs are unnecessarily high: the port is inefficient and most garment producers are not located in Mombasa. Port efficiency can be tackled by the approach taken to reduce costs in Dar es Salaam: once the port was run under management contract, costs rapidly fell to East Asian levels. The way to bring distances down is to concentrate firms in a few giant export processing zones (EPZs) located around Mombasa. To date, Kenya has not used its EPZs for a policy of clustering. Although it has created many of them, the zones are not, in fact, clusters. There are forty-three such zones with a total of only seventy-two firms in them. The typical zone is a single firm, awarded the status of being an EPZ in order to benefit from favourable tax treatment. Currently, the zones are located all over the country.

Although breaking into the global garments industry is difficult, Kenya already has an export industry, and so it must already be around the threshold of competitiveness. Bangladesh, which is one of the weakest governance environments in the world on the international ratings, has nevertheless generated around 2.5 million jobs in garment exports. Success on this scale would be transformative for Kenyan society.

2.5.4 Services and manufactures for regional markets

Some products and services are more cost-effectively traded regionally than globally. Often, this is because of the advantage conferred by local knowledge. However, agglomeration economies still apply. Many economies of scale come from city size: a doubling in city size increases productivity by around 4–8 per cent. Kenya has the main city in Eastern Africa. However, by global standards, Nairobi is not a large city, its population being only around 4 million.[4] There is some evidence that this relatively small size is the result of Africa's political divisions into so many small countries. Collier and Venables (2010) compare the city size structure of Africa and India. India has two cities of over 20 million people. As such, the productivity difference between a city of 4 million and one of 20 million is substantial. They simulate the consequence of ten typical African countries having sufficient political union to erase the barriers to city growth. They find that there would be a substantial increase in the overall proportion of the population that is urban. As a result, nearly all cities expand, even those in countries that do not have one of the new mega-cities that they predict would emerge. Hence, urban expansion is not a zero-sum game between rival countries. However, were Kenya and Eastern Africa to form such a federation, which Kenya is now starting to do through the East African Community (EAC), Nairobi would probably be a major beneficiary. (Mega-cities have significant negative externalities and, unless the urban tax base grows sufficiently and the physical infrastructure is also supportive, they otherwise fail to generate widespread prosperity.)

2.6 Specific Kenyan initiatives

Finally, in options for accelerated growth, we consider some specifically Kenyan constraints and opportunities.

2.6.1 Easing infrastructural constraints

Infrastructural constraints, such as high costs in the telecommunications, energy, and transport sectors and Mombasa port inefficiencies, have been identified as key factors explaining Kenya's slow growth and low competitiveness. Since 2009, the government has successfully issued three infrastructure bonds, the proceeds of which are earmarked for roads, energy, and water. Fibre optic cables have already transformed the information technology (IT) sector in both coverage and cost. Road and railway networks, as well as closing the energy deficit, can work the same way and encourage enterprise growth. If bonds-for-infrastructure are properly implemented, the government balance sheet can improve rather than deteriorate. The bond liabilities are offset by new assets that are higher yielding. However, the strategy is critically dependent upon a scrupulous commitment both to use all funds for investment in infrastructure and to implement these investments efficiently. Other strategies to ease infrastructural constraints include contract management of Mombasa port to reduce costs and inefficiencies, and the adoption of regional solutions to power problems.

2.6.2 Mobilization of extra resources

A substantial increase in investment will require both higher national savings and more FDI. One strategy for raising domestic savings is to broaden financial inclusion. Here, mobile phone technology has great potential. Mobile phone banking is taking services to remote areas where conventional banks have been physically absent: extending outreach using 'bricks and mortar' branches is prohibitively expensive. Mobile subscribers can open accounts, check their balances, pay their bills, or transfer money through their phones. Although these transactions currently dominate mobile usage, it is possible to harness the potential for mobilizing savings. Most of the previously unbanked population has now been accessed by the major mobile companies: huge sums of money, which would otherwise not be available for lending, are held by mobile users. This financial service could now be expanded to facilitate financial intermediation for the many low-income Kenyans who have been unbanked.

A further strategy for domestic savings mobilization is to tap the long-term sources of funds from pension and insurance companies, channelling these savings into long-term investment. Strategies to increase FDI hinge on reducing political and macroeconomic risks. Further, the return on FDI will automatically be raised by improvements in complementary infrastructure. (As mentioned earlier, there is a policy decision to be made with respect to foreign ownership of domestic industry, which has to be addressed if we are to seriously encourage FDI. There is a concomitant problem if FDI is financing industry through loans rather than equity, giving rise to vulnerable industries due to the adverse gearing ratio.)

2.6.3 Strengthening institutions

Strong institutions are good for growth. Agenda 4 of the National Dialogue and Reconciliation Process that followed the disputed outcome of the 2007 general elections and created a Grand Coalition Government has identified institutions that need to be strengthened. Reforms are focused on the public service, the electoral body, the judiciary, the police, and parliament. Given the prevalence of public service corruption, helpful approaches are a reduction in the scope for discretionary decisions and the introduction of results-based management. A number of reforms have been implemented to improve the electoral process. The Electoral Commission of Kenya has been disbanded, and the government has formed a new Interim Independent Electoral Commission charged with responsibility for reforming Kenya's electoral process and management of elections in order to institutionalize free and fair polls. The new body is also mandated with the establishment of an efficient and effective secretariat and the creation of a new voters' register. The need for this move arose in order to safeguard against tendencies that were experienced in the 2007 general elections.

Two critical laws have been enacted, the Constitution of Kenya Amendment Act, 2008, and the Constitution of Kenya Review Act, 2008. These have paved the way for discussions on the new constitution by a new Committee of Experts on Constitutional Review and by members of parliament. The anticipated new constitution is expected to institutionalize an elaborate system of checks and balances throughout government structures. It is also expected to devolve power.

2.6.4 Reducing youth unemployment

Young people make up three-quarters of the unemployed. In addition to targeted job creation, it is important to re-examine the education system. Young people need to be better prepared for self-employment and their skills developed from an early age. The past emphasis upon preparation for white-collar jobs is likely to have been inappropriate for a country at Kenya's stage of development. As most jobs will be in the private sector, it should be more closely involved. The private sector might potentially organize youth empowerment levies and get directly involved in youth education, training, mentorship, and youth entrepreneurship.

2.6.5 Reinforcing macroeconomic stability

Macroeconomic stability depends on a comprehensive approach to managing public finances, expenditure programmes, and sound monetary policy. This entails efficient and predictable levels of taxation, well-prioritized composition of expenditures, high rates of return on public investments, low and predicable inflation rates, reasonable real interest rates, competitive real exchange rates, and good infrastructure. To attain such stability requires efficient domestic revenue mobilization, a decrease in government indebtedness, fiscal space, improved institutional mechanisms for selecting high-return projects, and undertaking deliberate measures to foster investor confidence by highlighting Kenya's strengths domestically and internationally.

2.6.6 Increasing total factor productivity (TFP)

Evidence from other countries has demonstrated that the efficiency of investment manifested in changes in TFP is critical to growth. Given the high costs of business and the relatively unexploited regional integration potential in Kenya, considerable scope for enhancing productivity still exists. Thus, reducing business costs and improving integration within the region and the global economy through trade and investment would provide sources for enhancing TFP. Deepening integration will also help in integrating fragmented markets, allowing economies of scale, and helping in developing new exports to third markets. However, there is a limit to regional trade because the countries in the region have similar resource endowments and produce similar products. Kenya exports 43 per cent to the EAC region and mostly manufactures. Nevertheless, there are seasonal differences and, until the internal infrastructure improves significantly, cross-border trade is perfectly possible even for identical products. Therefore, the Kenyan growth strategy would need to push and help the private sector in enhancing its competitiveness beyond the East Africa region. This would include further trade liberalization and improved trade facilitation, among other policy actions.

2.6.7 Reducing inequality

The preceding discussion is predominantly focused on strategies to raise the aggregate growth rate of the economy. However, growth is not an end in itself, but a means of reducing poverty. Different growth strategies will have different implications for poverty reduction. Strategies that generate employment while reducing population pressure on the land will tend to skew income to poor people. Policies that drive down food costs will tend to skew purchasing power to poor people. Chapters 9, 10, and 11 discuss such policies in detail.

Although growth is necessary for decisive poverty reduction in a poor society, policies that directly redistribute income can also be effective. In Kenya, the case for redistribution is particularly strong: measured income distribution is less equal than in most other low-income societies. Redistributive policies can be one-off, contingent, or continuous. The classic one-off redistributive policy is land reform. This is a highly sensitive political issue, but the coalition government is committed to considering it, under the agreement brokered by Kofi Annan. The classic contingent redistributive policy is famine relief; more generally, schemes such as food-for-work can provide a floor to incomes. As discussed in Chapter 5, a limitation with such policies is that they can have disincentive effects, which gradually make them fiscally unsustainable. For the same reason, in low-income societies, continuous redistribution policies are usually limited to the free provision of basic health care and education.

Redistribution has two important interactions with growth. One is that it enhances the poverty impact of growth. Expressed in technical terms, the elasticity of poverty with respect to growth is higher in more equitable societies. The other is that, in some circumstances, redistribution increases growth, and this is likely to be so in Kenya on account of both political sensitivities and the structure of economic opportunities. Politically, Kenyan society is now acutely sensitive to inequality: perceived ethnic inequality was at the core of the post-election violence in 2008. As the violence demonstrated, perceived injustice can derail growth, compounding the poverty problem. Nor can this be regarded as a momentary problem: the society has long been fragile (Kimenyi and Ndung'u, 2005). Turning to the structure of opportunities, in a highly unequal society, poor people cannot realize their productive potential. For example, if poor people are unable to access credit markets, capital will be misallocated and high-return opportunities for investment missed. The implication is that, both for enhanced growth and to increase the poverty reduction that growth can bring, Kenya needs to address its actual and perceived inequalities.

In addressing inequality questions in the recent past, the government has introduced a number of targeted strategies. First, the Constituency Development Fund (CDF) led to countrywide development projects ranging from bus parks and road improvements to classroom construction. The success of this strategy caused the Minister for Finance to introduce in his 2009/10 budget speech a fiscal stimulus package that distributed money to constituencies for a variety of purposes. Many of these were investment in nature and gave rise to significant rural multiplier effects due to local sourcing of inputs. Complementary to these broadly based strategies for reducing inequality were targeted interventions for women and young people who were particularly vulnerable in the economic downturn following the 2007 elections.

2.7 Conclusion

Kenya has good opportunities, but it is living dangerously. Although the demographic transition is well underway,[5] the growth of job seekers and limited natural endowments imply that the society has little choice but to transform the economy, with rapid expansion of employment-creating sectors. Such transformation will need integration into global and regional markets combined with new investment. Although the government has done much to reduce the costs of doing business, logistics costs remain very high by world standards and limit integration. Investment depends not only upon tackling such costs, but upon whether businesses are confident that reforms will not be reversed during future episodes of social tension. Especially in view of the unresolved social tensions in Kenya, it is important for confidence that economic reforms be embedded in institutions rather than being seen to depend upon individual politicians. Unfortunately, subsidiarity, which is very beneficial in the developed world, leads to precarious rent seeking through institutional capture where subsidiary institutions do not adequately identify with the national agenda.

Notes

1 Based on estimates from the 1999 population census.

2 The National Rainbow Coalition (NARC) lasted only until 2005, by which time internal tensions saw it split into various factions on account of the then new constitutional draft. The Government lost the referendum on this draft constitution. By the 2007 elections, these factions had reformed themselves as the Orange Democratic Movement (essentially the old Liberal Democratic Party), whose presidential

candidate was Raila Odinga, and the Party of National Unity (PNU), whose candidate was the incumbent President Mwai Kibaki.

3 The 'Harambee movement', which is reflected in the motto on Kenya's coat of arms, was initially a strong self-help system generating extensive development, often through voluntary contributions of time and produce. It later degenerated, taking a more coercive character and rationalizing rent extraction.

4 Estimated based on the 1999 population census.

5 The demographic transition describes the transformation of a high birth rate and high death rate society into a low birth rate and low death rate society. Typically, the fall in the crude death rate precedes the fall in the crude birth rate, with the result that the transition entails a period of rapid population growth. As the birth rate declines, the population stabilizes. The death rate in Kenya fell sharply in the first decades following independence; the birth rate has taken much longer to fall, so that overall population growth rate remains high at around 2.6 per cent per annum. However, with total fertility falling fast, the demographic transition is entering its final phase.

References

Ali, A. and I. Elbadawi, 1999, 'Inequality and the Dynamics of Poverty and Growth in Developing Countries', Presented at the AERC Conference on 'Explaining African Economic Growth Performance', Harvard University, March.

Azam, J. P., A. Fosu and N. Ndung'u, 1999, 'Explaining Slow Growth in Africa', Background paper for *Can African Claim the 21st Century*. World Bank, 2000.

Buffie, E. F. 2003, 'Tight Money, Real Interest Rates, and Inflation in Sub-Saharan Africa'. *IMF Staff Papers*, 50, 115–135.

Collier, P. and A. J. Venables, 2007, 'Rethinking Trade Preferences: How Africa can Diversify its Exports', *The World Economy*, 14 (2), 1326–1345.

Collier, P. and A. J. Venables, 2010, 'International Rules for Trade in Natural Resources', *Journal of Globalization and Development*, 1 (1), Article 8.

Commission on Growth and Development, 2008, *The Growth Report: Strategies for Sustained Growth and Inclusive Development*. Washington, DC: World Bank.

Fujita, P., M. Krugman and A. J. Venables, 1999, *The Spatial Economy: Cities, Regions, and International Trade*. Cambridge, MA: The MIT Press.

Government of Kenya, 2003, *Economic Recovery Strategy for Wealth and Employment Creation (2003–2007)*. Nairobi: Ministry of Planning and National Development.

Government of Kenya, 2007, *Kenya Integrated Household Budget Survey (KIHBS) 2005/06*, Vol. I. Basic Report. Nairobi: Kenya National Bureau of Statistics.

Government of Kenya, 2007, *Vision 2030*. Nairobi: National Economic and Social Council, Office of the President.

Government of Kenya, 2008, *Vision 2030, Medium-Term Plan, Strategy for National Transformation 2008–2012. Accelerating Equitable Economic and Social Development for a Prosperous Kenya*. Nairobi: Ministry of State for Planning, National Development and Vision 2030.

Government of Kenya, *Economic Surveys*, various issues. Nairobi: Government Printers.

KACC (Kenya Anti-Corruption Commission), 2007, 'Press Statement on the Performance of the Kenya Anti-Corruption Commission (KACC)'. Nairobi: KACC.

Kimenyi, M. and N. Ndung'u, 2005, 'Sporadic Ethnic Violence: Why has Kenya not Experienced a Full-blown Civil War?' in Collier, P and N. Sambanis (eds) *Understanding Civil War, Vol. 1: Africa.* Washington, DC: The World Bank.

Krugman, P., 1991, 'Increasing Returns and Economic Geography', *Journal of Political Economy*, 99 (3).

Marshall, A., 1920, *Principles of Economics*, 8th edn. London: Macmillan Publishers.

Mohamed A. E. and M. Spence, 2006, 'Growth Strategies and Dynamics: Insights from Country Experiences'. Working Paper No. 6. Commission on Growth and Development, 2008. Washington, DC: World Bank.

Ndulu, B. J., S. A. O'Connell, J. P. Azam, R. H. Bates, A. K. Fosu, J. W. Gunning and D. Nijinkeu, 2008, *The Political Economy of Economic Growth in Africa, 1960–2000*, Vol. 2. Country Case Studies. Cambridge: Cambridge University Press.

UNIDO, 2009, *The Industrial Development Report, 2009.* Vienna: UNIDO.

World Bank, 2008, 'Kenya: Accelerating and Sustaining Inclusive Growth'. World Bank Report No. 42844-KE, July 2008.

World Bank, 2009, 'Kenya Economic Update: Still Standing- Kenya's Slow Recovery from a Quadruple Shock', Edition 1.

World Bank, 2010, 'Fiscal Policies and Institutions for Shared Growth in Kenya: Lessons from the Global Financial Crisis'. April 2010. Nairobi.

3

Unlocking the Future Potential of Kenya – *Vision 2030*

R. Owino Otieno and Njuguna S. Ndung'u[1]

3.1 Introduction

Since Kenya's independence in 1963, growth has been uneven with high growth rates experienced in the 1960s and early 1970s followed by sluggish performance in the mid-1970s and 1980s. By the 1990s, the economy was contracting, and gross domestic product (GDP) per capita was declining fast, a situation that prevailed up to the year 2002. As a result, the socio-economic indicators deteriorated markedly: the proportion of people living in poverty was estimated to have increased from about 48.8 per cent in 1990 to about 56 per cent at the end of 2002; life expectancy declined from 57 years in 1986 to 47 years in 2000; infant mortality increased from 62 per 1,000 in 1993 to 78 per 1,000 in 2003; whereas under-five mortality increased from 96 per 1,000 births to 114 per 1,000 between 1993 and 2003.

Against this background, in 2003, the Kenyan government formulated the Economic Recovery Strategy for Wealth and Employment Creation (ERS) covering the period 2003–2007. By the end of the ERS period, 2007, the Kenyan economy had made a remarkable recovery with real GDP recording an impressive growth of over 7 per cent compared with 0.6 per cent in 2002. This marked the first time in several decades that a sustained growth spell of five consecutive years had been witnessed.

To consolidate the gains achieved under the ERS and move to an even higher growth and development path, the Kenyan government formulated a new long-term development blueprint for the country – the Kenya *Vision 2030*. The *Vision* is anchored on three key pillars: economic, social, and political governance. The motivation for *Vision 2030* is to have a development strategy to transform Kenya into a newly industrialized, middle-income country providing a high quality of life to all its citizens in a clean and secure environment by the year 2030. The *Vision*, therefore, not only aims to meet the Millennium Development Goals (MDGs), but also make the country globally competitive in the mould of countries such as South Korea and Malaysia, which created visions for development and galvanized the population around them with much success.

This chapter analyses the strategic thrusts of Kenya's long-term development strategy and offers an assessment of the feasibility of achieving *Vision 2030* objectives.

3.2 Setting the scene

3.2.1 Overview

During the first four decades of Kenya's independence, the economy experienced a chequered growth path with high growth rates in the 1960s and early 1970s followed by sluggish performance starting in the mid-1970s. Reflecting performance in the key industrial, agricultural, and services sectors, real GDP growth peaked at 8.0 per cent per annum in the 1970s before declining to about 4 per cent and 1.7 per cent in the 1980s and 1990s respectively (Figure 3.1). As a result, Kenya's per capita income, which grew at around

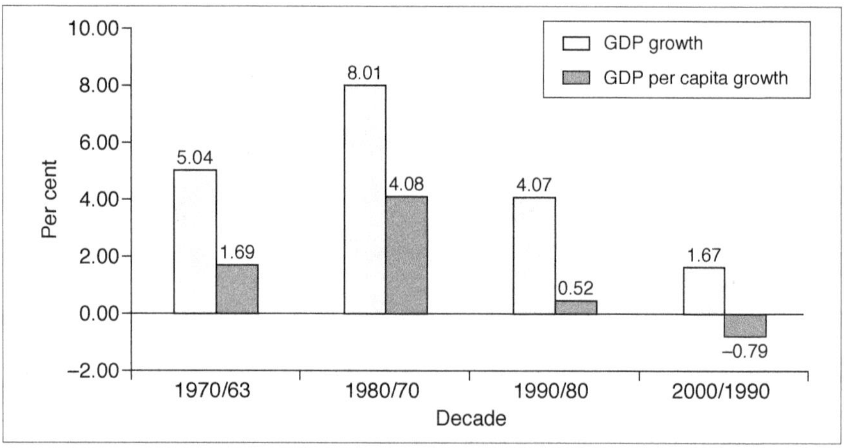

Figure 3.1 GDP growth per decade 1960s–1990s.
Source: Computed from data in Economic Surveys.

4.0 per cent annually in the 1970s, registered hardly any growth in the 1980s and even declined in the 1990s.

One of the principal causes of the disappointing economic performance in Kenya was the low level of investment. Kenya's gross domestic investment declined progressively from around 18 per cent of GDP in 1980 to less than 13 per cent of GDP by 2001 (Table 3.1), reflecting a massive decline in public sector investments from 10.1 per cent of GDP to 4.1 per cent, coupled with stagnation in private investments. The decline in public sector capital spending resulted in a serious decay in physical infrastructure such as roads and railways, driving up transport costs and further undermining the incentives for private investment.

The stagnation in private investment, which itself contributed to the poor economic performance in Kenya, could largely be attributed to sharply increasing operating costs, caused in part by the high and rising cost of energy, transport and telecommunications. By the late 1990s, these costs were much higher in Kenya than in its competitors such as Egypt, South Africa, and Mauritius. These rising direct costs exacerbated the deterioration in the general investment climate in Kenya at this time. Excessive business regulation and licensing procedures hindered new investment, while pervasive rent-seeking behaviour drove up the cost of doing business, stifling investment and growth.

Reflecting the slowdown in economic performance and in the growth of per capita income, the proportion of people living in poverty is estimated to have increased from about 48.8 per cent in 1990 to more than 56 per cent at the end of 2002, with some districts having much higher poverty levels. Furthermore, the social indicators worsened markedly between the mid-1980s and the year 2000: life expectancy declined; infant mortality increased; and under-five mortality also increased from 96 per 1,000 births to 114 per 1,000 during the same period. The different categories of mortality rate had declined progressively since the 1960s until the mid- to late-1980s when the trend reversed.

Table 3.1 Investment and savings in Kenya

	1980	1992	1993	1994	1995	1996	1997	1998	1999	2000	2001
Gross domestic investment	18.3	13.3	16.9	16.0	17.1	16.2	14.5	14.4	13.6	12.9	12.2
Private investment	8.2	6.2	8.9	7.5	9.7	9.2	8.1	9.4	9.3	8.5	8.1
Public investment	10.1	7.1	8	8.5	7.4	7	6.4	5	4.3	4.4	4.1
Gross domestic savings	13.4	13.7	23.8	19.6	11.3	13.2	7.9	7.4	8.9	3.8	4.2
External savings	4.9	–0.4	–6.9	–3.6	5.8	3.0	6.6	7.0	4.7	9.1	8.0

Source: The World Bank, African Development Indicators, 2003.

3.2.2 The Economic Recovery Strategy

Against this worsening economic background, in 2003, the government launched the Economic Recovery Strategy for Wealth and Employment Creation (ERS), aimed at: restoring high economic growth; enhancing equity and reducing poverty; and finally, improving governance and reducing corruption. To address the economic growth objective, the ERS envisaged achieving macroeconomic stability through fiscal discipline, increasing the role of the private sector in the economy and improving the physical infrastructure. To improve equity and reduce poverty, the strategy focused on providing access to universal primary education, improving access to basic health, expanding productive capacity in agriculture, developing hitherto overlooked arid and semi-arid areas and upgrading the living conditions for urban dwellers. And to strengthen governance, the strategy proposed extensive reforms of the judiciary, strengthening the rule of law and security and implementing reforms in public administration systems critical to improving government transparency and accountability.

Successful implementation of the strategy, centred on strong fiscal discipline, resulted in a rapid recovery in GDP growth from 0.6 per cent in 2002 to 7.0 per cent in 2007. The economic performance during the five-year period of the ERS exceeded the initial projections, with actual real GDP growth averaging 5.4 per cent per annum compared with a projected annual growth of 4.7 per cent in the ERS. In the social sector, implementation of free universal primary education in 2003 was a major achievement of the government.

To sustain this recovery and to build on the achievements of this period, the government formulated a new long-term development blueprint for the country – the Kenya *Vision 2030* – which emerged out of extensive consultations with stakeholders including business leaders, top public sector officials, parliamentarians, non-governmental organizations (NGOs), and the wider public, as well as local and international experts. The end result was a development strategy that seeks to build on the ERS and provide a strong continuation for the growth fundamentals.

In the next sections of this chapter, we outline the strategic thrusts of Kenya's long-term development strategy, anchored on three key pillars, economic, social, and political governance, which define the *Vision 2030*. Key objectives of each pillar and the strategic thrusts of sectors covered in each pillar are highlighted, followed by a section that provides an assessment of the capacity of *Vision 2030* to deliver Kenya's aspirations.

3.3 *Vision 2030*

The overarching vision of *Vision 2030* is for 'A globally Competitive and Prosperous Nation with a high quality of life by the year 2030'. The *Vision* is anchored on three pillars, namely economic, social, and political pillars, which are in turn underpinned by cross-cutting institutional reforms and infrastructure development interventions.

Each pillar has defined objectives to be achieved by 2030, as well as strategies and projects to be implemented in the first five-year phase. The projects are diverse, covering all social and economic sectors, and are widely dispersed to cover the whole country; but, more fundamentally, they are aimed at unlocking the potential of the economy and conferring benefits to a wider spectrum of Kenyans.

3.3.1 The economic pillar

Development of the economic pillar began with a diagnostic study of all sectors of the economy and benchmarking of the country's performance against its peers in the 1960s, which are currently more developed. This benchmarking led to the conclusion that, to achieve the people's aspirations, Kenya's economy needs a sustained high growth rate spanning at least two decades. This formed the basis for formulating the economic pillar's long-term objective and medium-term goals.

The objective of the economic pillar is 'To maintain a sustained economic growth of 10 per cent per annum for 25 years'. This is a daunting task as, historically, only a few countries (Oman, Botswana, Equatorial Guinea, and China) have achieved such a feat (Figure 3.2). More recently, between 2001 and 2007, Angola achieved an average annual GDP growth of 13.2 per cent.[2] Even the Asian tigers, whose performance Kenya aspires to emulate, never

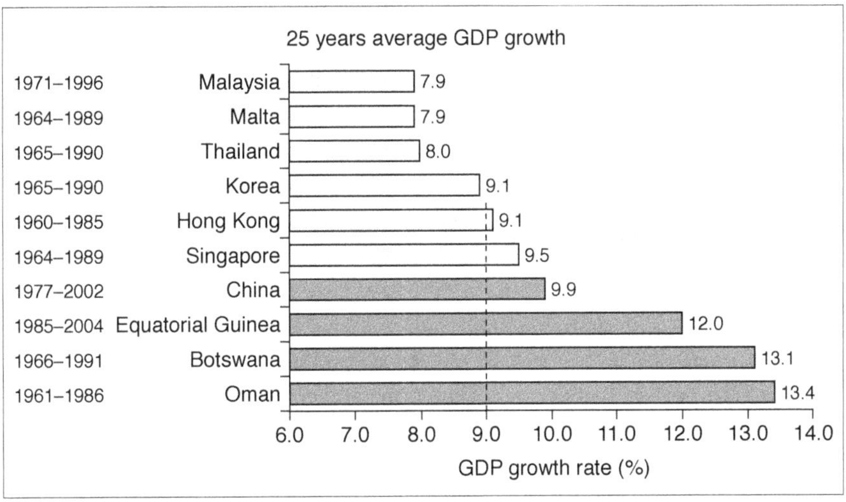

Figure 3.2 Average growth rates of selected countries.
Source: World Development Indicators, 2003.

achieved such growth rates for a sustained period of 25 years. In most of the cases where rapid growth was achieved in Africa, it reflected primarily the discovery and proper management of natural resources supported by appropriate macroeconomic and financial policies. For Kenya, achieving the economic pillar objectives requires an increase in savings and investment to more than 30 per cent of GDP. This will involve improving the business environment through regulatory reforms and increasing investments in infrastructure including roads, energy, and telecommunications in order to bring the costs of doing business in line with or below those of the benchmark countries.

Six priority sectors with the greatest potential to drive growth in the country have been identified.[3] They include tourism, agriculture, the wholesale and retail trade, manufacturing, business process outsourcing (BPO), and financial services. Achieving the growth target would entail implementing several flagship projects in the six priority sectors. These projects were carefully crafted to ensure that they are evenly distributed nationally, such that the parts of the country that are presently remote and underdeveloped could be opened up.

TOURISM

In the tourism sector, the vision is 'To be among the top 10 long-haul tourist destinations offering a high-end, diverse, and distinctive visitor experience'. This sector is one of the major employment drivers in the Kenyan economy, and has recorded more than 10 per cent growth per annum between 2004 and 2007. It remains one of the largest contributors to foreign exchange earnings. However, it remains underdeveloped compared with other top tourist destinations in terms of the number of tourists, yield, and diversity of experience. *Vision 2030* envisages a tourism sector that accounts for a significantly larger share of GDP based on a doubling of international visitors by 2012 and the development of the sector across the full range of tourism, from high-end niche markets and the conference business to coastal and safari tourism that exploits Kenya's natural environment.

AGRICULTURE

The *Vision's* objective for the agricultural sector is to transform it from the current practice of fragmented mixed crop farming to become more commercially oriented. The sector remains a key pillar of the Kenyan economy contributing about 25 per cent of GDP. However, productivity in the sector is two to three times lower than in international benchmark countries. The sector possesses additional opportunities to unlock the potential of Kenyan land with a strong need for legal and institutional reforms.

The sector vision, therefore, is 'Innovative, commercially oriented and modern farm and livestock sector', characterized by higher yields in key crops, greater specialization and the cultivation of currently idle and new land. Achieving these goals requires an emphasis on: institutional reforms to enable private sector agricultural growth; increased productivity of crops and livestock; transforming land use by strategically developing irrigable areas of arid and semi-arid lands for both crops and intensified livestock production; and finally, increasing access to markets particularly for smallholders.

WHOLESALE AND RETAIL

The wholesale and retail sector contributes about 30 per cent of GDP and 50 per cent of employment in both formal and informal establishments. It is extremely fragmented and highly informal as more than 90 per cent of its employment and 70 per cent of its value is informal. It has a very inefficient supply chain, and there is tremendous opportunity to formalize the sector.

The vision for the sector is, therefore, to 'Move towards a formal sector that is efficient, multi-tiered, diversified in product range, and innovative'. Specific targets to stimulate the sector include: developing producer business groups and large wholesale hubs to drive efficiency; creating small retail markets to locate informal players and help them grow; and attracting and developing large formal retail companies through joint and standalone domestic and foreign ventures.[4]

MANUFACTURING

The growth of the manufacturing sector, which comprises about 10 per cent of GDP, has been constrained by lack of competitiveness owing to high energy costs and heavy regulation. With improved competitiveness, there exists opportunity in the domestic and regional markets that can be exploited, and there is also the potential to develop global niches especially in agro-processed goods. The sector vision, therefore, is 'A robust, diversified and competitive manufacturing sector'.

The strategies for the sector have concentrated on three issues: encouraging local production by restructuring key industries that have local raw material availability but no competitive edge such as sugar and paper; exploiting opportunities to further process imports and capture the 'last step' in value addition (e.g. metals, plastics); and increasing the level of value addition in niche exports through, for example, agro-processing. One of the notable flagship projects in the sector would be the development of special economic clusters, initially focusing on select industries such as agro-processing and building materials, which would have all the necessary physical and economic infrastructure including energy, transport, and telecommunications. They would also be strategically located to ensure easy access to raw materials and markets.

BUSINESS PROCESS OUTSOURCING (BPO)

BPO is a new and promising sector with a significant niche opportunity for Kenya where location, language, and education hold the prospect of Kenya being a highly competitive environment. But for this potential to be realized, key inputs are required, in particular in the provision of reliable and low-cost energy and telecommunications and in key skills training for workers in the sector.

The vision for the sector is to be 'The top BPO destination in Africa'. The sector's goal for 2012 is to create at least 7,500 jobs with a corresponding increase in GDP. To achieve this objective, the government has set out to attract footloose international corporations, develop local capacity and establish clusters of activity – so-called 'BPO parks' – to concentrate marketing, training, incentives, and telecommunications infrastructure, to provide a one-stop shop for administration and talent and serve as a 'showcase' park to attract top foreign companies.

FINANCIAL SERVICES

Financial services play a critical enabling role in the economy and are expected to enable transformation of the economy through the mobilization of savings required for investment. As noted later in this volume, the sector experienced significant growth between 2004 and 2007. There is still, however, ample room for further development of all the segments of the financial sector including the securities and capital markets, banking, informal finance, and enhancing access to international capital markets. The vision for the financial services sector is to have 'A vibrant and globally competitive financial sector driving high levels of savings and financing Kenya's investment needs'. Such a financial sector would, it is hoped, improve access to financial services and products for a broader section of Kenyan society, especially small businesses; it would mobilize additional savings to support higher investment rates by creating a better financial environment that attracts investment and protects depositors' interests. Ultimately, the aim is to make Kenya a key regional financial services centre and one of the top ranked emerging market financial centres by 2030.

CROSS-CUTTING REFORMS

To support the priority sector strategies and projects, cross-cutting reforms and enabling infrastructure development will be required. The reforms will cover the public sector, infrastructure development, land reforms, and human resource development. Specifically, Kenya requires the creation of proactive delivery units in government to drive the implementation of flagship projects; aggressive pursuit of targeted investors to entice them into the country – a move from 'red tape' to 'red carpet'; the tying of budgets to performance; and the simplification and streamlining of taxes and other regulations that currently hinder informal firms from exploiting the returns and scale economies of the formal economy.

On infrastructure, successful implementation of the vision will require the building of key roads to support the proposed resort cities, revitalized tourist circuits, and wholesale hubs. The *Vision* also argues for reducing energy costs in key areas and within flagship projects, especially the Special Economic Clusters for manufacturing. There is also a need to support the development of transportation, construction, and telecommunications initiatives around flagship projects.

In the area of human resources development, the government will develop or provide incentives for the development of key training programmes to support the quantity and quality of talent needed in key sectors such as training around specific processes in BPO. The aim is to create a globally competitive and adaptive human resource base to meet the requirements of *Vision 2030*. Land reforms are also recommended, including the development of new land laws and a land use master plan using the land registry to identify and zone certain areas for specific types of activity. For instance, zoning could be done for crop specialization.

3.3.2 The social pillar

The social pillar of *Vision 2030* seeks to create 'a just, cohesive and equitable social development in a clean and secure environment'. It therefore presents comprehensive social interventions aimed at improving the quality of life of all Kenyans. The *Vision* classifies interventions in the social pillar into six broad areas of focus. These include education, health, water and sanitation, environment, housing and urbanization, and gender, youth and vulnerable groups.

MDG PRIORITIES: EDUCATION, HEALTH, WATER AND SANITATION

The vision for education and training is 'Globally competitive quality education, training and research for sustainable development', which embraces all levels of education from early childhood development education through primary, secondary, and vocational training up to university-level education, with a particular emphasis on increasing access and enrolment at all levels.

In the health sector, the vision is an 'Equitable and affordable health care system of the highest possible standards'. The key strategies to be pursued include: providing a functional, efficient, and sustainable health infrastructure network; improving the quality of health care delivery to international standards; and equitable financing of health care through the introduction of a purchaser provider system. The focus of all the interventions in the sector in the medium term will be in areas of preventive care.

These initiatives in health and education are supported by a commitment to improve and increase efficiency in water management and harvesting, water storage infrastructure and sanitation as a way of ensuring that water and sanitation are available and accessible to all Kenyans. Realizing this vision would entail the adoption of strategies in five broad areas: increasing fresh water availability and establishing water monitoring programmes; improving water storage capacity; upgrading supply in urban areas and expanding supply in rural areas; expanding sewerage coverage; and expanding the area under irrigation and drainage. The overriding objective in all these areas is to reverse the declining water availability per capita, increase access to safe water and sanitation, and increase the area under both irrigation and drainage.

ENVIRONMENT

Kenya's natural resource base is threatened by continued deforestation and poaching, human wildlife conflicts, increased occurrence of alien and invasive species, depletion of marine resources, lack of effective policy, regulatory and institutional frameworks, and environmental degradation and encroachment in fragile ecosystems.

The challenges in the area of climate change and desertification include the increased frequency and severity of droughts and floods, inadequate adaptation measures and the existence of knowledge gaps on the impact of climate change. Other environmental challenges include low innovation in the utilization of natural resources, inadequate capacity to apply scientific environmental research and the country's inability to adopt new technologies. Kenya's vision is to overcome these challenges through measures to address conservation, pollution and waste management, and environmental planning and governance.

HOUSING AND URBANIZATION

Kenya's rapid pace of urbanization is confronted by a shortage of urban infrastructure development. The housing sector in particular is faced with a myriad of challenges ranging from inadequate investment in housing and a low level of urban home ownership to weak enforcement of standards, codes, and policies. *Vision 2030* provides strategies and projects that will help to address these challenges and enable Kenya's urban centres to have adequate housing in a clean environment.

GENDER, VULNERABLE GROUPS, AND YOUTH

Finally, the *Vision* seeks to ensure that 'Men and women enjoy a high quality of life and equal opportunities'; improving 'livelihoods for the vulnerable persons at household, community and national levels'; and having 'A responsible, globally competitive and prosperous youth'. The strategies specified to move Kenya towards these goals are: increasing employment opportunities; affirmative action; and increasing social amenities and access to health care.

3.3.3 The political pillar

To meet the goals and aspirations of the economic and social pillars, Kenya needs to transform the national governance system. The Kenyan political system and governance structure seems to have promoted patronage rather than issue-focused and development-centred politics. The electoral and political processes are dominated by ethnic biases as opposed to consideration of issues being advanced by political parties, whereas the existing legal framework has also centred political authority and control of resources at the central government level.

The political pillar vision, therefore, is to have 'A democratic political system that is issue-based, people-centred, result-oriented and accountable to the public'. This will entail a complete overhaul of the current system dominated by tribal and regional political alliances with emphasis on patronage rather than issues.

The impetus behind this political vision is a desire to confront the current challenges concerning the rule of law and human rights in Kenya. The *Vision* seeks to develop a political system relevant to a modern, market-based economy in a human rights-respecting state. This means genuinely competitive and issue-based politics, a politically engaged and open society around which are built transparent, accountable, ethical, and results-oriented government institutions.

The first step in this process is the enactment of a new constitutional framework as the cornerstone of all the reforms necessary in the political arena. The new constitutional dispensation is expected to enshrine eight key governance principles including: constitutional supremacy; sovereignty of the people; equality of citizens (men and women, religion, tribes and races); national values, goals and ideology; strong and viable political party system; public participation in governance; separation of powers; and decentralization.

3.4 Assessment of *Vision 2030*

3.4.1 Kenya's growth opportunities

A key question that a growth strategy for Kenya cannot avoid is: What are Kenya's key growth opportunities that successive political and policy regimes have not successfully exploited? A great opportunity that the country has and which can be exploited in a growth strategy is its location. The country has access to a large coastline and can therefore adopt a coastal manufacturing strategy. This would drive export-led growth. Such a strategy would require targeted public investment in physical infrastructure that supports lowering of manufacturing costs not to mention the need to improve the investment environment to attract large-scale investors along the coastal strip.

Furthermore, the country's location makes it ideal for a growth strategy that takes advantage of its locational rents. The country's location places it where it can reap enormous benefits from tourism targeting its natural sandy beaches, the rich wildlife comprising the big five among other rare animal species, and beautiful and varying landscapes with mountains, coasts, lakes, and rivers that can attract sports such as mountain climbing and inland water sports. With a large inland water body in Lake Victoria that links the country directly with Uganda and Tanzania and puts it in close proximity to Rwanda and the Democratic Republic of Congo, Kenya could also be a trade hub in the region as it pursues an export-led growth strategy. In addition to the need for an appropriate road and railway network, this strategy could be supported by attracting investment in water transport infrastructure particularly for the inland waterways. With a major seaport in Mombasa and numerous landlocked neighbours, Kenya is well placed to serve as a major distribution hub and a gateway to the large East African market.

A development policy document should therefore take cognisance of these growth opportunities for the country. In our assessment, *Vision 2030* seems to have achieved this.

3.4.2 Vision assessment

The *Vision 2030* development process was quite consultative and comprehensive, and therefore covered the key issues facing Kenya. Relevant policies for consolidating economic recovery and driving Kenya to a higher growth and development path have therefore been brought forth. In our view, *Vision 2030* offers Kenya a very good framework for addressing growth-inhibiting factors in the markets, among private agents and the political economy. If fully implemented, *Vision 2030* would indeed propel the country to a higher development path.

Mwega and Ndung'u (2008) examine how much of Kenya's growth experience is explicable in terms of growth regressions and the extent to which the variables in these regressions can be used to explain the country's economic growth over the last 40 years or so. They look at the relative importance of factor accumulation and productivity, external shocks and domestic policies, among other factors, in explaining Kenya's growth experience. Their basic premise is that Kenya's economic performance over the period was to a large extent a function of the initial conditions – resource endowments and economic structure; economic policy; national political institutions; forms of economic organization – but above all a function of changing policy driven by political developments. *Vision 2030* therefore offers a framework for comprehensively addressing these growth factors.

With its financial sector strategies, the *Vision* will enable the country to rapidly accumulate savings and hence increase gross investment to levels that will increase growth and enhance the pace of development. Furthermore, by enabling massive infrastructure development, the interventions will improve the country's competitiveness and therefore not only maintain its regional market but also enhance its export volumes. Commercialization of agriculture, increased crop specialization and the creation of disease-free zones for livestock, and the opening up of new lands will greatly enhance productivity in the agriculture and livestock sector. Competitiveness for the manufacturing sector will also be greatly improved through the proposed special economic zones. The proposed location of these zones is intended to open up remote parts of the country and should greatly increase the productive capacity of the economy.

MANAGING RISK

One key omission in *Vision 2030* is the failure to address how Kenya can cushion itself against exogenous factors such as high oil and food prices and deteriorating terms of trade, which are currently affecting all developing countries, and persistent droughts that, among other things, drive inflation to high levels.

Furthermore, the macroeconomic framework underpinning *Vision 2030* does not contain any risk assessment of the framework in the form of alternative macroeconomic scenarios. The *Vision* document defined only a single economic growth and development path without offering an alternative or middle-ground path in case the high growth scenario is not achieved. For instance, at the time of formulating the *Vision 2030*, the impact of the post-election violence that erupted in 2008 and the drought experienced later that year was expected to be short-lived, and robust growth was expected to resume thereafter at a high level. The economic outlook has worsened as a result of the global financial and economic crisis, which gathered momentum in the second half of 2008 and is likely to have a negative impact on Kenya's exports of goods and services (such as tourism), remittances and foreign direct investments. This slowdown has definitely affected Kenya's growth momentum, and it is now highly unlikely that the 10 per cent growth target can be achieved by 2012. How quickly Kenya can return to the *Vision 2030* growth path will depend to a significant extent on the pace of the global economic recovery and the avoidance of major droughts in the next few years.

Although *Vision 2030* identifies clear goals, strategies, and projects, it needs to be supported by detailed sector-based implementation plans. For instance, although the health sector interventions clearly indicate the need to shift priority from curative to preventive measures, the *Vision* document does not have strategies for reorienting government health sector expenditure towards preventive health services. In the financial year 1996/97, about 67 per cent of Kenyan government's recurrent health budget went to curative services, whereas only about 21 per cent went to promotional and preventive care including rural health centres (Kimalu *et al.*, 2004). The need for detailed implementation plans has been partly addressed by the Medium-Term Plan for implementation of the *Vision*.

Numerous studies have identified infrastructure as key to unlocking Africa's development potential. Kenya is no exception. The proposed infrastructure sector projects in *Vision 2030* will provide Kenya with a key foundation for economic development and be a major contributor to employment creation in Kenya. Infrastructure development will not only have a greater impact in opening up remote parts of the country with high potential, but also create more employment, which would create higher demand in the economy with tremendous spillover effects. Aggressive expansion of the energy sector alone would create fairly high levels of employment in underexploited energy sources such as geothermal generation, wind power in parts of the Eastern and North Eastern provinces, and solar energy in most parts of the country.

With regard to the political pillar, the road map in the *Vision 2030* document that proposes enactment of a new constitutional dispensation together with enabling legislation is likely to comprehensively address the constraints on Kenya's political and governance system. However, the changing of laws alone will not resolve all the issues covered by the political pillar of the *Vision*. Kenya will have to undertake measures to encourage attitudinal change among the governing and the governed. The Kenyan people need to inculcate the values of tolerance and respect for divergence of opinion, particularly in the political arena.

3.5 Conclusion

Despite the minor gaps that have been observed, we are of the view that *Vision 2030* can deliver the growth and development that Kenya aspires to achieve, albeit with some delay given the global economic crisis and uncertainty about the timing of the recovery. Its success will, however, depend on maintaining macroeconomic stability and implementing key structural reforms and programmes in the social pillar, and managing political transitions and reform of institutions targeted by the political pillar of the *Vision* document. The recommended reforms of the pensions sector, insurance industry, capital markets and strengthening of the banking sector as spelt out in *Vision 2030* will be critical in allowing the country to achieve this shift, as these are the sectors critical for the mobilization of savings.

Notes

1 The authors greatly appreciate the insightful thoughts provided by Dr Kamau Thugge, former Economic Secretary of Kenya.

2 Source: International Monetary Fund, World Economic Outlook Database, October 2008.
3 The identification of the priority sectors was based on the sector's attractiveness and the feasibility. Attractiveness was based on the current size of the sector in GDP terms, whereas the feasibility was based on resources required for high-impact investments in the sector.
4 For additional details, see pp. 55–60, *Vision 2030* (Government of Kenya, 2007).

References

Bigsten, A., K. Lundvall and M. Söderbom, 1998, 'Constraints on Manufacturing Growth in Kenya'. Paper prepared for a Workshop on 'Firm Analysis and Competitiveness Surveys' at the World Bank, Washington, DC, 14–15 December 1998.

Central Bureau of Statistics, 2003, *Kenya Demographic and Health Survey*.

Gillis, M., D.H. Perkins, M. Roemer and D. R. Snodgrass, 1987, *Economics of Development*, 2nd edn. New York: N. W. Norton.

Government of Kenya, Ministry of Planning and National Development, 2007, *Kenya Vision 2030*.

Government of Kenya, Ministry of Planning and National Development, 2003, *Economic Recovery Strategy for Wealth and Employment Creation*. Nairobi: Government Printer.

International Monetary Fund, 2008, *World Economic Outlook Database*, October 2008.

Kenya Association of Manufacturers, 2008, 'Manufacturing in Kenya: Issues, Challenges and Opportunities'. A presentation at ESAMI Round Table, Nairobi, March 2008.

Kimalu *et al.*, 2004, 'A Review of Health Sector in Kenya'. KIPPRA Working Paper No. 11.

Mwega, F. M. and N. S. Ndung'u, 2008, 'Explaining African Economic Growth Performance: The Case of Kenya', in Ndulu, B. J., S. A. O'Connell, J.-P. Azam, R. H. Bates, A. K. Fosu, J. W. Gunning and D. Njinkeu (eds) *The Political Economy of Economic Growth in Africa, 1960–2000. Volume 2: Country Case Studies*. Cambridge: Cambridge University Press, 325–368.

Ndulu, B. J., S. A. O'Connell, J.-P. Azam, R. H. Bates, A. K. Fosu, J. W. Gunning and D. Njinkeu (eds) *The Political Economy of Economic Growth in Africa, 1960–2000*. Cambridge: Cambridge University Press.

UNAIDS/WHO, 2004, Update: Epidemiological Fact Sheet on HIV/AIDS and Sexually Transmitted Infections.

World Bank, 2003, *African Development Indicators 2003*.

4

Growth Analysis and Diagnostics for Kenya

Leonardo Garrido, Praveen Kumar, Njuguna S. Ndung'u, and John Randa

4.1 Historical perspective

Kenya's post-independence growth experience is characterized by a prolonged collapse after an initial period of relatively good growth that lasted until 1974. Mwega and Ndung'u (2004) divide Kenya's growth history during 1960–2000 into four subperiods: 1960–74, a period of improving economic performance based on an import substitution-driven industrialization strategy and supported by robust agricultural growth; 1975–84, a period of poor performance when the economy was hit by the oil shock in 1979, a military coup attempt in 1982, and a severe drought in 1983/84; 1985–89, a period of short-lived economic recovery led by a mini coffee boom and a decrease in oil prices and good weather; and the 1990s, a period of poor performance resulting from macroeconomic mismanagement, political uncertainty, and poor governance. The 1990s were indeed a lost decade as per capita income stagnated with growth rates hovering around zero in most years. The economy started to grow after 2002, however, and grew at an average rate of 2.0 per cent per capita during 2003–09.

Kenya's growth collapse after 1974 followed a pattern observed in most other sub-Saharan African (SSA) countries. Similar patterns have been observed by Pritchett (1998), who shows that a single main break in growth trends occurred for most SSA countries some time between 1973 and 1978 followed by persistent stagnation until the early 1990s. Where Kenya's growth experience stands out is in its persistent stagnation during the 1990s even as most SSA countries showed growth recovery, particularly during the second half of that decade (Table 4.1 and Figure 4.1).

The growth collapse, which lasted more than two decades, led to divergence in economic performance and level of development between Kenya and the rest of the developing countries outside SSA. Table 4.1 puts into perspective Kenya's growth performance, by decade, for the period 1965–2008 compared with benchmark groups (SSA, developing, and developed countries).[1] Kenya outperformed the average SSA country through part of the 1980s even as average output growth failed to keep pace with the developing and developed world. A period of stagnation followed, with Kenya's performance even falling slightly behind the average SSA country. In the 1990s, Kenya's economy shrank by an average 1 per cent per year, whereas that of the developing world expanded by 4 per cent. Although growth recovered to 1.7 per cent in the period 2000–08, the average growth in SSA was 3 per cent, whereas that of other developing economies was 5.9 per cent. Average growth in per capita gross domestic product (GDP) between 1960 and 2008 was just 1.2 per cent in Kenya, compared with an annual rate of 3.5 per cent in non-SSA developing countries and 2.7 per cent in the developed world.

A comparison of Kenya with selected resource-poor countries, coastal countries[2] with comparable per capita GDP around 1960 is depicted in Figure 4.2. This comparison is instructive given Kenya's potential for growth in view of its geography, endowments, and initial income. Countries such as Bangladesh, India, and Pakistan, which had a much lower per capita GDP in Kenya's independence year, went on to embark on a sustained growth path that has, in the case of Bangladesh, allowed it to close the income gap with Kenya, and in the case of India and Pakistan, to enjoy per capita income 50 per cent higher than the latter by 2008. In the case of Sri Lanka, the income gap has widened to 150 per cent of Kenya's per capita GDP in the same year.

Table 4.1 Per capita annual GDP growth rates (population weighted) by decade: Kenya and benchmark groups

	Kenya	Developing SSA	Developing world, excl. SSA	Rest of the world
1960s	1.1	1.3	1.6	4.7
1970s	4.1	0.7	2.4	2.8
1980s	0.3	-1.1	3.5	2.5
1990s	-1.0	-0.5	4.0	1.9
2000s	1.7	3.0	5.9	1.5
1960–2008	1.2	0.7	3.5	2.7

SSA, sub-Saharan Africa.
Source: Authors' calculations based on World Bank, World Development Indicators data.

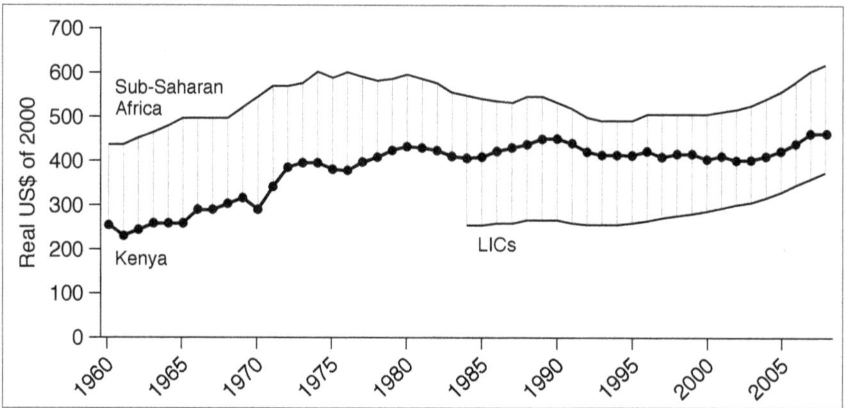

Figure 4.1 Kenya versus benchmark regions: real per capita GDP in US$ of 2000, 1960–2008.
LICs, low-income countries.
Source: Authors' calculations based on World Bank, Development Data Platform.

A deeper analysis of Kenya's growth experience shows that growth picked up again beginning in 2003, with the real GDP growth rate increasing from 0.5 per cent in 2002 to 2.9 per cent in 2003 and steadily increasing to 6.7 per cent in 2007. The abrupt reduction in the pace of growth to 3.5 per cent in 2008 and an estimated 2.7 per cent in 2009 resulted from successive shocks, including rising international prices (particularly of fuel, food, and fertilizers), poor rainfall, spillovers from the global financial crisis, and, on top of that, episodes of domestic post-election violence throughout the country. Average growth in the period 2003–09 was 4.8 per cent per year. Spurred by the economic success of the period 2003–07, the government set out in its *Vision 2030* document an ambitious target of 10 per cent annual real growth for twenty years from 2011 onwards in order to catch up with the East Asian

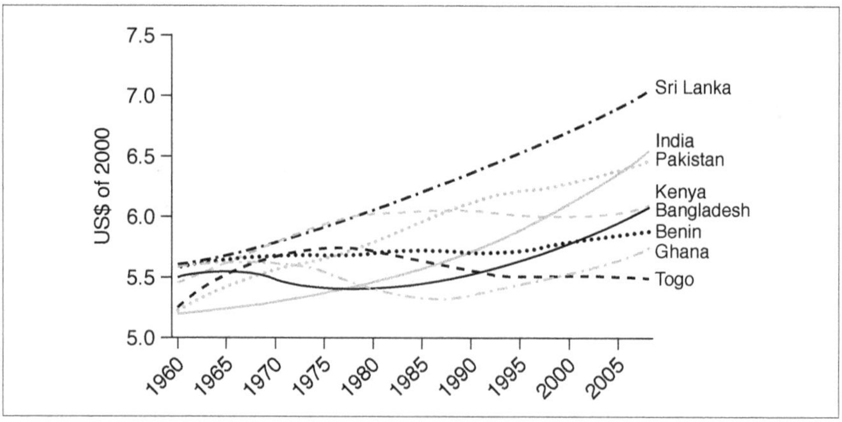

Figure 4.2 Trends in per capita real GDP, 1960–2008.

economies and become a middle-income country by 2030.[3] Kenya's *Vision 2030* plans remain unchanged, despite initial setbacks linked to the above-mentioned shocks in 2008 and 2009 and the moderate growth expectations for the period 2010–14, projected by the International Monetary Fund (IMF) at around 5.5 per cent per year (IMF, 2010).

4.1.1 What explains Kenya's growth experience – the need to understand private investment behaviour

What explains the collapse of growth after 1974, two decades of stagnation, and more importantly, the resurgence of growth after 2002? What are the constraints to further acceleration of growth? This section focuses on proximate determinants (sources) of growth – accumulation of physical and human capital – compared with deeper determinants of long-run sustained growth.[4]

Table 4.2 shows the result of an extended growth accounting decomposition for Kenya. It includes the customary decomposition of real GDP growth, by periods, from changes in inputs – physical capital and labour-adjusted skills – plus the residual, under assumptions for the functional form, competition, etc. It also includes a further decomposition of labour-adjusted skills to account for changes in human capital, employment, population, and the labour force. It shows the role of the sharp decline in physical capital accumulation during the 1980s and the 1990s (which was partly offset by gains in human capital accumulation) in the collapse of growth, and its resurgence in the 2000s. During the 1980s and 1990s, growth of physical capital *per worker* was negative, whereas human capital accumulation slowed, dragging down the performance of the economy. There was also a substantial decline in total factor productivity growth (TFPG) during this period attributable to a slowdown in the accumulation of human capital and a turning inward of the Kenyan economy (Azam and Daubreé, 1997). Azam and Daubreé (1997) also highlight the predominant role of insufficient private investment and its failure to match the progress of human capital accumulation as an important factor in slowing growth in Kenya during this period.

Table 4.2 Kenya's growth accounting decomposition, by periods (%)

Period	GDP growth	Physical capital	Labour-adjusted skills	TFPG	Population growth rate	Per capita GDP growth
1960s	4.5	1.5	2.1	0.8	3.3	1.1
1970s	8.0	2.1	2.9	3.0	3.7	4.1
1980s	4.1	0.8	2.6	0.6	3.7	0.3
1990s	1.9	0.8	2.8	–1.8	2.9	-1.0
2000–08	4.4	1.6	2.2	0.6	2.7	1.7

TFPG, total factor productivity growth.
Source: Authors' calculations.

Physical investment was on a trend decline until about 1995. It touched a post-independence historical low of 10.4 per cent in 1992. Although part of the decline came from diminished public investment, which peaked at more than 46 per cent of the total investment in 1978 (and 11.5 per cent of GDP), private investment stagnated as well. Microevidence from manufacturing confirms this picture. Firm-level data from the mid-1990s show that approximately half of firms undertook no investment, and the majority of firms reported modest investment rates (Söderbom, 2001). In 2002, only 15 per cent of the existing manufacturing firms reported investment rates (investment expenditure as a share of replacement value of capital stock) above 10 per cent, and a third of all firms reported zero investment (World Bank, 2004).

Investment picked up particularly after 2002, as evident in Table 4.3. The investment ratio returned to levels above 20 per cent after 2005. The IMF (2010) estimates that this figure will remain at around 19–20 per cent of GDP until 2014, of which more than half would correspond to private capital formation.

It is instructive to compare Kenya's investment rates across countries as well. Despite the recent pickup in investment, Kenya remains a low-investment economy by international standards. During 1960–2008, Kenya's average investment to GDP was 18.5 per cent (Table 4.3), just above the SSA average (17.8 per cent) and below the average for other low-income countries (20.9 per cent). In the current decade, despite the pickup, it still lags behind the average of low- and middle-income countries.

Table 4.3 Ratio of gross fixed capital formation to GDP, current US$ (%)

	1960s	1970s	1980s	1990s	2000s	1960–2008
Sub-Saharan Africa	–	18.8	18.3	17.2	16.6	17.8
Kenya	15.9	20.9	18.8	17.6	18.5	18.5
Middle East and North Africa	22.9	31.7	30.1	25.5	25.4	27.7
Europe and Central Asia	–	–	27.6	21.7	20.4	21.4
East Asia and Pacific	21.2	26.2	27.2	31.9	34.8	28.9
Latin America and Caribbean	20.5	23.2	21.5	19.0	18.7	20.6
Low income	–	–	18.6	19.5	22.9	20.9
Middle income	20.5	24.2	24.9	23.5	25.5	24.0
High income	21.8	23.2	22.2	21.6	20.4	21.9

Source: Authors' calculations based on World Bank, World Development Indicators data.

The above discussion points us towards the main issue in understanding Kenya's growth experience. It suggests that, in trying to understand the reasons behind the slow growth in Kenya, one must understand the reasons behind the behaviour of physical investment. The following section applies the growth diagnostic approach developed by Hausmann *et al.* (2004; HRV hereafter) to systemically look for reasons that would be consistent with the observed investment pattern. The chapter limits its focus to the 1990s and subsequently for two main reasons: (i) the structure of the Kenyan economy changed considerably after the initiation of structural reforms in 1987; and (ii) constraints that act as binding could change from one point in time to another. Going too far back into history is not likely to advance our insights into what needs to be done in the future to accelerate growth.

4.2 Growth diagnostics applied to Kenya

4.2.1 The HRV framework of growth diagnostics

Growth diagnostics is a heuristic approach that is motivated by three considerations: (i) that reform strategies should be growth strategies; (ii) that growth strategies are likely to differ according to domestic opportunities and constraints, so considerable knowledge of local specificities is required; and (iii) that capital for reforms is limited, hence they need to be prioritized. Therefore, all reform efforts should be focused on the main bottlenecks to growth, as opposed to what has been dubbed a 'wholesale' or 'spray-painting' reform approach.

HRV motivate the framework by arguing that, along a balanced growth path, consumption (c) and capital per capita (k) grow at the same rate, which in turn depends upon private returns to accumulation. The private returns to accumulation are a function of social returns (ρ), the private appropriability of social returns ($1-\tau$) (think of τ as taxes), and the cost of financing accumulation (r).[5]

$$\frac{\dot{c}_t}{c_t} = \frac{\dot{k}_t}{k_t} = \sigma \times \{\rho \times [(1-\tau] - r)$$

In line with the above thinking, HRV group the factors (constraints) behind inadequate levels of private investment (both physical and human) and entrepreneurship into two sets: (i) *Financing constraints* (low savings, poor intermediation in domestic financial markets, high country risk, or poor integration with external financial markets); and (ii) *Low private returns*. Low private returns could, in turn, result from *low social returns* (for example, due to insufficient investment in complementary factors such as human capital, technical know-how, infrastructure, or poor geography) or *poor private appropriability* (high taxation, macro risks such as instability, poor property rights and contract enforcement, high corruption and crime, labour–capital conflicts/rigid labour market, or poor learning and co-ordination externalities leading to low product diversification).

The above constraints are normally organized in a decision tree (Figure 4.3).[6] All the factors contained in the decision tree are likely to matter for growth and welfare, including the existence of market distortions and policy wedges. The growth diagnostics challenge consists of identifying constraints, the relaxation of which provides large positive direct effects, so that even after taking into account second-best interactions and indirect effects, the net impact of a policy change is beneficial and sizeable.[7]

The following discussion starts by focusing on the branch dealing with financing constraints first. This allows us to examine how far observed investment levels were constrained by the availability of finance. A conclusion is reached that availability of financing may not have been a binding constraint to investment until 2002. Yet it could become a binding constraint in the fu-

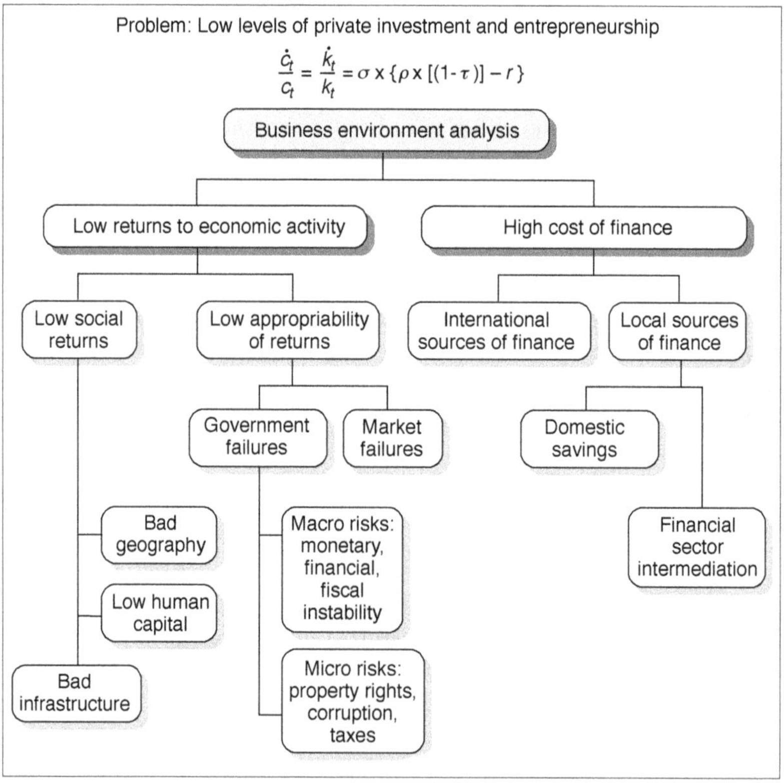

Figure 4.3 Growth diagnostics.

ture. The discussion then moves on to the other major section of the decision tree dealing with reasons for low private returns to economic activity, and comes to the conclusion that poor private appropriability of returns to investment appears to be the main reason behind low private investment rates in Kenya.

4.2.2 Financing constraints – are the high cost of capital and limited access to financing behind the low private investment rate?

The first important question to decide upon is whether the relatively low level of private investment rates in Kenya has been a result of financing constraints and whether such financing constraints are likely to be binding in the medium term. The objective would be to see whether the cost of finance in Kenya is high, which would deter investment. High cost of finance could result from low domestic savings or poor intermediation. Alternatively, access to finance could be constrained, which would lead to rationing out of investors.

To answer the above question, we first look at the historical relationship between real lending rates and gross fixed capital formation during the 1990s and after.[8] Figure 4.4 presents a scatter plot of a smoothed (three-year) moving average of the gross private investment to GDP ratio and real lending interest rates for the period 1998–2009.

During the first half of 1990, real interest rate increases resulted from a worsening of the economic environment.[9] Nominal lending rates peaked at 36 per cent in 1994 and began to decrease thereafter; and real interest rates fell from a historical post-independence high of 26 per cent in 1995 to nearly zero in 2009. The decline in real interest rates was accompanied by a slightly higher share of private investment in GDP, as shown in the scatter plot, which

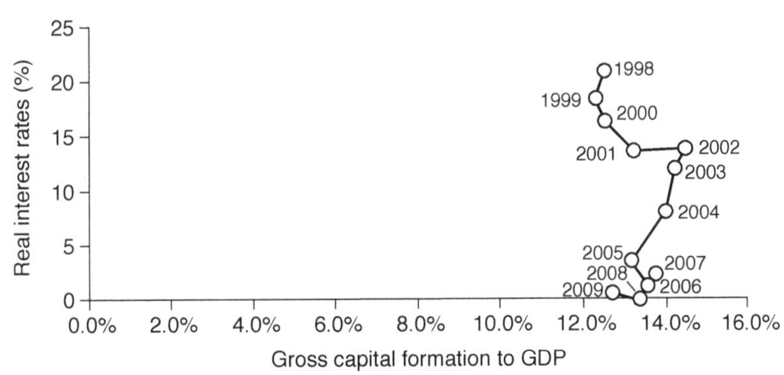

Figure 4.4 Kenya, ratio of gross fixed capital formation from private sector to GDP versus real interest rates (three-year averages), 1998–2009.
Source: Authors' calculations based on World Bank, Development Data Platform.

was however reversed after 2008. What is remarkable about the scatter plot is the narrow band of 13–15 per cent within which the private investment ratio has stayed in Kenya during the period under discussion. This has happened despite a steep fall in lending rates. This is indicative of a very weak relationship between the price of capital and the demand for it.

FIRM-LEVEL EVIDENCE ABOUT ACCESS TO CAPITAL

In an Investment Climate Assessment carried out by the World Bank in 2003 (World Bank, 2004), firms were asked about the cost and availability of finance. About 71 per cent of those in manufacturing cited the cost of finance as a major or severe constraint to their businesses, and access to credit was ranked as the second most important constraint to business. These data need to be treated with caution because they mix investment capital needs with working capital needs. In a repeat survey in 2007 (World Bank, 2008), however, only 26 per cent of the firms perceived that access to credit was a major constraint. Survey data allow us to isolate firms that had (i) applied for a loan or credit/line and were rejected, or (ii) did not apply for a loan because of a financial constraint. Figure 4.5 shows the percentage of firms with and without a loan and a credit line, and the reasons why firms did not apply for one. For 2007 data, about 17 per cent of firms that wanted credit did not manage

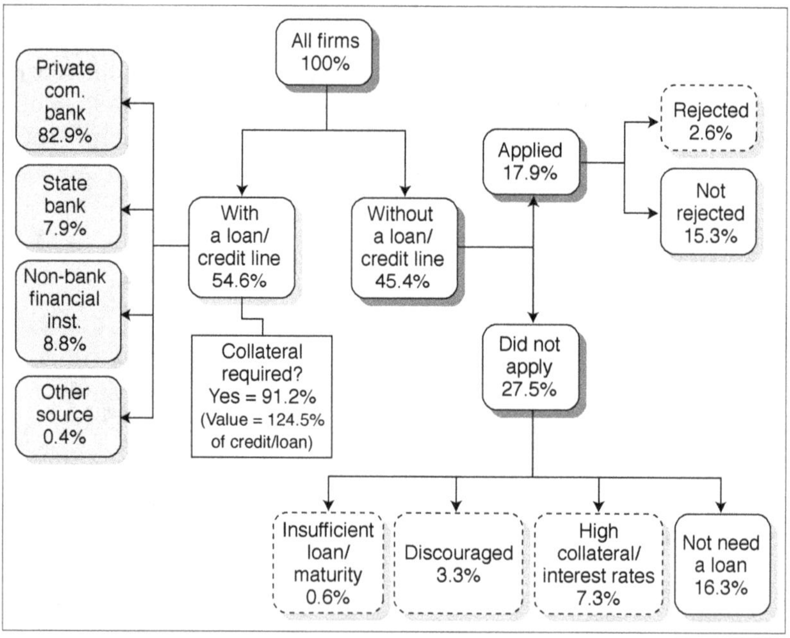

Figure 4.5 Are the high costs of capital and limited access to capital constraining Kenya's investment?

to get it. This percentage is at the low end across SSA countries (Figure 4.6), and comparable to averages for the Latin American region (13 per cent) and Europe and the Central Asia region (15 per cent).

The above discussion shows that the cost of finance or access to finance may not be a major problem for Kenyan firms. There are pockets of poor access, however. Surveys show that smaller firms and firms in rural areas suffer in a disproportionally greater way from credit rationing or restricted access to financial services.

DOES KENYA'S LOW DOMESTIC SAVING RATE EXPLAIN LOW INVESTMENT?

Given that investment generally shows home bias, policy discussion has centred on whether the savings rate is adequate to meet investment demand in Kenya. The gross domestic saving rate has been low in Kenya, generally below 20 per cent with a dip in the late 1990s to below 10 per cent. An observation is also made in the *Vision 2030* document that acknowledges the low and inadequate saving rate and aims to raise it if higher growth rates are to be achieved.

How would excess demand for domestic savings show up in an economy? One would expect that banks will try to attract savings with high deposit rates. Interest rates on government bonds could also be high in such a situation. To the extent that domestic and international savings are substitutes, one would see a high demand for international savings, which would show up in high levels of external debt and concomitantly high levels of current account deficits.

Kenya does not show any of the above signs, however. Deposit rates have been historically low (around 5 per cent in the 2000s). Kenya's external debt has been moderate, despite a very low inflow of external grants after 1993.

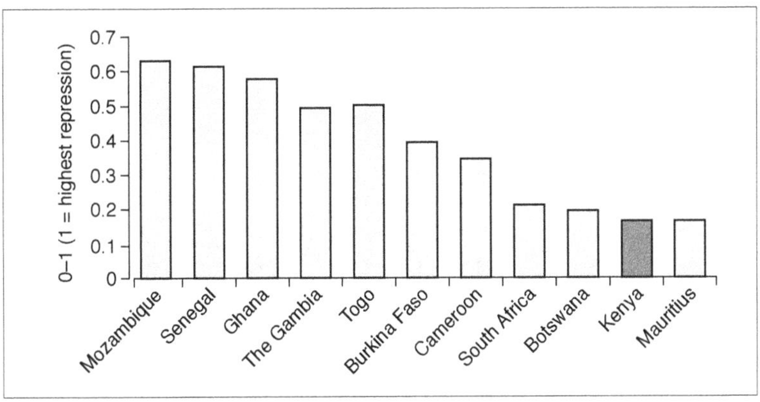

Figure 4.6 Index of financial access, Kenya and benchmark regions.

The average external debt in nominal terms as a ratio of GDP in the 1990s was 85 per cent and fell significantly in the 2000s. Table 4.4 shows the savings–investment balance during the period 1996–2008. It shows that the current account balance has remained a low share of GDP, an average of –2.3 per cent in the current decade.

The discussion above indicates that low savings rates have not translated into high current account deficits, high debt, or high deposit rates.

EXCESS LIQUIDITY IN THE BANKING SYSTEM

In Kenya, as in large parts of Africa, banks have built up high liquidity that private credit cannot soak up (Saxegaard, 2006). Since 2003, when the demand for funds to finance public expenditure through government securities declined as revenue collections by the Kenya Revenue Authority (KRA) improved, there have been excess investible funds with the banks. The oversubscription of KenGen and Safaricom shares divested by the government in 2007 provided strong evidence of excess liquidity in the banking system waiting for productive investment opportunities.

SUMMARY AND CONCLUSION OF EVIDENCE ON FINANCING CONSTRAINTS

How should the above evidence be interpreted? We argue that, after the mid-1990s, market signals do not support the hypothesis that a low investment

Table 4.4 Kenya current account, investment, and savings, 1996–2008

	Current account balance		Gross capital formation[a]			Gross national savings[b]	Statistical discrepancy[c]
Year	(US$ billion)	(% of GDP)	Public	Private	Total	(% of GDP)	(% of GDP)
1996	–0.21	–1.7	3.7	12.9	16.6	9.9	5.0
1997	–0.47	–3.6	3.4	12.7	16.0	9.1	3.4
1998	–0.55	–3.9	3.7	12.0	15.7	10.6	1.2
1999	–0.23	–1.8	2.9	12.3	15.2	12.0	1.4
2000	–0.38	–3.0	2.5	13.3	15.8	13.0	–0.2
2001	–0.49	–3.8	2.1	14.1	16.2	13.1	–0.6
2002	–0.12	–0.9	2.6	16.1	18.6	13.2	4.5
2003	0.13	0.9	3.2	12.6	15.8	13.5	3.2
2004	–0.13	–0.8	3.2	13.5	16.7	16.2	–0.3
2005	–0.26	–1.4	3.4	13.5	16.9	16.1	–0.6
2006	–0.48	–2.1	4.3	13.8	18.1	16.2	–0.2
2007	–1.10	–4.1	4.6	13.9	18.5	17.2	–2.8
2008	–1.29	–3.7	6.6	12.5	19.1	17.6	–2.2

a Gross capital formation=gross fixed capital formation +change in inventories.
b Gross national savings=GDP+net income from abroad+net transfers from abroad–total consumption.
c Statistical discrepancy=current account balance–gross national savings–gross capital formation).
Source: World Bank, World Development Indicators; IMF (2010).

rate resulted from financing constraints. We found that the cost of capital has not been very high, access to finance has been reasonable, and the low saving rate did not create pressures to borrow from abroad. Low demand for investment capital has led the banking system to build up high liquidity. All these findings point towards the same conclusion – that the investment rate is not low because of financing constraints. This conclusion, in turn, suggests that broad reforms aimed at improving access to finance, reducing the cost of capital (through say reducing intermediation costs), or improving the saving rate will not necessarily lead to higher growth, at least in the short run.

What does the above discussion not tell us? The above discussion does not tell us if finance will not become a binding constraint in future. According to the World Bank (2008), although Kenya's financial systems are well developed by regional standards, they lack the depth and efficiency to deliver high levels of growth. In 2006, the ratio of financial system deposits to GDP was 34.6 per cent, whereas the ratio of bank deposits to GDP was 33.1 per cent. Those figures compare favourably with other African countries, where average bank deposits/GDP hover near 25 per cent, but they remain substantially below the averages for higher growth regions such as East Asia Pacific (51.4 per cent) and South Asia (46.3 per cent). Therefore, development of the financial system would probably remain a longer term goal. Further, targeted efforts to improve access to finance in rural areas and to small businesses could improve the private investment rate.

4.2.3 Low social returns – are they behind the low private investment rate?

This section investigates whether low returns to economic activity are acting as a constraint to private investment. Private returns could be low if economic activities are intrinsically low-return activities (low social returns) or if appropriability of returns is low, thereby lowering private returns. First, we focus on investigating whether Kenya shows symptoms of low social returns. That is, whether Kenya's growth is being constrained by lack of complementary factors of production such as its infrastructure, its location in the world economy (i.e. geography), or its low level of human capital.

Kenya's location in terms of its geography cannot be seen to be a problem as it is not landlocked. It has a port at Mombasa located on a major shipping route in the Indian Ocean. It also has good airports mid-distance from Europe and the Far East where its major export markets are. On human capital, Kenya has an educated workforce. Much of its labour force have a university degree, and a good proportion of the adult population have at least twelve years of education and are amenable to further training. The English language is used in the education system. In Investment Climate Assessment surveys conducted by the World Bank, the percentage of firms who identified an inadequately educated labour force as a constraint declined from 31 per cent in 2003 to

11 per cent in 2007. It should be noted that firms still complain that highly skilled manpower is lacking in some sectors, especially manufacturing. Despite this, human capital is not recognized as a binding constraint in Kenya.

The World Bank (2008) argues that Kenya has high costs of business compared with other countries such as India, China, and South Africa. Table 4.5 shows that selected business costs in Kenya add up to three times more than in China and almost twice as high as in India. These high costs of business reduce the profitability of businesses and thus act as a disincentive to investment. The following sections first focus on infrastructure services. Low returns to capital appear to have their roots in an insufficient supply of complementary factors of production such as infrastructure services.

INSUFFICIENT AND UNRELIABLE ELECTRICITY SUPPLY

Kenya, surprisingly, presents a picture of a country with an insufficient and unreliable supply of electricity. Only 13 per cent of the population has access to electricity; this is more than 10 percentage points below the average for SSA.[10] Investment Climate Assessment data from 2007 show that electricity is cited among the top three constraints to business in Kenya. The problem worsened between 2003 and 2007 as the economy experienced a pick up in growth, hinting at increased binding constraints from an unreliable power supply (see Table 4.6). Some 85 per cent of firms in Kenya reported experiencing power cuts (World Bank, 2008). Over two-thirds of firms have generators, which are costly to obtain and operate.[11] In growth diagnostics terms, high shadow prices of electricity constraint are represented by this high proportion

Table 4.5 Costs of crime, security, bribes, and lost production are several times higher in Kenya than in other countries

	Kenya	China	India	South Africa	Senegal	Tanzania	Uganda
	(2007)	(2002)	(2006)	(2003)	(2003)	(2006)	(2006)
Production lost due to crime	3.9	0.3	0.2	0.6	1.0	1.1	1.0
Payment for security	2.9	0.8	1.3	0.9	1.5	2.3	1.4
Bribes	3.6	1.9	2.1	0.3	0.4	3.4	3.7
Production lost in transit	2.6	1.2	0.8	0.8	NA	1.6	1.2
Production lost due to power cuts	7.1	2.0	7.8	0.9	5.1	10.7	10.2
Total selected costs	20.1	6.2	12.2	3.5	NA	19.1	17.5

NA, not available.
Source: Enterprise surveys.

Table 4.6 Ratings and ranking of business constraints in Kenya (percentage of firms perceiving issues as being a major constraint): panel of firms in the manufacturing sector

	2003		2007	
	% of firms	Ranking	% of firms	Ranking
Crime, theft, and disorder	69	4	59	1
Tax rates	69	3	56	2
Electricity	47	8	55	3
Corruption	73	1	54	4
Transportation	36	12	53	5
Practices of competition in informal sector	64	5	50	6
Tax administration	52	6	50	7
Customs and trade regulations	40	11	42	8
Telecommunications	45	10	28	9
Business licensing and permits	13	16	28	10
Macroeconomic stability	50	7	26	11
Access to finance	71	2	26	12
Political instability	47	9	18	13
Access to land	23	14	16	14
Labour regulations	22	15	16	15
Inadequately educated labour force	31	13	11	16

Source: World Bank, Kenya ICA (2003, 2007).

of firms that have decided to incur costs acquiring power generators to get around the problems caused by the lack of reliable electricity services. Power disruption costs Kenyan firms approximately 7 per cent of sales. According to the World Bank (2008), these losses were among the highest in cross-country comparisons.

TRANSPORTATION

Infrastructure problems are not restricted to electricity. Transportation was quoted as a major bottleneck to business by 53 per cent of firms interviewed in the 2007 investment climate survey, with 25 per cent ranking it as one of the top three constraints (Table 4.7). As explained in Kenya's Investment Climate Assessment of 2007, over 60 per cent of manufacturing firms transport their own goods and, in 2007, more than half of them reported transportation as a major problem, up from only 37 per cent in 2003. *Doing Business* (2009) places Kenya in the bottom quintile in the area of trading across borders, with costs

Table 4.7 Ease of doing business: *Doing Business* (DB) ranking, 2009 (out of 181 economies)

Ease of...	DB 2009 rank	DB 2008 rank	Change
Doing business	82	78	–4
Starting a business	109	115	6
Dealing with construction permits	9	9	0
Employing workers	68	71	3
Registering property	119	116	–3
Getting credit	5	5	0
Protecting investors	88	84	–4
Paying taxes	158	158	0
Trading across borders	148	152	4
Enforcing contracts	107	106	–1
Closing a business	76	79	3

Source: *Doing Business* (2009).

to exports and imports being twice as large as those registered in Organization for Economic Co-operation and Development (OECD) countries, and almost three times longer on time wait to clear customs (Table 4.8).

Kenyan firms have to bear high direct and indirect costs because of the quality of the transportation infrastructure. High lead times and unreliability of transportation services are reflected in the disproportionately high number of days of inventory held by Kenyan firms, particularly in the manufacturing sector. Inland transport costs in the country are much higher than in China and India and among the highest of all comparator countries. Shipping a 40-foot container costs Kenyan firms much more than firms in all other comparator countries, except Uganda.

Kenyan companies lose 2.6 per cent of their sales to spoilage and theft during transportation. This is the highest value of all comparator countries. China, India, and South Africa lose half that amount. About 50 per cent of the transportation losses reported by Kenyan firms result from transport delays, whereas the other half are due to theft during transportation.

From an economic point of view, the size and quality of infrastructure provision affects variable as well as fixed costs. An increase in variable costs – say from transportation costs – reduces the scale of production, and also directly affects the firm's price-setting decisions. The high costs of internal transportation within Kenya appear to be neutralizing much of the country's location advantage. For example, the cost of transporting export goods from Nairobi or Kisumu to the Mombasa port is about 25–30 per cent of the total cost of transportation to Europe. Other examples are: Shanghai to Mombasa costs Ksh 5,400 per ton (distance 5000 km) whereas Mombasa to Nairobi costs Ksh 3,000 per ton (distance 500 km); corresponding costs for edible oil imports from Malaysia are almost at par (World Bank, 2008).

Table 4.8 Trading across borders, 2009 versus 2008 ranking 148/181

Trading across borders category	Kenya	SSA	OECD
Documents for export (number)	9	7.8	4.5
Time for export (days)	29	34.7	10.7
Cost to export (US$ per container)	2,055	1,878.80	1,069.10
Documents for import (number)	8	8.8	5.1
Time for import (days)	26	41.1	11.4
Cost to import (US$ per container)	2,190	2,278.70	1,132.70

Source: Doing Business (2009).

SUMMARY AND CONCLUSION OF EVIDENCE ON FACTORS BEHIND LOW SOCIAL RETURNS

The discussion above clearly demonstrates that infrastructure costs, especially resulting from the unreliability of the electricity supply and high transportation costs, are a big share of business costs in Kenya. Not only do they add to the cost of doing business, they also prolong the production process in terms of time, leading to productivity losses. As such, the lack of sufficient provision of complementary factors such as electricity and transport works to reduce the profitability of Kenyan businesses and thus acts as an impediment to private investment.

4.2.4 Does poor private appropriability explain the low private investment rate?

In this section, we explore whether the low investment rate observed in Kenya could be a result of high risks of appropriation of potential returns. Low or poor private appropriability can occur in an environment of high taxation, corruption, crime, macroeconomic risks including policy uncertainty, weak enforcement of contract and property rights, labour capital conflicts, and poor learning and co-ordination of externalities. This section examines some of these issues in turn.

AVERAGE TAX BURDEN COULD BE HIGH IN KENYA

Are taxes so high in Kenya as to discourage investment? The corporate income tax rate at 35 per cent and value added tax (VAT) at 16 per cent are comparable to those in the neighbouring countries that might compete with Kenya for domestic investment (Table 4.9). An IMF analysis in 2004 on comparative taxation in the East African Community concluded that Kenya's marginal effective tax rate (on new investment in manufacturing) is almost zero, which gives it considerable advantage over Uganda and Tanzania as a destination for investment.

Table 4.9 Comparative tax rates for residents in Kenya and comparators

	Kenya	Uganda	Tanzania	Rwanda	South Africa	Mauritius	Burundi	Zambia
Corporate tax rate (%)	30	30	30	35	28	22.5	35	35
(PAYE) top income tax rate	30	30	30	30	40	–	35	35
VAT rate	16	18	20	18	14	0	–	17.5
Excise on petrol (p)/diesel (d)	Ks 19.8/l	Ush 530/l	Tsh 200/l	Frw 116/l (p)	–	–	–	–
	10.3/l (d)			Frw 100/l (d)				
Excise duty on spirits	Ksh 250/l	–	–	70%	43%	–	–	–

Source: Kenyan authorities.

Despite objective indicators showing that the marginal tax rates in Kenya are comparable to those of its neighbours, perception surveys show that businessmen consider tax rates as burdensome. Some 56 per cent of those surveyed in the 2007 assessment indicated that tax rates were a constraint to their business. It is true that Kenya raises more than 20 per cent of GDP in tax revenues, which is almost 6–7 percentage points more than in Uganda and about 4–5 percentage points more than in Tanzania. Therefore, it is a possibility that the average tax burden in Kenya is relatively high, particularly when all the levies and fees are included. One approach to counter the negative perception of businesses about taxation would be to ensure higher efficiency – both in an allocative sense and in a value for money sense –in government spending. Businesses are less likely to resent taxation when they can see the benefits of taxes accruing in the form of efficient public goods and services, particularly those related to infrastructure.

CORRUPTION HAS HINDERED GROWTH IN THE PAST AND CONTINUES TO BE A PROBLEM

Corruption was ranked as one of the top obstacles to doing business in the 2007 assessment (World Bank, 2008), although its ranking had improved somewhat since the 2003 survey. Nearly 70 per cent of firms that reported corruption as a binding constraint ranked it as a top constraint (Figure 4.7). Three-quarters of firms reported having to make informal payments to 'get things done'. This costs Kenyan firms approximately 4 per cent of annual sales. Firms in comparator countries face a lower level of informal payments, with firms in China, India, and South Africa paying less than half that amount.

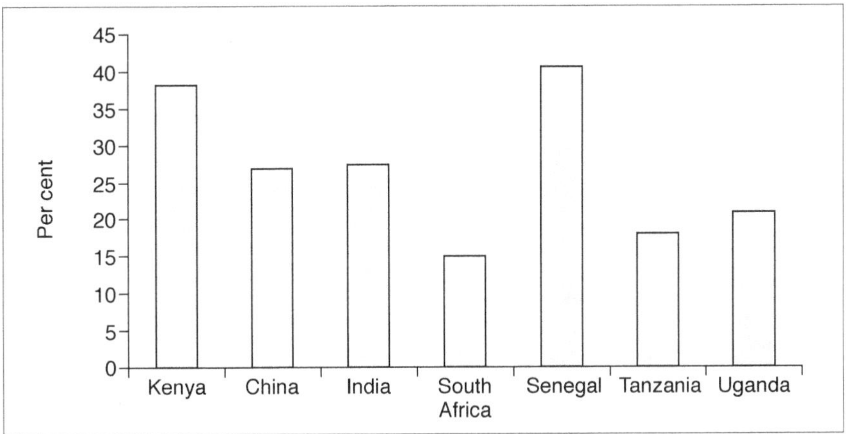

Figure 4.7 Firms perceiving corruption as a severe or major constraint: international comparison (%).
Source: ICA Survey.

The results of the 2007 survey are confirmed by other data sources. Both the Transparency International Corruption Perception Index and the World Bank's Governance Indicators show an improvement in Kenya's ranking over the last few years. Nevertheless, Kenya's corruption rating remains one of the worst among all comparator countries.

CRIME AND PRIVATE APPROPRIABILITY ARE DETERRENTS TOO

Crime and theft were quoted as the single most important obstacle to doing business in Kenya; in 2007, 59 per cent of Kenyan firms rated crime as a major constraint. This is much higher than in all comparator countries; China and India enjoy a much lower level of crime with 20 per cent and 9 per cent of firms complaining about it respectively (Figure 4.8). Kenyan firms reported having suffered losses from crime averaging almost 4 per cent of annual sales. Such costs seem to be significantly higher than costs experienced by firms in all other comparator countries, including South Africa, where losses were less than 1 per cent. Similarly, in China and India, objective cost data show a much lower incidence of crime on sales (one-tenth of the cost suffered by Kenyan firms).

Shadow costs from crime-related problems can be measured by the payments made by firms on security measures. About three-quarters of firms incurred extra costs to pay for security services (equipment, personnel, or professional security services) or to extend protection payments to organized crime. Kenyan firms spend much more on crime prevention than comparator countries. In addition to the costs of security, firms in Kenya also make informal payments to organized crime operators to prevent thefts and arson. Adding

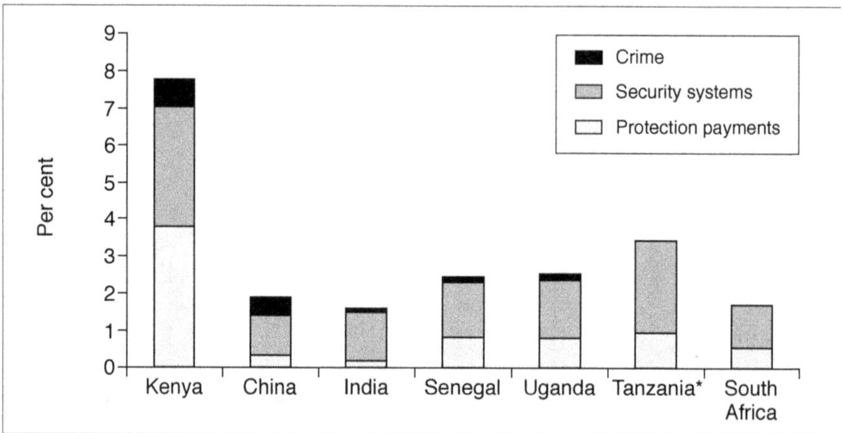

Figure 4.8 Total costs of crime, international comparison (%).
*Data on organized crime not available.
Source: ICA Survey.

the direct costs from criminal acts (theft and arson) to the costs of security services (both legal and illegal) yields a total value equivalent of over 8 per cent of sales from firms interviewed in 2007, much higher than in the comparator countries of SSA, China, and India (World Bank, 2008).

MACROECONOMIC RISKS – INSTABILITY AND POLITICAL UNCERTAINTY

Macroeconomic instability or expectations of instability can discourage investment. Collier and Patillo (2000) argue that the rate of return in Africa is one-third below that of anywhere else because of higher risks related to political instability, price volatility, policy reversals, and an uncertain macroeconomic environment. Historically, Kenya has suffered from macroeconomic instability, particularly during the period from 1992 to 1994 when it built up external arrears and was hit by the Goldenberg scandal. However, the onset of growth after 2002 coincided with improved macroeconomic outcomes evident in a significant decline in interest rates. We argue below that, currently, macroeconomic instability may not be a serious deterrent to investment. At the same time, political uncertainty is likely to continue to provide disincentives to investors.

Bandiera *et al.* (2008) argue that the positive macroeconomic outcomes after 2002 were driven by two main factors: (i) the lagged effects of price, trade, exchange rate, and interest rate liberalization; and (ii) macroeconomic stability based on reduced indebtedness. The first half of the 1990s was the period when all the major structural reforms initiated in the previous decade were concluded.[12] However, the reforms were accompanied by some policy actions that increased uncertainty. In 1992, the money supply was inflated by 80 per cent to finance elections. This was followed by an export incentive scandal that cost the treasury an estimated US$400 million.

After 1993, macroeconomic outcomes reflect a transition to cautious macroeconomic management, except closer to the 1997 elections. Monetary policy has generally been tight, resulting in falling and steady inflation, a buildup of reserves, and a steadily (market-determined) depreciating exchange rate. Between 1995 and 1997, heavy domestic borrowing resulted in high interest rates, but fiscal discipline has been generally tight – particularly after 1997.

Starting in 2003/04, there was a perceptible change for the better in Kenya's macroeconomic outcomes. The data suggest a 'break point' that year, manifested in a large decline in domestic real interest rates, a rise in growth, and a marked improvement in government debt dynamics. Over the past three years, domestic real interest rates have dropped to levels of 1.5–3 per cent compared with a range of 9–18 per cent over the preceding seven years (*ex post* real interest rates on government domestic debt). This drop is indicative of a drop in the country risk premium.

The view that emerges from the above discussion is that, although macroeconomic instability might well have discouraged investment or hurt productivity in the first half of the 1990s, in the past decade, macroeconomic outcomes have been indicative of improving economic policies. It also appears that the private sector has been developing increased confidence in the government's economic management.

At the same time, political risk, which measures uncertainty associated with policy decisions, continues to remain a major disincentive to investment in Kenya. The World Bank (2008) argues that part of the reason for the shift in Kenya's economic outcomes after 2002 was the peaceful change in political leadership. The change in leadership was seen by economic agents as an event that signalled that economic policies thenceforth were unlikely to change drastically with political leadership. The World Bank report noted that:

> The reduction in political risk that accompanied the change in political leadership in 2002 fuelled an improvement in sovereign creditworthiness and the private investment climate, thus permitting Kenya to begin reaping the benefits of political and economic reforms that date back to at least 1986. Improved sovereign creditworthiness has resulted in a reduction in country risk that showed up in a fall of real interest rates and greater willingness of firms to invest without concerns about political interference.

However, the 2007 elections brought policy uncertainty resulting from political instability to the fore again. Moreover, the source of political instability in 2007 appears to be deeper. It appears to be rooted in inequalities in income and wealth, which, in turn, appear to coincide with regional and ethnic disparities. It appears that policy uncertainty resulting from Kenya's regional inequalities within the country and ethnic fragmentation would provide a disincentive to private investors for quite some time to come.

SUMMARY AND CONCLUSION OF EVIDENCE ON PRIVATE APPROPRIABILITY OF RETURNS

The evidence produced in this section strongly suggests that Kenya has appropriability issues. The average tax burden could be high, particularly when seen against the level and quality of public services; corruption and crime appear to add significantly to the cost of businesses and also hurt their productivity; and although macroeconomic risk has abated, political risk continues to remain high. The high level of efforts made, and costs incurred by private agents, to relieve these constraints are an indication of the shadow price of these constraints.

4.3 Conclusions

This chapter organized the discussion on constraints to private investment, hence growth, in Kenya using the growth diagnostics framework of HRV. The discussion drew upon various types of evidence such as market outcomes, perceptions surveys, and behaviour of private agents to develop a sense of the extent to which a constraint is binding. It concluded that financing constraints such as the cost of capital, access to finance, or the relatively low saving rate do not appear to have been binding in the recent past. Thus, it is expected that they will not bind growth acceleration in the near future. At the same time, the level and quality of infrastructure services and various constraints to private appropriability appear to be holding back private investment. The appropriability constraints refer to corruption, crime, and political instability. Along with infrastructure services, they need to receive the urgent attention of policy-makers.

Notes

1 Following Collier and O'Connell (2006) regional/group average growth rates have been obtained by weighting country growth rates by their share in the overall regional/group population.
2 Following the Collier and O'Connell (2006) idea of 'opportunities'.
3 Theoretically, this is a feasible statement. If Kenya grows at a sustained rate of 10 per cent per year (7.5 per cent in per capita terms), it will reach a lower middle-income status around 2017. According to the World Bank Atlas Method, countries with a per capita income under US$935 are classified as low income. Lower income countries have a per capita income between US$935 and US$3,705. Upper middle-income countries have a per capita income between US$3,705 and US$11,455. Above the latter figure are high-income countries. The average income of economies classified as lower middle income was US$1,331 in 2008. Growing at 10 per cent per year, Kenya would reach this income by 2023. And it would reach the East Asian and Pacific 2008's income level (US$1,759) by 2027.
4 Deeper determinants refer to geography (see Collier and O'Connell, 2006), institutions (see Rodrik *et al.* 2002), and the extent of a country's integration into the global economy.
5 σ is a measure of the intertemporal elasticity in consumption, which affects how households allocate resources over time in order to maximize welfare.
6 Actually, a *decision tree* does not constitute a proper representation of how constraints determine low levels of private investment and entrepreneurship, in that moving down one branch does not exclude all others from consideration. Branches cross each other, as there may exist a complex interaction between different constraints. In other words, the economic problems that may be restraining investment cannot be classified in a simplistic way in the categories suggested by HRV (see Hausmann *et al.*, 2008). However, the *tree* does help to organize one's ideas when thinking.
7 The growth diagnostic approach supports relaxing the most binding constraint rather than attempting to relax several constraints at the same time. There is no doubt that reform efforts need to be reasonably focused because public resources, managerial capacity, and political will are scarce. From a theoretical viewpoint, there is merit in relaxing constraints that have the highest shadow price in order to get maximum value for reform. Also, theoretical possibilities exist for one set of pol-

icy reforms to run counter to another in a second-best world. However, we believe that an approach that aims to relax several constraints simultaneously has practical merit. In the real world, shadow prices of constraints are difficult to estimate. Also, welfare-reducing interactions between policy reforms are difficult to predict *ex ante*. And importantly, transformational changes such as skills development and institutional development take time to be put in place and therefore need to be pursued in parallel with other shorter term growth-accelerating measures.

8 As already noted, prior to this period, since around the mid-1970s, the ratio of gross investment to GDP was on a declining trend, even as real lending rates were relatively flat and close to zero. This period coincided with price controls, financial repression in which interest lending and savings rates were fixed by the authorities, directed credit to selected priority sectors of the economy such as agriculture and manufacturing, the trade regime supported huge tariff walls to protect domestic industry, i.e. import substitution strategy, and the exchange rate and the capital account were controlled. Despite these measures, average gross investment to GDP declined. This behaviour is consistent with a conclusion that, until the early 1990s, the equilibrium level of investment was determined by a low level (actually shrinking) of investment demand and a relatively stable and flat supply schedule mostly driven by government policy.

9 As explained by Mwega and Ndung'u (2004): 'There was a drought in 1991/92, the oil price increased due to the Gulf War, compounded by the aid embargo of 1991–1993 and "ethnic clashes" in 1992. These exogenous shocks were accompanied by an increase in the budget deficit and money supply with the rate of inflation rising rapidly alongside large exchange rate depreciations, as the foreign exchange market was liberalized in the context of large macroeconomic imbalances in the run-up to the 1992 elections'.

10 World Bank (2010). This study constitutes part of the Africa Infrastructure Country Diagnostic (AICD), a project designed to expand the world's knowledge of physical infrastructure in Africa. The AICD will provide a baseline against which future improvements in infrastructure services can be measured, making it possible to monitor the results achieved from donor support.

11 According to the Investment Climate Assessment survey of 2007 (World Bank, 2008), Kenyan firms experienced approximately eight power cuts per month in 2007, each lasting approximately 4.5 hours. As a result, firms in Kenya lost on average the equivalent of approximately four days of production a month due to power cuts. Given the dimensions of this problem, two out of three firms in Kenya own or share a generator and use it for 16 per cent of their electricity needs.

12 For example, the tariff structure was further simplified in 1994, import licensing was largely removed by 1991, foreign exchange controls were abolished in 1993, floating exchange rate mechanisms were adopted in 1994, and the authority of the Central Bank of Kenya was enhanced in 1997.

References

Acemoglu, D., S. Johnson and J. Robinson, 2001, 'The Colonial Origins of Comparative Development: An Empirical Investigation', *American Economic Review*, July 2001.

Africa Private Sector Group and Kenya Institute for Public Policy Research and analysis (KIPPRA), 2004, *Investment Climate Assessment. Enhancing the Competitiveness of Kenya's Manufacturing Sector: The Role of the Investment Climate.* Africa Regional Program on Enterprise Development.

Appleton, S., A. Bigsten and D. Manda, 1999, 'Educational Expansion and Economic Decline: Returns to Education in Kenya, 1978–1995'. The Centre for the Study of African Economies Working Paper 90.

Azam, J.-P. and C. Daubrée, 1997, *Bypassing the State : Economic Growth in Kenya, 1964–90.* Paris, London: Development Centre of the Organization for Economic Co-operation and Development.

Bandiera, L., P. Kumar and B. Pinto, 2008, 'Kenya's Quest for Growth: Stabilization and Reforms – But Political Stability?' World Bank Policy Research Working Paper WPS 4685.

Barro, R. and J.-W. Lee, 2000, *International Data on Educational Attainment: Updates and Implications.* CID Working Paper 42. Harvard University: Center for International Development.

Bosworth, B. and S. Collins, 2003, 'The Empirics of Growth: An Update'. Brookings Papers on Economic Activity. Brookings Institution.

Calvo, S., 2005, 'Growth Diagnostics and the Binding Constraints to Growth', in 'Bolivia Country Economic Memorandum: Policies to Improve Growth and Employment'. PREM Unit, LACR.

Collier, P. and S. O'Connell, 2006, *Opportunities and Choices.* Synthesis volume, Chapter 2. African Economic Research Consortium's project: Explaining African Economic Growth (forthcoming).

Collier, P. and C. Pattillo, 2000, *Investment and Risk in Africa.* Basingstoke: Macmillan; and New York: St Martin's Press.

Doing Business, 2009, Database available at http://www.doingbusiness.org/CustomQuery/.

Easterly, W. and R. Levine, 1995, *Africa's Growth Tragedy. A Retrospective, 1960–1989.* The World Bank, Policy Research Department. Macroeconomics and Growth Division, and Finance and Private Sector Development Division.

Easterly, W. and R. Levine, 1997, *Africa's Growth Tragedy. Policies and Ethnic Divisions.* The World Bank.

Gallup, J., J. Sachs and A. Mellinger, 1999, 'Geography and Economic Development'. Harvard University, Center for International Development. Working Paper No. 1.

Hausmann, R. and B. King, 2006, 'Structural Transformation and Patterns of Comparative Advantage in the Product Space'. CID Working Paper No. 128. Center for International Development at the Kennedy School of Government, Harvard University.

Hausmann, R. and D. Rodrik, 2006, 'Industrial Policy as Predicament'. Draft. Center for International Development at the Kennedy School of Government, Harvard University.

Hausmann, R., L. Pritchett and D. Rodrik, 2004, 'Growth Accelerations'. Working Paper 10566. Harvard University, John F. Kennedy School of Government.

Hausmann, R., D. Rodrik and A. Velasco, 2005a, 'Growth Diagnostics'. Harvard University, John F. Kennedy School of Government.

Hausmann, R., J. Hwang and D. Rodrik, 2005b, 'What You Export Matters'. Working Paper 11905. NBER.

Hausmann, R., B. Klinger and R. Wagner, 2008, 'Doing Growth Diagnostics in Practice: A "Mindbook"'. CID Working Paper No. 177. Harvard University.

Heston, A., R. Summers and B. Atten, 2002, *Penn World Table Version 6.1*. Center for International Comparisons at the University of Pennsylvania.

Ianchovichina, E. and P. Kacker, 2005, 'Growth Trends in the Developing World. Country Forecasts and Determinants'. World Bank PREM, Policy Research Working Paper No. 3775.

International Monetary Fund (IMF), 2010, 'Kenya: Staff Report for the 2009 Article IV Consultation'. IMF Country Report No. 10/26.

Kaufmann, D., A. Kraay and M. Mastruzzi, 2005, *Governance Matters IV: Governance Indicators for 1996–2004*. World Bank.

King, B. and D. Lederman, 2004, 'Discovery and Development: An Empirical Exploration of "New" Products'. World Bank Policy Research Working Paper 3450.

Loayza, N., P. Fajnzylber and C. Calderon, 2004, 'Economic Growth in Latin America and the Caribbean: Stylized Facts, Explanations and Forecasts'. World Bank Study, World Bank and Central Bank of Chile Working Paper No. 265.

Manda, D., G. Mwabu and M. Kimenyi, 2004, 'Human Capital Externalities and Private Returns to Education in Kenya'. University of Connecticut, Department of Economics Working Paper 2004-08.

Mogaka, H., S. Gichere, R. Davis and R. Hirji, 2006, 'Climate Variability and Water Resources Degradation in Kenya: Improving Water Resources Development and Management'. World Bank Working Paper No. 69.

Mwega, F. and N. Ndung'u, 2004, 'Explaining African Economic Growth Performance: The Case of Kenya'. Working Paper No. 3. African Economic Research Consortium.

Ndulu, B. and S. O'Connell, 2000, 'Africa's Growth Experience: A Focus on Sources of Growth'. World Bank. Paper presented at AERC Growth Project Conference, Nairobi, December 1999.

Ndulu, B. J., L. Chakraborti, L. Lijane, V. Ramachandran and J. Wolgin, 2006, *Challenges of African Growth: Opportunities, Constraints and Strategic Directions*. World Bank.

Ng, F. and A. Yeats, 2005, 'Kenya: Exports Prospects and Problems'. Africa Region. Working Paper Series No. 90.

Patillo, C., S. Gupta and K. Carey, 2005, 'Sustaining Growth Accelerations and Pro-Poor Growth in Africa'. Working Paper WP/05/195. International Monetary Fund.

Pritchett, L., 1998, 'Patterns of Economic Growth: Hills, Plateaus, Mountains and Plains'. World Bank Policy Research Working Paper 1947.

Psacharopoulos, G. and H. Patrinos, 2002, 'Returns to Investment in Education. A Further Update'. Policy Research Working Paper 2881. The World Bank.

Rodrik, D., 2004a, *Rethinking Growth Policies in the Developing World*. Harvard University, Kennedy School of Government.

Rodrik, D., 2004b, *Growth Strategies*. Harvard University, Kennedy School of Government.

Rodrik, D., A. Subramanian and F. Trebbi, 2002, *Institutions Rule: The Primacy of Institutions over Geography and Integration in Economic Development*. Harvard University and International Monetary Fund.

Saxegaard, M., 2006, 'Excess Liquidity and Effectiveness of Monetary Policy: Evidence from Sub-Saharan Africa', IMF Working Paper WP/06/115.

Söderbom, M., 2001, 'Constraints and Opportunities in Kenyan Manufacturing: Report on the Kenyan Manufacturing Enterprise Survey 2000'. Available from http://www.economics.ox.ac.uk/CSAEadmin/reports/main.html.

Svensson, J., 2005, 'Eight Questions About Corruption', *Journal of Economic Perspectives*, 19 (3), 19–42.

World Bank, 2003, 'Kenya: A Policy Agenda to Restore Growth'. Report No. 25840-KE. PREM 2. Country Department AFC05, Africa Region.

World Bank, 2004, 'Kenya Investment Climate Assessment: Enhancing the Competitiveness of Kenya's Manufacturing Sector: The Role of the Investment Climate'. RPED Africa Private Sector Group.

World Bank, 2006, 'Searching for the Binding Constraints to Growth in Morocco', in *Kingdom of Morocco. Country Economic Memorandum. Fostering Higher Growth and Employment with Productive Diversification and Competitiveness*. Volume II: Background Studies. PREM–MENA.

World Bank, 2008, *Kenya Investment Climate Assessment*, RPED Africa Finance and Private Sector Group.

World Bank, 2010, *Africa's Infrastructure: A Time for Transformation*. Foster, V. and C. Briceño-Garmendia (eds). The International Bank for Reconstruction and Development/The World Bank.

II

The Macroeconomic Environment

5

Fiscal Policy in Kenya: Looking Towards the Medium to Long Term

Kamau Thugge, Peter S. Heller, and Jane Kiringai

5.1 Introduction

Kenya is in many respects now at an important juncture, with its fiscal policy influencing the pace at which the economy will grow and its capacity to deal with the key challenges that will arise over the next several decades. Fiscal policy will not only shape whether overall macroeconomic policies are sustainable in a low-inflation context, but also whether the preconditions for a transition to a high-growth path are met and whether Kenya's substantial income, asset, and regional inequalities as well as high poverty rate are fundamentally addressed. Not only will fiscal discipline be required, but also a careful balancing among these alternative policy objectives and an awareness of the potential risks inherent in the domestic and external policy environment, particularly in the wake of the current global recession.

This chapter will examine whether Kenya's medium-term fiscal policy strategy is responsive to the challenges Kenya is likely to face in the next two decades and the scope of its policy goals for this period. Section 5.2 will briefly identify both the domestic policy challenges that Kenya's fiscal policy-makers must address in the coming years as well as the different potential external policy environments within which these policies must be formulated. Section 5.3 reviews the Government of Kenya's (GOK) fiscal policy strategy, as broadly embodied in its recently issued long-run perspective (*Vision 2030*), but more concretely in the Medium-Term Plan for 2008/09–2012/13 and the Medium-

Term Budget Strategy Paper (MTBSP) for 2009/10–2011/12. In particular, it will examine the economic and institutional assumptions underlying this strategy; the policy choices made in terms of the balance between the roles of the public and private sectors; the choice among alternative public spending priorities; the way in which possible downside risks are addressed; the approach to financing fiscal initiatives; and the sustainability of the fiscal and debt strategy. Section 5.4 will then assess whether the GOK's chosen policy strategies appear both responsive to the long-term policy challenges identified in Section 5.2 and robust to the downside risks in the external economic environment.

5.2 Medium- to long-run challenges

In *Vision 2030,* Kenya aspires to achieve middle-income status by 2030 through the realization of a 10 per cent per annum real growth rate for the period 2012–30. This is a highly ambitious objective, although not an unreasonable aspiration, given the importance of Kenya to the regional economy of East Africa and the many assets that Kenya possesses in terms of its human capital and its industrial, service, and tourism potential. But achieving this goal will require that Kenya successfully pursues disciplined and ambitious policies that will confront the many domestic and external policy challenges it now faces. It will also require a bit of luck and a bit of skill by Kenyan policymakers in adapting to the uncertain global economic policy environment that will undoubtedly emerge in the next two decades.

Fiscal policy will need to be finely balanced if Kenya is to achieve the *Vision 2030* objectives. It must facilitate rapid growth – through both the provision of needed infrastructure and human capital – while still being responsive to both the demands of the population for basic public services and the potential downside risks that may emerge. Yet fiscal policy must also be sustainable. Fiscal space will be precious if the various expenditure objectives are to be met without compromising macroeconomic stability or raising doubts about Kenya's solvency. If growth proves less than anticipated – as occurred in 2008 and as expected in 2009 – the needed fiscal space may prove inadequate to finance the required government outlays. Under these circumstances, unrestrained recourse to additional borrowing could jeopardize Kenya's solvency and crowd out its private sector.

5.2.1 Domestic policy challenges to which fiscal policy should respond

There are several important obstacles that could impede Kenya's progress towards achieving the high growth rate targeted until 2030. First, after years of neglect, Kenya has only recently begun to address the inadequacy of its infrastructure for the realization of a modern, twenty-first-century economy. Deficiencies exist in terms of Kenya's port facilities, its trunk and secondary roads, its railway system, its energy plant, and in the availability of clean water and sanitation facilities. While telecommunications has been the bright light of the last several years, there is still much to be done to make the system fully accessible, and the proposed undersea fibre-optic cable, the East Africa Marine System, should help in this regard. *Vision 2030*'s emphasis on rebuilding and creating a productive infrastructure is rightly supported by international observers (e.g. in the International Monetary Fund (IMF)'s 2009 staff report) and appears responsive to this challenge.[1] But creating this infrastructure will be costly and could easily outstrip the domestic financial capacity of the government if it were to go it alone, justifying the government's interest in seeking public–private partnerships as well as external financial support.

Second, while Kenya is blessed with a relatively high-quality and deep base of human capital, it has yet to find ways to deploy it more efficiently. Among African countries, Kenya has always been known for the high aspirations of its population for education and the drive of its citizens for self-betterment. But the productivity of Kenya's educational system has long been a source of concern, and the continuing weaknesses in the health system have meant that infant and mortality rates are still too high, that malaria still poses a heavy health burden, and that the AIDS epidemic has cost Kenya significant losses among its most productive citizens.[2] The success of many Asian countries in realizing high growth rates when they were at Kenya's stage in the demographic transition derived from their ability to productively employ the rising share of the working-age population. Strengthening the quality and exploiting the productive use of Kenya's human capital, particularly looking forward, must thus be a high policy priority.

Third, governance concerns remain an obstacle to Kenya fully exploiting its growth potential through foreign investment inflows. Although the World Bank's 'Doing Business Indicators' suggest some improvements in creating the conditions for a receptive foreign investment climate (with Kenya ranking among the world's top ten reformers in 2006/07), Kenya still ranks only eighty-second on this index out of 181 countries, and ranks 147 out of 180 countries in terms of Transparency International's index of perceptions of corruption for 2008.[3] Prioritizing and effectively carrying out the necessary institutional reforms, while not requiring substantial fiscal resources, may still prove costly and difficult in political economy terms. More important, it may play a critical role in determining whether Kenya can meet its ambitious investment goals in infrastructure, given that they are to be primarily financed from private sources through public–private partnerships.

Fourth, to achieve its target growth, Kenya will need not only to raise its pace of investment significantly (from an average of 19 per cent of gross domestic product (GDP) in 2005/06–2007/08 to over 30 per cent by 2012/13), but also to maintain the relatively low incremental capital output ratio (ICOR) of about 3 that it has experienced over the last few years. The latter may prove difficult. Among low- and low/middle-income countries, an ICOR of about 4 seems the norm (see World Bank, 2008). For the few non-oil-based countries in the world that have experienced growth rates as high as 10 per cent for a sustained period, investment rates have been in the range of 40 per cent of GDP plus (e.g. China), reflecting a loss of efficiency in capital investment (and thus a higher ICOR).

For Kenya to realize more efficiency from its investments, it must demonstrate a concomitant capacity to mobilize human capital resources effectively (e.g. rectifying both the under- and overstaffing of different public service activities), efficiency in the utilization of capital inputs, adequate attention to routine and periodic maintenance of existing infrastructure, and a focus on investments that are of particularly high return (the last influencing the appropriate structure of Kenya's public and private investment programme). Linked to these issues is the low absorptive and implementation capacity in the key infrastructure line ministries, particularly for foreign-financed projects. A key challenge that will determine whether the desired change in the composition of expenditure materializes will be the actual implementation rate of the development budget. In the past, actual expenditures have fallen well short of budget estimates and, in particular, absorption of donor development assistance has been very low – usually below 50 per cent of budgeted amounts. Increasing the implementation capacity of the infrastructure ministries, and especially that of the Ministry of Roads and Public Works, will therefore be critical.

Fifth, generating the required financing for a higher level of investment will be a further challenge. A sound fiscal policy will constrain how much can be provided directly from the budget, leading to the acknowledged need to rely on the private sector, domestic and external, for the remaining financing. The modalities by which Kenya provides incentives and deals with the risks associated with public–private partnerships, and improves governance, will determine the extent of foreign capital participation in Kenya's investment programme.

Sixth, despite the progress made in reducing poverty incidence from 57 per cent in 2002 to 46 per cent in 2006 (MTBSP, para. 14), Kenya still faces high income and asset inequality as well as significant regional inequality in incomes and assets. Whereas rapid growth over the next two decades would do much to reduce absolute poverty levels, the number of absolute poor will still remain substantial. Together with continued high inequality, this would constitute a significant drag, in political economy terms, on Kenya's ability to obtain popular support for an ambitious resource mobilization and savings effort. Certainly, unless addressed, income inequality will constrain growth in the country, dampen the scope for poverty reduction, and create an environment for social and political unrest.

Seventh, and linked to the previous point, current fiscal decentralization efforts to address regional inequality through the use of a devolved funds mechanism are subject to potential vulnerabilities. In principle, through community-based projects, such an approach can have a positive impact on grassroots[4] support. However, slippages in governance and accountability, efficiency, or effectiveness in the use of devolved funds could undermine their potential impact, with political pressures engendering spending programmes that would not normally meet benefit–cost criteria or address the existing regional maldistribution of resources. In the medium term, three potential threats to the effectiveness of a devolved funds approach require attention. First are the poverty-weighted allocation criteria, which effectively incentivize constituencies to be ranked poor in order to qualify for a higher share of the devolved resources. Second, the provision of such 'free' budgetary resources may dampen revenue generation efforts at the local level. Third, the disconnect between community-based projects and the provision for operations and maintenance within the central budget can limit efficiency and effectiveness in the use of these funds.[5]

All of the above factors might be considered as relevant in formulating current budgetary policies. But Kenya also confronts other *future* developments that can easily undermine the long-term capacity of the economy to sustain rapid growth. These include:

- *The rapid rate of urbanization*: By 2025, Nairobi and Mombasa will have to invest in urban infrastructure (e.g. housing, water, sewage, transport, schools, and health facilities) to accommodate a virtual doubling of their populations.[6] The size of other urban centres will more than double by 2025 (from 3.8 million to 9.3 million).[7] Overall, the urban population is projected to triple to 21–22 million. Such urban infrastructure investments are likely to be of a lower overall productivity (thus implying a higher ICOR), further constraining the prospects for achieving the high efficiency level required to realize a 10 per cent annual growth rate.
- *The continued high overall population growth rate*: Kenya's fertility rate of 5 is high. The population aged 5–14 – the prospective primary and secondary school age groups – is anticipated to rise during the period 2005–30 by at least 60 per cent (more than 5.2 million children). This highlights both the prospective increase that will be needed in spending on Kenya's primary and secondary school system and the substantial expansion that is likely to be needed for tertiary education facilities. The latter will be particularly costly, and will put enormous pressure on the education budget (with one tertiary student costing the equivalent of forty primary students). Without policies that will encourage a reduced fertility rate, Kenya's capacity to

create fiscal space by shifting the composition of government expenditure towards growth-enhancing investments will be severely limited.

- *The pressures for job creation arising from population growth*: In the next six years, Kenya's education system will produce at least 14 million new school leavers seeking jobs. While the public sector cannot be responsible for their employment, government expenditure policies will need to be sensitive to the job creation possibilities associated with the realization of the government's expenditure programme. This burgeoning employment challenge also highlights the importance associated with a successful transition to a high-growth policy framework, as this will be the key to meeting the continuing pressure for job creation over the medium to long term.
- *Cost pressures in the public sector*: As with most middle-income and industrial economies, rapid productive growth in the economy will typically outpace productivity growth in the government sector. As wages in the public sector respond to market wage developments in the private sector, this will create cost-push pressures on public service delivery (particularly in the social sectors) (the so-called 'Baumol effect'), pushing up the recurrent cost budget and generating further need for a higher revenue share.
- *The looming costs of climate change*: Recent World Bank reports suggest that Kenya is among the countries most at risk from an increased frequency and intensity of drought conditions. Addressing the potential deleterious effects on agricultural productivity will require a combination of intensified investment in water-control systems that promote enhanced efficiency in the use of water resources; a further shift in the role of non-agricultural outputs (and thus a capacity to become competitive in earning the foreign exchange required for a higher level of food imports); and new R&D efforts at promoting agricultural techniques robust to drought and uncertain precipitation conditions.

  Given the importance of Mombasa as Kenya's principal port, the probability of a rise in sea level raises the question of when it will become necessary for Kenya to undertake the investments required to cope with the potential longer term damage to Mombasa and what alternative approaches might be needed to ensure a continued viable port capacity.

  Less of a challenge and more of an opportunity is the possibility that Kenya might be able to exploit its comparative advantage with respect to solar and geothermal energy generation, and earn additional export and fiscal revenues from selling carbon credits to other high-emission countries.
- *The budgetary risks associated with recognized contingent liabilities*: The most obvious include those associated with the pay-as-you-go budgetary funding of civil service pensions; the potential for the National Social Security Fund (NSSF) to be relatively unfunded; and the possibility of losses associated

with the parastatal sector. The anticipated effort by the government to seek public–private partnerships in a number of infrastructure projects carries with it the potential for additional contingent liabilities.

5.2.2 External policy challenges

Kenya's ability to achieve its *Vision 2030* objectives is not wholly subject to its own making. The global financial crisis that commenced in 2008 has adversely affected Kenya, and highlighted the importance of external factors in influencing the growth of an economy. Kenya is vitally integrated within the global economy, being dependent on external commodity markets for its exports and critical energy imports, sensitive to the state of global tourism markets, significantly reliant on remittances, a recipient of aid flows, and ambitious in its pursuit of both direct foreign investment flows and possible external credits. In geopolitical terms, it has already experienced terrorist incidents and is a vital transport hub for many important countries in Central Africa. But of course the future is uncertain, particularly if one is considering policy options looking out more than twenty years. There is, thus, an important argument for seeking a policy programme that is robust to potential downside risks and the possibility of very different external environments.

One approach to exploring the robustness of the *Vision 2030* fiscal strategy is to examine its viability in the context of alternative scenarios of the future. In 2005, the World Bank undertook just such an exercise to consider alternative scenarios for how the global economy might evolve to 2020. Each of the three scenarios elaborated was meant to constitute 'relevant, compelling, plausible, and logically consistent', but importantly, divergent stories of what the global economy might look like in 2020. As emphasized by the Bank, 'no single scenario will ever come true in its entirety, but if it is to be a valuable stone against which to sharpen one's strategy, one must believe it just might!'. Box 5.1 provides a brief summary of these three different worlds, and Section 5.4 will examine more concretely the robustness of *Vision 2030* in the context of these scenarios. At this point, what is important to emphasize are the key external policy factors to which the success of *Vision 2030* might prove sensitive, and the way in which these scenarios highlight potential issues to which Kenyan policy-makers might need to be responsive.

Among the key factors that could affect Kenya's prospects, the following appear most relevant:

- *Robustness of global growth*: Kenya's capacity for mobilizing the fiscal resources required to implement its public investment programme (and equally the prospect for the private sector also to achieve the targeted growth in its investment share) will be strongly influenced by the pace and structure of global growth. Given its dependence on external commodity

Box 5.1 Alternative scenarios for the world of 2020

The following provides a brief summary of how these different worlds will appear, with our focus principally on the character of the alternative potential external economic environments facing Kenya.

Affluence, Ltd (AL)

Years of rapid, US-centred, economic growth will nearly double world GDP, an annual increase of more than 4 per cent. States have shifted their focus from guaranteeing outcomes to providing opportunities. Rapid innovation and new technologies enable continuous improvements in productivity, which global corporations spread around the world as they expand. But economic success is not universal. Forty less competitive countries have been left behind because of geographical isolation, poor governance, small market size, or lack of strategic relevance. For most major economies, however, the USA has guaranteed political stability and open trade conditions that have encouraged the creation of massive amounts of wealth.

Globalization Unwinding (GU)

Up until 2020, economic growth has been slow worldwide, averaging less than 2 per cent for more than a decade. Weaker states have collapsed, as economic pressure translates into domestic unrest, while other state governments have resorted to authoritarianism or populism in order to stay in power. Costs of military interventions, energy price volatility, and years of deficits brought a sharp contraction in the US economy, and the consequent dollar crisis triggered a global economic downturn. Europe and Japan lacked the dynamism to lead the world out of recession, while the growth engines of China, India, Korea, and other 'emerging economies' all sputtered, as did those of Russia and Latin America. Most developing countries have proven unable to mitigate the worst effects of the downturn. A deep-seated cynicism about the value of free markets prevails in the world, and economic decisions are generally focused on short-term returns. Protectionism grew rapidly following the downturn, and the path to recovery looks difficult.

Competing Horizons (CH)

Large emerging markets of China, India, Brazil, Indonesia, and much of Southeast Asia have sustained rapid long-term growth – particularly in comparison with older industrialized economies – and a second wave of developing countries has joined their ranks. The developing world accounted for almost two-thirds of global GDP growth between 2005 and 2020. Regional economic powers have started to contest US primacy in their regions and in global forums. Poles of cutting-edge R&D have emerged, with growing numbers of firms from these high-growth countries rivalling the multinational companies from the USA, Europe, and Japan. Many other developing countries have grown rapidly following improved policies and governance and benefiting from rising volumes of global trade. However, rising tensions between Old World and New World powers seem inevitable in the medium term. Despite strong networks of trade and continued rising demand for raw materials and basic commodities, growth in parts of the developing world – particularly in parts of Africa – remains low. In addition, the environmental costs of broad-based growth are significant: accelerating environmental degradation and severe resource constraints for water, strategic minerals, and energy are the order of the day.

Source: World Bank, 2006, *Rehearsing for the Future: the World and Development in 2020*, World Bank, Washington, DC (www.worldbank.org/2020).

and tourism services, a slower global growth scenario (such as in the GU scenario in Box 5.1) would probably be reflected in slower Kenyan growth, lower fiscal revenues, and the need for a smaller budgetary envelope. How would the budget be prioritized in such circumstances? Would the same infrastructure and human capital investment priorities be relevant under a lower global growth scenario? Certainly, with the pace of population and urban growth (not to mention climate change) *not* affected by external factors, the pressure would be to cut back on precisely those investments most likely to generate additional growth and employment!

Moreover, if global growth were to be dominated by a higher share derived from emerging markets, would this adversely affect Kenya (perhaps through reduced tourism from industrial countries)? Would reduced dynamism in the US and European economies imply a lower level of concessional financing, or would Kenya be able to obtain such assistance from alternative sources (e.g. China and India)? With changes in the pace or sources of global growth, would Kenya still be able to realize the currently anticipated level of direct foreign investment flows? Would these derive from different sources and, if so, would they be directed to the same sectors?

- *Scale of security threats*: The alternative scenarios highlight the potential for different degrees of ethnic, terrorist, and regional security tensions.

Kenya may thus need to be prepared for the possibility of a higher level of security-related military outlays than presently envisaged under *Vision 2030*. Depending on the extent of external financial support to deal with terrorism and regional security threats, this may prevent the realization of the current strategy to shift funding away from such 'other sectors' for the purpose of creating fiscal space for social or growth-oriented outlays.

- *Nature of the trade environment*: The extent to which further global trade barriers are reduced, or rather shifted towards bilateral or regional trading arrangements, may potentially influence the pace of growth and potentially the sources of Kenya's principal comparative advantage, again influencing both the prospects for revenue mobilization and the focus of the investment programme.
- *Importance of governance concerns*: Were there to be a shift in the global economic centre more towards emerging market countries, there might be a reduced incentive for Kenya to focus as much on governance issues. However, given the possibility of the AL scenario (Box 5.1) also arising, and given the merits on political economy grounds for strengthening Kenya's governance and regulatory system (particularly given the increased role envisaged for public–private partnerships), current strategies would appear robust to the alternative possible scenarios.
- *Pace of technological change*: Alternative scenarios also suggest differences in the future pace of technological change. This could be important, particularly with respect to certain kinds of infrastructure (e.g. in the energy and possibly the information and communications technology (ICT) sectors). Would the nature of infrastructure investment decisions be influenced by the possibility that newer and more advanced technologies might make existing infrastructure or technologies inappropriate?

All of these uncertainties raise the question of whether fiscal policy, to be robust under alternative scenarios, should be more conservatively managed, particularly with respect to the level of non-concessional borrowing that would be appropriate in financing the investment programme (or, more pointedly, in the level of any fiscal debt anchor that might be considered in managing fiscal policy). They also raise questions as to the core investment programme that would appear appropriate, given the uncertainty as to which scenario might occur.

5.3 Kenya's fiscal strategy underpinning the *Vision 2030*

5.3.1 Background and macroeconomic assumptions

Under the Economic Recovery Strategy (ERS) covering the period 2003/07, Kenya made significant progress in macroeconomic management and in implementing key structural and governance reforms. As a result, the economy staged a remarkable broad-based recovery as growth in real GDP accelerated from 0.5 per cent in 2002 to 7.0 per cent in 2007. In the aftermath of the post-election violence (PEV) in early 2008 and the global economic slowdown, growth fell sharply in 2008 to 1.7 per cent. In 2009, the economy is projected to rebound only slightly to 2.5 per cent.

Underpinning the good economic performance of recent years was the implementation of sound macroeconomic policies and, in particular, until 2007, the pursuit of a prudent fiscal stance in which the overall budget deficit (on a commitment basis, including grants) was contained to an average of about 2 per cent of GDP compared with a target of 3.2 per cent in the ERS. As a result, there was a net domestic repayment of 0.7 per cent of GDP in 2007/08, relative to a net borrowing of 3.6 per cent of GDP in 2002/03, thereby contributing to a decline in the ratio of net domestic debt to GDP from 23 per cent in 2002/03 to roughly 17 per cent in June 2008. This facilitated a reduction in interest rates and an expansion of credit to the private sector in support of productive activities.

With the conclusion of the ERS at end-2007, the Kenyan government elaborated a medium-term development plan, the national *Vision 2030*, aimed at achieving rapid economic growth and poverty reduction. The vision had three pillars:

- an *economic* pillar, the goal of which was to achieve and then sustain annual real GDP growth of 10 per cent by 2012 with a view to making Kenya a middle-income country by the year 2030;
- a *social* pillar aimed at creating a cohesive society enjoying equitable social development. This pillar would address inequality and poverty challenges faced by many Kenyans and move Kenya towards achieving some of the Millennium Development Goals (MDGs); and
- a *political* pillar calling for an issues-based, accountable, and democratic political system.

Achieving the *Vision 2030* growth target would require Kenya to increase its investment share in GDP from about 22 per cent in 2007/08 to 33 per cent by 2012/13. Over the same period, domestic savings would need to increase from about 16 per cent of GDP to 28 per cent. Details of the key indicators underpinning the macroeconomic framework of *Vision 2030* and the Medium-Term Plan are provided in Table 5.1.

The fiscal framework underpinning the *Vision 2030* scenario called for increased spending on the critical 'flagship' projects, while at the same time ensuring that the overall fiscal deficit (after grants) would progressively narrow from 6.2 per cent of GDP in 2007/08 to a sustainable level of around 4 per cent of GDP over the medium term. This would allow net domestic debt to decline substantially from 17.8 per cent of GDP to 14.3 per cent by 2012/13. The strengthened fiscal position would be supported by the implementation

Table 5.1 Key macroeconomic indicators underpinning *Vision 2030* and the Medium-Term Plan

		2008/09	2009/10	2010/11	2011/12	2012/13
	2007/08	Medium-term projections				
(Annual percentage change)						
National accounts and prices						
Real GDP	5.7	6.2	8.3	9.1	9.7	10.0
CPI (end of period)	28.5	7.5	5.0	5.0	5.0	5.0
(As a percentage of GDP)						
Investment and savings						
Investment	21.9	21.9	23.3	27.3	29.9	32.6
o/w central government	8.2	8.6	8.4	8.6	9.0	9.5
Gross domestic savings	15.9	15.1	17.4	21.8	24.6	27.5
o/w central government	0.4	1.6	2.7	2.9	3.2	3.5
Central government budget						
Total revenue	21.3	21.6	21.8	21.8	21.9	22.0
Total expenditure and net lending	29.4	28.6	27.6	27.6	27.8	28.0
Overall balance (incl. grants)	–6.2	–5.6	–4.2	–4.0	–4.0	–4.0
Domestic debt, net (eop)	17.8	16.8	16.5	15.7	15.0	14.3
Total public sector debt	41.6	43.0	40.2	41.3	38.0	38.9
External sector						
Current account (incl. official transfers)	–6.0	–6.8	–5.9	–5.5	–5.3	–5.1
Reserves (months of import cover)	3.2	3.5	3.7	3.9	4.2	4.5

Source: Ministry of Finance, Medium-Term Budget Strategy Paper, 2008/09–2010/11.

of revenue administration measures by the Kenya Revenue Authority (KRA), which would sustain the revenue-to-GDP ratio at around 22 per cent throughout the medium term.

Under *Vision 2030*, public expenditure was to be restructured in favour of development spending and other priority social interventions. Improved management of public sector finances was expected to lead to a positive shift in investor and creditor confidence as well as to boost growth by providing the fiscal resources to raise public development spending from 8.2 per cent of GDP in 2007/08 to 9.5 per cent of GDP by 2012/13.

5.3.2 The Medium-Term Plan, 2008–12 (MTP)[8]

To understand how the Kenyan government envisaged the role of fiscal policy in its broad vision for development in the coming two decades, it is useful to begin with the first five-year development strategy, the Medium-Term Plan (MTP), issued in 2008 and intended to be the instrument for implementing the *Vision 2030* development strategy. Two important elements underpin the MTP.

First, the MTP clarified how overall resources in the economy would be allocated among the three pillars and the enabling sectors (i.e. the Foundations for National Transformation) during the course of the first five years of the *Vision 2030* (see Appendix Figure 5.A1 and Appendix Table 5.A1). In particular, it highlighted the overwhelming importance that would be played by investments in infrastructure projects, particularly beginning in 2010/11.[9] While in 2008/09 and 2009/10, 21 per cent of overall resources was to be on infrastructure,[10] this share was to rise in the three subsequent years to about 60 per cent with a heavy emphasis on roads (reflecting the inadequate maintenance and limited construction on new roads during the 1990s and earlier). The MTP also indicated that (with the exception of a short burst in 2009/10), the social sector would absorb about 20 per cent of available resources. Spending on the economic sector pillar was to drop sharply after 2008/09 (being replaced by infrastructure spending), but would then be held roughly constant for the remaining four years of the MTP period (see Appendix Table 5.A1).[11]

Second, given the limited resources available to the government, the MTP emphasized that the financing of infrastructure should rely heavily on the private sector through the use of public–private partnership (PPP) financing initiatives. For the five-year period, at least 80 per cent of infrastructure spending should expect to be financed through PPPs, particularly starting in 2010/11. Thus, the success of infrastructure financing would be predicated on two important fundamentals: first, that domestic savings could be increased from about 16 per cent of GDP in 2007/08 to reach 28 per cent of GDP in 2012/13; and second, that a legal and regulatory framework for PPPs could quickly be put in place so investors would feel comfortable about investing in this strategy. Regarding the latter, we note that a PPP framework has been developed but has yet to be made operational.

5.3.3 Medium-Term Budget Strategy Paper, 2009/10–2011/12 (MTBSP)

Each year, the MTBSP provides much more detail on the government's fiscal framework over the next three budget years, not only in terms of the allocation and financing of the budget for the different government ministries, but more importantly with regard to the key policy objectives. The most recent MTBSP was issued in June 2009 at the time of the Budget Speech for fiscal year 2009/10. Unlike the MTP, the MTBSP is guided by the need to be prudent on growth prospects to mitigate the risk of being overly optimistic. In the event that higher than expected growth rates were to be achieved, the medium-term macroeconomic framework could be modified accordingly, with the higher revenues allocated to priority expenditures.

Table 5.2 summarizes the main macroeconomic indicators underpinning the more cautious fiscal framework in the 2009 MTBSP, and recognizing the preliminary estimates of the outcome for 2008/09. Table 5.2 reveals the striking contrast between what had been assumed in the MTP for the next few years and the new assumptions dictated by recent domestic and external developments. Reflecting the domestic and external shocks of 2008 and 2009 – the violence following the December 2007 election and the global economic slowdown – real GDP growth over the next three years is now projected to average under 5 per cent, much lower than the 6.8 per cent projected in the 2008 MTBSP and half the 10 per cent targeted under *Vision 2030*.

With respect to the saving–investment balance, there is also a significant divergence between the MTP's medium-term targets and the revised targets in the 2009 MTBSP. For example, the saving-to-GDP ratio is projected to reach 19 per cent compared with 24.6 per cent in the MTP in 2011/12 – a shortfall of 5.6 percentage points of GDP. Similarly, the investment-to-GDP ratio is now projected to reach only 23.3 per cent in 2011/12 compared with 29.9 per cent in the MTP – a shortfall of 6.6 percentage points of GDP. Virtually all the projected shortfalls in both saving and investment are associated with the private sector, as public sector saving and capital spending are broadly as envisaged in the MTP.

The large projected shortfalls in private sector saving and investment suggest that the *Vision 2030* growth objectives are unlikely to be met within the timeframe originally envisaged for 2012/13. Moreover, unless the level of productivity rises sharply (or the ICOR is reduced markedly compared with the target in the MTP) in the next few years, achieving the growth objectives of *Vision 2030* with a lower investment rate is unlikely to be realized. Therefore, to avoid a prolonged divergence between actual outcomes and the *Vision 2030* objectives, it is critical for Kenya to fast track the implementation of key

Table 5.2 Key macroeconomic indicators underpinning the MTBSP

	2007/08	2008/09 Prelim. est.	2009/10	2010/11	2011/12
			Medium-term projections		
(Annual percentage change)					
National accounts and prices					
Real GDP	4.0	2.5	3.1	5.2	6.4
CPI (end of period)	29.3	18.0	10.1	5.9	5.0
(As a percentage of GDP)					
Investment and savings					
Investment	19.1	18.1	19.2	22.1	23.3
o/w central government	8.2	7.6	10.2	8.9	9.1
Gross national savings	13.5	11.9	14.1	17.3	19.0
o/w central government	1.7	1.7	2.3	3.1	3.5
Central government budget					
Total revenue	22.0	22.6	22.3	22.5	22.6
Total expenditure and net lending	27.2	28.5	30.3	28.4	28.3
Overall balance (incl. grants)	–3.5	–4.9	–6.6	–4.5	–4.2
Domestic debt, net (eop)	16.9	18.5	20.6	21.1	21.1
Total public sector debt	39.3	42.6	44.5	44.3	43.8
External sector					
Current account incl. official transfers	–5.6	–6.2	–5.1	–4.8	–4.3
Reserves (months of import cover)	3.4	2.8	2.9	3.1	3.5

Source: Ministry of Finance; and the MTBSP, 2009/10–2011/12.

reforms aimed at rapidly improving the investment climate. In particular, the authorities must put in place the institutional framework to facilitate private sector participation in infrastructure projects through PPPs. Without these reforms, the timeline for achieving the *Vision 2030* growth objectives will not only be delayed substantially but could be seriously compromised.

As in the previous year, the 2009 MTBSP also aims at maintaining revenue collection at around 22 per cent of GDP over the medium term. This is quite reasonable by historical Kenyan standards and high by sub-Saharan African standards, and reflects the assumption that revenue collection will keep up with growth in nominal GDP. No major tax rate increases are envisaged in line with Kenya's intention to maintain a competitive climate for foreign and domestic investors by reducing the cost of doing business (see the recent budget speech of the Minister of Finance; Kenya, Government of, 2009b). Avoiding higher taxes seems, at this time, to be a reasonable policy position, although the issue of a further increase in the overall tax share will become more important to consider as one moves further into the next decade (as discussed below).

The MTBSP rightly takes a cautious view on the availability of grants and concessional loans, which are projected at roughly 3.5 per cent of GDP annually until 2011/12. However, even for this amount of financing to become available, the MTBSP recognizes that improving public expenditure and financial management will be critical in order to give assurance to development partners that their resources are being used efficiently to support economic growth and poverty reduction. The decision to exclude budget support in formulating the medium-term framework is informed by the recent success of having more predictability in budget execution by ensuring that resources allocated to line ministries are not disrupted by the ups and downs of donor relations and conditionalities. This practice has been highlighted positively by Standard and Poor's and Fitch ratings. However, as the 2008 MTBSP emphasized, the exclusion of budgetary support should not suggest a slowdown in implementing reforms in public expenditure management, in the financial sector, and in the restructuring and/or privatizing of public enterprises. Indeed, the assumed lower donor inflows should be accompanied by an intensification of the pace of structural reforms, especially in the modernization of tax and customs administration, to ensure that Kenya's recent financial independence is sustained in line with KRA's motto of 'Tulipe Ushuru–Tujitegemee'.

On the expenditure side, the 2009 MTBSP proposes an increase in overall spending from 28.5 per cent of GDP in 2008/09 to 30.3 per cent followed by a gradual reduction thereafter to about 28 per cent by 2011/12, while simultaneously effecting a slight shift in the composition of expenditure towards development projects. As a result, the share of recurrent outlays in total outlays will have declined from a high of 90 per cent in 2002/03 to 80 per cent in 2006/07 and to 67 per cent by 2010/11. This is consistent with *Vision 2030*'s objective of increased funding for the flagship infrastructure projects while still maintaining macroeconomic stability.

Reflecting the importance of the other pillars of *Vision 2030*, the proposed expenditure profile in the 2009 MTBSP provides for spending on education and health to remain broadly unchanged at around 30 per cent of total spending over the medium term (Appendix Figure 5.A2 and Table 5.3).[12] This follows significant increases in resource allocation to both sectors in recent years. Nevertheless, it may still be necessary to provide more resources to both sectors (see below), and this will require careful prioritization of spending to create the fiscal space for the shift in budget priorities. In particular, spending on other parts of the budget (including public administration, defence, internal security, etc.), which is currently projected to remain broadly stable at around 46 per cent of total spending, may need to be rationalized in order to release more resources for the social sectors as well as physical infrastructural investments. Although government spending on the economic sector has fallen, as earlier anticipated, the drop in the share of planned physical infrastructural spending appears inconsistent with development needs.

Based on the projected revenue and expenditure, the overall budget deficit (after grants) is estimated to rise initially from 4.9 per cent in 2008/09 to about 6 per cent of GDP in 2009/10 – reflecting the impact of the fiscal stimulus package – and then decline to 4.2 per cent by 2011/12 (see Table 5.2). It is an-

Table 5.3 Spending on the social and economic sectors (as a percentage of total expenditure)

	2007/08	2008/09	2009/10	2010/11	2011/12
Social sectors	28.1	29.1	30.4	30.6	29.7
Health	6.1	5.7	6.8	6.0	6.0
Education	22.0	23.6	23.6	24.7	23.7
Economic sectors	29.2	24.8	22.9	23.6	24.8
Productive, incl. agriculture	7.0	4.3	3.5	4.3	4.4
Physical infrastructure	22.2	20.5	19.5	19.3	20.4
Other	42.7	45.9	46.7	46.3	45.6
Total	100.0	100.0	100.0	100.0	100.0

Source: The Medium-Term Budget Strategy Paper, 2009/10–2011/12.

ticipated that concessional financing, mainly from multilateral institutions, non-concessional borrowing through the issuance of sovereign bonds, and domestic borrowing will cover the deficits. The projected domestic borrowing (including the issuance of domestic infrastructure bonds) would result in a gradual increase in the stock of outstanding net domestic debt from 17 per cent of GDP in 2007/08 to about 21 per cent in 2011/12. This increase, although necessary in the context of the economic slowdown and government policy response, carries with it the risk of potentially crowding out the private sector. This could pose difficulties in allowing the private sector to play its role in financing economic activities consistent with achieving the higher growth path.

5.3.4 Overall fiscal and debt sustainability

The projected medium-term fiscal deficits are broadly consistent with fiscal and debt sustainability. Throughout the period covered by the MTBSP, the ratio of public sector debt-to-GDP fluctuates within a narrow range of 40–44 per cent of GDP, implying that the net present value of debt-to-GDP ratio is well below 35 per cent.[13] It should be noted that the issuance of sovereign bonds to fund high-return infrastructure projects does carry some debt sustainability risks arising from the exchange rate, making it important that the projects be subjected to rigorous cost-effectiveness analysis. Also, some caution may be needed with regard to the timing of issuance of these bonds, given the increased borrowing spreads currently facing many developing countries, as well as the recent and potential further depreciation of the Kenya shilling against the euro and the US dollar.

Regarding contingent liabilities, a significant amount has already been taken into account in the context of the financial restructuring of the National Bank of Kenya (over Ksh 21 billion) and during the course of privatizing

Kenya Telecom. However, owing to lack of data, not all potential contingent liabilities from the parastatal sector and from the pension scheme have been included in the debt sustainability analysis. Including such contingent liabilities would increase the official public debt and the risk of the overall public debt becoming unsustainable.

Another potential source of contingent liabilities is the government's planned heavy reliance on PPPs to finance many of the infrastructure projects for *Vision 2030*. It will be critical to ensure that increased use of the PPP framework is well managed and minimizes potential contingent liabilities. Reliance on PPPs in some instances involves some assumption of the government ultimately in the future financing the purchase of the privately built assets. Moreover, depending on the terms of an individual PPP, the government could bear a number of potential risks associated with each project (demand risk, financing risk, political risk, supply risk, legal risk, etc.). The government appears to be cognizant of this danger, and intends to establish a PPP unit in the Ministry of Finance to vet all new PPP-funded projects. In the meantime, the government should avoid any new PPP projects before the finalization of the PPP legal and regulatory framework.

5.3.5 The potential role of PPPs

Can and should Kenya realistically rely on PPP mechanisms? First, there are some areas of public infrastructural spending where the private sector may potentially be willing to invest and provide services *without* the need for a PPP (e.g. as has already been demonstrated in the telecommunications sector). In other sectors, the challenge is for the government to ensure that the same public policy factors that originally motivated public sector investment and provision, e.g. equity factors, natural monopoly conditions, or externalities, are taken into account in the way in which the private sector produces and delivers services. Here, the government's task is to ensure that a clear and well-designed regulatory structure is in place, particularly with regard to pricing policy.

Second, private financing in the form of a PPP entails both opportunities and risks to a government, and management of these risks is essential if there is to be a genuine sharing of both the gains and the associated risks between the public and private sectors. What makes a PPP attractive to a government is the ability to harness the potential of the private sector to construct and operate a facility with greater efficiency than would be the case for the public sector, with such efficiency gains offsetting the presumably higher borrowing or equity costs associated with private as opposed to government borrowing. Such efficiency gains are particularly relevant when the private sector can bundle the construction and operating phases of a project, thus allowing for internalization of cost-reducing incentives (Scandizzo and Sanguinetti, 2009).

At the same time, by substituting the private sector for public provision, the government can also save scarce public funds and relieve strained budgets. But PPPs can also be used inappropriately to bypass spending controls and move public investments off budget and debt off the government's balance sheet. This could leave governments bearing most of the risks involved and facing large fiscal costs over the medium to long term.

Experience in other countries suggests that, to work effectively and for a PPP to be an appropriate approach, several key prerequisites should be satisfied: the quality of services should be contractible; there should be competition or incentive-based regulation; as noted, there should be an appropriate distribution of risks; the institutional framework should be characterized by political commitment, good governance, and clear supporting legislation (including with regard to pricing); and a transparent procedure should be in place for the award of performance incentives and enforcement of sanctions throughout the concession period. Finally, a government needs to have a capacity, in both the finance and sector ministries, to effectively appraise and prioritize public infrastructure projects; design PPPs; evaluate affordability, value for money, and risk transfer; correctly select those projects that are appropriate to undertake as PPPs; draft and scrutinize contracts; monitor, manage, and regulate ongoing projects; and undertake periodic performance evaluations (see IMF, 2004; Tchakarov, 2007; Scandizzo and Sanguinetti, 2009; Sutherland *et al.*, 2009). This underlines the importance of Kenya moving at a deliberate pace to put in place a strengthened management capacity in the Ministry of Finance and, given past governance failures, to exhibit caution so as to ensure that the government sector is not burdened with excessive risks that ought legitimately to be borne by the private sector.

In terms of negotiating the distribution of risk, the experience of Latin American countries with PPPs suggests that some are appropriately borne by the private partner – those associated with the construction or the operation of the project in particular. Others, such as political and regulatory risk, should clearly be borne by the government. Others – such as market demand risk, some supply-side risks (the cost of foreign exchange, some factor cost risks) – may be influenced by government but not fully under its control. How such risks are shared is obviously an important and sensitive aspect in the negotiation of a PPP with a private partner, as it will bear on how large are the contingent risks to which a government is exposed.

Experience has also taught that governments entering into PPPs need to be aware that there is a strong tendency for contracts to be renegotiated. Tchakarov (2007) notes that, in Latin America and the Caribbean, over 30 per cent of PPPs were renegotiated (particularly in transportation and water projects), often within the first two to three years of the award of a PPP. Key factors forcing renegotiation have included the fixed term nature of concession contracts, the challenges posed by demand risk, poor decisions at the design stage, government acceptance of aggressive bidding, and changes in the rules of the game by the government after the contract award. Tchakarov also notes that an 'improper regulatory framework and poor regulatory oversight [can] increase the chances of conflict, rent capture by operators, or opportunistic behavior by government'.

In sum, private sector financing offers important opportunities for Kenya to augment its fiscal space for infrastructure, but successful exploitation of this source requires important capacity building within the government in order to ensure both fiscal savings and efficiency gains relative to public provision.

5.3.6 Risks

The MTBSP recognizes that the underlying medium-term assumptions are not without risks, and that the projected rate of economic growth may not be achieved. Under such circumstances, the MTBSP indicates that the government would take appropriate measures to mitigate the risks to macroeconomic stability, such as by delaying or scaling back on expenditure on non-priority programmes. However, the MTBSP does not identify which programmes would be curtailed should revenues fall short of the projected amounts.

5.4 Assessing the *Vision 2030* and the MTBSP

5.4.1 Do Vision 2030 and the MTBSP address the key challenges facing Kenya?

In assessing Kenya's fiscal policy going forward, it is probably best to work from the plans indicated in the recent MTBSP, primarily because *Vision 2030* and the MTP provide less detail on the macroeconomic and fiscal policy framework. *Vision 2030* is also of course more ambitious in its objectives for growth, so that any doubts raised about the MTBSP would only be more the case concerning *Vision 2030*.

At the outset, it is worth pointing out that the fiscal framework in the MTBSP appears to be based on fairly conservative assumptions and has introduced some degree of flexibility that can accommodate several alternative scenarios. In particular, the assumed lower growth in the MTBSP compared with *Vision 2030* is, regrettably, realistic in the light of recent global developments. However, the projected constant revenue-to-GDP ratio also comes at a time when KRA is undertaking significant reforms in the customs and tax administration. This means that there is likely to be some revenue windfall.

The projected disbursement of concessional loans in line with GDP assumes no improvement in absorption capacity in the key line ministries from the low levels of between 40 and 50 per cent, and the authorities have underlined this as an objective to pursue in coming years. With the recent enhanced monitoring of project implementation, the absorption of donor funds should increase. The exclusion of donor budget support from the framework at a time when public financial management (PFM)/public expenditure management (PEM) reforms are ongoing also suggests a potential upside in donor support. Finally, even with the increase in government spending associated with the fiscal stimulus, the level of public sector debt-to-GDP ratio still provides some scope for additional domestic borrowing to fund key infrastructure projects, if warranted, without jeopardizing Kenya's debt sustainability status. All in all, with the exception of the growth scenario, most of the other assumptions appear fairly cautious and leave room for some overperformance.

However, several observations can be made on the MTBSP. First, both it and *Vision 2030*, as noted above, articulate sensible and thoughtful strategies as to the key sectors that need to be emphasized if Kenya is to significantly accelerate its growth path and as to the critical importance of the role to be played by the private sector. Equally, the macrofiscal strategy is prudent, being fiscally sustainable and consistent with long-term solvency and a low-inflation environment, both attributes being critical for providing appropriate incentives for private sector investment, both foreign and domestic. In other words, the 'words' make sense and the strategy is appropriate. The question is whether the words can be matched by both actions, in terms of *budget priorities* in individual sectors and specific projects, and in the *implementation* of programmes and policies.

Second, an examination of the budgetary projections highlights the difficult fiscal realities that Kenya confronts as it seeks to realize the MTBSP's assumptions (and even more the *Vision 2030*'s policy objectives). The projected high spending on education and health between 2007/08 and 2010/11 underlines the importance that the government places on these two sectors as cornerstones for achieving its *Vision 2030* objectives. Nevertheless, for education and health, the proposed spending for the three-year period may still not be enough to accommodate the increase in the number of prospective students resulting from population growth, projected inflation, and the need for wage increases for teachers and health professionals that roughly correspond with wage growth in the private sector, the so-called 'Baumol effect'. Once these factors are taken into account, there are very few resources still available for improving the quality of teaching, financing increased availability of educational materials, and for redirecting outlays towards new initiatives (such as is suggested in the MTBSP with regard to higher development spending on higher education, and in particular on science and technology). The tight fiscal position will also limit movement towards expanded enrolments in tertiary education and the use of the budget to foster job creation efforts for school enrolees (other than what is already envisaged with regard to the Youth Fund, the Women's Fund and, more recently, the *Kazi kwa Vijana*).

As indicated earlier, however, additional resources to fund an increase in spending in these sectors could be generated from rationalizing spending in other non-critical ministries or from within the sectors themselves. For example, in the health sector, the ongoing efforts supported by the Millennium Challenge Corporation (MCC) to improve the procurement process should generate additional savings. As for the education sector, recent World Bank studies suggest that the real issue there is not the availability of resources, but the efficient deployment of available resources. Fiscal space created from these reforms can be used to improve the quality of health and teaching, finance increased availability of educational materials, and redirect outlays towards new initiatives on science and technology.

Third, the MTBSP projects a reduction in spending on wages and benefits from 7.4 per cent of GDP in 2007/08 to 6.7 per cent in 2011/12. Certainly, with the expected growth in social sector spending, this implies containing nominal wage increases and some important cutbacks in other areas of government employment associated with the provision of goods and services. This could be a positive development, if it implies a tightening of the public sector workforce through shedding of unproductive employees (although there is little allocation indicated for civil service reform during the period beyond that for the Voluntary Early Retirement Scheme), a reallocation of the existing workforce to those areas critical for energizing higher productivity in the government, and a shift towards key spending areas critical for facilitating private sector investments and activities. However, unless a civil service reform agenda is planned and fully implemented, then one can express some unease as to whether the projected decline in the wage bill will actually materialize.

In a similar vein, the cutback in 'other' spending revealed in the economic classification of government expenditures in the MTBSP – from 7.9 per cent of GDP in 2009/09 to 6.9 per cent in 2011/12 – may represent the effort of the authorities to tighten and rationalize budget spending, cutting back on unproductive expenditures (a point emphasized by the Minister in his Budget Speech). But there must be a concern as to how to strengthen what has heretofore been a weak complement of non-wage spending in a number of sectors, contributing to low productivity and poor upkeep of public infrastructure. A reallocation of 'other' outlays may be included in the details of the budget, but one would need to see this reflected in hard budgetary allocations to the sectors targeted in the MTBSP and *Vision 2030* as the critical growth sectors. What is important to underline is the criticality of ensuring that investments in infrastructure financed by so-called infrastructure bonds are complemented by the provision of adequate recurrent resources for the operation and maintenance of the newly created infrastructure. In the absence of such spending, the longer term productivity of the infrastructure will be compromised, raising questions about its potential contribution to the objective of a sustained high growth rate for the economy.

Fourth, now is the time to begin to develop a strategic plan for raising Kenya's tax share, as would be compatible with its goal of middle-income status, and weaning itself from reliance on external assistance flows. Over time, particularly as one moves into the next decade, Kenya will need to consider ways to strengthen the revenue potential from its personal and corporate income tax, reflecting the growing size of its middle- and upper-income groups. Perhaps even more important, as trade liberalization is pursued within the framework of the East African Customs Union, there will be scope for a gradual increase of a few percentage points (over the next several decades) in the value added tax (VAT). As the government policy machinery strengthens, there may equally be room to move to a uniform VAT rate, replacing the zero rate with alternative transfer schemes to target and assist the low-income groups that are the principal policy target of the zero-rated commodities.

Fifth, the MTP calls for a sharp increase in overall investment in order to achieve the planned 10 per cent real GDP growth. However, in light of the sharply lower medium-term levels of saving and investment now projected in the MTBSP, the government needs to move with deliberate speed to implement structural reforms and improve the investment climate in order to raise productivity rapidly. Without a significant increase in total factor productivity, achieving the *Vision 2030* growth objectives could be seriously impaired. One implication of the limited amount of resources available to the government for the needed additional spending on infrastructure is the criticality of the institutional policy changes that must occur if the increased role of the private sector in terms of higher savings and investment rates is to be realized. As we have noted earlier, it will be essential to put in place an adequate institutional and policy framework to give confidence to private sector investors considering PPPs in infrastructure.

Sixth, both the current global economic situation and the variability implied under the three World Bank scenarios presented in Section 5.2 suggest the heightened vulnerability of the MTBSP to global downside risks. On the expenditure side, Kenya faces challenges that are insensitive to the external context and demand higher and more efficient outlays – still rapid population growth, climate change, pressures for urbanization, and a need to rehabilitate and modernize its basic infrastructure for the twenty-first century. In contrast, on the resources side, Kenya's prospects for financing expenditure are still constrained by whether it can access cheaply external resources, and whether it can realize a sufficiently rapid level of economic growth (in response to external demands) so that it can generate sufficiently high levels of domestic revenue as well as private sector income growth that can facilitate an increase in the private sector savings rate.

Thus, one can envisage downside risks on the external side that could have significant adverse effects on the Kenyan economy. For example, since the publication of the *Vision 2030* medium-term fiscal framework, there has been a dramatic change in the external environment. The subprime problem, which originated in the USA and spread to other developed countries, has resulted in what the Governor of the Bank of England has called the 'worst financial crisis since the great depression!'. The expected global economic slowdown, and especially the recession in industrial countries, has already affected Kenya's growth prospects negatively in several ways: (i) reduced demand for Kenya's exports of goods and services, particularly tourism; (ii) a decline in export prices – although lower international import prices, including for oil, have reduced inflationary pressures; (iii) lowered remittances from Kenyans in the diaspora; (iv) a reversal of portfolio inflows as foreign investors with heightened risk aversion flee from developing countries; (v) reduced donor assistance in light of the potential large budgetary deficits among donor countries arising from an ageing population and actions to deal with the international credit crunch; and finally (vi) increased the budgetary cost associated with the planned flotation of a sovereign bond of US$500 million, in light of the dramatic increase in spreads for developing countries' sovereign bonds. Even if the issuance does not take place, the financing shortfall would necessitate a rephasing of some of the infrastructure projects that had been planned.

Scenarios that highlight potential security tensions could also put pressure on Kenya to increase further the share in GDP of its internal security and defence spending from the 2006/07 levels. So, whereas the pressure for higher spending – both recurrent and investment – is great for Kenya, both to meet pressing social needs and to facilitate a high growth strategy, there is far more downside risk that the fiscal situation may prove far tighter than envisaged, notwithstanding the cautious assumptions underpinning the fiscal framework in the MTBSP. Given these obvious uncertainties as to the full impact and durability of the global financial crisis, Kenya will need to be monitoring the situation closely and, as more and more information becomes available, the medium-term fiscal framework should be adjusted in order to reflect the new realities.

Although the MTBSP does highlight the potential downside risks to the budget framework and indicates how the government would respond to protect the hard-won achievement in macroeconomic stability, there is not much discussion on how the GOK would respond in terms of the structure of government spending programmes. In some respects, Kenya may be hobbled by the effort of responding to both the challenge of meeting the MDGs (which calls for an extensive effort to address deficiencies in access to education, health, and environmental conditions among the poor) and its ambition to move to a higher growth trajectory through focused outlays on infrastructure and on the segment of its potential workforce with the greatest potential for attracting and facilitating investment that can yield high growth in the economy. Which investments and which areas of recurrent spending should be seen as critical and necessary, even if there is to be a lower trajectory of revenues?

And which parts of the budget should be seen as possibly 'expendable' or, at a minimum, able to be postponed in the event of such a slowdown? In this context, much remains to be done to prioritize the long list of projects identified in the implementation matrix of the MTP.

In order to crystallize this issue, in the event that some of the aforementioned external risks materialize, it would be prudent to identify and scale back non-priority expenditures, rather than risk triggering macroeconomic instability. At the same time, the government may wish to seek a slower phased implementation of some of the flagship projects. Such a strategy would avoid putting pressures on prices, which are already high, and will contribute to the maintenance of sustainable low interest rates, which are a key determinant of the private sector investment needed to generate the 10 per cent growth envisaged in *Vision 2030*.

While it is tempting to focus wholly on the current conjunctural crisis, the scenarios in Section 5.2 illustrate further the potential for external developments to be very different from what might be suggested presently. For example, the scenarios illustrated in Section 5.2 offer the possibility of positive external developments in the event that growth proves stronger than anticipated outside the western industrial countries. If this were to happen, it would require Kenyan exporters and tourism providers to adapt and focus on new markets. Equally, Kenya may find it useful to diversify its export markets and enhance its dialogue with potential aid donors from both Asia and the Middle East so as to offset any shortfalls in aid from the west.

In conclusion, Kenya's policy framework is rightfully ambitious. Given that Kenya's population is still rapidly growing and urbanizing, and that the level of poverty and shortfalls in MDG realization remain large, an ambitious policy strategy for growth is a prerequisite if Kenya is to move further on its transition to a middle-income position. Such a strategy must be predicated on a scaling up of the rate of investment, high efficiency in the use of investment resources, and a focus on the key areas of infrastructure that are necessary if there are to be incentives for the private sector to view Kenya as an attractive growth pole in the East Africa region.

Fortunately, owing to the recent improvement in fiscal management, which has resulted in a reduction in net domestic debt, the budget framework in the MTBSP appears sufficiently flexible to address several downside risks, particularly if one also takes into account the cautious assumptions underlying the medium-term revenue estimates and external budgetary support. This flexibility is critical as it provides the government with some scope to meet its *Vision 2030* spending priorities without causing macroeconomic instability or raising concerns about debt sustainability. A necessary condition for creating a favourable investment climate is macroeconomic stability, and Kenya must ensure that this is maintained.

Nevertheless, reliance on external private capital investment inflows will necessarily be a critical component of this strategy. This is because there are limits as to the role that the public sector investment programme can play, given the need to maintain a disciplined macroeconomic posture and the competing demands for public resources for addressing poverty-related gaps in terms of the MDGs and the central role of the public sector in financing human capital formation. This is now particularly the case as the budget is likely to be tighter if real growth is slower and revenue performance suffers. Although Kenya is entering the early stages of the demographic transition, and thus can potentially obtain some increase in the domestic savings rate with the slight projected decline in its demographic dependency burden, the potential for domestic private savings to fully finance the projected investment targets is still limited. So there is justification in Kenya's emphasis on the use of PPPs to finance the required higher infrastructure spending. This implies two important imperatives. The new PPP framework must be put in place with all due speed if it is to begin to influence positively private sector incentives for infrastructure investment. But equally, the framework must reflect 'best practices' in the approach to PPPs (from the experience of emerging market countries in Latin America and Asia) so that the new PPPs do not jeopardize long-term fiscal sustainability. But to meet these imperatives and thus to attract external capital successfully (particularly in a world where global investors are now particularly risk averse), Kenya will need to address boldly the persistent concerns that have arisen in the past about governance and the investment climate.

Appendix

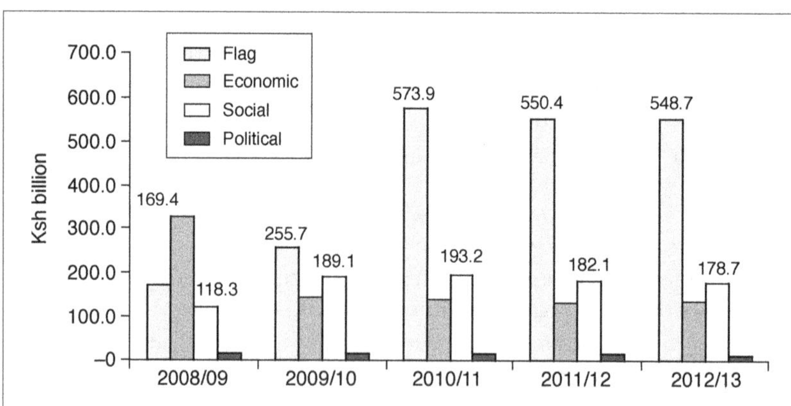

Appendix Figure 5.A1 Resource requirements for *Vision 2030* MTP 2008/09–2012/13 *(Ksh billion).*

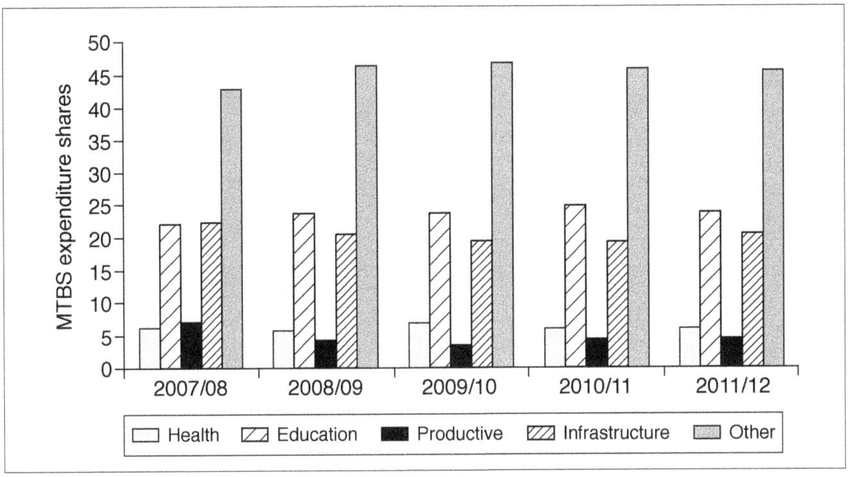

Appendix Figure 5.A2 Medium-Term Budget Strategy 2007/08–2011/12: sector shares.

Appendix Table 5.A1 Resources for implementing *Vision 2030* MTP (2008/09–2012/13)

(Ksh million)	2008/09	2009/10	2010/11	2011/12	2012/13
Foundations for National Transformation	169,376.0	255,652.0	573,916.0	550,442.0	548,709.0
Infrastructure	73,917.0	185,241.0	518,992.0	514,935.0	518,433.0
ICT	5,830.0	5,425.0	2,020.0	820.0	1,015.0
Science and technology	3,772.0	7,893.0	5,971.0	9,050.0	5,382.0
Land reforms	610.0	761.0	762.0	614.0	416.0
Human resource development	21,326.0	9,545.0	8,005.0	6,140.0	4,930.0
Security and peace	63,921.0	46,787.0	38,166.0	18,883.0	18,533.0
Economic	324,636.0	143,492.0	140,791.0	130,429.0	133,601.0
Tourism	27,991.0	24,189.0	26,340.0	24,485.0	27,798.0
Agriculture	52,258.0	49,270.0	46,240.0	42,050.0	42,050.0
Wholesale and retail trade	235,177.0	54,638.0	54,638.0	54,138.0	54,138.0
Manufacturing	3,902.0	9,874.0	9,338.0	9,331.0	9,330.0
Business process outsourcing	4,253.0	5,171.0	3,945.0	150.0	80.0
Others	1,055.0	350.0	290.0	275.0	205.0
Social pillar	118,283.0	189,060.0	193,177.5	182,147.5	178,746.5
Education	58,410.0	57,625.0	68,473.0	74,185.0	78,878.0
Health	5,490.0	3,066.0	3,717.0	1,025.0	986.0
Environment, water, and sanitation	12,788.0	44,368.0	40,186.0	33,541.0	23,836.0

Appendix Table 5.A1 (cont.)

(Ksh million)	2008/09	2009/10	2010/11	2011/12	2012/13
Population, urbanization, and housing	13,080.0	43,350.0	29,430.0	24,885.0	24,870.0
Gender, vulnerable groups, and youth	28,122.0	40,296.0	50,981.5	48,071.5	49,686.5
Equity and wealth	393.0	355.0	390.0	440.0	490.0
Political	16,778.0	13,814.0	16,814.0	17,214.0	13,506.0
Governance	14,628.0	11,594.0	14,984.0	16,064.0	12,886.0
Decentralization	2,150.0	2,220.0	1,830.0	1,150.0	620.0
Total	629,073.0	602,018.0	924,698.5	880,232.5	874,562.5

Notes

1 The IMF report also highlighted the extent to which Kenya's competitiveness has been hampered by higher 'costs related to infrastructure, taxation, security, and bribes' relative to most of its competitors.

2 Despite the historic zeal of the Kenyan people for education (dating from the Harambee movement of the 1960s) and the substantial expansion of its primary, secondary, tertiary, and vocational school network, Kenya remains a country where the quality of the education provided for substantial numbers of students requires significant improvement. Pupil–teacher ratios in many parts of the country can be shockingly high, teacher quality is of great variance, available educational materials are limited, and dropout and repetition rates are still too high. The provision of free secondary education, although an important step in facilitating access to education, should complement and not substitute for providing the quality of teaching and education materials necessary to foster the creation of the necessary human capital.

3 According to the World Bank's 'Doing Business' report, Kenya has launched an ambitious licensing reform programme. In the past three years, a total of 315 licences were eliminated and another 379 simplified out of a total of 1,325 licences that had been identified as hindering the growth of small and medium-term enterprises. In addition, in 2007/08, key regulators such as the Communications Commission of Kenya, the Betting Control and Licensing Board, and the Ministry of Tourism further reduced the number of licences from 390 to 46 licences.

4 The Constituency Development Fund (CDF), earmarked at 2.5 per cent of ordinary revenue, and the Local Authority Transfer Fund (LATF), which takes up 5 per cent of income taxes, are good examples.

5 Recent evidence indicates that some of the health facilities constructed using CDF resources are yet to be utilized because no provisions were made for the operational costs of the facilities.

6 Mombasa's population will rise from 0.82 million in 2005 to 1.76 million by 2025; Nairobi's population will rise from 2.8 million to 5.9 million.

7 This will include two urban centres – Nakuru and Kisumu – which are presently under 0.5 million but which will exceed 0.5 million by 2025, as well as other urban

centres whose population will rise from 3.8 million to 8.2 million (UN 2007 Urbanization Prospects).

8 The Medium-Term Plan (2008/09–12/13) (MTP) is the first in a series of successive five-year medium-term plans intended to implement Kenya's *Vision 2030*. It was designed to provide the implementation matrix for the high-return, flagship projects intended to begin the structural transformation of the Kenyan economy and engineer a more ambitious growth potential. In turn, the Medium-Term Budget Strategy Paper (MTBSP) was designed to implement the MTP.

9 Over the five-year period, roughly 85 per cent of resources devoted to the 'Foundation for National Transformation' would be dominated by investments in infrastructure. But there are flagship projects in other sectors, including ICT, science and technology, land reforms, human resource development, and security and peace.

10 The figure of Ksh 235.2 million under wholesale and retail trade for 2008/09 is distorted by the unrealistic assumption that Ksh 227.5 million will be spent on a free port project in Mombasa under a PPP framework in 2008/09.

11 It is worth noting that many of the projects identified in the MTP for funding under a PPP framework may not be of interest to the private sector. Just to give a few examples, 'Operationalizing the New Labor Laws' (p. 156) and 'National Security and Policing Reforms', as well as 'Peace Building and Conflict Resolution' (p. 157) are put under the PPP financing framework. A thorough review of projects that are amenable to the PPP framework should be undertaken and the matrix attached to the MTP revised accordingly. Only then will a more accurate picture emerge of the relative shares of resources going to the different pillars.

12 The sectoral allocation of resources shown in the MTBSP is based solely on the resources envelope derived from government revenues, project grants and loans from development partners, and domestic and foreign (sovereign bonds) borrowing. Resources to be mobilized through the PPP framework are not included.

13 A joint debt sustainability analysis for Kenya done by the IMF and the World Bank (see the 2009 Staff Report discussed by the IMF Board in May 2009) concluded that Kenya faces only a low risk of external debt distress. According to the report, the net present value (NPV) of central government debt over the period 2008/09–2012/13 will range between 32 and 34 per cent of GDP – for external debt only, the ratio of NPV declines from 14.0 per cent of GDP in 2007/08 to 13.8 per cent in 2012/13. The indicative threshold for external debt sustainability for a medium-term performer such as Kenya (based on the World Bank's classification) is an NPV of debt-to-GDP ratio of 40 per cent, an NPV of debt-to-exports ratio of 150 per cent, and an NPV of debt-to-revenue ratio of 250 per cent, a debt service-to-exports ratio of 20 per cent, and a debt service-to-revenue ratio of 30 per cent.

References

International Monetary Fund, 2004, *Public Investment and Fiscal Policy*. Washington, DC: IMF.

International Monetary Fund, 2008a, *Ex Post Assessment of Longer-Term Program Engagement*. Washington, DC: IMF.

International Monetary Fund, 2008b, *Kenya: Staff Report for the 2008 Article IV Consultation* as well as *Selected Issues Paper* (2008).

International Monetary Fund, 2009, Request for Disbursement Under the Rapid-Access Component of the Exogenous Shocks Facility: Staff Report (June), IMF Country Report No. 09/191. Washington, DC: IMF.

International Monetary Fund and World Bank, 2008, *Joint IMF/World Bank Debt Sustainability Analysis.*

Kenya, Government of, 2008a, *Medium-Term Plan, 2008/09–2012/13.*

Kenya, Government of, 2008b, *Medium-Term Budget Strategy Paper, 2008/09–2010/11* (May).

Kenya, Government of, 2008c, *Vision 2030.*

Kenya, Government of, 2008d, *Medium-Term Expenditure Framework Reports, 2008/09–2010/11*, by sector, with sector reports issued for the following sectors: Information Communication Technology; Physical Infrastructure; Public Administration; the Productive Sector; the Health Sector; the Education Sector; Manpower and Special Programmes; Governance, Justice, Law and Order.

Kenya, Government of, 2009a, *Medium-Term Budget Strategy Paper, 2009/10–2011/12* (June).

Kenya, Government of, 2009b, *Budget Speech of the Minister of Finance, Uhuru Kenyatta, for FY 09/10.*

Scandizzo, S. and P. Sanguinetti, 2009, *Infrastructure in Latin America: Achieving High Impact Management* (discussion draft of 2009 Latin America Emerging Markets Forum).

Sutherland, D., S. Araujo, B. Égert and T. Kozluyk, 2009, 'Infrastructure Investment: Links to Growth and the Role of Public Policies', Economics Department Working Paper No. 686, ECO/WKP(2009)27 (16 March).

Tchakarov, I., 2007, 'Public Investment in Thailand: Macroeconomic Effects and Implementation', in *Thailand: Selected Issues,* IMF Country Report 07/231. Washington, DC: IMF.

World Bank, 2008, *Kenya: Accelerating and Sustaining Inclusive Growth,* Report No. 42844-KE (July).

6

Trade Policy in Kenya[1]

Maureen Were, Moses Sichei, and Chris Milner

6.1 Introduction

For Kenya to become a globally competitive and prosperous nation by 2030, it will require international trade policies that support export expansion of manufactured and non-traditional goods and services in both regional and extra-regional markets. Exports of textiles mainly to the US market have increased in recent years, thanks to the African Growth Opportunity Act (AGOA). However, despite trade liberalization and a number of export promotion incentive schemes and programmes, manufacturing and service exports from Kenya and Africa in general are still relatively low in comparison with those from East Asian countries. Trade has to become the foundation upon which Kenya's development and industrialization strategy rests.

6.1.1 Kenya's trade policy challenges

Some of the key challenges for Kenya's trade policies in the coming decades are:

- Designing and implementing trade and other related domestic policies to facilitate growth and diversification of export capacity and supply.
- Formulating and negotiating effective trade strategies regionally and internationally to bring about deeper regional and international integration and improve market access for Kenyan exports and access to competitive inputs and services.

- Increasing the capacity of the Kenyan economy to adapt and respond to the challenges and opportunities associated with globalization, including the further fragmentation of international production and growth of 'trade in tasks' (see UNIDO, 2009).

This chapter analyses trade policies and trends in Kenya's export performance, with a view to drawing lessons for the country's trade strategies. It also examines the rapidly evolving institutional framework for regional and international trade in Kenya, with a particular focus on the new East African Customs Union and the European Union (EU) Economic Partnership Agreement (EPA). Regional arrangements, complemented with appropriate policies, can play a critical role in the growth of manufacturing sector exports and services. At the same time, there has been concern that the North–South arrangements under the EPA could lead to trade imbalances and further polarization given development disparities between the EU and African countries. Any coherent growth strategy for Kenya built on trade should, thus, take into account the implications of such trade arrangements.

The remainder of the chapter is organized as follows. Section 6.2 reviews the evolution of trade policy in Kenya from import substitution to trade liberalization, and the associated trade performance. Section 6.3 outlines Kenya's multilateral, regional, and bilateral trade policy issues and commitments. In Section 6.4, an assessment of the impact of trade policy is offered, while the need for a broad concept of trade policy space to improve its export performance is set out in Section 6.5. The overall conclusions of the chapter are summarized in Section 6.6.

6.2 Evolution of Kenya's trade policies and trade performance

6.2.1 Trade reforms

Kenya's trade reforms can be categorized into three phases: the import substitution period (1960s and 1970s), the period of Structural Adjustment Programmes (SAPs) with emphasis on the removal of quantitative controls and export promotion programmes, and the later period of comprehensive trade liberalization, starting from the early 1990s.

IMPORT SUBSTITUTION PERIOD

On attaining independence in 1963, the new Kenyan government continued with the import substitution policy from the colonial era aimed at industrial development (Were *et al.*, 2002). Several public enterprises enjoyed monopoly status. The 1960s and 1970s saw the introduction of regulatory and protectionist policies in virtually all key sectors of the economy. Manufacturing production was skewed towards consumer goods, with industrial output geared in general towards the captive domestic market. The incentive structure was biased against exporting. In the first decade of independence, import-substituting manufacturing grew rapidly, supported by expansionary fiscal policy and export growth to Tanzania and Uganda under the East African Community (EAC) common market (Wagacha, 2000).

The inefficiency and inadequacy of the import substitution policy became apparent in the 1970s. The first oil crisis (1973) and the collapse of the EAC in 1977 adversely affected the performance of import substitution enterprises. The impact on gross domestic product (GDP) growth was cushioned by sharp increases in international prices of tea and coffee. In contrast, the growth of non-traditional exports was discouraged by high levels of protection, cumbersome administrative procedures, and an overvalued currency (Were *et al.*, 2002). According to Lall and Pietrobelli (2002), the indiscriminate and open-ended protection distorted resource allocation, reduced foreign competition, and restricted technology inflows from abroad.

STRUCTURAL ADJUSTMENT AND EXPORT PROMOTION

As the import substitution development strategy became untenable, coupled with budgetary constraints, the government reluctantly began embracing trade reforms under Structural Adjustment Programmes (SAPs) in the early 1980s.[2] A major component of reform was a shift to export promotion, and conversion of quantitative restrictions to tariff equivalents. However, little reform was achieved in the 1980s and neither, unsurprisingly, was there an export response. By the end of 1983, some policy reversals had been witnessed and, to the extent that quantitative restrictions were removed, tariffs were raised, in some cases by over 100 per cent (Were *et al.*, 2006). According to Swamy (1994), this episode of import liberalization was not successful because it coincided with a period of macroeconomic crisis.

Tariff reform made some progress during the second half of the 1980s (see Table 6.1).[3] By 1991, quantitative restrictions affected only 5 per cent of imports compared with 12 per cent in 1987 (Swamy, 1994). However, the level of progress was still limited,[4] and the import licensing system and foreign exchange restrictions were still in place with considerable executive discretion.

A number of new export incentive and promotion programmes were initiated. These included the introduction of Manufacturing under Bond (MUB) in 1988, Export Processing Zones (EPZs) in 1990, and the revival of the Kenya Export Trade Authority, as well as a duty and value added tax (VAT) exemption scheme administered under the Export Promotion Programmes Office (currently TREO) for tax rebates on imported inputs for exporters and essential products such as drugs. In addition, the Export Promotion Council (EPC) was established in 1992 to address bottlenecks faced by exporters.

Table 6.1 Economy-wide average tariffs, fiscal years 1984–90 (%)

All schedules	1984/85	1985/86	1986/87	1987/88	1988/89	1989/90
Unweighted	40	39.6	41.3	41.0	38.8	39.0
Import weighted	–	29.6	27.3	24.5	22.0	20.4

Source: Department of Economics, University of Nairobi and University of Gothenburg (1993), Table 3.5, p. 36.

The incentives for EPZs included a ten-year tax holiday, exemption from import duties on machinery and intermediate inputs, and exemption from VAT. Under MUB, firms exporting their total output are exempted from payment of import duties and VAT on inputs. The export promotion programmes were mainly geared towards promoting manufactured exports – mainly labour-intensive manufactures. However, the export incentive schemes had limited impact on industrial exports. This can be attributed partly to weaknesses in implementation and co-ordination of the promotion schemes.

Rolfe *et al.* (2004) observed that poor infrastructure and other investment barriers may eliminate potential benefits from tax holidays. According to Rolfe *et al.* (2004), two problems hindered the development (of MUB) in the mid-1990s: revocation of Kenya's quotas on some apparel products by the USA and the appreciation of the exchange rate coupled with a rise in real wage costs at the time when Southeast Asian currencies were devalued and their labour costs fell. Exports from EPZs and MUB factories accounted for only slightly more than 1 per cent of total exports from 1993 to 1998 (Glenday and Ndii, 2000).

COMPREHENSIVE TRADE LIBERALIZATION REFORMS

Comprehensive trade reforms came rapidly in the early 1990s, after the suspension of balance of payment (BOP) support.[5] The economy was in crisis: economic performance had deteriorated (real GDP growth fell from 5 per cent in 1989 to 2.1 per cent and 0.5 per cent in 1991 and 1992 respectively); budgetary and financial constraints deepened following curtailment in donor funding; and the country experienced serious macroeconomic instability.[6] This gave the multilateral donor institutions leverage to push for quick and comprehensive reforms (Were *et al.*, 2006).

The introduction of Foreign Exchange Bearer Certificates (Forex-Cs) in October 1991 marked the first step towards liberalization of the foreign exchange market. The Forex-Cs could be used for automatic import licensing. A series of other reform measures were hastily implemented. In April 1992, for instance, a secondary market for Forex-Cs was established, while in August, retention schemes were introduced allowing 100 per cent retention of foreign exchange earnings from non-traditional exports such as manufactured goods and horticulture.

Although some policy reversals were witnessed, 1993 is considered as the year when Kenya opened up in earnest (Sachs and Warner, 1995; Were *et al.*, 2006), with the abolition of trade licensing requirements and, more importantly, foreign exchange controls. In October 1993, the official exchange rate under the dual exchange rate system was finally abolished, paving the way for a freely floating exchange rate. During 1993–94, all current account and virtually all capital account restrictions were lifted. Additionally, the tariff structure was harmonized and tariff dispersion lowered. The adoption of the EAC common external tariff (CET) in January 2005 led to a further reduction in Kenya's applied tariffs – the simple average fell from 16.8 per cent in 2004 to 12.7 per cent. The CET has three tariff bands: 0 per cent for meritorious goods, raw materials, and capital goods; 10 per cent and 25 per cent for intermediate and consumer goods, respectively.

Following trade liberalization reforms, the exchange rate, inflation, and interest rates stabilized and, by the end of 1995, economic growth had resumed. But lack of fiscal adjustment delayed the return to stability, inducing broad uncertainty, and hence reducing incentives for private sector, export-led growth (Levin, 1998).

From the various trade policy reforms undertaken since independence, it is evident that Kenya has made substantial progress towards a more liberal and outward-oriented trade regime. The manufacturing sector is still largely inward oriented, however, with part of the production largely targeted at regional export markets. There has been little response to trade reforms in the form of large-scale investments, as most of the new investments seem to have come from small and micro enterprises. The structure of the manufacturing sector has not changed very significantly in the last twenty years or so – it accounts for about 10 per cent of GDP. The sector is import dependent in terms of raw materials, capital, and intermediate goods. Kenya's industrial base is still narrow and tilted in favour of agro-based activities, showing that the country is still at the lower end of the industrial transformation towards a service-dominated economy. Nonetheless, Kenya's manufacturing sector is relatively more developed and open by regional standards. That notwithstanding, Kenya has yet to position itself as a major exporter of manufactures and services in sub-Saharan Africa (SSA). This raises the question of whether more trade reforms alone are sufficient to induce a major, non-traditional export response.

6.2.2 Trade performance in more detail

There was a marked increase in exports and imports following the implementation of trade liberalization reforms in the early 1990s. Deeper regional integration, i.e. the revival of EAC and the wider Common Market for Eastern and Southern Africa (COMESA), also added an impetus to export performance, particularly manufactured exports. On average, the value of total exports and imports of goods and services to GDP ratio as a broad measure of trade openness rose from 42.5 per cent a decade before liberalization (1980s) to 51.2 per cent in the 1990s and 60 per cent for the period 2001–07 (Figure 6.1).[7] Average growth in total exports of goods and services increased from 11.7 per cent in the 1980s to 19.4 per cent in the 1990s before declining to 12.3 per cent for the period 2000–07.

In general, growth in imports of goods and services has outstripped that of exports, resulting in trade deficits. However, the country has had a trade surplus in services since 1980 (UNCTAD, 2008). Merchandise exports account for over 50 per cent of Kenya's total export earnings. Although the diversification of exports, particularly the introduction of horticultural exports in the 1990s, was a major boost to Kenyan exports, the level of export concentration is still high. Figure 6.2 shows the percentage share of exports of goods for the top five, ten, and twenty products or subcategories (at SITC three-digit level) from 2000 to 2007. The top five and top ten products accounted for about 50 per cent and 61 per cent of merchandise exports in 2006–07, respectively. However, the level of concentration has been declining, notably for the top twenty products, which accounted for 73.8 per cent of exports in 2006–07, down from 81.3 per cent in 2000–01. Tea (and maté) alone accounted for about 21 per cent of total domestic exports. Other top five export products are crude vegetable materials not elsewhere specified (i.e. cut flowers), vegetables (fresh, chilled, and frozen), coffee and coffee substitutes, and petroleum oils. These are all primary commodities, which illustrates the dominance of agricultural

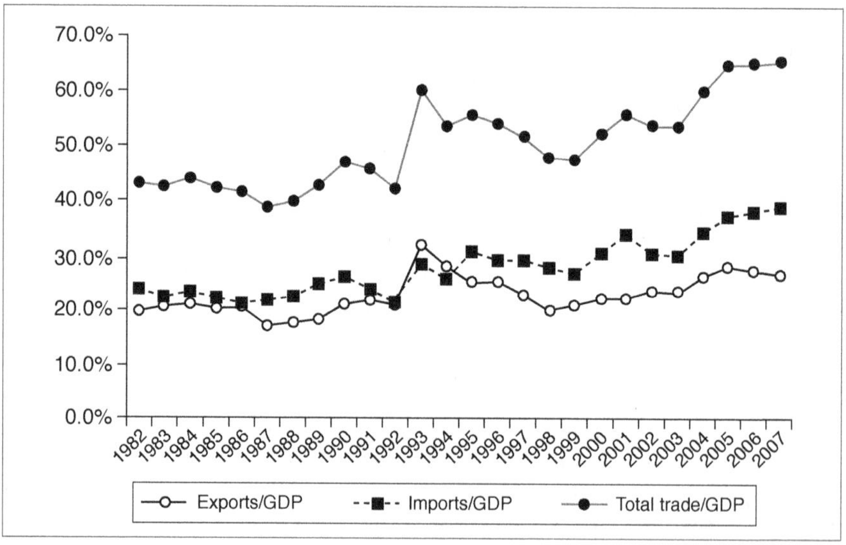

Figure 6.1 Value of exports and imports of goods and services as a percentage of GDP.

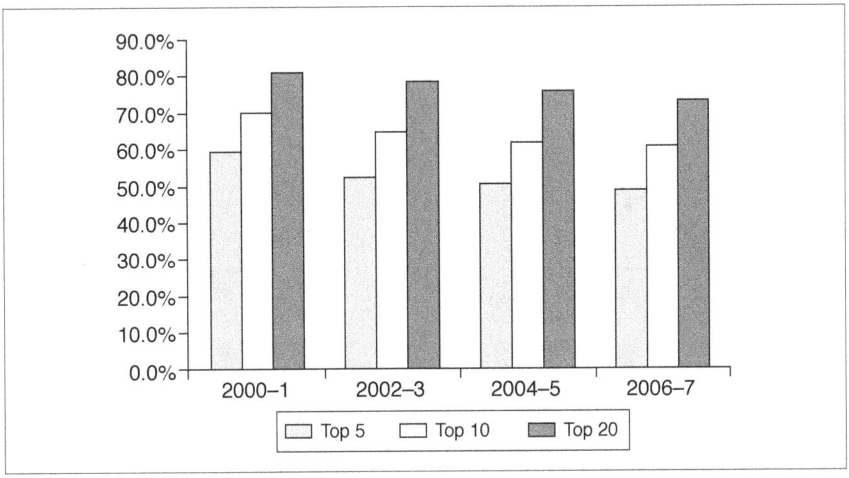

Figure 6.2 Share of top five, ten, and twenty export products (SITC three-digit level).

primary products in Kenya's exports. Manufactured exports (SITC one-digit level) accounted for only 14 per cent of domestic exports in 2006–07.

Table 6.2 shows the share of Kenya's key export products (at HS four-digit level) in the world market for the respective products in the period 2003–07. On average, Kenya's tea exports account for 16 per cent of total export value in the world market, whereas coffee accounts for only 1 per cent. Kenya has made a considerable impact in the horticulture industry, accounting for about 4.2 per cent and 1.3 per cent of the world's exports of cut flowers and fresh vegetables, respectively. The market share for most of the other key export products is very small. In total, Kenya's domestic exports account for only 0.03 per cent of the world's merchandise exports.

Regionally, however, Kenya has carved itself a niche within the East African market, with the highest percentage of its exports going to Uganda. In 2007, for instance, exports to Uganda accounted for 12 per cent of Kenya's domestic exports, followed by the UK (10.5 per cent), Tanzania (8 per cent), and the Netherlands (8 per cent). Table 6.3 shows the share of Kenya's exports to various regions for selected years. The African continent accounted for the largest share, rising from 36 per cent in 2001 to 45 per cent in 2007. Exports to African countries have increased over time, thanks to regional trading arrangements, namely the EAC and COMESA. The COMESA region has overtaken the European Union (EU) as the main trade partner and, more importantly, trade is dominated by non-traditional and manufactured goods. Overall, despite efforts to diversify away from the traditional European markets, Kenya's export market is concentrated in a few countries – six countries accounted for 50 per cent of Kenya's domestic exports in 2007 (i.e. Uganda, the UK, Tanzania, the Netherlands, the USA, and Pakistan).

Table 6.2 Kenya's top export products as a percentage of world export value for the product

HS code	Product	2003	2004	2005	2006	2007
0902	Tea	16.15	13.86	15.20	17.04	17.69
0603	Cut flowers and flower buds for bouquets, fresh or dried	3.55	4.35	4.04	4.44	4.48
0709	Vegetables, fresh or chilled	1.12	0.88	1.15	1.76	1.86
0901	Coffee	1.20	1.02	0.95	0.93	0.93
2710	Petroleum oils, not crude	0.27	0.24	0.16	0.05	0.03
2401	Tobacco unmanufactured; tobacco refuse	0.49	0.43	0.82	1.19	1.08
6204	Women's suits, jackets, dresses, skirts, etc. and shorts	0.0001	0.003	0.16	0.21	0.16
2836	Carbonate: peroxocarbonate, commercial ammonium carbonate	0.03	0.02	2.26	1.43	1.91
7210	Flat-rolled production of iron, clad, plated, or coated	0.18	0.22	0.22	0.24	0.18
0604	Foliage, branches, etc.	0.41	0.33	0.39	3.79	5.86
2523	Cements: Portland, aluminous, slag, supersulphate, and similar hydraulic cement	0.61	0.47	0.49	0.61	0.76

Source: ITC trade statistics.

In the service sector, exports have mainly been dominated by travel (tourism), but the trend had changed by 2006, with transport services taking the lead, followed by travel, communications, royalties and licence fees, and insurance (UNCTAD, 2008). The contribution of service exports to total exports increased from about 32 per cent in 1980 to 40 per cent in 2007 (UNCTAD, 2008). Export of services is an avenue of export expansion, as Kenya has the potential (e.g. wildlife, beaches, and coastal scenery as well as skilled manpower). Indeed, Kenya's *Vision 2030* is a good starting point, as tourism and business process and outsourcing (BPO) are identified as strategic sectors (Republic of Kenya, 2007a).

6.3 Multilateral and regional trade agreements and Kenya's policy space

6.3.1 World Trade Organization (WTO) rules and negotiations

Kenya is a long-standing member of the General Agreement on Tariffs and Trade (GATT) and now the WTO. Its trade policy sphere is affected by the multilateral trading rules and by the negotiated reforms of tariffs and other trade policy instruments.

Table 6.3 Kenya's export shares (%) to various destinations

	2001	2004	2007
Africa	**35.9**	**42.8**	**45.1**
Uganda	29.2	41.0	27.1
Tanzania	19.9	18.6	18.0
Egypt	16.4	7.3	7.4
Rest of Africa	34.6	33.1	47.5
Europe	**37.9**	**29.3**	**28.7**
United Kingdom	41.7	35.9	36.6
Netherlands	23.5	28.4	27.8
Germany	11.3	7.7	7.6
Rest of Europe	23.6	28.0	28.1
Asia	**21.1**	**15.9**	**17.1**
Pakistan	35.1	33.8	28.8
United Arab Emirates	12.3	7.0	18.3
Afghanistan	11.2	8.6	5.4
India	9.1	11.9	12.4
Rest of Asia	32.3	38.7	35.1
America	**3.5**	**2.4**	**7.5**
USA	76.0	73.8	93.7
Canada	8.3	8.2	3.2
Mexico	5.6	0.6	0.9
Rest of America	10.1	17.4	2.2
All other countries	**1.6**	**9.5**	**1.7**
Total	100.0	100.0	100.0

Source: Computed from ITC trade statistics data.

SAFETY VALVES

This principle argues that, in specific circumstances, governments can restrict trade. There are three types of provisions in this connection: articles allowing for the use of trade measures to attain non-economic objectives (protection of public health, national security, and policies to protect industries that are substantially injured from imports); articles aimed at ensuring 'fair competition' (countervailing or anti-dumping duties on subsidized or dumped imports); and provisions permitting intervention in trade for economic reasons (e.g. balance of payment or infant industry support).

DISPUTE SETTLEMENT

The WTO Dispute Settlement Mechanism (DSM) was designed to secure rules-based international trade. As pointed out by Alavi (2007), there are obstacles to the use of DSM by countries in SSA. Litigation costs are prohibitively high. DSM has inadequate and inappropriate retaliatory mechanisms for SSA: an insignificant share of international trade; historical and colonial ties with specific developed countries; and dependence on developed countries for donor funds. Finally, there is the lack of a development component. The only instance where development considerations feature in the DSM is the special and differential treatment provisions, which oblige DSM panels to consider any development issue raised by a developing country in a dispute.

The above difficulties deter countries such as Kenya from using the DSM. Indeed, apart from a few instances where Kenya has been enjoined in WTO cases as a third party,[8] the country has resolved trade disputes by other means. Examples include the fish and fish products dispute with the EU in the mid-1990s and the Kenya–Mauritius trade dispute on Kenya's ban on day-old chicks in April 2006 due to fears of avian encephalomyelitis.

ACCESS FOR AGRICULTURAL EXPORTS

Agriculture contributes about 23 per cent of Kenya's GDP. It is also a source of employment for about 70 per cent of the total labour force. The sector earns about 60 per cent of the total foreign exchange, provides raw materials to agro-based industries, and is the main source of the country's food requirements (Nyangito and Nzuma, 2005). In this regard, improved market access for Kenya's agricultural exports through multilateral trade liberalization is critical for the country. Kenya is concerned about the increased use of non-tariff barriers (NTB) and technical barriers to trade (TBT) by its trading partners. It is also concerned about tariff peaks in industrial countries against Kenya's primary export products and about the prospect of erosion in key industrial export markets of the tariff preference it benefits from, under preferential schemes such as AGOA in the USA or the EU if WTO negotiations lower non-preferential tariffs.

NON-AGRICULTURE MARKET ACCESS (NAMA)

NAMA negotiations are based on the Doha mandate of 2001, which calls for reduction or elimination of tariff peaks, tariff escalation, high tariffs, and non-tariff barriers for industrial products. A key element is tariff cuts according to some general formula, although there will be some flexibility proposed for developing countries to shelter their most sensitive sectors. Developed countries have been pushing for more market access for their industrial goods in the developing countries' markets in return for reducing their 'trade-distorting' farm subsidies. They want the developing world to bring down their industrial tariffs significantly. But this would require developing countries such as Kenya to undertake larger tariff cuts overall than developed countries.

GENERAL AGREEMENT ON TRADE IN SERVICES (GATS)

Services in Kenya play a critical developmental role and have both forward and backward linkages with other sectors of the economy. Low-cost and high-quality services are potentially exportable, but they are also required for successful exporting by other sectors. Kenya lacks adequate basic infrastructure – roads, power supply, telecommunications, and public transport. Open services trade regimes may help the country to access such services at competitive prices.

Developed countries have been the main 'demanders' in the services negotiations. This gives rise to several difficulties for Kenya. First, like most African countries, it has weak service sector infrastructure. Second, it does not have an accurate assessment about the domestic legal, administrative and regulatory capacities to support service liberalization. It is therefore difficult for Kenya to precisely identify its strategic interest on GATS issues. Third, negotiations require more human, financial, and institutional capacity in Geneva and at home than it can currently muster.

Most SSA countries have identified the movement of natural persons as one constituting export interest to them, as they have endowments of types of workers who are seeking employment. However, the Annex on Movement of Natural Persons Supplying Services under the Agreement for GATS (WTO, 2002) excludes any worker seeking employment in another WTO member state. Horizontal commitments that link access to commercial presence to benefit semi-skilled workers are required.

6.3.2 Bilateral and regional trade policy issues

Kenya is a member of both COMESA and the EAC. COMESA is a preferential trade agreement (PTA) but has yet to launch a customs union. It has nineteen member states with a population of over 389 million (Figure 6.3). In 2008, COMESA signed an agreement with the Southern African Development Committee (SADC) and EAC for an expanded free trade zone covering a population of 527 million people.

Regional co-operation facilitates access to wider markets, which in turn enables the exploitation of economies of scale and, consequently, the attraction of foreign investment. Kenya's exports to the COMESA region increased from an average of 15 per cent for the period 1990–92 to 34 per cent in 1996–98 (Glenday and Ndii, 2000). In 2007, the value of exports to the region increased to approximately Ksh 86.2 billion from Ksh 45 billion in 1997, whereas imports increased to Ksh 28.6 billion from Ksh 1.7 billion in 1992. Therefore, the country has a large trade surplus with other COMESA countries.

Having collapsed in 1977, the EAC was officially revived in July 2000. It aims at widening and deepening economic, political, and social co-operation among the partner states (membership increased to five after Rwanda and Burundi joined in July 2007). The EAC established a customs union from January 2005. Under the terms of the customs treaty, Kenyan exports continue to be subject to duty in the other four countries until 2010. Common external tariffs (CETs) apply to all goods imported from third-party countries. A political

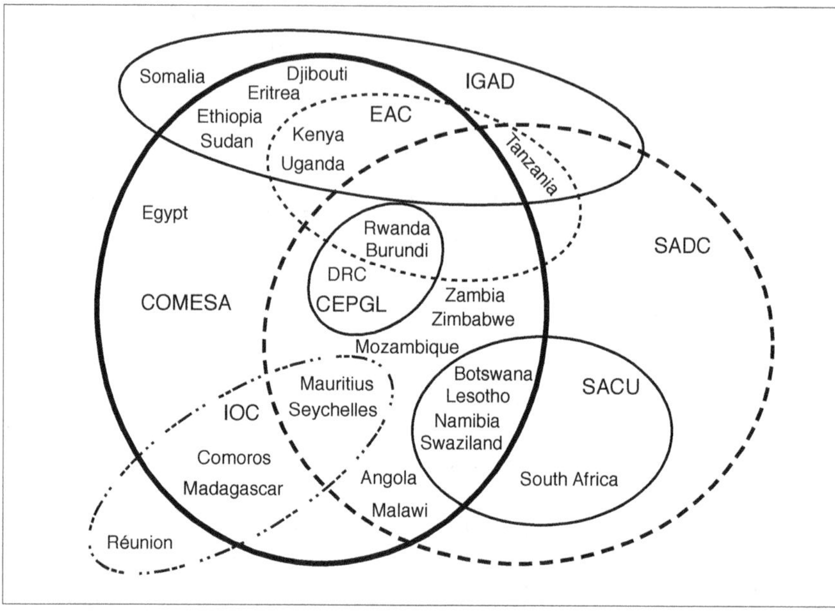

Figure 6.3 'Spaghetti bowl' of overlapping regional integration agreements in Eastern, Central, Northern, and Southern Africa.
CEPGL, Economic Community of the Great Lakes Region; SADC, South African Development Community; SACU, Southern African Customs Union; IOC, Indian Ocean Commission; EAC, East African Community; COMESA, Common Market for Eastern and Southern Africa; IGAD, Intergovernmental Authority on Development.
Source: Adapted from the Economic Commission for Africa (2006: 51).

federation is envisaged in 2015. It is hoped that experience gained in exporting to regional markets will increase the capacity and prospects for penetrating extra-regional markets.

CHALLENGES FOR REGIONAL INTEGRATION AGREEMENTS (RIAS)

There is a general consensus that RIAs in Africa have been unsuccessful in achieving their objectives (Geda and Kebret, 2008). The key challenges for RIAs are overlapping memberships, lack of trade complementarity among member states, and unwillingness of governments to surrender sovereignty on macroeconomic policy-making to a regional authority (Johnson, 1995).

The patchwork resulting from the multiplicity creates a 'spaghetti bowl' effect (Figure 6.3), which has several drawbacks: fragmented economic spaces and approaches to regional integration; increased cost of membership in RIAs; unhealthy rivalry for donor funds; contradictory obligations and loyalties for member countries; inconsistent objectives and conflicting operational mandates.

Despite the above challenges, some progress has so far been made within EAC and COMESA that suggests optimism. COMESA achieved free trade area

(FTA) status in 2000 as a step towards a customs union, and currently most countries have achieved a tariff reduction rate of 80–90 per cent on goods originating from member states (Geda and Kebret, 2008). The EAC member states have agreed to pool their sovereignty and pursue a common international trade policy.

KEY NORTH–SOUTH RELATIONSHIPS

For about thirty-two years, until 31 December 2007, most of Kenya's exports, like those of other African, Caribbean, and Pacific (ACP) countries, entered the EU market duty free. The legality of this non-reciprocal preferential market access to the EU was challenged at the WTO. The WTO Ministerial Meeting of 2001 granted the ACP and EU countries until 31 December 2007 to rectify this, which led to the development of an alternative trade regime in the form of Economic Partnership Agreements (EPAs), which requires Kenya to substantially open its market to EU imports.

Kenya had the option of going for the EPA or settling for the Generalized System of Preferences (GSP) plus (available to developing countries). It opted for the EPA for two reasons. First, GSP plus is not contractual and could be amended by the EU periodically without consulting beneficiary countries. According to Republic of Kenya (2008a), EPAs offer a contractually secure trade regime that Kenya can use for stimulating investments targeting the EU market. Second, under the GSP plus, there are some products that attract import duty in the EU and yet they are duty free under the EPA. These include agricultural products such as dairy.

Kenya, along with other EAC member states, negotiated the EPA under the auspices of Eastern and Southern Africa (ESA). Tanzania, on the other hand, pursued an EPA under SADC configuration. This posed a major policy challenge. Under the EAC customs union, the countries were bound to sign an EPA as a customs territory. At the same time, Kenya, not being a least developed member state in the EAC, faced the possibility of preference erosion if an EPA was not signed as it does not enjoy the benefits under the Everything But Arms (EBA) agreement within the GSP framework. As a result, only an 'interim' goods-only EPA was signed up to by the EAC group in late 2007. The framework was due to be (but has still not been) replaced by a comprehensive EPA with effect from 1 July 2009, covering services, investment, and co-operation in other related areas such as competition and government procurement.

It is evident from this review of multilateral and regional trade policy issues facing Kenya that its trade policy space could be both constrained and enhanced in the coming years through its international trade negotiations. It is also evident that there are growing demands on Kenya's trade negotiating capacity, and an associated need to increase this capacity if the appropriate balance between policy constraint and enhancement is to be achieved. In the final section, we return to the key trade policy choices and actions Kenya needs to take.

6.4 Assessment of the impact of trade policy

Trade policy can affect household welfare via three broad channels that work through the following institutions: enterprises, retail and wholesale distribution system, government, and households (Winters, 2000). This takes place by inducing changes in the prices of consumption goods and services (distribution channel); factor prices, income, employment, incentives for investment and innovation; short-run risks and adjustment costs faced by economic agents (enterprise channel); and government revenue (government channel). The transmission process is presented in Figure 6.4.

6.4.1 Distribution channels

PRICE TRANSMISSION TO CONSUMERS

Trade policy interventions (tariffs and NTBs) plus other international trade costs (international transport, insurance, and port handling) raise the inside-the-border price of importable goods in Kenya. The prevailing exchange rate also contributes to the post-tariff border price. Once inside Kenya, the goods face domestic taxes and distribution costs from the entry port to major wholesale distribution centres, which may add costs. The resulting price is the wholesale price. From the wholesale depot, the goods are distributed to the retail centres and, hence, potentially face similar costs (Figure 6.4). Individuals and households buy the goods at the retail price, with all the accumulated costs.

The extent to which the world import price signal is translated into economic welfare depends on a number of factors, which mitigate or amplify the effects of trade policies on households. These include: the nature of intermediate organizations in the distribution chain; a household's endowment of time, skills, land, and technology; the quality of infrastructure in the country; and the completeness of markets. The distribution and wholesale sector is quite important and accounts for 15.7 per cent of the GDP and 10 per cent of formal employment in Kenya (Republic of Kenya, 2008b). However, the subsector faces a number of challenges, which include: weak and fragmented supply chains; an unconducive licensing and regulatory framework; high transportation costs; inadequate business management skills; and inadequate logistics and information and communications technology capabilities.

Poorer households spend a relatively large proportion of their income on tradable products, including food, beverages, clothing, and textiles (Republic of Kenya, 2007b). As a consequence, poorer households are bound to pay a disproportionate share of the tariff burden relative to their share of expenditure. However, although tariff liberalization is expected to reduce the cost of

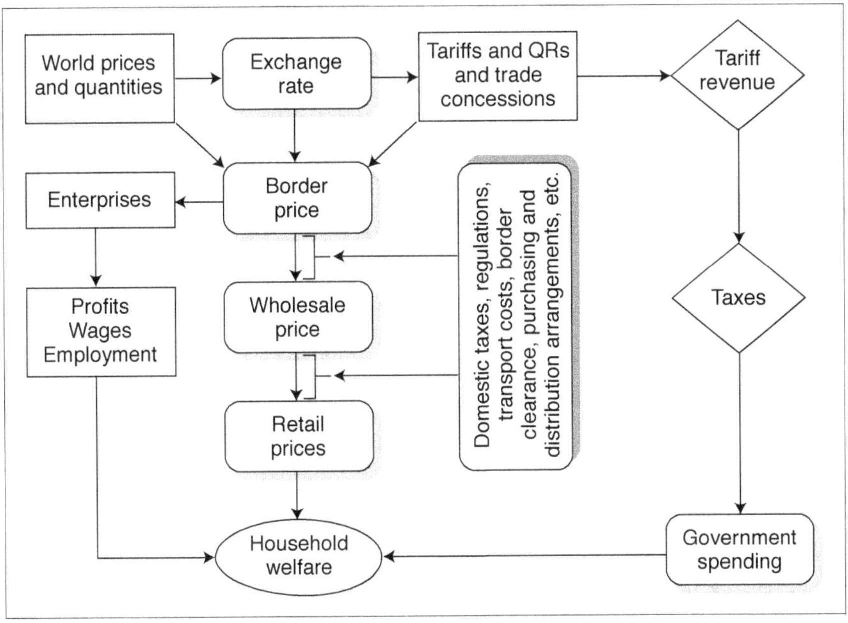

Figure 6.4 Transmission channels from trade policy to welfare. QR, quantative restriction
Source: Adapted from Figure 2 of Winters (2000: 58).

living of poor households, the lower border prices are not transmitted to the poor because of the excessive intermediate costs.

TRANSMISSION FROM DOMESTIC PRODUCERS TO THE EXPORT MARKET

On the export side, the effects of trade policy can be analysed starting at the bottom of Figure 6.4. As illustrated by the World Bank (2005), the coffee farming value chain is dominated by spraying using imported agrochemicals (33.4 per cent) followed by plant maintenance (26.4 per cent). The coffee is sold to the co-operatives, whose value chain is dominated by processing (68.3 per cent). The processed coffee is then sold to the secondary processors, comprising hulling (61.5 per cent) and handling (38.5 per cent). At the final stage is the dealers and exporters, where the activity is statutory charges (98 per cent) and auction fees (2 per cent). At each stage, the institutions incur costs and add mark-ups, all of which enter the final export invoice price. In the export market, the coffee faces the trade policies of the importing country (regional trading arrangements, import policies and procedures, standards, etc.), all of which add costs. Thus, the production and transaction costs to coffee farmers have been overly high. As the international price is fixed, the costs are netted off the farm-gate price that determines the coffee farmer's welfare.

Price transmission can be explored using information on relative unit value (RUV) of exports, i.e.the ratio of the average unit value of exports for a country to the world average unit value. If the RUV is below 1, then the country exports its product at a lower price than the world average unit price. Alternatively, if the RUV is above 1, then the country exports its product at a higher price than the world average unit price. According to trade map data from the International Trade Centre (ITC),[9] there are some products in Kenya, such as transport equipment, minerals, fresh food, processed food, chemicals basic manufactures, and electronic components, that are exported at higher than the average world price. Other exports, such as wood products, leather products, non-electronic machinery, information technology and consumer electronics, clothing, and miscellaneous manufacturing, are exported at prices below the world average.

6.4.2 The enterprise channel

This channel provides the link from trade policy to welfare arising through its effects on enterprises. Enterprises here refer to any unit that produces and sells output and employs labour from outside its own immediate household. Trade comes in through the fact that inputs are acquired and outputs sold through market transactions. This is the most important channel through which trade can alleviate poverty (McCulloch *et al.*, 2001).

The demand for factor inputs and the supply of output by the enterprises is determined by the export, import, and domestic prices. The net effect is that operations at the enterprise level determine profitability, wages, and employment. Price changes affect the incentives for enterprises to produce particular goods and adopt technologies.

TRADE AND EMPLOYMENT

Theoretically, any trade-induced change in a country's product prices shifts resources towards the industries in which relative profitability has increased, which in turn leads to an increase in demand for factors used intensively – abundant unskilled labour in the case of a developing country such as Kenya. However, Wood (1997) argues that international trade may have adverse effects on wages and the employment of unskilled workers by bringing about technological change that leads to a displacement of unskilled workers and/or by increasing the own price employment elasticity of unskilled workers, hence making such workers more vulnerable to economic shocks. Trade liberalization has had an impact on employment in Kenya, with levels declining in some sectors. Within manufacturing, there are labour-intensive sectors that have contracted such as soft drinks and carbonated waters, cotton ginneries, tanneries and leather finishing, manufacture of footwear except plastic, manufacture of electrical appliances and machinery, manufacture of rail equipment, manufacture and assembly of motor vehicles, and ship repairing.

Growth in total wage employment declined from an average of 3.8 per cent for the period 1964–89 to a mere 1.2 per cent for the period 1990–2002. Although the decline can be attributed to factors such as poor economic performance and public sector reforms in the 1990s, it was partly due to the collapse of private firms and retrenchment resulting from stiff competition from imports following trade liberalization (Manda, 2002; Republic of Kenya, 2002). At the same time, the informal sector increased, and casual employment as a proportion of total wage employment has been on the rise since around 1994. There has been concern that trade liberalization has led to the casualization of employment and low wages for the unskilled in most firms (Were, 2007). Thus, while employment has increased in exporting sectors such horticulture and EPZs, the quality of jobs is still an issue – casual workers often operate without job security, with low pay, and non-wage employment benefits, with implications for poverty. Arguably, trade should promote human dignity besides simply spurring economic growth. At the same time, the high cost of living, particularly in the urban centres (food, housing, transport, utilities), leads to pressure for higher real wages in Kenya, which is a disincentive for foreign direct investment in exporting sectors. The other challenge is the footloose investors with limited forward and backward linkages. With trade liberalization, services have become the key source of employment, accounting for over 50 per cent of total wage employment in Kenya.

6.4.3 The government channel

The right hand side of Figure 6.4 refers to the link between trade and poverty via government tax and spending. In most developing countries, trade taxes form a significant part of government revenue, and the impact of tariff liberalization on the fiscus in general, and social expenditure in particular, is an important consideration. In Kenya, trade taxes now account for about 24 per cent of total revenues with some decline in recent years. Trade taxes have declined mainly due to trade liberalization and tariff harmonization measures within the EAC. However, other reforms have countered the possible effect of loss of international trade revenue on the poverty alleviation initiatives. These include improvement in tax administration, which led to an increase in domestic tax revenues (VAT, income tax, and others), as well as the pro-poor expenditure programmes under the Medium Term Expenditure Framework (MTEF) and the Investment Programme for the Economic Recovery Strategy covering the period 2003–07.

6.5 On the need for a broad concept of trade policy space

Thus far, the focus of the discussion and analysis has been on a traditional, narrow view of trade policy. It is increasingly recognized, however, that trade policy is only one source of trade costs. Indeed, in the context of a country such as Kenya, the other sources of trade costs besides those induced by trade policies (tariffs, NBTs, etc.) may be a more dominant element of overall trade costs. Consider for example the information in Table 6.4 taken from the 2007–08 Global Competitiveness Index for Kenya on infrastructure and goods market efficiency, for which Kenya is ranked 93rd and 74th out of 134 countries.

It is clear from this information that the costs of trading both domestically and internationally are likely to be much higher for Kenyan traders and producers than in many other countries. For road quality (95th), port infrastructure (83rd), and burden of customs procedures (100th), Kenya is shown to be lagging by international standards. This means that producers' own costs of production and those of their suppliers are higher than they would be in more competitive conditions. It also means that the costs of acquiring (intermediate and capital) goods and services from domestic and foreign suppliers are higher than they would be in an environment with a better infrastructure and more efficient institutions (e.g. customs authority). Exporters are similarly faced with higher trading costs, with foreign buyers having the option to source their goods from lower trade cost sources.

Clearly, it is desirable to create a generally competitive business environment in which the costs of production and trading are relatively low and in

Table 6.4 Global competitiveness rankings for Kenya in subindices of infrastructure and goods market efficiency

Infrastructure	(Rank/134)	Goods market efficiency	(Rank/134)
Quality of overall infrastructure	88	Intensity of local competition	71
Quality of roads	95	Extent of market dominance	77
Quality of railway infrastructure	68	Effectiveness of anti-monopoly policy	62
Quality of port infrastructure	83	Extent and effect of taxation	111
Quality of air transport infrastructure	68	Total tax rate	91
Available seat kilometres	56	Number of procedures required to start a business	103
Quality of electricity supply	94	Time required to start a business	99
Telephone lines	121	Agricultural policy costs	28
		Prevalence of trade barriers	120
		Trade-weighted tariff rate	80
		Prevalence of foreign ownership	57
		Business impact of rules on foreign direct investment	79
		Burden of customs procedures	100
		Degree of customer orientation	33
		Buyer sophistication	96

line with international standards. The creation of such an environment is about the whole gamut of government policies and, ultimately, about the success of development policies overall. It would be unrealistic to view trade policy so broadly, but it is equally inappropriate and unhelpful to view trade policy as simply being about the policy instruments of import control (tariffs, NTBs) and of export promotion (e.g. export processing zone support measures). As in many other SSA countries, the lowering of trade costs through narrow trade policy reform is unlikely to be sufficient to support deep international and regional integration and substantial trade growth (see Milner, 1998; Milner and Zgovu, 2006).

HIGH TRADE COSTS AND TRADE REGIME BIAS

Trade costs, whether associated with trade policy interventions or not, have explicit or implicit taxing and subsidizing effects on local producers of traded goods. A local producer whose production competes with imports can raise his prices without losing competitiveness as a result of anything that raises the trading costs of the imports, whether that is a higher tariff or non-tariff barrier against the competing imports or higher international shipping costs or higher costs of moving the imports through the port or from the port to the domestic centres of consumption. These implicit or explicit subsidization or taxation effects are not identical, however, for production for the local market (importables production) and production for the export market (exportables production). The key message is that the higher the trade costs are, the greater the incentive to produce importables for the domestic market and, correspondingly, the greater the disincentive to produce exportables for the export market.

Consider Table 6.5, which summarizes the pattern of subsidization and taxation associated with policy and other sources of trade costs. It represents the pattern of effects on the price of final goods (output effects) and the cost of intermediate goods (input effects) associated with a typical trade policy regime (positive tariff and some non-tariff import barriers, but approximately zero, nominal export subsidies and taxes). The output of importables production is implicitly subsidized by policy and other trade costs, but exportables output is not. An exportables producer cannot raise prices in export markets because of a tariff that only affects conditions in the local market. An exportables producer does, however, have to bear the cost of higher trade costs (resulting from, for example, port inefficiency, poor domestic road links to the port, or uncompetitive international shipping conditions). The potential buyers of these goods in the foreign market will typically not absorb these higher trade costs because they have the option to buy from many sources, including those with lower trade costs. On the input side, higher trade costs (irrespective of source) must raise the cost of inputs; policy or other trade costs explicitly raise

Table 6.5 Explicit and implicit subsidization and taxation effects of policy and other sources of trade costs

	Importables (M)	Exportables (X)
Output effects		
(a) Policy (s_j^p) Import tariffs and NTBs (on competing imports)	Positive subsidization (25%)[a]	Neutral (0%)
(b) Other trade costs (s_j^o)	Positive subsidization (23%)[b]	Positive taxation (23%)[b]
Input taxation		
(a) Policy (t_i^p) Tariffs and NTBs (on importable inputs)	Positive taxation (6.5%)[c]	Positive taxation (0%)[d]
(b) Other trade cost (t_i^o)	Positive taxation (23%)[b]	Positive taxation (23%)[b]

a Maximum tariff typically charged on competing imports.
b Equals 1.05 (domestic transport costs) times 1.0525 (port handling fee plus efficiency and customs delays) times 1.115 (international freight costs) minus 1.
c Simple average of simple average applied tariff (12.9 per cent) and zero rate.
d Assuming exporting from export processing zone with exemption from duties on imported goods. This is an extreme assumption, given that locally produced goods may be absorbed by EPZ firms and they are increased in price because of trade barriers.

the cost of imported inputs and, by implication, the cost of locally produced inputs competing with more highly 'taxed' imported inputs. This positive taxing effect on inputs of any type of trade costs is now symmetrical across importables and exportables production, unless exporters are exempted from tariffs on imported inputs.

The net or overall effect of these output and input tax and subsidy effects is ambiguous in the case of importables, but not in the case of exportables. For importables, there are positive output subsidies and negative input taxes, and the net effect will depend on the relative rates of subsidy and taxation (although as we will shortly see it is likely to result in net subsidization under normal conditions). In contrast, the net impact for exportables is clear: positive output and input taxation must result in net overall taxation. We have strong a priori expectations of an anti-exportables bias induced by both trade policy and other sources of trade costs, one that will not be eliminated by lowering trade policy-induced trade costs.

A THOUGHT EXPERIMENT?

Without conducting a detailed empirical investigation, it is possible to attach some credible orders of magnitude to the rates of subsidy and taxation applying in Kenya and to the net effects on incentives to produce. Even if we restrict ourselves to transport (international and domestic) and some border-related costs (trade policy, port handling, customs procedures), which is only a subset of the total trade costs (which also includes domestic distribution costs and other border-related costs associated with language, information, security, and currency barriers) on which some commentators focus (Anderson and Van Wincoop, 2004), the importance of trade costs can still be demonstrated.

The policy-induced trade costs imposed on the production of any particular good will depend on the specific duty applied and on any NTBs applying. Here, we assume there are no NTBs but that the maximum tariff rate (the EAC maximum common external tariff rate) will be applied to competing imports of final products. Intermediate inputs will typically be subject to lower tariff rates or be exempt. Here, we assume an average or typical duty on intermediates that is a simple average of a zero rate and the average applied rate overall for Kenya in 2006.

The other trade costs rate assumed for both tradable final and intermediate goods is 23 per cent. This is a modest estimate of other trade costs, based on the average international freight costs for Africa (reported by Perez and Wilson, 2008) and compounded by the actual port handling fee reported by the WTO for Kenya plus assumed additional costs associated with domestic transportation, port handling, and customs delays.

We estimate the indicative rates of net or effective protection (e_j) using a simplified estimation framework suggested by Milner (1997), as follows:

$$e_j = \left[\frac{s_j^p - a_{ij}t_i^p}{1-a_{ij}}\right] + \left[\frac{s_j^o - a_{ij}t_i^o}{1-a_{ij}}\right] + \left[\frac{s_j^p s_j^o - a_{ij}t_i^p t_i^o}{1-a_{ij}}\right] \tag{6.1}$$

where $s_j^{p(0)}$ = the nominal rate of subsidy on final good *j* induced by trade policy (other trade costs)

$t_i^{p(0)}$ = the nominal rate of tax on composite intermediate input *i* induced by trade policy (other trade costs)

a_{ij} = the share of intermediate inputs in the total value of good *j*.

(For the present purposes, we take the average share of intermediate goods in the value of gross output in the manufacturing sector in 2007, i.e. we set a_{ij} equal to 0.71.) The expression in Equation (6.1) is arranged so that total net protection can be decomposed into that associated with trade policy (s^p and t^p terms), with other trade costs (s^o and t^o terms) and the interaction effect between the trade policy and other trade costs.

Applying the indicative tax and subsidy rates for the typical Kenyan importable and exportable product recorded in Table 6.5, we obtain the estimated overall net rates of protection and components as set out in Table 6.6. There is a larger overall net subsidy effect for importables (+109.5 per cent) and a net tax or disprotection effect for exportables (135.6 per cent), with the bulk of the net subsidization of importables being induced by trade policy and the whole of the net taxation of exportables being due to non-trade policy sources of trade costs. Note also that, even if there was to be complete liberalization of imports in Kenya (i.e. import tariffs and NTBs eliminated), there would still be a very large regime bias in favour of production for the home market and against exporting (this rate of net subsidization of importables falling to +23.0 per cent, but the rate of net subsidization of exportables remaining at –135.6 per cent). Indeed, given the short- to medium-term constraints on trade policy reform (internal political economy or fiscal constraints on lowering tariffs), the only way of lowering the taxation of exportables is to focus reforms on this broader set of trade costs. Export promotion policies need to have this broad concept of trade costs if they are to be effective.

COMPLEMENTARY POLICIES AND A BROAD CONCEPT OF TRADE FACILITATION

Trade policy reforms have been necessary to initiate integration into the global economy, but they have often not been sufficient. The costs of imported goods and the competitiveness of their products in export markets depends as much if not more on international transport and other natural trade costs than on their own or other countries' trade policies. There is growing recognition (Milner, 2006) that trade policy, narrowly defined, has been overemphasized at the expense of complementary trade-related measures. Such measures include domestic and international transport policy reforms, national or regional infrastructure developments, or a wider range of services (e.g. insurance, banking) affecting the cost of international transactions. Manufacturing is transaction intensive, and with the growing fragmentation of international production and creation of international production networks – what we referred to earlier as 'trade in tasks' – it is important that developing countries have access to competitive trade and trade-related services.

Viewed narrowly, trade facilitation enables the movement of goods and services across national barriers. Improving transport systems by investing in infrastructure or changing policies to increase competition and efficiency are broader facilitation measures. Improving customs clearance procedures, supporting the capacity to meet the technical or health standards in export markets, and strengthening support for marketing export products is also required. Trade facilitation might also extend to the availability and efficiency of financial and other business services. Uncompetitive local conditions and barriers to offshoring may allow costly and lengthy administration procedures

Table 6.6 Indicative rates of effective protection induced by trade costs in Kenya (%)

	Due to:			
	Trade policy (a)	Other trade costs (b)	Interaction of (a) and (b)	Total
Importables	+70.3%	+23.0%	+16.2%	+109.5%
Exportables	0%	–135.6%	0%	–135.6%

to persist in service sectors. The cost of credit, including trade credits, and of working capital can be much higher in developing countries than in countries with more developed and competitive service sectors. Many developing countries have made progress in reducing administrative procedures, bureaucracy, and corruption. Changing the ethos of institutions and administrative systems and restoring confidence in them, however, is often difficult and slow. There is still considerable scope for improving the business environment in many developing countries and for reducing the costs of doing business. Kenya, like many SSA countries, needs a comprehensive strategy to promote a competitive domestic economy, and to increase the integration of the economy into the regional and international economy by reducing trade costs.

6.6 Summary conclusions and policy options

Since the early 1980s, Kenya has shifted away from import substitution towards a more outward-oriented strategy of export promotion. It has done this through a mixture of providing more direct incentives for export promotion through, for example, incentives to operate in EPZs, and indirectly by reducing the incentive to produce for the domestic market by lowering tariff and non-tariff sources of protection from competing imports. The import regime has been significantly liberalized and rationalized with tariffs now the dominant source of protection, the number of tariff rates much reduced, and tariff peaks in general significantly reduced. These import policy reforms have been implemented as part of both unilateral (e.g. structural adjustment) programmes and implementation of the common external tariff of the EAC and the WTO framework. The simple average applied tariff is now only about 13 per cent, although there are marked variations in sectoral averages and substantially higher tariff peaks in some sectors. Given the significantly escalating structure of tariffs (with lower, even zero tariffs on intermediate inputs and new materials and above average tariffs on the final stages of production), the effective protection for local (in particular manufacturing) production remains far from negligible. The trade liberalization process is not necessarily complete, although the pace of further liberalization will be dependent on the capacity of the economy to adjust and to develop further export capability.

Except for a sharp rise in the export to GDP ratio in 1993 (coinciding with currency depreciation), the effects of trade policy reform are as yet more evident on the import than the export side. There has been some recovery (following the post-1993 fallback and steady growth in horticultural exports) in the decade since the late 1990s, but import growth has in general outstripped export growth. The resulting deterioration in the trade balance is not necessarily a source of concern for an economy in need of investing (in excess of savings) at this stage of development. What is of greater concern is the rather limited response of exports in growth and diversification terms (in particular non-traditional exports) that has been experienced following the substantial trade reforms.

A key question for Kenyan policy-makers is 'why has substantive trade policy reform in Kenya produced to date a limited response in terms of the growth and diversification of exports?'. This chapter has concentrated on a number of issues relevant to answering this question and to the formulation and implementation of future policy: the issue of export market access, possible further trade policy reform, and complementary measures to support trade policy reform. All are shown to be necessary, but probably not sufficient, to turn Kenya into a competitive, export-oriented economy.

Improved market access needs to be gained through targeted bilateral, regional, and multilateral trade negotiations. This will require enhanced human and institutional capacity at the national level, and improved co-ordination across the agencies of trade policy. A new National Trade Policy is currently being drafted to meet this need. It will, however, also require greater co-operation and co-ordination across national governments within the region. The current 'spaghetti bowl' of overlapping regional integration arrangements is not conducive to improved co-ordination and co-operation in the region. Kenya's membership of two customs unions (EAC and COMESA) is not sustainable in the long term. The immediate prospects for deeper integration are higher in the narrower EAC grouping, but the potential benefits from wider economic integration in COMESA and Africa in general need also to be recognized. Those benefits are on the import side (greater competition in the home market, access to wider choice, and cheaper inputs, etc.) as well as on the export side. The mutual benefits of reciprocal opening up within the wider region, of resource sharing, and increased bargaining power and capacity beyond the region need to be embraced by Kenya, and the phased deepening and broadening of regional economic integration and policy co-operation needs to be embedded in Kenya's vision for the future. Similarly, the greater integration of the economies within the region should be seen as supporting greater international economic integration. Improving access for Kenya's exports (through the multilateral trade negotiations or through the implementation of bilateral opportunities associated in the USA with AGOA or the EPA with the EU) should be viewed as also requiring increased competition in Kenya (appropriately sequenced and phased in, and supported by adjustment support measures and investments). Increased import competition should not ultimately be viewed as the price to be paid for increased export opportunities but as a necessary ingredient for improved export performance. Kenya, for instance, could position herself as the BPO destination of choice given the existence of a pool of highly educated and skilled manpower. BPO has great potential to provide employment opportunities at call centres, but will require reduced costs of internet connectivity and adherence to international quality standards.

Other necessary ingredients for improved export performance are improved competitiveness of business and financial services and intermediate input suppliers in Kenya, and reduced trade costs in general. This chapter has set out in broad terms the type of complementary policies and trade facilitation measures required. Trade policy should not only be viewed as occupying the narrow range of policy space associated with border policy instruments (tariffs, export promotion agency activities, etc.), but as occupying a much broader space. Competitive Kenyan exporters need competitive suppliers, competition in local and regional markets, effective institutions (customs, etc.), and a good functioning infrastructure (transport, telecommunications, etc.). The agenda and investment needs for Kenya's future trade policy are substantial.

Notes

1 We thank the participants of the trade session at the CSAE 2009 conference at St Catherine's College, Oxford University, for useful comments on the version of the chapter that was presented at the conference. All remaining errors are the authors' responsibility.

2 Kenya was the first sub-Saharan Africa country to receive funds under structural adjustment lending from the World Bank in 1980.

3 It was not possible to extend the table to later years due to non-availability of directly comparable data.

4 See Swamy (1994) for details.

5 Quick disbursing BOP support was suspended in 1991 on account of what was described as rising levels of corruption, failure to correct macroeconomic imbalances caused by fiscal indiscipline, slow pace of reforms particularly public sector reforms, and political democratization. Substantive market-oriented reforms were implemented in other sectors such as public, financial, agriculture, and social sectors (see Were *et al.*, 2006 for details).

6 The macroeconomic instability was partly triggered by financial scams and fiscal indiscipline in the run-up to the first multiparty general elections of December 1992. Interest rates, inflation rate, and exchange rate rose to unprecedented levels in 1993.

7 The data on the GDP measures are based on the 1993 System of National Accounts (SNA), which Kenya adopted in 2004. This switch led to a slightly higher GDP value than was previously recorded under the 1968 SNA.

8 See details at www.wto.org/english/thewto_e/countries_e/kenya_e.htm.

9 RUV of Kenyan export data from the trade map of the International Trade Centre at http://www.intracen.org.

References

Alavi, A., 2007, 'African Countries and the WTO Dispute Settlement Mechanism', *Development Policy Review*, 25(1), 25–42.

Anderson, J. E. and E. Van Wincoop, 2004, 'Trade Costs', *Journal of Economic Literature*, 42, 691–751.

Department of Economics, University of Nairobi and University of Gothenburg, 1993, *Economic Development and the Manufacturing Sector in Kenya*. The African Regional Programme on Enterprise Development, Country Background Paper. Washington, DC: World Bank

Economic Commission for Africa, 2006, *Assessing Regional Integration in Africa II: Rationalising Regional Economic Communities*. Addis Ababa: Economic Commission for Africa.

Geda, A. and H. Kebret, 2008, 'Regional Economic Integration in Africa: A Review of Problems and Prospects with a Case Study of COMESA', *Journal of African Economics*, 17 (3), 357–394.

Glenday, G. and D. Ndii, 2000, 'Export Platforms in Kenya'. African Economic Policy Discussion Paper Number 43.

Hoekman, B., 2002, 'The WTO: Functions and Basic Principles', in Hoekman, B., M. Aaditya and P. English (eds) *Development, Trade, and the WTO*. Washington, DC: The World Bank, 41–60.

Ikiara, M. M. and L. K. Ndirangu, 2003, 'Prospects of Kenya's Clothing Exports under AGOA after 2004', KIPPRA Discussion Paper Series DP/24/2003. Nairobi: Kenya Institute for Public Policy Research and Analysis.

Johnson, O. E. G., 1995, 'Regional Integration in Sub-Saharan Africa', *Journal of European Integration*, 18 (2–3), 201–234.

Lall, S. and C. Pietrobelli, 2002, *Failing to Compete: Technology Development and Technology Systems in Africa*. Cheltenham, UK: Edward Elgar.

Levin, J., 1998, 'Structural Adjustment and Poverty: The Case of Kenya'. PhD thesis. Department of Economics, Götenborg University, Sweden.

Manda, D. K., 2002, 'Globalisation and the Labour Market in Kenya', Discussion Paper 6. Globalisation and Poverty. A paper prepared as part of the DFID-funded research project, 'Globalisation, Production and Poverty'.

McCulloch, N., L. A. Winters, and X. Cirera, 2001, *Trade Liberalization and Poverty: A Handbook*. London: CEPR and DFID.

Milner, C. R., 1997, 'On Natural and Policy-Induced Sources of Trade Regime Bias', *Review of World Economics*, 132, 740–752.

Milner, C. R., 1998, 'Trade Regime Bias and the Response to Trade Liberalisation in Sub-Saharan Africa', *Kyklos*, 51, 219–236.

Milner, C. R. 2006. 'Making NAMA Work: Supporting Adjustment and Development', *The World Economy*, 29, 1409–1422.

Milner, C. R. and E. Zgovu, 2006, 'A Natural Experiment for Identifying the Impact of "Natural" Trade Barriers on Exports'. *Journal of Development Economics*, 80, 251–268.

Nyangito, H. O. and J. M. Nzuma, 2005, 'Kenyan Agriculture's Domestic Trade Regime and External Market Access Conditions 1980–2000', in Mwega, F. M. and H.O. Nyangito (eds) *African Imperatives in the World Trade Order*. AERC Collaborative Project, 23–87.

Perez, A. and J. S. Wilson, 2008, 'Lowering Trade Costs for Development in Africa: A Summary Overview', Mimeo, World Bank.

Republic of Kenya, 2002, *National Development Plan 2002–2008*. Nairobi: Government Printer.

Republic of Kenya, 2007a, *Kenya Vision 2030*. Ministry of Planning and National Development and the Kenya National Economic and Social Council, Office of the President. Nairobi: Government Printer.

Republic of Kenya, 2007b, 'The New Urban Consumer Price Index: Derived from the Kenya Integrated Household Budget Survey (2005/2006)'. Kenya National Bureau of Statistics, Ministry of Planning and National Development. Nairobi: Government Printer.

Republic of Kenya, 2008a, 'Policy Brief on Background to EPAs: Why Kenya Needs to Conclude EPAs With the EU and EAC–EU EPA Negotiation Progress November 2008'. Office of the Deputy Prime Minister and Ministry of Trade. http://www.trade.go.ke/images/stories/pdf/brief_on_epa_latest.pdf (accessed 17 December 2008).

Republic of Kenya, 2008b, 'Draft National Trade Policy'. Office of the Deputy Prime Minister and Ministry of Trade. http://www.trade.go.ke (accessed 26 February 2009).

Rolfe, R. J, D. P. Woodward and B. Kagira, 2004, 'Footloose and Tax Free: Incentive Preferences in Kenyan Export Processing Zones', *South African Journal of Economics*, 72 (4), 784–807.

Sachs, J. and A. Warner, 1995, 'Economic Reform and the Process of Global Integration'. *Brookings Papers on Economic Activity*, 1, 1–118.

Swamy, G., 1994, 'Kenya: Patchy, Intermittent Commitment', in Husain, I. and R. Faruqee (eds) *Adjustment in Africa: Lessons From Country Case Studies*. Washington, DC: World Bank.

UNCTAD, 2008, *UNCTAD Handbook of Statistics*. http://stats.unctad.org/handbook (accessed 29 March 2009).

UNIDO, 2009, *Industrial Development Report 2009*. Vienna: UNIDO.

Wagacha, M., 2000, 'Analysis of Liberalization of the Trade and Exchange Regime in Kenya since 1980'. IPAR Discussion Paper Series: DP No. 023/2000. Nairobi: Institute of Policy Analysis and Research (IPAR).

Were, M., 2007, 'Employment Outcomes and Export Orientation of Firms in Kenya's Manufacturing Sector'. KIPPRA Discussion Paper No. 78. Nairobi: Kenya Institute for Public Policy Research and Analysis.

Were, M., G. Alemayehu., N. S. Ndung'u and S. N. Karingi, 2002, 'Analysis of Kenya's Export Performance: An Empirical Evaluation'. KIPPRA Discussion Paper Series, DP No. 22. Nairobi: The Kenya Institute for Public Policy Research and Analysis.

Were, M., R. W. Ngugi and P. Makau, 2006, 'Understanding Reform Process in Kenya', in Mensah, J. (ed.)*Understanding Economic Reforms in Africa: A Tale of Seven Nations*. Basingstoke: Palgrave Macmillan.

Winters, A, L., 2000, 'Trade, Trade Policy and Poverty: What are the Links?' Draft Paper, Centre for Economic Policy Research, London and Centre for Economic Performance, London School of Economics.

Wood, A., 1997, 'Openness and Wage Inequality in Developing Countries: The Latin American Challenge to East Asian Conventional Wisdom', *World Bank Economic Review*, 11, 33–57.

World Bank, 2005, 'Summary of Kenya Value Chain Analysis'. Note Number 8 of Africa Region Private Sector Unit.

World Trade Organization, 2002, *The Legal Texts: The Results of the Uruguay Round of Multilateral Trade Negotiations*. Geneva: WTO.

World Trade Organization, 2008, *World Tariff Profiles 2008*. Geneva: WTO.

7

Building a Kenyan Monetary Regime for the Twenty-first Century

Christopher S. Adam, Benjamin O. Maturu, Njuguna S. Ndung'u, and Stephen A. O'Connell

7.1 Introduction

This chapter asks: what sort of monetary framework is appropriate for Kenya as it seeks to establish itself as a full-fledged emerging market economy in the twenty-first century? Now is a particularly good time to consider the choices facing the authorities, and the Central Bank in particular, as the transformation of the macroeconomic landscape in Kenya, as elsewhere in Africa, has so altered conditions that the redesign of the monetary framework is now both pressing and meaningful. This transformation is not just in terms of economic conditions, but also of perceptions of the scope and limits of monetary policy. As recently as the early 1990s, the prevailing orthodoxy across much of Africa was that monetary policy could and should be deployed as a purposive instrument in the broader development process. Thus, Honohan and O'Connell (2008) describe post-Independence monetary frameworks in Africa as being largely geared towards the (cheap) financing of government activities, the extension of subsidized credit to favoured sectors, and active pursuit of an exchange rate target (often reflecting the interests of powerful urban consumers at the expense of producers), rather than the control of inflation.[1] Moreover, weak fiscal control – informed to a degree by the same orthodoxy – meant that monetary policy was conducted in an environment of substantial fiscal dominance, so that even basic macroeconomic policy coherence was achieved only by recourse to progressively tighter controls on the capital account and other policies that repressed the development of domestic financial markets. This cocktail of fiscal dominance and the overburdening of monetary policy with multiple objectives led to the inevitable outcome that African monetary regimes neither delivered low inflation nor posted sustained gains on the other policy objectives. This history is broadly consistent with the post-Independence monetary history of Kenya.

By the early 1990s, however, the evident failure of an (over)activist monetary policy encouraged moves to dismantle control regimes, liberalize foreign exchange markets, and establish more robust fiscal regimes (often in the context of International Monetary Fund-supported stabilization programmes). As a consequence, although a number of African countries still remain in the grip of severe macroeconomic instability, most African central banks today are under less pressure to accommodate large domestic fiscal deficits, while the dismantling of systems of financial repression, the widespread elimination of exchange controls, and a tendency towards the adoption of flexible exchange rates has opened up the space for genuinely independent central banks to function.

To frame our discussion, we start, in Section 7.2, by describing the characteristics of the monetary frameworks in floating exchange rate regimes such as Kenya's, focusing specifically on monetary targeting and inflation targeting. We pay particular attention to the latter, however, explicitly recognizing the strengthening consensus view that formal inflation targeting (IT) offers a coherent framework for the conduct of monetary policy, not only for industrialized and established emerging market economies but also, with some modification, for pre-emerging market economies such as Kenya (see O'Connell, 2010). This consensus view has, of course, been challenged recently in some quarters by those who see narrow IT frameworks as culpable in contributing to the global financial crisis. Nonetheless, we concur with the dominant view that the basic architecture of the formal inflation targeting framework is sound and is likely to remain in place in the future. Thus, this chapter presumes a move in this direction by the monetary authorities in Kenya (and elsewhere in the East African Community (EAC)): we therefore concentrate on the challenges faced by the authorities as they seek to build an IT framework that is consistent with supporting sustained investment and growth in the real economy. The key message from this chapter is that the authorities should be focused on developing the institutional structures that will support this anchor to domestic inflation.

Section 7.3 then provides a brief review of the conduct of monetary policy since the mid-1990s, focusing principally on the quest to establish price stability, while Section 7.4 returns to a set of practical policy and design challenges that, we feel, confronts Kenyan policy-makers as they seek to develop their monetary policy framework. A number of the issues discussed in this chapter dovetail closely with those addressed in Chapter 8, which directly addresses the design of monetary policy in the context of an increasingly open capital account where concerns about nominal and real exchange rate volatility figure large.

7.2 Choosing a monetary regime: some considerations[2]

A monetary regime defines the institutional framework to deliver monetary policy and the constraints under which monetary policy-makers operate. Today, most governments, and certainly most central bankers, would subscribe to the view that the role of monetary policy can be reduced to three core functions. The first, overriding, function is the delivery of low and stable inflation. Exactly how low this should be is an unresolved question, especially in developing countries, but crucially, whatever the target, the prevailing consensus sees this function as being best pursued through some form of policy rule. The case for rule-based policy is twofold. First, as argued by Milton Friedman, policy rules (in his case, a constant growth rate for money) are desirable when the authorities do not have the information or capability to know when or how much to stimulate or dampen the economy. Without this capacity, activist stabilization policies can end up exacerbating the very economic volatility they seek to reduce. The second is that rules tie hands and help to minimize or eliminate the incentives of the monetary authorities to operate in a time-inconsistent manner.[3]

The second function, conditional on targeting inflation, is to moderate fluctuations in the path of domestic output by judicious tightening or loosening of the stance of monetary policy as circumstances dictate. This is fundamentally a discretionary function and hence, to the extent that the output stabilization objectives may run counter to inflation stabilization objectives and vice versa, this potentially sets up a tension between rules and discretion at the heart of monetary policy. It is this tension that a coherent monetary framework must resolve. Contemporary monetary theory sees the reconciliation of these objectives emerging from a system of 'constrained discretion' such as embodied in an inflation targeting framework, where the institutional constraints defining the credible public commitment to an inflation target create the space for the authorities to pursue output stabilization. The management of this trade-off between inflation and output stabilization is particularly challenging in small open economies subject to large supply-side shocks, such as Kenya. We consider this issue in some detail in Section 7.4.

The final function of monetary policy is less direct. It is to support the smooth functioning of the payments system and the financial system more generally, so as to promote the efficient market-based allocation of credit and pricing of risk in support of efficient investment and growth. As above, this objective may not necessarily be consistent with price and output stabilization and, again, a coherent monetary framework must reconcile and prioritize these competing objectives. We say little about this function in this chapter; later chapters focus specifically on issues of capital market development.

7.2.1 Money targeting versus inflation targeting in emerging markets

Virtually all contemporary monetary regimes can be thought of as 'inflation targeting' in the strict sense that a central – if not the dominant – objective of monetary policy is to establish a credible anchor for domestic prices. Frameworks differ in terms of how they operationalize this objective; in other words, how they choose the nominal anchor.[4] This choice is not unconstrained, however; rather, it has implications for how the authorities address the other concerns competing for their attention. This tension is encapsulated in the notion of the 'impossible trinity' or 'trilemma', which states that, beyond the short run, no country can simultaneously maintain an open capital account, target the exchange rate, and pursue an independent monetary policy. One of the three must be abandoned even though each is desirable in its own right: open capital accounts to the extent that they support the efficient global allocation of capital to high-return investment opportunities; exchange rate targeting to support trade and sustain a stable external value of the currency; and an independent monetary policy to pursue domestic output stabilization objectives.[5]

Although debate continues on the case for limiting short-run cross-border capital flows through either tax or other restrictions, and even though this debate has, if anything, become more strident in the wake of the global financial crisis, it is reasonable to expect that capital flows have become permanently more responsive to cross-border return differentials (see Chapter 8 for evidence). Hence, for most countries, including those in East Africa, the resolution of the trilemma has become a simple choice over the nominal anchor: does it make better sense in terms of the other objectives of monetary policy to fix the exchange rate to a reference currency and adopt that country's anchor (and thus its monetary policy) or to let the exchange rate float and use domestic policy instruments to anchor inflation? At least since the early 1990s, Kenya has chosen the latter path and has used the growth of broad money as the anchor.

MONEY TARGETING

The rationale for money targeting as an anchoring mechanism builds on two assumptions, both of which are verifiable. The first is that the manner in which the private sector manages its wealth portfolio, of which the demand for money is one crucial element, induces a predictable relationship between money and prices. If this relationship is stable, then a policy that targets the growth of nominal money has some prospect of stabilizing inflation at desired levels and at reasonable cost in terms of other objectives. Specifically, starting with the definition of the velocity of circulation $v=Py/M$ where P is the price level, y a measure of real economic activity, and M broad money, then if the change in velocity and the level of real economic activity can be predicted, these can be used to generate an inflation-consistent path for broad money growth. Using a hat (^) to denote the growth rate of a variable, π the rate of inflation, the superscript p for projection, and a star (*) for a target, we obtain the following relationship relating the intermediate target (M) to the ultimate objective (inflation), given projections about the demand for real balances (the term in parenthesis):

$$\hat{M}^* = \pi^* + (\hat{y}^p - \hat{v}^p) \tag{7.1}$$

The second assumption is that there is a stable and exploitable relationship between the intermediate target, money, and the central bank's policy instrument, which, in the case of Kenya and most other African economies, is currently base (or reserve) money, denoted here as H, which consists of the currency in circulation in the economy plus the reserves of the banking systems lodged with the central bank. This relationship, the money multiplier, is defined as $m=M/H$. Using this expression, we can rewrite Equation (7.1) as a simple control rule linking base money growth to the target inflation rate conditional on the evolution of the real demand for base money (as proxied by the growth in output and velocity) and the money multiplier:

$$\hat{H}^* = \pi^* + (\hat{y}^p - \hat{v}^p - m^p) \tag{7.2}$$

Assuming the stability, or at least predictability, of m ensures that a given intermediate target for M (from Equation (7.1)) implies a path for H and a corresponding constraint on the evolution of the central bank's balance sheet. Placing H on this path is the central bank's task. The asset-side counterparts to base money on the bank's balance sheet are net international reserves (NIR) and net domestic assets (NDA), principal among which are central bank claims on government.[6] Conventionally, and certainly under IMF-supported programmes, the path for NIR is bounded below by the need to maintain sufficient foreign exchange liquidity to meet unanticipated shocks to the balance of payments. When this constraint binds, overall control of the growth in reserve money devolves to setting a ceiling on the growth of NDA, which in turn is dominated by central bank lending to government. Monetary targeting, in this sense, is therefore a programme built around quantitative money supply targets that constrains fiscal choices (it also limits the extent to which foreign reserve accumulation, which may be undertaken to meet an exchange rate objective, can proceed unsterilized because, at the margin, any growth in

NIR needs to be offset or sterilized by a corresponding reduction in NDA to satisfy a given target for reserve money).

INFLATION TARGETING

Inflation targeting pursues the same fundamental objective, but here the nominal anchor is *expected inflation.* The instruments at the disposal of the central bank (be they interest rates or quantitative instruments) are set not to influence a tangible quantity or price but rather to *directly* influence the private sector's expected or forecasted rate of inflation at some horizon. The rationale is that future expected inflation feeds into current price- and wage-setting behaviour; a credible inflation target thus leads to target-consistent price and wage-setting behaviour today, thereby validating the forecast.

The essence of IT is that the authorities' policy actions and announcements credibly influence the evolution of the private sector's inflation expectations. Three elements therefore define contemporary IT regimes. The first is an explicit public commitment to a target inflation rate, defined in terms of either overall 'headline' inflation or 'core' inflation, where the latter excludes specific items such as food and fuel of which prices are determined principally by supply-side effects or world market conditions (we return to this issue below). This public commitment to the target establishes as the focal point for public scrutiny the inflation rate itself, rather than an intermediate indicator such as money, the measurement of which is difficult and the intrinsic relevance of which may be obscure.

Second, the policy instrument (typically the policy interest rate) is set to guide the economy towards this target on the basis of a forward-looking reaction function of the form:

$$i_t = r + E\pi_{t+i} + \gamma_1[E\pi_{t+i} - \pi^*] + \gamma_2[y_t - \bar{y}_t] \tag{7.3}$$

Equation (7.3) is known as a Taylor rule after John Taylor (Taylor, 1993) who observed that federal policy after 1980 was well approximated by a reaction function of this form. Here, r is the long-run equilibrium (or neutral) real interest rate, assumed to be constant and defined as the rate that would equate aggregate demand with aggregate supply if wages and prices were flexible, and $E\pi_{t+i}$ is expected inflation i periods in the future.[7] Policy responds both to deviations in the inflation forecast from the target and to deviations in output from its potential (i.e. to the output gap). There is no requirement that the feedback parameters γ_1 and γ_2 are equal. Rather, the parameter values reflect the nature of the transmission mechanism and the relative weights given to inflation and the output gap in the monetary authority's preferences. However, achieving the inflation objective does require a positive coefficient on the inflation deviation term in Equation (7.3). This is the so-called 'Taylor principle', which says that, holding the output gap constant, the monetary authorities must respond to an increase in observed inflation by increasing the expected short-term *real* interest rate $i_t - E\pi_{t+i}$ (see Woodford, 2003).

A key distinction between money targeting and inflation targeting approaches is that there appears to be no role for money in the latter. However, even though the Taylor rule is written in terms of a policy interest rate, it could equally have been derived in terms of reserve money (by using an expression for the demand for money to substitute reserve money for the interest rate). In other words, the same ultimate policy reaction could be accomplished either directly, by controlling the interest rate, or indirectly, by controlling the supply of central bank balances. As other countries, such as Mexico, have shown, a fully consistent IT framework can be implemented with the quantity of reserve money serving as the policy instrument. Indeed, unavailability of a policy interest rate does not rule out the setting of available policy instruments to target expected inflation to whatever degree desired.

The third element is a structured approach to deliberation and communication on the part of the central bank. In part, this requires that the relevant inflation index is publicly understood and that the public has confidence in its measurement. But more generally, the objective is to make public, in a timely fashion, the central bank's own information and analysis to ensure that its actions are verifiable and its own expectations of future developments are revealed, thereby resolving the problems of asymmetric information, which can create incentives for time-inconsistent behaviour on the part of the monetary authorities.

In practice, this has seen IT central banks publish the evidence and analysis that informs their rate-setting decisions; publish the voting records of the members of interest rate-setting committees; and devote substantial resources to public information and direct engagement with key stakeholders. This comprehensive communication strategy applies both when inflation is on target and, *a fortiori*, when it is off target, in which case additional disclosure requirements may be placed on the central bank to explain deviations and specify remedial action to return inflation to target.[8] Important in establishing the credibility of this structure is the reliance on independent external membership of key decision-making bodies and the pressures these bodies exert on the national statistics offices to produce timely and accurate data.[9]

When successful, these characteristics – the explicit inflation target, the 'Taylor principle', and the associated public disclosure and explanation of policy decisions and outcomes – deliver the credibility required to defuse the time inconsistency problem inherent in monetary policy by validating the belief in the private sector's mind that the central bank will (eventually) bring inflation back on track and will do so in a transparent manner. Moreover, theory suggests, as inflation expectations firm around the target, the pass-through from current price developments to expected future inflation reduces, allowing the authorities to use monetary instruments to pursue other ultimate targets of policy, which may include competitiveness or stabilization of short-run output around its potential.

This textbook description of a full-fledged IT regime sets the bar high and, in practice, only a few countries demonstrate all these characteristics. Stone (2003) has coined the term 'inflation targeting lite' (ITL) to describe countries – and Kenya would count among these – whose frameworks are gravitating towards an IT configuration but where, operationally, the conduct of monetary policy may still lack clarity of objectives and transparency of communication. In such regimes, the authorities often announce a target for inflation and publically commit to a flexible exchange rate but, in practice, they tend to actively manage the exchange rate, often to the point where the prioritization of the competing constraints of an independent monetary policy and the desire to influence the path of the exchange rate is obscure.[10] Moreover, structures for communication and verification are only beginning to be established; domestic asset markets remain relatively thin and central bank balance sheets are often still too weak to allow effective deployment of interest-rate-based policy instruments; and, in some cases, core analytical capacity – in inflation forecasting and developing robust models of the transmission mechanism, for example – are only just being built.

7.2.2 Summary and the challenges of translating IT for low-income countries

The spread of inflation targeting after 1990 was influenced in large measure by the successful performance of adopters (see Mishkin and Schmidt-Hebbel, 2007). No inflation targeting country has yet abandoned this approach to conducting monetary policy, whereas more and more countries, in addition to those already classified as pursuing ITL regimes, are moving closer to embracing IT frameworks. This remains the case even after the approach came under heavy criticism from some quarters for being responsible, in part, for the global financial crisis that erupted in 2008. Critics argued that the narrow mandate and relatively short horizon over which targets were defined led policy-makers to pay insufficient attention to asset price inflation, and contributed to excessively lax monetary and credit conditions and the build up of financial imbalances that preceded the crisis. From this followed calls for reform, ranging from the operational, for example, that central banks should seek to 'lean against the wind' of asset price movements, to the radical redesign of the framework of monetary policy, including even calls to abandon IT regimes in favour of more discretionary regimes (there have been no sustained calls, however, for a return to monetary targeting).[11]

Although aspects of the critique have grabbed headlines, the case against inflation targeting has not attracted widespread support in academia or from central banks themselves. On the contrary, the prevailing view – certainly among industrialized countries and mature emerging market economies – is that the essential framework of IT remains a robust and pragmatic solution to the problem of assigning responsibility for inflation control and – subject to that – for the stabilization of output around the natural rate. Central banks remain the appropriate institution and interest rates the appropriate instrument. In the context of the crisis, however, the key point is that inflation control and output stabilization were only part of the assignment problem and, although operational errors were probably made in the conduct of monetary policy at this time, the crisis owed much more to failures elsewhere, specifically in the areas of financial sector regulation and fiscal policy. As the Governor of the Bank of England, Mervyn King, has noted: '. . .inflation targeting is a necessary but not sufficient condition for stability in the economy as a whole. When a policy is necessary but not sufficient, the answer is not to abandon, but to augment it' (King, 2009).

This confidence is probably well grounded. But we must also recognize that IT is the outcome of industrialized countries' generally unsuccessful attempts to address their own specific stabilization problems in the late 1970s and 1980s, following the collapse of the Bretton Woods exchange rate arrangements. The intellectual underpinning and, indeed, the implementation of IT regimes thus reflect a set of economic structures and institutions very different from those in developing countries and especially low-income countries.

Making a robust case for adopting IT in Kenya, and for other low-income countries, therefore obliges us to address a number of key issues. O'Connell (2010) outlines some of these challenges:

> Does it make sense to target inflation when exchange rates, food prices, and public-sector prices (utilities, fuel, and public sector wages) are more prominent – and verifiable – in the public eye? Can the framework be deployed successfully when supply shocks are dominant and the GDP gap is difficult to measure? Is there a role for exchange rate targets, given imperfect capital mobility and the importance of export promotion? What operational policy rules can be used when there is not a strong transmission from policy interest rates to aggregate demand, and where (as in almost all African cases) central banks use balance sheet instruments rather than interest rates?

We take up some of the challenges in Section 7.4, but before doing so, we provide some context by offering a brief description of monetary conditions and developments in Kenya over the last decade.

7.3 Monetary policy in Kenya: recent performance and institutional change

7.3.1 Macroeconomic stabilization

The early 1990s represented a watershed for the Kenyan economy. The impetus towards economic liberalism, first laid out in the famous Sessional Paper No. 1 of 1986, which saw Kenya turn its back on its post-Independence *dirigisme*, gained momentum as a sequence of events forced the pace of reforms. A standoff with the IMF in 1992 and the general hardening of donor attitudes towards corruption – responding in particular to the recently exposed Goldenberg scandal – saw the external budget constraint tighten substantially and prompted government to move rapidly to establish fiscal control and allow the exchange rate to float relatively freely. By the mid-1990s, *de jure* capital controls had been substantially eliminated (Bandiera *et al.*, 2008). These changes in the policy regime laid the foundations for a decade of solid if not spectacular performance lasting until the end of 2007. Output growth increased from around 2 per cent per annum in the late 1990s to around 4 per cent in the first half of the 2000s and to close to 7 per cent per annum in 2007. Underpinning this was a monetary framework that was successful in taking advantage of the 'great moderation' in the global economy to bring domestic inflation back under control. This regime – which remains substantially in place today – was configured rather conventionally around a broad money anchor, with reserve money functioning as the operational target.

With this framework in place, and with government maintaining a relatively tight fiscal stance, inflation fell sharply from its peak of around 60 per cent per annum in early 1994 and remained in single digits throughout the remainder of the decade (see Figure 7.1). By the mid-2000s, however, inflation was once more starting to drift upwards and accelerated from 2007. Most of this latter increase is accounted for by the accommodation of sharply rising food and fuel prices, which, in turn, reflected developments in global commodity markets combined with a severe drought at home. Given the weight of food and fuel in the overall consumer prices index (CPI), these developments drove headline inflation higher. Recent work by the IMF and the Kenyan National Bureau of Statistics suggests that some of this sharp rise in food and overall inflation from the mid-2000s may have been spurious, stemming from methodological errors in the calculation of price indices. A new inflation series was introduced in November 2009, at which point year-on-year headline inflation was revised downwards from 17.5 per cent per annum to 6.5 per cent.[12]

Nonetheless, inflation – including core inflation, which was less affected by external cost-push factors – had started drifting upwards before 2007, and

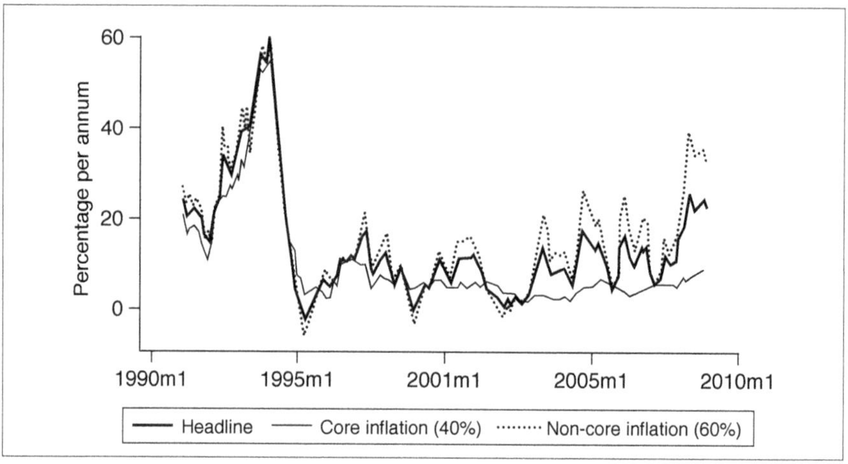

Figure 7.1 Year-on-year inflation, 1990–2009.

concerns were being expressed that, compared with the immediate post-1994 period, the monetary targeting framework was becoming less effective, even after allowing for the effect of measurement bias in the inflation data.

At a technical level, concerns also focused on the efficacy of the money targeting approach and, in particular, the increasing difficulty in accurately predicting the velocity of circulation and the money multiplier. The consequences of these prediction errors can be seen if we use the reserve money growth identity (Equation (7.2) above) to decompose, *ex post*, the inflation error. Recalling that a *p* superscript denotes a prediction and a star (*) a target, the deviation of inflation from its target can be defined as:

$$(\pi - \pi^*) = (\hat{H} - \hat{H}^*) - (\hat{y} - \hat{y}^p) + (\hat{v} - \hat{v}^p) + (\hat{m} - \hat{m}^p) \tag{7.4}$$

Overshooting the inflation target can thus be attributed to (some combination) of four factors: (i) excess growth in reserve money, possibly reflecting a loss of fiscal control or unsterilized exchange rate targeting; (ii) lower than predicted output growth; (iii) higher than predicted velocity (i.e. a *lower than predicted* demand for money given the path of real income); and (iv) a higher than predicted money multiplier. The converse also holds so that, for example, overprediction of the velocity of circulation (in other words, money demand pessimism) will lead to an overtightening of monetary conditions and an undershoot of the inflation target.

We can use Equations (7.2) and (7.4) to evaluate the performance of the reserve money programme in Kenya over the last decade. Figure 7.2 compares the actual growth in reserve money against a counterfactual 'inflation-consistent' path. The latter is computed from Equation (7.2) on the basis of a target

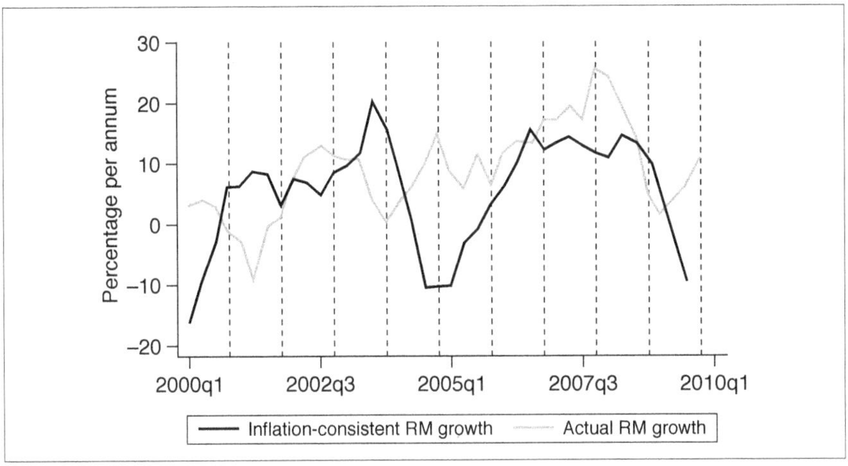

Figure 7.2 Actual versus inflation-consistent growth in reserve money (RM).

inflation rate of 5 per cent per annum, and assumes that year-on-year real output growth is projected without error. The projected growth rates for velocity and the multiplier are computed at each point in time by extrapolating the growth rate over the past three years.[13]

A number of features emerge from Figure 7.2. The first is that the average 'excess' money growth, although positive, is relatively low, with the mean deviation at just less than 1 percentage point per quarter, against a mean growth in reserve money of approximately 7 per cent per quarter. Second, however, the standard deviation around this mean is large (8 per cent per quarter). Deviations (in growth rates) from the target are, however, short-lived, their half-life of around four months suggesting a relatively strong 'error correction' element to the authorities' policy reaction function. This is consistent with recent econometric work by Maturu (2007) and Rotich *et al.* (2008) showing that deviations in actual reserve money from its inflation-consistent path have a significant feedback effect on overall inflation, and that over this period, the Central Bank of Kenya (CBK) responded aggressively to such deviations in accordance with the 'Taylor principle'. An important implication of these papers is that, over the 2007–09 period when the 'inflation bias' in the CPI was increasing sharply, the progressively tighter monetary stance shown in Figure 7.3 was, *ex post*, tighter than required, arguably pulling the economy towards its inflation target more rapidly and at a higher cost in terms of other objectives than was desirable.

Building on Figure 7.2, Table 7.1 decomposes the inflation error in Equation (7.4) in terms of the different components of the money targeting programme.

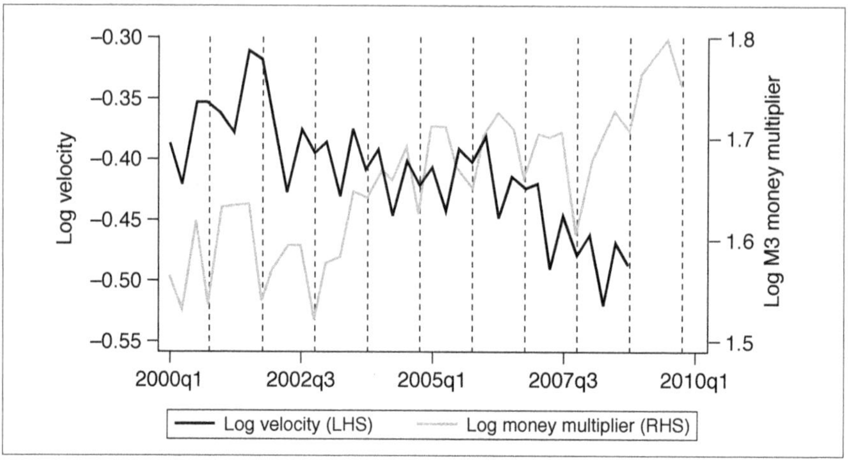

Figure 7.3 Velocity of circulation and M3 money multiplier.

Prediction errors in both velocity and the multiplier account for between 0.7 and 1.2 percentage points of the inflation error, but this is relatively small compared with the 'residual' component, which consists of the contribution of overpredicting the growth in real GDP plus the effect the prediction errors have for the inflation-consistent growth of reserve money. The single largest factor in play is the difficulty in predicting real output growth. As our later

Table 7.1 Decomposition of excess inflation 2000q1 to 2008q4

	2000q1–2008q4	2000q1–2004q4	2005q1–2008q4
Inflation error: $(\pi - \pi^*)$	6.3	3.1	10.4
Represented by:			
Excess money growth $(\hat{H} - \hat{H}^*)$ (relative to *ex ante* inflation-consistent path – Figure 7.2)	0.7	–0.8	2.6
Plus:			
Prediction error in:			
Velocity $(\hat{v} - \hat{v}^p)$	0.3	0.2	0.5
Money multiplier $(\hat{m} - \hat{m}^p)$	0.4	0.4	0.7
Residual	-4.9	-3.3	-6.6
o/w prediction error in real GDP growth	-4.1	-2.7	-5.4

Errors in percentage points of inflation. See text for calculation of predicted velocity and money multiplier values; 'excess money growth' is defined relative to *ex ante* inflation-consistent path, which assumes zero prediction errors in velocity, money multiplier, and real GDP. The residual is therefore the net effect of the deviation between the *ex ante* and *ex post* inflation-consistent growth in reserve money, the principal component of which is the prediction error in the growth of real GDP, $(\hat{y} - \hat{y}^p)$.

discussion emphasizes, forecasting output accurately (and determining the nature of output shocks) is, and will continue to be, a first-order challenge for any economy, such as Kenya, undergoing rapid structural transformation. As Table 7.1 suggests, the returns to improved forecasting of output are likely to be high: this should be a priority research activity of the central bank.

Although forecast errors in velocity and the money multiplier are somewhat smaller, their importance should not be understated. Since 2002, velocity has been steadily declining, although with marked quarter-on-quarter variation. This falling trend in velocity – which increases the inflation-consistent growth of broad money – has been accompanied by a sharp trend increase in the money multiplier, which, for a given target growth rate of broad money, reduces the inflation-consistent growth rate of reserve money. More significantly, however, both have been relatively volatile, which makes prediction difficult. Under strict financial programming – meaning that the short-run path for reserve money is aggressively error-corrected to keep inflation on target – mistakes in forecasting velocity and the multiplier (and, indeed, errors in forecasting real output) are transmitted to the real economy via swings in the liquidity conditions facing banks, causing them to maintain a more liquid asset book, which adversely affects the cost and quantity of their long-term lending.

Setting aside the challenges in controlling reserve money itself, predicting velocity and the multiplier is increasingly difficult. In Kenya, as elsewhere in Africa, there has been a systematic tendency towards underprediction of money demand growth during periods of favourable structural reforms, which have tended both to increase the 'monetary intensity' of economic activity (thereby exogenously raising money demand) and to support a step-decline in inflation expectations.[14] Failure to recognize this means excessive monetary restraint and excessively high domestic interest rates. In addition, as Berg and Borensztein (2000) and Buffie *et al.* (2008) have argued, currency substitution and dollarization will tend to increase the instability of money demand, thereby exacerbating the risk of unpredictable shifts in velocity.

The money multiplier is equally difficult to predict with accuracy in times of rapid financial innovation (see, for example, Saxegaard, 2006). First, aside from increasing the instability of money demand, dollarization may have similar effects on the money multiplier if the intermediate target is defined solely in terms of domestic monetary liabilities. In Kenya, the monetary target, M3, includes foreign currency deposits, which internalizes such portfolio shifts (although the stability of the multiplier is now influenced in part by the effect of exchange rate revaluation operating on foreign currency deposits).

Second, however, rapid financial innovation is transforming financial markets, both in the large-scale formal end and, perhaps most dramatically, with the rapid expansion of M-Pesa mobile phone banking, which is beginning to

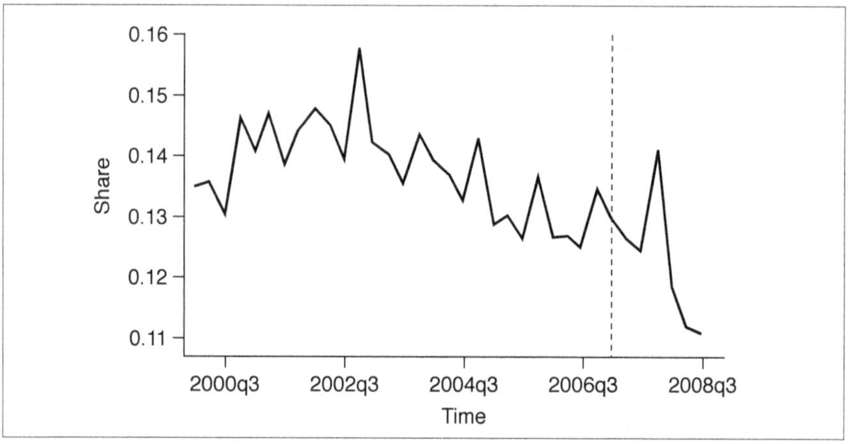

Figure 7.4 M-Pesa and the cash ratio.

have important consequences for the nature of money demand in Kenya (see Chapter 13 and Jack *et al.*, 2010). Figure 7.4 plots the currency-to-deposit ratio over the period from 2000 to 2008, where the vertical line marks the introduction of M-Pesa. This ratio – which is one of the key components in the money multiplier – shows a marked decline in the cash-to-deposit ratio as M-Pesa has been rolled out. Such innovation may also be expected to feed back onto banks' own behaviour, altering their own liquidity preference, which, in turn, will be reflected in movements in the bank reserve ratio.[15]

Finally, maintaining a focus on money growth rather than on inflation itself may lead to a bias in favour of excess tightness even when inflation is correctly predicted to fall, for example because money demand is rising. This can arise because of a fear that warranted rapid nominal money growth cannot be explained to the public without undermining confidence about inflation, or perhaps, and more correctly, it will not be understood properly, precisely because the public would like to focus on indicators that bear directly on their lives, such as exchange rate movements, interest rates, and food prices.

Although problems of accurate measurement of inflation and output (and the output gap) are also present under inflation targeting, the direct focus on the ultimate target of inflation, rather than on an intermediate target such as money, means the difficulties presented by shifts in velocity and the multiplier are obviated. Inflation targeting bypasses movements in intermediate aggregates, and hence accommodates structural shifts in and shocks to money demand, either through discretionary adjustment of quantitative policy instruments (reserve money) or automatically once interest rates emerge as the main policy instrument. A virtuous circle may emerge as the greater the stabilizing effect of policy on inflation expectations, the more stable becomes the demand for money itself and the lower the expected volatility from this source.

7.3.2 Institutional reforms: same framework, evolving institutional architecture

These challenges in conducting monetary policy have taken place against the background of important and far-reaching institutional and structural changes to the monetary framework, through which the Central Bank of Kenya has gained greater operational independence. Allied to continued fiscal control and the progressive deepening of domestic money and capital markets, this has endowed Kenya with an institutional structure conducive to building a coherent inflation targeting monetary framework. Successive revisions to the Central Bank of Kenya Act have served to define the objectives of monetary policy, help develop price-based instruments of monetary policy, and support a consistent strategy for communication and engagement.[16]

The 1996 revision to the Act gave the Central Bank a clear mandate to 'formulate and implement monetary policy directed at achieving and maintaining stability in the general level of prices' while fostering 'the liquidity, solvency and proper functioning of a stable market-based financial system'. This mandate was made concrete in the form of an inflation target announced by the Minister of Finance in the annual Finance Bill. This target has remained at 5 per cent per annum since the first Monetary Policy Statement issued in 2007. This unambiguous mandate was, however, modified in 2007 with the introduction of a less precise requirement that, *conditional on the Bank meeting its core requirements*, the Bank should seek to 'support the economic policy of the Government, including its objectives for growth and employment'.

But perhaps the landmark change was the introduction in the 2007 revisions of an executive committee on monetary policy – the Monetary Policy Committee (MPC). The MPC formulates monetary policy and is accountable to the Board of the CBK. In addition to its advisory and policy formulation functions, the MPC, which consists of both internal and external members, plays a central role in the communication of policy decisions and their rationale, thereby serving to co-ordinate market expectations and communicate the likely future path of the economy.

7.4 Challenges

In terms of structure and conduct, the Kenyan monetary regime is, at present, a hybrid. The authorities publish an explicit inflation target, but concerns about the level and volatility of the exchange rate remain ever present, and the debate on the extent to which monetary policy can and should be used to address concerns about external competitiveness is active (see Chapter 8). The language of monetary policy emphasizes the role of indirect instruments in influencing the price of credit, but practice is resolutely anchored in a conventional quantity-based approach, where M3 remains the principal intermediate target and the volume of reserve money the operating instrument. Thus, although, for the moment, the Kenyan authorities have stopped short of implementing a full-fledged formal inflation targeting structure, there are pressures to move decisively in this direction. These pressures have been both technical and political. At a technical level, as noted above, concerns have been mounting that, although the current money-based programme performed exceptionally well in establishing price stability in the decade from the mid-1990s, it has been performing less well as the economy develops and financial markets deepen and become more open. These new sources of instability alter the transmission mechanism and challenge the basis for a simple money-based programme. Meanwhile, monetary policy continues to contend with both substantial supply-side shocks to agriculture, the terms of trade and aid, and periodic portfolio shocks, with the most recent being the shift away from the Kenyan shilling at the time of the election-related violence in early 2008. Not all of these challenges relate solely to the use of money targeting however. We have already alluded to the problems of forecasting output, and the errors in the official measurement of inflation, which recently placed the programme under strain, would have led to a 'deflation bias' in any monetary framework where the ultimate policy objective is an inflation target.

On the political side, there is pressure towards increased economic integration under the auspices of the EAC. Some of this is in the domain of trade policy, but it is being accompanied by moves towards monetary union (echoing the African Union (AU)'s Abuja Declaration on economic integration of 2005). In August 2007, the heads of state of the EAC (Kenya, Uganda, Tanzania, Rwanda, and Burundi)[17] committed themselves to full monetary union in 2012. Although significant doubts surround the feasibility of meeting this target date – a view reinforced by the recently endorsed ECB report – the central banks of the EAC, including the CBK, have committed themselves to move, with deliberate speed, towards revising the current framework to accommodate changing policy challenges and emerging wisdom in inflation targeting (including, as an important first step, harmonization of methods for measuring inflation).

Other than South Africa, the only African economy that has sought to implement full-fledged inflation targeting is Ghana, which embarked on this path in May 2007. Implementation has been difficult (Sowa and Abradu-Otoo, 2009) and, as O'Connell (2010) notes:

> ...the Bank of Ghana had yet to achieve a target range that was already higher and wider than that of any other targeter. Its struggles with trans-

parency are palpable and it remains to be seen whether the distortions implied by committing to a target that is rarely met, of unclear salience, and difficult to forecast, are fundamentally damaging to economic stability – or are more than compensated by committing the fiscal authorities to self-restraint and forcing the pace of institutional maturation within the central bank.

These same concerns must, of course, figure large if Kenya were to move in the same direction. In this final section, we consider some of these in more detail. We focus on four issues: (i) the efficacy of IT regimes in environments subject to supply-side shocks; (ii) reconciling IT with competing policy objectives, specifically those concerning the exchange rate and competitiveness; (iii) the challenge of a weak monetary transmission mechanism; and finally (iv) whether an IT regime can form a buttress against future fiscal indiscipline. The importance of investing in the research capacity of the CBK and its MPC and the data generation capacity of the statistical authorities is an obvious fifth challenge. We do not treat this separately here, not least because our discussion of the other challenges effectively defines the relevant research agenda.

7.4.1 Inflation targeting when supply-side shocks predominate

All economies are exposed to both aggregate demand and aggregate supply shocks. For demand-side shocks – for example, unanticipated public expenditure – the impact on the output gap on the one hand and inflation on the other is positively correlated (excess demand drives up both the output gap and inflation), whereas this correlation is negative for supply-side shocks.

As Figure 7.5 shows, as per capita incomes rise, the correlation of output and inflation flips from negative to positive. This is consistent with the interpretation that, in an industrialized country environment shocks tend to come predominantly from the demand side, whereas in developing and emerging market countries, supply-side shocks tend to play a much larger role. An obvious, indeed perennial, example of the latter would be the effect of unanticipated variations in rainfall on agricultural output. Kenya's location in Figure 7.5 is consistent with the prevalence of this type of shock. It turns out that this simple distinction poses a major challenge for the conduct of monetary policy, as it undermines one of the features that have made inflation targeting so attractive to industrialized economies. Moreover, pursuit of aggressive inflation targeting in the presence of supply-side shocks may, in fact, be counterproductive by leveraging up this output volatility. And to make matters worse, the obvious solution to the problem – the one adopted in other settings – turns out to be quite unattractive for low-income countries such as Kenya.

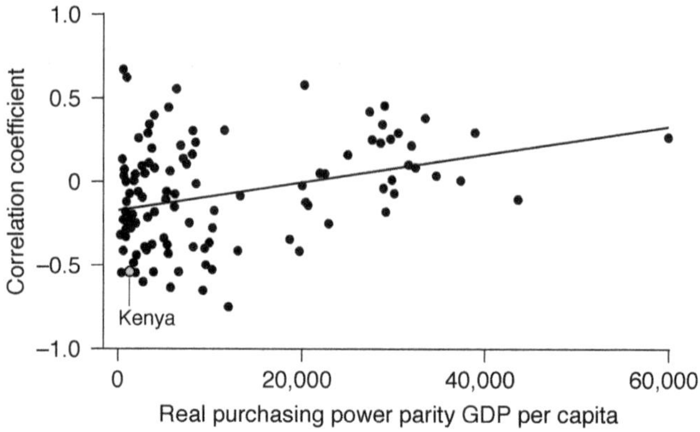

Figure 7.5 Demand-side versus supply-side shocks.
The figure plots the correlation between output and inflation 'shocks' against per capita income for 118 countries for which continuous data exist over the period 1990–2008. Shocks are measured as the deviation of actual inflation (output) from a Hodrick–Prescott trend.

The essential problem is as follows: with demand shocks moving output and inflation in the same direction, a policy reaction, for example an interest rate rise, designed to bring inflation back on track will simultaneously serve to eliminate excess demand. This 'divine coincidence' – the fact that demand shocks dominate and that a policy reaction targeting inflation also targets output – goes a long way to explaining the attraction of IT in industrialized countries. With supply-side shocks – for example an increase in the cost of imported oil, which drives up production costs, thereby reducing output, and simultaneously adds to inflationary pressures – output and inflation will move in opposite directions. One instrument is now no longer sufficient: acting to stabilize the inflationary consequences of a supply shock risks exacerbating the adverse output effects and vice versa. This brings to the fore the essential problem of monetary policy: with a single instrument, policy-makers must confront the trade-off between competing objectives (in this case inflation and output stabilization).

This is, of course, a generic 'instruments and objectives' problem, and will occur under any choice of anchor but, as Frankel *et al.* (2007) show, the appeal of IT over other policy rules – most notably a money targeting rule – as a means of delivering lower inflation volatility and lower output volatility only holds true when demand shocks dominate. When supply shocks dominate, strict IT continues to deliver lower inflation volatility but at the cost of higher output volatility.[18] In these circumstances, a conventional money-based anchor will result in lower output volatility (although inflation volatility will be higher), and the unambiguous welfare-based argument in favour of IT disappears. Frankel *et al.* (2007) present these results in the context of very simple policy rules in which IT is strict (such that no weight is placed on output stabilization) and where money targeting is concerned exclusively with the intermediate target (money) and not with either inflation or output itself. Nonetheless, the fundamental point remains under more general policy rules such as the Taylor rule specified in Equation (7.3) above.

It is certainly not the case that the tension thrown up by supply-side shocks is restricted to developing countries only. It is just much more pervasive. Industrialized country central banks did, however, face exactly this trade-off in the first half of 2008 when the sharp increase in fuel and other input costs began to simultaneously squeeze output and stoke inflationary pressures. (Admittedly, this episode was short-lived as the global financial crisis and the massive deleveraging that occurred subsequently turned this incipient supply-side shock into a negative demand shock of much greater proportions, in which central banks were confronted by falling output and the threat of deflation: in this case, there was no trade-off and the conventional 'Taylor rule macro' response by central banks was rapid and decisive, and was only limited by the fact that the policy instrument, the interest rate, hit its zero lower bound.)

But it is important to reflect on what these countries did in 2008 in order to understand the implications it has for the implementation of IT in countries such as Kenya where supply-side shocks are comparatively common. The conventional argument for handling supply shocks – which was employed in industrialized economies in 2008 – recognizes that such shocks typically emanate from developments in markets in which prices are outside the direct control of the domestic authorities. In most small open economies, these are the markets for food and fuel, where prices of the former are driven to a large extent by weather conditions[19] and of the latter by world market conditions. The appropriate response of (IT) policy-makers, therefore, is to distinguish between 'core' components of inflation – those where domestic policy has leverage – and these 'non-core' components of inflation and to bring to bear the apparatus of IT only on the core component of inflation, reacting to movements in non-core prices only to the extent that they have second-round feedback effects on core inflation.[20] This leads to a strategy of accommodating the first-round effects of non-core price movements but bearing down on any second-round effects. This is why most industrialized country inflation targeters allowed their headline inflation rates to stray outside its target zone in the first half of 2008.

This approach makes sense in developed countries where non-core components account for a relatively small share of the overall CPI, so that focusing monetary policy on the stabilization of core inflation goes a long way towards stabilizing overall inflation without drawing the authorities into destabilizing responses to supply-side shocks.[21] In Kenya, as in other low-income countries, however, non-core items account for a large share of the CPI. As noted in Figure 7.1, the combined food and fuel share in Kenya's CPI basket has been in excess of 60 per cent, and even following the revisions to the CPI weights in March 2010, the food share in the CPI is still around 40 per cent and fuel a further 18 per cent. In other words, targeting core inflation would mean that the authorities will end up targeting less than half the overall consumption basket. Even if an IT regime was extremely successful in stabilizing core inflation, this may still co-exist with high volatility in headline inflation if the evolution of prices of non-core items is volatile. If, as seems reasonable, we believe that private agents set prices and wages not in terms of the evolution of expected *core* inflation – as IT theory suggests – but on actual headline inflation, the efficacy of monetary policy is likely to be undermined as inflation expectations will be less securely anchored by any given policy action. Stated slightly differently, trying to control overall inflation in these environments would require the authorities to lean much more heavily on their policy levers, with the attendant risk of greater volatility in output and interest rates.

These are uncomfortable but unavoidable truths. As we have noted above, there are good arguments for believing that targeting inflation directly may be preferable to targeting money, *at least from the perspective of anchoring inflation.* But we may also need to recognize that this may come at the cost of higher output volatility, and that this volatility may be greater the broader the measure of inflation we seek to stabilize. Having said this, it is reasonable to expect that, over time, the process of economic growth and structural transformation will ease the severity of this trade-off, both as the share of non-core goods in total consumption declines and as diversification and innovation reduce the likely scale and frequency of supply-side shocks.

7.4.2 Reconciling exchange rate objectives

As stressed in the introduction, the incoherence brought about by the overburdening of monetary policy with multiple objectives meant that monetary regimes often delivered on none of them. But, even though a new understanding of the limits of monetary policy has emerged, the multiple objectives have not entirely disappeared, with concerns about the path and volatility of the exchange rate still playing a dominant role. This is certainly true for Kenya, as shown clearly in Chapter 8.

One strand of the IT literature (for example Batini and Laxton, 2007) argues for a clear and unambiguous prioritization of the inflation target with the authorities forgoing any attempt to manage the exchange rate. This argument does not imply that they should ignore the exchange rate – not least because it plays a central role in forecasting inflation – but rather that it should be made clear that the authorities are not beholden to any specific value of the currency. Moreover, the argument goes, a non-interventionist stance creates positive incentives for the private sector to develop the capacity to price and manage exchange rate risk.

Evidence – from Kenya and elsewhere – suggests otherwise. As Edwards (2007) and others have shown, intervention in support of the exchange rate is the norm rather than the exception among IT as well as non-IT countries. Theory also lends support to this view. Buffie *et al.* (2008), for example, suggest that, when fiscal policy reacts to variations in aid or commodity price flows, some degree of exchange rate intervention may be desirable, particularly where dollarization is widespread. These arguments are particularly powerful in environments where domestic prices are sticky or where other forms of market imperfection (e.g. credit rationing) mean that the effects of exchange rate volatility on real resource allocation are highly geared.

Responding at least indirectly to movements in the exchange rate is unavoidable in an IT setting in a small open economy such as Kenya's, even if stabilizing the exchange rate is not a separate policy objective (see O'Connell, 2008). With imports accounting for around 30 per cent of total absorption, there is inevitably a strong pass-through from the exchange rate to domestic prices and output (see, for example, Cheng, 2006). Any framework that focuses on inflation and the output gap will therefore respond indirectly to exchange rate movements, even when the authorities profess adherence to a pure float.[22]

But navigating these considerations requires coherence both at the level of policy and in terms of communication. The key issue for the success of IT is probably not that the authorities pursue a pure float but rather that they establish a credible commitment that the inflation target will take precedence when there is a conflict. In reality, the recent history of low global inflation combined with the steady fall in velocity in many post-stabilization economies allowed unsterilized exchange rate intervention aimed at limiting the appreciation of the domestic currency to be absorbed by rapid non-inflationary growth in money demand, so that the two objectives were rarely in conflict. With global inflation now rising more rapidly and the growth in real money demand easing, the risk of conflict is rising, not least because letting the exchange rate appreciate uncompetitively may be the easiest way of hitting an inflation target in an import-dependent economy.

The favourable experience of emerging market inflation targeters over the last decade, including over the recent global crisis period, suggests that these concerns have been manageable. But as O'Connell (2008) notes, the literature offers very little guidance on how multiple instruments, e.g. a policy interest rate and foreign exchange intervention, ought to be deployed when imperfect capital mobility allows the monetary authority some scope to reconcile domestic with external objectives. Little is known, for example, regarding the appropriate scale of intervention or the degree to which intervention should be sterilized (Edwards, 2007). Analytical work on these issues is likely to begin emerging as the group of inflation targeters gets wider; meanwhile, an appropriate presumption is probably that the degree of capital mobility is increasing rather than decreasing, and that although some scope for active exchange rate management probably exists, overemphasizing exchange rate objectives may carry significant risks.

7.4.3 Weak transmission channels

The effectiveness of monetary policy and the credibility of any regime will depend on how reliably and how quickly observable policy actions influence inflation and other real variables; in other words, on the nature of the transmission mechanism. Critically, and especially in the context of an IT regime, effectiveness also depends on how well the transmission mechanism is understood, as the ability of the monetary authorities to deploy their instruments to anchor expected inflation requires demonstrable results. Credibility will be undermined if observed policy actions are perceived to be ineffective or even have persistently perverse outcomes.

The textbook macroeconomic model, which underpins both IT frameworks and, with little modification, the more conventional monetary frameworks employed in Africa, fundamentally derives from the research and experience of the Organization for Economic Co-operation and Development (OECD).[23] This model emphasizes the interest rate channels of transmission, in which short-run interest rate decisions are transmitted directly to long-term interest rates, which, in turn, influence the interest-sensitive components of aggregate demand and hence moderate expected and actual inflation. In the open economy setting, this effect is augmented by the exchange rate channel: higher interest rates appreciate the exchange rate, which reduces net exports and thus the output gap. In addition, exchange rate appreciation directly reduces the domestic cost of imports.

For less mature emerging markets and for pre-emerging markets where the financial sector is often much less developed, these traditional channels may be less powerful, although others may dominate. Moreover, transmission effects are also likely to be much less stable. We have already discussed how the processes of structural transformation and innovation in financial markets generate shocks to velocity and the money multiplier, which can substantially alter the short- to medium-run link between money growth or nominal depreciation and domestic inflation and output. In the rest of this section, we consider some other areas where the transmission mechanism in Kenya is likely to differ from the textbook characterization. This is necessarily speculative as one of the major gaps in our knowledge about many contemporary African economies is a robust quantitative assessment of the relative strengths of alternative channels of monetary transmission.

In industrial countries, short-term market interest rates are the main instrument of monetary policy, operating directly through interest-sensitive components of absorption and indirectly through wealth effects, by altering collateral conditions and thereby expanding or contracting bank lending. An implicit assumption is that the banking system is relatively competitive and fully lent out so that changes in the short-run policy rate are rapidly transmitted through the length of the yield curve. In less developed economies, including Kenya, where monetary policy still tends to be exercised through operations on the central bank's own balance sheet – domestic credit policy, bond operations, and foreign exchange sales – and where the banking sector has been dominated by oligopolistic commercial banks, interest rates tend to play a less important role. Although Kenya is home to one of the most developed banking systems on the continent, levels of intermediation are still significantly lower than elsewhere in the world. Banks have, historically, tended to be highly liquid, suggesting little intermediation at the margin, with excess funds often invested not in private enterprises but in government securities, foreign deposits, and non-remunerated excess reserves (Cihak and Podpiera, 2005; Sacerdoti, 2005; Saxegaard, 2006), suggesting that the bank credit channel in the transmission of monetary policy has been weak. The absence of a strong interest rate or credit channel effects is a feature of the few empirical studies of the transmission mechanism in Africa. This feature emerges from studies of Kenya (for example, the work by Cheng, 2006), although, importantly, the most recent work focusing on bank performance over the 2000s suggests that the bank lending channel is becoming significantly stronger (see Sichei and Njenga, 2010).

The exposure of domestic banks to capital gains and losses from exchange rate movements also strengthens the exchange rate channel. Although dollar-denominated deposits are widely available, commercial banks rarely hold substantial open positions, due to a combination of regulatory restrictions and caution; nor do domestic firms, given the reluctance of banks to lend domestically in foreign currency. Nonetheless, the widespread use of foreign currency and foreign currency deposits in private portfolios increases the sensitivity of domestic money demand to interest rates and inflation.

Finally, although conventional interest rate channels may not be strong, interest rate effects may operate more powerfully through domestic debt markets on to the fiscal accounts. Domestic asset markets in most African economies, including Kenya, are still relatively thin and oligopolistic, while the CBK still conducts much of its open market operations using government debt instruments. The level and volatility of interest rates thus places considerable stress on the consolidated fiscal accounts, so that monetary policy actions can exert powerful real effects through the fiscal burden of interest payments. These effects may be magnified when the domestic fiscal balance is also sensitive to movements in the exchange rate, as is the case in economies where revenues are highly dependent on commodity prices and/or aid flows (see O'Connell *et al.*, 2007). These fiscal channels of transmission tend not to feature in the textbook model, but understanding them is of critical importance for implementing effective monetary policy in most emerging and pre-emerging market economies.

We started this section by noting that policy effectiveness requires a credible understanding of the monetary transmission mechanism. In reality, although our understanding is improving, we still lack a robust calibration of the relative strength of the key channels from policy instruments to outcomes and, arguably, less than is required to implement a full-blown and credible IT regime. Addressing this gap in knowledge must be a priority for the central bank.

7.4.4 Guarding against the re-emergence of fiscal dominance

A major achievement of the Kenyan authorities over the last decade has been the elimination of fiscal dominance, allowing a coherent monetary policy to emerge. The dragon of fiscal indiscipline is, of course, never completely slain, so an important consideration becomes the capacity of alternative monetary regimes to offer an effective bulwark against recurring fiscal indiscipline. Under conventional monetary targeting, and particularly that practised in many Africa countries under the aegis of IMF-monitored programmes, this disciplining role centred on quantitative ceilings on the domestic credit to government component of reserve money growth and was policed by IMF programme performance criteria.

As the IMF's role in Africa changes, with fewer countries engaged in prolonged lending arrangements (Kenya's last IMF programme expired in 2007, for example),[24] debate has turned to the question of how best to fill the external agency of restraint role played by the IMF. Here, a well-established IT regime may contribute in a positive manner. First, and most obviously, the explicit commitment to an agreed inflation target – especially one that the authorities are seen to converge towards – combined with an increasingly transparent public role for the MPC in explaining policy choices helps to reinforce the credibility and independence of the central bank. But this may be reinforced by another mechanism, first described by Bean (1998) in the context of the UK. Bean characterized the relationship between the central bank and the ministry of finance as a so-called 'Stackleberg game', in which a credible monetary policy regime allowed the central bank to act as a 'Stackleberg follower', which set monetary policy so as to deliver the inflation target, *given the fiscal policy stance being adopted by the Treasury* (*Ministry of Finance*).[25] Recognizing this, the fiscal authorities, as the 'Stackleberg leader', would not be tempted to overexpand the economy, as it would know that if it did the monetary authority would just raise interest rates and activity would not actually increase: more precisely, the central bank's interest rate action would ensure that a fiscal expansion directly crowded out private activity.

This strong disciplining perspective may need to be tempered, however, if the underlying political economy constraints generating excessive fiscal pressures have not been fully addressed. As countries such as Zambia and Uganda discovered as they sought to implement 'cash budgets' in the 1990s, tight commitments on inflation, and therefore on monetary finance in circumstances where underlying spending pressures are not concomitantly reined in can result in inefficient fiscal adjustments elsewhere or costly domestic or international borrowing. In other words, monetary policy cannot on its own 'solve' structural problems of fiscal control: this requires deeper political considerations, even though a credible and transparent monetary regime may play an important role in securing fiscal discipline on an ongoing basis. In such circumstances, O'Connell (2008) suggests that, when fiscal problems are serious:

> ...a more accommodative policy at the outset might share the adjustment burden more efficiently between seigniorage and distortionary adjustments in fiscal policy, such that greater flexibility on inflation outcomes early on would more than repay itself in the medium run in terms of smoother adjustment, lower inflation, and better performance of the real economy.

7.5 Conclusions

The achievement and maintenance of macroeconomic stability has been an important feature of Kenya's economic performance since the mid-1990s. This has helped lay the foundations for structural change and innovation in financial markets and in the real economy, many of which are discussed elsewhere in this volume. In this chapter, we have argued that, although the current money targeting regime was both well suited to and effective in delivering macroeconomic stability, it is less obvious that it still constitutes the most effective regime as Kenya seeks to establish itself as an emerging market economy in the twenty-first century. We have argued that the IT regimes that have been adopted widely across industrialized and middle-income emerging markets offer a potentially attractive alternative, but we have also identified some of the pitfalls and challenges the Kenyan authorities are likely to encounter as they move in this direction. For Kenya, the transition from one monetary framework to another will be neither abrupt nor taken in isolation. Many of the elements of full-fledged inflation targeting are already in place, and the CBK is actively engaged in developing the capacity required to underpin new operational procedures with credible technical analysis. Many of these developments will be undertaken in concert with the other countries of the EAC. The successful development of coherent monetary frameworks across the member states holds out the prospect of better macroeconomic management at the country level, and of supporting broader economic convergence and more effective macroeconomic policy co-ordination at the regional level.

Notes

1 Masson and Pattillo (2005) offer a similar diagnosis of the post-Independence monetary history of Africa.

2 This section draws extensively on papers presented by two of the authors at a conference on monetary frameworks and inflation targeting hosted by the Central Bank of Nigeria in Abuja, Nigeria, in January 2008. See O'Connell (2008) and Adam (2008).

3 The notion of time inconsistency dates back to the Nobel prize-winning work of Kydland and Prescott (1977), subsequently developed in the context of monetary policy by Barro and Gordon (1983). The essential idea is that when the authorities set their policy instrument only after the private sector has formed its expectations about inflation (possibly based on some prior announcement about the stance of policy), they will have an incentive to renege on their announcement. Specifically, a monetary authority concerned about output as well as inflation will have an incentive to announce a commitment to low inflation and then renege on this commitment to exploit the short-run Phillips curve so as to boost aggregate demand. Anticipating this incentive, the initial policy announcement will no longer be credible and private sector expectations will adjust accordingly. This creates an *inflation bias*, locking the economy into a higher long-run inflation rate. In this situation, to make their announcements credible and eliminate, or at least reduce, the inflation bias, the monetary authorities may seek to commit to a fixed and verifiable policy rule.

4 The nominal anchor is some quantity or price in the economy targeted by the monetary authorities. The anchor determines the path for average prices around which all relative prices are determined and, in the long run, the growth rate of nominal aggregates (nominal wages, nominal debt) will converge to the growth rate of the anchor (plus any real growth in the underlying real variables).

5 To illustrate, consider the economy being subject to a positive external shock that raises the *ex ante* return to domestic assets (this may be an exogenous fall in the country risk premium or some technology shock that improves prospects in the domestic economy). With an open capital account, foreign private capital will flow in, thereby generating an incipient appreciation of the currency. Attempts to stabilize the exchange rate will draw the central bank into foreign exchange intervention, thereby undermining the autonomy of domestic monetary policy through the effect of intervention on the domestic money stock. Restoring monetary autonomy through bond sterilization may work but only by driving up domestic interest rates relative to world rates, thereby exacerbating the original pressure on the exchange rate. Eventually one of the objectives must be abandoned.

6 Choices over the path of NIR will have implications for the exchange rate, and the two together influence the local currency value of this component of base money. This creates a direct link between net foreign capital inflows, the authorities' re-

sponse to these, and the pursuit of money targets. To the extent that the inflows drive actual base money and broad money away from targets, this places additional pressure on monetary policy instruments.

7 How 'forward-looking' this rule should be depends on the lags in the monetary policy transmission process describing how quickly output and prices respond to policy actions. This in turn reflects, among other things, the extent to which economic agents form their price expectations on a forward-looking basis as opposed to relying on a backward-looking or 'rule of thumb' method. Maturu *et al.* (2007) derive results for Kenya suggesting that forward-looking expectations formation weakly dominates 'rule of thumb' methods.

8 The Bank of England Governor's obligation to write an 'Open Letter' to the Chancellor (Minister of Finance) if inflation strays outside its target range is a good example of this approach.

9 Members of the Bank of England MPC have also stressed the importance for policy credibility of developing a 'culture of intellectual dissent', in which the central bank governor and his or her executive can find themselves in a minority on interest rate decisions.

10 Low-income or pre-emerging economies are not alone in this respect. As Edwards (2007) and Blanchard *et al.* (2010) note, many industrialized countries act in a very similar manner, declaring an inflation target but actively targeting the path for the exchange rate. What matters, in the end, appears to be how these potentially conflicting actions are reconciled.

11 See White (2009) for a flavour of this critique.

12 See Kenya National Bureau of Statistics: http://www.knbs.or.ke/sectoral/cpi/cpi102009.html.

13 The simple rolling trend extrapolation represents a rule of thumb frequently used in negotiations with IMF mission teams. At each quarter, the projected growth in velocity is the extrapolation of a linear trend estimated using the last twelve quarters' data; likewise for the multiplier.

14 Adam *et al.* (2010) show, for the case of Tanzania, how structural reforms in that economy since the mid-1990s contributed to a substantial increase in the demand for money.

15 The money multiplier can be written as follows: $m = \frac{M}{H} = \frac{C+D}{C+R} = \frac{1+c}{c+r}$ where C denotes currency in circulation, R bank reserves, and D deposits, so that c is the cash-to-deposit ratio and r the reserves-to-deposit ratio.

16 Since its promulgation in 1966, the CBK Act has been revised sixteen times. Eleven of these revisions have occurred since 1996 and six since 2000. The 1996 revisions established the nature and term of the Governor's appointment (by presidential appointment and for a maximum of two terms of four years), prescribed that the external value of the shilling would be market determined, and articulated clear and specific objectives for monetary policy (see text).

17 The Treaty for the Establishment of the East African Community was signed on 30 November 1999 and entered into force on 7 July 2000 following its ratification by the original three partner states: Kenya, Uganda, and Tanzania. The Republic of Rwanda and the Republic of Burundi joined the EAC on 18 June 2007 and became full members of the community with effect from 1 July 2007.

18 The intuition is as follows. In a money targeting environment, policy is anchored by a rule (i.e. a rate of growth for the money supply) that does not allow the instrument to respond to output and inflation developments (the 'Friedman principle' noted above). In an inflation targeting environment, however, the instrument does respond. A supply-side shock, which puts upward pressure on inflation, will elicit a contractionary policy reaction, and if this policy reaction feeds back on output (for example through the IS curve), the original output volatility is amplified.

19 Or, in recent years, by policy decision on, for example, the US government subsidy programme for biofuels.

20 The argument for excluding these items from the target derives from the view that the role of monetary policy is to influence 'sticky' prices to bring the economy as close as possible to its notional real business cycle path (i.e. the path that would be followed if all prices were perfectly flexible). By this argument, prices that are in fact fully flexible, as is the case of imports where variations in world prices are allowed to pass through instantly to domestic prices, should be excluded from the target. Failure to exclude them would lead to placing excess weight on the policy levers. For example, seeking to lean against a positive oil price shock – which would be the case if policy was geared to targeting headline inflation – would lead to an inefficiently tight squeeze on the non-oil price component of the headline index, serving to 'overdeflate' the economy.

21 For example, food shares account for around 10 per cent of CPI for the OECD (Euromonitor).

22 Some authors have argued that, if the exchange rate pass-through and capital mobility are sufficiently high, an inflation target may reduce to the virtual equivalent of a pegged exchange rate regime: shocks that otherwise depreciate the exchange rate and put upward pressure on inflation will draw forth an increase in the interest rate, which, in turn, will appreciate the exchange rate. Caballero and Krishnamurthy (2005) note that, if market participants anticipate this reaction *ex ante*, they will treat their domestic currency claims as effectively insured against depreciation, and will take open positions that expose the economy to a greater likelihood of capital account crises.

23 Labelled the 'new Keynesian open economy model', this model consists of four basic elements: (i) an open economy IS curve characterizing aggregate demand in which the output gap responds to movements in real interest rates and the real exchange rate; (ii) on the supply side, a Phillips curve in which the conventional inflation–output relationship is augmented by a pass-through effect from the exchange rate; (iii) an interest parity condition; and (iv) a policy rule summarizing central bank interest rate-setting behaviour (Berg *et al.*, 2006). As Adam *et al.* (2009) note, this model can be readily adapted to reflect an environment in which the policy instrument is the money supply rather than the interest rate.

24 This is not counting the Rapid Access Exogenous Shocks Facility credit extended in 2009 at the onset of the global financial crisis.

25 The Stackleberg game is a concept in economics and game theory used to characterize the strategic interaction between parties, typically firms competing in a market, in circumstances in which each understands the other's reaction function (i.e. how they will react to any action taken by the other player) and where one player, the 'Stackleberg leader', has some sort of market power, first-mover, or other informa-

tional advantage. A key insight is that the Stackleberg leader's best outcome will be that which internalizes the follower's reaction function.

References

Adam, C., 2008, 'Factors in the Choice of Monetary Policy Regime'. Paper prepared for the Central Bank of Nigeria Conference on the Transition to Inflation Targeting, Abuja, Nigeria, January 2008.

Adam, C., S. O'Connell, E. Buffie and C. Pattillo, 2009, 'Monetary Policy Rules for Managing Aid Surges in Africa', *Review of Development Economics*, 13 (3), 464–490.

Adam, C., P. Kessy, J. Nyella and S. O'Connell, 2010, 'The Demand for Money in Tanzania'. Bank of Tanzania and International Growth Centre Working Paper No 2.

Bandiera, L., P. Kumar and B. Pinto, 2008, 'Kenya's Quest for Growth: Stabilization and Reforms – But Political Stability? ' World Bank Policy Research Working Paper WPS 4685.

Barro, R. and D. Gordon, 1983, 'A Positive Theory of Monetary Policy in a Natural Rate Model', *Journal of Political Economy*, 91 (4), 589–610.

Batini, N. and D. Laxton, 2007, 'Under What Conditions can Inflation Targeting be Adopted?' in Mishkin, F. and K. Schmidt-Hebbel (eds) *Monetary Policy Under Inflation Targeting*. Santiago: Central Bank of Chile.

Bean, C., 1998, 'The New UK Monetary Arrangements: A View from the Literature', *The Economic Journal*, 108, 1795–1809.

Berg, A. and E. Borensztein, 2000, 'The Choice of Exchange Rate Regime and Monetary Target in Highly Dollarized Economies'. IMF Working Paper WP/00/29

Berg, A., D. Laxton and P. Karam, 2006, 'Practical Model-Based Monetary Policy'. IMF Working Paper WP/06/80.

Bernanke, B. and F. Mishkin, 1997, 'Inflation Targeting: A New Framework for Monetary Policy', *Journal of Economic Perspectives*, 11 (2), 97–116.

Blanchard, O., G. Dell'Ariccia and P. Mauro, 2010, 'Rethinking Macroeconomic Policy'. IMF Staff Position Note, February, SPN/10/03.

Buffie, E., C. Adam, S. O'Connell and C. Pattillo, 2008, 'Riding the Wave, Monetary Responses to Aid Surges in Low-income Countries', *European Economic Review*, 52 (8), 1378–1395.

Caballero, R. and A. Krishnamurthy, 2005, 'Inflation Targeting and Sudden Stops', in Bernanke, B. and M. Woodford (eds) *The Inflation-Targeting* Debate. Chicago: University of Chicago Press.

Cheng, K., 2006, 'A VAR Analysis of Kenya's Monetary Policy Transmission Mechanism: How does the Central Bank's REPO Rate affect the Economy? ' IMF Working Paper WP/06/300.

Cihak, M. and R. Podpiera, 2005, 'Bank Behavior in Developing Countries: Evidence from East Africa'. IMF Working Paper WP/05/129, June.

Edwards, S., 2007 'The Relationship between Exchange Rates and Inflation Targeting Revisited', in Mishkin, F. and K. Schmidt-Hebbel (eds) *Monetary Policy Under Inflation Targeting*. Santiago: Central Bank of Chile.

Frankel, J., B. Smit and F. Sturzenegger, 2007, 'South Africa: Macroeconomic Challenges After a Decade of Success'. RWP 07-121, John F. Kennedy School of Government, Harvard University.

Honohan, P. and S. O'Connell, 2008, 'Contrasting Monetary Regimes in Sub-Saharan Africa', in M. Ncube (ed.) *Financial Systems and Monetary Policy in Africa*. Nairobi: AERC.

Jack, W., T. Suri and R. Townsend, 2010, 'Monetary Theory and Electronic Money: Lessons from the Kenyan Experience' (mimeo).

King, M., 2009, Mansion House Speech, June. http://www.bankofengland.co.uk/publications/speeches/2009/speech394.pdf.

Kydland, F. and E. Prescott, 1977, 'Rules rather than Discretion: the Inconsistency of Optimal Plans', *Journal of Political Economy*, 85 (3), 473–491.

Masson, P. and C. Pattillo, 2005, *The Monetary Geography of Africa*. Washington, DC: Brookings Institution.

Maturu, B. O., 2007, 'The Money–Inflation Nexus in Kenya'. Unpublished paper presented during the Working Retreat of the Monetary Policy Advisory Committee of the Central Bank of Kenya, Rift Valley Lodge, 3 August.

Maturu, B. O., K. Kethi and I. Maana, 2007, 'A New Keynesian Phillips Curve for Kenya'. Paper presented during the 12th Annual International Conference of the African Econometric Society, Cape Town, South Africa, 4–6 July. http://www.africametrics.org/conference-papers.html.

Mishkin, F. and K. Schmidt-Hebbel, 2007, 'Does Inflation Targeting Make a Difference?', in Mishkin, F. and K. Schmidt-Hebbel (eds) *Monetary Policy Under Inflation Targeting*. Santiago: Central Bank of Chile.

O'Connell, S., 2008, 'Inflation Targeting as a Monetary Framework: Issues and Concerns'. Paper prepared for the Central Bank of Nigeria Conference on the Transition to Inflation Targeting, Abuja, Nigeria, January 2008.

O'Connell, S., 2010, 'Inflation Targeting in Africa', in Aryeetey, E., S. Devarajan, R. Kanbur and L. Kasekende (eds) *The Oxford Companion to the Economics of Africa*. Oxford: Oxford University Press.

O'Connell, S., C. Adam, E. Buffie and C. Pattillo, 2007, 'Managing External Volatility: Central Bank Options in Low-Income Countries', in Batini, N. (ed.) *Monetary Policy in Emerging Market and Other Developing Countries*. New York: Nova Science Books and Journals.

Rotich, H, M. Kathanje and I. Maana, 2008, 'A Monetary Policy Reaction Function for Kenya'. Paper presented during the 13th International Conference of the African Econometric Society, Pretoria, South Africa. http://www.africametrics.org/documents/conference08/day2/session6/rotich_katanje_maana.pdf.

Sacerdoti, E., 2005, 'Access to Bank Credit in Sub-Saharan Africa: Key Issues and Reform Strategies'. IMF Working Paper WP/05/166, August.

Saxegaard, M., 2006, 'Excess Liquidity and the Effectiveness of Monetary Policy: Evidence from Sub-Saharan Africa'. IMF Working Paper WP/06/115.

Sichei, M. and M. Njenga, 2010, 'Does the Bank-Lending Channel Exist in Kenya? Bank-Level Panel Data Analysis'. AERC Final Report.

Sowa, N. K. and P. Abradu-Otoo, 2009, 'Inflation Management and Monetary Policy Formation in Ghana', in Hammond, G., R. Kanbur and E. Prasad (eds) *Monetary Policy Frameworks for Emerging Markets*. Cheltenham, UK: Edward Elgar.

Stone, M., 2003, 'Inflation Targeting Lite'. IMF Working Paper WP/03/12

Taylor, J. B., 1993, 'Discretion versus Policy Rules in Practice'. Carnegie-Rochester Conference Series in *Public Policy* 39 (December), 195–214

White, W., 2009, *'Should Monetary Policy be "Lean or Clean"?'*. Globalization and Monetary Policy Institute Working Paper 34. Dallas, TX: Federal Reserve Bank of Dallas.

Woodford, M., 2003, *Interest and Prices: Foundations of a Theory of Monetary Policy*. Princeton, NJ: Princeton University Press.

8

Capital Mobility, Monetary Policy, and Exchange Rate Management in Kenya

Stephen A. O'Connell, Benjamin O. Maturu, Francis M. Mwega, Njuguna S. Ndung'u, and Rose W. Ngugi[1]

8.1 Introduction

This chapter examines a pair of challenges that will confront the Central Bank of Kenya (CBK) as the country enlists foreign capital flows in support of *Vision 2030*. The first is maintaining macroeconomic stability – a pillar of *Vision 2030* – in a context of increasing capital mobility. The second is supporting export competitiveness in the context of large capital inflows and a major infrastructure push.

Private capital flows can be a source of stability by promoting credit and risk-sharing across borders. They can also undermine macroeconomic stability, however, by exposing domestic markets to external volatility and sharpening the trade-offs between competing objectives of monetary policy. The first half of this chapter takes a descriptive and empirical approach to capital mobility in Kenya. We characterize in turn the *de jure* and *de facto* openness of Kenya's capital account, the degree to which private capital flows already influence the environment for monetary policy, and the determinants of vulnerability to a costly reversal of inflows. Our findings are consistent with a situation of imperfect capital mobility, in which monetary policy can pursue multiple targets over the short run. This scope can rapidly disappear, however, when targets are sharply inconsistent or when economic or political shocks interact with pre-existing vulnerabilities. Anticipating a potentially sharp increase in capital inflows, we emphasize the looming importance of the celebrated trilemma of monetary policy and the importance of prudential and regulatory instruments in achieving a favourable balance of expected returns and macroeconomic risks. These include adjustments in the exchange control regime, policies to facilitate private markets for foreign exchange risk, and policies to monitor and limit macroeconomic vulnerabilities.

The second half of the chapter addresses the role of monetary policy in supporting export competitiveness – a more controversial issue, both from a theoretical perspective and from the viewpoint of Kenya's current monetary framework. Policy-makers in Kenya have historically avoided severe exchange rate overvaluation, and the cross-country evidence suggests that continuing this record will be important in achieving the ambitions of *Vision 2030*. But should the CBK actively target an undervalued shilling? Given the importance of export growth for employment and economy-wide productivity, the question deserves debate. We review the issues and conclude that, for Kenya, the policy instruments that matter most for export success lie outside the realm of monetary policy. These include the reliable provision of productivity-enhancing public inputs and the protection of private economic returns from investment – policies emphasized in the economy-wide growth diagnostics of Chapter 3. There may nonetheless be episodes during which resisting appreciation pressures is fully consistent with maintaining a strong inflation anchor.

8.2 Maintaining macroeconomic stability

Kenya adopted a unified and flexible exchange rate in the early 1990s, as part of a market-based reform programme designed to improve the investment environment and spur economic growth (Mwega and Ndung'u, 2008). By 1995, these reforms went beyond the abandonment of exchange controls on exports and imports to include the removal of a number of long-standing restrictions on capital flows. Taking a comparative approach, we briefly document the opening of the capital account and consider its implications for investment and macroeconomic management in Kenya. We then turn to evidence on the degree of capital mobility and its interaction with monetary policy.

8.2.1 Opening the capital account

Ndung'u and Ngugi (1999) describe the liberalization of exchange controls in detail. Following the removal of interest rate controls in 1991, the CBK introduced tradable foreign exchange bearer certificates, effectively creating a dual exchange rate system in which the bulk of foreign exchange transactions continued to take place at the official rate. The free exchange rate started to acquire greater importance as exchange controls were liberalized, but in late 1992, relations with external donors deteriorated during the run-up to the country's first multiparty presidential election. During the first half of 1993, reforms were temporarily reversed in the midst of a banking sector and balance of payments crisis. The Moi government then renewed the process in mid-1993, and received new commitments from donors. Exchange rate unification then proceeded rapidly: during 1994, the government removed all restrictions on current account transactions, and accepted Article VIII status in the International Monetary Fund (IMF).[2] By the middle of 1995, the government had removed many of the remaining restrictions on the capital account. In June 1995, Parliament repealed the Exchange Control Act.

The appropriate combination of regulations and restrictions on private capital movements remains a topic of vigorous debate among economists (Edwards, 2007; Obstfeld, 2008). How open is Kenya's capital account a decade and a half after the reforms of the mid-1990s? Figure 8.1 adopts a cross-country perspective, comparing a *de jure* measure based on official restrictions with a *de facto* measure based on observed transactions. Panel 1 shows that Kenya was an early and substantial capital account liberalizer, especially within sub-

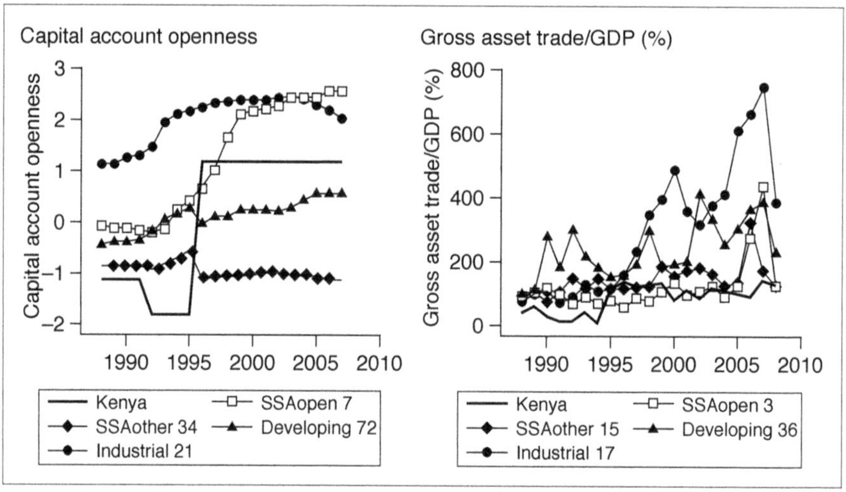

Figure 8.1 Capital account openness, 1988–2008: *de jure* and *de facto*.
We report cross-country averages for various country groups; see the legends for group sizes, which are smaller in panel 2 because of data limitations. Panel 1 includes all countries with a full set of annual observations; panel 2 allows at most one missing observation. The SSAopen 7 includes all countries with a capital account openness index at least as high as Kenya's in 2007 (see text). The 'Developing' category excludes transition economies and SSA. In panel 2, gross capital account trade is the sum of the absolute values of debit and credit entries in the capital and financial accounts of the balance of payments, including errors and omissions and excluding derivatives trade. Balance of payments data are from the IMF's *International Financial Statistics* online.
Sources: panel 1, Chinn and Ito dataset, 2008; panel 2, IMF and CBK.

Saharan Africa (SSA). We use the measure developed by Chinn and Ito (2008), which relies on the detailed annual assessments of exchange restrictions in the IMF's *Annual Report on Exchange Controls and Exchange Restrictions*.[3] By this measure, Kenya vaulted in 1996 from the most closed 7 per cent of developing countries to the most open 25 per cent in terms of capital account openness. As of 2007, Kenya remained one of only eight countries in SSA to fall within the most open 30 per cent of the developing country distribution.[4] Of these eight, however, Kenya's regime was the least liberal, retaining a variety of controls on the ability of non-resident investors to acquire assets and issue liabilities in the local market (see IMF, 2007).

As a measure of *de facto* openness, panel 2 of Figure 8.1 shows the ratio of gross trade in assets – purchases plus sales of financial claims between Kenyans and foreign residents – to gross domestic product (GDP).[5] We emphasize two observations. First, Kenya experienced a substantial once-for-all increase in the volume of capital flows in the mid-1990s, coinciding with its relaxation of restrictions on the capital account. Their trajectory since the mid-1990s is flat, by comparison with increases elsewhere, an observation that corroborates the impression of partial liberalization suggested by the Chinn and Ito measure. Second, however, gross capital flows remain relatively low even by the standards of Kenya's comparatively liberal policy regime. In recent years, gross flows in Kenya have been well below the non-African developing country average and below even the average among countries of SSA with tighter *de jure* restrictions on capital movements. This may in part reflect perceptions of country risk; we provide a rough estimate below of Kenya's risk premium and show that it is above that of a set of comparator countries. Although the sources of this are various, it is likely that perceptions of political instability play a role. Of the large number of international comparisons reported by Kenya Institute for Public Policy Research and Analysis (KIPPRA, 2009) in its comprehensive study of national competitiveness, Kenya's relative performance was weakest by far on investor perceptions of government stability.[6] Below, we show evidence of turmoil in the foreign currency markets around the time of national elections.

8.2.2 Financing investment

Net financial trade can provide an important source of investment financing even if two-way financial trade remains relatively modest as a share of GDP. Figure 8.2 relates investment in Kenya to its ultimate sources in national saving and net financial inflows. Foreign financing – the total amount of which, including the use of official foreign exchange reserves, equals the current account deficit – has indeed played an important role during the period of an open capital account. This is particularly so over the past half decade, during which time a sharp increase in the investment rate has been almost fully matched by an increase in the current account deficit.

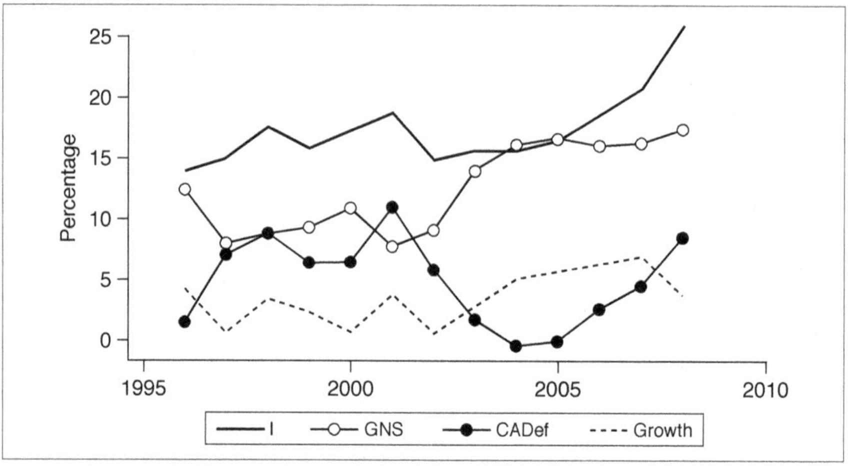

Figure 8.2 Investment, saving, current account deficit, and economic growth, 1996–2008.
National accounts data in national currency at constant 2001 prices are from the World Bank, *World Development Indicators* online. Gross domestic investment (I), gross national saving (GNS), and the current account deficit (CADef) are measured as percentages of gross national disposable income. The identity I=GNS+CADef holds. The current account deficit equals the trade deficit minus the sum of net current transfers and net factor income. Growth is the growth rate of GDP.

The recent confluence of external inflows with increasing rates of investment and growth reflects, at least in part, a vote of confidence by internal and external investors in Kenya's economic prospects. The implied increase in overall net foreign liabilities is nonetheless substantial, and is projected to continue under *Vision 2030*. Although Kenya's external debt position is favourable (see below), this depends in part on a combination of official debt relief and growth rates of exports and GDP that have exceeded the real interest rates on external debt. The global recession and financial crisis have tended at least temporarily to reverse the latter ranking, raising questions of the sustainability of continued current account deficits. Aizenman *et al.* (2007) find that net capital inflows continue to constitute a limited source of investment finance for developing countries despite the sharp increases in global gross capital flows during the 1990s. This suggests that the very substantial further increases in domestic investment being anticipated under *Vision 2030* – the investment target is 30 per cent of GDP – will have to be financed mainly through increases in national saving.

8.2.3 The composition of capital flows

Openness to foreign capital flows provides domestic residents with opportunities for diversification and may contribute to investment by reducing the country's overall cost of capital. It also alters the environment for monetary policy, however, by increasing the degree of *de facto* capital mobility. One of the central propositions of international monetary economics is that an increase in capital mobility sharpens the trade-off between internal and external objectives of monetary policy. An extreme version of this proposition – the so-called trilemma – states that, when capital mobility is perfect, a country cannot simultaneously pursue an exchange rate target (an external objective) and an interest rate target (an internal objective). One of three elements must be sacrificed: capital mobility must be restricted, the exchange rate must be freed, or domestic policy objectives must be ignored.

Our evidence on gross capital flows suggests that monetary policy in Kenya is in an intermediate position – capital mobility is substantial but far from perfect, so that the CBK has at least limited scope for pursuing interest rate and exchange rate objectives simultaneously. However, the environment for monetary policy is also strongly influenced by the composition of external flows. Liquid short-maturity flows – particularly short-term debt – are widely regarded as more constraining of monetary policy than long-term flows. Their attractiveness to investors, whether domestic or foreign, can depend sensitively on interest rates and exchange rate expectations. Their easy reversibility, moreover, increases the risk of a 'sudden stop': a shift in market sentiment that creates a flight away from domestic assets, such as occurred during the Asian financial crisis of 1997–98 and in a number of emerging market economies during the recent global financial crisis. A sudden stop generates an unpleasant menu of policy choices. The monetary authority can stand aside and allow the shilling to depreciate; it can defend the shilling by raising interest rates; it can finance the outflow by spending international reserves; or it can attempt to stop outflows directly, by tightening exchange controls. The trilemma is at work here, because each of these strategies requires the sacrifice of some domestic or external objective. Depreciation contributes to inflation and may provoke a populist outcry from import-dependent groups including urban wage earners; and it increases the debt burden of domestic entities – banks, firms, or government – that have net foreign currency liabilities. Interest rate increases may contract aggregate demand and endanger the solvency of net debtors, including prominently the public sector; and they can weaken the banking sector, given the maturity mismatch between assets and liabilities. International reserves are limited and costly to rebuild, and as long as interest rates remain low, any perception that the central bank cannot tolerate depreciation may redouble speculative pressures against the currency. Tighter controls may undermine the confidence of portfolio holders further, creating renewed pressure for outflows and discouraging subsequent inflows once the crisis is over; and they may be difficult to remove.

Figure 8.3 provides a summary view of Kenya's external position as it has evolved over the period since 1996. Panel 1 shows that exports of goods and services have doubled in real terms since 2002, and that imports have grown even faster. Aid flows began to recover in the late 1990s following a long decline, but they remain low as a share of overall imports. Panel 2 shows the

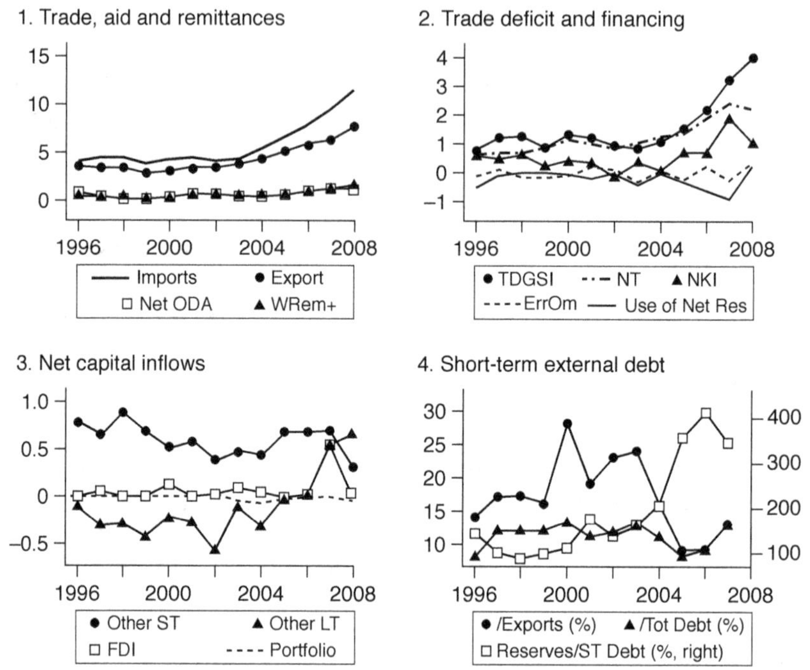

Figure 8.3 Balance of payments, 1996–2007/8.

All variables in panels 1–3 are deflated using the USA GDP deflator. Balance of payments data are from the CBK. Imports and exports are of goods and non-factor services, and TDGSI is the trade deficit on goods, services, and income. The NT and NKI variables are our own constructs: NT (=net transfers) is the sum of net current transfers from the current account and 'capital account, net' from the capital account; we call this variable net transfers because the 'capital account, net' is composed mainly of debt forgiveness and other capital grants. NKI (=net capital inflow) is the sum of net direct investment, net portfolio flows, and net other investments; it corresponds to the financial account of the balance of payments. ErrOm denotes errors and omissions. Use of NetRes (=use of net reserves) is the overall balance, with a minus sign; over this period, it is composed almost exclusively of the reduction in net foreign exchange reserves of the monetary authority. The following balance of payments identity holds: TDGSI=NT+NKI+ErrOm+Use of NetRes. Net ODA is net official development assistance, from the OECD's DAC data online. Debt ratios (panel 4) are from World Bank, *World Development Indicators* online.

trade deficit in goods, services, and income, along with its financing. We construct a broad measure of net transfers from abroad, NT, by combining official transfers with capital grants and net worker remittances; this variable is larger than private capital flows and large enough in some years to cover the entire deficit. Net private capital inflows are also substantial, however; they reach a trough in 2002 and then rise sharply until 2007, consistent with our discussion above. Note that the appropriate classification of remittances is unclear here: they may well have some of the characteristics of a financial flow, including responsiveness to perceived investment returns.

Panel 3 shows the composition of net capital inflows, and leaves us with a puzzle. Short-term non-equity flows are by far the dominant form of financing, and in fact long-term debt flows show net repayment over most of the period. The balance of payments data therefore suggest that the average maturity of Kenya's external liabilities has shortened considerably over the past decade, a worrying trend from the perspective of exposure to sudden stops. But, as shown in panel 4, Kenya's official external debt situation is in fact highly favourable, both with respect to maturity structure and according to standard measures of debt burden (see also Republic of Kenya, 2009). As of late 2007, moreover, international reserves were well above the 1:1 ratio to short-term external debt that is now regarded as a minimally prudent rule of thumb for emerging market countries.[7] An important question from a monetary policy perspective, therefore, is whether the short-maturity obligations implied by the balance of payments (panel 3) present a risk of reversal that could be activated by a change in relative yields, business expectations, or political conditions in Kenya. The nature of these claims – including their origin and currency of denomination – is the subject of an ongoing study by the Kenya National Bureau of Statistics and the CBK. We take an indirect approach to these questions in the following section.

8.2.4 Capital flows, exchange rates, and monetary policy in Kenya

The volume and maturity structure of private flows suggests a relatively modest level of rollover risk, but there are numerous conduits for portfolio substitution including the dollarization of domestic bank liabilities, the circulation of foreign currency in the tourist and informal economies, and the accumulation of offshore deposits by Kenyan residents. Rather than focus on the size and composition of annual flows, we look in this section for the imprint of capital mobility on monthly interest rates and exchange rates. Following a brief review of exchange rate policy in Kenya, we begin with the most conventional approach, examining the evidence for an uncovered interest parity relationship between short-term interest rates in Kenya and the world capital market. We then construct a measure of exchange market pressures that combines exchange rate movements with changes in international reserves, in order to accommodate variations over time in how the CBK has responded to balance of payments pressures. An analysis of the time pattern of exchange market pressures suggests that national elections have been an important source of balance of payments volatility in the past, perhaps reflecting uncertainties in the electoral process and working through remittance flows as well as through capital account transactions. We study the two-way relationship between our exchange market pressure variable and domestic interest rates, showing that each affects the other, as expected in a world in which market participants respond to interest rate differentials and the monetary authority must take cognizance of the capital account in setting domestic interest rates. Finally, we use the September 2008 demise of Lehman Brothers, widely viewed as the event that converted a global recession into a global financial crisis, to shed light on the determinants of *ex ante* vulnerability of the capital account to external shocks.

EXCHANGE RATE POLICY

Table 8.1 documents key transitions in Kenya's exchange rate regime. Focusing on the most recent period, the IMF classifies Kenya as operating an independent float between 1992 and 1997 and a managed float since 1998. Reinhart and Rogoff (2004) note that developing country central banks tend to pursue exchange rate targets with considerably more determination than their official pronouncements suggest – so that a managed floater might in fact be operating a fixed exchange rate or a crawling peg for extended periods. Their *de facto* empirical classification, based on observed exchange rate movements and updated to 2007, characterizes the Kenyan regime as a crawling band with margins of ±2 per cent or smaller.

Figure 8.4 shows the basis for this view. Following Eichengreen *et al.* (1994), we calculate a monthly measure of exchange market pressures – denoted EMP – by adding the percentage loss in reserves during the month to the percentage depreciation of the shilling:

$$EMP = 100 \bullet \left(\frac{E_t - E_{t-1}}{E_{t-1}} \right) + 100 \bullet \left(\frac{R_{t-1} - R_t}{R_{t-1}} \right) \tag{8.1}$$

Here, E_t is the nominal exchange rate in Kenya shillings (Ksh) per US dollar, and R_t is the dollar value of total international reserves (excluding gold, which is virtually never used for exchange rate management). This measure is robust to differences in a country's allegiance to any particular target path for the nominal exchange rate. A favourable shock to the balance of payments, for example, will induce reserve accumulation when the exchange rate is heavily managed, and exchange rate appreciation when the exchange rate is allowed to float freely; in both cases, the reduction in exchange market pressures produces a decline in EMP.

Figure 8.4 shows the two components of EMP along with a smoothed version of EMP itself, for the period of an open capital account. Consistent with a *de facto* narrow band, exchange rate movements are generally small and tend to be accompanied by reserve losses that are larger in magnitude and in the same direction. This evidence of active pursuit of exchange rate targets is not definitive, however, because balance of payments conditions were favourable over most of the period, and reserve accumulation was desirable on prudential grounds in the wake of the 1993 balance of payments crisis and subsequent global events (including the Asian financial crisis). Moreover, the external sit-

Table 8.1 Transitions in Kenya's exchange rate regime, 1966–2009

	Exchange rate regime			
Year	Ndung'u *et al.*	IMF *de jure* classification	RRI *de facto* classification	Exchange controls (M&N 2001)
1966	Peg to UK pound; switch to US$ in 1971	Peg	Pre-announced peg	
1970				Administrative controls tightened (1970/1)
1975	Peg to IMF Special Drawing Rights (SDR)			
1982	Crawling peg to trade-weighted basket			
1987			Managed floating	
1991	Market-determined rate[b]			FEBCs introduced[a]
1992		Independently floating	Freely falling	Export retention scheme introduced
1993	Float (official rate merged with interbank rate)			All exchange control regulations suspended
1994			Managed floating	Article VIII status
1995				Foreign Exchange Control Act repealed
1996			*De facto* crawling band that is narrower than or equal to ±2%	
1998		Managed floating		
2009				

Cells show regimes starting in the year they were introduced.
a FEBCs are Foreign Exchange Bearer Certificates of Deposit; see Ariyoshi *et al.* (2000).
b Ndung'u (2000) characterizes the exchange rate regime from 1990 to 1992 as a dual system characterized by an official rate and a market-determined interbank rate.
Source: M&N (2001) refers to Mwega and Ndung'u (2001). 'Ndung'u *et al.*' refers to M&N (2001) and Ndung'u (2000). RRI refers to the Reinhart and Rogoff (2004) classification, as updated by Reinhart and Ilzetski (http://terpconnect.umd.edu/~creinhar/Papers.html); this is an empirically driven classification based mainly on observed exchange rate movements; Reinhart and Rogoff (2004) had previously characterized Kenya's regime as managed floating from 1994 to 2001. The IMF classification is as recorded by RRI.

uation reverses itself sharply in 2008, in the face of global food and fuel price shocks and in the midst of post-election violence. During this episode, the balance of payments adjustment is more evenly shared between reserve losses and exchange rate depreciation. On balance, the evidence suggests that, during periods of relative quiescence in foreign exchange markets, the CBK can smooth out exchange rate volatility with relatively modest fluctuations in its intervention. During periods of greater pressure, the CBK has been prepared to allocate a more substantial burden to exchange rate movements.

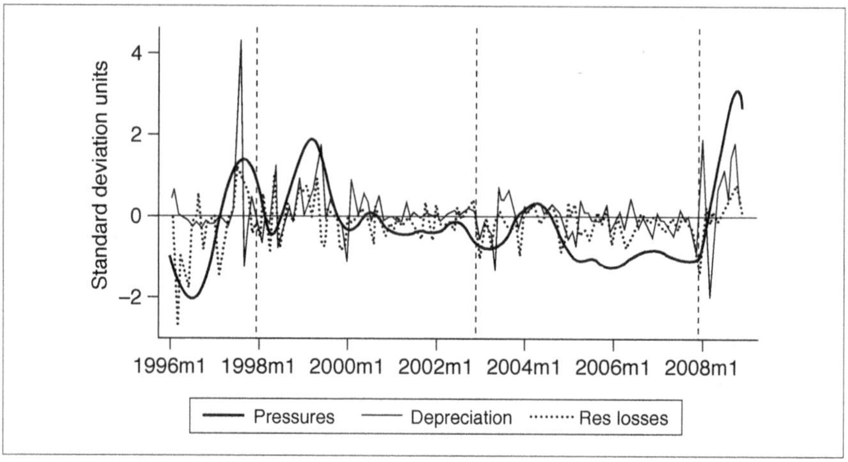

Figure 8.4 Exchange market pressures, 1996–2008.
Pressures=EMP (smoothed). Vertical lines show presidential and parliamentary elections.
Source: CBK.

UNCOVERED INTEREST PARITY

When capital movements are perfectly free and investors can diversify away exchange risk, a version of the 'law of one price' should hold for debt securities: the expected return on claims of similar maturity, liquidity, and default risk should be the same when measured in a common currency. This benchmark is known as *uncovered interest parity* (UIP). As the expected yield on a dollar-denominated three-month US Treasury bill, when measured in Kenya shillings, is approximately the interest rate on that security plus the rate of expected deprecation of the shilling against the US dollar during the three-month holding period, the UIP condition can be stated as:

$$i_t = i_t^* + Expected\ Ksh/\$\ depreciation\ from\ t\ to\ t+3 \qquad (8.2)$$

where i_t and i_t^* are the Kenyan and US interest rates. Under UIP, the trilemma is in full force: the country can either choose the path of its interest rate (e.g. on domestic policy grounds) by letting its exchange rate float freely, or choose the path of its exchange rate and leave its interest rate to be determined by international arbitrage. It cannot act independently on the two variables, for example by raising interest rates in order to keep inflation low while simultaneously using foreign exchange intervention to avoid an appreciating exchange rate.

Cross-country deviations from interest parity reflect imperfect capital mobility. These can in principle go in either direction; effective controls on outward capital movements, for example, may support a captive market for domestic bonds in a low-income country even when the interest rate they pay is below the uncovered yield on similar foreign bonds.[8] If controls are absent or ineffective, however, an emerging market interest rate would be expected to exceed a similar uncovered industrial country yield by a 'risk premium' that reflects the less attractive liquidity, default risk, or other characteristics of the emerging market instrument:

$$i_t = i_t^* + Expected\ Ksh/\$\ depreciation\ from\ t\ to\ t+3 \\ + Risk\ premium \quad (8.3)$$

Table 8.2 shows uncovered interest parity deviations – estimates of the risk premium – on three-month Treasury bills in Kenya and a set of comparator economies, using US Treasury bills as the foreign asset. We employ two alternative measures of exchange rate expectations. One is the *ex post* rate of depreciation itself. The assumption here is that market participants base their behaviour on an unbiased forecast of upcoming depreciation. As the forecast is unbiased, the *ex post* rate equals the forecast plus a forecast error that has an expected value of zero at the time the forecast is made. By construction, therefore, the average *ex post* yield equals the average yield expected by market participants, and the difference between this and the home interest rate is the average risk premium. As an alternative, we use a simple backward-looking rule of thumb, whereby market participants assume that annualized depreciation over the next three months will be the same as the observed rate of depreciation over the previous year.

Kenya's premium is the highest of the comparison group – close to 400 basis points when *ex post* depreciation is used and well over 500 basis points

Table 8.2 Uncovered interest parity deviations

	Unbiased forecasts (%)			Static forecasts (%)		
Country	No. of obs.	Mean	Std dev.	No. of obs.	Mean	Std dev.
Uganda	156	–0.60	20.09	144	1.60	9.83
Tanzania	159	-2.07	16.20	147	–0.93	7.16
Ghana	146	1.94	42.43	134	1.88	27.59
Kenya	156	3.71	23.58	144	5.37	8.43
Vietnam	133	0.23	6.94	133	–0.02	3.78
Philippines	144	-2.01	26.86	132	-2.02	13.14
Thailand	98	2.16	12.20	99	1.79	7.20
South Africa	159	-5.70	44.65	147	–0.51	18.42
Mexico	159	3.15	28.00	148	4.24	8.45

In the 'unbiased forecasts' columns, expected depreciation equals actual *ex post* depreciation over the three-month holding period of the bond (*t* to *t*+3). In the 'static forecasts' columns, expected depreciation is the observed rate of depreciation between months *t* and *t*–12.

using the rule-of-thumb forecast. Although this may in part reflect strong prudential limitations on inward investment, it may also reflect concerns about political stability, or other sources of reluctance by foreign investors – including, possibly, expectations of currency depreciation that have not materialized over the course of the sample.

Although the size of the risk premium has implications for Kenya's debt burden and also for the domestic cost of capital, the implications of portfolio behaviour for monetary policy depend less on the size of the risk premium than on the time period over which monetary policy can influence the premium. If the markets demand a non-zero but constant premium from month to month, then in practice the trilemma is at work: movements away from the average premium will tend to be brief, and the scope for influencing the interest rate and exchange rate separately will be limited. How tightly, then, are domestic interest rates tied to changes in the foreign uncovered yield? In Table 8.3, we report a set of bivariate regressions using our two proxies. The dependent variable is the domestic interest rate. The explanatory variable is the sum of the US interest rate and expected depreciation, using our rule-of-thumb depreciation in the upper panel and observed *ex post* depreciation in the lower panel. In the latter case, forecast errors generate a simultaneity bias even if market forecasts are unbiased; to handle this, we employ four lags of the independent variable, dated periods t–3 to t–6, as instruments. Under the hypothesis of uncovered interest parity, the coefficient on the uncovered yield in these regressions should be 1 and the constant should be zero.

At the bottom of each panel in Table 8.3, we show an approximate 95% confidence interval for the coefficient on the uncovered yield. The empirical record of UIP is weak even among industrial and emerging market countries (Flood and Rose, 2002), and our results are consistent with this: in no case does the confidence interval include 1. In most cases, however, the confidence interval also excludes zero, allowing us to reject the hypothesis that domestic interest rates are unrelated to the uncovered US yield.

The upper panel performs significantly better statistically, and in some cases the differences are sharp. Kenya's is one of these – in the upper panel, the Kenyan T-bill rate seems strongly tied to the foreign uncovered yield, suggesting that capital movements are sensitive to relative yields and that exchange rate developments may influence interest rates through an expectations channel. In the lower panel, however – where the maintained assumption is that exchange rate expectations are fully forward-looking – there is little evidence that private capital movements exert a constraint on monetary policy; we cannot reject the possibility that the coefficient is zero. In the next subsection, we develop some further evidence on the policy environment by examining the bivariate relationship between Kenyan interest rates and exchange market pressures.

Table 8.3 Interest parity regressions

Variable	UGA	TZA	GHA	KEN	VNM	PHL	THA	ZAF	MEX
Panel 1: OLS regressions on backward-looking expected yields									
UNCYLD	0.079***	0.099**	0.210***	0.343***	0.348***	0.184***	–0.021	0.048***	0.350***
	2.71	2.38	8.12	6.20	11.09	16.58	–1.57	3.68	3.42
Constant	9.039***	8.030***	20.627***	8.920***	4.600***	6.382***	2.583***	10.103***	9.187***
	31.79	17.57	20.5	16.86	13.49	27.61	21.42	40.29	14.82
N	144	147	134	144	133	132	99	147	148
R^2	0.043	0.034	0.333	0.222	0.355	0.637	0.017	0.086	0.193
RMSE	3.701	3.609	9.725	5.922	2.213	2.221	1.152	2.994	6.282
95% confidence interval:									
Lower	0.019	0.019	0.150	0.223	0.288	0.164	–0.041	0.028	0.150
Upper	0.139	0.179	0.270	0.463	0.408	0.204	–0.001	0.068	0.550
Panel 2: Instrumental variables regressions on *ex post* yields									
UNCYLD	0.112	–0.150	0.145***	–0.420	0.501***	0.201**	–0.010	–0.055	–0.062
	1.02	–1.50	4.05	–1.54	3.06	1.99	–0.34	–0.93	–0.62
Constant	8.629***	10.802***	22.728***	14.692***	3.635***	6.258***	2.587***	11.673***	13.151***
	7.26	9.49	17.49	6.57	3.7	6.68	22.63	11.73	10.14
N	150	153	140	150	133	138	98	153	153
RMSE	4.352	3.871	12.45	12.09	3.802	5.586	1.139	3.995	7.582
95% confidence interval:									
Lower	–0.108	–0.350	0.065	-0.960	0.181	0.001	–0.070	–0.175	–0.262
Upper	0.332	0.050	0.225	0.121	0.821	0.401	0.051	0.065	0.138

The table shows estimated coefficients and robust t-statistics (***denotes significance at the 1% level, **at the 5% level). In panel 1, the uncovered yield (UNCYLD) is the annualized interest rate on US three-month Treasury bills in month t plus the percentage depreciation of the average Ksh/$ exchange rate between month t and month t–12. In panel 2, the interest rate is the same, but we use the annualized *ex post* depreciation between months t and t+3. As a proxy for expected depreciation, the *ex post* value is subject to a measurement error (the forecast error) that is correlated with the proxy and therefore a source of simultaneity bias. As instruments, we use annualized depreciation in months t–3, t–4, t–5, and t–6. If forecasts are conditionally unbiased, these are valid instruments because they are in the market's information set at the time forecasts are made. The 95% confidence intervals for the coefficient on UNCYLD are approximate: the table shows the estimated coefficient minus and plus 2 standard errors. RMSE denotes root mean squared error.

INTEREST RATES AND EXCHANGE MARKET PRESSURES

When capital mobility is appreciable and the monetary authority seeks to avoid excessive volatility in the exchange rate and/or international reserves, we expect to see a two-way relationship between exchange market pressures and domestic short-term interest rates. On the one hand, monetary policy actions, to the degree that they operate directly or indirectly through short-term domestic interest rates, should provoke a portfolio response that manifests itself as a change in exchange market pressures. On the other hand, we should see monetary policy instruments, again reflected directly or indirectly in short-term interest rates, responding to exogenous changes in exchange market pressure with a view to moderating the impact on the exchange rate and/or reserves. The latter relationship underlies the 'interest rate defence' of a currency facing speculative outflows.

In this section, we estimate reduced form dynamic models to characterize the relationship between Kenyan interest rates and exchange market pressures, conditional on foreign interest rates. These bivariate vector autoregressions (VARs) take the form:

$$x_t = \Sigma_{j=1}^{k} A_j x_{t-j} + \Sigma_{j=0}^{k} C_j i_{t-j}^{*} + \varepsilon_t, \tag{8.4}$$

where x_t is a 2×1 vector composed of the Kenyan interest rate and EMP, A_j (2×2) and C_j (2×1) are matrices of reduced form coefficients, and ε_t is a 2×1 vector of shocks or 'innovations' to the dependent variables. We are interested, first, in patterns of causality between the two variables, which we assess using tests of Granger causality. These tests ask whether lagged values of the Kenyan interest rate add predictive power to lagged values of EMP in forecasting future EMP – in this case, the Kenyan interest rate is said to 'cause' EMP – and similarly for lagged values of EMP in forecasting future interest rates. We then use the estimated equations to trace out the time path of how each variable responds over time to an unexpected one-time change or 'innovation' in the other. Under the assumption that the innovations correspond to shocks to monetary policy and the balance of payments, respectively, these impulse responses indicate the direction, magnitude, and persistence of influences from monetary policy shocks to the balance of payments – given the high frequency of our data, most probably through portfolio effects – and from balance of payments shocks to monetary policy.

We estimate two separate VARs, involving in turn the three-month T-bill rate and the repo rate in Kenya. We estimate with twelve monthly lags, and in each case we include the relevant US interest rate – the three-month T-bill rate, and the Federal Funds rate respectively – as an exogenous variable in the VAR.

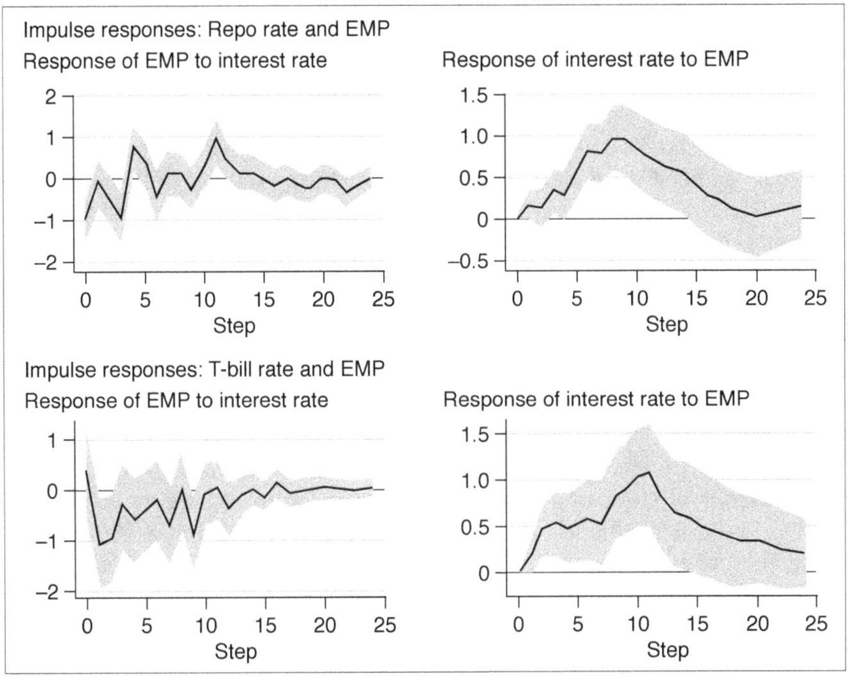

Figure 8.5 Impulse responses: interest rates and exchange market pressures in Kenya. The figures show responses to a shock equal to one standard deviation of the relevant innovation; steps are in months. Upper and lower bounds show the estimated effect plus and minus two standard deviations. The underlying bivariate VARs have twelve monthly lags and include as exogenous variables a set of centred monthly dummy variables and the current value and twelve lags of the relevant US interest rate (the Federal Funds rate in the repo case and the three-month T-bill rate in the T-bill case). We assume in both cases that the interest rate innovation is causally prior to the EMP innovation, so that innovations in the domestic interest rate affect EMP in the month they occur, whereas the interest rates respond to EMP only with a one-month lag (the qualitative results are not sensitive to the choice of ordering).

In both cases, the causality evidence is very strongly consistent with a two-way relationship between the interest rate and exchange market pressures. We reject the hypothesis of no Granger causality from the interest rate to EMP, and also from EMP to the interest rate, and in both cases the significance level is well below 1 per cent. Figure 8.5 shows the impulse responses, using the repo rate in the upper panel and the T-bill rate in the lower. These indicate a statistically significant short-run response of each variable to the other. The direction of these responses is consistent, on the one hand, with a conventional portfolio response to changes in domestic monetary policy: a monetary tightening produces a short-run reduction in exchange market pressures. In the other direction, the impact of exchange market pressures on the interest rate is consistent with a monetary policy that seeks to reduce exchange rate volatility by responding to shocks to the balance of payments. The second of these effects is stronger and more persistent, and is estimated more precisely.[9]

DETERMINANTS OF VULNERABILITY: SOME EVIDENCE FROM A GLOBAL FINANCIAL SHOCK

Monetary policy has two very different responsibilities with respect to the exchange market volatility associated with capital inflows. The responsibility for handling shocks as they occur falls within the domain of conventional monetary policy. The evidence we have provided thus far suggests that capital flows already exert a significant impact on the conduct of monetary policy in Kenya. An important complement to this *ex post* responsibility, however, is the challenge of managing the country's *ex ante* vulnerability to shocks. What factors determine a country's vulnerability to a costly reversal in capital flows? An extensive literature investigates this question in the case of industrial and emerging market countries: we have already mentioned short average maturities, currency mismatches, a preponderance of debt liabilities over equity liabilities, and inadequate reserve coverage as potentially important correlates of vulnerability (Obstfeld, 2008). Less is known, however, about the relevance of these and other determinants for pre-emerging economies such as Kenya's. In this section, we treat the collapse of Lehman Brothers on 15 September 2008 as an exogenous shock to global capital markets, and ask what variables helped to determine the vulnerability of developing countries to a sharp increase in exchange market pressures. Our purpose here is narrow; we are not seeking to determine the overall impact of the global crisis, which emerged over a longer period and, within Africa, primarily via export markets. We are instead exploiting the unanticipated and dramatic nature of the Lehman Brothers collapse to isolate asset market pressures on the exchange rate and infer the sources of vulnerability to such pressures.

Rose and Spiegel (2009) find that most of the variables suggested by the literature have little or no success in predicting which countries were hit hard, and which were not, by the global financial crisis. Our exercise differs from that of Rose and Spiegel in some important ways, however, most notably in focusing on a well-defined and limited aspect of the crisis – its immediate short-run impact on the foreign exchange market (Rose and Spiegel construct a 'crisis' variable that combines changes over the course of 2008 in real GDP, the stock market, country credit ratings, and exchange rates). Reflecting our focus on emerging and pre-emerging economies, moreover, our sample excludes the industrial countries altogether and includes all of the non-industrial countries for which data are available. Nonetheless, the Rose and Spiegel results suggest that modest expectations are appropriate in this exercise, which we view as an exploratory first cut.

To construct our dependent variable, we make three important changes to EMP. First, consistent with our earlier results for Kenya, we expand the definition of exchange market pressure to include the change in the domestic discount rate, i_t:

$$\mathrm{EMP}^{+} = 100\bullet(i_t - i_{t-1}) + 100\bullet\left(\frac{E_t - E_{t-1}}{E_{t-1}}\right) + 100\bullet\left(\frac{R_{t-1} - R_t}{R_{t-1}}\right) \tag{8.5}$$

We do this to avoid masking the effect of the shock in countries that adopted an interest rate defence, raising domestic rates in order to contain the impact on reserves and/or the exchange rate.[10] Second, we study the change in EMP+ rather than its level, in order to avoid confounding the impact of the global crisis with pre-existing country-specific trends in exchange market pressure. Finally, to control for structural differences in exchange market volatility across countries, we normalize each country's change in exchange market pressure by the historical standard deviation of such changes for that country. Our dependent variable, denoted LBE for 'Lehman Brothers effect', is therefore:

$$\mathrm{LBE}_i = \Delta\mathrm{EMP}_i^{+}(\text{October 2008}) / \sigma_i(\Delta\mathrm{EMP}^{+}) \tag{8.6}$$

where $\sigma_i(\mathrm{EMP}^{+})$ is the country-specific standard deviation of EMP+ calculated over the period 2000–07.

Note that we focus on changes over the course of October rather than September 2008.[11] Although the Lehman Brothers event is widely viewed as a turning point, this is with the benefit of hindsight. Figure 8.6 shows the distribution of exchange market pressures among emerging market countries, and shows that the global recession became a global crisis only in October. Our regressions seek to uncover the determinants of this shift at the country level.

To avoid reverse causality, we restrict attention to initial conditions that were established by or before 2007. We therefore run a set of cross-sectional regressions of the form:

$$\mathrm{LBE}_i = \alpha + \beta\bullet x_i(2007) + \gamma'\mathrm{controls}_i(2007) + \varepsilon_i \tag{8.7}$$

where x_i is a variable suggested by the literature as a measure of *ex ante* vulnerability. All regressions include the log of real GDP per capita, to control for level of development, and the log of population, to control for country size. Table 8.4 reports the estimated values of β along with robust *t*-statistics.

Table 8.4 tentatively confirms the potential relevance of a number of the vulnerability measures suggested in the literature. The ratios of M2 and short-term external debt to international reserves are alternative measures of implicit claims on the central bank's liquid reserves. Higher values of these in 2007 predict the Lehman Brothers effect at a significance level of 10 per cent or better. The capital-to-asset ratio of banks in 2007, and an indicator of the rate of expansion of bank balance sheets between 2005 and 2007 (the increase in the domestic credit to GDP ratio) also predict balance of payments pressure at close to conventional levels of significance. The Kraay–Nehru debt distress

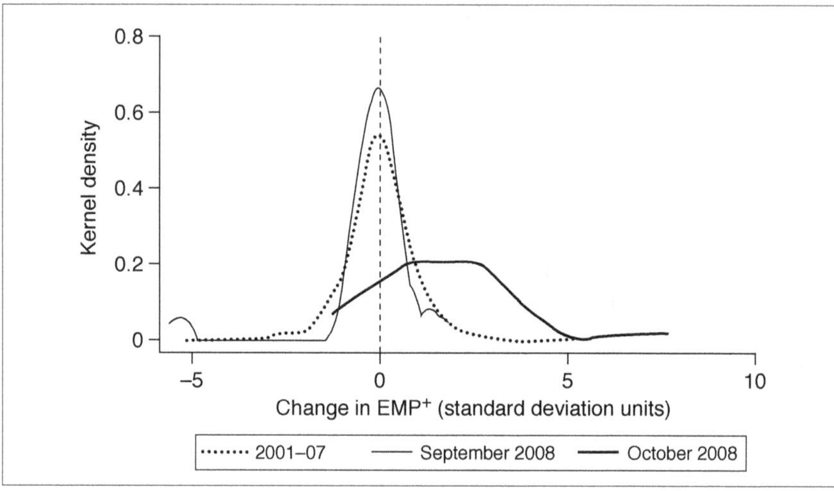

Figure 8.6 Lehman Brothers and the global distribution of EMP+, non-industrial countries.
The kernel densities are smoothed histograms of the cross-country data for twenty-one emerging market countries.

indicator is particularly relevant for the pre-emerging countries in the sample. It defines a distress episode as one during which the country had substantial arrears on external debt, received debt relief from the Paris Club group of bilateral creditors, or received substantial balance of payments support from the IMF.[12] This variable is available only to 2002, and as a predictor we use the proportion of years between 1990 and 2002 classified as distressed. In principle, this variable operates both as a predictor of continuing exposure to debt distress and as a proxy for adverse reputational effects from earlier episodes. Higher values were associated with larger exchange market pressures. Finally, the size of net capital inflows immediately preceding the crisis – captured by the current account deficit – carries a positive point estimate, but not a significant one at conventional levels. Results for the two control variables are of varying statistical significance but consistently positive in sign; they suggest that richer and larger countries tended if anything to be harder hit, consistent perhaps with their more sophisticated financial systems.[13]

A number of variables identified as potentially relevant in the literature did not prove significant in predicting EMP+. These include measures of real exchange rate overvaluation; World Bank assessments of the quality of economic policy; ratios of bank liquid reserves to assets; non-performing loans; and the ratios of debt and debt service to exports or GDP. The Chinn and Ito capital account openness indicator enters with a positive but statistically insignificant coefficient.

Table 8.4 Determinants of the Lehman Brothers effect

Dependent variable: September 2008–October 2008 change in normalized EMP+ calculated using US$ exchange rates

		Individual OLS regressions on x_i variables:						
		Ratio of M2 to international reserves	Ratio of short-term external debt to international reserves	Share of short-term debt in total external debt	Increase in domestic credit as share of GDP	Commercial banks' capital/ asset ratio	Average value of Kraay–Nehru (2006) debt distress indicator	Current account deficit
Result	Control variables only	2005–07	2007	2007	2007	2007	2007	1990–2002
log(y per capita)	0.3399	0.2794	0.0848	0.0286	0.3876	0.4209	0.2046	0.4137
robust *t*-stat	2.24	1.90	0.61	0.15	2.39	1.51	1.40	2.25
P value	0.03	0.06	0.55	0.88	0.02	0.14	0.17	0.03
log(population)	0.112	0.2003	0.1798	0.0778	0.1273	0.1201	0.0646	0.1639
robust *t*-stat	1.24	2.56	3.20	0.86	1.65	0.81	0.66	1.80
P value	0.22	0.01	0.00	0.39	0.10	0.42	0.51	0.08
Coefficient on x_i	–	0.2135	0.0035	0.0336	–0.0246	–0.1342	0.0177	–0.0146
robust *t*-stat	–	1.66	19.02	1.27	–1.51	–1.60	1.72	–1.34
P value	–	0.10	0.00	0.21	0.14	0.12	0.09	0.19
N	68	67	57	57	67	38	60	62
R^2	0.0765	0.1962	0.4126	0.1392	0.1215	0.1196	0.1756	0.0870
RMSE	1.403	1.329	1.097	1.328	1.390	1.329	1.275	1.433
Standardized Kenya residual	0.2136	0.0326	0.0371	0.1393	0.1804	0.5786	–0.4620	0.2648

Sample sizes are determined by data availability, and industrial countries are excluded. For Kenya, we use the repo rate as a discount rate is not available. The standardized Kenya residual is Kenya's residual divided by the RMSE of the regression. The domestic credit variable is the increase in the percentage ratio of total commercial banks' domestic credit to GDP between 2005 and 2007. The Kraay–Nehru variable is the proportion of years from 1990 to 2002 when the country was classified as debt distressed by Kraay and Nehru (2006). Real GDP per capita is in constant international dollars. All variables except the Kraay–Nehru indicator are from World Bank, *World Development Indicators* online. RMSE denotes root mean squared error.

8.2.5 Summarizing

Vision 2030 anticipates a substantial contribution from foreign capital inflows. The period from 2003 to 2007 illustrates the favourable interactions that are central to sustaining such a strategy: domestic reforms supported a combination of inflows and rising investment; strong growth in exports and GDP produced stable or improving creditworthiness despite a buildup of foreign liabilities; and the central bank was able to pursue price stability while limiting the short-run volatility of the exchange rate. The global financial crisis, however, illustrates the urgency of some of the concerns we have raised in this section. First, the composition of Kenya's external liabilities is an important determinant of the country's exposure to macroeconomic instability from sudden reversals. Given ongoing uncertainties in international financial markets and in the domestic political realm, it is a priority that the facts in this area be better established. Second, *Vision 2030* anticipates a central role for foreign direct investment (FDI), both in the infrastructure area and in supporting export diversification. In the absence of direct restrictions on FDI, aspects of the overall investment environment are the most crucial determinants of the rate of inward investment.[14] We have nonetheless noted that, although the reforms of the mid-1990s removed direct restrictions on FDI, the impact of lingering controls on financial transactions by non-residents may be substantial. In contrast with controls on short-term international borrowing, which are largely absent, these do not have an obvious prudential justification. Adequate justification may of course lie elsewhere, but on macroeconomic grounds, the balance between these two types of control should perhaps be revisited. Third, the cross-country evidence emphasizes the overriding importance of domestic saving, even in a world of high capital mobility; we return to this point below. Finally, the degree of capital mobility has an important effect on the environment for monetary policy. We have taken a variety of approaches to assessing the relevance of the trilemma in Kenya, recognizing that balance of payments flows are difficult to measure and classify with precision. Our results suggest that short-run capital mobility is imperfect but substantial in Kenya; we believe it is likely to be even greater in the years ahead. This places a premium on central bank activities that lie outside of conventional stabilization policy, including effective prudential oversight of the banking system and regular assessment of the capital controls regime.

8.3 Supporting external competitiveness

Central banks worldwide have placed increasing emphasis over the past two decades on the objective of price stability. In theory, at least, this is not a choice of stability over development. Instead, it reflects an intellectual consensus that monetary policy makes its best contribution to long-run development by maintaining relatively low inflation and a strong financial system. As outlined in Chapter 7, this consensus favours a system of 'constrained discretion' in which the pursuit of short-run goals by the central bank is subordinated to the maintenance of an anchor for private sector expectations of inflation. According to this consensus, market participants must understand that, when conflicts arise between price stability and competing 'real' objectives – including low public sector borrowing costs, high employment, or a competitive real exchange rate – the central bank will give first priority to price stability. These principles are strongly reflected in a succession of Central Bank Acts in Kenya, dating from 1996, and also in the *Vision 2030* documents with their prominent emphasis on macroeconomic stability.

We saw in Section 8.2 that, although private capital mobility is considerable in Kenya, the CBK is not yet in the throes of the trilemma. A combination of imperfect asset substitutability, prudential regulations, and residual capital controls appears to give the CBK scope to target inflation while also exerting some influence over the path of the nominal exchange rate. As domestic wages and prices move more slowly than the exchange rate in the absence of intervention, the CBK has a handle – certainly in the short run and perhaps for extended periods – not just over the nominal but over the *real exchange rate*, defined here as the domestic relative price of non-traded to traded goods.[15] Calvo *et al.* (1995) characterize the real exchange rate as 'probably the most popular real target [of monetary policy] in developing countries' (p. 98).[16] They also warn, however, that targeting the real exchange rate typically comes at a cost in terms of other objectives. How aggressively should the CBK pursue real exchange rate targets?

8.3.1 Reducing volatility

It is important to distinguish two types of exchange rate objective. The first – and less controversial – is limiting extreme short-run appreciations or depreciations. In thin markets, these can be driven by large temporary shocks to the current or capital account. As capital mobility rises, however, the capital account looms larger: herd behaviour may amplify the response to news of any kind, and exchange rates may overshoot when adjusting to changes in monetary policy whether at home or abroad.

There are good reasons to intervene to limit short-run volatility. These include avoiding excessive instability in aggregate demand, especially when banks or other domestic residents may have open positions in foreign exchange (Obstfeld, 2008); avoiding severe liquidity problems for firms when credit markets are weak and costs and revenues are on different sides of the traded/non-traded divide (e.g. for exporters of labour-intensive goods or services); and limiting exchange rate risks when foreign exchange markets are thin and instruments for hedging these risks are absent. The last two considerations are particularly relevant when domestic financial markets are poorly developed. This may help to explain our earlier observation that central banks in emerging market and low-income countries routinely intervene to limit exchange rate volatility, even when the official stance of policy is that the exchange rate is floating (Calvo and Reinhart, 2002). We have seen evidence of this phenomenon in Kenya throughout this chapter, including the *de facto* classification of Reinhart and Rogoff (Table 8.1), which suggests a narrow crawling band rather than the official stance of a managed float.[17]

Of course, any volatility reduction strategy faces the practical problem of deciding when to intervene and for how long. Capital mobility makes this more difficult, because on top of the difficulty of distinguishing transitory from permanent shocks, the central bank must contend with private sector expectations about the onset and abandonment of intervention. Too great an allegiance to any predetermined path for the exchange rate risks activating the trilemma. When pressures push the currency to the weak side of the central bank's notional band, a targeting policy can produce a currency crisis. The key issue from the viewpoint of the monetary framework, as emphasized in Chapter 7, is that, when conflicts arise between the provision of a nominal anchor and exchange rate objectives, the nominal anchor comes first.

Particularly in low-income countries, central banks with flexible exchange rates also face a tension at the level of policy design, in determining the degree of volatility they are prepared to tolerate. We emphasized above that the welfare benefits of reducing volatility may be greatest when domestic financial markets are weak. Consistent with this, Aghion *et al.* (2006) find that the impact of real exchange rate volatility on economy-wide productivity growth is essentially zero for countries with highly developed financial markets, but negative and statistically significant for countries at low levels of financial development.[18] The gains from limiting volatility may therefore be strong, particularly for activities that the government finds it difficult to support via other means, including non-traditional exporters and/or small to medium-sized enterprises who lack access to existing financial markets. But a reduction in exchange rate volatility also undermines the incentive for private agents to develop the financial markets and instruments for managing that volatility.[19] The short-run benefit may therefore come at the cost of a less vibrant and growth-oriented financial sector. The appropriate balance is a matter of judgement, and in any case exchange rate policy should be complemented with direct efforts to foster the development of efficient and well-regulated financial markets.

8.3.2 Real exchange rate trends

Our main focus, however, is on strategies that target an undervalued real exchange rate. In an appendix,[20] we develop a simplified version of the workhorse non-traded goods/traded goods model to illustrate the influence of the real exchange rate on export competitiveness. A real appreciation increases the profitability of firms producing for the domestic market, drawing labour and other mobile resources out of the production of exports. If the export sector is already too small from the perspective of long-run growth, real appreciation worsens this distortion and creates potentially serious welfare losses (Rodrik, 2008). Any impact on the investment environment for exports compounds these losses over time.

Real exchange rate targets are an active source of discussion in Kenya, where export performance has improved since 2002 but continues to fall short of the ambitions of *Vision 2030*. Pollin and Heintz (2007) have recently called for a reassessment of monetary policy with a view to achieving a more depreciated shilling. The underlying argument is that the sectors favoured by real depreciation – those that produce either directly (exports) or indirectly (import substitutes) for the world market – include some that are 'special' from a development perspective, due to the quantity and quality of jobs they create and, perhaps especially, the productivity spillovers they deliver to the rest of the economy. These sectors are suboptimally small, it is argued, in the absence of a real exchange rate policy: their expansion, even at the cost of other activities, would generate economy-wide gains.

The 'principle of policy assignment' states that the best approach to a market failure is generally to attack the problem at its source. Examples include removing the labour market rigidities that generate underemployment, and directly subsidizing industrial activities that generate learning-by-doing. The argument for a weak real exchange rate is therefore what economists call second best: its validity is context specific and depends not just on the presence of a market failure but on the absence of a viable first-best policy approach. Hausmann and Rodrik (2003) interpret an undervalued currency as a second-best form of industrial policy, for countries with relatively weak government institutions and with potential comparative advantage in manufactured exports. The argument is that the manufacturing sector is a source of productivity spillovers that are external to the firm and therefore subject to market failure. The 'first-best' or optimal policy is to subsidize exports directly, and particularly non-traditional exports; but this requires both ample fiscal resources and institutions that are capable of combining subsidies with strong pressures to succeed. A weak but unified exchange rate, they argue, delivers incentives for export diversification without promoting rent-seeking or requiring an unrealistic degree of public sector capability for industrial policy.

Panel 1 of Figure 8.7 suggests the locus of concerns over exchange rate competitiveness in Kenya. We show three concepts of the real exchange rate. The most commonly used is the multilateral real effective exchange rate (REER), calculated as a trade-weighted average of bilateral external real exchange rates with Kenya's main trading partners (of which the USA and the Euro zone are

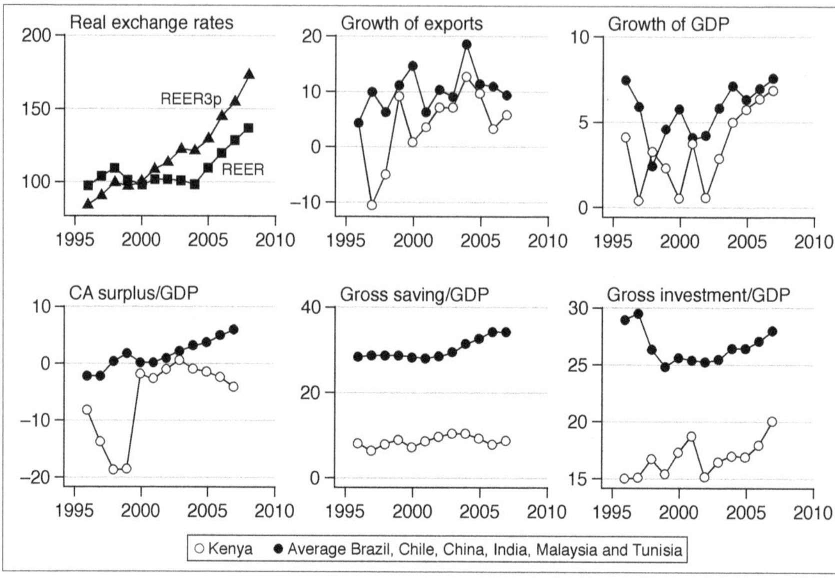

Figure 8.7 Kenya and third-party exporters.
Panel 1: REER is the CBK's trade-weighted real exchange rate, built up from country-level real exchange rates of the form $r_i = CPI_{KENYA}/(E_i \cdot CPI_i)$, where E_i is the bilateral nominal exchange rate in Ksh per unit of currency of country *i* (each bilateral index is converted to 2000=100). The CBK applies separate weights to imports and exports for Kenya's eight largest trading partners (USA, the Euro area, South Africa (imports), the UK, India, Japan, Uganda (exports), and Tanzania (exports)). REER3p is a simple average of Kenya's CPI-based bilateral real exchange rate indices *vis-à-vis* Brazil, Chile, China, India, Malaysia, and Tunisia.
Panels 2–6: Growth of nominal dollar exports; growth of constant local currency GDP. Gross (domestic) saving=GDP–private consumption–government consumption. Gross investment=gross fixed capital formation. CA surplus=trade surplus+net factor income+net unilateral transfers received. The number of third-party exporters in panels 2–6 varies depending on data availability.
Source: World Bank, *World Development Indicators* online.

by far the largest). The underlying bilateral real exchange rates are measured here as Kenya's consumer price index divided by the foreign consumer price index, converted to Kenya shillings at the relevant bilateral official exchange rate. As the price indices refer to different baskets of goods, only changes in the REER, not its level, are meaningful; we have arbitrarily set the level to 100 in 2000. Figure 8.7 shows that the REER has appreciated substantially since 2002, in line with the deterioration in the trade balance over the same period (recall Figures 8.2 and 8.3). These two phenomena are of course closely related. There is ample evidence that trade flows respond to the real exchange rate, both across developing countries and in Kenya (Ghei and Pritchett, 1999; Mwega and Ndung'u, 2001; Were *et al.*, 2002). It is also well established empirically that a surge in net capital inflows tends, in the short run, to produce an excess demand for non-traded goods and a real appreciation (the label 'Dutch disease' applies to the resulting loss in competitiveness of dynamic export sectors; see Edwards, 1989; Hinkle and Montiel, 1999).

Panel 1 of Figure 8.7 also examines Kenya's exchange rate competitiveness *vis-à-vis* a set of six third-party exporters, using this term to refer to developing countries whose exports have grown rapidly in recent years and may pose formidable challenges to Kenyan exports in major industrial country markets. These include some of the economies routinely cited in support of the positive externalities to producing manufactured goods for world markets. Some of these countries, e.g. China and Tunisia, are known not just for their export success but also for their aggressive pursuit of real exchange rate targets. Kenya shares some important features with these economies, including labour abundance, a coastal location, and a tradition of relative macroeconomic stability. In some other respects, including relative endowments of human capital versus natural resources, the credibility of government commitments to export competitiveness, and perceived political stability, Kenya's situation appears to differ substantially.

Panel 1 shows the average bilateral external real exchange rate index against these third-party competitors, again set arbitrarily to 100 in 2000. This measure is directly comparable to the REER except in its country composition and its use of a simple rather than a weighted average. It is clear that Kenya's real exchange rate has appreciated even faster relative to the third-party group than it has with respect to its trading partners.[21]

8.3.3 Targeting an undervalued shilling: strategic considerations

Globally, country episodes of sustained rapid growth since 1960 have typically been accompanied by sharp increases both in the share of manufacturing in exports and GDP and in the share of exports in GDP (Eichengreen, 2008). What role does monetary policy have in achieving this outcome?

We briefly develop four points. First, although Kenya has judiciously avoided acute overvaluation over the years, the empirical literature has become increasingly favourable to the view that undervalued exchange rates are good for growth. Second, however, the real exchange rate is only one of many determinants of export performance in Kenya, and probably not the most important. Third, the issue of appropriate policy assignment is important. Fiscal policies are far more prominent than monetary policies in determining the real exchange rate in the medium to long run, and within the domain of monetary policy, regulatory policies should not be overlooked in the midst of debate over policies that operate directly on the exchange rate. Finally, both theory and evidence suggest that using conventional monetary policy instruments to target a depreciated real exchange rate requires the central bank to accept a higher rate of inflation.

THE REAL EXCHANGE RATE AND GROWTH

In a recent survey of the evidence on real exchange rates and growth, Eichengreen (2008) concludes that an undervalued exchange rate can *facilitate* growth, particularly in the early stages of a growth acceleration. Rodrik (2008) takes a stronger position, arguing on the basis of panel evidence that undervaluation positively promotes growth. Both authors acknowledge that, although the underlying mechanisms are not fully understood, the observed correlations rely strongly on the expansion of manufactured exports in a succession of fast-growing Asian economies, both before and after the Asian financial crisis of 1997. The most prominent recent example is China. Dooley *et al.* (2007) interpret China's currency policy as an attempt to attract FDI in a situation of rural labour surplus. The strong currency keeps the cost of labour low in dollar terms, encouraging inward investment, which generates rapid growth of employment, exports, and GDP.

These assessments are less agnostic than earlier literature, which argued that, although acute overvaluation was damaging to growth, modest levels of over- or undervaluation had little systematic impact (e.g. Razin and Collins, 1999). The classic form of acute overvaluation arises in a managed exchange rate regime when the monetary authority attempts to maintain a non-inflationary path for the exchange rate while providing the government with easy monetary finance. As long as the rate of inflation implied by the government's demand for monetary finance exceeds the rate of crawl of the exchange rate, the situation is unsustainable. The domestic relative price of non-traded goods rises relative to the prices of traded goods, which are held down by the nominal exchange rate; the booming non-traded goods sector draws labour and other productive resources out of the increasingly non-competitive export sector, and exports fall; imports rise, particularly as the private sector comes to understand that the period of cheap imports is likely to be temporary. The trade balance worsens, and external liabilities accumulate. The central bank may tighten exchange controls in the hope of stemming reserve losses, but unless the macroeconomic fundamentals are corrected – in this case, via fiscal adjustment – a currency crisis ensues, forcing the central bank to give up its exchange rate objective and accept higher inflation.

Although we have argued that the CBK pays attention to the path of the exchange rate, the danger of an acute overvaluation driven by fiscal accommodation and aversion to devaluation seems remote. In contrast to its neighbours, Kenya did not allow its exchange rate to become sharply overvalued during the 1970s and 1980s. This in turn reflected, in part, a stronger tradition of fiscal discipline – as witnessed, for example, in the substantial adjustment of the fiscal balance and domestic saving in the face of declining external capital flows during the 1980s. But it also reflected a willingness to devalue the official exchange rate – and tolerate the resulting open inflation in the prices of traded goods – rather than allowing the parallel premium to get extremely large and suffering the attendant distortions.[22] This commitment was buttressed in 1994 by Kenya's acceptance of the obligations of Article VIII status in the IMF. Moreover, any existing willingness to allow necessary exchange rate adjustments to take place, rather than resisting them, has become progressively easier since the mid-1990s, as firms and financial markets have come to expect some degree of exchange rate adjustment in response to shocks.[23]

SOURCES OF EXPORT COMPETITIVENESS

Although the growth evidence is somewhat more favourable than previously to the positive impact of undervaluation, the real exchange rate is only one of many determinants of export performance. We develop this point in the appendix (see note 20), by analysing the investment environment for exports within a version of the classic traded goods/non-traded goods model. Along with the real exchange rate, the model emphasizes a wide range of determinants of costs and productivity, including tariff rates on imported equipment, explicit taxes and bureaucratic predations on the export sector, and the cost and quality of public infrastructure capital and public services.

KIPPRA (2009) adopts a holistic perspective that is fully consistent with our analysis. Of the four key competitiveness priorities stressed in the KIPPRA report – education and training, the business environment, technology and innovation, and infrastructure development – monetary policy enters only in the second, and there not through the value of the shilling but through the favourable impact of macroeconomic stability on the business environment. We return below to whether targeting a weak shilling will enhance macroeconomic stability; the answer is much less clear than in the case of avoiding acute overvaluation. But a targeting policy should always be viewed (if at all) as a complement to action in these microeconomic and institutional arenas, not as a substitute. Inappropriate sequencing – real depreciation before the establishment of key preconditions for an investment response – could expose the economy to a spiral of weak supply responses and macroeconomic instability.

POLICY ASSIGNMENT

We turn now to the policy objective of achieving an undervalued shilling over periods longer than the short term (e.g. a year or more). The central point is that the real exchange rate is an endogenous variable. The full range of macroeconomic shocks and policies affects its value over time. Fiscal policy is among the most important determinants of the equilibrium real exchange rate at all horizons, operating primarily on the demand side in the short to medium run, via the size and non-traded/traded composition of government spending (Edwards, 1989).[24] Monetary policy, in contrast, is generally viewed as incapable of affecting the level of any real variable in the long run. This suggests that cases of successful real exchange rate targeting are highly likely to have involved fiscal actions that eventually bore the brunt of sustaining target values for the real exchange rate.

A return to Figure 8.7 underlines this point. The most dramatic difference between Kenya and the third-party group is in the levels of saving and investment. Moreover, this difference operates not just on average – year in and year out – but also over the period since 2002, when Kenya's real exchange rate diverges from that of the third-party group. Kenya's investment boom over this subperiod was financed externally, whereas a similar investment boom among third-party competitors was financed internally. To the degree that *Vision 2030* anticipates a continued strong contribution from foreign financing, it does not look like a 'weak exchange rate' strategy, at least in the early stages. Avoiding an equilibrium real appreciation that undermines export competitiveness will require a policy environment that is conducive to a high rate of saving out of income growth.

A final point on policy assignment relates to the distinction we made in the previous section between regulatory policies and the use of traditional stabilization instruments. Above, we emphasized the concept of *ex ante* vulnerability to reversals of capital flows and provided some corroboration of indicators proposed in the literature. Regulatory actions that reduce vulnerability can reduce the macroeconomic risks associated with episodes of real exchange appreciation or depreciation. This responsibility should not be overlooked in the midst of debate over policies that operate directly on the real exchange rate.

RECONCILING REAL EXCHANGE RATE TARGETS WITH INFLATION TARGETS

Finally, what are the macroeconomic consequences of using conventional monetary policy instruments to maintain a weaker real exchange rate than would otherwise be the case? Both theory and experience suggest that, when the capital account is relatively open, using monetary policy in this mode requires the central bank to accept a higher rate of inflation than would otherwise prevail, at least at the outset (Calvo *et al.*, 1995). A weak shilling policy could therefore come into sharp tension with the CBK's existing framework, with its long-standing inflation target of 5 per cent.

The logic of this view is straightforward, and relies on demand-side effects of the type featured in the Dutch disease literature. Achieving a persistent effect on the real exchange rate requires altering the equilibrium real exchange rate, which in turn means altering the demand-and-supply balance in the market for non-traded goods. A fortuitous move in the fundamentals – a shock to foreign financing, for example, or to commodity export prices

– can of course generate the required effect. During the 1990s, for example, conflicts with external donors led to sharp reductions in official development assistance (ODA) in Kenya; other things being equal, these reductions drove down overall spending; part of this fell on non-traded goods, generating a real depreciation.

If monetary policy alone is going to achieve a similar effect, however, monetary instruments must be capable of reducing national spending on non-traded goods. How this is done depends on the degree of capital mobility. When capital mobility is low, a period of tight money and high real interest rates does the job, provided that the fiscal impacts of the higher public debt service can be handled through higher taxes. But when capital mobility is high, monetary policy has little traction over the real interest rate. In this case, the mechanism emphasized by Calvo *et al.* (1995) is a temporary increase in the rate of crawl of the nominal exchange rate, for the duration of the undervaluation episode. This produces a temporary increase in the nominal interest rate and therefore – as cash is needed for purchasing consumer goods – in the effective price of consumption. Consumption falls, and with it the demand for non-traded goods and the real exchange rate.[25]

The likelihood of an increase in inflation suggests that actively targeting an undervalued shilling would require a substantial adaptation in Kenya's monetary framework, which is currently constructed around an inflation target of 5 per cent or below. Widening the inflation band would re-pose the nominal anchor issues discussed in Chapter 7, and the cost of this might reasonably be viewed as too great. Like any consensus about a complex issue of institutional design, however, the consensus that continues to support inflation targeting among emerging market economies reflects the environment that produced it, most notably the Great Inflation among the industrial countries and the rise in global capital mobility. Two broadly competing visions exist – one largely discredited by experience, and the other likely, in our view, to remain a focus of debate. The discredited vision is that central banks can reconcile price stability with competing objectives – including providing ample finance to government – through the use of direct controls in credit and foreign exchange markets. Even Malaysia, widely cited for its use of capital controls in the wake of the Asian financial crisis of 1997, retains a strong preference for fiscal stability, prudential regulations over direct controls, and the maintenance of convertibility for current account purposes (Edwards, 2007). The second competing vision is over how tightly countries should commit to themselves to very low inflation. Even before the global financial crisis of 2008, this issue was more clearly resolved for industrial countries than it was for developing countries. The global evidence suggests that high inflation – 40 per cent was the benchmark used by Bruno and Easterly (1998) – is clearly damaging to long-run growth, and that for industrial countries, the optimal range for inflation, in terms of long-run growth, is quite low (positive but below 5 per cent). But for low-income countries, the growth benefits of moving from an inflation rate of 10–15 per cent to one of 5 per cent or below (for example) appear to be small, and may even be slightly negative. This debate is likely to be renewed with vigour if one or more industrial countries choose an inflationary exit from burdensome domestic currency debts.

In practice, of course, there may be propitious episodes during which developments in the macroeconomic fundamentals allow the CBK to lean heavily against the shilling while satisfying inflation targets. A resolution of political uncertainties in Kenya, for example, would not only reduce the cost of external finance for Kenya and enhance the prospects of achieving *Vision 2030*, but also potentially generate a sustained increase in the demand for shilling-denominated assets, including bank deposits. In such a situation, a policy of reserve accumulation may be well justified within an inflation targeting framework, even at the risk of violating preset money growth targets, as an alternative to an overshooting appreciation that harms exports and growth (Buffie *et al.*, 2004). The role of the real exchange rate in export competitiveness suggests that the CBK should be alert to such opportunities.

8.4 Conclusions

Kenya embraced an open capital account in the hope of widening portfolio opportunities for domestic residents, attracting foreign finance, and spurring financial development. The trilemma was broadly acknowledged from the outset, in the realization that, if monetary policy was to have any scope for domestic objectives, an open capital account was inconsistent with the maintenance of a heavily managed exchange rate. As outlined in Chapter 7, the framework introduced in the mid-1990s has reproduced itself successfully over time: an inflation target pursued via money base targeting, a market-determined exchange rate, and an intervention policy geared towards containing short-run market volatility rather than guiding the path of the real exchange rate.

Vision 2030 anticipates a substantial increase in private external capital flows, and we have focused in this chapter on two related challenges for monetary policy. The first of these, managing macroeconomic volatility, is central to the CBK's stated mission and to the macroeconomic stability pillar of *Vision 2030*. The second, supporting export competitiveness, is suggested by the role of exports in high-growth countries and the prominence of national competitiveness in *Vision 2030*. These broad concerns will be inherited by a regional central bank should currency union proceed on a fast track, and for this reason, we have not dealt separately with issues of monetary integration.

Our overriding message is that there are limitations to what monetary policy can accomplish without compromising its central roles of maintaining a nominal anchor and supporting a competitive and robust financial system. This is clearest with respect to real exchange rate targets, where Rodrik (2008) and others have argued that an undervalued exchange rate provides a market-based substitute for industrial policy in promoting non-traditional exports and productivity-enhancing FDI. If, however, other determinants of the investment environment are the binding constraints on these activities, as we believe they are, then the macroeconomic costs of subordinating exchange rate targets to inflation targets are likely to be high. We have also argued that the truly indispensable interventions to support a competitive real exchange rate are those that increase national saving, which is fundamentally a task of fiscal rather than monetary policy.

With respect to macroeconomic stability, we have focused on the degree of capital mobility and its implications for monetary policy. The evidence suggests that capital moves less readily into Kenya than might be expected given its largely open capital account. This is particularly worrisome with respect to FDI, where direct restrictions are absent and the potential advantages in terms of an employment- and export-promoting growth profile are large. Although most of the determinants of FDI are outside the CBK's control, restrictions on non-residents may serve to discourage long-term commitments even in the absence of direct controls on FDI itself. Restrictions on short-term borrowing by banks, in turn, are more readily justified on macroeconomic grounds given the economic costs of a sudden reversal.

Although the evidence we have presented places Kenya well short of the trilemma, we find that capital flows respond to interest rate differentials, exchange rate expectations, and uncertainties about the domestic political process. These effects may well be non-linear, allowing the CBK to achieve considerable short-term smoothing of the exchange rate during normal times but proving illusory in the presence of large shocks. A strategy for keeping these interventions selective and temporary has the advantages of avoiding confusion regarding the CBK's nominal anchor, allowing necessary real exchange rate adjustments to take place, and providing ongoing incentives for the development of private markets for exchange risk. Within such a strategy, however, the CBK should be alert to opportunities to resist large and transitory real appreciations when this can be done without compromising the inflation anchor. The first such opportunity may come as global markets emerge from the financial crisis, if a resolution of political uncertainties in Kenya produces a large portfolio adjustment in favour of the shilling.

Notes

1 We are grateful to Christopher Adam for extensive guidance and suggestions, and to Aart Kraay for providing us with data from Kraay and Nehru (2006). Any errors are our own responsibility.

2 Article VIII status embodies a commitment not to impose exchange controls on current account transactions.

3 Like most measures of *de jure* openness, the IMF indicators reflect only the presence or absence of controls, rather than their intensity. Chinn and Ito (2008) try to capture intensity indirectly, by including controls on the current account (often a conduit for unrecorded capital movements) and adjusting for the duration of capital account restrictions.

4 The other seven are Botswana, Djibouti, Gambia, Liberia, Mauritius, Uganda, and Zambia.

5 These data should be treated with care. Capital flows are notoriously difficult to measure, particularly where they are illegal. Accounting conventions can also differ substantially across countries.

6 Table D12.8, p. 222 reports the ICRG index of government stability for 2006. At 5.9, Kenya's value was the lowest in the table, 2.4 standard deviations below the average of 9.4 for the other sixteen emerging market comparators.

7 This is sometimes referred to as the 'Guidotti–Greenspan rule'.

8 If domestic interest rates are market determined, however, it is unlikely that capital controls alone can explain a persistently negative risk premium. The reason is that domestic investors have the alternative of investing in other domestic assets. Low market-determined rates on government securities may reflect, at least in part, regulations that compel banks and other financial firms to hold these securities.

9 A more sophisticated approach would incorporate the transmission channel from the repo rate to the T-bill rate. The evidence regarding policy transmission from policy to market rates is mixed. Cheng (2006) finds that the interest rate channel is weak, and attributes this to structural limitations in Kenya's financial sector. Maturu (2007) finds greater evidence of effective transmission from the repo rate to money market rates including the T-bill rate.

10 Countries may of course have felt compelled to do the opposite – to cut interest rates in order to act as lender of last resort to the banking sector. In either case, the interest rate response belongs in the dependent variable.

11 In Equation (8.6), reserves and the exchange rate are both measured in US dollars and at the end of the month. The discount rate is a monthly average.

12 By these criteria, Kenya experienced eighteen years of debt distress between 1975 and 2002, the most recent associated with a combination of arrears and Paris Club debt relief in 2000–02 (Kraay and Nehru, 2006).

13 Rose and Spiegel (2009) report a similarly mixed result for the significance of size and income. In their sample, which includes the industrial countries, there is some evidence that the smaller countries were harder hit.

14 From this perspective, the impressive rate of FDI into Tanzania and Uganda by Kenyan firms raises questions about the overall investment environment in Kenya, as these firms could serve the regional market from Kenya.

15 The real exchange rate is sometimes defined as the price of domestic goods relative to foreign goods, measured in a common currency. These parallel concepts are known as the 'internal' and 'external' real exchange rate (see Hinkle and Montiel, 1999).

16 They mean the most popular *formal* real target, for example via announced or unannounced purchasing power parity (PPP) rules that adjust the rate of crawl *vis-à-vis* a currency or basket to the difference between domestic and foreign inflation.

17 The Reinhart and Rogoff classification is based solely on observed exchange rate movements, and therefore does not distinguish sharply between regimes that implement PPP rules or other formal approaches to real exchange rate targeting (the topic of Section 8.3.3), and regimes that limit short-run exchange rate volatility while allowing considerable medium- to long-term movement in the real exchange rate. Kenya maintains a formal target of four months of imports, and the CBK is therefore in the foreign exchange markets intermittently for reserve management purposes. This may provide cover for modest interventions that smooth out extremes, without implying any sustained commitment to a particular path for the real exchange rate.

18 Eichengreen (2008) surveys the empirical literature on real exchange rate volatility and growth and finds mixed results; some studies find a negative relationship between the two variables, and others conclude that exchange rate variability has no impact. Causality is often unclear, he argues, because macroeconomic crises tend to be associated with large real exchange rate changes.

19 Eichengreen (2008) notes the rapid development of these markets following the Asian financial crisis and the transition to greater exchange rate flexibility in affected countries.

20 The appendix can be downloaded from http://www.swarthmore.edu/SocSci/soconne1/research.html.

21 In the appendix (see note 20), we develop a second comparison versus the third-party group based on a measure of absolute price competitiveness developed by Johnson *et al.* (2007). This measure has the advantage of being directly comparable across countries. It evolves similarly over time to REER3p, and indicates that Kenyan prices were overvalued by roughly 20 per cent *vis-à-vis* the third-party group in 2007.

22 Consistent with this, Maturu (2002) finds that the degree of exchange rate misalignment during the mid- to late 1990s, following financial sector liberalization and adoption of the market-determined exchange rate, was not substantially different from patterns observed in the pre-liberalization period of the 1980s.

23 Recent studies of real exchange rate misalignment in Kenya have generated mixed results. Mwega (2007) reports an overvaluation of 40.8 per cent in 2005, with updated results suggesting a continued large overvaluation in 2006 and 2007. But Pollin and Heintz (2007) find milder degrees of misalignments in the mid-2000s, and the IMF (2008) shows an undervaluation in 2006–07. Where these authors agree is on the importance of non-monetary determinants of export performance.

24 The medium- to long-term impact of fiscal policy on the real exchange rate operates primarily via the supply side and is much less well understood. Adam and Bevan (2006) emphasize the importance of how public infrastructure investment affects sectoral productivities.

25 Lizondo (1991) and Montiel and Ostry (1991) develop models in which the monetary authority can engineer a *permanent* real depreciation by increasing the inflation rate. In these models, however, it is ultimately a fiscal rather than a monetary effect that generates the real depreciation. The increase in inflation generates a transfer of seigniorage revenues to the government, which is assumed to spend less intensively on non-traded goods than the private sector does.

References

Adam, C. and D. Bevan, 2006, 'Aid and the Supply Side: Public Investment, Export Performance, and Dutch Disease in Low-Income Countries', *World Bank Economic Review*, 20 (2), 261–290.

Aghion, P., P. Bacchetta, R. Ranciere and K. Rogoff, 2006, 'Exchange Rate Volatility and Productivity Growth: The Role of Financial Development'. NBER Working Paper No. 12117, March.

Aizenman, J., B. Pinto and A. Radziwill, 2007, 'Sources for Financing Domestic Capital – Is Foreign Saving a Viable Option for Developing Countries?' *Journal of International Money and Finance*, 26, 682–702.

Ariyoshi, A., K. Habermeier, B. Laurens, I. Otker-Robe, J. I. Canales Kriljenko, and A. Kirilenko, 2000, 'Capital Controls: Country Experience with their Use and Liberalization'. IMF Occasional Paper No. 190.

Bruno, M. and W. Easterly, 1998, 'Inflation Crises and Long-Run Growth', *Journal of Monetary Economics*, 41 (1), 3–26.

Buffie, E., C. Adam, S. O'Connell, and C. Pattillo, 2004, 'Exchange Rate Policy and the Management of Official and Private Capital Flows in Africa'. *IMF Staff Papers*, 51 (Special Issue), 126–160.

Calvo, G. A. and C. M. Reinhart, 2002, 'Fear of Floating', *Quarterly Journal of Economics*, 47, 379–408.

Calvo, G., C. Reinhard and C. Vegh, 1995, 'Targeting the Real Exchange Rate: Theory and Evidence', *Journal of Development Economics*, 47, 97–133.

Cheng, K., 2006, 'A VAR Analysis of Kenya's Monetary Policy Transmission Mechanism: How Does the Central Bank's REPO Rate Affect the Economy?'. IMF Working Paper WP/06/300, December.

Chinn, M. and H. Ito, 2008, 'A New Measure of Financial Openness', *Journal of Comparative Policy Analysis*, 10 (3), 309–322.

Dooley, M. P., D. Folkerts-Landau and P. Garber, 2007, 'Direct Investment, Rising Real Wages, and the Absorption of Excess Labor in the Periphery', in R. H. Clarida (ed.) *G7 Current Account Imbalances: Sustainability and Adjustment.* Chicago: University of Chicago Press: 103–126.

Edwards, S., 1989, *Real Exchange Rates, Devaluation, and Adjustment.* Cambridge, MA: MIT Press.

Edwards, S. ed., 2007, *Capital Controls and Capital Flows in Emerging Economies: Policies, Practices, and Consequences.* Chicago: University of Chicago Press.

Eichengreen, B., 2008, 'The Real Exchange Rate and Economic Growth'. World Bank, Commission on Growth and Development, Working Paper No. 4.

Eichengreen, B., A. K. Rose and C. Wyplosz, 1994, 'Speculative Attacks on Pegged Exchange Rates: An Empirical Exploration with Special Reference to the European Monetary System', in Canzoneri, M., P. Masson and V. Grilli (eds) *The New Transatlantic Economy.* Cambridge: Cambridge University Press.

Flood, R. P. and A. K. Rose, 2002, 'Uncovered Interest Parity in Crisis'. *IMF Staff Papers*, 49 (2), 252–266.

Ghei, N. and L. Pritchett, 1999, 'The Three Pessimisms', in Hinkle, L. E. and P. J. Montiel (eds) *Exchange Rate Misalignment: Concepts and Measurement for Developing Countries.* Oxford: Oxford University Press.

Hausmann, R. and D. Rodrik, 2003, 'Economic Development as Self-Discovery', *Journal of Development Economics*, 72, 603–633.

Hinkle, L. E. and P. J. Montiel, 1999, *Exchange Rate Misalignment: Concepts and Measurement for Developing Countries*. Oxford: Oxford University Press.

IMF, Monetary and Capital Markets Department, 2007, *Review of Exchange Arrangements, Restrictions, and Controls*. Washington, DC: International Monetary Fund.

IMF, 2008, 'Kenya: Ex Post Assessment of Longer-Term Program Engagement'. 4 August. http://www.imf.org/external/pubs/cat/longres.cfm?sk=22423.0.

IMF, 2009, 'Kenya: Selected Issues and Statistical Appendix'. IMF Country Report No. 09/192, June.

Johnson, S. H., J. Ostry and A. Subramanian, 2007, 'The Prospects for Sustained Growth in Africa: Benchmarking the Constraints'. IMF Working Paper 07/52, March.

Kenya Institute for Public Policy Research and Analysis (KIPPRA), 2009, *Kenya Economic Report 2009: Building a Globally Competitive Economy*. Nairobi: KIPPRA.

Kraay, A. and V. Nehru, 2006, 'When is External Debt Sustainable?' *World Bank Economic Review*, 20 (3), 341–365.

Lizondo, J. S., 1991, 'Real Exchange Rate Targets, Nominal Exchange Rate Policies, and Inflation', *Révista de Análisis Económico*, 6, 5–22.

Maturu, B. O., 2002, 'Modeling the Real Exchange Rate for Kenya, 1980–1998'. Unpublished PhD thesis, Jomo Kenyatta University of Agriculture and Technology, Institute for Human Resource Development.

Maturu, B. O., 2007, 'Channels of Monetary Policy Transmission in Kenya'. Paper presented during the 12th Annual African Econometric Society Conference in Cape Town, South Africa; http://www.africametrics.org/conference-papers.html (Day 2, Session 6, Track 1).

Montiel, P. J. and J. Ostry, 1991, 'Macroeconomic Implications of Real Exchange Rate Targeting in Developing Countries'. *IMF Staff Papers* 39, 58–78.

Mwega, F. M., 2007, 'The Exchange Rate, External Balance and Economic Growth in Kenya'. Prepared for the School of Economics Workshop on Policy Options in Achieving the Kenya Vision 2030, 30 May.

Mwega, F. M. and N. S. Ndung'u, 2001, 'Kenya's Recent Exchange-Rate Policy and Manufactured Export Performance', in Fosu, A. K., S. M. Nsouli and A. Varoudakis (eds) *Policies to Promote Competitiveness in Manufacturing in Sub-Saharan Africa*. Development Centre Seminars with the IMF and the AERC OECD. Paris: OECD, 33–56.

Mwega, F. M. and N. S. Ndung'u, 2008, 'Explaining African Economic Growth Performance: The Case of Kenya', in Ndulu, B. J., S. A. O'Connell, J.-P. Azam, R. H. Bates, A. K. Fosu, J. W. Gunning and D. Njinkeu (eds) *The Political Economy of Economic Growth in Africa, 1960–2000. Volume 2: Country Case Studies*. Cambridge: Cambridge University Press, 325–368.

Ndung'u, N. S., 2000, 'The Exchange Rate and Monetary Policy in Kenya', *African Development Review*, 12 (1), 24–51.

Ndung'u, N. S. and W. R. Ngugi, 1999, 'Adjustment and Liberalization in Kenya: The Financial and Foreign Exchange Market', *Journal of International Development*, 11 (3), 465–491.

Obstfeld, M. 2008, 'International Finance and Growth in Developing Countries: What Have We Learned? ' Commission on Growth and Development, Working Paper No. 34. Washington, DC: The World Bank.

Pollin, R. and J. Heintz, 2007, 'Expanding Decent Employment in Kenya: The Role of Monetary Policy, Inflation Control, and the Exchange Rate'. International Poverty Centre Country Study No. 6, March.

Razin, O. and S. M. Collins, 1999, 'Real Exchange Rate Misalignments and Growth', in Razin, A. and E. Sadka (eds) *The Economics of Globalization: Policy Perspectives from Public Economics*. Cambridge: Cambridge University Press, 59–81.

Reinhart, C. M. and K. S. Rogoff, 2004, 'The Modern History of Exchange Rate Arrangements: A Reinterpretation', *Quarterly Journal of Economics*, 119 (1), 1–48.

Republic of Kenya (ROK), 2009, *Annual Public Debt Management Report, July 2007–June 2008*, Office of the Deputy Prime Minister and Ministry of Finance (Debt Management Department); http://www.treasury.go.ke.

Rodrik, D., 2008, *The Real Exchange Rate and Economic Growth*. Cambridge, MA: John F. Kennedy School of Government, Harvard University.

Rose, A. K. and M. M. Spiegel, 2009, 'Cross-Country Causes and Consequences of the 2008 Crisis: Early Warning'. Unpublished draft, Haas School of Business and FRB San Francisco, 22 September.

Were, M., N. S. Ndung'u, A. Geda and S. N. Karingi, 2002, 'Analysis of Kenya's Export Performance: An Empirical Evaluation'. KIPPRA Discussion Paper No. 22. Nairobi: Kenya Institute for Public Policy Research and Analysis.

III

The Environment for Private Market Activity

9

Policy Options for Agriculture Growth in Kenya

Joseph Karugia, Lydia Ndirangu, Hezron Nyangito, and Tavneet Suri

9.1 Introduction and background

The agricultural sector in Kenya is large in terms of the population involved, yet it contributes less than its proportionate share to gross domestic product (GDP), a feature that is common among many developing economies. The World Development Report (henceforth WDR; World Bank, 2007) categorizes developing countries into three distinct types according to the share of overall growth that comes from agriculture and the share of total poverty in rural areas.

The first of these types the WDR calls agriculture-based economies, where agriculture is a major source of growth (it accounts for an average of 32 per cent of growth across these countries, mostly because agriculture contributes a large share of GDP) and where most of the poor are in rural areas (70 per cent on average). Such economies have about 417 million rural inhabitants and account for 82 per cent of rural sub-Saharan Africa. The second type is transforming economies, where poverty is mostly rural but agriculture contributes only an average of 7 per cent to growth; examples include China and India, and such economies encompass 2.2 billion rural inhabitants. The third type are urbanized countries, where poverty is mostly urban and agriculture contributes only 5 per cent to growth on average (these economies have 255 million rural inhabitants, and examples include Latin America, Europe, and Central Asia).[1]

The role of the agricultural sector in the development process (in terms of both growth as well as poverty reduction) will vary across these types. Kenya lies in the first of these categories with agricultural value added at 23 per cent of GDP, manufacturing value added at 12 per cent of GDP, and services value added at 58 per cent of GDP in 2008. At this time, 79 per cent of Kenya's population was rural. This large agricultural sector has persisted for decades in Kenya – 93 per cent of Kenya's population was rural, agricultural value added contributed 38 per cent of GDP, and manufacturing value added only 9 per cent to GDP in 1960. Figure 9.1 shows the trend in the total and the rural population for the Kenyan economy since 1960, and Figure 9.2 shows the trends in agricultural, manufacturing, and services value added (all as a fraction of GDP) over the past 45 years.

Agriculture is currently high on the policy agenda (World Bank, 2008). In an economy such as Kenya, where agriculture is dominated by low-income smallholder farmers, it is an open question as to how much potential such a sector will play in the growth of the economy, especially when compared with economies where historically the role of agriculture has been crucial (such as Japan). This debate has moved further to the front of the policy agenda recently given the fluctuations in food prices that have been witnessed in the recent past. However, there is little argument that, for Kenyan small-scale farmers to survive the world market, they need accelerated technological change and ways of expanding the markets for high-value commodities to mitigate the increasingly binding land constraint.

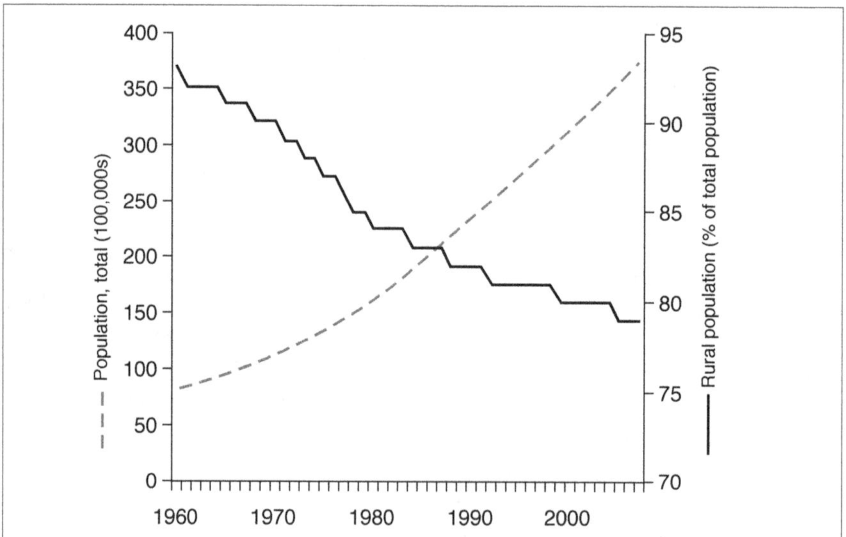

Figure 9.1 Total population and rural population (% total population), 1960–2007.
Source: World Development Indicators (online database).

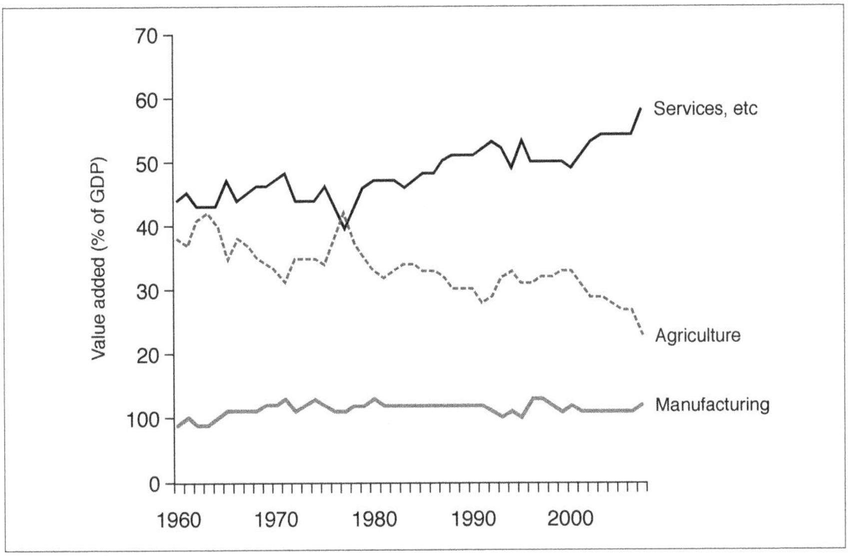

Figure 9.2 Sectoral value added (% GDP), 1960–2007.
Source: World Development Indicators (online database).

Often, a distinction is drawn between the main food staples and non-food crops (such as coffee, tea, and flowers). In terms of a strategy for achieving food security, the focus is often on self-sufficiency in domestic production of staple crops. On the other hand, most non-food crops are produced for export or for the manufacturing sector for the goals of foreign exchange earnings or employment creation. From a national perspective, the goals pursued in agricultural production can be competing for resource use if emphasis is put on the production of food crops compared with export crops or vice versa. The challenge for policy at the national level then becomes developing a policy framework that enhances agricultural production to increase household incomes while at the same time providing readily accessible sources of food and other consumer goods. The Kenyan government appreciates this challenge and focuses on the intensification and commercialization of the agricultural sector in many of its development strategies, e.g. Kenya *Vision 2030* (GOK, 2008). This approach is consistent with a strategy that ensures food security through increased availability, and access to food through increased incomes rather than a narrow focus on self-sufficiency.

The aim of this chapter is to bring together some analysis and the literature on the role of agriculture in poverty reduction as well as its role in the overall growth process of the Kenyan economy. The WDR (2008) highlights how, for the poorest people, GDP growth in the agricultural sector is about four times more effective in poverty reduction than GDP growth from other sectors. We would therefore like to address two broad themes when discussing the agricultural sector in Kenya. First, what are the prospects for growth of the agricultural sector itself and how will this raise the standards of living for the households involved in this sector? The Kenya Poverty and Inequality Assessment (henceforth KPIA, 2009) reports high poverty rates in rural areas (where four out of five Kenyans live) on the order of 50 per cent, compared with 34 per cent in urban areas. Rural poverty rates have declined over the past decade (KPIA, 2009), but are still extremely high. So, understanding how agriculture can be harnessed to improve livelihoods in this sector is of first-order importance.

Second, we need to better understand the role of the agricultural sector in the growth prospects of the Kenyan economy as a whole. With the exceptions of Singapore and Hong Kong (which did not have an agriculture sector to begin with), few countries have been able to sustain a rapid transition out of poverty without raising productivity in their agricultural sector. We therefore need to think about Kenya's transition process during which the relative importance of agriculture to the overall economy declines as industry and services grow rapidly. However, this is not possible unless agriculture itself grows rapidly to provide investment and effective demand for rural non-farm goods and services.

In this chapter, we address these questions by analysing in detail both what has happened in Kenya over the last decade and what may help the economy going forward. During the course of the chapter, we will draw on the large recent literature on the agricultural sector in Kenya (much based on the Tegemeo rural panel survey of about 1,300 households across most of rural Kenya between 1997 and 2007), as well as analysis from the KPIA (2009), which also draws on the Tegemeo data and the Kenya Integrated Household Budget Survey (KIHBS), 2005/06. We also draw evidence from the internationally referenced Food and Agriculture Organization (FAO stat) and World Development Indicators (2008) databases.

This chapter is organized as follows. The next section outlines ways of thinking about the transition of an agricultural sector along an economy's growth path and the role of policy in such environments. In Section 9.3, we discuss trends in the performance of the Kenyan agricultural sector, focusing on the last decade. We discuss the main changes that have taken place, the successes, and the failures in this sector. In Section 9.4, we discuss the evidence on where Kenya is in its transition path. Finally, we discuss the policy agenda for Kenya going forward.

9.2 Frameworks of analysis and the role of policy

As mentioned, there are two main questions to be addressed. First, given the large part of Kenya's population in agriculture, what role is there for policy in improving the sector's general performance so as to improve livelihoods in the sector. Second, and of course related, is what role this sector can play in the growth and transition of the economy more generally.

To understand some of these questions, we will be drawing on the frameworks of agricultural transition, as described by Lewis (1954), Fei and Ranis (1964, 1997), and more recently Timmer (1988, 1997a) and Mellor (2000). One component of these frameworks is an increase in agricultural productivity that is a key ingredient and driver of the welfare improvements in the sector as well as transitions to a more developed economy as a whole. Agriculture often plays a key role in the transition process, and it accounts for a smaller fraction of aggregate output as growth proceeds. The agricultural sector is a source of labour, capital, and foreign exchange for the growing industrial and service sectors, as well as a source of food, fibre, and oils. It also provides a market for consumer goods and services produced in the non-agricultural sector.

Timmer (1988) identifies four phases to a transition. The first phase is a rise in agricultural productivity, which will generate surpluses that can be used in the non-agricultural sector in the second phase (similar to Lewis, 1954 and others).[2] The third stage is the subsequent integration of markets and the development of infrastructure from better rural markets (especially capital and labour markets). The final stage is when agriculture has become a small share of GDP and occupies a small proportion of the population. His research also identifies the broader steps that define a successful agricultural transformation based on these stages.

Timmer (1997a) discusses how the process of agricultural transformation can be understood through the trends in household diversification and specialization in the agricultural sector. Initially, at the start of the transformation, there is more diversification in the sources of income for agricultural households, for example through different types of crops or through different income sources. This is then followed by agricultural specialization as the economy continues its process of transition. Diversification is a benefit to households in the short to medium term as it enables them to diversify risk (for example, there is evidence that more diversification in rural Kenya is associated with less poverty, see Suri *et al.*, 2008). In the long term, however, there are stronger benefits to specialization as the economy transitions into a state where agriculture contributes less to GDP and accounts for much less of the labour force. We will use this idea to analyse where in the transformation process Kenya is by looking at what has happened to diversification over the last decade in Section 9.4.

All this involves, in some form, modernizing the agricultural sector. Agricultural modernization or commercialization[3] has been a subject of debate in the literature. For example, Schultz (1964) argued that farmers, in responding to new events that impinge on their farm enterprises in traditional agricultural settings, do in fact allocate their limited resources efficiently, but traditional agriculture is relatively stable and the few adjustments required tend to be small. Nerlove (1988) referred to Schultz's work as focusing on transforming traditional agriculture in an environment where changes in technology, infrastructure, and markets have not occurred for a long time, where productivity is low, and the ratio of human to non-human capital in the production process is low. On the other hand, Nerlove defines modern agriculture as a state where it is a relatively small sector of the economy, it is characterized by a high degree of competition, it is highly commercialized, and the use of purchased inputs is high with non-purchased inputs valued at opportunity cost. In terms of productivity, marginal productivity to human capital is high, returns to all forms of investment are high, and farmers are responsive to price incentives. Agricultural transformation or commercialization therefore requires a transition from traditional agriculture, which according to Nerlove (1988) is at a state of disequilibrium in growth, to modern agriculture, which is at a state of equilibrium in growth.

Mellor (2000) presents a framework that builds on similar ideas to those of Fei and Ranis (1964), but focuses on the non-farm sector, drawing on his work in India and Egypt (Mellor, 1976, 2000). For poor rural economies such as Kenya, the non-farm sector output is demand constrained. Expanding the sector, and the number of jobs it creates, depends on the local purchasing power (Besley and Cord, 2007). Mellor's model emphasizes the role of the rural non-tradable sector in pulling underemployed workers out of agriculture and into the non-agricultural rural economy. The model explicitly integrates manufactured export performance (the source of dynamism in East Asia's economies since the 1960s) and the rural non-tradable sector (which includes a wide array of local agro-processing) to explain subsequent reductions in poverty.

This explains how countries with substantial agricultural sectors that experienced rapid growth from labour-intensive manufactured exports had such good records of economic growth and poverty reduction. The framework stresses the role of producing locally consumed rural non-tradables that are the 'ladder' for underemployed workers in agriculture to move to modern jobs at higher wages. Thriving farmers in low-income countries spend about 20 per cent of incremental income on labour-intensive livestock and horticulture and 40 per cent on rural non-farm goods (Bell and Hazell 1980; Hazell and Roell 1983; Mellor 1995), whereas rich landowners typically spend incremental income on imports and capital-intensive manufactures (Timmer, 1997b).

As mentioned above, a key consideration in all this is the policy framework, which broadly includes macroeconomic policies that affect incentives in all sectors, agricultural sector policies that affect productivity and commodity, and input prices and policies that could affect agricultural productivity indirectly. Many governments agree on the need to strengthen incentives in the sector to deal with slow agricultural growth relative to population growth, declining food production per capita, leading to rising food imports, and a declining share of world exports for many primary agricultural exports (World Bank, 1981, 1986, 2007). In addition to the prices of agricultural inputs and outputs, real farm profits are influenced by factors such as farm subsidies, taxes, research, extension, road infrastructure, cost and accessibility of consumers and services such as marketing and credit.

The impact of agricultural policies and their role in transforming agriculture through farmers' responses to production are often analysed as responses to price (producer and input prices, taxes, exchange rates, subsidies) and non-price factors (technological innovations, input delivery systems, infrastructure, output markets, access to resources, and research and extension systems). It is generally accepted that farmers respond to price factors and that individual crop supply elasticities can be responsive to changes in relative prices, as farmers switch between crops (Beynon, 1989). This finding often forms the basis for policy reforms based on using exchange rates, taxation, subsidies, and input and output prices to raise producer prices as incentives for increasing production. However, it has also been observed in the literature, particularly for sub-Saharan Africa, that the aggregate supply response to price factors is disappointingly low (Beynon, 1989; Jaeger and Humphreys, 1989; Mosley and Smith, 1989). Other studies (Delgado and Mellor, 1984; Binswanger, 1989) have shown that non-price factors are important in determining farmers' supply response.

As agricultural growth responds to both price and non-price factors, when formulating policies for agricultural development, it is important to look at the broader picture regarding the dynamics of agricultural growth. There is a need for strategies that make smallholder agriculture more competitive and sustainable by improving the asset position of the rural poor and diversifying income sources towards the labour market and the rural non-farm economy; facilitating successful migration out of agriculture; improving price incentives through macro and micro price policies that improve farm profitability; increasing the quality and quantity of public investment in technology development and infrastructure to allow product and input markets to work better; and improving access to financial services to reduce exposure to risks.

These are some of the issues analysed in this chapter to determine whether and how they have played a role in the performance of Kenyan agriculture in the last decade. This will allow us to identify policies that could enhance agricultural growth for the Kenyan economy going forward.

9.3 What has been happening in Kenya?

This section first describes the broad changes in policy and the environment for Kenyan agriculture over the last few decades. It then describes the state of affairs as regards the agricultural sector, mostly discussing the trends in agricultural productivity and identifying successes and failures over the last decade. We discuss these mostly in the framework of effects on the welfare of households in the agricultural sector, and we leave Section 9.4 to discuss the transition process.

9.3.1 Evolution of agricultural policy

Kenya has had major policy changes governing the agricultural sector dating back to the colonial period. Before independence, policies were aimed at supporting agricultural production through the use of subsidized finance, low taxation, administered pricing mechanisms, and public investment in infrastructure as well as agricultural research. Trade was restricted via import licensing regulations. The government had strict control of the economy. This situation continued after independence for two decades, and the policies implemented supported both smallholder and large-scale producers.

The early 1990s marked a big change in Kenya with waves of liberalization across various sectors of the economy. The initial attempts to liberalize actually came in the form of structural adjustment in the 1980s (Nyangito and Karugia, 2002; Karanja *et al.*, 2003), but most of this liberalization happened in the 1990s (Mwega and Ndung'u, 2002) when foreign exchange and interest rates were liberalized, input and commodity prices were deregulated, trade barriers removed, and some state-owned enterprises sold. In addition, maize meal prices were deregulated, subsidies eliminated and, in 1992, all price controls on food and agricultural inputs were removed (Nyangito and Karugia, 2002). The role of the National Cereals and Produce Board (NCPB) also changed over this period as the private sector took over sales of maize and the NCPB was left to manage strategic reserves and be a buyer of last resort (Nyangito and Karugia, 2002; Karanja *et al.*, 2003). There were also reforms in the tea and coffee sectors at this time, with the removal of foreign exchange controls and the floating exchange rate helping export crops. These policy changes greatly affected the agricultural sector, especially given the liberalization of internal trade and prices. Using the nominal rate of assistance (NRA), Winter-Nelson and Argwings-Kodhek (2009) show that, during the pre-liberalization era of the 1990s, the trend was to support exportables and tax importables. In the post-liberalization era, the NRA for most commodities has tended towards zero, indicating a reduction in price distortions. The exception has been sugar, which is still highly protected.

9.3.2 Agricultural productivity growth

Even though the levels of labour productivity in agriculture are relatively low compared with the other productive sectors, there have not been systematic improvements in productivity in Kenyan agriculture, as has happened in other developing countries in Asia and Latin America (the Kenyan trend is similar to that for some other African countries). Figure 9.3 shows the stagnating growth of agricultural production per capita over the last 45 years. Although agricultural production has grown, it has been slower than population growth. When looking at cereals (see Figure 9.4), the trends are markedly worse, with per capita cereal production declining to almost half of what it was in 1960.

Some of the major reasons cited for the poor performance of agriculture have included the fragmentation and unequal distribution of land (due to lack of a comprehensive land use policy), agricultural price instability, overreliance on rain-fed agriculture, limited diversification of production, limited development and exploitation of the livestock sector, inadequate funding for agricultural R&D, and poor and inadequate rural infrastructure. We now discuss these in detail through the lens of discussing successes and challenges for Kenyan agriculture.

9.3.3 Successes in the last decade

In the last decade, there have certainly been significant improvements in agricultural productivity in terms of yield, at least for a subset of crops.[4] For example, Kibaara *et al.* (2008) looked carefully at the changes in agricultural productivity by crop using the Tegemeo panel survey. These data are a representative survey of non-pastoralist farmers in Kenya. They show that there has been a consistent growth in maize productivity between 1997 and 2007 for both pure stand and intercropped maize. Overall, maize productivity rose from about 597 kg/acre in 1997 to 839 kg/acre in 2007. Improvements are apparent across most agro-ecological zones and, in fact, the improvements have

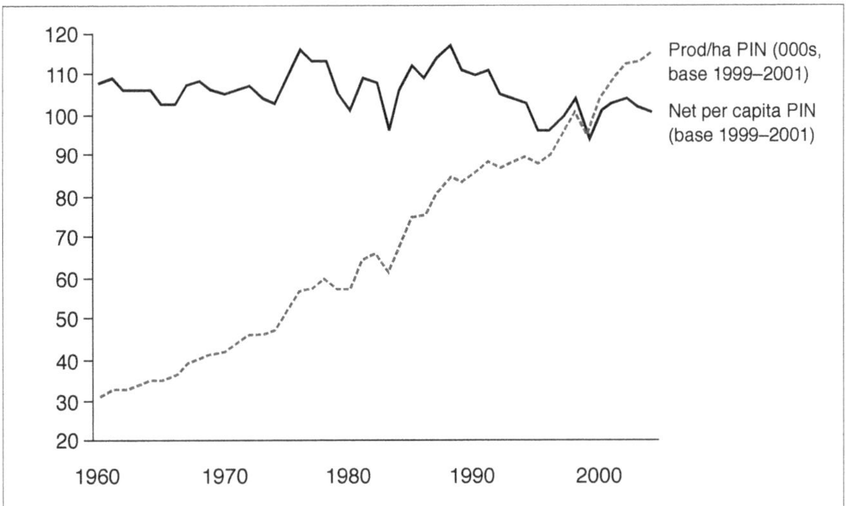

Figure 9.3 Total agricultural and per capita production indices (PIN): 1961–2005.
Source: FAO stat (base year: 1999–2001).

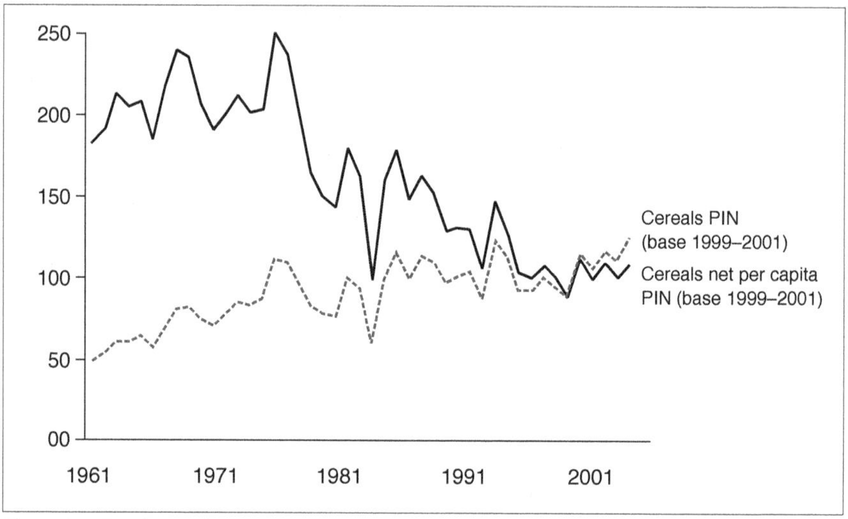

Figure 9.4 Total cereal and per capita cereal production indices (PIN): 1961–2005.
Source: FAO stat (base year: 1999–2001).

been higher in the lower maize productivity areas. Maize contributes about a third of crop income. They also show that for tea there have been marginal improvements in productivity, and declines for coffee and sugar cane.

The reasons Kibaara *et al.* (2008) give for these recent positive trends in maize productivity include increased use of improved seed and fertilizer, better access to fertilizer suppliers, and better access to credit. For example, in the Tegemeo panel, the fraction of households using both fertilizer and high-yielding maize varieties rose from 51 per cent in 1997 to 61 per cent in 2007; the distance to the closest fertilizer stockist for households fell from 8 km in 1997 to 3 km in 2007, and such decreases were seen across all regions of the country; and the fraction of households that received agricultural credit rose 26 per cent to 33 per cent. The improvements in the fertilizer market are critical to policy on fertilizer subsidies in Kenya. Government distribution of subsidized fertilizers may reverse the gains made and successes in fertilizer market development and incentives to the private sector to continue participating in the market.

Ariga *et al.* (2008) looked at the role of fertilizer over this period using the Tegemeo panel data. They show that the fraction of farmers using fertilizer on maize has risen from 55 per cent in 1996 to 70 per cent in 2007 (with a lot of variation across the country). In addition, they found that the rates of application for those who use fertilizer have stayed relatively stable or shown very slight increases over the period at close to 60 kg/acre for maize. In their empirical analyses, they show that education, wealth, and access to fertilizer suppliers drive differences in the use of fertilizer as well as the amount used. As the authors explain, the improved access to fertilizer sellers has been driven by a large increase in entry and investment in the wholesaling of fertilizer – they cite IFDC estimates that there are over 500 wholesalers and 7,000 retailers across the country. This is indeed an impressive success story in the private sector over this period.

The livestock sector has also seen growth, with the dairy sector improving and milk productivity rising. Kibaara *et al.* (2008) document a rise in average milk productivity from 1,164 litres per cow in 1997 to 1,371 in 2007, improvements that are greatest for the wealthiest quintile in the sample. They pinpoint the following reasons for this change: increased investment in dairy production and in producing fodder crops (for example, the fraction of households growing fodder rose from 16 per cent in 1997 to 53 per cent in 2007, and the proportion of cultivated land that was allocated to fodder rose from 3 per cent in 1997 to 12 per cent in 2007), increased adoption of improved breeds, and investment in knowledge and technology, improvements in access to markets and access to credit.

Looking at the diversification of rural household incomes, Suri *et al.* (2008) illustrate the breakdown of household income using the Tegemeo rural panel data over the period 1997 to 2007, which is replicated in Figure 9.5. Crop income contributed more than 40 per cent of total income in 1997, and this declined slightly over the period. At the same time, the role of livestock grew, and the fraction of income from business/informal sources rose over the period. We discuss diversification in more detail in the next section when discussing the transition process.

Suri *et al.* (2008) bring together the implications of these changes. They document how changes in access to credit, fertilizer suppliers, and markets more generally were associated with reductions in rural poverty as well as with transitions out of poverty, findings similar to those of KPIA (2009). In addition, they show how the source of income really matters for poverty over the decade. For example, in their econometric analyses, they find that, among other factors, the main source of cash income being farm *kibarua* (casual work) is strongly correlated with poverty. They find that cultivating more land, using fertilizer, belonging to a producer group, and having access to credit remain important correlates with not being in poverty.[5]

9.3.4 Challenges

LAND FRAGMENTATION AND INEQUALITY OF ACCESS

The World Bank (2008) reports that, when looking at regions within countries, two-thirds of the rural population in sub-Saharan Africa live in less favoured areas, areas they define as being arid and semi-arid, with poor market

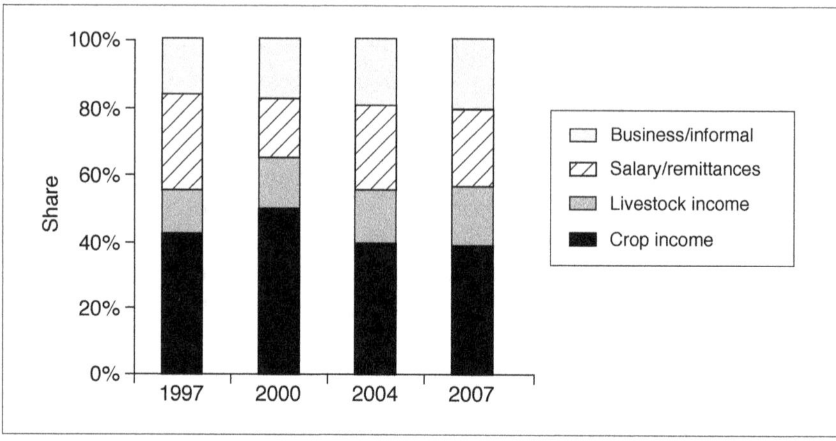

Figure 9.5 Trends in sources of rural income, 1997–2007.
Source: Suri *et al.* (2008) (based on the Tegemeo rural panel data).

access. In the case of Kenya, close to 80 per cent of the population is settled on the 17 per cent of the land area categorized as high and medium potential. The population dependent on agriculture has tripled in the last three decades, whereas cultivated land has only increased by 50 per cent. The consequence has been a steady decline in land per capita, from 0.42 hectares per capita in 1960 to 0.15 hectares per capita in 2005 (FAO, 2008). Microeconomic data sets attest to these macro trends. According to the KIHBS (2005/06), the average per capita holding is about 0.17 hectares, 0.29 hectares for the landed. Kibaara *et al.* (2008) present similar evidence with per capita owned land and per capita cultivated land declining over the last decade. They highlight how more than 30 per cent of smallholder farms in their sample control less than 1 acre of land, and just over half of cropped land is allocated to maize.

This masks substantial inequality in land holdings, even among smallholder farmers. Figure 9.6 presents the Lorenz curve for land distribution among those households with land. About 65 per cent of the population own 20 per cent of the land. The Gini coefficient is estimated at 0.50 among smallholder farmers and 0.59 for the country. KPIA (2009) also documents the change in the land Gini coefficient for Kenya between 1997 (using the WMS data) and 2005/6 (using the KIHBS data). The KPIA points out how a lot of earlier work (such as Deinenger and Squire, 1998) has looked at inequality among landholders, but as Erickson and Vollrath (2004) point out, it is important to consider the landless.[6] The KPIA documents a 36 per cent increase over the period in land inequality for the national population. Among the landowners, inequality levels are of course lower, although still high, with lower increases in inequality over the period for this sample of households.[7]

As a key asset for rural livelihoods, land access determines both income and expenditure. Figure 9.7 shows a kernel regression of land per capita against

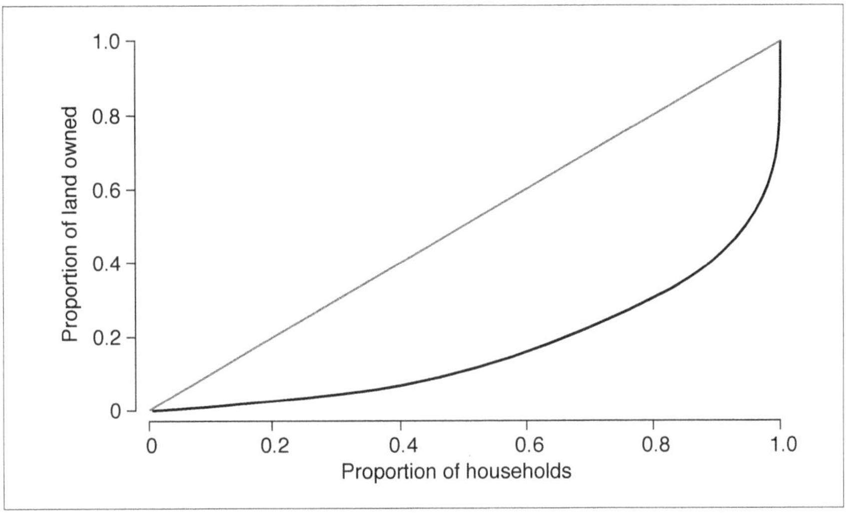

Figure 9.6 Lorenz curve for land distribution in Kenya.
Source: Authors' calculations, KIHBS (2005/06).

welfare as measured by per capita expenditure. Welfare increases at an increasing rate between 1 and 1.5 hectares per capita, beyond which the curve starts to flatten. For example, an increase in landholding from 1 to 1.5 hectares is correlated with a 40 per cent increase in per capita consumption. Noting that the basic poverty line for rural areas (Ksh 1,562) corresponds to the flat region of the graph, the graph seems indicative of a threshold level of land size for poverty reduction at around 1 hectare.

Using income as the measure of welfare, Jayne *et al.* (2003) observed that an increase in land access from zero to 0.25 hectares is associated with a 40 per cent increase in per capita income. The rise in income with land size also seems to be associated with participation in the market. Table 9.1 shows that the proportion of households who marketed their farm produce varies by landholding quartile, in particular from 37 per cent in the lowest landholding quartile to almost 60 per cent in the highest landholding quartile. Table 9.1 also shows that the average income from crop sales in the lowest quartile of landholdings is less than a quarter of that in the highest quartile.

In a similar vein, Figure 9.8 shows the composition of household earnings by quartile of landholdings. The highest proportion (47 per cent) of income for the lowest quartile households is from off-farm work. However, from Figure 9.9 and from the evidence in Suri *et al.* (2008), these are low-wage and low-return enterprises. This category of households could be simply responding to a distress–push type of diversification. This is in stark contrast to the highest quartile households who, although they earn a lower proportion (27 per cent) of their income from off-farm work, are probably engaged in much higher return activities. These are demand–pull activities, which typically require high-

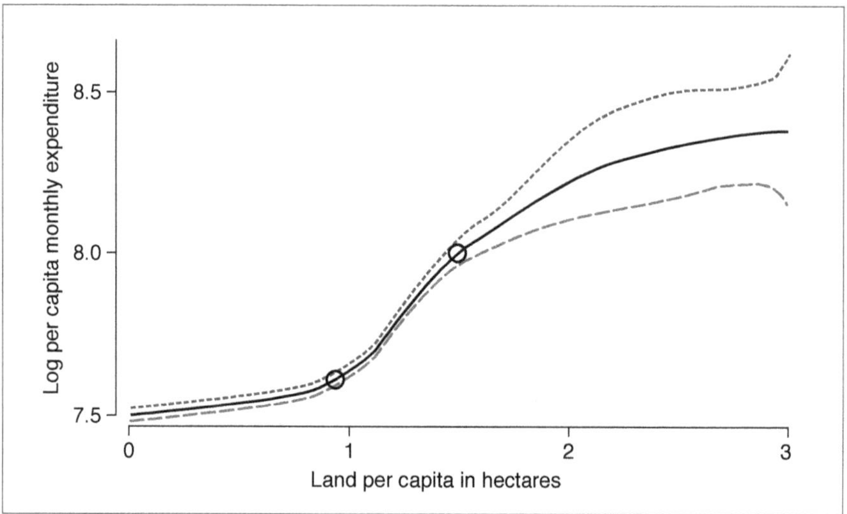

Figure 9.7 Kernel regression of per capita land holding and consumption.
Source: Authors' calculations, KIHBS (2005/06).

er investments and hence activities that only the well-endowed households can afford. The evidence in Suri *et al.* (2008) on the correlation of poverty rates and participation in *kibarua* (casual labour) activities also supports this.

The evidence from Figures 9.8 and 9.9 conforms to the Reardon *et al.* (1998) observation that African farm households are essentially firms that have multi-sectoral activities. The different members of any given household participate in a variety of different economic activities and across a variety of economic sectors. We come back to this aspect below and discuss it further in the context of the policy agenda.

AGRICULTURE GROWTH AND URBANIZATION

Kenya is urbanizing rapidly (Kenya, 2008). Although an estimated 19 per cent of the population lived in urban areas in 1999, urban population was estimated at 26 per cent in 2007 and is projected to reach 60 per cent by 2030 (Kenya, 2008). For example, Figure 9.10 from Kenya *Vision 2030* (GOK, 2008) predicts an impressive growth in the fraction of the labour force that is urban over the next twenty years.

Table 9.1 Fraction of households selling crops and crop sales by land quartile

	Quartile 1	Quartile 2	Quartile 3	Quartile 4
% selling crop produce	0.37	0.50	0.55	0.60
Income from crop sales	6,236	7,713	1,0737	2,7452

Source: Authors' calculations, KIHBS (2005/06).

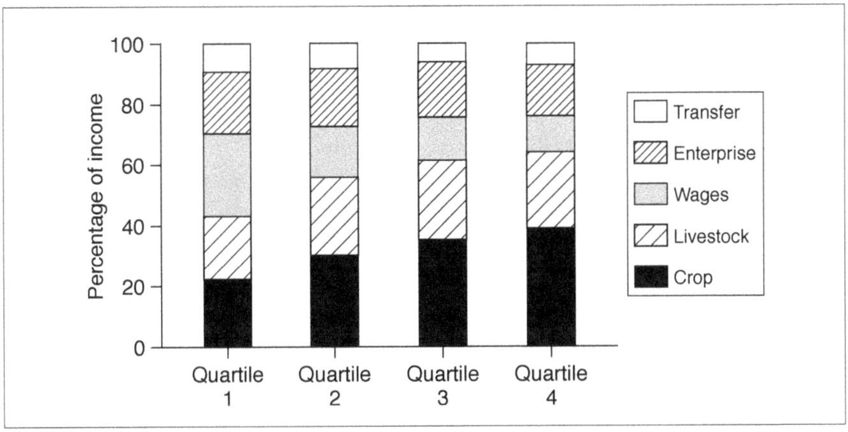

Figure 9.8 Proportion of rural earnings from crop, livestock, off-farm activities.
Source: KIHBS (2005/06).

A growing urban and non-farm population represents a huge demand for food. This is even more so if backed by purchasing power. Purchased food constitutes a large portion of the food budget for most Kenyan households. From analysis of the KIHBS (2005/06) database, the proportion of food purchased by rural and urban households was 57 per cent and 80 per cent respectively.[8]

Assuming these proportions of food shares hold for most years, weighting the proportions by the urban and rural shares of the population allows estimation of the share of food that is purchased. According to these estimates, about 60 per cent of food was marketed in 2007, with rural households purchasing about 72 per cent of all marketed food (see Table 9.2). Assuming that the 2005/06 consumption pattern is sustained, the rural share would be expected

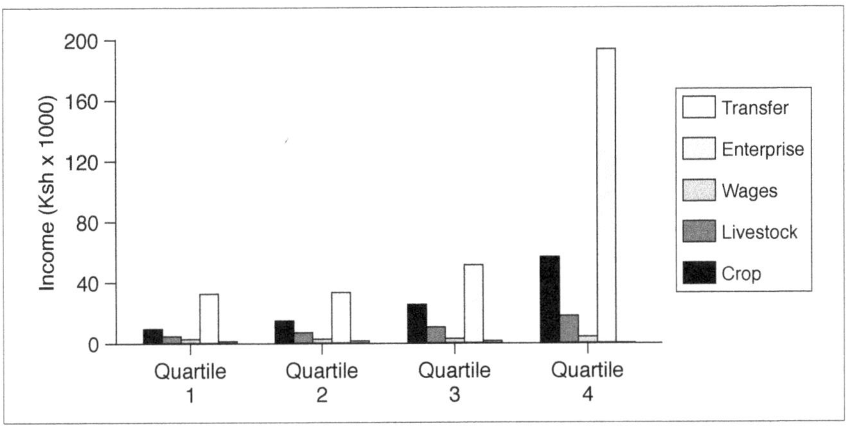

Figure 9.9 Income by activity and land holding quartile.
Source: KIHBS (2005/06).

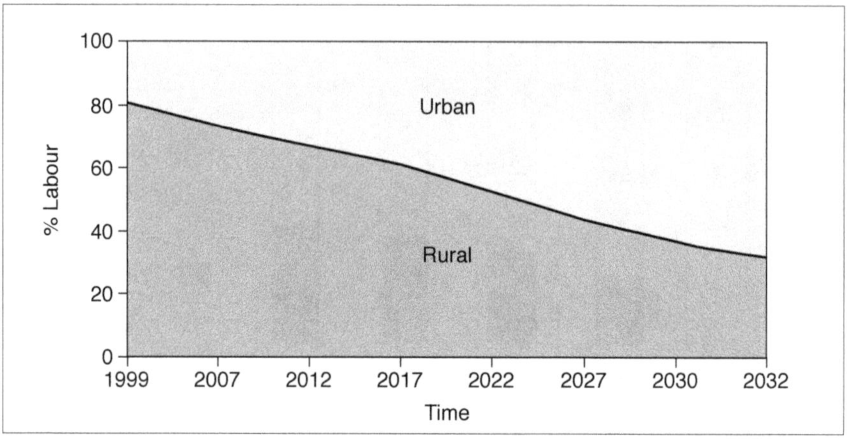

Figure 9.10 Projected growth in the urban labour force.
Source: Kenya *Vision 2030* (Kenya, 2008).

to decline to only 50 per cent by the year 2030 when about 60 per cent of Kenya's population is expected to live in urban areas.

Collier (2008) attributes the high proportion of purchased food among low-income African farmers to the stagnation of agriculture combined with growing populations (see Figures 9.3 and 9.4). Despite the predominance of subsistence agriculture, Collier notes that most African countries have remained net food importers and food accounts for over half of the budget of low-income households. This high share of purchased food implies that rising food prices hurt both agricultural and non-agricultural households.

HIGH AND VARIABLE FOOD PRICES

The recent trends in food prices have renewed the problem of price variability for agricultural commodities. Food is a major component of inflation, contributing on average about 55 per cent of monthly inflation. Kenya has seen an increase in price instability with the advent of market liberalization in the 1990s (Nyangito *et al.*, 2005). Although there is evidence that the market has been good for growth in some sectors (Kibaara *et al.*, 2008), markets may not have been very good at providing stability, and in some cases, equity. Rising food prices may erode the gains of relatively high growth rates. Economic growth and development can be undermined in the face of inflationary pressure and unsustainable food import bills.

Farmers who are net sellers would experience rising incomes, and this could raise their incentives for production and improving productivity. This could have positive consequences, but needs to be balanced by the effects of high and variable food prices on the poor segment of the population, who cannot easily respond to high prices through production (given poor access to

Table 9.2 Estimates of urban and rural shares of marketed food (2005/06)

	% of food consumed that is purchased by household	Weighted by % of total population	Purchased food as % of total food consumption	% of all purchased food
Rural	54[a]	80[b]	43	72
Urban	82[a]	20[b]	17	28
		100	60	100
Projected estimates for year 2030				
Rural	54[a]	60[b]	32	50
Urban	82[a]	40[b]	33	50
		100	65	100

Source: a KIHBS (2005/06); b Authors' calculations.

markets and inputs). This has implications for both the transformation process and inequality. Although price movements are necessary for trading, some stability is important for households to have confidence in the markets and move away from subsistence.

TECHNOLOGY IMPROVEMENTS AND MORE GENERAL INVESTMENT IN AGRICULTURE

Although there is evidence of improved agricultural technology use, there are still challenges here. Land and labour productivity levels in Kenya have stagnated over the past four decades. International comparisons show that productivity is far from the frontier, especially when compared with Asia. As noted above, agricultural productivity improvements are of key importance.

Suri (2010) uses the Tegemeo panel data between 1997 and 2004 to show that there is immense spatial variation in both the costs and the benefits for farmers to using agricultural technologies such as hybrid seed and fertilizer. She illustrates how the technology adoption decisions of farmers are well described by the variations in benefits and costs. She finds that, for a group of farmers who do not use hybrid seed at all over this period, the benefits in using this seed could be immense, higher than the average gain to hybrid for the sample of users. However, she also shows that these famers face significant constraints: larger distances to fertilizer distributors and poorer infrastructure. She concludes that this group of farmers would benefit greatly from infrastructure improvements to improve access to seed and fertilizer and markets in general.[9] On the other hand, farmers who consistently use hybrid seed would benefit from the introduction of new improved varieties.

Figure 9.11, drawn from Suri (2010), shows the average return to hybrid seed for four groups of farmers: non-hybrid users (did not use hybrid seed in both 1997 and 2004), leavers (used hybrid seed in 1997 but not in 2004), joiners (used hybrid seed in 2004 but not in 1997), and hybrid users (used hybrid seed in both 1997 and 2004). There is a wide variance in the returns across these groups, with the joiners and leavers having essentially no gain to using hybrid seed. Her analysis shows that these differences are correlated with the cost measures described above.

In addition to crops, another important biological resource is livestock. From Figures 9.5 and 9.8, households tend to derive at least a fifth of their income from livestock activity. Anecdotal evidence shows that, when population densities are high and markets, technology, and inputs are not readily available, intensity of land use increases, and mixed crop livestock production becomes the most efficient and sustainable mode of food production because of complementarities between crops and livestock raising. The successes in this sector have been mostly in the high-potential cropping areas and among the high-income households, where the private sector has played an important role. The livestock sector has not received consistent policy support.

More generally, there has been a lack of investment (on the part of households, governments, etc.) in agriculture in Kenya over the last two decades. Empirical evidence shows that government spending on agriculture has positive impacts on productivity and poverty reduction (e.g. Fan *et al.* 2000; Fan and Rao, 2003). The rates of return to public investment in agriculture exceed those from health and education (Fan *et al.*, 2009). However, the World Bank (2007) reports that 75 per cent of the world's poor live in rural areas, but only 4 per cent of overseas development assistance goes to agriculture in developing economies. In sub-Saharan Africa, public spending on farming is only 4 per cent of total government spending.

Thurlow and Benin (2008) use the government financial statistics obtained from the International Monetary Fund (IMF, 2007) to show that the share of total government resources allocated to agriculture in Kenya has been declining steadily (see Table 9.3). The share reached a low of about 4 per cent in 2003

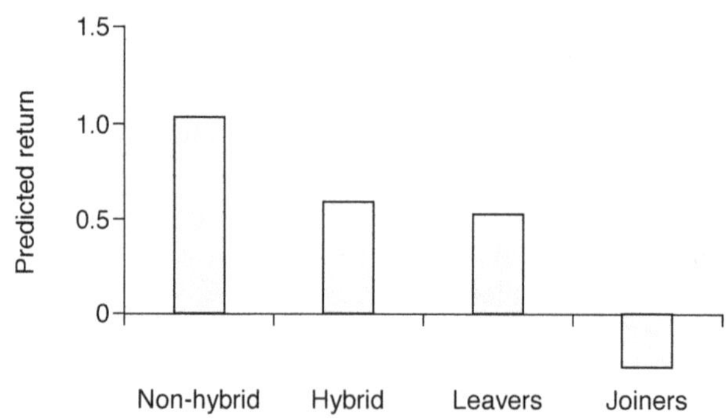

Figure 9.11 Predicted returns (1=100%) to hybrid maize across farmer types.
Source: Suri (2010).

and then started to rise again. Non-agricultural and total spending grew at about 4.3 per cent and 4.6 per cent per year in real terms, respectively, whereas public agricultural expenditure grew by about 9.1 per cent per year. Of the total spending in agriculture, almost two-thirds is spent on recurrent activities (dominated by salaries for employees, including extension officers[10]). Less than 30 per cent is spent on development, including agricultural research and information, animal health, crop protection, seed inspection, mechanization, etc. (World Bank, 2005).

Figure 9.12 shows the amount across the six ministries involved in the sector – 38 per cent of the resources were spent on crops, 22 per cent on livestock and fisheries, and 20 per cent on forestry and other natural resources. Figure 9.13 shows how the expenditures on agricultural R&D in Kenya have grown over the last two decades, including expenditures by non-government organizations (NGOs), although it is rather striking that this matches expenditure by the government. The government's share in the total is also rather low. All these figures show immense room for improvement in terms of public investment in various aspects of the agricultural sector in Kenya.

Furthermore, Thurlow and Benin (2008) show that it is not only important to increase public spending but also to prioritize investments on the basis of their potential returns on agricultural growth. Using estimated expenditure–growth elasticities, they estimate that the bulk (60–70 per cent) of additional resources to agriculture should be allocated to infrastructure (or improving market access and information services, etc.), followed by agricultural research (about 30 per cent), and then extension and other technical services (about 6 per cent). Rural roads increase farmers' access to agricultural inputs and product markets and enable farmers to participate in higher value-added market chains. Research generates improved technologies that increase agricultural production, reduce the costs of production, and protect the environ-

Table 9.3 Government spending by sector, 1975–2006

	1975	1980	1985	1990	1995	2000	2005	2006
Expenditure (2006 Ksh, bn)								
Total	115.3	182.7	211.2	294.7	331.9	265.4	365.7	386.0
Agriculture	8.7	15.4	21.9	17.8	18.3	18.1	24.2	22.8
Non-agriculture	106.5	167.4	189.3	276.9	313.5	247.3	341.5	363.2
Expenditure shares (%)								
Agriculture/total expenditure	7.6	8.4	10.4	6.0	5.5	6.8	6.6	5.9
Ag/Ag-GDP	5.4	7.6	9.3	6.5	6.0	4.9	6.6	5.8
Non-ag/Non-ag GDP	28.6	32.0	32.4	34.4	36.5	26.7	28.9	29.1
Total/total GDP	21.6	25.3	25.8	27.3	28.5	20.5	23.6	23.5

Source: Thurlow and Benin (2008) from Government Finance Statistics (IMF, 2007) and Public Expenditure Review (World Bank, 2005).

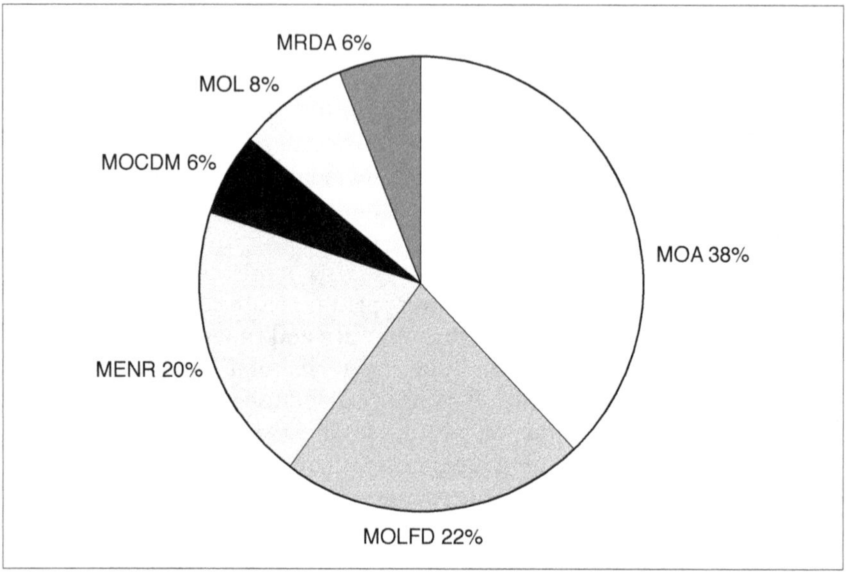

Figure 9.12 Spending on the agriculture sector by ministry, 2002/03 to 2004/05.
MENR, Ministry of Environment & Natural Resources; MOLFD, Ministry of Livestock & Fisheries Development; MOA, Ministry of Agriculture; MRDA, Ministry of Regional Development Authorities; MOL, Ministry of Lands; MOCDM, Ministry of Cooperative Development & Marketing.
Source: Thurlow and Benin (2008) Public expenditure review (World Bank, 2005).

ment for sustainability. The effectiveness of public extension systems has been a controversial issue with some studies showing large positive returns (Bindish and Evenson, 1997; Evenson and Mwabu, 1998) and others showing possible negative returns (Gautam and Anderson, 1999).

9.4 Rural transformation for the prosperity of agriculture

As outlined in Section 9.2, in Mellor's framework, a turning point[11] is reached when the absolute size of the agricultural labour force starts to decline. The speed at which this turning point is reached is highly dependent on policies aimed at increasing agricultural productivity and non-farm employment. The higher the initial agricultural share in employment, the longer the time it takes to reach the turning point. In addition, the greater the difference between the growth rates of the total labour force and of non-farm employment, the less time is required to reach the turning point.

For Kenya, the growth rate of wage and self-employment has averaged about 4.5 per cent in the last ten years, which is higher than the growth rate of the total labour force (about 2.5 per cent). And the growth rate of the agricultural labour force was 1.9 per cent over the same period. This implies that the

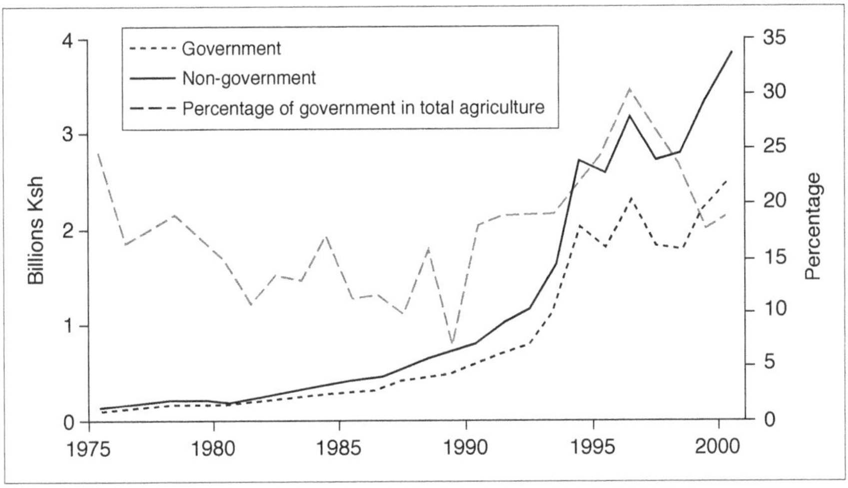

Figure 9.13 Spending on agricultural R&D.
Source: Thurlow and Benin (2008) from ASTI (IFPRI, 2007) and Government Finance Statistics (IMF, 2007).

share of agricultural labour is in decline. According to the World Bank (2007), the agricultural labour force constitutes close to 73 per cent of the total labour force. If the above rates of growth for farm, off-farm, and total labour force are maintained, the process of structural transformation will be extremely slow, and it will take close to 50 years for the non-farm sector to overtake agriculture in employment. This predicted transition is shown in Figure 9.14, which illustrates the time path for the agricultural labour force, the non-agricultural labour force, and the total labour force until 2041.

Other data sources, however, provide different estimates for sector employment. For instance, KIHBS (2005/06) shows only 41 per cent of employed people to be in small-scale agriculture, and the KNBS (2008) shows that, for the same year as KIHBS, large-scale agriculture accounted for about 18 per cent of the labour force, giving a total of 59 per cent of the labour force in agriculture. Figure 9.15 shows a possible growth path with this share of employment in agriculture, assuming similar growth rates for the total and off-farm labour force as above. With this estimate, structural transformation will be faster, with a turning point at about 2024, which is close to the Kenya *Vision 2030* estimate of 2027 when urban dwellers will exceed half the country's population and overtake rural dwellers.[12]

The challenge for Kenya, however, will be how to maintain a growth rate in the non-farm labour force of 4.5 per cent. Very few countries have sustained a growth of this magnitude (Gabre-Madhin and Johnson, 1999). Quoting Chairman Mao, Timmer and Akkus (2008) observe that 'unless the non-agriculture economy is growing, there is little long-run hope for agriculture'. But agriculture plays an important role in stimulating the non-agricultural economy, as

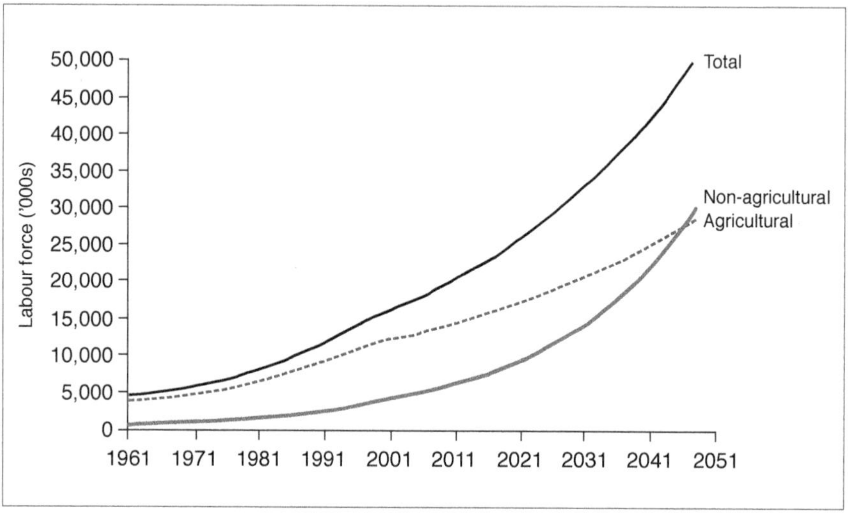

Figure 9.14 Growth scenario for farm, non-farm, and total labour force with initial share of agriculture employment at 70%.
Source: Authors' calculations (data from WDI, KNBS).

history shows (Haggblade and Hazell, 1989; Todaro, 2001; Timmer, 2002). As agriculture is the largest rural employer and may be the largest supplier of raw materials, it plays a strong early role in influencing the size and structure of the non-farm sector.

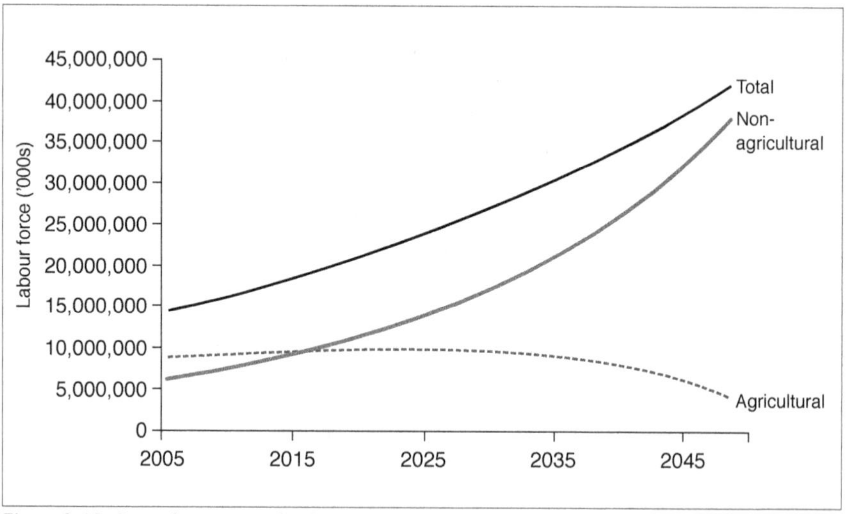

Figure 9.15 Growth scenario for farm, non-farm, and total labour force with initial share of agriculture employment at 59%.
Source: Authors' calculations (data from WDI, KNBS).

Finally, on the microeconomic side, Timmer (1997a) identified the implications for diversification at the household level. Kimenju and Tschirley (2008) document Kenya's progress in this transformation using the Tegemeo data. As described above, we would initially expect diversification to increase, especially as there tend to be different rates of market development for staple and export/cash crops.[13] However, as this progresses, the level of diversification will peak and then start to decrease as the economy moves towards specialization. Kimenju and Tschirley (2008) find that Kenya is in the early part of the transformation, with diversification on the rise, but specialization is yet to begin. Table 9.4 (drawn from their paper) shows the trends in crop, agricultural (both crops and livestock), and livelihood (across all income sources) diversification using the Herfindahl index (zero under complete specialization in one activity and 1 when there is no dominant activity). They show that diversification seems to be driven by better infrastructure and better access to markets. They document how areas with higher population density, those closer to urban areas, and those with agro-ecological potential have seen some specialization by 2007. Finally, they find that the poorest households tend to be the most diversified, whereas the richer households tend to be more specialized.

9.5 Policies and implications for growth

This section brings together all the above analysis and frameworks to really try to understand what may be some of the ways forward for Kenya. More specifically, we highlight policy steps that could help the process of welfare improvements in agriculture and the transformation of this sector and the economy as a whole.

Given the importance of agriculture in Kenya's economy and its potential to contribute to poverty reduction, there is a need to provide incentives to boost both agricultural production and private investment in the sector. Steps should be taken to enhance macroeconomic stability. Macroeconomic policies have a systemic impact on the investment climate through the confidence they stimulate (or demoralize) in prospects for growth and the outlook for exchange rates, prices, wages, and interest rates, and the availability of credit. Exchange rate overvaluation taxes the agricultural sector and hence should be avoided. Inflation rate and external debts should be kept to a mini-

Table 9.4 Crop, agricultural, and livelihood diversification indices, 1997–2007

	1997	2000	2004	2007
Crop diversification	0.49	0.57	0.60	0.59
Agricultural diversification	0.60	0.60	0.65	0.65
Livelihood diversification	0.59	0.62	0.63	0.66

Source: Kimenju and Tschirley (2008) (using the Tegemeo panel survey).

mum to reduce domestic financing, which in turn reduces both interest and taxation rates.

Policies for transforming agriculture need to consider the status of agriculture in various parts of the country. Given that Kenya's smallholder agriculture is characterized by farm sizes that are likely to remain small for decades, given population pressures, diversification from the production of staple grains to higher valued commodities is the first step in the process. Kimenju and Tschirley (2008) and Omiti *et al.* (2008) identify high input costs, poor input quality, and poor transport infrastructure as constraints to this step. Therefore, there should be a commitment to increasing public investment in rural infrastructure to reduce the high levels of transport and transaction costs.

There is need for a focus on improving agricultural productivity in general to provide an impetus to the transition. Policy needs to account for the riskiness of rain-fed agriculture. Current high-yielding varieties perform well only for a subsample of farmers in the country (Suri, 2010); others have poor access to technologies. And yet there is still a need to develop varieties that are specific to the different environments in Kenya (especially given the advent of climate change). The importance of research and development for agriculture is clear. India, for example, releases more new seed varieties a year than Kenya does over a decade.

In efforts to boost agricultural productivity, the country has taken a positive step towards the adoption of improved crop varieties developed through biotechnology by passing the Biosafety Bill in December 2008. The legislation will govern research, field testing, commercialization, and imports of bioengineered crops. The long-term benefits of this legislation will be realized only if the country installs the relevant regulatory capacity to pacify interests that oppose the use of genetically modified organisms on the basis of risks to human health and the environment. AGRA (Alliance for a Green Revolution in Africa) is certainly set to play an important role in this agenda.

In addition to the research side, access to technologies still needs to be improved through improvements in infrastructure as well as improving access to credit. In the case of the former, investment in infrastructure, more efficient ports, rural information systems, and reductions in transactions costs are all important components. In the case of the latter, an example is the $50m facility launched by Equity, the International Fund for Agricultural Development (IFAD), and the Ministry of Agriculture in May 2008 to get better credit to farmers. In September 2008, the government announced a plan to partially subsidize fertilizer for farmers. As Ariga *et al.* (2008), Morris *et al.* (2007) and Minde *et al.* (2008) point out, the government needs to be careful in designing and implementing any subsidy programme. The findings by Kibaara *et al.* (2008) that distance to a fertilizer market declined by close to 60 per cent is a signal that the design of a fertilizer subsidy policy in Kenya needs to take account of the gains in access Kenya has experienced from market reforms and the future potential of the private sector.

In this vein, to help this process and encourage investment by households themselves in agricultural land and assets, the land issues need to be addressed, and the increasing inequality is of great concern. Access to land through better functioning markets is needed. Economies with highly concentrated land distributions tend to grow more slowly than the more egalitarian ones (Deininger and Squire, 1998). Given the difficulties in land distribution facing Kenya and sustainability issues, increased land productivity via intensification seems to be the more viable option of connecting the poor with the growth process. The country should implement a comprehensive land policy that ensures efficient utilization of land by those who hold it, particularly the absentee landlords.

The second step in this transformation process will be to move beyond basic commodity production to access value-added supply chains for the modern retail sector, especially supermarkets, where the value-added element comes in the form of quality, timeliness, food safety, and labour standards in production. These are highly management-intensive factors and can contribute to production economies of scale (Timmer, 2004; Neven and Reardon, 2008). Using the Kenyan case of horticulture, Neven and Reardon (2008) show that key success factors in accessing the high-value supply chains include: a focus on quality products with a pre-identified market; the catalysing involvement of private and/or public organizations with a commercial basis; and sustainable group formation among farmers. Kimenju and Tschirley (2008) show how the richest households have started to specialize and are therefore furthest along the poverty spectrum.

The horticulture sector in Kenya provides more evidence of this. The sector has been an impressive success over the last few decades. Over Ksh 73 billion was earned from exports for the year ending 31 December 2008. Kenya exports about 450,000 tons of vegetables, fruit, and flowers to Europe, with 80 per cent of its flowers going to the European cut flower trade. The growth in this sector of Kenya's economy has been immense over the past decade, with horticulture growing from 13.6 per cent of Kenya's total exports to about 21 per cent between 2001 and 2007 (over the same period, tea exports fell from 24 per cent of total exports to 17 per cent and coffee from 5.1 per cent to 3.8 per cent). This immense success in horticulture has been attributed to investment in infrastructure in the major horticultural production and processing areas. There have, however, been more recent challenges in this sector, especially with the recent drought and the fall in demand due to the financial crisis of 2009.

However, as Muendo *et al.* (2004) point out, exports of horticulture are still only a small fraction of the overall horticultural sector in Kenya. They show how, for the last decade, more than 90 per cent of all Kenya's production of fruit and vegetables were consumed in the domestic market, and the domestic market accounted for 90 per cent of the total growth in their production. They also state that less than 2 per cent of smallholder farmers produce horticultural products directly for export. This underlines the importance of keeping a focus on improving productivity and lowering the costs of production for the domestic market. Minot and Ngigi (2004) also demonstrate the success of small-scale horticulture producers in terms of household income generation, export earnings, and area expansion. Critical policy areas for this success include limited public sector involvement, institutional innovations, and linking smallholder farmers to high-value urban and export markets. As Steve Wiggins puts it '...when small farmers are given the incentives to produce more and the means to do so, they invest, innovate and respond to opportunity' (FAC, 2009). The horticulture case may be proof that it is lack of conditions that allow small farmers to fulfil their potential that is behind the disappointment of agriculture in Kenya and elsewhere in Africa. Minot and Ngigi (2004) find that the horticultural production of large-scale farmers is, in fact, no more commercially oriented than that of the small-scale farmers.

Nevertheless, declining farm size among small-scale Kenyan farmers remains a challenge. Ellis (2005) notes that, for small farm agriculture to prosper in sub-Saharan Africa, rapid rural–urban transitions must take place to reverse declining farm size, provide robust domestic markets for farm produce, increase cash in circulation in rural areas, and take the pressure off overexploited natural resources. Figures 9.8 and 9.9 suggest that Kenyan households are essentially firms that have multisectoral activities. As such, they are sensitive to the terms of trade across sectors and would therefore shift resources among them. Policy needs to be attentive to such opportunities especially when they are driven by pull factors.

The final step in the transformation is the diversification of the rural economy itself, from being primarily driven by agriculture to depending more on industrial and service sectors for rural growth. This step seems feasible only when population densities permit substantial clusters of activities that feed on themselves for inputs and demand for output (Lanjouw and Lanjouw, 2001). The effectiveness of Mellor's model of demand for labour-intensive, rural nontradables as the vehicle for pro-poor growth, driven by agricultural profitability and wages from labour-intensive exports, seems to be dependent on good rural infrastructure and human capital. In the current state of infrastructure in Kenya, this is largely limited to parts of the coastal and highland areas. Public investments in education and infrastructure are essential.

Clearly, opportunities do exist to enhance agricultural productivity. But Kenya does need to develop a strong intersector labour market in which workers can move from rural agricultural jobs to rural and urban industry and service jobs. To do so, it must follow a land-saving technology path, improving investment in agriculture and agricultural technology, just as the East Asian countries have done. However, it is important to remember that the environment, climate change, and fluctuating food prices (and the Dutch disease effects of exports such as horticulture) will pose important constraints, and policy needs to react accordingly. Finally, the financial crisis in the USA and Europe may have big impacts on agricultural exports from Kenya. As demand has fallen in Europe, a big market for horticultural produce from Kenya, it is having impacts on horticulture that are still yet to be completely felt in the Kenyan economy.

Notes

1 Of course, countries can move between these types, for example China and India have moved from agriculture based to transforming economies. Similarly, countries can also have disparities within them, for example transforming countries can have agriculture-based regions such as Bihar in India.

2 Fei and Ranis (1997) document the process of agricultural transformation for a number of countries historically, such as Japan and Taiwan. They find that a lot of the transitions are preceded by large increases in agricultural productivity when wages are still low. The extra surplus in agriculture is invested in non-agriculture, which then draws in labour from the rural areas, where wages then rise. The key to generating the transition is improvements in agricultural productivity.

3 Agricultural commercialization is often measured by the percentage of value of marketed output to total farm production (Haddad and Bouis, 1990).

4 For example, Kibaara *et al.* (2008) document how coffee and sugar cane productivity declined over this period. They attribute the trends in coffee to declines in world prices, mismanagement of the co-operatives, high production costs, and few new varieties (Nyoro *et al.*, 2001). In the sugar cane industry, they point to poor equipment, poor varieties, and the state of the infrastructure as the culprits. In addition, they look at a few other crops such as cabbages and Irish potatoes, but do not find any real systematic trends in these other crops.

5 Interestingly, they also find that primary education is not always enough to keep a household out of poverty. However, education levels higher than primary have much more robust correlations with a lack of poverty and poverty mobility.

6 Note that, as reported in KPIA (2009), about half the poor are landless, whereas about two-thirds of the non-poor are landless.

7 The KPIA (2009) also points out how the levels of land inequality as measured by land Ginis are higher than the consumption Ginis or the earnings Ginis. In addition, these levels of land inequality in Kenya are higher than in South and East Asia, and approaching those in Latin America. Relative to other African countries, levels of land inequality are lower in Uganda and higher in Tanzania.

8 The proportion purchased by agricultural households coincides with that of rural households.

9 Suri also provides the following evidence from the Tegemeo data. Farmers who use non-hybrid seed were asked why they do not use improved seed varieties, and

14 per cent blamed unavailability of seed as one of the top two reasons for this; 65 per cent put high costs as one of the top two reasons. The 2000 survey showed that one of the common fertilizers (MAP) was not used at all. Studies done by CIMMYT cited unavailability of inputs, issues discussed at the Africa Fertilizer Summit in 2006.

10 Agricultural extension services are provided by both government and non-governmental entities, including private companies, NGOs, community-based organizations, and faith-based organizations (Muyanga and Jayne, 2008).

11 In the Fei and Ranis (1964, 1997) model, a turning point is reached when wages start to increase to match productivity increases in the agricultural sector. Remember that this framework is based on a labour market in the rural agricultural sector that is not neoclassical, such that wages are low and do not increase in line with productivity improvements in this sector. As productivity improves, the extra surplus is invested in non-farm activities, with the result that labour is drawn into that sector. Eventually, the wages in the agricultural sector begin to rise and move in line with productivity increases – this is the turning point in this framework. We cannot look for a turning point according to this methodology as a consistent time series of data on agricultural wages for Kenya is not easily available.

12 The census conducted in 2009 will provide a more accurate estimate of the actual labour force in the various sectors of the Kenyan economy.

13 The markets for staple crops may develop more slowly for a number of reasons. First, they have lower value for weight due to a lower scope for trade and high transport costs. These staple crops are often mostly traded domestically. And governments can often intervene in the markets for staples for political reasons or over food security concerns.

References

Ariga, J., T. S. Jayne, B. Kibaara and J. K. Nyoro, 2008, 'Trends and Patterns in Fertilizer Use by Smallholder Farmers in Kenya, 1997–2007'. Tegemeo Conference Paper, 2008.

Bell, C. L., and P. B. R. Hazell, 1980, 'Measuring the Indirect Effects of an Agricultural Investment Project on its Surrounding Region', *American Journal of Agricultural Economics*, 62, 75–86.

Besley, T., and L. Cord (eds), 2007, *Delivering on the Promise of Pro-poor Growth: Insights and Lessons from Country Experiences*. London: Palgrave Macmillan and World Bank.

Beynon, J. G., 1989, 'Pricism versus Structural Adjustment in African Agriculture', *American Journal of Agricultural Economics*. 40 (3), 323–335.

Bindlish, V. and R. E. Evenson, 1997, 'The Impact of T&V Extension in Africa: the Experience of Kenya and Burkina Faso', *World Bank Research Observer*, 12 (2), 183–201.

Binswanger, H., 1989, 'The Policy Response in Agriculture'. Proceedings of the World Bank Annual Conference on Development Economics. Washington, DC.

Collier, P., 2008, '6 Responses to Food Crisis is a Chance to Reform Global Agriculture: Comment', *Economist Forum*, 30 April 2008.

Deininger, K. and L. Squire, 1998, 'New Ways of Looking at Old Issues: Inequality and Growth', *Journal of Development Economics*, 57, 259–287.

Delgado, C. L. and J. W. Mellor, 1984, 'A Structural View of Policy Issues in African Agricultural Development', *American Journal of Agricultural Economics*, 66 (5), 665–670.

Ellis, F., 2005, 'Small-farms, Livelihood Diversification and Rural–Urban Transitions: Strategic Issues in sub-Saharan Africa'. Paper, Research Workshop on the Future of Small Farms, organized by IFPRI, Imperial College and ODI, Wye, June 2005.

Erickson, L. and D. Vollrath, 2004, 'Dimensions of Land Inequality and Economic Development'. IMF Working Paper 04/158. Washington, DC: International Monetary Fund.

Evenson, R. E. and G. Mwabu, 1998, 'The Effects of Agricultural Extension on Farm Yields in Kenya'. Economic Growth Center Discussion Paper 798, New Haven, CT: Economic Growth Center, Yale University.

FAC, 2009, Futures Agriculture e-debate. Downloaded on 22 November 2009. Available from http://www.future-agricultures.org/EN/e-ebates/Big_Farms/farm_debate.html.

Fan, S. and N. Rao, 2003, 'Public Spending in Developing Countries: Trend, Determination and Impact'. Environment and Production Technology Division Discussion Paper 99. Washington, DC: International Food Policy Research Institute.

Fan, S., P. Hazell and S. Thorat, 2000, 'Government Spending, Agricultural Growth and Poverty in Rural India', *American Journal of Agricultural Economics*, 82(4), 1038–1051.

Fan, S., T. Mogues and S. Benin, 2009, 'Setting Priorities for Public Spending for Agricultural and Rural Development in Africa'. IFPRI Policy Brief 12, April 2009.

Fei, J. and G. Ranis, 1964, *Development of the Labour Surplus Economy: Theory and Policy*. Homewood, IL: Richard D. Irwin.

Fei, J. and G. Ranis, 1997, *Growth and Development from an Evolutionary Perspective*. Malden, MA, and Oxford, UK: Blackwell Publishers.

FAO (Food and Agricultural Organization), 2008, FAOSTAT database. Available at http://faostat.fao.org/.

Gabre-Madhin, E. and B. F. Johnston, 1999, 'Accelerating Africa's structural transformation: Lessons from East Asia'. MSSD Discussion Paper 34. Washington, DC: International Food Policy Research Institute, Market and Structural Studies Division.

Gautam, M. and J. R. Anderson, 1999, *Reconsidering the Evidence on the Returns to T&V Extension in Kenya*. Washington, DC: Operations Evaluations Department, World Bank.

GOK (Government of Kenya), 2008, *Kenya Vision 2030. A Globally Competitive and Prosperous Kenya*. Nairobi; Ministry of Planning, National Development and Vision 2030.

Haddad, L. J. and H. E. Bouis, 1990, *Agricultural Commercialization, Nutrition and the Rural Poor. A Study of Philippine Farm Households*. Washington, DC: International Food Policy Research Institute.

Haggblade, S. and P. Hazell, 1989, 'Agricultural Technology and Farm-Nonfarm Growth Linkages', *Agricultural Economics*, 3, 345–364.

Haggblade, S., P. Hazell and J. Brown, 1989, 'Farm–Non-Farm Linkages in Rural Sub-Saharan Africa', *World Development*, 17, 1173–1201.

Haggblade, S. P., B. R. Hazell and T. Reardon (eds), 2007, *Transforming the Rural Nonfarm Economy: Opportunities and Threats in the Developing World*. New Delhi: Oxford University Press.

Hazell, P. and A. Roell, 1983, 'Rural Growth Linkages: Household Expenditure Patterns in Malaysia and Nigeria'. Research Report 41. Washington, DC: International Food Policy Research Institute.

IMF (International Monetary Fund), 2007, *Government Finance Statistics*. Washington, DC: IMF.

Jayne, T. S., T. Yamano, M. Weber, D. Tschirley, R. Benfica, D. Neven, A. Chapoto and B. Zulu, 2003, 'Smallholder Income and Land Distribution in Africa: Implications for Poverty Reduction Strategies', *Food Policy*, 28, 253–275.

Karanja, A. M., A. Kuyvenhoven and H. Moll, 2003, *Economic Reforms and Evolution of Producer Prices in Kenya: An ARCH-M Approach*. African Development Bank.

Kenya Integrated Household Budget Survey (KIHBS), 2005/06, *Database*. Nairobi: Kenya National Bureau of Statistics.

Kibaara, B., J. Ariga, J. Olwande and T. S. Jayne, 2008, 'Trends in Kenyan Agricultural Productivity: 1997–2007'. Tegemeo Conference Paper, 16–17 September, 2008, Nairobi, Kenya.

Kimenju, S. and D. Tschirley, 2008, 'Agriculture and Livelihood Diversification in Kenyan Rural Households'. Tegemeo Conference Paper, 2008.

KNBS, 2008. *Economic Survey*. Nairobi: Kenya National Bureau of Statistics.

KPIA, 2009, *Kenya Poverty and Inequality Assessment: Executive Summary and Synthesis Report*. Poverty Reduction and Economic Management Unit, Africa Region, The World Bank.

Lanjouw, J. and P. Lanjouw, 2001, 'The Rural Non-Farm Sector: Issues and Evidence from Developing Countries', *Agricultural Economics*, 26 (1), 1–23.

Lewis, A., 1954, 'Development with Unlimited Supplies of Labour', *The Manchester School*, 22, 139–191.

Maxwell, S, 2004, 'Launching the DFID Consultation "New Directions for Agriculture in Reducing Poverty"'. Available from http://dfid-agriculture-consultation.nri.org/launchpapers/simonmaxwell.html.

Mellor, J. W., 1976, *The New Economics of Growth: A Strategy for India and the Developing World*. Ithaca, NY: Cornell University Press.

Mellor, J. W., 1995, *Agriculture on the Road to Industrialization*. Baltimore, MD: Johns Hopkins University Press.

Mellor, J. W., 2000, 'Agricultural Growth, Rural Employment, and Poverty Reduction – Non-tradables, Public Expenditure, and Balanced Growth'. Paper presented at the World Bank Rural Week 2000, Poverty or Prosperity: Rural People in a Globalised Economy, 28–31 March 2000.

Minde, I., T. Jayne, E. Crawford, J. Ariga and J. Govereh, 2008, 'Promoting Fertilizer Use in Africa: Current Issues and Empirical Evidence from Malawi, Zambia, and Kenya'. Working Paper for Re-SAKSS/Southern Africa, Pretoria, South Africa.

Morris, M., V. A. Kelly, R. Kopicki and D. Byerlee, 2007, *Promoting Increased Fertilizer Use in Africa: Lessons Learned and Good Practice Guidelines*. Washington, DC: World Bank.

Minot, N. and M. Ngigi, 2004, 'Are Horticultural Exports a Replicable Success Story? Evidence from Kenya and Côte d'Ivoire'. IFPRI EPTD DP No. 120 and MTID DP No. 73.

Mosley P. and L. Smith, 1989, 'Structural Adjustment and Agricultural Performance in Sub Saharan Africa 1980–1987', *Journal of International Development*, 1 (3), 321–355.

Muendo, K., D. Tschirley and M. Weber, 2004, 'Improving Kenya's Domestic Horticultural Production and Marketing System: Current Competitiveness, Forces of Change, and Challenges for the Future'. Vol. 3, Tegemeo Institute Working Paper No. 08C/2004.

Muyanga, M. and T. S. Jayne, 2008, 'Private Agricultural Extension System in Kenya: Practice and Policy Lessons', *The Journal of Agricultural Education and Extension*, 14 (2), 111–124.

Mwega, F. M., and N. S. Ndung'u, 2002, 'Explaining African Economic Growth Performance: The Case of Kenya'. African Economic Research Consortium Report. Nairobi: African Economic Research Consortium.

Nerlove, M., 1988, 'Modernizing Traditional Agriculture'. Occasional Paper No. 16. International Centre for Economic Growth, San Francisco, CA, USA.

Neven, D. and T. Reardon, 2008, 'The Rapid Rise of Kenya Supermarkets: Impacts on the Fruit and Vegetable Supply System', in McCullough, E. B., P. L. Pingali and K. Stamoulis (eds) *The Transformation of Agri-food Systems: Globalisation, Supply Chains and Smallholder Farmers*. London: Earthscan and FAO, 189–206.

Nyangito, H. and J. Karugia, 2002, 'The Impact of Globalization and Internal Policy Changes on the Agricultural Sector in Kenya', in Bigman, D. (ed.) *Globalization and Developing Countries: Economic Potential and Agricultural Prospects*. Wallingford, UK: CABI Publishing.

Nyangito, H., W. Odhiambo, S. Mwakubo and L. Ndirangu, 2005, 'Effects of Market Price Volatility on Production Patterns and Apparent Retreat into Subsistence Farming by Kenyan Smallholders'. Cornel University, Strategies and Analysis for Growth and Access (SAGA) Policy Brief, February 2005.

Nyoro, J., M. Wanzala and T. Awour, 2001, 'Increasing Kenya's Agricultural Competitiveness: Farm Level Issues'. Tegemeo Institute Working Paper No. 4, Tegemeo Institute, Nairobi, Kenya.

Omiti, J. D., O. T. Nyanamba and E. B. McCullough, 2008, 'The Transition from Maize Production Systems to High-value Agriculture in Kenya', in McCullough, E. B., P. L. Pingali and K. Stamoulis (eds) *The Transformation of Agri-Food Systems: Globalisation, Supply Chains and Smallholder Farmers*. London: Earthscan and FAO, 235–257.

Reardon, T., C. Delgado and P. Matlon, 1992, 'Determinants and Effects of Income Diversification among Farm Households in Burkina Faso', *Journal of Development Studies*, 28, 264–296.

Reardon, T., K. Stamoulis, A. Balisacan, M. E. Cruz, J. Berdegue and B. Banks, 1998, 'Rural Nonfarm Income in Developing Countries'. Special Chapter in *The State of Food and Agriculture 1998*. Rome: Food and Agricultural Organization of the United Nations.

Schultz, T. W., 1964, *Transforming Traditional Agriculture*. New Haven, CT: Yale University Press.

Suri, T., 2010, 'Selection and Comparative Advantage in Technology Adoption', *Econometrica*, forthcoming.

Suri, T., D. Tschirley, C. Irungu, R. Gitau and D. Kariuki, 2008, 'Rural Incomes, Inequality and Poverty Dynamics in Kenya'. Tegemeo Institute of Agricultural Policy and Development WPS 30/2008, Tegemeo.

Thurlow, J. and S. Benin, 2008, 'Agricultural Growth and Investment Options for Poverty Reduction in Kenya'. Preliminary report prepared for Kenya's Comprehensive Africa

Agricultural Development Programme (CAADP) Roundtable Discussion. International Food Policy Research Institute.

Tiffen, M., 2003, 'Transitions in Sub-Saharan Africa: Agriculture, Urbanization and Income Growth', *World Development*, 31 (8), 1343–1366.

Timmer, C. P., 1988, 'The Agricultural Transformation', in Chenery, H. and T. N. Srinivasan (eds) *The Handbook of Development Economics, Vol. I*. Amsterdam: North-Holland, 275–311.

Timmer, P., 1997a, 'How Well do the Poor Connect to the Growth Process?' Harvard Institute for International Development for the USAID/CAER project, December.

Timmer, C. P., 1997b, 'Farmers and Markets: The Political Economy of New Paradigms', *American Journal of Agricultural Economics*, 70, 621–627.

Timmer, P., 2002, 'Agriculture and Economic Growth', in Gardner, B. and G. Rausser (eds) *Handbook of Agricultural Economics, Vol. IIA*. Amsterdam: North-Holland, 1487–1546.

Timmer, P., 2004, 'Food Policy in the Era of Supermarkets: What's Different?' *Journal of Agricultural and Development Economics*, 1 (2), 50–67.

Timmer, P. and S. Akkus, 2008, 'The Structural Transformation as a Pathway out of Poverty: Analytics, Empirics and Politics'. Working Paper no. 150. Center for Global Development.

Todaro, M., 1997, *Economic Development*, 6th edn. New York: Addison Wesley.

Winter-Nelson, A. M. and G. Argwings-Kodhek, 2009, 'Kenya', in Anderson, K. and W. A. Masters (eds) *Distortions to Agricultural Incentives in Africa*. Washington, DC: The World Bank, 282–283.

World Bank, 1981, *Accelerated Development in Sub-Saharan Africa: An Agenda for Action*. Washington, DC: The World Bank.

World Bank, 1986, *Financing Adjustment with Growth in Sub Saharan Africa 1986–1990*. Washington, DC: The World Bank.

World Bank. 2005, *Kenya Public Expenditure Review, 2004*. Washington, DC: The World Bank.

World Bank, 2007, *Agriculture for Development*. World Development Report, Washington, DC: The World Bank.

World Bank, 2008, World Development Indicators database.

10

The Manufacturing Sector

Arne Bigsten, Peter Kimuyu, and Måns Söderbom

10.1 Introduction

Kenya is a resource-poor country with rapid population growth and, in terms of employment, a large agricultural sector. With limited access to fertile land, the agricultural sector may not be able to deliver sustained growth in per capita income in the future. As land is not an important factor for manufacturing production, this is much less of a constraint for manufacturing growth. Unless there is a high rate of growth in the formal manufacturing sector generating job opportunities for the rapidly growing Kenyan labour force, Kenya risks remaining a low-skill, low-capital economy with low incomes and increasing distributional tensions. At present, the informal sector absorbs most of the newcomers to the labour market, but this sector offers low wages and contributes little to exports and technological progress in the country. For reasons to do with technology and costs, manufacturing may benefit from economies of scale, so that average production costs fall as firms grow. Policy-makers in Kenya recognize the importance of the manufacturing sector for long-term economic development. Indeed, the growth targets for manufacturing stated by the government in its *Vision 2030* document are ambitious and require rapidly increasing investment levels, eventually reaching levels above 30 per cent of gross domestic product (GDP) (Kenya, 2007).

Against the backdrop of these ambitious government plans, we discuss in this chapter the experiences of and prospects for the Kenyan manufacturing sector. Our discussion consists of two main parts. The first, provided in Section 10.2, focuses on industrialization strategies. After a brief overview of the period between 1960 and 2000, we provide a detailed account of recent industrial policies in Kenya. We note that the current industrial policies are no longer rooted exclusively in ideas related to the Washington consensus, which revolved around stabilization, privatization, and liberalization. Instead, improving the investment climate more broadly is seen as the general means of achieving significant investment and growth in the industrial sector. We examine recent reforms in trade policy that may affect manufacturing firms' ability to export and benefit from technological spillovers, and discuss the government's far-reaching plans for improving the infrastructure. We also discuss the thorny issue of instability and political uncertainty and the implications for manufacturing performance. In this context, the damage caused by the clashes following the disputed presidential election results in December 2007 may be long term. We end our policy discussion by noting some difficult choices for Kenya concerning the potential trade-off between efficiency and equity in the context of implementing policies. The second part of our discussion, provided in Section 10.3, provides an overview of the performance of Kenya's manufacturing sector and a comparative study of the constraints to business. Drawing on firm-level data obtained from manufacturing surveys and official aggregate data, we show how key outcome variables such as growth, productivity, investment, and exports have developed in the last few years, and discuss the leading business constraints. Our conclusions are provided in Section 10.4.

10.2 Strategies for industrialization: past and present

10.2.1 The 1960s and 1970s: import substitution

Kenya pursued a strategy of import substitution following independence in 1963, similar to many other African countries at the time. Most of the manufacturing investment in the 1960s went into heavily protected import-substituting industries, such as footwear, leather, rubber, petroleum, industrial chemicals, paints, soft drinks, cement, and metal products. Whereas import substitution ensured the domestic availability of products previously imported, it distorted industrial development in Kenya by encouraging the creation of excess capacity, low technical efficiency, and subsequent inability to penetrate external markets (Bigsten, 2001). At the beginning of the 1970s, Kenya faced a foreign exchange crisis, and the government tightened administrative controls on the economy further by means of higher tariffs, stricter import licensing procedures, and widespread price controls. These interventions reduced export incentives, and the share of manufacturing exports shrank from 40 per cent of the value of manufacturing output in 1964 to about 10 per cent in the mid-1980s. In spite of the poor export performance, manufacturing in

Kenya increased its share of GDP during the 1970s. At the same time, there was a rapid expansion in informal manufacturing production of mainly simple consumer goods and services for low-income households. Informality resulted from efforts to avoid high compliance costs and low opportunity costs for self-employment due to a mismatch between high labour force growth rates and formal sector employment opportunities.

10.2.2 The 1980s and 1990s: unstable transition

In the early 1980s, there were growing concerns about the distortionary effects of the import substitution policy, in the form of reduced competition, discrimination of export production, and low capacity utilization. Several Structural Adjustment Programmes were implemented to deal with these structural problems as well as macroeconomic imbalances. This started an unstable transition towards a more open policy stance. During the 1980s and in the early 1990s, the government introduced a series of reforms to support export production. These included export processing zones, manufacturing under bond, an export compensation scheme, and a duty/VAT drawback scheme. There was also a series of international agreements to increase regional trade and collaboration. In 1983, Kenya entered the Preferential Trade Area (PTA) of Eastern and Southern Africa and, in 1993, the Common Market for Eastern and Southern Africa (COMESA) was established. In 1993, most of the administrative controls purporting to protect local industry from competition and consumers from high prices were abolished, including import licensing and foreign exchange controls. The official and the interbank exchange rates were harmonized and, since then, the foreign exchange market has been fully liberalized for commercial transactions. Import tariffs became the main trade policy instrument. Tariff structures were simplified gradually following the initial reforms in 1993.

10.2.3 The new millennium: beyond liberalization

By the end of the 1990s, the general policy discussion of the problems facing the private sector in poor countries had begun to shift. Two of the world's leading development economists, Joseph Stiglitz and Dani Rodrik, argued that the development policies implied by the Washington consensus were flawed, and the idea that stabilization, privatization, and liberalization were insufficient for growth and development became widespread.[1] Instead, the 'investment climate', which can be thought of as 'the institutional, policy, and regulatory environment in which firms operate—factors that influence the link from sowing to reaping' (Dollar *et al.*, 2005), was highlighted by many economists and policy-makers as the key reason for the poor private sector performance in many developing countries (World Bank, 2004). Three development blueprints capture the main thrusts of the policy reforms in Kenya since 2000: the Poverty Reduction Strategy Paper 2001–2004 (PRSP), the Economic Recovery Strategy for Wealth Creation and Employment 2003–2007 (ERS), and Kenya *Vision 2030*. These documents presented numerous policy proposals aimed at improving the productivity and performance of industry in Kenya. Some of the policy proposals address general concerns about governance and infrastructure, whereas others address problems specific to industry. Following the World Bank's recent Commission on Growth and Development (2008), our discussion of these proposed, and in some cases implemented, policies will revolve around five factors thought to underlie sustained growth: accumulation, innovation, stabilization, allocation, and inclusion.

ACCUMULATION AND INNOVATION

Private and public investment in Kenya has long been too low to enable the manufacturing sector to take off. Private investment is essential for firms to upgrade their technology and become efficient producers. Public investment, notably in infrastructure, is important to reduce transaction costs. Without significant progress in these areas, Kenyan firms will not be able to compete internationally on a significant scale. This seems to be recognized politically. A major increase in private sector investment is a key goal in *Vision 2030*, for example. Proposed policy interventions include strengthening small and medium-sized enterprises (SMEs) to improve their productivity and innovativeness, boosting science, technology, and innovation in manufacturing by increasing R&D investment, increasing key infrastructure, namely ports, rail, and major roads and energy distribution systems, and carrying out efficiency-improving institutional reforms. The financial service strategy has focused on improving access to funds for investment through better management of specialized agencies, promotion of access to finance through different capital market segments, enactment of a microfinance bill, and maintaining low interest rates (Kenya, 2008b).

Technological progress is driven by research and development (R&D). Although the government wishes to increase R&D in Kenya, this is a very costly activity and requires a solid basis of skills in the country. Realistically, the main source of technological progress in Kenya will be foreign R&D, which will benefit Kenya through spillover effects. Importantly, empirical evidence (based on data from developed countries) indicates that technological spillovers are geographically limited in scope. Countries located far away from the centre of technological advances benefit much less from these than countries close to the centre (Keller, 2002). In this regard, Kenyan firms are clearly at a disadvantage, on account of the great distances between Kenya and the technologically most advanced countries. However, research also shows that the distance effect has weakened over time, a result attributable to globalization.

This suggests that trade is an important conduit for technological spillovers. Indeed, the Commission on Growth and Development argues that increasing trade is a good way of spurring technological progress (World Bank, 2008).

TRADE POLICY

Access to a larger market and exposure to new technology are two fundamental reasons why Kenya's manufacturing sector would benefit from becoming more trade oriented. The core of Kenya's trade policy consists of agreements with the other members of the East African Community (EAC), the European Union (EU), and the USA. There have been significant developments with regard to these relationships in the last decade. In 2005, the EAC introduced a Common External Tariff (CET), which resulted in a reduction in the average applied tariff rate from 16.8 per cent to 13.2 per cent. This is positive. Other developments have been less favourable, however. The CET has implied an increase in tariff dispersion, and it has preserved a pattern of tariff escalation, so that tariffs increase with the stage of processing.[2] This is intended to protect final stage producers, but this path towards vertical integration is hardly appropriate. Instead, Kenya should seek to become involved in global production chains, as it is this type of trade that is growing the fastest. Protecting producers of final goods is no longer a viable strategy to support manufacturing. Kenya should instead seek out its comparative advantages in the new structures of production along the whole production chain.

The three-band CET is generally relatively simple and transparent, but it has an extensive exception regime. There are problems with the phasing in of rules of origin within the EAC customs union, as it implies barriers to certain imports from Kenya. We may also note that several new tariffs were introduced or increased on specific items, whereas they were reduced on other selected items (Kenya, 2008a: 24). The tariff policy is still used selectively to support specific industries.

As is well known, non-negligible tariffs on imports result in an anti-export bias as firms find it profitable to focus on the domestic market. To counter this, Kenya has used a range of incentive schemes for exporters in an attempt to rectify the implied bias through the tariffs. Arguably, lowering tariffs would be a more direct way of eliminating this bias (World Bank, 2007a: 52). Another important effect of trade restrictions on manufacturing performance may be through food prices and wages. Specifically, if the wages of factory workers are based on the cost of obtaining food, they will be higher if food prices are kept high because of import restrictions. Thus, if tariffs imply high food prices, the tariffs are effectively undermining Kenyan firms' ability to compete internationally. Real wages in Kenya have been on an upward trend since 1993 without a corresponding increase in productivity. For manufacturing, this may seriously reduce its competitiveness.

The EAC, including Kenya, has entered into an interim agreement about commodity trade with the EU, while the negotiations for a full Economic Partnership Agreement (EPA) continue. Since January 2008, the EAC including Kenya has tariff- and quota-free access to the EU market for all commodities except for temporary restrictions on sugar and rice. This agreement holds for the interim agreement and will also hold for the full EPA. The agreement offers chances to advance areas that are important for Kenya's trade agenda, such as rules of origin, standards recognition, aid for trade, trade diversion, and worker migration. Reductions in Kenyan import tariffs will probably take place during the later part of the transition period, that is 2015–23. The EU currently has rather strict rules of origin. Collier and Venables (2007) argue that more liberal rules of origin would be beneficial for the ability of African firms to export. Rules of origin are more favourable under the African Growth and Opportunity Act (AGOA), initiated in the USA in 2000. AGOA meant that all restrictions on imports into the USA were dropped for a range of industrial products, including apparel. Frazer and van Biesebroeck (2008) show that this has had a positive effect on exports from the African countries that were involved. With regard to apparel, there was a large and robust impact on imports to the USA, and the impact on exports was greatest in Kenya. According to the World Bank, AGOA has led to the creation of new jobs and exports in Kenya (World Bank, 2007a: 61).

POLICIES FOR BETTER INFRASTRUCTURE

It is often argued that the poor investment climate in Africa results in high transaction costs and particularly disadvantages the manufacturing sector and its ability to export, because manufacturers are intensive users of investment climate services (Collier, 2000). This is problematic, because exporting may present a promising route to growth and development. In Kenya, improving the infrastructure is high on the political agenda. Recent policy actions in transport and communications have included the privatization of Telkom Kenya, contracting out the management and operations of Kenya Railways, strengthening the management of ports, modernizing container terminals, port equipment, and facilities, and privatizing selected operations of the Kenya Ports Authority. The ERS contained proposals for updating road designs and specification, making roads and other civil engineering works more cost effective, deepening the control of the quality of roads during construction, maintenance, and rehabilitation, dualling the Mombasa–Malaba highway, using an East African Road Network Project to develop internal roads, improving the quality of rural access roads by implementing the Roads 2000 programme, and constructing bypasses to decongest traffic in the cities of Nairobi and Mombasa. Policies to improve rail transport have included privatizing Kenya Railways. In order to improve air transport, the government under the ERS sought to upgrade smaller airports to make them capable of accommodating medium-range jets, privatize commercial and non-regulatory airport services, and modernize the management of air traffic. On marine transport, the port of Mombasa was to be converted to a landlord port and complemented with a range of new facilities.

On energy, the main recent policy step has been to strengthen the rural electrification programme and increase private sector participation in generation, transmission, and distribution. Kenya was also to expedite the implementation of planned generation plants and explore alternative sources of power. Policy proposals targeting telecommunications included the restructuring of Telkom Kenya to improve performance prior to privatization, licensing of four additional internet gateway service providers and a third mobile operator (in addition to Safaricom and Celtel), and liberalizing the use of very small aperture terminal (VSAT) services. A whole range of reforms was instituted to improve the water and sanitation services, including the encouragement of private sector participation in the financing and management of water and sanitation services.

Improved infrastructure is thus a major policy objective, but so far the results have been modest. A recent budget strategy paper (Kenya, 2008b) reports that there has been considerable progress in the development of roads and other infrastructure, but that very much remains to be done, not least when it comes to the maintenance of the existing infrastructure.

STABILIZATION AND POLITICAL UNCERTAINTY

Most economists agree that a stable macroeconomic framework is important for private sector growth. This is especially true for the manufacturing sector, where irreversible investments combined with high uncertainty may result in firms postponing their investments until confidence in future profitability is restored (Dixit and Pindyck, 1994). Impressionistic evidence on the association between investment and instability is provided in Figure 10.1. This graph, based on firm-level data for Kenya's manufacturing sector from 2007, shows how average investment rates and perceived macroeconomic instability across regions, categories of firm size, and manufacturing subsectors are correlated. There is a clear negative relationship between investment and perceived macroeconomic instability.

Even though reforms with regard to monetary and budget policy have improved the Kenyan setting, lack of stability remains a significant problem in the country. There are both external and internal reasons for this. Most significant at present is probably the uncertainty over how and when the developed world is to emerge from the current financial crisis, which means future demand for exports is difficult to predict. Of course, there is only so much a poor African country can do to manage instability caused by global

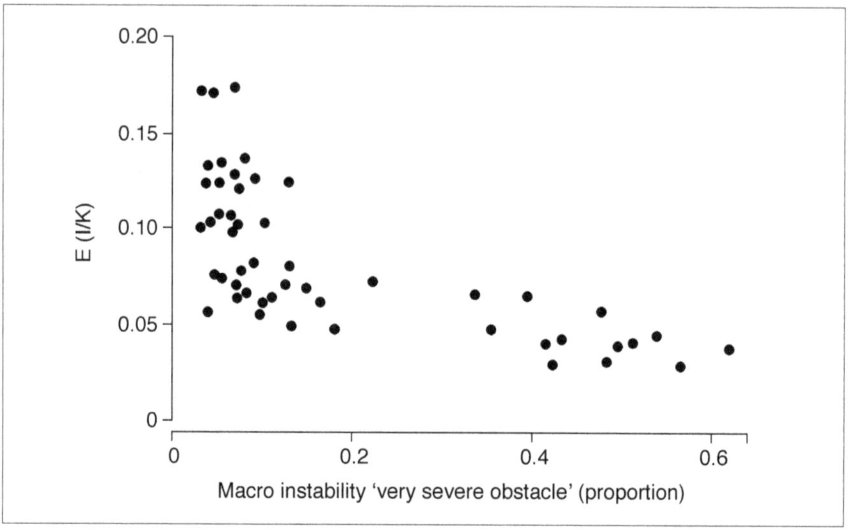

Figure 10.1 Investment and perceived macroeconomic instability: impressionistic evidence from Kenyan survey data, 2007

The data were collected as part of the World Bank's Investment Climate Survey in Kenya in 2007. Each data point in the graph represents an average across firms in a particular location, size category, and manufacturing industry. The vertical axis shows average investment rates, i.e. investment expenditures divided by the value of the capital stock. The horizontal axis shows the proportion of firms in a particular location–size–sector cell that rate macroeconomic instability as a 'very severe obstacle'.

events. Traditional stabilization policies, focusing on inflation and exchange rates, do play their part, but in the context of the global financial crises, these instruments do little to reduce uncertainty. That is true, of course, for most countries. For Kenya, however, stability is further rocked by the home-grown political problems, recently evidenced by the turmoil and clashes in January 2008 and beyond, following the presidential elections. These events will have caused significant damage to investor confidence. Real options models of investment predict that the response of investment to demand growth is weak if uncertainty is high (see e.g. Bond *et al.*, 2007). This suggests that, when the global business cycle recovers and export markets start to grow again, firms in Kenya will be slower to respond than firms in more politically stable countries.

If the political uncertainty persists, it is hard to see how Kenya will be able to achieve the ambitious growth rates set out in the policy documents discussed above. Some measures aimed at tackling a range of governance problems hindering industrial development have been implemented. In May 2003, the parliament passed the Anti-Corruption and Economic Crimes Act that led to the creation of the Kenya Anti-corruption Commission charged with responsibility for dealing with economic crimes and corruption. A second legislation was the Public Offices Ethics Act that spelt out codes of conduct for public servants. Other governance-related administrative and policy reforms with a bearing on industry include the establishment of a task force to review contracts for government jobs for which payment was still pending, and programming of legislation of governance-related bills including the Public Procurement and Disposal of Public Assets and Financial Management and Accountability Bill.[3] The ERS suggested measures to facilitate the creation of alternative dispute resolution mechanisms (such as arbitration), ensuring that these are entrenched in law and establishing regional commercial courts for expeditious determination of commercial disputes. The government also undertook to review industrial and labour relations frameworks to support dispute resolutions, encourage productivity and new investment, and prepare an export development strategy to address the necessary measures for diversification of export markets and reduce the likelihood of unilateral decisions.

IMPLEMENTATION OF POLICIES: A TRADE-OFF BETWEEN EFFICIENCY AND EQUITY?

We end this section with a brief discussion of some potentially difficult policy choices for Kenya. To improve the investment climate and reduce transaction costs facing manufacturers, large public investments are required. However, not everything can be done at once. What are the policy options and the priorities? A common argument in the current policy discussion is that targeted and intensive policy measures may be more effective than spreading out reforms thinly across a wide range of activities. This argument was widely discarded in the 1990s on the grounds that you can't 'pick winners', but appears to be back in vogue now. In Kenya, there is, for example, talk of supporting the development of niche products in which the country has a global competitive advantage, such as the agro-based industries. In the medium term, the government wishes to promote the establishment of special economic clusters, as well as small and medium-sized industrial parks, to support manufacturing (Kenya 2008b: 14). There is clearly a potential tension between these types of steps, which are motivated by efficiency arguments and equity concerns. For example, there is an obvious conflict between attempts to decentralize and the clustering strategies, especially in the short term. It may therefore be politically very difficult to implement policies that, while raising incomes in certain sectors or areas, are seen to increase inequality. In Kenya, the rural–urban aspect of development has long been a contentious issue, and given the clashes following the December 2007 elections, the importance of regional equity and inclusiveness is clearer than ever. Moreover, most of the poor live in rural areas and so, if manufacturing growth is to have an impact on poverty, the sector needs a stronger presence in rural areas than presently. Some policy steps have recently been taken to facilitate this. For example, the government has introduced tax incentives for investors locating outside the major cities to increase employment opportunities in rural Kenya. The government also plans to improve infrastructure in rural areas to attract local and foreign investors. The policy proposals designed under the PRSP included decentralization of justice and the creation of commercial courts away from Nairobi. This would make it easier for manufacturing firms outside Nairobi to enforce contracts and resolve other types of conflicts with suppliers or buyers, thus reducing transaction costs in such areas.[4] Overall, however, the policy-maker is walking a fine line here. Measures designed to stimulate the production of a wide range of manufacturing goods in many parts of the country may enhance equity but result in low efficiency; narrow policy steps may have the opposite effects.

10.3 Performance and constraints on business

In this section, we draw on official aggregate data and firm-level survey data in order to review the performance of the Kenyan manufacturing sector and to identify the main constraints on business.

10.3.1 Macro data on growth, employment, and capital formation

After a long period of virtual stagnation, the Kenyan economy went through a strong phase over the period 2003–07, as the rate of economic growth accelerated up to 7 per cent (see Table 10.1). During the same period, total factor productivity (TFP) in manufacturing increased by as much as 20 per cent (World Bank, 2007b). Aggregate capital formation increased up to 19.5 per cent, which is high by Kenyan standards, but of course pales in comparison with that of its Asian competitors. And it is a long way away from the long-term target of investments of 30 per cent of GDP. The positive development was (temporarily) halted by the post-election conflicts in 2008. Manufacturing growth followed more or less the same pattern as GDP, which meant that its share of GDP remained at slightly below 10 per cent of GDP. There has thus not been any major take-off for manufacturing production in Kenya.

The growth of overall formal employment has been very slow, while there has been an explosion in (estimated) informal employment. This shows that the formal sector is not able to absorb the increase in the labour force and the outflow of labour from the agricultural sector. The share of formal manufacturing employment in total formal employment increased over the seven years from 13.0 per cent to only 13.7 per cent. We may note, however, that the number of manufacturing workers in the informal sector is several times larger than the number of people in formal jobs. Still, to get some indication

Table 10.1 Economic indicators 2000–07

	2000	2001	2002	2003	2004	2005	2006	2007
GDP growth (at constant 2001 prices) (%)	0.5	4.5	0.5	2.9	5.1	5.8	6.4	7.0
Gross fixed capital formation share of GDP (%)	16.8	18.2	17.4	15.8	16.3	18.7	19.1	19.5
Manufacturing growth (%)	1.0	1.6	0.1	6.0	4.5	4.7	6.3	6.2
Manufacturing share of GDP (%) (current prices)	10.1	9.9	9.7	9.7	10.9	10.5	10.3	9.7
Wage employment formal ('000)	1,678.4	1,677.1	1,699.7	1,727.3	1,763.7	1,808.7	1,859.7	1,907.3
Informal employment ('000)	4,150.9	4,624.4	5,086.4	5,717.4	6,168.2	6,628.3	7,048.7	7,475.6
Manufacturing quantum index	281.4	283.6	287	290.6	310	334.1	353.5	381.5
Manufacturing employment ('000)	218.7	216.6	229.7	239.7	242	248.7	254.9	261.3
Index manufacturing output/empl. (year 2000=1)	1	1.018	0.971	0.928	1.057	1.0487	1.032	1.053

Sources: Economic Survey (Kenya, 2003, 2008), Statistical Abstract (Kenya, 2003, 2008), Central Bank of Kenya Annual Report (2008), Central Bureau of Statistics homepage. Kenya National Bureau of Statistics, 2008.

of the development of labour productivity in manufacturing, we compute a measure of output (the quantum index) per formal sector employment (Table 10.1). These estimates suggest that the productivity increased by only 5.3 per cent over the period. This is an extremely modest level compared with emerging Asian markets, but it is also poor compared with South Africa, which had a labour productivity growth of 4 per cent per year between 1988 and 2003 (Harding and Rattsö, 2009).

The growth of the subsectors in manufacturing since 2003 is shown in Appendix Table 10.A1. For the textiles and clothing sectors, AGOA meant that there was a rapid expansion in exports to the USA, but there was a concern that the preference obtained would be eroded with the abolition of the Multi-Fiber Agreement in 2004. It is noteworthy that at least clothing production has continued to increase after 2004, so the concerns for the case of Kenya seem to have been exaggerated.

Investment peaked at 25.1 per cent of GDP in 1978, but then followed a long period of lower investment. Bigsten and Durevall (2008) have measured the availability of three factors of production in Kenya between 1980 and 2000, and show that over this period capital investments in Kenya were not large enough even to maintain the capital–labour ratio. It was thus even harder at the end of the period to achieve a shift out of labour-intensive sectors (including informal manufacturing) towards more capital-intensive formal manufacturing. This also explains why the labour that has been pushed from the land has had to be absorbed by the low-capital informal sector. There was a recovery from 2003 onwards, making the investment rate go up to close to 20 per cent of GDP in 2007. Still, by international standards, Kenya is not a high-investment economy. The growth in investment in recent years has been strong in transport equipment and machinery and equipment, which seems to indicate increased investment in manufacturing as well.

The government has the ambition to try to attract more foreign direct investment (FDI), but so far it has not been very successful. There was a huge increase in FDI in 2007 with inward FDI equivalent to 13.1 per cent of GDP, whereas the normal inflow before that was less than 1 per cent of GDP. The big increase was mainly due to a telecom privatization and investments in railways (UNCTAD, 2008), whereas not much has happened in terms of manufacturing FDI.[5]

10.3.2 Large firms are more productive than small ones because of higher capital intensity

Using firm-level data, we can investigate how firm performance varies across firms within the manufacturing sector. Table 10.2 shows sample averages of value added per employee and capital per employee, both in natural logarithms, for 2000 and 2003.[6] To highlight the role of firm size, we distinguish between three size categories: small (10–49 employees); medium (50–99 employees); and large (100+ employees). It is clear from these data that labour productivity increases with firm size, a rather general finding for African manufacturing (see e.g. Lundvall, 1999, for evidence on Kenya 1992–94; Söderbom and Teal, 2004, for evidence on Ghana). One frequently cited reason for this result is that large firms are much more capital intensive than small firms, so that each worker in a large firm has access to more machinery than do workers in small firms. The data in Table 10.2 are clearly consistent with this explanation. The figures for 2002, for instance, imply that the capital–labour ratio among large firms is about 80 per cent higher than among small ones.[7] Investing in equipment is therefore crucial in increasing the productivity of labour. Further statistical analysis of the firm-level data indicates that returns to scale in the sector are either constant or mildly increasing.[8] Productivity tends to be higher in Nairobi than in other areas, and in the food sector compared with other manufacturing subsectors. Other firm characteristics, such as foreign ownership and firm age, are not typically associated with large productivity differences.

Table 10.2 Firm size, labour productivity, and capital intensity

	log Value added per employee		log Physical capital per employee	
	2003	2000	2003	2000
Small: 10–49 employees	8.13 [49]	8.12 [56]	8.94 [49]	8.97 [56]
Medium: 50–99 employees	8.58 [27]	8.62 [22]	9.20 [27]	9.58 [22]
Large: 100+ employees	8.90 [60]	8.79 [53]	9.54 [60]	9.90 [53]
All categories	8.56 [136]	8.47 [131]	9.26 [136]	9.45 [131]

The table reports sample means of log value added per employee and log physical capital per employee. The figures in square brackets show the numbers of observations.
Source: Authors' calculations based on firm-level survey data.

10.3.3 Which types of firms invest in new machinery and technology?

Firm-level data reveal big differences in investment patterns across firms. Table 10.3 is based on data collected in 2007 as part of the World Bank's Investment Climate Analysis (World Bank, 2007b). Table 10.3 shows mean values of a range of firm-level characteristics, distinguishing between firms that have made at least some new investment in the last year and firms that have not (column 1), and between firms that have recently introduced new technology and those that have not. It is clear that exporting, having International Standards Organization (ISO) certification, and being part of a global production network are much more common activities among investing firms. These numbers indicate a strong positive association between operating in the international market and investing. We see exactly the same pattern when we look at the introduction of new technology. Unsurprisingly, the more dynamic class of firms (with more investment, exports, and international operations) tends to contain larger enterprises than the comparison group. More surprisingly, however, there is no evidence that firms with foreign ownership invest or innovate more than domestically owned firms.

10.3.4 Kenya and the world economy

Kenya's share of world exports had fallen from 0.085 per cent in 1980 to 0.035 per cent by the year 2000; thus Kenya became increasingly marginalized in the world market during this period (Table 10.4). Over the same period, its share of world GDP fell at a slightly slower rate from 0.066 per cent to 0.040 per cent. However, Kenya's share of world exports has increased since 2000, as has its share in the world export of manufactures. In fact, export of goods and services was the fastest growing component of final demand during 2001–05. The World Bank (2007b: 12) finds that Kenya gained in competitive-

Table 10.3 How investors and non-investors differ

	1. Bought fixed asset?		2. Introduced new technology?	
	No	Yes	No	Yes
Proportion exporters	0.31	0.39	0.32	0.45
Proportion with ISO certificate	0.05	0.15	0.08	0.28
Proportion part of global production network	0.05	0.10	0.03	0.12
log Employees	2.27	2.54	3.49	4.35
Employees	25.62	50.48	65.81	183.95
Firm age (years)	12.85	19.99	23.90	22.45
Proportion of foreign ownership	0.06	0.06	0.18	0.17
Nairobi	0.51	0.62	0.76	0.82
Mombasa	0.21	0.22	0.10	0.12
Kisumu	0.12	0.09	0.02	0.05
Nakuru	0.16	0.07	0.11	0.01
Observations	171	225	171	225

Source: Authors' calculations based on firm-level survey data.

ness between 2002 and 2005. Although there has been some diversification in terms of export destinations, there has not been any significant diversification of Kenyan exports in terms of products.

Although Kenya has been quite successful in terms of increasing its export of textiles and clothing in the last decade, agricultural commodities still dominate Kenyan exports overall. The government is seeking to support the diversification of exports into labour-intensive manufacturing through its National Export Strategy initiated in 2004. There are also attempts to develop the EAC and to increase trade within the region. Kenya's regional export of manufactured goods consists of rather simple products, where its comparative

Table 10.4 Percentage shares of Kenya in world trade and of exports in GDP

	2000	2001	2002	2003	2004	2005	2006
Export share of GDP (%)	26.55	26.54	23.87	23.87	26.40	27.95	27.20
Share of Kenya in world exports of goods and services (current US$) (%)	0.034	0.039	0.040	0.038	0.037	0.041	0.040
Share of Kenya in world GDP (current US$) (%)	0.040	0.041	0.040	0.041	0.039	0.043	0.047
Share of Kenya in world export of manufactures (%)	0.023	0.023	0.023	0.023	0.023	0.026	

Source: Central Bank of Kenya Annual Report (2008), Economic Survey (2003), World Bank (2008).

advantage is mainly that it is an international communications hub with better transport and communications networks than its partners.

10.3.5 Why further expansion of manufactured exports may be challenging

The main constraints to trade expansion in Kenya identified by the World Bank (2007a: xii) are 'Kenya's commercial and investment climate, i.e. the cost of doing business, the weakness of the legal framework, licensing, complex rules and regulations for exports, and the poor quality and high cost of business services in Kenya'. It is also noted that the state of infrastructure and utility services hampers exports, e.g. the high costs of telecommunications services, power, transport, plus poor trade logistics and standard compliance. The inefficiency of the Port of Mombasa, including the slow pace of customs clearance, is a problem. The government has initiated a Private Sector Development Strategy, an Investment Climate Action Plan, and a Regulatory Reform to deal with these challenges. The last has led to the removal of many licences that were found to be unnecessary and inefficient.

Much of the growth in world trade in recent years has been in the form of international production sharing, but here Kenya and most of Africa are lagging behind. There has been some expansion of this type of trade between Kenya and South Africa, however. Kenya has recently become Africa's third largest importer of components, so there are signs of improvement in this area (World Bank, 2007a: 22). We may also note that Kenya's export of machinery and transport equipment had increased to 4.5 per cent of its exports by 2007 (UN, 2008), more than doubling its share in four years. Still, Kenya's export profile continues to be concentrated on commodities and raw materials, and it is thus not yet developing along lines similar to those of the emerging economies in Asia. Kenya still has a low level of intra-industry trade, which means that the country is not yet well integrated into outsourcing operations. We note that the escalating tariffs in Kenya – favouring vertical integration rather than outsourcing – are likely to be counterproductive if the country wants to move towards participation in the new international division of tasks.

One reason why it is hard for Kenyan firms to become reliable suppliers of inputs in international production chains is that the domestic supply chains are inefficient and uncertain. This manifests itself for example in the sizeable inventories held by Kenyan firms. On average, manufacturing enterprises hold 47 days of production of their most important inputs in stock (World Bank, 2007b: 46). The time to clear customs has gone down significantly in recent years, but the 12 days it now takes on average is still high by international standards. This is not only a time cost, but predictability is also a concern. If firms are to be able to be part of a supply chain, where timely deliveries are crucial, they must know how fast they can receive inputs and deliver outputs.

10.3.6 The labour market: informal employment continues to grow

Total employment has increased fast, but most of it has been in the informal sector (Table 10.1). Formal employment has only increased slowly. The lion's share of the manufacturing workforce is in the informal sector. There are some drawbacks to being an informal producer, e.g. getting access to finance and land can be difficult. On the other hand, it reduces the burden of taxation, inspections, and licensing. Obviously, many entrepreneurs feel that on balance the benefits of informality outweigh the costs.

Real wages began to increase in the mid-1990s and their increase continued longer in the private than in the public sector (Table 10.5). We note that manufacturing real wages peaked in 2005 and then declined, and we also note that they are substantially lower than in the whole of the private (and public) sector.[9] This may suggest that manufacturing labour is relatively cheap in Kenya, but we must note that we are not controlling for skill composition here. Still, there are estimates of unskilled labour costs that have been found to be relatively low in Kenya compared with China for example. However, the World Bank (2007a: 4) believes that the costs of unskilled labour in Kenya are not matched by labour productivity to make Kenyan firms competitive with those in Asia. Interestingly, few firms in Kenya report that they are concerned with access to skills. Only 8.9 per cent are concerned in Kenya, compared with 30.7 per cent in China and 35.5 per cent in South Africa for example (World Bank, 2007b: 78). This could be due to good access to high-quality labour, but it could also be because the firms have chosen to adjust their input mix of product choice away from activities requiring high-skilled labour. In any case, the main constraints on competitiveness in Kenya appear to be related to transaction costs rather than to lack of skills.

10.3.7 Transaction costs and constraints on business

The indirect costs of doing business in Kenya have been reduced in the last few years, but they are still in the range of 13–20 per cent of total sales, which

Table 10.5 Real average wage earnings per employee (2003–07) (thousands of Ksh per annum)

	2003	2004	2005	2006	2007
Manufacturing	83.5	90.2	90.5	89.3	86.0
Private sector	159.7	177.7	186.7	191.3	190.2
Public sector	144.2	154.4	149.1	145.7	143.3

Source: Economic Survey (2008: 75).

is quite high. The level of indirect costs computed for Kenya in 2006 was 20.1 per cent of sales, which can be compared with those of China at 6.2 per cent and South Africa at 3.6 per cent. Kenya's costs are higher than those of neighbouring Tanzania and Uganda (World Bank, 2007b: Table 2.6). In Kenya, this was made up of 7.1 per cent for electricity,[10] 3.6 per cent for bribes, 2.6 per cent for production lost in transit, 3.9 per cent for theft or arson, and, finally, 2.9 per cent for security costs. The World Bank (2007a: 32) further notes that 'as a result of dilapidated infrastructure and complicated procedures, especially at Mombasa port, trade facilitation indicators for Kenya are poor'. The country was also ranked as the least logistically friendly of seventy countries in the 2004 Logistics Perception Survey (World Bank, 2007a: 33). Air logistics are good, however, and the road transport and forwarding industries are among the best organized in Africa (World Bank, 2007a: 36). In face-to-face interviews with entrepreneurs and company owners, tax rates, access to finance, and corruption are rated as the top three problems.

TAXES

Firms in Kenya pay more than half of their corporate income in taxes, with a profit tax rate of 32.5 per cent. Taxes have been reduced in recent years, but it is still estimated that firms in Kenya are required to pay 50.9 per cent of corporate income in taxes (World Bank, 2007b: 32). This is high by international standards. Despite the fact that the number of tax payments has been reduced in recent years, firms feel they pay a lot and describe the procedures involved as cumbersome and time consuming. On the positive side, they find that VAT refunds function fairly smoothly.

FINANCE

Costly and inaccessible external financing is often argued to be a key constraint on the growth and competitiveness of enterprises in developing countries. The Africa Competitiveness Report 2007 (World Economic Forum, 2007), for example, argues that access to finance remains a 'critical constraint', and that 'improvements in the regulatory environment [. . .] represent a necessary step for unleashing the potential impact of finance on firm competitiveness in Africa' (World Economic Forum, 2007: xi). Indeed, data based on interviews with entrepreneurs, senior managers, and chief executive officers in African companies suggest that finance is a severe and widespread constraint: across all thirty-four African countries surveyed, 50 per cent of the respondents indicate that finance is a 'major or very severe' constraint and, in Kenya, more than 70 per cent said so (World Economic Forum, 2007).

In recent years, the lending regime in Kenya has improved, resulting in lower direct costs of credit and many firms having good information available. This is reflected in the survey data, which indicate that the proportion of firms feeling financially constrained has fallen recently. Still, many firms still rate finance as a serious obstacle, and firm size remains an important determinant of access to finance. Small firms in particular have a hard time accessing credit for start-up and expansion. Of microenterprises, only 31 per cent of loans obtained were from private commercial banks, whereas the corresponding number for the remaining firms was 82 per cent. Still, Kenyan firms finance about 51 per cent of working capital and 59 per cent of new investment with retained earnings.

Using the Kenyan survey data collected by the World Bank (2007b), we can assess whether there is any evidence that investment is lower among firms that operate in environments where credit appears to be particularly problematic. We begin by estimating the proportion of firms belonging to a certain sector, size group, and location, for which a given constraint is 'very severe'. We then investigate how this variable – referred to as quality of finance – correlates with observed average investment across locations, size groups, and sectors. Figure 10.2 illustrates the relationship between average investment in different sector–size–location cells (on the vertical axis) and our quality of finance variable (on the horizontal axis). There is a very clear negative relationship between sector–size–location investment and access to finance in the data: sector–size–location cells with a relatively *high* proportion of firms indicating that financing is a very severe obstacle, have a relatively *low* proportion of firms recording positive investments.

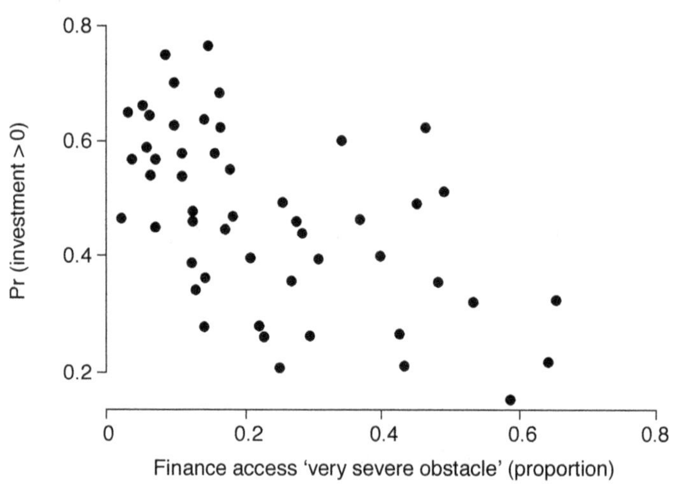

Figure 10.2 Investment and access to finance
The data were collected as part of the World Bank's Investment Climate Survey in Kenya in 2007. Each data point in the graph represents an average across firms in a particular location, size category, and manufacturing industry. The vertical axis shows the proportion of firms with positive investments. The horizontal axis shows the proportion of firms in a particular location–size–sector cell that rate finance access as a 'very severe obstacle'.

CORRUPTION

Corruption remains a fact of life in Kenyan manufacturing. The survey data collected by the World Bank (2007b) indicate that about 75 per cent of firms have made informal payments to 'get things done'. A similar survey in 2003 reported that manufacturing firms spent 7.5 per cent of the total value of their annual sales on unofficial payments. Those who succeeded in getting government contracts paid 14.2 per cent of the contract value as kickbacks. Licences and utilities were all subject to these unofficial payments. In total, these firms lost more than 14 per cent of their total annual sales to corruption, theft, and arson. See Kimuyu (2007) for further details.

REGULATION AND RED TAPE

In an effort to cut red tape, a process of reform of the licensing system was started in 2006. As a result, the number of licences has fallen. Although this has started to reduce the burden of licensing, corruption in obtaining licences is still high in Kenya and partly accounts for the continued existence of some of the unnecessary licences. Kenya is now the best performer among the countries that the World Bank (2007b: 59) compares, in terms of the number of procedures, time, and cost to deal with new licences. Still, even if Kenya has seen some improvements, much remains to be done to make the environment attractive for investors. We may also note that several new tariffs have been introduced recently, and some existing ones have been increased, whereas others have been reduced (Kenya, 2008a: 24). Tariff policy is clearly still used selectively to support specific industries.

10.4 Policy lessons

The world economy has become more and more integrated, and many developing countries have been able to benefit from this and break into the export market. So far, outsourcing has largely bypassed Kenya, however. Kenya has certainly liberalized its foreign trade regime, but the export response as far as manufacturing is concerned has been limited (there has been some success with regard to, for example, horticulture and flowers). Still, it is hard to know what the counterfactual scenarios would have been without liberalization. Maybe the reforms at least set in motion a process of restructuring, preparing the ground for future export expansion. The slow growth of the sector may hide the replacement of firms set up behind high tariff walls by firms that are viable in an open environment. As there is evidence that there are learning externalities in African manufacturing (Bigsten *et al.*, 2004), it is particularly important that this sector grows.

To break into export markets, Kenyan firms can benefit from market advantages provided by richer countries. For example, AGOA has provided one form of advantage that has been very beneficial for Kenyan apparel production. Trade agreements with the EU have not been as effective as presumed, because it has tough and complicated rules of origin. The EU had the idea that one should seek to stimulate the production of complete products, but the situation has changed in recent decades. Competition in international markets is less and less in terms of products and more and more in terms of tasks. Therefore, the rules of origin become particularly critical. It is important that this is taken into account in the (slow) ongoing negotiations about an EPA with the EU.

To speed up growth in Kenya's manufacturing sector, substantive investment is required. Why has investment been so low in Kenya for so long? Insufficient credit may be part of the story (especially for small firms), but is, we think, unlikely to be the whole answer. Evidence based on survey data, for example, indicates that the share of profits invested is very low in African manufacturing firms (Bigsten *et al.*, 1999). If external financing is so expensive, why then do the firms not invest more once they have access to internal capital? Another possible explanation is the comparative advantage story, suggesting that Kenya is a resource-abundant country that does not have its natural comparative advantage in manufacturing. There may be some validity in this argument, and the expansion of horticultural and flower exports is consistent with this. But comparative advantages are not given once and for all. Leamer (1987) argues that countries change their pattern of specialization as their factor abundance changes. The normal pattern identified by this author is one of capital deepening, which leads to a change in the product mix towards more capital-intensive goods. So Kenya should be able to shift towards manufacturing if it manages to have high enough investments.

So again, a key question is why investors (domestic and foreign) do not invest in Kenya to any large extent. We think it is fair to say that the explanation is essentially internal. Export markets for Kenyan manufacturing are quite open, even if there are technical issues with regard to the import content of products and the like. Still, we think that the main limitations are, first, the perception of the environment for investors as risky and, second, the rather high costs (relative to productivity) of doing business in Kenya. One explanation as to why manufacturing investment has not been forthcoming is that much foreign investment and international trade is now related to outsourcing and, when that is the case, timely delivery is absolutely essential. This is an issue in Kenya. The modern system requires goods to arrive when they are needed as an input in a product or as goods to go into a marketing campaign that starts on a certain date. If African countries cannot set up their systems so that this is possible, they will have a hard job to capture a large share of the modern production structure. To get into international value chains, firms in Kenya need to be able to meet international standards. Programmes to strengthen competence in this area would seem important.

It should also be possible to design policies that would enable Kenyan firms to take better advantage of externalities. Bigsten *et al.* (2008) report empirical results suggesting that agglomeration economies matter for manufacturing in the case of Ethiopia. Locating close to other firms tends to have a positive effect on productivity and competitiveness. Similar mechanisms may hold for Kenya (although we are not aware of any empirical work on this). This may suggest that, for example, export processing zones (EPZs) can have a positive effect. For EPZs to work well, however, they need good management, good infrastructure, and efficient supporting institutions. Kenya has pursued an EPZ policy to cluster firms and to make export production easier. It has established forty-three EPZs but, as they only contain about seventy-two firms, there are only 1.5 firms per cluster on average. And this is hardly enough to create cluster economies. Location policy may matter as we suggested. The building of modern industrial areas may make sense, for example.

Overall, Kenya needs to address both cost and risk issues if it is to become an attractive arena for international investors in manufacturing. It seems reasonable to hypothesize that money is available if the country can offer stability, good institutions, as well as an efficient and cheap export infrastructure. One may ask whether manufacturing production should receive extra subsidies. It seems reasonable at least to argue that it would make sense to provide extra support for attempts to break into the export markets, as there is evidence that firms improve productivity and competitiveness as a result of exporting ('learning-by-exporting'; Bigsten *et al.*, 2004). In the medium and long term, it may also make sense to support the supply of technical and other relevant skills (inducing R&D) in specific areas. This could be done within firms or in external institutions. Whether Africa will manage to break into the world markets will ultimately depend on the cost–productivity trade-off. As costs go up in Asia, Africa may become a relatively more attractive location for investors, if it can keep costs under control.

Appendix

Appendix Table 10.A1 Quantum index of manufacturing production (1976=100)

Industry	2003	2004	2005	2006	2007
Meat and dairy products	89.8	104.8	118.7	125.3	153.4
Canned vegetables, fruits, fish, oils, and fats	405.3	466.7	469.2	556	680.5
Grain mills products	177.7	193.3	231.2	253.6	246.9
Bakery products	284.3	185.1	202.6	212.8	204.6
Sugar and confectionery	218.9	250.9	237.7	232.4	251.3

Appendix Table 10.A1 (cont.)

Industry	2003	2004	2005	2006	2007
Miscellaneous foods	250.8	269.1	271.1	257.6	295.4
Food manufacturing	211.1	233.5	235.6	239	268.9
Beverages	176	200.6	232.6	259.5	314.7
Tobacco	126.7	142.6	195.2	273.5	324.8
Beverages and tobacco	170.3	193.8	229.2	263.8	319
Textiles	106	89.3	97.1	102.3	104.1
Clothing	188.1	187.3	269.4	379.1	396.6
Leather and footwear	80.4	75.2	116.6	124.4	124.1
Wood and cork products	51.2	40.5	39.2	39.2	39.5
Furniture and fixtures	55.1	56.9	57.6	58.1	58.7
Paper and paper products	362.7	336.3	427.5	414.2	403.4
Printing and publishing	428	422.4	419.8	286.8	295.1
Basic industrial chemicals	145.8	150.1	123.1	108.8	78.2
Petroleum and other chemicals	865.7	982.7	947.6	1027	1237.3
Rubber products	712.8	707.3	760.3	682.3	895.3
Plastic products	969.3	972.9	1,270.5	1,656.3	1,674.8
Clay and glass products	1,142.7	1,172.9	1,472.8	1,836.1	1,791.9
Non-metallic mineral products	190	166.9	187.5	222.2	237
Metallic products	238.2	246.8	257.9	282.1	314.5
Non-electrical machinery	87.1	87.1	87.9	90	83
Electrical equipment	216.8	259	268.8	245.5	180.2
Transport equipment	483.5	1,109.6	975.7	1,281.7	1,309.9
Miscellaneous manufactures	1,148.2	1,052	1,058.6	1,442.6	1,412.7
Total manufacturing	**290.6**	**310**	**334.1**	**353.5**	**381.5**

Source: Economic Survey 2008 (Kenya, 2008b).

Notes

1 Rodrik (2007) notes that successful countries have prioritized economic growth, followed market-friendly policies, and maintained economic stability, but the way in which these general principles are put into practice can vary and needs to be context specific.
2 Measures were taken to reduce import duties on raw materials and capital equipment in order to lower production costs and enhance competitiveness.
3 The establishment of a commission to investigate and report on the Goldenberg scandal to pave the way for prosecution and recovery of public funds was also part of the raft of proposals for dealing with governance challenges.
4 Survey data on Kenyan manufacturers indicate that entrepreneurs have a hard time dealing efficiently with business disputes. There is little reliance on more formal dispute resolution avenues such as lawyers and courts of law. Court cases are pro-

tracted and outcomes are uncertain even when the evidence is compelling. As a result, when faced with business disputes, most manufacturers use either negotiators or arbitrators.

5 The FDI inward stock in 2007 stood at US$1,892 million, up from US$668 million in 1990 and US$931 million in 2000.

6 Value added is defined as the value of output minus the value of inputs excluding labour and capital. All financial variables are expressed in constant US$ 2002.

7 Calculation: exp(9.54–8.94)–1=0.82.

8 This result is obtained by estimating a production function using ordinary least squares.

9 Real wages in agriculture and mining are lower than those in manufacturing, but wages in utilities and services are much higher.

10 Kenya's electricity prices are among the highest in the region (World Bank, 2007a: 46). Estimates of productivity determinants show that electricity losses have the largest impact (World Bank, 2007b: 101).

References

Bigsten, A., 2001, 'History and Policy of Manufacturing in Kenya', in Bigsten, A. and P. Kimuyu (eds) *Structure and Performance of Manufacturing in Kenya*. London: Palgrave.

Bigsten, A. and D. Durevall, 2008, 'Factor Proportions, Openness and Factor Prices in Kenya, 1965–2000', *Journal of Development Studies*, 44 (2), 289–310.

Bigsten, A., P. Collier, S. Dercon, B. Gauthier, J. W. Gunning, A. Isaksson, A. Oduro, R. Oostendorp, C. Pattillo, M. Söderbom, M. Sylvain, F. Teal and A. Zeufack, 1999, 'Investment in Africa's Manufacturing Sector: a Four Country Panel Data Analysis', *Oxford Bulletin of Economics and Statistics*, 61 (4), 489–512.

Bigsten, A., P. Collier, S. Dercon, M. Fafchamps, B. Gauthier, J. W. Gunning, A. Oduro, R. Oostendorp, C. Pattillo, M. Söderbom, F. Teal and A. Zeufack, 2004, 'Do African Manufacturing Firms Learn from Exporting? ', *Journal of Development Studies*, 40 (3), 115–171.

Bigsten, A., M. Gebreeyesus and M. Söderbom, 2008, 'Agglomeration Effects in Ethiopian Manufacturing', mimeo, University of Gothenburg.

Bond, S., N. Bloom and J. Van Reenen, 2007, 'Uncertainty and Investment Dynamics', *Review of Economic Studies*, 74, 391–415.

Central Bank of Kenya, 2008, *Annual Report 2008*. Nairobi: Central Bank.

Collier, P., 2000, 'Africa's Comparative Advantage', in Jalilian, H., M. Tribe and J. Weiss (eds) *Industrial Development and Policy in Africa*. Cheltenham, UK: Edward Elgar.

Collier, P. and A. Venables, 2007, 'Rethinking Trade Preferences: How Africa Can Diversify its Exports', *World Economy*, 30 (8), 1326–1345.

Commission on Growth and Development, 2008, *The Growth Report: Strategies for Sustained Growth and Inclusive Development*. Washington, DC: The World Bank.

Dixit, A. K. and R. S. Pindyck, 1994, *Investment under Uncertainty*. Princeton, NJ: Princeton University Press.

Dollar, D., M. Hallward-Driemeier and T. Mengistae, 2005, 'Investment Climate and Firm Performance in Developing Countries', *Economic Development and Cultural Change*, 54 (1), 1–31.

Frazer, G. and J. Van Biesebroeck, 2010, 'Trade Growth under the African Growth and Opportunity Act', *Review of Economics and Statistics*, forthcoming.

Harding, T. and J. Rattsö, 2009, 'Industrial Labor Productivities and Tariffs in South Africa: Identification based on Multilateral Liberalization Reform", Discussion paper No. 585, Research Department, Statistics Norway.

Keller, W., 2002, 'Geographic Localization of International Technology Diffusion', *American Economic Review*, 92 (1), 120–142.

Kenya, annual, *Economic Survey*. Nairobi.

Kenya, annual, *Statistical Abstract*. Nairobi.

Kenya, 2001, *Poverty Reduction Strategy Paper for the Period 2001–2004*. Nairobi.

Kenya, 2003, *Economic Recovery Strategy for Wealth Creation and Employment 2003–2007*. Nairobi.

Kenya, 2007, *Kenya Vision 2030: A Globally Competitive and Prosperous Kenya*. Nairobi: Government of Kenya, Ministry of Planning and National Development, the National Economic and Social Council and the Office of the President.

Kenya, 2008a, *Budget Speech for the Fiscal Year 2008/2009*. Nairobi.

Kenya, 2008b, *The Medium Term Budget Strategy Paper 2008/09–2010/11*. Nairobi.

Kenya National Bureau of Statistics, 2008, *Gross Domestic Product 2nd Quarter 2008*. Nairobi: National Bureau of Statistics.

Kimuyu, P., 2007, 'Corruption, Firm Growth and Export Propensity in Kenya', *International Journal of Social Economics*, 34 (3&4), 197–217

Leamer, E. E., 1987, 'Paths of Development in the Three Factor n-Good General Equilibrium Model', *Journal of Political Economy*, 95 (5), 961–999.

Lundvall, K., 1999, 'Essays on Manufacturing Production in a Developing Economy: Kenya 1992–94'. PhD Thesis, University of Gothenburg.

Rodrik, D., 2007, *One Economics, Many Recipes*. Princeton, NJ: Princeton University Press.

Söderbom, M., and F. Teal, 2004, 'Size and Efficiency in African Manufacturing Firms: Evidence from Firm-Level Panel Data', *Journal of Development Economics*, 73, 369–394.

UN, 2008, *COMTRADE database 2008*.

UNCTAD, 2008, *World Investment Report 2008*. Geneva: UNCTAD.

World Bank, 2004, *World Development Report 2005: A Better Investment Climate for Everyone*. Washington, DC: The World Bank.

World Bank, 2007a, *Kenya: Unleashing the Potential for Trade and Growth*. Washington, DC: The World Bank.

World Bank, 2007b, *Kenya: Investment Climate Assessment*, draft. Washington, DC: The World Bank.

World Bank, 2008, *World Development Indicators*, CD-ROM. Washington, DC: The World Bank.

World Economic Forum, 2007, *Africa Competitiveness Report 2007*. Geneva: World Economic Forum.

11

Kenyan Labour Market Challenges

Arne Bigsten and Anthony Wambugu

11.1 Introduction

Classical analyses in development economics have focused on structural change, and the presumption has been that there will be a gradual shift of labour from the traditional agricultural sector to the modern sector (Lewis, 1954; Harris and Todaro, 1970). The development in Kenya in recent decades has not worked as expected, however. There has been a shift of labour out of agriculture but into the non-agricultural informal sector rather than the formal sector.

To capture the essential elements of this process of structural change and its employment implications, we take a three-factor model based on Leamer (1987) as our starting point. The model provides an analytical framework for the analysis of development paths, that is an analysis of the impact of the accumulation of factors and changes in policy on factor returns and allocation. We present the main features of the model in Section 11.2. Section 11.3 presents data on changes in Kenya's factor endowments 1950–2000. Section 11.4 discusses changes in the Kenyan labour markets, while Section 11.5 looks at Kenya's labour market policies. Section 11.6 presents our policy conclusions.

11.2 Paths of development

All capital-poor countries have started from a similar pattern of specialization and low wages. To understand how the pattern of employment has developed in Kenya, we need a model that explains the change in the pattern of specialization in production. Leamer (1987) proposes a three-factor model, which allows for a richer menu of development paths than simple two-sector models. If the three factors are labour (L), capital (K), and land (T), the impact of capital accumulation on employment structure and wages (and other factor rewards) depends on what happens to both labour abundance and land abundance.

In the model, one can enter different sectors of production, with varying production characteristics. The factor use of those sectors depends on production technology used for the various goods. The economy will move between patterns of specialization as factor abundance changes. In the case of Kenya, we may broadly divide the economy into four sectors. The non-agricultural part of the economy, where we assume that only capital and labour are used, consists of a less capital-intensive or informal sector and a more capital-intensive or formal sector. Then we distinguish between two agricultural sectors, a smallholder sector using only land and labour, and a modern agricultural sector using all three factors. The pattern of production that actually materializes will be determined by the relative availability of factors of production in Kenya. When factor endowments change, the pattern of specialization will change, as will the factor price structure. Both production structures and the pattern of factor prices will change in a systematic fashion as the endowment vector and the goods price structure change.

First, we may consider what changes in factor endowments do to the production structure. When capital is accumulated (other factors given), capital-intensive goods will increase their share of production. An increase in labour supply instead leads to a more labour-intensive mix of products. The amount of arable land has changed very little in Kenya, which means that land is getting increasingly scarce relative to the other two factors. A move towards a more capital-intensive mix of production will (in a setting with equilibrium wages and rentals at least) lead to higher wages (and higher land rentals). Thus, an increase in K/L will in the long run yield sustainable increases in wages, whereas on the other hand, premature increases in wages will delay the process of structural transformation and the transfer of labour to better paying jobs.

Our second concern is to understand how changes in the character of the relationship with the world market affect factor rewards and the economic structure. The link to the world market comes via the goods prices. These can change autonomously, or the government can intervene with trade policies to change the domestic price structure. The development pattern that Leamer considers to be 'normal' is one where countries climb the ladder of development, and by this he basically means an increase in capital relative to labour (and land). For an economy that starts from a labour-abundant point, this would generally lead to higher wages and lower capital rentals, and a shift in the pattern of specialization towards a more capital-intensive mix of goods. Should the government seek to change domestic relative prices or let them be determined from the foreign market? By having high tariffs on manufacturing imports, the government has changed domestic relative prices in a way that has helped manufacturing at the expense of the rest of the economy. There may be good reasons to support a sector if it has positive external effects, but there is ample evidence that import substitution policies have not worked well in Africa. It would be better to use more direct ways (with fewer negative side-effects) to support industry.

A third force that may change the economic structure is technical progress. The effects depend on the character of the technical progress, that is the extent to which it saves or uses labour, land, and capital, and it also matters in which sector it occurs. If technological change is labour augmenting, it can help to increase wages and to some extent compensate for a slow rate of capital accumulation. Generally, technical progress naturally contributes to overall gross domestic product (GDP) growth.

Fourth, Leamer's model does not explicitly allow for factor market distortions, but the structure of factor prices could of course also be affected by the integration of the domestic factor markets with the international factor markets. This could be particularly relevant for the capital market, although Wood (1994) argues that global capital markets throughout the world are so integrated that capital abundance is no longer a basis for comparative advantage. We do not think that this is the case for Kenya as yet, although there certainly has been a movement towards closer integration with the world markets in recent years. The wages in Kenya are of course not determined in a perfect market. Different segments of the labour market are not fully integrated. For example, there are barriers to mobility between the informal and the formal labour markets, which implies that labour with similar skills will be paid differently in the two markets. Within the formal market, there exist minimum wage legislation and trade union contracts that may generate wages that are different from equilibrium wages. As they generally are above equilibrium, they will hold back production and employment growth in the formal sector.

We may thus distinguish four different types of determinants of changes in the production structure. These are, first, changes in the factor endowment of the economy. The key to growth in better paid formal sector jobs is capital deepening, which will occur if there is a higher rate of investment. We would argue that this factor is the most important one for a government to focus on if it wants to see substantial modern sector growth. Second, there are the effects that come from changes in goods prices. These are largely exogenous. Government interventions to push up prices of import-competing manufacturing goods have not had the predicted positive impact so the move towards less draconian protection should be continued. Third, there are the effects of technical progress. Such effects are very important for growth and make it possible for the economy to pay higher factor rewards, e.g. wages. Finally, there may be changes in the level of distortions. Some of these are hard for the government to change in the short run, and it should be careful not to use interventions that push factor costs too high. Interventions that compensate for externalities are of course not distorting, but they need to be carefully thought out before being put in place. Implementation of detailed interventions is problematic in environments where there is an abundance of rent seeking. Thus, high-quality governance is also a key factor in this area.

11.3 Changes in factor endowments

We argue that factor abundance is a crucial determinant of the pattern of specialization and factor prices, although market distortions may make factor prices diverge from the equlibrium values. Bigsten and Durevall (2008) have constructed estimates of factor availability for the period 1964–2000, and used these to compute the endowment ratios shown in Figure 11.1. The K/L ratio is very important for the pattern of specialization and the factor price outcomes. We see that the ratio increased until around 1980, but that the trend was then reversed. As expected, the capital–land ratio grows during most of the period, whereas the land–labour ratio declines continuously.

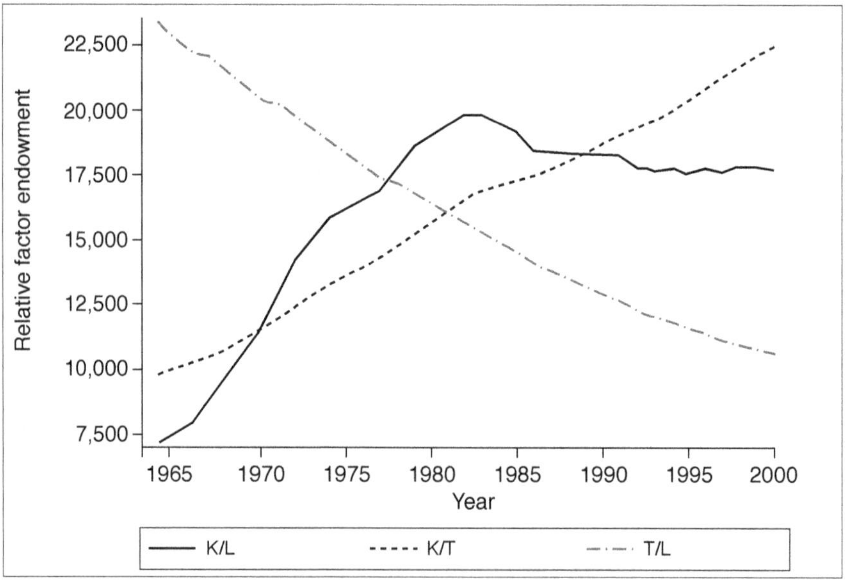

Figure 11.1 Relative factor endowments in Kenya, 1964–2000.
The variables have been mean and variance adjusted to increase the readability of the graph.
Source: Bigsten and Durevall (2008).

The most noteworthy development is thus that labour force growth has outpaced the growth of capital from the 1980s onwards. The development path with an increasing capital–labour ratio that was the essence of Leamer's analysis was reversed. This is a serious indication of the failure of Kenya to move towards sustainable growth. And it also has great implications for how the reallocation of labour in the economy evolves. The labour pressure on land in agriculture increases, continuously pushing labour off the land. This labour could be absorbed by captial-intensive agriculture or capital-intensive (formal) non-agriculture if capital had been accumulated at a sufficiently rapid rate. But as this has not happened, the labour pushed off the land has had to move into activities that use little capital, that is the informal sector and various forms of self-employment. This analysis thus implies that one would expect that labour leaving agriculture will have to be absorbed by the informal sector. We will look at the data in the following section. There we will also touch upon the impact of the other factors mentioned in the theory review, but our bottom line is that it is the changes in factor endowments that largely drive strucutural change in the Kenyan economy. For the growth pattern to change, it is particularly the rate of capital accumulation that must be faster.

11.4 Kenyan labour market trends

In this section, we examine changes in the labour force, participation rates, employment patterns, and unemployment rates, and consider whether the changes in the Kenyan labour market are consistent with the theoretical predictions.

11.4.1 Labour force

Kenya uses the International Labour Organization (ILO) definition of the labour force, and classifies the working-age population (15–64 years) into three categories: the employed, the unemployed, and those not in the labour force (individuals who are neither working nor looking for work).[1] Most of the inactive population are students. Table 11.1 is based on the two most recent large-scale labour force surveys, and it shows the key measures of labour force activity in 1998–99 and in 2005–06. In 1998–99, 12.3 million individuals were in the labour force, consisting of approximately 10.5 million employed and 1.8 million unemployed persons. By 2005–06, the labour force had expanded to over 14 million with 12.7 million employed and 1.9 million unemployed (Republic of Kenya, 2003a, 2008a). These estimates imply that the labour force grew by approximately 2.4 per cent per annum.

The increase in the labour force may be attributed to three factors: increase in the working-age population, increased labour force participation, and net

Table 11.1 Kenya's working-age population (15–64 years) by activity status, 1998–99 and 2005–06

	Employed		Unemployed		Inactive		Total	
Age (years)	1998–99	2005–06	1998–99	2005–06	1998–99	2005–06	1998–99	2005–06[a]
15–19	0.08	0.08	0.15	0.19	0.65	0.61	0.22	0.23
20–24	0.14	0.15	0.30	0.33	0.13	0.19	0.15	0.18
25–29	0.15	0.16	0.16	0.21	0.05	0.06	0.13	0.14
30–34	0.15	0.15	0.10	0.08	0.03	0.03	0.11	0.11
35–39	0.15	0.12	0.08	0.07	0.03	0.02	0.11	0.09
40–44	0.11	0.11	0.06	0.05	0.02	0.02	0.08	0.08
45–49	0.09	0.08	0.05	0.03	0.02	0.02	0.07	0.06
50–54	0.07	0.06	0.04	0.02	0.02	0.02	0.05	0.05
55–59	0.04	0.05	0.04	0.01	0.02	0.02	0.04	0.04
60–64	0.03	0.03	0.03	0.01	0.03	0.02	0.03	0.03
Total	10,525,609	12,708,035	1,800,623	1,856,294	3,599,231	5,266,112	15,925,463	19,830,441

a Totals for 2005–06 exclude about 0.2 million individuals whose activity status is reported as undetermined.
Source: Republic of Kenya (2003a, 2008a).

in-migration. While in-migration and out-migration are difficult to quantify, such flows are unlikely to be a major factor in Kenya's labour force growth. On the other hand, the working-age population (15–64 years) has grown considerably. In Table 11.1, we find the distribution of the working-age population split into three categories: employed people, unemployed people, and inactive people. First, we see that in 1998–99, the working-age population was about 16 million and rose to about 20 million in 2005–06, equal to an annual rate of growth of 3.2 per cent. Second, the data reveal that the expansion in working-age population is concentrated among persons below 30 years, with those aged 15–24 years comprising 37 per cent of the working-age population in 1998–99 and 41 per cent in 2005–06. These facts have led the government to consider policies and programmes to address the youth unemployment challenge.

11.4.2 Labour force participation

We have seen that the working-age population has increased in the recent past. However, only a proportion of these are actively involved in the labour force. The percentage of the working-age population in the labour force is known as the labour force participation rate. These figures are reported in Table 11.2, where we find that the total labour force participation rate declined from 73.6 per cent in 1998–99 to 72.6 per cent in 2005–06. The decline was mainly due to a decline in female labour force participation rates (from 72.6 per cent to 69.7 per cent), while the male labour force participation rate actually rose (from 74.7 per cent to 75.7 per cent). We saw in Table 11.1 that the fraction of the inactive working-age population increased between 1998–99 and 2005–06. An increase in school attendance among people above the age of 14 contributed to declining participation.

11.4.3 The nature of unemployment

Open unemployed are those individuals who are without work but are available for work and are actively searching for work during the reference period. The unemployment rate is measured as the number of unemployed people divided by the labour force. Table 11.3 shows open unemployment rates derived from the two most recent labour force surveys.

We can identify three features of the structure of unemployment in Table 11.3. First, the total open unemployment rate decreased from 14.6 per cent in 1998–99 to 12.7 per cent in 2005–06. Part of this period coincided with economic recovery – GDP growth rose from 2.9 per cent in 2003 to 6.1 per cent in 2006. Second, young labour market participants (15–29 years) have the highest unemployment rate. Third, unemployment rates for women are generally higher than those for men.

Table 11.2 Labour force participation rates in Kenya by gender and age (1998–99 and 2005–06) (%)

	1998–99			2005–06		
Age (years)	Male	Female	Total	Male	Female	Total
15–19	28.1	30.5	29.3	30.3	29.9	30.1
20–24	66.6	69.8	68.3	73.2	67.6	70.2
25–29	91.5	87.7	89.4	92.6	82.0	87.0
30–34	96.6	91.6	94.1	97.3	85.5	91.5
35–39	97.4	92.3	94.8	97.7	90.1	93.7
40–44	97.5	92.9	95.2	97.9	89.9	93.7
45–49	95.6	90.7	93.4	95.8	89.1	92.5
50–54	94.0	86.9	90.3	93.1	85.2	89.2
55–59	87.8	82.5	85.1	91.9	82.3	87.2
60–64	85.0	77.4	80.9	88.9	76.0	82.0
Total	74.7	72.6	73.6	75.7	69.7	72.6

Source: Republic of Kenya (2003a, 2008a).

Generally, it is harder for women to get into remunerative employment. They are disproportionately engaged in unpaid home production, and they are more likely to be discouraged workers (workers who have given up searching for work). As many of the opportunities open to women are in the informal sector or other sectors where earnings are low, the incentive to seek external employment is less for women than for men.

11.4.4 Workforce by sector

A distinction can be made between three workforce categories in Kenya: the modern (or formal) sector, the informal sector, and the small-scale agriculture and pastoralist sector. The formal sector comprises the public sector and all formally registered private enterprises and institutions. This is the sector (comprising both agriculture and non-agriculture) that Leamer (1987) and many others have assumed would grow and absorb an increasing share of the labour force as countries develop. For this process to be realized, the rate of capital accumulation needs to be high. But the higher the amount of capital that is required to employ one more worker, the harder it will be for the sector to absorb the labour released from agriculture. The choice of capital intensity in production is influenced by the costs of factors of production, and if the government pursues policies that make capital artificially cheap, the producers will choose techniques that are too capital-intensive. So what is required is a combination of non-distorted capital prices and other measures that stimulate investments. The aim is to increase aggregate K/L rather than to increase the capital intensity in the production. Higher labour costs resulting from

Table 11.3 Unemployment rates in Kenya, by age group and sex, 1998–99 and 2005–06 (%)

	1998–99			2005–06		
Age (years)	Total	Males	Females	Total	Males	Females
15–19	24.3	21.8	26.4	25.0	22.4	27.7
20–24	27.1	19.0	33.9	24.2	21.0	27.3
25–29	15.5	8.2	21.6	15.7	13.5	17.9
30–34	10.8	4.8	16.8	7.5	6.1	9.2
35–39	8.4	5.0	11.8	7.6	6.9	8.3
40–44	9.1	7.8	10.6	6.4	6.4	6.4
45–49	8.2	4.9	12.5	5.7	4.9	6.5
50–54	8.7	6.3	11.1	4.7	4.9	4.4
55–59	13.5	14.2	12.7	4.0	4.8	3.2
60–64	11.7	7.5	15.7	2.5	4.2	0.8
Total	14.6	9.8	19.3	12.7	11.2	14.3

Source: Republic of Kenya (2003a, 2008a).

policy interventions will also hold back employment. The sector is also subject to labour market regulations that increase labour costs, and which might hinder flexibility to adjust to shocks. Kenya has not been able to achieve rapid capital accumulation, nor has it been able to keep wage costs low relative to productivity in the formal sector. These factors jointly explain why formal sector employment expansion has been slow.

The informal sector comprises all unregistered and unregulated enterprises. It is a sector that is heterogeneous with respect to type of business, premises, and individual characteristics. In addition, while some segments are easy to enter, others require greater amounts of capital. Typically, the labour costs (including the costs of meeting regulations, paying taxes, etc.) are lower here than in the formal sector, which means that firms in this sector will find it easier to increase employment.

In Table 11.4A, we find the total employment and sectoral employment shares for 2001–06. We can see that total employment increased by 2.3 million, which implies a faster rate than that implied by the two labour force surveys used above.[2] We also see that many of the new jobs were created in the informal sector where total employment grew by 2,146,200, equal to an increase of 46 per cent compared with the increase of 183,100, equal to 10.5 per cent in formal sector employment over the five-year period. Self-employment and unpaid family workers contributed only a small share of total employment growth over this period.

The figures shown in Table 11.4A are remarkable! Total formal sector wage employment as a share of total employment (outside smallholder agriculture and pastoralism) fell from 27.2 per cent to 22.0 per cent over a period as short

Table 11.4A Formal and informal sector employment in Kenya, 2001–06

	2001	2002	2003	2004	2005	2006
Formal sector						
Wage employment	0.262	0.247	0.235	0.225	0.219	0.213
Self-employment and unpaid family workers	0.010	0.010	0.009	0.008	0.008	0.008
Total formal employment	0.272	0.257	0.244	0.234	0.227	0.220
Informal sector	0.728	0.743	0.756	0.766	0.773	0.780
Total employment	6,411,200	6,873,500	7,339,400	7,822,800	8,271,500	8,740,500

Source: Republic of Kenya, Economic Surveys (2006, 2007).

as five years, whereas the share of total informal sector employment increased from 72.8 per cent to 78.0 per cent. This is a really dramatic change in the employment structure outside agriculture, and it confirms the picture we drew initially about a process of structural change that pushes labour out of agriculture into informal sector employment. The modern formal sector is unable to absorb the outflow of labour. To deal with this problem is one of the key challenges of Kenyan development policy.

The rapid growth of informal sector employment is an indication of the flexibility of this sector in terms of labour absorption, and the employment expansion there is clearly made possible by the very limited capital requirements for new jobs. The ease of entry into the informal sector explains why the open unemployment rates are not as high as in some other countries such as South Africa (29 per cent in 2002), where the informal sector has not expanded much (see Kingdon and Knight, 2004). In the absence of any unemployment compensation schemes and bearing in mind the high incidence of poverty, remaining openly unemployed for an extended period of time in Kenya is not an attractive or feasible option. These people must find some way to earn at least some income. In this situation, the problem is not only open unemployment but also that of the working poor (ECA, 2005), that is workers who are counted as employed but with earnings that are very low for decent living conditions.

A more detailed picture of wage employment emerges in Table 11.4B, where we see that total formal wage employment grew by 10.8 per cent between 2001 and 2006. The share of private sector employment grew from 60.7 per cent in 2001 to 65 per cent in 2006, while the public sector employment share fell from 39.3 per cent to 35 per cent in the respective years. Still, we find from detailed statistics in the Economic Surveys (Republic of Kenya, 2006, 2007) that the overall structure of formal employment has not changed much over the period. In particular, the sector that is emphasized in the long-term development strategy of Kenya, that is manufacturing, has just managed to maintain its share of about 18 per cent of formal private and about 5 per cent of formal public employment over these five years.

Table 11.4B Wage employment shares by industry in Kenya

	2001	2002	2003	2004	2005	2006
Private sector	0.607	0.612	0.618	0.627	0.638	0.650
Public sector	0.393	0.388	0.382	0.373	0.362	0.350
Total	1,677,100	1,699,500	1,727,200	1,763,700	1,807,700	1,858,500

Source: Computed from Republic of Kenya, Economic Surveys (2006, 2007).

11.4.5 Development of real wages by sector

Table 11.5 shows how real average wage earnings per worker by formal sector have evolved over the period 2002–06. Real wages in the public sector increased by 3.6 per cent in 2002–04 but decreased thereafter. In the private sector, average real wages per worker increased by 13.2 per cent in 2002–04. However, unlike in the public sector, real wage earnings continued to rise and, by 2006, private sector workers earned 24.6 per cent more on average than they had earned in 2002.

It is clear from Table 11.5 that, throughout this period, real wage growth in the private sector exceeded that in the public sector. By 2006, the wage levels were considerably higher in the private sector. The relative public–private wage fell from 1.047 in 2002 to 0.839 in 2006. As we do not control for possible differences in labour force composition, the estimates may not be wholly comparable. Still, the trend is clear and one would not expect that there would have been dramatic changes in the composition in only five years. Therefore, increasing wage differences may eventually lead to skill shortages in the public sector as experienced and high-quality workers increasingly exit the public sector to go to the private sector. If productivity in the public sector can be increased, it will be possible to pay higher wages and thus retain high-quality workers for public service delivery. Alternatively, higher public sector wages can be realized if the government is able and willing to increase taxation to finance them. This may come into conflict with other goals, however, such as maintaining an investor-friendly economic environment.

Significant wage differentials also exist in Kenya by firm size (Manda, 2002), with large firms paying considerably more than smaller firms. This is

Table 11.5 Estimated real wage earnings (public, private sectors, and total) 2002–06, Ksh p.a.

Year	2002	2003	2004	2005	2006
Public sector	165,466.2	159,014.8	171,416.1	164,279.5	165,259.2
Private sector	158,036.6	160,572	178,892.3	188,677.6	196,942.7
Relative public/private wage	1.047	0.990	0.958	0.871	0.839
Total	160,952.1	159,974.4	175,905.8	179,846.9	185,862.3

Source: Republic of Kenya (2007).

a reflection of higher productivity in larger firms, and then it would be counterproductive to push for higher wages in small firms, which might then go out of business. An increase in the number of large firms is desirable, but that requires that the investment climate is good enough to attract investors. This is not primarily a labour market issue, although labour costs relative to labour productivity are certainly also an important factor. Again, we can conclude that a good labour market outcome requires higher capital investments.

Eifert *et al.* (2005) showed that total factor productivity of Kenyan manufacturing firms is much below that of Chinese manufacturers when looking at firms' related costs only. When the impact of indirect costs such as the cost of transport is included, the gap increases a great deal, and Kenya's total factor productivity (TFP) is then only about 40 per cent of China's. For Kenya's firms to be competitive relative to China, the cost of labour would have to be lower, even if they still suffer from high indirect costs that must also be dealt with. It is hard to compare costs of labour across counties, but a recent estimate by the World Bank (2009: 83) suggests that the median wage for production workers in Kenya is about 30 per cent above that of China! Kenyan producers thus face a wage cost problem relative to China apart from the problem of much higher indirect costs.

11.4.6 Changing labour force composition

The quality of labour supply depends on a range of factors, but we focus on changes in the quality of labour by education level. The education system remains the main initial source of skills in Kenya. Table 11.6 shows labour force participation rates for various categories of education. In 1998–99, the participation rate of individuals with no education was 83.7 per cent compared with 97.6 per cent for university graduates. The pattern in 2005–06 is similar except that participation rates are somewhat lower. Thus, there is positive correlation between education and labour force participation. Individuals who invest more in education require greater participation to recoup their costs, and earnings from market work increase with education, thus increasing the opportunity cost of non-participation.

Table 11.7 shows the educational composition of employed individuals in 1998–99 and 2005–06. One important change is the decline in the proportion of employees with no education and the increase in the proportion with primary education. This reflects the near universal primary education in Kenya. The proportion of employees with secondary education is constant, but there was an increase (from 24.1 per cent to 26.5 per cent) in the proportion of female employees with secondary education, whereas that of males declined (from 37.6 per cent to 35.2 per cent). The proportion of female employees with a university education is still small compared with that of males.

Table 11.6 Labour force by education attainment

	1998–99			2005–06		
Education level	Male	Female	Total	Male	Female	Total
Primary	85.0	83.1	84.0	72.6	69.5	71.0
Secondary	94.6	90.1	92.7	78.5	69.4	74.3
University	96.7[a]	100.0[a]	97.6[a]	75.1	63.5	71.5
None	86.0	82.7	83.7	51.6	73.8	60.6
Other	–	–	–	89.0	74.9	82.5
Not stated	50.8	65.2	59.7	82.9	71.0	75.1
Total	74.7	72.6	73.6	75.7	69.7	72.6

a Combines undergraduate and postgraduate levels.
Source: Republic of Kenya (2003a, 2008a).

Wages differ very much by levels of education (Bigsten, 1984; Knight and Sabot, 1990; Söderbom *et al.*, 2006) and on-the-job training in Kenya (Rosholm *et al.*, 2007). Consequently, investment in education and training coupled with employment opportunities improves earnings. However, one must keep in mind that an increased supply of skilled labour tends to push earnings down, unless there is at the same time a sufficient increase in labour demand. Once again, higher earnings depend on growth, which depends on investments. To get investments up is a key challenge for Kenya if it is to achieve the ambitious targets of poverty reduction in its development strategy.

11.4.7 Labour mobility patterns

Labour mobility is essential if workers are to take advantage of opportunities generated by economic growth. And mobility is important for growth, as it contributes to the achievement of an efficient allocation of the labour force. Table 11.8 shows three measures of lifetime migration, out-migration, in-migration, and net migration, constructed from the 1998–99 Labour Force

Table 11.7 Employed individuals by education attainment, 1998–99 and 2005–06

	1998–99			2005–06		
Education level	Male	Female	Total	Male	Female	Total
Primary	49.5	51.6	50.5	51.6	53.4	52.4
Secondary	37.6	24.1	31.2	35.2	26.5	31.0
University	2.7	0.9	1.8	2.3	0.9	1.60
Nursery	0.4	0.4	0.4	–	–	–
None	9.7	22.9	16.1	0.1	0.1	0.1
Other	–	–	–	0.6	0.5	0.5
Not stated	0.0	0.1	0.1	10.2	18.8	14.4
Total	100	100	100	100	100	100

Source: Republic of Kenya (2003a, 2008a).

Table 11.8 Distribution of out-migrants and in-migrants in Kenya by region and province

Region/province	Out-migration rate[a] (%)	In-migration rate[b] (%)
Region		
Rural	13.7	5.7
Urban	11.1	34.9
Total	13.2	13.2
Province		
Nairobi	25.3	61.1
Central	18.8	7.0
Coast	4.8	14.7
Eastern	10.0	5.3
North Eastern (urban)	3.4	13.8
Nyanza	15.1	5.3
Rift Valley	6.0	16.1
Western	21.5	7.4
Total	13.2	13.2

a Out-migration rate is computed as the percentage of out-migrants to the population born in the area.
b In-migration rate is computed as the percentage of in-migrants to the enumerated population in the area.
Source: Republic of Kenya (2003a).

Surveys (Republic of Kenya, 2003a). The overall out-migration rate was 13.2 per cent, and out-migration from rural areas outweighed out-migration from urban areas. Conversely, the rate of in-migration into urban areas strongly outweighed the in-migration rate in rural areas. Several provinces (Nairobi, Western, Central, and Nyanza) recorded relatively high out-migration, over 15 per cent of the population born in the province. Provinces with relatively low out-migration are Coast (4.8 per cent) and North-Eastern (urban) (3.4 per cent), and Rift Valley (6 per cent). The Nairobi, Rift Valley, and Coast provinces recorded relatively high in-migration rates.

Economic theory suggests that migration flows respond to relative costs and benefits in the source area and the destination. Potential migrants consider the net benefit and then decide to move or not to move. Nairobi is the capital city and the centre of commerce and industry. Consequently, the probability of gaining employment and hence income is likely to be relatively higher there than in other places. In addition, the concentration of population provides demand for goods and services and for self-employed individuals such as those in the informal sector. Thus, movers have obviously predicted that the net benefit of a move to Nairobi is positive. The Rift Valley has abundant farmland, which raises the potential benefits of in-migration given that many Kenyans rely on smallholder agriculture for their livelihood. Overall, we can conclude that labour in Kenya has been relatively mobile, which is essential for the efficient allocation of labour. However, the post-election violence might have changed the benefit–cost analysis of movers.

11.5 The policy environment

This section discusses recent changes in labour market policies in Kenya as well as what is required for the future. We focus on labour market regulations and institutions and labour market policies.

11.5.1 Minimum wage legislation

A system of minimum wages has existed in Kenya since 1932 (see Bigsten, 1984). The country currently operates a set of minimum wages differentiated by sectors, occupations, and regions. As we noted earlier, the bulk of the labour force in Kenya is engaged in informal activities, whereas formal sector employment has grown very slowly. This has implications for the coverage of minimum wage laws and compliance because, although workers in the formal sector are covered by minimum wages, those in the informal sector are not covered and non-compliance within the formal sector is also a problem.

In the past, the government adjusted the minimum wage upwards annually, usually on Labour Day. The main factor considered for many years was the cost of living. However, since 1994, the government has also taken other factors into account, in particular the need for increased employment by keeping wage rates in line with worker productivity and employers' ability to pay (Republic of Kenya, 2000).[3] There were no minimum wage increments in 2007 and 2008, a decision that did not go down well with the trade unions. Another change that has occurred is that the tripartite partners have established the Productivity Centre of Kenya, whose aim among others is to measure productivity levels to enable wage setting to be linked to productivity. However, because this is still in its formative stages, it is likely that minimum wages will continue to be set by the government for some time yet following the practice in the recent past.

The main argument against minimum wage laws is that minimum wages impede job creation. The evidence as to whether minimum wages negatively affect job creation in Kenya is thin. It should also be noted that difficulties with enforcement and the presence of a large informal sector that is not covered complicate analysis of the impact of minimum wages. Thus, the minimum wage might de facto play a rather limited role. In Kenya, Omolo and Omiti (2004) estimate that, although average labour productivity declined by 0.8 per cent per annum in the period 1992–2001, minimum wages grew by approximately 6.2 per cent per annum.[4] They conclude that this adversely affected job creation in the formal sector. Manda *et al.* (2005a) investigated the long-term impact of minimum wages in Kenya and found a negative impact of minimum wages on private sector employment in the long run. Overall, it is likely that minimum wage legislation has at least some negative effects on employment growth in the formal sector.

As Kenya pursues *Vision 2030*, the government should exercise caution with regard to revisions of the minimum wage to avoid pricing out low-skilled workers whom minimum wages are supposed to protect. Moreover, high wage costs would make sectors that are earmarked to drive *Vision 2030*, such as manufacturing, less competitive and more slow growing. The present system of minimum wages is too differentiated, making implementation cumbersome and enforcement difficult. Consolidation of the number of minimum wages should be considered as a way to ease implementation and improve compliance. In addition, given the large numbers of unemployed youth, whose productivity at entry to the labour market is likely to be low, the government should consider a minimum wage regime differentiated by age with lower minimum wages for youth to encourage employers to hire them.

11.5.2 Job security regulations

Job security regulations in Kenya cover a wide range of labour market outcomes and practices including hiring, firing, hours of work, and leave, among others. While some regulation is needed to protect workers from unfair dismissal and facilitate efficient contracting, excessive regulation may serve to entrench insiders – those already having a job – at the expense of outsiders – the unemployed and those in the informal sector. The challenge is to establish a balance between employment protection and labour market flexibility.

Before 1994, employers in Kenya had to follow a cumbersome procedure to lay off workers. It was lengthy and involved approval from the minister in charge of labour. Such regulation can make it difficult to lay off workers and discourages job creation because employers are reluctant to hire permanent workers whom they cannot easily lay off (World Bank, 1995). However, with liberalization of the product market and financial markets, it was considered necessary to liberalize the labour market too, to enable employers to adjust their workforces in the liberalized economic environment. In 1994, the procedure to lay off workers was made easier. The aim was to encourage employers to hire by reducing the costs of firing. A key change in this area is the enactment of a new law in 2008: *The Employment Act, 2007*.

Although job security regulations may have reduced job creation in Kenya, the available evidence is not conclusive. The strictness of employment regulation in a country depends on many aspects. The World Bank has constructed four labour market-related *Doing Business* indicators to measure the strictness of employment protection in member countries (World Bank, 2008). The difficulty of hiring index measures how difficult it is to hire a new employee, the rigidity of hours index measures the degree of rigidity in working hours regulations, and the difficulty of firing index measures how difficult it is to fire redundant employees. The rigidity of employment index is the average of the three indices. Each index takes values between 0 and 100, with higher values indicating more rigidity. These indicators are shown in Table 11.9 together with an estimate of firing costs (in terms of weeks of salary).

The best practice for rigidity of employment index is in Hong Kong (0) and for firing costs is in New Zealand (0). On the former measure, Kenya, at 17.4, shows lower levels of job protection than the comparator countries. However, on the latter measure, firing costs in Kenya, at 47, are relatively high. Overall, compared with best practice, Kenya still needs to reduce rigidity in hiring and firing as well as firing costs. Similar indices reported by Azam *et al.* (2005) indicate that the rigidity of employment index was 22 and the rigidity of hours index was 20. The other indices were at the same level in 2009.

It is noteworthy that, although Kenya's indices were below the sub-Saharan average, sub-Saharan Africa had the most rigid labour markets in the world. So, in comparison with major Asian competitors, the Kenyan labour market is still rigid. This suggests that Kenya still requires to relax job security regulations in order to reduce the costs of firing workers and encourage employers to hire new workers. This would ensure that job security regulations do not

Table 11.9 Indices of employment laws, 2009

	2009	Best practice	Comparator countries
Rigidity of employment[a]	17.4	Hong Kong: 0.00 United States: 0.00 Singapore: 0.00	Botswana: 20 Mauritius: 23 Mozambique: 49 Namibia: 20 Seychelles: 38
Difficulty of hiring[b]	22.2		
Rigidity of hours[c]	0.00		
Difficulty of firing[d]	30		
Firing costs[e]	47.2	New Zealand: 0.00	Botswana: 90 Mauritius: 35 Mozambique: 134 Namibia: 24 Seychelles: 39

a The rigidity of employment index is the average of three subindices: difficulty of hiring, rigidity of hours, and difficulty of firing.
b The difficulty of hiring index measures the flexibility of contracts and the ratio of the minimum wage to the value added per worker.
c The rigidity of hours index covers restrictions on weekend and night work, requirements relating to working time and the working week, and mandated days of annual leave with pay.
d The difficulty of firing index covers workers' legal protections against dismissal, including the grounds permitted for dismissal and procedures for dismissal (individual and collective): notification and approval requirements, retraining or reassignment obligations, and priority rules for dismissals and re-employment.
e The firing costs indicator measures the cost of advance notice requirements, severance payments, and penalties due when terminating a redundant worker, expressed in weeks of salary.
Source: World Bank (2008).

act as a source of competitive disadvantage as Kenya seeks to increase exports. Further liberalization of the labour market would also reduce the power of incumbent workers (insiders) to demand higher wages, which would otherwise be detrimental to the unemployed (outsiders) willing to work at lower wages. Moreover, because Kenya envisages that small and medium-sized businesses will be critical in achieving *Vision 2030*, relaxing job security regulations would reduce the fixed costs associated with frequent hiring and firing of workers by formal small and medium-sized enterprises (SMEs).

11.5.3 Trade unions

Trade unions have been a key institutional force in Kenya's formal labour market since before independence (see Bigsten, 1984). In the past, the Kenyan government has sought to reduce the role and power of trade unions partly for political reasons but also out of the belief that trade union activity might reduce employment by pushing up the wage levels. Legislation limits the grounds on which unions can legitimately undertake industrial action (e.g. strikes and go-slows), and the process of engaging in a legal strike is cumbersome and time consuming. Strikes by workers in essential services (e.g. health services and the police) are prohibited by law.

The influence of trade unions on the labour supply also depends on their ability to organize a substantial proportion of workers for joint action to fight for better working conditions and pay. In Kenya, union membership has been declining over time. Azam *et al.* (2005) note that union membership in African countries is low compared with developed countries. They report that, in Kenya, union membership declined by 38 per cent between 1985 and 2000. The liberalization of the economy that led to the exit of major employers such as textile firms might have contributed to declining union density. In recent years, most of the job creation in Kenya has occurred in the informal sector, where few workers if any are unionized. With declining union density, the financial base of many unions has become weak, which restricts their ability to offer support to striking workers or in collective bargaining. A recent study by Manda *et al.* (2007b) suggests that union membership in Kenya's manufacturing sector is associated with higher wages. Still, it is important to note that trade unions could also influence other important variables such as employment, investment, profitability, and productivity.

The conduct of industrial relations and collective bargaining in Kenya is governed by law. The major policy development in this area is the enactment of new legislation: the *Labour Relations Act, 2007*. The main areas addressed in the Act are: (i) freedom of association and rights of workers and employers; (ii) establishment and registration of workers' and employers' associations; (iii) governance of such associations; (iv) recognition of trade unions and collective bargaining agreements; and (v) strike action and dispute resolution.

Trade unions and collective bargaining are likely to remain important in the Kenyan formal sector. First, the new law supports collective bargaining in that it requires employers or an employers' organization in any sector, including the public sector, to recognize a trade union for the purposes of collective bargaining if the union represents a simple majority of unionizable employees. This is important given that recognition is a precondition for unions to have a say in collective bargaining. Second, trade unions, through their umbrella organization, the Central Organization of Trade Unions (COTU), are often consulted by the government on labour-related issues such as salary reviews for public sector workers and adjustment of the minimum wage. Moreover, unions are represented in running key institutions related to labour such as the Productivity Centre of Kenya (PCK) and the National Social Security Fund (NSSF). The challenge is to strengthen the tripartite relationship between the government, unions, and employers. In addition, unions face the challenge of organizing workers in an environment characterized by unemployment and informal sector expansion. So trade unions will remain an important feature of the modern sector labour market in Kenya, and it is not desirable that they should disappear. They may contribute to an orderly wage-setting process and the protection of workers' rights. Still, the government should continue to follow the outcomes of the wage-bargaining process, as rapidly increasing wages may hinder the realization of the expansion in formal sector jobs that is envisaged in *Vision 2030*.

11.5.4 Employment and unemployment policies

Next, we review policies and programmes aimed at the unemployment challenge and job creation in Kenya. In theory, four reasons can be advanced for government intervention in the labour market (World Bank, 1995): uneven market power, labour market discrimination, insufficient information, and inadequate insurance against risk.

Policy-makers in Kenya are concerned about the difficulties that those in the labour force face in obtaining gainful employment, and they recognize the adverse impact of unemployment, especially unemployment among the youth. The government's response to the challenge of job creation and reduction in unemployment aims at: (i) expanding employment opportunities for income generation; (ii) investment in education; and (iii) special attention to individuals who, for one reason or another, have not acquired adequate skills.

POLICIES TO ACCELERATE AND SUSTAIN HIGH ECONOMIC GROWTH

Economic growth is the key to expanding employment opportunities but, as is discussed elsewhere in this book, growth in Kenya has been slow. Therefore, the formal sector has not been able to absorb a substantial proportion of the labour force. The government that came to power in December 2002 developed an economic recovery strategy, the *Economic Recovery Strategy for Wealth and Employment Creation (ERSWEC)* (Republic of Kenya, 2003b), to address the challenges of poverty, employment, and economic growth. The *Sessional Paper No. 7* of 2005 on *Employment Policy and Strategy for Kenya* (Republic of Kenya, 2005d) also addressed employment issues. Looking ahead, the government has launched *Vision 2030*, a long-term development blueprint for 2008–30 to transform Kenya into 'a globally competitive and prosperous nation'. *Vision 2030* has three pillars: the economic pillar, the social pillar, and the political pillar (Republic of Kenya, 2008b). The First Medium-Term Plan (2008–12) for the *Vision 2030* emphasizes rapid employment growth to address unemployment, especially among the youth. It proposes initiatives to develop human resources and tackle unemployment: revitalization and expansion of youth polytechnics; increases in the Youth Enterprise Fund; and deliberate efforts to boost labour-intensive infrastructure projects including road projects and tree planting programmes. However, the objectives can only be realized if the government implements the initiatives on a substantial scale given the extent of youth unemployment documented earlier in this chapter. This will be a challenge, both financially and administratively.

MICRO AND SMALL ENTERPRISES/INFORMAL/JUA KALI SECTOR POLICY

In recognition of the role of SMEs in meeting demand for goods and services, broadening job opportunities, and income generation, the government formulated a SME development policy in 2005. In the *Sessional Paper No. 7* of 2005 on *Employment Policy and Strategy for Kenya* (Republic of Kenya, 2005d), the government spelt out policy measures to encourage entrepreneurship. These include: increasing funding to training institutions; promoting greater private sector involvement; and formulating job restructuring and redeployment programmes to provide credit, guidance, counselling, skills, and entrepreneurship training.

The *Sessional Paper 2* of 2005 on *Development of Micro and Small Enterprises for Wealth and Employment Creation for Poverty Reduction* (Republic of Kenya, 2005b) outlines a policy framework with the goal of providing a favourable environment for the sector to flourish. The specific policy measures were to: (i) create a favourable environment through reducing the costs of doing business in a stable economic environment, better infrastructure, provision of business development services; (ii) improve and develop effective linkages between institutions and business; (iii) provide access to financial services; (iv) establish an enabling legal and regulatory environment; (v) encourage learning institutions to offer entrepreneurial and business training; (vi) promote gender equality by pursing policies that would empower women; (vii) create an information centre for SMEs; (viii) promote good governance, ethical trading, and the rule of law; (ix) improve working conditions for SMEs; and (x) address the issue of HIV/AIDS in the sector. These policy issues related to the expansion of SMEs will be dealt with elsewhere in this volume. Still, here we may note that these firms will play an important role in short-term employment generation and poverty alleviation. But for Kenya to achieve an economic take-off, there most be expansion in larger scale enterprises that can compete on the international market. There is thus a need for a two-pronged strategy. On the one hand, there must be policies that handle the short-term poverty issues, at the same time as there must be policies that open up the country for a breakthrough à la Asia in the longer run.

POLICY FOR YOUTH EMPLOYMENT

As we saw in Section 11.2, youth unemployment is of particular concern, more so after the post-election violence that rocked Kenya in late December 2007 and early 2008. The government has developed the National Youth Policy (Republic of Kenya, 2005c) outlining measures to address the youth unemployment challenge. These include: (i) encouraging firms to offer temporary employment, internship, and volunteer opportunities to the youth; (ii) encouraging the establishment of agricultural production and cottage industries, and informal sector employment; (iii) encouraging the government, civil society organizations, and the private sector to provide friendly microfinance credit facilities and to develop business incubators and mentorship for the youth; (iv) imparting accessible and affordable education and vocational skills; and (v) protecting *Jua kali* innovations through patents.

To broaden employment opportunities for young Kenyans (aged 18–35 years), the government set up a Youth Enterprise Development Fund in 2006. The objectives of the fund are: (i) to provide funds to microfinance institutions for lending on to youth enterprises; (ii) to attract and facilitate investment in SME-oriented commercial infrastructure such as business and industrial parks and business incubators; (iii) to support SMEs established by young people to develop linkages with large firms; (iv) to facilitate marketing of products and services of youth enterprises in domestic and international markets; and (v) to facilitate the employment of youth in the international labour market.

IMPROVING THE OPERATIONS OF THE LABOUR MARKET

To the extent that unemployment is due to information problems, improved collection and dissemination of labour market information is needed. Kenya has several firms that offer employment services to employees (e.g. CV banks) and employers (e.g. recruitment). The number of beneficiaries is likely to be small given the location of such firms mainly in the capital. For this reason, public employment services have been set up at district labour offices. However, the offices have not played their role adequately because of inadequate resources and staff. Where labour market information is costly to acquire, counselling and job search assistance programmes would help to broaden employment opportunities.

The government and other stakeholders have implemented or plan to implement public works programmes to hire some of the unemployed to work on public infrastructure projects (roads, public buildings, water, and sanitation) on a temporary basis. The jobs may provide an avenue to acquire work experience, which could enable them to secure jobs upon exiting the programmes. Such projects also provide an opportunity to target other programmes (e.g. training). But although such programmes can offer temporary relief, the longer term solution is for the economy to generate adequate jobs. Without external funding, the fiscal burden that such programmes entail means that the scale has to be kept small, yet many individuals seem to want to work. The management of such programmes must also be strengthened. As a means to achieve social equity and poverty reduction in line with *Vision 2030*, public works programmes should be institutionalized as a safety net.

POLICIES FOR BUILDING SKILLS AND CAPABILITIES

To ensure accessible and affordable social services to facilitate human capital formation, the Economic Recovery Strategy (ERS) paper had several social sector objectives. The education sector objectives were: (i) to raise primary school enrolment rates to 100 per cent; (ii) to improve access to and quality of education; (iii) to expand bursaries at secondary school level; and (iv) to rehabilitate laboratories and classrooms. To attain the objectives, the government increased the number of staff and textbooks, in-service training for teachers, and the bursary allocation. Further, the *Sessional Paper No. 7* of 2005 on *Education and Training* (Republic of Kenya, 2005a) emphasizes the provision of vocational training, apprenticeships, internships, attachments, mentorship, and coaching programmes being incorporated into the education system. A strategy has been developed to guide the revitalization of technical and vocational education and training. Such a strategy finds support in a recent study (Rosholm *et al.*, 2007) of the impact of on-the-job training on wages in Kenyan manufacturing. They found that on-the-job training improves wages, and the effect is larger for longer duration training and training in large firms.

Poor health reduces the ability of workers to take advantage of employment opportunities. A number of studies have found that better health enhances productivity. Consequently, the government policy to make health care accessible and affordable through rehabilitation of public health facilities and reduction in the costs of drugs by overhauling the drugs procurement and distribution system should take on added urgency. In addition, ensuring food security and improved nutrition especially in children and improving health care and awareness with regard to HIV/AIDS will be critical in the development of human resources required to achieve *Vision 2030*.

11.6 Policy conclusions

The main message of this chapter is that the Kenyan economy has adjusted to the rapid growth in labour supply and the slow pace of capital accumulation by shifting towards the labour-intensive informal sector. This has helped to cushion the effect on unskilled labour. Still, the long-term growth prospects of the economy will be dismal unless capital accumulation can again outpace labour force growth. There were some signs of investment acceleration before the clashes in conjunction with the 2007 election, but the challenge is now to revive that again. We saw that the rate of unemployment declined when the economy was growing faster. This also improved the situation for women in the labour market. Still, they continue to work much less than men outside the household, and young people still have a hard time entering the labour market.

An important change in the Kenyan labour market is the rapid educational upgrading of the labour force. This should lead to higher wages but, for these to be realized, there has to be an expansion in the demand for labour. This will again depend on what happens to investments. If wages are pushed up prematurely, the process of growth and employment creation may be seriously constrained.

The speed of employment creation also depends on the set of labour market policies and institutions that are in place. Generally, the situation in Kenya is better than in neighbouring countries in these areas. Like most countries, Kenya has minimum wages that tend to hold back employment, but overall we do not think they bite very hard in the Kenyan case. This does not mean that it would be costless to push them up. Furthermore, there is always a need for some job security legislation, but it can be so extensive that it makes firms reluctant to hire labour. One may therefore need to consider how strict the regulations can be, given that Kenya is competing for internationally mobile investment capital.

Trade unions are part of the negotiation machinery for wages in the formal sector and, as such, they are important for the orderly functioning of that market. They are able to affect the level of wages in the formal sector to some extent, thereby influencing the rate of employment creation. Still, one would not think that the trade unions can push wages up very much, given the structure of the Kenyan labour market. It may be reasonable to argue that the unions are an essential ingredient in a well-functioning system of wage negotiations.

The government also has a set of special policies to create more jobs for young people, as well as public works to employ people who struggle to find work. These measures can help to reduce unemployment somewhat but, in the longer term, the economy can only create more jobs via economic growth.

The main objective of the government is to improve the living standards of Kenyans through job creation, which would in turn lead to poverty reduction. The key assumption is that economic growth would generate adequate and well-paid employment. The main conclusion of our review of the situation is that this requires faster economic growth. How to achieve this is discussed further in other chapters in this volume.

Notes

1 The Kenya National Bureau of Statistics (KNBS) definition of employment includes all persons who reported that they performed some work during the reference period or that they held a job even if they were not actually performing the work at the time of the survey.

2 As we are primarily interested here in finding out how the overall employment pattern has changed over time, and there were some anomalies in the labour force survey data, we use these data from *Economic Surveys*.

3 On Labour Day 2006, the minimum wage was increased by 12 per cent under the General Wages Order and 11 per cent for workers in the agricultural sector. In 2005, the increases were 7 per cent and 9 per cent respectively. In 2004, the increases were 11 per cent and 10 per cent respectively (Republic of Kenya, 2006).

4 Some evidence of the impact on actual wages is provided by Pollin *et al.* (2007) based on data from the *Kenya Integrated Household Budget Survey* (KIHBS), 2005–06. They could not compare actual wages with actual minimum wages, but they compared actual wage levels for workers in the formal private sector as a whole with the average minimum wage level. They found that 43–50 per cent of formal private sector workers had wages below the average minimum wage and concluded that minimum wage laws had limited influence on wage setting.

References

Azam, J. P., P. Alby and S. Rospabe, 2005, 'Labour Institutions, Labour Management Relations, and Social Dialogue in Africa'. http://siteresources.worldbank.org/INTLM/Resources/390041-1134749230121/Alby_LaborInstitutions.pdf.

Bigsten, A., 1984, *Education and Income Determination in Kenya*. Aldershot, UK: Cower Publishing Company.

Bigsten, A. and D. Durevall, 2008, 'Factor Proportions, Openness and Factor Prices in Kenya 1965–2000', *Journal of Development Studies*, 44 (2), 289–310.

ECA, 2005, *Economic Report on Africa 2005: Meeting the Challenges of Unemployment and Poverty in Africa*. Addis Ababa, Ethiopia: ECA.

Eifert, B., A. Gelb and V. Ramachandran, 2005, *Business Environment and Comparative Advantage in Africa: Evidence from the Investment Climate Data*, Working Paper No 56. Washington, DC: Centre for Global Development.

Harris, J. and M. Todaro, 1970, 'Migration, Unemployment and Development: A Two Sector Analysis', *American Economic Review* , 60, 126–142.

Kingdon, G. and J. Knight, 2004, 'Unemployment in South Africa: The Nature of the Beast', *World Development*, 32 (3), 391–408.

Knight, J. and R. Sabot, 1990, *Education, Productivity, and Inequality: the East African Natural Experiment.* New York: Oxford University Press.

Leamer, E., 1987, 'Paths of Development in the Three-Factor, n-Good General Equilibrium Model', *The Journal of Political Economy*, 95 (5), 961–999.

Lewis, W. A., 1954, 'Economic Development with Unlimited Supplies of Labour', *The Manchester School*, 22 (2), 139–191.

Manda, D. K., 2002, 'Wage Determination in Kenyan Manufacturing', in Bigsten, A. and P. Kimuyu (eds) *Structure and Performance of Manufacturing in Kenya*. London: Palgrave.

Manda, D. K., G. Kosimbei and B. Wanjala, 2005a, 'Impact of Minimum Wages on Formal Employment in Kenya'. Kenya Institute of Public Policy Research and Analysis Discussion Paper No. 67.

Manda, D. K., A. Bigsten and G. Mwabu, 2005b, 'Trade Union Membership and Earnings in Kenyan Manufacturing Firms', *Applied Economics*, 37 (15), 1693–1704.

Omolo, J. and J. Omiti, 2004, 'Is Minimum Wage Policy Effective in Kenya?' Institute of Policy Analysis and Research Discussion Paper 54, Nairobi.

Pollin, R., Mwangi wa Gĩthĩnji and J. Heintz, 2007, *An Employment Targeted Economic Program for Kenya*. UNDP Country Study supported by the International Poverty Centre. Amherst, MA, USA: Political Economy Research Institute.

Republic of Kenya, 2000, *Economic Survey*. Nairobi: Government Printer.

Republic of Kenya, 2003a, *Report of 1998–99 Labour Force Survey*. Nairobi: Government Printer.

Republic of Kenya, 2003b, *Economic Recovery Strategy for Wealth and Employment Creation, 2003–2007*. Nairobi: Government Printer.

Republic of Kenya, 2005a, *Sessional Paper No. 1: Education Training and Research*. Nairobi: Government Printer.

Republic of Kenya, 2005b, *Sessional Paper No. 2: Development of Micro and Small Enterprises*. Nairobi: Government Printer.

Republic of Kenya, 2005c, *Sessional Paper No.4: Youth Policy*. Nairobi: Government Printer.

Republic of Kenya, 2005d, *Sessional Paper No.7: Employment Policy and Strategies*. Nairobi: Government Printer.

Republic of Kenya, 2006, *Economic Survey*. Nairobi: Government Printer.

Republic of Kenya, 2007, *Economic Survey*. Nairobi: Government Printer.

Republic of Kenya, 2008a, 'Labour Force Analytical Report', based on the *Kenya Integrated Household Budget Survey: 2005/06*. Nairobi: Government Printer.

Republic of Kenya, 2008b, *Kenya Vision 2030*. Nairobi: Government Printer.

Rosholm, M., H. Nielsen and A. Dabalen, 2007, 'Evaluation of Training in African Enterprises', *Journal of Development Economics*, 84 (1), 310–329.

Söderbom, M., F. Teal, A. Wambugu and G. Kahyarara, 2006, 'The Dynamics of Returns to Education in Kenyan and Tanzanian Manufacturing', *Oxford Bulletin of Economics and Statistics*, 68 (3), 261–288.

Wood, A., 1994, 'Give Heckscher and Ohlin a chance! ' *Review of World Economics*, 130 (1).

World Bank, 1995, 'Workers in an Integrating World', World Development Report 1995. New York: Oxford University Press.

World Bank, 2008, 'Doing Business 2009: Country Profile for Kenya'. Washington, DC: The World Bank.

World Bank, 2009, *Kenya ICA 2009*. Washington, DC: World Bank. http://siteresources.worldbank.org/INTAFRSUMAFTPS/Resources/KENYA_ICA_2009_Book.pdf.

12

Education for Prosperity: Improving Access and Quality

Tessa Bold, Justin Sandefur, Mwangi S. Kimenyi, and Germano Mwabu

12.1 Overview

A daunting challenge in the quest to achieve prosperity in any country concerns improving the stock of human capital. It is now well established in both theoretical and empirical literature that increasing the stock of human capital is pivotal to the achievements of accelerated economic growth and overall human development. An important component of human capital is education. Increasing this dimension of human capital entails higher school enrolments at all school levels and also raising the quality of education. Increasing access (quantity) without improving quality (achievement) means that the contribution of such investments is unlikely to be effective in improving economic and social prosperity. Of course, the task of raising the stock of education must begin at the primary level.

Since independence, the Government of Kenya's policy on education has been geared to universal education as stipulated in Sessional Paper No. 10 of 1965 on *African Socialism and Its Application to Planning in Kenya*. This focus on access to primary education is evidenced by the rapid growth in gross primary school enrolment rates especially between 1965 and 1990. However, in the 1990s, school enrolment rates declined. For example, the gross enrolment rate (GER) declined from 92.10 per cent in 1990 to 87.84 per cent in 1993 and to 86.91 per cent in 1999 (Kimalu *et al.*, 2001; Bedi *et al.*, 2002; Vos *et al.*, 2004).

The declining enrolment has been attributed to several factors including a general deterioration of the economy, the school fees charged to students, and perceived low returns to education (Bedi *et al.*, 2002). Thus, by the turn of the twenty-first century, Kenya was doing poorly in terms of access to primary education.

As a response to the problem of declining primary school enrolment, the newly elected government of Kenya introduced free primary education (FPE) nationwide in 2003. An immediate impact of this policy response was a surge in school enrolments. Although the access goal of FPE was quite successful, it is not certain that the same was true about quality, and there might have been a trade-off between increased enrolments and quality of education. We investigate the impact of FPE on student achievement with a view to identifying how best to design education policies that meet both the access and the quality goals.

Although FPE has succeeded in increasing the quantity of children enrolled in school, there is widespread concern that school quality has suffered – particularly in a subset of districts. We assess three common explanations for this alleged decline: (i) the failure of school budgets and staffing levels to keep pace with enrolment in some areas; (ii) changes in the composition of students; and (iii) the loss of local accountability as school management and funding has become centralized in the Ministry of Education since the introduction of FPE.

As it is well documented, an important determinant of service delivery outcomes relates to the accountability relationships across the service delivery chain. In addition to scrapping all fees paid by students, the FPE policy altered the relationships between the clients and the school administration and teachers as the role of the parents was constricted. Prior to the introduction of FPE, parents and local communities were heavily involved in the decision-making about their schools, construction of classrooms, and so on. Thus, one concern is that FPE might have weakened the client power with consequential deterioration in learning outcomes.

Briefly, we find that FPE has led to a 22 per cent increase in enrolment with no appreciable decline in Kenya Certificate of Primary Education (KCPE) scores at the national level, although there is substantial variation at the district level. Overall, FPE has been a successful pro-poor policy. Poorer districts have seen larger increases in enrolment compared with richer districts and are also to some extent catching up in terms of achievement. However, staffing levels have not kept pace, and increases in enrolment are associated with larger class sizes and lower KCPE scores. Moreover, both the potential decline in parental support as the composition of students changes as well as the crowding out of local accountability in the wake of FPE are reasons for concern, as both these factors are found to be important correlates of educational achievement.

12.2 Motivation and hypotheses

Understanding the effects of FPE on educational attainment is important because educational attainment and human capital accumulation are linked to economic well-being via two important avenues. First, higher levels of enrolment and education are linked to higher per capita income and economic growth. According to Psacharopolous and Patrinos (2004), an additional year of schooling increases wages by an average of 7.3 percentage points in sub-Saharan Africa. Moreover, although traditional wisdom has held that returns to education are concave (Psacharopolous and Patrinos, 2004), more recent evidence indicates that the returns to education are convex with most of the benefits accruing at secondary and tertiary level (Schultz, 2003; Rankin *et al.*, 2007). This is certainly confirmed in Kenya where Kimenyi *et al.* (2006) have found rates of return of 7.7 per cent at primary level, 23.4 per cent at secondary level, and 25.1 per cent at tertiary level. The evidence of the impact of education on growth is more mixed, however, with something of a micro–macro paradox, meaning that high effects from schooling on individual wages are not necessarily mirrored when regressing incomes on aggregate enrolment in cross-country regressions. However, there is some evidence that the aggregate enrolment does impact positively upon the growth rate (albeit not the level) of per capita income (see Benhabib and Spiegel, 1994). Second, higher levels of educational attainment are linked to increased civic participation. However, if education is not free, then the poor may be prevented from participating in education. Abolishing fees under FPE is therefore an important step towards increasing enrolment rates and educational achievement.

In this chapter, we identify and investigate three channels linking FPE to student performance. In particular, we examine what happens to student performance when:

1 Sources and total amount of funding in the education sector are affected:

- Government funding is increased.
- Increased government funding may have an ambiguous effect at the school level because local fund-raising may be reduced.

2 There are changes in the pool of students:

- Fees are abolished, so more children can access education.
- These children may differ from existing students in terms of socio-economic background, age, and ability.

3 Increased centralization may lead to a loss of accountability:

- School Management Committees no longer raise funds for the school and, as a result, their governance power is undermined.

- Parents no longer pay for the school, so they may lose a sense of ownership.
- Finally, the authority over hiring of teachers is held by the central government leaving little power to local school management.

12.3 Data

We examine the determinants of educational achievement since the introduction of FPE in 2003 using a panel data set based on a census of Kenyan primary schools, spanning all provinces and districts of the country. The data set combines a variety of administrative data sources collected by the Ministry of Education, the Teacher Service Commission (TSC), and the Kenya National Examinations Council (KNEC). The data cover the population of primary schools in Kenya – roughly 18,000 public and private schools in total – on an annual basis, both before and after implementation of FPE. Basic school characteristics such as enrolment and staffing are drawn from the Education Management Information System (EMIS), whereas our primary performance measure is the school average score in the KCPE examination, administered to all students completing Standard eight. In addition, we use detailed school-level information on parental and community involvement prior to the introduction of FPE from a nationally representative sample of 200 primary schools surveyed by the Southern African Consortium for Monitoring Educational Quality (SACMEQ) in 2000. Finally, school-level data have been linked to poverty indicators from the 2006 Kenyan Integrated Household Budget Survey (KIHBS).

12.4 Enrolment and achievement under FPE

The most obvious anticipated effect of FPE is a surge in enrolment. The EMIS database allows us to look at nationwide enrolment and KCPE score patterns, and determine how enrolment patterns and KCPE scores have changed in the wake of FPE.

Since the introduction of FPE, there has been a clear upward trend in enrolment. Figure 12.1, which is based on enrolment data from the EMIS database, presents the average gross enrolment rate before and after FPE. The data are at the school level, but have been summarized in province-level averages in the figure. To compare performance measures before and after FPE, the data are collapsed into just two periods: the before FPE period runs from 2000 to 2002, whereas after FPE spans the period from 2003 to 2005. Total enrolment in public primary schools in Kenya increased by 22.4 per cent from 2000–02 to 2003–05, while private primary enrolment rose by 37.0 per cent. Despite

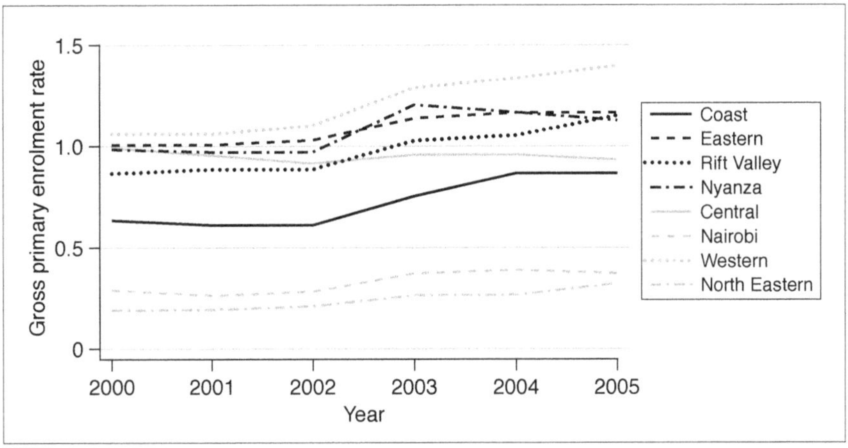

Figure 12.1 Enrolment trends by province. Enrolment increased in all eight provinces after FPE.

growing more rapidly, private enrolment accounted for just 3.6 per cent of the nationwide total in the period after the introduction of FPE.

Although FPE has succeeded in increasing the quantity of children enrolled in school, there is widespread concern that school quality has suffered. However, there is little evidence that these concerns are well founded at least in terms of performance in the KCPE. Figure 12.2 presents the averages of school-level KCPE scores before and after FPE by province. Across the country, the average score has remained more or less constant – in fact, even showing a

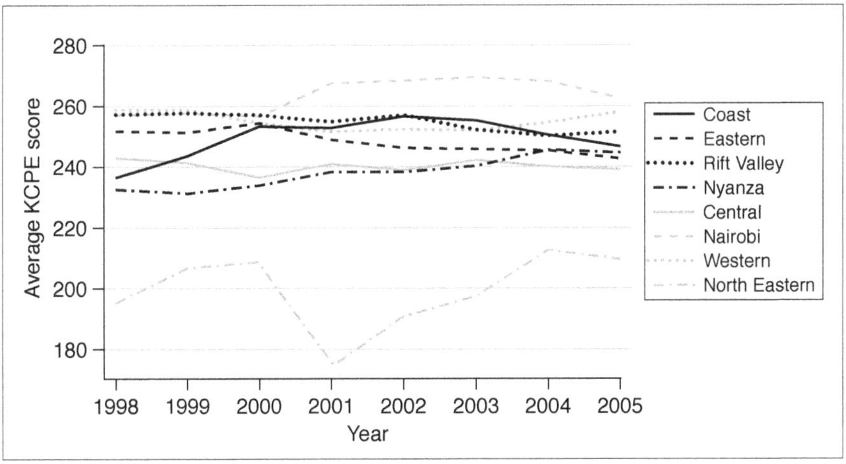

Figure 12.2 KCPE trends by province. KCPE scores have remained relatively stable – perhaps due to normalization of scores.

small increase of 0.3 per cent in these examinations – between 2000–02 and 2003–05, although there is some concern that scores are normalized and so between-district and -school comparisons are likely to be informative.

Increases in enrolment have not been uniform across all districts. The first part of Figure 12.3 shows a map of Kenyan districts coded by changes in enrolment. Although enrolment has increased across the board, districts in the north-east and along the western border have seen the largest increases, whereas increases in the central districts have been more modest.

A common concern is that performance in the KCPE examinations has suffered because of the influx of marginal students. However, inspection of the second part of Figure 12.3, which shows a map of Kenyan districts colour coded by changes in KCPE scores, indicates that there is little evidence for this. Comparing the two parts of Figure 12.3, we find no clear correlation between increases in enrolment and a deterioration in KCPE performance. If anything, districts that have experienced the largest increases in enrolment are also seeing bigger improvements in their KCPE scores.

12.4.1 Funding and resources

A necessary precondition for FPE to have a positive impact on access and quality is that central budgets are large enough to fund the influx of new students. Education spending in Kenya since the introduction of primary education has certainly been impressive. Table 12.1 shows public expenditure from 2000–01 to 2003–04, spanning the period before and after the implementation of FPE in 2003. As seen in Table 12.1, in absolute terms, the primary education budget rose roughly ninefold over this period, and increased roughly sevenfold as a share of public expenditure.

Although these increases have been impressive, it is important to ascertain how these funds have been distributed among the general populace. Overall, we find that the introduction of FPE has been an impressive pro-poor policy. Poorer districts have seen larger increases in enrolment compared with richer districts as students who could previously not afford schooling enter the education system. Poorer districts are also to some extent catching up in terms of achievement. However, increases in enrolment are associated with larger class sizes and concomitantly lower KCPE scores.

These findings are based on combining EMIS, KIHBS, and KNEC data. Figure 12.4 plots increases in Standard eight enrolment against the district-wide poverty head count. There is a clear positive relationship, indicating that poorer districts have been catching up in terms of participation since the introduction of FPE. The relationship between changes in enrolment rates and the poverty head count is statistically significant at the 5 per cent level: a district with one standard deviation higher poverty (16.8 percentage points) will on average have experienced an increase in enrolment of 4.8 percentage points.

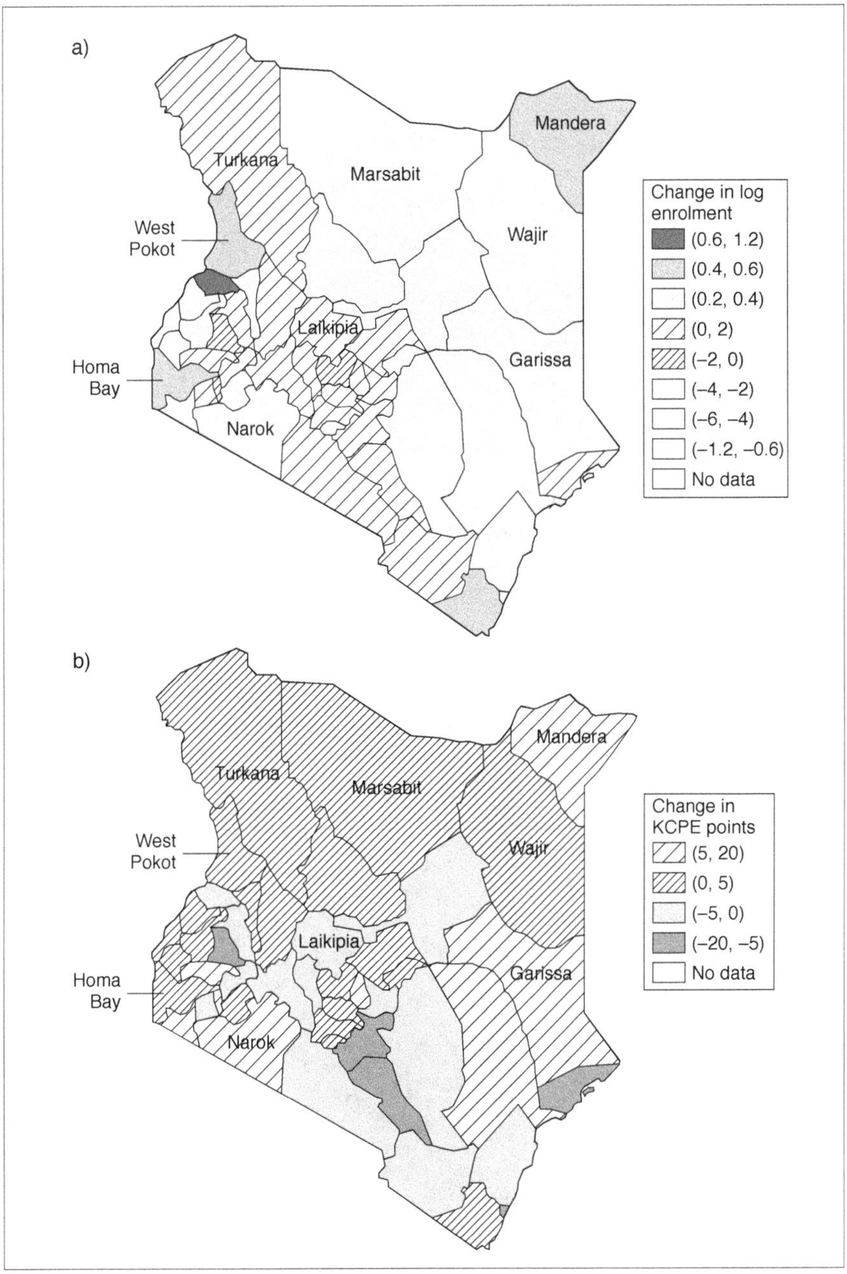

Figure 12.3 Maps before and after FPE.

Top, changes in enrolment since FPE. Values represent the changes in the log of public school enrolment. Bottom, Change in KCPE scores since FPE. KCPE scores measured by the sum of English, maths, and science examinations. Data are based on averages from 2000–02 and 2003–05; changes refer to the difference between these three-year averages.

Table 12.1 Public spending and aid for primary education (millions of Kenyan shillings).

	2000/01	2001/02	2002/03	2003/04
Primary education				
Actual expenditure	941	933	3,423	8,661
Aid receipts	207	319	231	1,262
Total Ministry of Education				
Actual expenditure	48,499	53,992	63,715	74,066
Aid receipts	288	559	272	1,529
Total national budget				
Actual expenditure	181,667	186,845	203,635	229,392
Aid receipts	34,116	35,072	32,658	33,244

Figures in the table represent the sum of the recurrent expenditure and development accounts, i.e. the sum of Votes D31 and R31 for the Ministry of Education, and within these, the sum of Votes D311 and R311 related to primary education.
Source: Republic of Kenya, Report of the Controller and Auditor-General.

Figure 12.5 shows that poorer districts have also caught up in terms of KCPE scores, but less so. Although this increase is not significant, there is in any case no evidence that poorer districts are falling behind in terms of achievement despite a surge in student numbers.

However, there is evidence that staffing levels have not quite kept up with the increases in enrolment. On average, pupil–teacher ratios have increased from 30:1 in 2001 to 44:1 in 2008. Class sizes have increased more in poorer districts where enrolment has been high as can be seen in Figure 12.6, which plots changes in Standard eight enrolment against district-level poverty rates. Moreover, higher class sizes for those taking KCPE exams are associated with

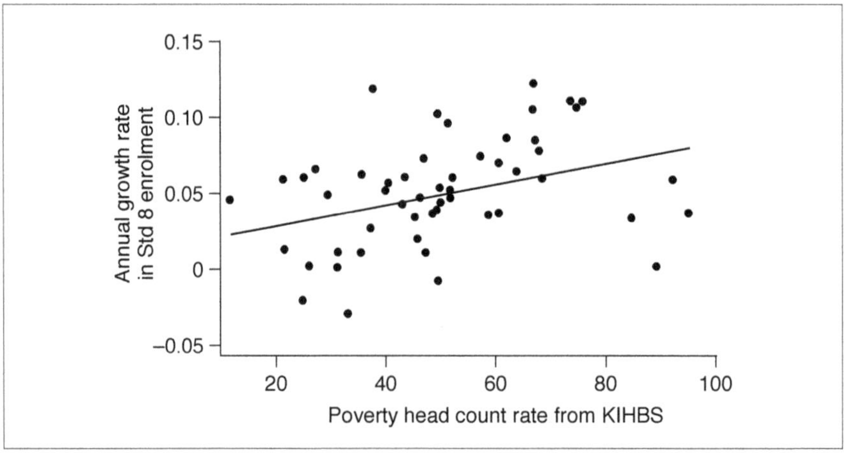

Figure 12.4 Enrolment growth by poverty rate. FPE is a pro-poor policy.

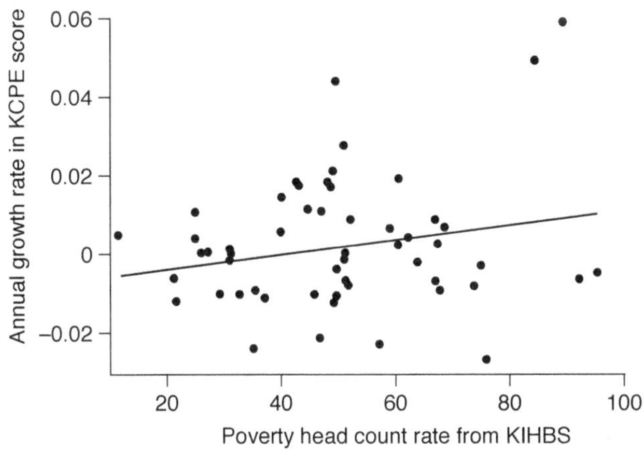

Figure 12.5 Growth in KCPE scores by poverty rate. KCPE scores increased faster in poorer districts.

lower performance, as seen in Figure 12.7, although the effect is relatively small.

12.4.2 Composition of students

Our results show that the composition of students entering education has indeed changed since the introduction of FPE. In particular, the age profile of students has been affected by the introduction of FPE, with older students

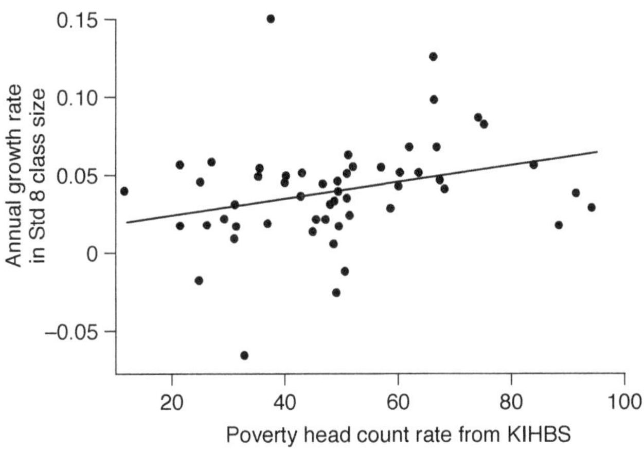

Figure 12.6 Growth in class size by poverty rate. Class sizes grew faster in poorer areas.

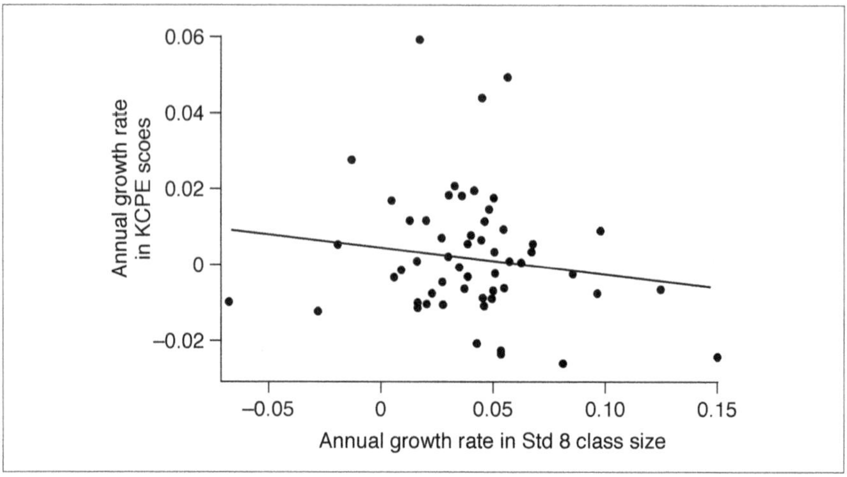

Figure 12.7 Growth in KCPE scores by growth in class size. Higher class sizes are associated with lower growth in KCPE scores.

entering or returning to school. For example, the proportion of students who are at least one year older than the regular age in Standard eight has increased from 28 per cent to 48 per cent between 2002 and 2004, and there is at least anecdotal evidence from teachers that this leads to disciplinary problems.

We cannot say how the parental background of students has changed, as previously not enrolled students enter the education system. However, Bold *et al.* (2009) find that the introduction of FPE has led wealthier parents to move their children into the private sector. Their study finds that the number of children in the private sector has tripled with a concomitant threefold rise in the price of private education.. If these are the parents who previously gave a lot of external support to schools – which is certainly plausible given that their decision to move to the pricier private sector reveals a strong preference for their children's education – then the introduction of FPE may well have drained schools of parental support and supervision. Moreover, this is of concern if parental support is an important input to educational achievement, and we do indeed find evidence that this is the case. Based on a nationally representative sample of 200 schools that were included in the SACMEQ survey in 2000, we have created an index of parental support in a school prior to the introduction of FPE. We find that high levels of initial parental support prior to FPE are associated with persistently higher KCPE scores between 2001 and 2005 in the 200 sample schools. This is seen in Figure 12.8, where we graph the average KCPE scores by initial level of parental support. Schools where parents were on average more involved and supportive prior to the introduction of FPE are achieving KCPE scores, which are 15 points higher on average, but this relationship may not be causal.

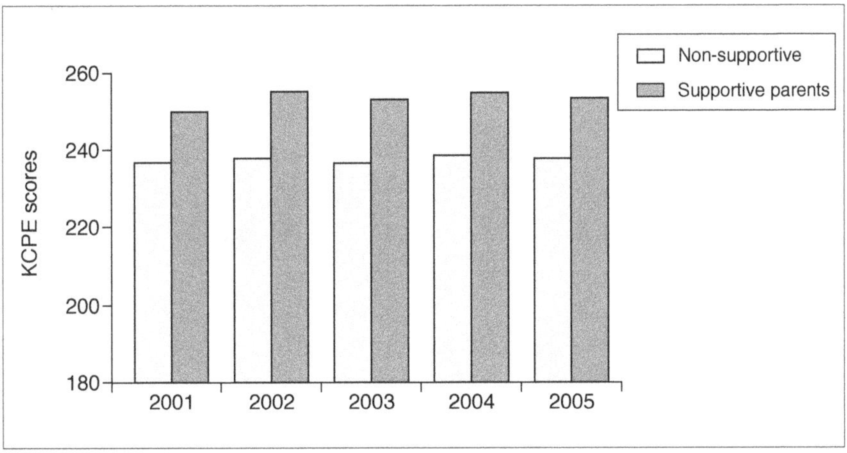

Figure 12.8 Parental support is an important input.

12.4.3 Accountability, incentives, and monitoring

Following the introduction of FPE, there has been some concern that centralized funding and monitoring has undermined local accountability and ownership. Based on combining EMIS, KIHBS, SACMEQ, and KNEC data, we find that high levels of community fund-raising and local monitoring and incentive provision prior to the introduction of FPE are indeed associated with persistently better performance in KCPE examinations.

Based on the SACMEQ sample of 200 schools surveyed in 2000, we have created indices of community fund-raising and monitoring. These include involvement in building and maintaining school facilities, and providing textbooks and stationery. As seen in Figure 12.9, we find a moderate relationship between initial levels of community fund-raising and KCPE scores in the 200 sample schools. Communal fund-raising activities are associated with a five-point increase in KCPE scores. These include activities such as organizing local *harambees* and providing bonus payments to teachers. We find a moderate relationship between levels of community fund-raising prior to FPE and KCPE scores in the 200 sample schools.

More importantly, schools in communities that provided bonus payments to teachers prior to the introduction of FPE do persistently better than those in communities that did not engage in this activity. As can be seen from Figure 12.10, communities that provide some bonus payments to teachers who performed well have KCPE scores that are on average 17 points higher.

Finally, in Figure 12.11, we explore the impact of communities being involved in extracurricular activities based on the SACMEQ data. Schools situated in communities that are active in this regard achieved KCPE scores that

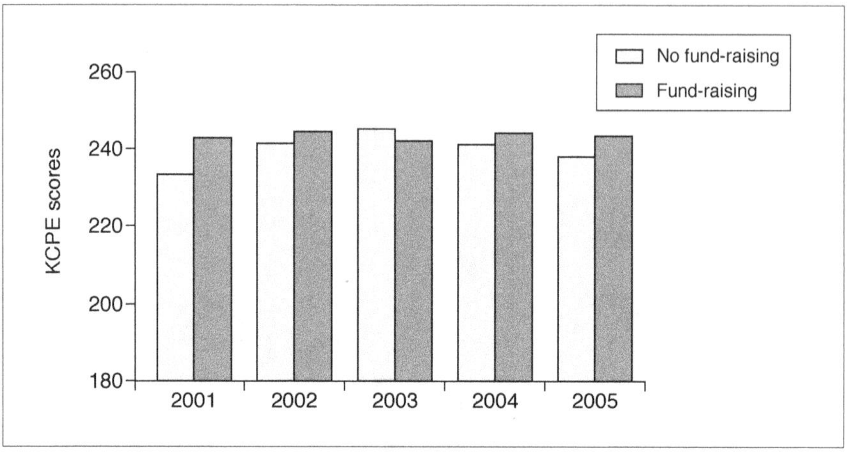

Figure 12.9 Community fund-raising is associated with higher KCPE scores.

were 30 points higher in 2001 and 2002. However, this difference has decreased markedly since the introduction of FPE.

Of course, these findings could be driven by differences in poverty levels, in the sense that richer districts can afford to be more active in fund-raising. We find no significant relationship between district poverty levels and the propensity to engage in fund-raising activities, however. Taken together, this suggests that the impact on test scores is not just driven by socio-economic variables, but that local accountability and incentive provision in themselves may increase academic achievement.

Given the potential crowding out of bottom-up monitoring in the wake of FPE, centralized, top-down monitoring and supervision by the Ministry of

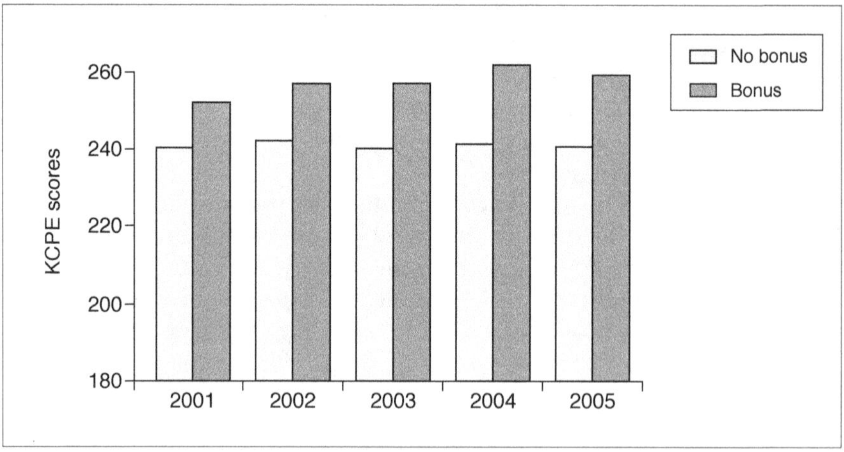

Figure 12.10 Teacher bonus pay is associated with higher KCPE scores.

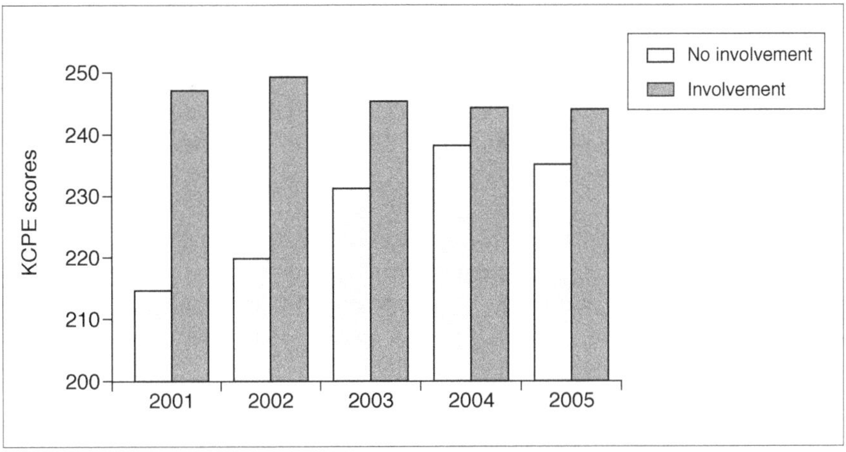

Figure 12.11 Extracurricular activities are associated with higher KCPE scores.

Education and its subsidiaries becomes more important. Combining the EMIS and KNEC database, we find evidence that school inspections are positively correlated with improvements in educational quality. First, the likelihood of an inspection is sensitive to the performance of the school. As shown in Figure 12.12, districts with below average test scores have almost 10 per cent more inspections than districts with above average test scores. Second, following an inspection, schools tend to improve. Districts with a high percentage of inspections see their test scores increase by an average of three points compared with districts with a low percentage of inspections.

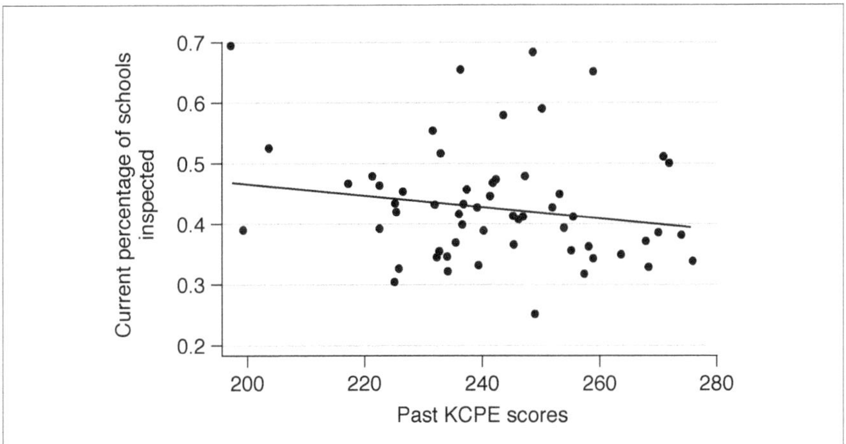

Figure 12.12 Inspections are responsive to past KCPE scores.

12.5 Conclusion and looking ahead

FPE has been an impressive pro-poor policy. There have been immediate gains in enrolment especially in poorer districts. But challenges remain: high pupil–teacher ratios have only begun to be addressed. However, although there is some association between class sizes and examination performance, the correlations are not strong enough to explain all of the variation in test scores. The effective use of inputs to achieve educational gains seems to require something else. The evidence presented in this chapter suggests that systems of accountability and monitoring – both internal and external – and the interaction and co-operation between schools, parents, and communities are the core drivers of educational achievement.

What are the implications of these findings as regards education policies for prosperity? In particular, how can the country improve both education access and quality?

It is of course difficult to 'engineer' community involvement and support. However, the evidence generated in this work suggests that the drop in communal and parental support may be largely due to a change in the composition of students in the private sector rather than those parents who have always remained in the private sector changing their behaviour in the wake of FPE. From this, we can deduce a clear policy prescription: the government of Kenya should aim to make the public sector as attractive as the private sector in terms of resource inputs. This policy might entice back high-income parents who have abandoned public primary schools in search of quality education for their children, enabling them to reduce the education burden. In particular, the questions of high pupil–teacher ratios and lack of resources to monitor schools need to be addressed. Currently, two government initiatives are planned that may have some success in doing so. According to recent newspaper reports, the government of Kenya is planning to hire an additional 16,000 relief teachers to address the high pupil–teacher ratios (*The Standard*, March 2009), but there are political challenges to this initiative. It is also planning to move to a system of performance contracts, in which teacher promotions are at least in some part dependent on past performance. Moreover, there is a feeling within the Ministry of Education (Minutes, meeting 20 March 2009) that school management committees were not sufficiently integrated into the process of making primary education freely available and that central administration needs to devolve more responsibilities to them. These are all steps in the right direction, which should directly improve the quality of public education. These two effects may well reinforce each other in bringing about improvements in education quality. In any case, the lessons learned from introducing FPE may well prove useful as the government moves to do the same for secondary education.

Achieving both access to and quality in primary education lays an important foundation for the country's long-term development agenda. Kenya's *Vision 2030* seeks to transform Kenya into a middle-income status economy by 2030. The cornerstone of this *Vision* is the achievement of a globally competitive economy, and a key prerequisite to make the *Vision* a reality is a skilled labour force that can adapt to new technologies and innovations. This requires improving access and quality at secondary and tertiary levels of education. Currently, the transition rates from primary to secondary schooling remain quite low and are not consistent with generating the type of labour force necessary to meet the *Vision*. The government has initiated a programme to provide free secondary education, but it has faced major problems of financing, and students are still expected to pay significant out-of-pocket fees and charges. Furthermore, the same concerns over quality experienced with the provision of FPE are likely to emerge as teacher training lags behind the consistently increasing student population, which is likely to increase even faster with the new initiative. Thus, achieving access to quality secondary and tertiary education remains a challenge to the country's quest to become globally competitive.

References

Bedi, A. S., P. K. Kimalu, D. K. Manda and N. N. Naful, 2002, 'The Decline in Primary School Enrolment in Kenya'. KIPPRA Discussion Paper No. 14.

Bedi, A. S., P. K. Kimalu, D. K. Manda and N. N. Naful, 2004, 'The Decline in Primary School Enrolment in Kenya', *Journal of African Economies*, 13, 1–43.

Benhabib, J. and M. M. Spiegel, 1994, 'The Role of Human Capital in Economic Development: Evidence from Aggregate Cross-country Data', *Journal of Monetary Economics*, 34, 143–173.

Boissiere, M., J. Knight and R. Sabot, 1985, 'Earnings, Schooling, Ability, and Cognitive Skills', *American Economic Review*, 75 (5).

Bold, T., M. K. Kimenyi, G. Mwabu and J. Sandefur, 2009, 'Free Primary Education in Kenya: Enrolment, Achievement and Local Accountability'. Presentation at CSAE Conference, March 2009, Oxford.

Government of Kenya, 1965, *Sessional Paper No. 10 on African Socialism and Its Application to Planning in Kenya*. Nairobi: Government Press.

Kimalu, P. K., N. Nafula, D. K. Manda, A. S. Bedi, G. Mwabu, and M. S. Kimenyi, 2001, 'Education Indicators in Kenya', KIPPRA Working Paper No. 4.

Kimenyi, M. S., G. Mwabu and D. K. Manda, 2006, 'Human Capital Externalities and Private Returns to Education in Kenya', *Eastern Economic Journal*, 32 (3) (Summer), 493–513.

Krueger, A. and M. Lindahl, 2001, 'Education for Growth: Why and for Whom?' *Journal of Economic Literature*, 39 (4), 1101–1136.

Lucas, R. E. (1988) 'On the Mechanics of Economic Development', *Journal of Monetary Economics*, 22, 3–42.

Manda D. K., G. Mwabu and M. S. Kimenyi, 2004, 'Human Capital Externalities and Private Returns to Education in Kenya'. Department of Economics Working Paper, University of Connecticut.

Mankiw, N. G., D. Romer and D. N. Weil, 1992, 'A Contribution to the Empirics of Economic Growth', *Quarterly Journal of Economics*, 107 (2), 407–437.

Minutes, 2009, Ministry of Education, Relief Teacher Programme, 20 March 2009.

Psacharopoulos, G. and H. A. Patrinos, 2004, 'Returns to Investment in Education: A Further Update'. World Bank Research Paper 2881.

Rankin, N., J. Sandefur and F. Teal, 2010 'Learning and Earning in Africa: Where are the Returns to Education High?'. CSAE Working Paper 2010-02.

Schultz, T. P., 2003, 'Evidence of Returns to Schooling in Africa from Household Surveys'. Yale University Economic Growth Center, Discussion Paper No. 875.

The Standard, March 2009.

Vos, R., A. Bedi, P. Kimalu, D. K. Manda, N. Nafula and M. S. Kimenyi, 2004, 'Achieving Universal Primary School Education in Kenya'. KIPPRA Discussion Paper No. 46.

13

Securing Property Rights in Land in Kenya: Formal Versus Informal

Joseph Kieyah and Patricia Kameri-Mbote

13.1 Introduction

Land is the centrepiece of Kenya's development and has often dictated the pulse of nationhood since independence. The essence of the land question confronting Kenya is insecure and unclear property rights for over two-thirds of 144 million hectares. Furthermore, the enforcement of private property rights for over 28 million hectares has not been forthcoming because of institutional factors. Clear and well-defined enforceable property rights to land will induce landowners to invest resources in productive activities instead of spending them on defending their claims. The absence of clear and secure property rights might inhibit the ability of the Kenyan government to deal adequately with new emerging issues. For example, global warming and climate change are expected to affect land use.

Since independence, the land issue has remained contentious. Although Kenya has developed since independence, a majority of the population continue to depend on the land for their livelihoods and economic well-being, making it increasingly complex. New land-related problems due to rapid population growth have added to historical legacies resulting in a labyrinth of problems that require focused and serious attention (Government of Kenya, 2002). However, failure by the government to adequately address the problem continues to threaten the social, political, and economic well-being of the nation (Kameri-Mbote and Kindiki, 2009). Indeed, land is the fulcrum of Kenya's development as rightly recognized by recent government publications (Government of Kenya, 2007). It is worth noting that land has emerged as one of the issues that needs to be dealt with if the underlying causes of violence, such as that sparked by the disputed presidential election in 2008, are to be avoided (Government of Kenya, 2008). Thus, any debate on Kenya's prosperity must incorporate the land issue. Land commissions have been established since colonial times to address the land question, and the main recommendations have been the call for urgent overall land reform and the singling out of lack of a national land policy as the root cause of land problems in Kenya (Government of Kenya, 2002). The report on Illegal/Irregular Allocations of Public Land (Government of Kenya, 2004) implicitly attributed the haphazard dealing over land to the absence of a land policy.

Through a widely consultative process, the Ministry of Land completed drafting the National Land Policy (NLP) in 2007 to address the land problem and fill the identified gap. The policy was adopted by Cabinet in 2009, and the National Land Policy was passed as Sessional Paper No. 3 of 2009. The overall objective of the policy is to secure property rights in land to provide for sustainable growth, investment, and the reduction of poverty in line with the government's development objectives. Although it has correctly diagnosed the land problem, it does not offer prescriptive measures on how to resolve these issues, leaving these to be spelt out in laws that will implement the policy. The provisions of the policy have sparked controversy, which is expected to continue in the implementation phase. It sets out long-term goals and principles of land management that enable the achievement of a socially optimal utilization of land.[1]

Vision 2030 acknowledges land reform as a critical ingredient in socio-economic transformation. Based on the current land debate, the land problem has gained a national importance.[2] Agenda four of the *Agreement on the Principles of Partnership of the Coalition Government* signed on 28 February 2008 deals with long-term solutions to the conflict that was witnessed in Kenya pursuant to the disputed 2007 presidential election. The land question comprises a major issue in Agenda four. Given that the land problem is not monolithic, it is difficult to recommend a one-size-fits-all solution. As one of the commission's reports points out, the land question has, over time, been shaped by economic, political, social, and legal parameters (Government of Kenya, 2002). These include the dependency of the economy on land, making the issues of tenure, access, distribution, and regulation critical. The political nuance of the land question is pegged to the administrative and political control of the economy based on land. The land–social structure nexus is clearly discernible in the African economy where the communities remain largely dependent on land for their livelihoods as well as economic activities (Government of Kenya, 2002). Each issue must be examined on its merits.

Conventional economic theory maintains that secure property rights in land, especially individual property rights, are a prerequisite for land development and economic growth (Demsetz, 1967; Ellickson, 1993). Secure rights comprise rights defined with sufficient precision and enforceable with least cost (Deininger, 2003). One important legal institution used for protecting those rights is land title registration. Attempts to institute land title registration on a voluntary basis have not succeeded in most parts of the world. De Soto (2000) argues that the reason why developing countries have not enjoyed the fruits of capitalism is the failure to institute formal title systems. He argues that lack of formal title is what prevents poor landowners from using their considerable land holdings as collateral for the purposes of 'unlocking' capital value.

In a review of De Soto's book, Woodruff (2001) questions why the gains from formal property rights are so great, and why formal property rights have not emerged as economic theory suggests they should have (Demsetz, 1967). However, he argues there exists an externality:

> An individual owner internalizes some of the gains from formal title – an increase in land value, increased access to credit, for example. But other gains are external to the person receiving the title. The ability to trade with strangers has network characteristics – I gain from you being formalized. Property registration systems help utilities collect from their customers. My cost will be lower if you are forced to pay. Thus, the benefit of universal titling might exceed the costs and the system may fail to develop spontaneously. Indeed, this is the case in the contemporary developing world, in De Soto's view.
>
> Woodruff (2001: 1217)

Based on empirical studies, the general consensus is that security of land tenure has no effect on agricultural productivity of land in Africa. Migot-Adholla *et al.* (1991) found no significant relationship between land rights and productivity at farm level based on cross-sectional data from Kenya, Ghana, and Rwanda. Place and Hazell (1993) reached similar results based on further examination of the same data set. Carter *et al.* (1994) found that land title in Kenya had no impact on yield output, income, and profit per acre. Pinckney and Kimuyu (1994) compared land use practices in two similar coffee-growing communities: Kenya, where individual land title has been promoted by the government; and Tanzania, where the state owns all the land. Consistent with the above studies, they found that land title has had little effect on land investment and the use of credit markets. In a detailed re-examination of the World Bank data set, Migot-Adholla *et al.* (1993) and Besley (1995) essentially reinforced the above conclusion. Using the conceptual model of Feder (1991), Place and Migot-Adholla (1998) tested the effects of land title in

Kenya on productivity as a function of exogenous factors and obtained similar results. However, using a district-level cross-sectional data set, Miceli *et al.* (2001) found that demand for land title registration in Kenya is influenced by economic factors. These results contrast with studies that have used farm-level data to suggest that title registration in Africa does not seem to have produced the sort of increases in productivity and capital investment that proponents of the system promised.

However, other comparable studies of countries such as Brazil demonstrate that secure titles enhance property values and promote farm-specific investment (Alston *et al.*, 1996). In Thailand, Feder and Onchan (1987) confirmed that security of landownership has substantial effects on agricultural productivity.

The conventional view that land titling has no or little impact on productivity is problematic because it is contrary to economic theory, which states that secured property rights in land are a prerequisite for land development and economic growth. Notwithstanding methodological concerns, one possible explanation for the failure of land title registration to affect productivity in Kenya is that the expected gains from registration have not yet been fully realized for various reasons.

There has been empirical evidence linking land reform and growth around the world. For example, Besley and Burgess (2000) used the general equilibrium framework to explain the linkages between land reform and poverty in India. Land reform in India aimed to increase tenure security through tenancy reforms, abolish intermediaries, implement ceilings on land holdings and consolidate disparate land holdings. Empirical work done in Nepal (Adhikari and Chatfield, 2008) has indicated that conventional redistributive policies, such as the redistribution of agricultural land through land reform programmes, has a direct impact on the incomes of the poor who benefited from these transfers. The aim of land reform in Nepal was redistribution of property rights in cultivatable land. Using time series data from Thailand, Byamugisha (1999) has shown that there is a positive and significant long-term effect between land titling and economic growth. In Zimbabwe, Moyo (1995) has shown that land reform in the form of redistribution has improved the well-being of resettled households dramatically over the last twenty years. The land redistribution reforms have not had negative impact on large-scale commercial farm outputs given the underutilization of arable land in the large-scale commercial farm sector in Zimbabwe. Chirwa (2004) has shown that land reforms, through land redistribution in Malawi, which led to access to land, are important factors that can translate to poverty reduction. Kieyah and Kivuti (2009) have empirically demonstrated that ownership of titled land affects household poverty. The data used for the analysis in this study are from the Kenya Integrated Household Budget Survey (KIHBS), which was conducted in 2005/06 by the Kenya government and consists of 13,430 observations in 1,343 clusters. Using consumption expenditure as a proxy for poverty and controlling for household characteristics, they found that ownership of titled land is positively and significantly related to poverty. These findings are consistent at both national and provincial level with the exception of the Western, Rift Valley, Nairobi, and North Eastern provinces due to data collection problems.

It is important, however, to consider the social side of the property institution, which nuances the economic aspect: property deals with value-enhancing relationships regarding assets. Consequently, legal enforcement of property rights enhances the owner's probability of retaining possession. It could mesh with assets that are not capable of being commodified,[3] such as property belonging to a group for a bereaved widow, kinship, and other familial ties. Indeed, the value of property increases with each additional subscriber, and the utility of property draws from the network of subscribers who can keep away the free-riders. The state provides the mechanism for public enforcement of property as a public good, ensuring that the law standardizes forms of property and reduces the costs of investigations. An effective title registration system needs to relate to the social side of property because the acceptance by one's neighbours of the legitimacy of a property owner's claim is quintessential to the enjoyment of that property. It is this acceptance that makes people keep off and, where people perceive some inalienable rights in the *res* that is claimed as property by another, the costs of protecting the property rise exponentially.

This chapter suggests that a definition of property rights and the formulation of mechanisms for protecting these rights are critical for both individuals and communities. Assuming clarity of land property rights, the chapter examines the formal and informal options for property rights protection. Section 13.2 traces the history of land reform in Kenya during the colonial and post-Independence period. Section 13.3 provides a comparative analysis of informal and formal mechanisms of protecting land rights. It examines the weaknesses and strengths of informal institutions. The benefits of the formal system notwithstanding, the section provides a simple economic model to explain the failure of land title reform in Kenya. Section 13.4 concludes.

13.2 Background information

This section explores the history of land reform in Kenya. During the colonial period, land policy was skewed in favour of European settlement at the expense of African reservation. The post-Independence Kenya government vigorously pursued the inherited land tenure reform coupled with its own land reform initiatives including land redistribution as embodied in settlement schemes and group ranches.

13.2.1 Colonial land policy

Kenya inherited colonial land laws that are a hybrid of English and African customary law. The colonial government viewed African customary land tenure as an impediment to greater agricultural production and proper land use. The newcomers proposed replacing the customary system with an English-style system based on individual land rights. Implementation of this remedy became a stated part of the colonial government's land policy in 1933 through the recommendation of the *Report of the Kenya Land Commission*. The inability of the colonial government to meet domestic food demands after the Second World War coupled with the Mau Mau revolt of the early 1950s created an urgent need for land reform (Okoth-Ogendo, 1976). In the wake of the revolt, an appointed Royal Commission published the *East Africa Royal Commission Report 1953–1955*, which became the blueprint for subsequent land reform policy. At the same time, the colonial government published the Swynnerton Plan, which called for the intensified development of African agriculture (Swynnerton, 1955). Both reports recommended the replacement of customary land tenure with private, titled property as a means of increasing agricultural productivity and redistributing land to efficient farmers (Kiamba, 1989). Pursuant to the recommendations of the two reports, the colonial government embarked on a major social engineering agenda to facilitate the formalization of African land tenure and institute a land title registration framework in the native 'reserves' (Government of Kenya, 1966; Coldham, 1979). More specifically, the Swynnerton Plan recommended the consolidation of land holdings of families into one, followed by the adjudication of property rights in that land and the registration of individuals as absolute owners of land adjudicated as theirs. This process was to end the perceived uncertainty of customary tenure already considerably modified by years of European contact (Okoth-Ogendo, 1991).

Following the publication of the Swynnerton Plan, the colonial government established a commission to consider specific legislation to implement the recommendations of the plan. As a result of the commission's report, the Native Land Tenure Rules were enacted in 1956.[4] This formalized the administrative process of consolidation, adjudication, and registration. To ensure that the rights granted through the process were not disturbed, the African Courts (Suspension of Land Suits) Ordinance was passed in 1957 to bar all litigation to which the 1956 Rules applied.[5] The net effect of these laws was to close avenues available to aggrieved land holders and dispossessed peasants. Three years later, two more comprehensive statutes, the Native Lands Registration Ordinance and Land Control Ordinances, were passed. The Native Lands Registration Ordinance of 1959 spelt out the rights of the registered proprietor at §37(a), namely an estate in fee simple in such land together with all rights and privileges belonging or appurtenant thereto.[6] These three pieces of legislation established the legal framework for formalizing the African land tenure system, which was to be implemented on an ad hoc basis.

13.2.2 Post-Independence land policy

At the time of independence, there were three substantive regimes in property law[7] and five registration systems[8] supported by administrative institutions to effect the objects of the regimes. The net effect of this was to perpetuate a dual system of economic relationships consisting of an export enclave controlled by a small number of European settlers and a subsistence periphery operated by a large number of African peasants. The duality was manifest in:

- Systems of land tenure based on principles of English property law and a largely neglected regime of customary property law;
- A structure of land distribution characterized by large holdings of high potential land and highly degraded and fragmented small holdings;
- An autonomous and producer-controlled legal and administrative structure for the management of the European sector, as opposed to a coercive control structure for the African areas; and
- A policy environment designed to facilitate the development of the European sector of the economy by underdeveloping its African counterpart (Government of Kenya, 2002).

To structure the inherited land tenure reform, the newly elected government enacted the Registered Land Act (RLA), which adopted many of the provisions of the Native Lands Registration Ordinance of 1959. In addition to addressing the competing interests between Kenyan Africans and the European settlers, the Kenyan government instituted land redistribution through land settlement schemes. The colonial authorities had initiated the Million Acre Scheme to resettle Africans. In the post-Independence period, the government offered to finance private people, both Kenyans and Europeans, to purchase large farms outside the settlement areas (Leo, 1989).

The intention in promulgating the RLA was to bring all land under this statute and thus achieve two sets of objectives (Kagagi, 1992). First, the Act set out to unify the multifarious systems of land registration in Kenya. This process entailed voluntarily bringing previously registered land in compliance with the RLA (Jackson, 1988). Specifically, land titles privately held under the Government Lands Act, Land Titles Act (LTA) and the Registered Titles Act (RTA) were to be converted and transferred to the new register in compliance with the RLA (Jackson, 1988; Kagagi, 1992). This has not been achieved.

The second objective involved converting land that was formerly held under African customary law into the modern tenure system of the Act through consolidation, adjudication, and registration. Under the adjudication, existing land rights and interests under African customary law in a particular parcel are finally and authoritatively ascertained under the Land Adjudication Act (LAA). Once ownership is determined, consolidation of the land holdings is allowed whenever appropriate, according to the Land Consolidation Act. It entails owners giving up their adjudicated fragmented plots in exchange for a single plot with the same acreage as the fragmented plots (Onalo, 1986). The final step includes recording the interest of the land in the public register and the issuance of land title deeds under the RLA.

TRUST LAND

Areas that were classified as native reservation and non-scheduled were reclassified as Trust land. The notion of Trust land was a way of giving recognition to group and native rights. Trust land consists of areas that were occupied by the natives during the colonial period and which have not been consolidated, adjudicated, and registered in individual or group names, and native land that has not been taken over by the government.[9] It is governed by the Trust Lands Act, Chapter 288, of the Laws of Kenya. Trust land is divided into two: that which should be registered under the RLA and that which is not for registration. Currently, Trust land falls within three broad categories: adjudicated, unadjudicated, and public land. Although a small part of the country has undergone the process of consolidation, adjudication, and registration, most of the Trust land has remained unadjudicated. The ownership of the Trust land is constitutionally vested in the local government on behalf of residents within its jurisdiction. The occupiers of Trust land that is unregistered land have rights that are in limbo and awaiting confirmation through registration. These rights are, in some cases, guaranteed under some form of customary tenure. Tenure of Trust land is increasingly changing from the trust status to ownership by individuals, legally constituted groups and the state, with the application of customary law being ousted and land removed from the ambit of local government control (Kameri-Mbote, 2002).

GOVERNMENT LANDS

Colonization, it has been argued, introduced a novel and alien concept of property relations in Kenya, namely the state–land relationship, with the assertion of the protectorate as a political entity owning land and granting property users subsidiary rights (Okoth-Ogendo, 1991). The 1901 East Africa (Lands) Order in Council defined Crown Lands as

> all public lands within the East African Protectorate which for the time being are subject to control of His Majesty by virtue of any Treaty, Convention or Agreement, or of His Majesty's Protectorate, and all lands which have not been or may hereafter be acquired by His Majesty under the Lands Acquisition Act, 1894, or otherwise howsoever.[10]

This was followed by the Crown Lands Ordinance No. 21 of 1902, which vested power in the Commissioner to sell freeholds in Crown land to any purchaser in lots not exceeding 1,000 acres.[11] These regulations conferred enormous discretionary power on the colonial authorities, which had a virtually free hand to determine what was 'waste and unoccupied' land. The tendency was to treat all native rights to land as temporary and only exercisable if the native is in actual occupation of the land.

The 1915 Crown Lands Ordinance ended the official pretence of concern for the interests of the natives by declaring all land within the protectorate is Crown land whether or not such land was occupied by the natives or reserved for native occupation.[12] The Ordinance mandated the colonial authorities to grant 999-year leases, although the settlers clamoured for perpetual leases.[13] Chief Justice Barth's interpretation of the provisions of this Ordinance in the case of Isaka Wainaina & Another v Murito wa Indagara & Ors. was to the effect that Africans were mere tenants at will of the Crown with no more than temporary occupancy rights to land.[14] Upon independence, Crown land was renamed government land governed by the Government Lands Act, Chapter 280 of the Laws of Kenya. Section 3 of this Act gave the President, like the Governor before him, power to make grants or dispositions of any estates, interests, or rights in or over unalienated government lands (Kameri-Mbote, 2002). Although some of the original land has been retained, some has been reserved for railways and allocated to private owners. Land previously owned by Europeans through grants became private land under freehold or leasehold.

SETTLEMENT SCHEMES

At independence, the Kenyan government adopted a market-based land distribution strategy to address landlessness and stimulate agricultural production (Government of Kenya, 2004). The struggle for independence was centred principally on the quest to regain control of land that had been taken by the colonial authorities. By the late 1940s, there was widespread discontent among Africans about colonial occupation of their land. Following independence, the new government embarked on settling its citizens who had been displaced from their ancestral land through discriminatory colonial policies of land alienation.

The objective of the strategy was to facilitate the transfer of large-scale European farms to Africans through settlement schemes. To start with, the Kenyan government financed the settlement through loans and grants from the British government and other international agencies (Leo, 1989). Upon acquisition of the European farms, based on a willing seller and buyer principle, the government subdivided them into economic units and mortgaged them to Africans. The Settlement Fund Trustees (SFT) was established to execute the programme. The beneficiaries purchased land on mortgage from SFT by paying periodically until the purchase price had been fully paid.

GROUP RANCHES

Formalizing land title in Maasailand posed several challenges to the new government: the area was dry with poor soil and bad landscape. Since Maasai land tenure was based on customary law, it was impractical to formalize land rights (Coldham, 1979); and international forces exogenously pressured the government to induce development by increasing livestock productivity while protecting Maasai communal ownership rights. Indeed, the *Report of the East Africa Royal Commission of 1953–1955* on the policy on land tenure in the East African Protectorate noted that, although individualization of land ownership should be the main aim, it should not be confined to individuals but should also be extended to groups such as companies, co-operatives, and customary associations of Africans.[15]

The Kenyan government introduced the concept of the group ranch as a compromise between conflicting communal ownership and private ownership interests. The concept is a hybrid of Maasai customary land tenure and private land tenure (Galaty, 1994). It involves setting aside a piece of land that is communally owned by a group of people who are recorded and registered as legal owners of that land in a ranch (Rutten, 1992). Although the Maasai had previously resisted various forms of development that would change their way of life, the concept of group ranches was attractive to the educated members of the community. It offered them security of title and protected them from land loss to other tribes (Government of Kenya, 1966).

A group ranch consists of members who hold group land title in common. Elected group representatives co-ordinate and implement ranch development projects including the management of resources and community organization (Galaty, 1994). The conventional view is that group ranches have failed to meet their intended objectives. Instead, most group ranches have been subjected to ongoing rapid subdivision, driven in part by their members. The inefficiency of group representatives in management, together with government pressure to privatize the ranches, has increased demand for subdivision (Kieyah, 2007). These inefficiencies are rooted in the original establishment of the group ranches, which disregarded Maasai customary laws. For instance, the territorial boundaries of these ranches were arbitrarily created and did not correspond with each group's previous boundaries.

13.3 Analysis

This section analyses the two options for the protection of property rights that are currently in place: informal and formal systems.

13.3.1 Informal protection

Some of the benefits of the informal system embodied through customary laws include protection of individuals' security of tenure and limited unsustainable use and dissipation of rents. However, the scope of its enforcement tends to be narrow and restricted to small communities. As the informal system lacks legal legitimacy, it is difficult to enforce against outsiders of a given community. Furthermore, the system remains vulnerable to break down if the custodians of customary law behave opportunistically as the resources rise in value.

As a means of protecting property rights in land, informal systems have not worked in Kenya. The post-Independence land laws have retained an element of hostility to the informal system, which was inherited from colonial land policy. The assumption was that the customary systems would fall into disuse and be replaced by modern/formal tenure systems. This has not happened, and those whose claim to land draws from informal systems have not received sufficient legal protection, leaving many vulnerable to legal usurpations and evictions (Lynch, 1996).

Although the existing Kenyan national laws recognize and protect customary land rights, the government's failure to enforce the law continues to undermine these rights. For instance, the Kenyan Constitution recognizes African customary law as the guiding legal principle under which the rights, interests, or other benefits of local residents over Trust land in a given county are held. However, subsequent provisions of the Constitution undermine these rights by imposing, in some instances, restrictions or extinguishment. First, under the repugnancy clause, 'no right, interest or other benefit under African customary law shall have effect ...so far as it is repugnant to any written law' (Government of Kenya, 2002). This makes indigenous peoples' land rights in Trust land subject to the vagaries of national politics. Any arbitrary legislation could be enacted that may explicitly contradict the African customary law and thereby supersede it. This is because of the assumption that customary tenure needs to be modernized and that, being the principle guiding land policy and law in Kenya, there is very little documented information on customary tenure norms, values, and institutions. Attempts to recognize and protect customary tenure have been through organizational forms, the institutional norms and values of which clash with those of the community. Group ranches and local authorities are cases in point.

Second, the Kenyan Constitution, through an Act of Parliament, grants the local government and the President eminent domain power to 'set apart an area of Trust land' for public use.[16] Appropriation under this section extinguishes all the interests previously held under the informal system. Anecdotal evidence indicates that councillors have illegally allocated Trust land set apart for public purposes to individuals and to themselves (Government of Kenya,

2004). With regard to group ranches, there is evidence of parcellation into individual holdings, thus negating the intentions that informed this form of land holding. Indeed, one could argue that such titling seeks to lock in the benefits of formalized tenure in a situation in which the land holders perceive their holdings as unsecured.

13.3.2 Formal protection

Kenya's experimentation with formalization of land title through registration is a mixed bag. Methodological issues of evaluating the impact of the registration process notwithstanding, it might be the case that expected gains from registration have not yet been fully realized for various reasons. Since its inception, the title registration process has been predicated on voluntary adoption, which might have been the main reason why the process failed.

This section provides a verbal description of a simple model showing that title reform, based on voluntary adoption of a new system, will most likely result in underutilization (Miceli and Kieyah, 2003). The model is developed in the Appendix.

The fundamental question the model seeks to answer is whether the voluntary policy may have contributed to its failure. Title registration is a necessary condition for economic development, yet economists and policy-makers often assume that the demand for it will arise spontaneously. Suppose the government decides to formalize ownership through title registration in a region where ownership is predominantly protected by informal means. Assume economies of scale of administrative costs of title registration per parcel depend on the number of parcels in the new system. Costs per parcel decline as the number of parcels in the system increases. Given the cost, only landowners whose parcels' net values exceed those of the prevailing system voluntarily demand title registration. In so doing, they ignore the benefit that their entry confers on all other entrants by lowering costs. As a result, few owners may choose to enter the system.

The anecdotal evidence on the assessment of Kenya's land title registration supports the model. The first objective of land title reform is to unify the multifarious systems of land registration under a single act. This process is costly where landowners whose titles are governed by the pre-Independence registration laws are expected to voluntarily bring them into compliance with the RLA (Jackson, 1988). Since enactment of the RLA, not a single title has been converted (Kagagi, 1992).

The second objective entailed formalization of African land tenure through a land title registration process where land claims are filed voluntarily during the adjudication phase. The rate of formalization has been slow, protracted and stalled in some regions. Moreover, in some other cases, gains of title registration have been reversed. For instance, in regions where land registration has been completed, land transactions have continued to be conducted informally (Coldham, 1979). Out of 144 million acres, only 4 million titles have been issued, and about 18 per cent of all land available for title registration countrywide has been entered into the system (Syagga, 2006).

One other contributory factor is institutional reforms such as the regulation of agricultural land transactions, which have generated unintended consequences in impeding land title reform. Through the Land Control Act (LCA) of 1967, the government established a legal framework under which the transactions of agricultural lands were to be administratively regulated. Specifically, the Act provided for efficient use of agricultural land by controlling fragmentation, landlessness, and speculation. It establishes a three-tier land control board system with unimpeachable statutory powers to grant or deny consent for the controlled transactions of agricultural lands. Controlled transactions as defined in the LCA are not capable of conferring any interest and right to land without the board's consent. Evidence shows that the land board control system has not been operating inefficiently, but that the administrative nature of the system propagates rent-seeking behaviour, which raises the transaction costs of dealing with agricultural land (Government of Kenya, 2002).

Another reason why the benefits of formalization may not have been realized is the disconnection between the objects of formalization and its actual operations on the ground. As Nyamu-Musembi (2006) and Bromley (2008) aver, the benefits of formalization may be overrated compared with the actual results. Bromley asserts that 'formalisation erodes and displaces existing social networks and arrangements that do offer security' and that 'formalisation offers little assurance that beneficial outcomes are inevitable' (Bromley, 2008).

13.4 Conclusion

This chapter offers two options of property rights protection on land: formal and informal systems. The informal system offers security of tenure with minimal costs; however, its effectiveness is localized, which severely impedes the development of a land market. Furthermore, although the existing national laws recognize the informal system, they provide weak legal enforcement mechanisms, which are sometimes contradictory. From anecdotal evidence, individuals and communities whose claims to land draw from informal systems do not have sufficient legal protection. This leaves many of them vulnerable to legal usurpations and evictions including land grabbing and illegal takings.

On the other hand, formal protection through land title registration offers maximum security of tenure but it is costly. Kenya's experimentation with land title registration has not produced the sort of increases in productivity and capital investment the proponents of the system promised. Formal title systems are essential to economic development; however, economists and policy-makers often assume that they simply exist or will arise spontaneously.

This chapter shows that, even in the extreme case where all landowners would gain from the institution of a new system, equilibrium usage may fall short of the optimal level due to a fundamental externality. Of course, it is impossible to determine the importance of this effect relative to a myriad of other factors that contribute to the success or failure of title reform. Even under the most favourable conditions for reform, policies based on voluntary reform are unlikely to achieve their full potential. Therefore, Kenyan government provision and maintenance of a title system is a necessary, although perhaps not a sufficient component of a successful economic development policy.

Land remains the fulcrum of Kenya's development. It forms a critical link between the three pillars of development: political and legal, economic, and social, as envisaged by *Vision 2030*. *Vision 2030* acknowledges the implementation of the draft as a key ingredient to socio-economic transformation that the country envisages by the year 2030. Land is a critical input in the productivity of the agriculture and tourism sectors, which *Vision 2030* has identified as major drivers of overall economic growth. Clear property rights in agriculture will increase revenues through taxation as well as reduce incidences of poverty. Proper management of public land would provide for other land uses such as manufacturing, mining, and urban planning. Socially, protection of property rights may positively affect the reduction in poverty incidence.

Appendix

Simple model

Suppose there are N parcels of land in a given region. Let v be the value of a given parcel under the prevailing land title system, where, for simplicity, differences in v across parcels solely reflect varying title risks. Let F(v) be the distribution of these values over the range $[0, v_{max}]$.

Suppose that, by bringing a parcel into the new title system, a landowner can eliminate all (or nearly all) existing defects, resulting in a value of V that is the same for all parcels (reflecting the fact that the parcels are identical, apart from title defects). Further, $V>v_{max}$, implying that all parcels attain a higher value under the new system. Thus, if the new system was costless to operate, all landowners would rationally enter it.

However, the new system is not costless. Specifically, let t(n) be the cost per parcel of operating the new system as a function of the number of parcels in the system, n. The key assumption is that there are scale economies in these administrative costs. That is, $t'(n)<0$, or costs per parcel decline as the number of parcels in the system increase. Decreasing average cost might reflect, for example, high fixed costs associated with the establishment of a title registry, coupled with low variable costs.

Compulsory title reform would require that all N landowners enter the new system and assess each at a cost of t(N). Such a reform would therefore constitute a Pareto improvement if

$$V - t(N) \geq v_{max} \tag{13.A1}$$

which means that the net value of the land is higher under the new system for the parcel with the highest value under the prevailing system. Although this need not be true, we assume that it is in order to show that, even when it is in the interest of all owners to enter the new system, a policy of voluntary entry may nevertheless fail to achieve this outcome.

Now, suppose that the entry into the system is voluntary, and that individual landowners take the cost of entering the system, t, as given. An owner whose land is worth v under the prevailing system will therefore enter the new system if

$$V - t \geq v \tag{13.A2}$$

According to this condition, owners with the most serious defects will be the most willing to enter the new system. For a marginal landowner, $V-t=v$. We therefore define

$$v^*(n) = V - t(n) \tag{13.A3}$$

as the highest valued parcel that enters the system under a voluntary regime when n parcels are in the system. In equilibrium, therefore, it must be true that

$$n = N\, F(v^*(n)) = G(n) \tag{13.A4}$$

where $F(v^*(n))$ is the fraction of parcels entering the new system as implied by Equations (13.A2) and (13.A3). To determine the implication of Equation (13.A4), note first that

$$\partial G/\partial n = NF'(\partial v^*/\partial n) = -NF't'(n) > 0 \tag{13.A5}$$

where the positive sign reflects the scale economies in administrative cost.

Now, suppose that n=0, or no parcels are in the new system. In that case, $v^*(0)=V-t(0)$. If this is positive, then the owners of the lowest valued parcels under the prevailing system would find it privately optimal to enter the new system. In that case, G(0)=NF(v*(0))>0. Alternatively, if v*(0)<0, no individual owners would find it optimal to establish the system, in which case G(0)=0. It follows that G(0)≥0. Now suppose n=N, or all parcels are in the new system. From Equation (13.A1), v*(N)≥0, which implies that F(v*(N))=1 and G(N)=N.

Note that, although n=N, the efficient outcome, is one equilibrium, there may exist others with n<N (including n=0 in the case where G(0)=0). The reason for the existence of these suboptimal equilibria is the externality embodied in the t(n) function. Specifically, in a regime of voluntary entry, individual landowners take the entry cost, t, as given and enter according to Equation (13.A2). In so doing, however, they ignore the benefit that their entry confers on all other entrants by lowering t(n). As a result, too few owners may choose to enter the system.

Figure 13.A1 indicates that multiple interior equilibria may exist, depending on the particular shape of the G(n) function. Some of these equilibria are stable and some are not. The stable equilibrium are those in which G(n) cuts the 45° line from above, i.e. where the slope G(n) is <1. In Figure 13.A1, there are two stable equilibria, namely the interior point A and the efficient point n=N.

General model

Suppose the cost of registering a property in the new title system is given by t(v, n) where $t_v < 0$ and $t_n < 0$. The fact that $t_v < 0$ implies that it is costlier to repair more serious title defects. From Equation (13.A2), the condition for an owner with property value v to enter the new system is

$$V \geq t(v, n) + v \equiv A(v, n) \tag{13.A6}$$

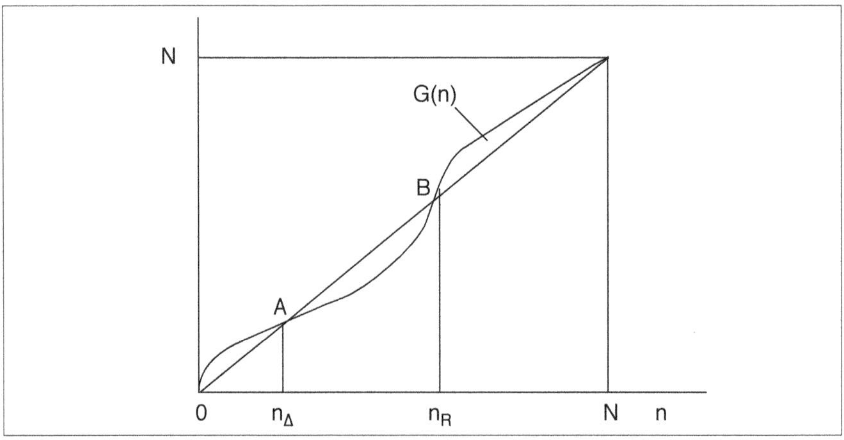

Figure 13.A1 Equilibrium adoption of the new title.

Note that $A_v=t_v+1 \geq 0$ or $A_v=t_v+1 < 0$. Thus, it is no longer necessarily true that the owners with the lowest values of v will be the first to enter the new system.

Let us define S(n) to be the set of parcels for which it is profitable to enter the new system for given n, that

$$S(n)=\{v: A(v, n)\} \leq V \tag{13.A7}$$

The number of parcels in the system is therefore given by

$$G(n)=N \int dF(v) \tag{13.A8}$$

It follows that, in equilibrium,

$$N=G(n) \tag{13.A9}$$

The fact that $A_n=t_n < 0$ implies that S(n) is non-decreasing in n. Thus, $G'(n) \geq 0$, and the conclusions in the text carry through.

Finally, we need to revise Equation (13.A1), which ensures that it is socially optimal for all parcels to enter the new system. Define v*(N) to be the parcel for which entry into the new system is least desirable when all parcels are in the system. From Equation (13.A1), it follows that $v^*(N)=\arg_{max} A(v, n)$. Thus, Equation (13.A1) is replaced by

$$V \geq A(v^*(N), N) \tag{13.A10}$$

Note that if A(v, n) is increasing in v for all n, then $v^*(N)=v_{max}$ as in the text.

Notes

1 Paul Syagga, 'Objectives Principles and Key Recommendations of the Draft National Land Policy', a paper presented at the Workshop on Land Reforms for Sustainable Peace, Stability and Development by the Institution of Surveyors of Kenya at Nairobi Safari Club on 10 June 2008.

2 Kofi Annan's Recommendation. Recent Safari Park Workshop convened by the Minister of Land.

3 See Margaret Jane Radin (2001) explaining the distinction between fungible property (not unique and not linked to persona), which is easily amenable to transaction in the market, and non-fungible property (unique and personal as part of the owner's personality; sentimental, emotional link), the value of which to the owner is beyond the market.

4 These rules empowered the Minister for African Affairs to set up machinery for the adjudication of areas of 'native' lands within which private rights to land were considered to exist.

5 The Kikuyu districts of Kiambu, Nyeri, and Fort Hall (now Murang'a) (comprising Central Province) and Embu and Meru (comprising part of Eastern Province) were among the first areas where tenure reform was carried out. See examples from figures given in J. D. MacArthur, 1961, Land Tenure Reform and Economic Research into African Farming in Kenya, *East African Economic Review*, 82. Consolidation consisted of the process of amalgamating all the pieces of land owned by one person to determine the acreage to which the person was entitled. It would be followed by adjudication, namely determination of the rights of each person to that land, and then registration, which vested absolute rights in the registered proprietor to the land.

6 See Colony and Protectorate of Kenya, Native Lands Registration Ordinance No. 27 of 1959 (1959) (hereinafter the NLRO, 1959). The aim of this ordinance as stated in the Preamble was 'to provide for the ascertainment of rights and interests in, and for the consolidation of land in the native lands; for the registration of title to and transactions and devolutions affecting such land and other land in native lands and for purposes connected therewith and incidental thereto'. It was the precursor to the current Registered Land Act, Chapter 300 of the Laws of Kenya (hereinafter the RLA).

7 The Transfer of Property Act of India, 1882, the Registered Land Act, Cap. 300 of the Laws of Kenya and customary law.

8 Registration of Documents Act (Cap. 285), the Registration of Titles Act (Cap 281), the Government Lands Act (Cap. 280), the Land Titles Act (Cap. 282) and the Registered Land Act (Cap. 300).

9 See §115 of the Constitution of Kenya (1983).

10 See §1 of the East African Order-in-Council, 1901, passed at the Court of St James on 8 August 1901.

11 See §4 of the Crown Lands Ordinance, 1902.

12 See §5 of the Crown Lands Ordinance, 18 May 1915.

13 See §34 of the Crown Lands Ordinance, 18 May 1915.

14 (1922–23) Kenya Law Reports, Vol. IX, 102.

15 See Report of the East Africa Royal Commission of 1953–1955, Cmd 9475 (1955).

16 Ibid. at §117, cl 1.

References

Adhikari C. and P. Chatfield, 2008, 'The Role of Land Reform in Reducing Poverty Across Nepal'. Himalayan Policy Research Conference, Nepal Study Centre, Madison, WI.

Alston, L. *et al.*, 1996, 'The Determinants and Impact of Property Rights: Land Title on the Brazilian Frontier', *Journal of Law and Economics, Organization*, 12, 25–61.

Besley, T., 1995, 'Property Rights and Investment Incentives: Theory and Evidence from Ghana', *Journal of Political Economy*, 103, 903–937.

Besley T. and R. Burgess, 2000, 'Land Reform, Poverty Reduction and Growth: Evidence from India', *Quarterly Journal of Economics*, 115 (2), 389–430.

Bromley, D. W., 2008, 'Formalising Property Relations in the Developing World: The Wrong Prescription for the Wrong Malady', *Land Use Policy*, 26 (1), 20–27.

Byamugisha, F. K., 1999, 'The Effects of Land Registration on Financial Development and Economic Growth: A Theoretical and Conceptual Framework'. World Bank Policy Research Working Paper No. 2240.

Carter, M. *et al.*, 1994, 'Tenure Security for Whom?: Differential Effects of Land Policy in Kenya', in Bruce, J. W. and S. Migot-Adholla (eds) *Searching for Land Tenure Security in Africa*. Dubuque, IA: Kendall/Hunt Publishing Company.

Chirwa, E. W., 2004, *Access to Land, Growth and Poverty Reduction in Malawi*. University of Malawi. Available at http://www.g24.org/chirwa.pdf (accessed 4 November, 2009).

Coldham, S., 1979, 'Land-Tenure Reform in Kenya: The Limits of Law', *Journal of African Modern Studies*, 17, 615–627.

Deininger, K., 2003, *Land Policies for Growth and Poverty Reduction*. Washington, DC: World Bank and Oxford University Press.

Demsetz, H., 1967, 'Toward a Theory of Property Rights', *American Economic Review*, 57, 347–359.

De Soto, H., 2000, *The Mystery of Capital: Why Capitalism Triumphs in the West and Fails Everywhere Else*. New York: Basic Books.

Ellickson, R., 1993, 'Property in Land', *Yale Law Journal*, 102, 1315–1400.

Ensminger, J., 1997, 'Changing Property Rights: Reconciling Formal and Informal Rights to Land in Africa', in Dobrak, J. and J. Nye (eds) *The Frontiers of the New Institutional Economic*. San Diego: Academic Press.

Feder, G., 1991, *Land Policies and Farm Productivity in Thailand*. Baltimore, MD: Johns Hopkins University Press.

Feder, G. and T. Onchan, 1987, 'Land Ownership Security and Farm Investment in Thailand', *American Journal of Agricultural Economics*, 69, 311–320.

Galaty, J., 1994, 'Ha(l)ving Land in Common: Subdivision of Maasai Group Ranches in Kenya', *Nomadic Peoples*, 34, 110.

Government of Kenya, 1966, *Report of the Mission on Land Consolidation and Registration in Kenya*. Nairobi: Government Printer.

Government of Kenya, 2002, *Report of the Commission of Inquiry into the Land Law System of Kenya on Principles of a National Land Policy Framework, Constitutional Position of Land, New Institutional Framework for Land Administration*. Nairobi: Government Printer.

Government of Kenya, 2004, *Report of the Commission of Inquiry into Illegal/Irregular Allocation of Public Land*. Nairobi: Government Printer.

Government of Kenya, 2007, *Kenya Vision 2030*. Nairobi: Government Printer.

Government of Kenya, 2008, *Report of the Commission of Inquiry into the Post Election Violence*. Available at http://www.kenyalaw.org/Downwards/Reports/Commission_of_inquiry_into_Post_Election_Violence.pdf.

Jackson, T., 1988, *The Law of Kenya*. Nairobi: Kenya Literature Bureau.

Johnson, O., 1972, 'Economic Analysis, the Legal Framework, and Land Tenure Systems', *Journal of Law and Economics*, 15, 259–276.

Kagagi, D. N., 1992, 'The Law and Practise of the Registered Land Act 1963: A Comparative Study'. PhD Dissertation, University of Leeds Faculty of Law.

Kameri-Mbote, P., 2002, *Property Rights and Biodiversity Management in Kenya*. Nairobi: ACTS Press.

Kameri-Mbote, P. and K. Kindiki, 2009, 'Trouble in Eden: How and Why Unresolved Land Issues Landed "Peaceful Kenya" in Trouble in 2008'. Forum for Development Studies, Oslo, Norway, Vol. 2, 2008 (January 2009).

Kenya National Archives. BN/82/9, BN/81/16A, BN/82/9.

Kiamba, M., 1989, 'The Introduction and Evolution of Private Landed Property in Kenya', *Development and Change*, 20, 121–147.

Kieyah, J., 2007, 'Indigenous Peoples' Land Rights in Kenya: A Case of the Maasai and Ogiek People', *Penn State Environmental Law Review*, 15 (3), 397–437.

Kieyah, J. and R Kivuti, 2009, 'Land Reform and Poverty'. Working Paper Series 17. Global Development Networks.

Leo, C., 1989, *Land and Class in Kenya*. Harare, Zimbabwe: Nehanda Publishers.

Lynch, O., 1996, 'Legal Challenges Beyond the Americans: Indigenous Occupants in Asia and Africa', *St Thomas Law Review* , 9, 93.

Miceli, T. and J. Kieyah, 2003, 'The Economics of Land Title Reform', *Journal of Comparative Economics*, 31 (2), 246–259.

Miceli, T., Sirmans and J. Kieyah, 2001, 'The Demand for Land Title Registration: Theory with Evidence from Kenya', *America Law and Economics Review*, 3 (2), 275–287.

Migot-Adholla, S. *et al.*, 1991, 'Indigenous Land Rights Systems in Sub-Saharan Africa: A Constraint on Productivity? ' *World Bank Economic Review*, 5, 155–175.

Migot-Adholla, S. *et al.*, 1993, 'Security of Tenure and Land Productivity in Kenya', in Bruce, J. W. and S. Migot-Adholla (eds) *Searching for Land Tenure Security in Africa*. Dubuque, IA: Kendall/Hunt Publishing Company.

Moyo, S., 1995, *The Land Question in Zimbabwe*. Harare, SAPES Books.

Musembi, C. N., 2006, 'Breathing Life into Dead Theories about Property Rights: De Soto and Land Relations in Rural Africa'. IDS Working Paper No. 272. Brighton: Institute of Development Studies.

Okoth-Ogendo, H. W. O., 1976, *African Land Tenure Reform in Agricultural Development in Kenya: An Economic Perspective*, J. Heyer *et al.* (eds). Nairobi: Oxford University Press.

Okoth-Ogendo, H. W. O., 1991, *Tenants of the Crown: Evolution of Agrarian Law and Institutions in Kenya*. Nairobi: African Center for Technology Studies Press.

Onalo, P., 1986, *Land Conveyance in Kenya*. Nairobi: Heinemann Kenya.

Pinckney T. and P. Kimuyu, 1994, 'Land Tenure Reform in East Africa: Good, Bad or Unimportant? ' *Journal of African Economies*, 3, 1–28.

Place, F. and P. Hazell, 1993, 'Productivity Effects on Indigenous Land Tenure Systems in Saharan Africa', *American Journal of Agricultural Economics*, 75, 10–19.

Radin, M. J., 2001, *Contested Commodities*. Cambridge, MA: Harvard University Press.

Rutten, M. M. E. M., 1992, *Selling Wealth to Buy Poverty: The Process of the Individualization of Landownership Among the Maasai Pastoralists of Kajiado District in Kenya, 1890–1990*. Fort Lauderdale: Verlag Breitenbach Publishers.

Simpson, S., 1976, *Land Law and Registration*. Cambridge: Cambridge University Press.

Swynnerton, R. J. M., 1955, *A Plan to Intensify the Development of African Agriculture*. Nairobi: Government Printer.

Syagga, P. M., 2006, 'Land Ownership and Use in Kenya: Policy Prescriptions from an Inequality Perspective', in Society of International Development (ed.) *Readings on Inequality in Kenya: Sectoral Dynamics and Perspectives*. Nairobi: Regal Press Kenya Ltd.

Woodruff, C., 2001, 'Review of De Soto's *The Mystery of Capital*', *Journal of Economic Literature*, 39, 1215–1223.

14

Banking Sector Stability, Efficiency, and Outreach in Kenya

Thorsten Beck, Robert Cull, Michael Fuchs, Jared Getenga, Peter Gatere, John Randa, and Mircea Trandafir[1]

14.1 Introduction

The current crisis has put the financial sector again at the centre of policy-makers' attention across the developed and developing world. Although, in recent years, the financial sector debate across the African continent has been dominated by policies to increase access to financial services, minimizing the impact of the crisis currently tops the agenda. Financial systems across Africa have seen a deepening and broadening over the past years, partly benefiting from the Great Moderation and global liquidity glut, but also from improvements in macroeconomic policies and progress in institutional reforms (Beck *et al.*, 2009). This chapter discusses the recent development of the financial sector in the major East African economy of Kenya, in the context of recent reforms.

By African standards and in comparison with other East African economies, Kenya's banking sector has for many years been credited for its size and diversification. Private credit to gross domestic product (GDP) – a standard indicator of financial development – was 23.7 per cent in 2008, compared with a median of 12.3 per cent for sub-Saharan Africa (Table 14.1). Although this number is not higher than it was in 2005, the quality of lending has improved significantly, as can be seen from the increasing ratio of loans net of provision relative to GDP (Table 14.2).[2] Unlike most other countries in the region, Kenya

Table 14.1 Kenya's financial system in regional comparison

	Private credit to GDP (%)	Liquid liabilities to GDP (%)	Net interest margin (%)
Kenya	23.7	36.0	6.6
Tanzania	12.3	26.3	6.6
Uganda	7.2	20.7	11.7
Sub-Saharan Africa (median)	12.3	23.0	6.6

Source: Beck *et al.* (2010).

has a variety of financial institutions and markets – banks, insurance companies, stock and bond markets – that provide an array of financial products. Notwithstanding this relative advantage, Kenya's financial system has failed to provide adequate access to banking services for the bulk of the population. Whereas the larger proportion of savings comes from small depositors, lending is skewed in favour of large private and public enterprises in urban areas. Financial services are expensive, as evidenced by high interest rate spreads and account fees.[3]

Table 14.2 Growth and structure of the banking sector, 2000–07 (%)

	2000	2001	2002	2003	2004	2005	2006	2007
Private credit/GDP	25.6	24.1	23.5	23.1	23.2	23.8	24.3	22.4
Loans (net of provisions)/GDP	20.9	20.2	20.9	20.5	22.8	23.5	23.6	24.8
Real GDP growth	0.5	4.5	0.5	2.9	5.1	5.7	6.1	6.9
Share of banking sector assets								
Foreign	44.3	46.3	48.3	48.7	45.3	43.4	43.8	43.5
Private domestic	21.9	22.7	22.6	24.1	25.7	28.7	29.9	31.0
Government	7.1	7.1	6.6	6.0	6.2	5.6	5.3	4.8
NBK	6.1	5.9	5.7	5.2	5.5	5.2	4.8	4.4
Government-influenced	26.7	23.9	22.5	21.2	22.7	22.2	21.1	20.7
KCB	16.6	15.0	12.8	11.7	11.9	11.8	11.5	11.9
Co-operative	5.7	5.2	6.5	6.5	8.3	8.2	7.7	6.9
Share of total loans (net of provisions)								
Foreign	39.9	40.8	41.9	43.7	42.5	42.3	41.0	44.5
Private domestic	22.1	22.0	22.6	24.4	25.4	28.8	31.4	31.5
Government	10.0	9.8	10.0	9.7	8.4	7.7	7.3	2.0
NBK	9.2	8.9	9.0	8.7	7.6	7.3	6.8	1.6
Government-influenced	28.0	27.4	25.5	22.3	23.6	21.3	20.3	22.0
KCB	16.5	15.8	12.8	10.7	11.5	9.9	10.5	11.5
Co-operative	5.8	6.3	8.3	7.7	9.2	8.7	7.2	7.7

NBK, National Bank of Kenya; KCB, Kenya Commercial Bank.
Sources: For private credit/GDP, Beck *et al.* (2010). For real GDP growth and nominal GDP, World Development Indicators. Data for all other calculations are from the Central Bank of Kenya.

Kenya's sector faced major crises in the 1980s and 1990s, due to undercapitalization, high levels of non-performing loans, and weaknesses in corporate governance. Non-bank financial institutions (NBFIs) were most affected, but the number of failing commercial banks increased as well in the 1990s. The crisis culminated in 1992, when – according to Honohan and Laeven (2005) – Kenya formally suffered a systemic banking crisis.

In 2003, the Government of Kenya (GoK) published the Economic Recovery Strategy (ERS) paper on wealth creation and employment that defined certain critical high-level objectives underlying the reform efforts through 2007. In the ERS, the government acknowledged that the banking sector was experiencing difficulties that would undermine the achievement of the objectives set out in the ERS, including: a comparatively high ratio of non-performing loans in some major banks; inadequate competition in the banking sector; persistence of wide interest rate spreads leading to a high cost of credit; insufficient quantities of credit (and poor-quality credit assessments); absence of vibrant institutions for the provision of long-term finance; weak legal arrangements creating long delays in contract enforcement; and weak dispute resolution mechanisms.

In recent years, Kenya has made substantial progress in improving the stability and efficiency of its banking system. Upgrading of the supervisory framework was accompanied by write-off of non-performing loans and reductions in the government's role in the financial sector. Interest spreads, although still high, have come down recently as a result of lower loan loss provisions and overhead costs, but also lower profit margins, suggesting a certain degree of competition. This was accompanied by a reduction in inflation and the fiscal deficit and stable exchange rates, which in turn facilitated not only a drop in interest rates, but also improvements in the government-managed and -influenced financial institutions. Kenya's financial system, however, continues to face challenges. The banking system is still fragmented, with many small banks serving specific niches, but not contributing to competition in the sector. The outreach of the financial system is still limited.

In 2007, GoK published Kenya's *Vision 2030* as a long-term development plan for the country, which puts the provision of financial services at the centre of the planned economic growth trajectory through to the year 2030. The main objectives for the financial sector that were articulated in *Vision 2030* were to: (i) improve stability; (ii) enhance efficiency in the delivery of credit and other financial services; and (iii) improve access to financial services and products for a much larger number of Kenyan households. Delivery of these objectives requires the implementation of policies that would contribute to stable macro and fiscal positions aimed at lower inflation and financial sector stability.

The current global financial crisis has underlined the need for further and deeper reforms, while at the same time potentially undermining progress made so far. The drastic reduction in international capital flows forces most countries in the region to rely more on domestic resources and increase domestic intermediation efficiency. Beyond macroeconomic policies and institutional reforms, issues of market structure will become important in the coming years. Theory and international evidence are ambiguous on the relationship between bank concentration and stability. The experience in Nigeria is too fresh to draw inferences from, but has raised awareness of the issue across the region. As we will discuss below, there is no clear mapping from market structure to competition; attempts to consolidate the sector might increase efficiency and stability, with ambiguous implications for outreach, but the ultimate effect will depend on the future ownership structure of the Kenyan banking system and the underlying financial infrastructure, including the contractual framework and possible credit registry.

The remainder of this chapter is structured as follows. Section 14.2 discusses Kenya's financial safety net, including recent changes in the regulatory framework and the deposit insurance scheme. Section 14.3 addresses the stability of banks, in the context of the current market structure. Section 14.4 presents trends in interest rate spreads and their components over the past seven years. Section 14.5 discusses the outreach of Kenya's banking system, based on recent household surveys. Section 14.6 discusses the case for regulation-induced consolidation in the sector, based on the findings of the previous sections and international experience, and Section 14.7 concludes.

14.2 The regulatory framework for banking in Kenya

Given the critical role of banks in a modern market economy, the opacity of banks' balance sheets, the dispersion of banks' creditors – typically many small depositors – and the maturity transformation banks perform converting short-term deposits into medium- to long-term assets, there are limitations to market discipline and additional sources of fragility, compared with non-financial corporations. Banking has therefore historically been one of the most regulated sectors, with regulation ranging from licensing requirements to ongoing supervision to a bank-specific failure regime and deposit insurance.

In Kenya, the Central Bank (CBK) is responsible for the regulation and supervision of banks. Over the past decades, there have been numerous revisions to the Banking Act, the Central Bank of Kenya Act, and prudential guidelines aimed at strengthening CBK's supervisory role. The Banking Act has been reviewed over time to give more legal powers to the regulatory authority and to broaden the responsibilities and coverage of institutions. The first comprehensive review was made in 1985 following the rapid growth of NBFIs that was mainly attributed to weaknesses in the regulatory framework. In addition, there was a change in the licensing procedures for banks that introduced a clearer mandate for the Central Bank in the licensing process.

In 1995, further amendments were made to the Banking Act aimed at further strengthening supervision of the banking industry. Prudential guidelines were revised to encourage self-regulation and covered codes of conduct for directors, chief executives, and other employees; duties and responsibilities of directors, chief executives, and management; duties and responsibilities of external auditors; and the definition of bad and doubtful advances and loans.

In 1998, the Central Bank enhanced capital requirements to avoid a repeat of the banking crises experienced in the mid-1980s and early 1990s. To this end, the gearing ratio was raised to 7.5 per cent from 5 per cent. In 2000, the Central Bank adopted the Basel I standards on capital adequacy. This led to the introduction of additional capital adequacy ratios of 8 per cent and 12 per cent for core capital and total capital to risk-weighted assets respectively. These reforms were in tandem with the then-prevailing global trends that required financial institutions to maintain capital commensurate with the credit risk inherent in their business.

In response to gaps identified in the 2003 joint International Monetary Fund (IMF)/World Bank Financial Sector Assessment Program (FSAP), a series of legal and regulatory reforms have been undertaken. These have included significant changes to the Banking Act (Cap. 488) and to prudential guidelines to strengthen arrangements in relation to bank licensing, corporate governance, capital adequacy, risk classification of assets, and overall risk management.

Deposit insurance is often seen as an integral part of a financial safety net, in spite of significant risks shown by both case studies and cross-country comparisons (for an overview, see Demirgüç-Kunt and Kane, 2002). Although the initial purpose is to protect small savings and prevent bank runs, deposit insurance also reduces market discipline even further, as depositors have fewer incentives to properly monitor and discipline banks. This results in additional pressure on supervisors, which can result in deposit insurance leading to more rather than less fragility in countries with a weak regulatory and supervisory framework (Demirgüç-Kunt and Detragiache, 2002). Across countries with deposit insurance, structure, funding, and mandates vary a lot. Although some countries have pure paybox deposit insurance funds, such as in Brazil and Uganda, other schemes have wide-ranging supervisory powers, such as in Canada or the USA. Deposit insurers might be more likely to carefully monitor banks and intervene rapidly in failing banks as they have to carry the costs in terms of higher payouts to indemnified depositors. Cross-country comparisons indeed show that banks in countries where the deposit insurer has the responsibility in intervening in failed banks and the power to revoke membership in the deposit insurance scheme are more stable and less likely to become insolvent (Beck and Laeven, 2008).

Following the banking crisis of 1985/86, Kenya established a Deposit Protection Fund Board (DPFB) with a wide mandate. Specifically, the DPFB's main tasks are to manage the deposit insurance fund and carry out the liquidation of insolvent institutions once they have been closed by the CBK (by repaying protected deposits and dividends, carrying out debt recovery, and winding up the institutions under liquidation). The DPFB offers protection to small depositors up to Ksh 100,000 (US$1,250) against loss of their savings in case of a bank failure. Institutionally, the DPFB is part of the CBK and relies on staff from the CBK, but also on information from the CBK's supervisory department. It does not have any role in the supervisory process. Although having a broad mandate, the DPFB's responsibilities are thus not completely aligned with its incentive to minimize insurance fund losses.

In order to improve the role of the DPFB in enhancing depositor confidence, initiatives are under way to enact a new and separate Kenya Deposit Insurance Corporation Act that will give the Fund autonomy in its operations. Among other additional roles, the draft Act provides the DPFB with powers to request the Central Bank to carry out an inspection of a member institution and, where deemed necessary, to conduct the examination itself.

14.3 Soundness of the Kenyan banking sector

Since 2000, there has been a significant improvement in financial stability, as indicated by the financial soundness indicators in Table 14.3. The aggregate indicators, however, mask significant variation across different ownership groups.

Banks are generally well capitalized with an overall capital adequacy ratio of 18 per cent, comparable to or considerably above that in other emerging economies and above the 8 per cent recommended by Basel Core Principles (Table 14.4). Liquidity ratios have been maintained above the minimum statutory requirements, while earnings measures have improved steadily. Significant improvement in the stability of the banking sector has been reflected in asset quality. The banking sector experienced high levels of non-performing loans (NPLs) for many years averaging about 30 per cent of gross advances before the year 2003. However, the ratio declined significantly to stand at 8.4 per cent as of December 2008. Notwithstanding this improvement, this ratio is still significantly higher than in other emerging markets as of 2007 (Table 14.4). A large proportion of the NPLs are concentrated in a few government-owned and -influenced banks as well as other adequately capitalized banks. Banks have passed significant provisions onto their books, thanks to strict prudential requirements, and hence the high level of NPLs does not pose a systemic threat to the Kenyan banking system.

Table 14.3 Financial soundness indicators (%)

	2000	2001	2002	2003	2004	2005	2006	2007	2008
Regulatory capital to risk-weighted assets	17.5	17.1	17.4	17.2	16.6	16.4	16.5	18.0	18.4
Regulatory tier 1 capital to risk-weighted assets	14.2	14.5	14.1	14.7	16.3	16.0	16.4	16.8	16.2
Non-performing loans to gross loans	37.2	39.4	39.6	34.9	29.3	25.6	21.3	10.9	8.4
Non-performing loans net of provisions to total capital	78.7	78.8	77.8	60.7	52.7	40.1	28.6	15.1	10.8
Return on assets	0.5	1.6	1	2.3	2.1	2.4	2.8	3.0	2.9
Return on equity	4.9	15.7	10.9	23.2	22.0	25.0	28.6	27.5	28.6
Net interest income to gross income	42.1	43.6	43.8	50.5	50.7	50.2	50.2	50.1	48.3
Non-interest expenses to gross income	65.4	58.6	66.9	62.9	63.9	55.7	52.8	50.8	48.7
Liquid assets to total assets	29.5	34.4	33.7	33.2	32.4	33.1	30.5	35.1	34.6

Source: Central Bank of Kenya.

Stress tests confirm the resilience of Kenya's banking system. Table 14.5 shows stress tests conducted using individual bank data from December 2008 to assess the impact of credit risk using two shocks. The first evaluates a deteriorating loan portfolio that would result in an increase in provisions by 50 per cent and 100 per cent, whereas the second assesses the impact of migrating 25 per cent and 50 per cent of performing loans to the substandard category. The results indicate that, on the whole, banks appear to be resilient to the shocks measured. However, the most significant impact would be felt if a riskier client base resulted in a 100 per cent increase in provisions. Such a significant shock would result in seventeen banks (accounting for 24 per cent of assets) failing to meet minimum capital requirements. Four of these banks would be insolvent. These results could be seen as providing a justification for increasing minimum capital requirements.

Table 14.4 Comparator countries: financial soundness indicators, 2007 (%)

Country	CAR	NPLs ratio[4]	Return on assets (ROA)	Return on equity (ROE)
Brazil[5]	17.4	4.4	2.3	24.5
Indonesia[6]	19.2	16	2.6	28
Malaysia[7]	12.7	8.7	1.3	14.1
Nigeria	18.6	7.7	1.8	13.8
South Africa[8]	12.7	1.1	1.4	18.6
Kenya	18.0	10.9	3.0	27.5

[4–8] See Notes at the end of the chapter.
Sources: Central Bank of Kenya, Central Bank of Nigeria (CBN) and IMF, GFSR.

Table 14.5 Sensitivity to credit risk (regulatory capital to risk-weighted assets, %)

		Provisions increase by		Migration to NPLs of	
	Before the shock	50%	100%	25% of performing loans	50% of performing loans
Peer group: large	18.3	17.1	15.3	18.0	17.8
Peer group: medium	18.7	15.0	11.1	18.1	17.6
Peer group: small	35.2	32.5	29.6	34.7	34.2
Banks with CAR <12%	0	11	17	2	3
Share of assets	0	20	24.0	5.1	12.3
Banks with CAR <0%	0	1	4	0	0
Share of assets	0	0.99	2.2	0	0

Source: Central Bank of Kenya data.

14.4 Banking sector efficiency

In this section, we describe how interest spreads, our proxy for the efficiency of financial intermediation, have evolved over the past ten years in Kenya, and relate those developments to our discussion of government strategy for the development of the financial sector and the accompanying changes in the legal and regulatory framework discussed above. We then present simple arithmetical decompositions of the interest spreads to explain the factors that have contributed to their relatively high levels and also to their decline over time. We also examine how spread levels and their determinants differ by bank size and ownership type. Finally, we offer regressions that better enable us to test whether the determinants of spreads differ by bank ownership type and if such differences can be explained by the types of activities that different owners pursue.

Headline indicators produced by the Central Bank of Kenya indicate that spreads declined from 1999 to 2003 and have since remained stable (Figure 14.1). The relatively sharp decline in spreads in 2003 owes much to improvements in Kenya's fiscal situation and general macromanagement, which led to substantial declines in both the volume of government securities issued and the interest rates paid. As government securities became a less attractive investment option for banks, they turned to new lending opportunities, and the competition between banks for those opportunities coincided with lower spreads. However, the shift out of government securities was much swifter for some banks than for others, and most banks increased their holdings of those securities from 2004 to 2005. In addition, yearly average spreads in Figure 14.1 mask wide variation across banks, and our statistical analysis below indicates that the drivers of changes in spreads differ across bank ownership types. For

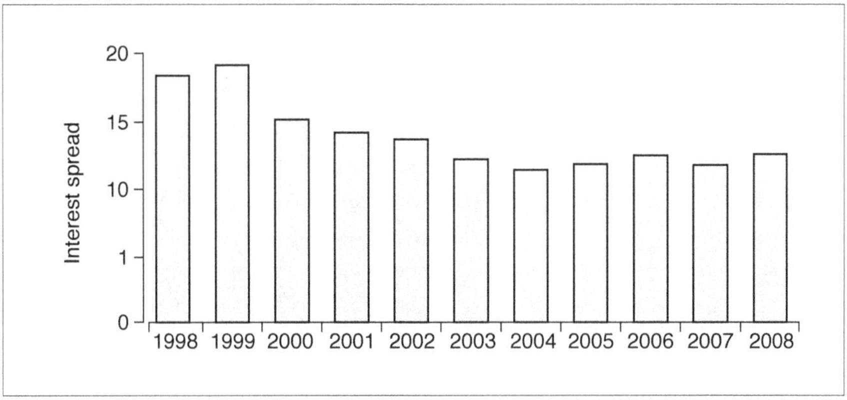

Figure 14.1 Interest spreads in Kenya over time.
Source: Data are from the Central Bank of Kenya Statistical Bulletin, June 2008. The lending rate is the weighted average of commercial banks' interest rates on loans and advances. Similarly, the deposit rate is the weighted average rate paid by commercial banks on savings deposits. For 2006 and 2007, we use the December figures. For 2008, we use the June figures (latest available).

these reasons, the reduction in government debt issuance does not provide a complete explanation for the evolution of spreads over this period.

Further indications that the decline in spreads is not wholly attributable to macroeconomic stability and improved management of government debt come from simple arithmetical decompositions of interest spreads. In the decomposition exercise, we follow the method used in Beck and Fuchs (2004), subtracting the interest rate paid for deposits from the interest rates charged on loans. To calculate the weighted average interest rate charged on loans, we add the interest income earned to interest in suspense, and divide that sum by total loans.[9] Because this measure captures interest income and interest that was accrued but not collected, it is our best proxy for the *ex ante* interest rates charged on loans by banks. The interest spread is then calculated as the difference between that figure and the interest expense paid on deposits (divided by total deposits). The spreads in our analysis are therefore a weighted average for the banking sector as a whole (rather than a simple average across banks).

We decompose the spreads into their different components. Banks charge higher interest rates to riskier borrowers in anticipation of defaults, and so we therefore account for loan loss provisions in the decomposition. We also account for overhead costs, taxes, and required reserves, all factors that contribute to higher spreads. The overhead costs are those attributable to loans, which we identify by calculating the share of loan interest revenue in total revenue. Profit margin is a residual after adjusting for loan loss provisions, the tax rate, reserve requirements, and overheads.[10]

Using the *ex post* constructed spreads across banks shows a different development over time from the headline indicators. Table 14.6A shows that spreads declined for the sector as a whole, but not until much later in the

Table 14.6 Decomposition of interest spreads over time

A. All banks	2000	2001	2002	2003	2004	2005	2006	2007
Average lending rate	25.03	24.47	25.89	24.64	21.45	22.75	12.22	12.19
Average deposit rate	5.79	4.62	3.53	2.00	1.36	2.60	2.57	2.41
Spread	19.25	19.85	22.36	22.64	20.10	20.16	9.66	9.78
Overhead costs	6.94	6.49	7.53	6.60	5.83	5.99	3.10	3.16
Loan loss provisions	4.28	2.66	3.43	2.68	2.02	1.68	1.64	0.85
Reserve requirement	0.64	0.51	0.39	0.22	0.15	0.29	0.29	0.27
Taxes	2.21	3.05	3.30	3.94	3.63	3.66	1.39	1.65
Profit margin	5.16	7.12	7.71	9.20	8.47	8.54	3.24	3.85
B. Private banks								
Average lending rate	20.72	19.63	17.65	15.77	12.92	13.78	13.77	12.98
Average deposit rate	5.29	4.60	3.36	2.14	1.47	2.78	2.88	2.79
Spread	15.44	15.03	14.29	13.64	11.46	11.00	10.89	10.19
Overhead costs	4.86	4.66	4.85	3.75	3.05	3.24	3.15	3.00
Loan loss provisions	3.01	1.89	1.76	2.77	1.93	1.32	1.08	0.68
Reserve requirement	0.59	0.51	0.37	0.24	0.16	0.31	0.32	0.31
Taxes	2.09	2.39	2.19	2.06	1.90	1.84	1.90	1.86
Profit margin	4.89	5.58	5.12	4.82	4.42	4.29	4.44	4.34

Source: Own calculations, based on CBK data.

period than was indicated in Figure 14.1, which is based on the *ex ante* interest rates charged by banks rather than the *ex post* interest earned and accrued that we rely on in this analysis. The reason for this discrepancy is that, until 2006, the interest in suspense for the government-owned banks (Cooperative, Consolidated, Kenya Commercial Bank (KCB) and National Bank of Kenya (NBK)) was much higher than for privately owned banks because of their huge overhang of non-performing loans. Our method for calculating interest spreads can yield misleading results for banks with large stocks of non-performing loans. When we drop those government-owned banks from the sample in Table 14.6B, the evolution of spreads looks very similar to that in Figure 14.1, except that declines occurred about a year later. This is because the *ex post* spreads reflect the *ex ante* rates charged on loans at a lag. In all, however, our *ex post* calculated spreads for private banks match up well with the headline indicators produced by the Central Bank of Kenya, which are based on *ex ante* interest rates charged by banks.

The effects of the government's programme for the development of the banking sector are reflected in the decline in both spreads and their determinants. The decomposition for privately owned banks (both domestic and foreign) in Table 14.6B shows a steady decline in the interest rates charged on loans and a substantial reduction in the interest rate paid for deposits. The decline in lending rates is consistent with greater competition, whereas the drop in deposit rates probably reflects the improvements in bank soundness indicators summarized in Section 14.3 and the increasing confidence of depositors.

The decomposition in Table 14.6B points to a number of specific factors that contributed to the reduction in the spreads of the private banks. First, productive efficiency appears to have improved, as reflected in the steady decline in overhead costs (relative to total loans). Second, the quality of loan portfolios improved, as reflected in lower provisions for bad debts. Reserve requirements and taxes have seen more moderate declines, although neither was among the more important components of spreads, as reflected in the decomposition. Despite the substantial declines in overhead costs and loan loss provisioning, which should improve profitability, banks' profit margins declined in the middle of the period and have remained more or less steady since. This too points to an increasingly competitive private banking sector.

Stratifying the sample of private banks based on size (total deposits) reveals that larger banks generally tend to have lower interest spreads, which in part reflects the gradual decline in overhead costs as bank size increases (Table 14.7). At the same time, the decompositions reveal that banks in the largest size quartile are distinct from those in the other three in important respects. For example, provisioning charges are very similar for banks in the lowest three quartiles, but less than half of that level for banks in the top quartile. Also, the banks in the top quartile charge substantially lower rates on their loans and pay much lower rates on deposits. Their spreads are lower than other banks, and so too are their profit margins, indicating that they operate in a relatively competitive market niche. Banks in the third largest size quartile have spreads and margins that are closest to those of the largest banks, whereas those in quartile 2 and, especially the bottom quartile, charge the highest rates on loans and interest spreads, but also have higher profit margins. Based on the available data, it is difficult to know whether those high margins result from a less competitive market niche or our less-than-perfect method for calculating spreads. Again, for banks with a large stock of non-performing loans, this method could yield misleading results.

The pattern in Table 14.7 suggests that the largest private banks are more efficient, as reflected in their overhead costs, and more stable, as reflected in their loan loss provisions. For these reasons, proposals to increase minimum capital requirements and thereby consolidate the sector by creating larger banks are being explored. Section 14.6 discusses this issue in greater detail.

Although the size of private banks appears to have an effect on the efficiency of financial intermediation, bank ownership plays at least as important a role in explaining the relative efficiency of Kenyan banks. Table 14.8 shows why, namely because the figures for government-owned and government-influenced banks are not reliable. Recall that our method for calculating spreads is less reliable for banks that have a large stock of non-performing loans. This

Table 14.7 Spread decomposition by size quartile; ranking based on 2007 deposits

	Smallest			Largest
	0–25th percentile	26–50th percentile	51–75th percentile	76–100th percentile
Average lending rate	28.97	14.21	18.91	10.46
Average deposit rate	4.23	3.79	4.63	2.16
Spread	24.74	10.42	14.28	8.30
Overhead costs	7.65	4.15	3.96	2.38
Loan loss provisions	1.33	1.26	1.19	0.45
Reserve requirement	0.47	0.42	0.51	0.24
Taxes	4.59	1.38	2.58	1.57
Profit margin	10.70	3.22	6.03	3.66

Co-operative, Consolidated, KCB, and NBK are excluded from these calculations.
Source: Own calculations, based on CBK data.

is probably because interest is accrued on the same non-performing loan multiple times. In short, our method makes sense for banks that are pricing loans to cover the expected future costs of defaults.

And so the enormous lending rates and spreads calculated for government banks is the first tipoff that they are not adhering even remotely to commercial banking principles, although we concede that the difficulties appear to be more severe for government-owned than for government-influenced banks. At the same time, our spreads were increasing for all government banks from 2000 to 2005. During this same period, spreads were declining substantially for the private domestic and foreign banks. So the general decline in spreads in Figure 14.1 cannot be attributable to the government banks.

In 2007, the spreads of the government-owned banks declined steeply, yet this was certainly due to the large injection of capital into the NBK, which was used to clean up its large overhang of non-performing loans. The NBK is by far the largest majority government-owned bank, and thus the injection has a sizeable effect on the spreads for that ownership category. Even with the injection, the spreads for government-owned banks remain substantially above those for private banks, whereas those for the government-influenced banks are roughly similar. And the spreads for the government-influenced banks were actually increasing from 2005 to 2007.

It is also worth noting that both types of government banks pay less for their deposits than do private banks. This suggests that depositors are certain that they will be bailed out regardless of problems with the loan portfolios of these banks. As these banks still comprise a large share of the banking sector (Table 14.2), this situation implies substantial misallocation of investable resources (savings). In addition, the existence of large government banks no doubt has a distortionary effect on the activities of private banks, which could

Table 14.8 Spread decomposition by ownership type

	Foreign			Private domestic			Government-owned			Government-influenced		
	2000	2005	2007	2000	2005	2007	2000	2005	2007	2000	2005	2007
Average lending rate	16.61	11.21	10.46	21.30	14.90	16.75	46.34	65.59	27.91	25.86	23.57	27.01
Average deposit rate	3.76	1.83	2.09	7.42	4.15	3.81	6.13	2.59	2.08	7.89	2.07	1.20
Spread	12.85	9.38	8.36	13.88	10.75	12.94	40.21	63.00	25.83	17.97	21.50	25.81
Overhead costs	4.11	2.50	2.40	4.37	3.68	3.80	20.92	18.32	9.37	8.71	8.31	9.25
Loan loss provisions	2.90	1.37	0.55	3.60	1.22	0.85	3.94	2.66	2.21	6.54	2.04	1.21
Reserve requirement	0.42	0.20	0.23	0.82	0.46	0.42	0.68	0.29	0.23	0.88	0.23	0.13
Taxes	1.62	1.59	1.55	1.53	1.62	2.36	4.40	12.52	4.21	0.55	3.28	4.56
Profit margin	3.79	3.71	3.62	3.57	3.77	5.50	10.27	29.21	9.81	1.29	7.65	10.65

Source: Own calculations, based on CBK data.

be effectively precluded from pursuing efficiency enhancement in some geographical areas or offering a wider array of services. For all of these reasons, ownership restructuring, including privatization, would appear to be a major remaining priority for the reform agenda of the Kenyan banking sector.

The general picture from Table 14.8 is that foreign banks have shown steady improvement in efficiency (lower spreads and overhead costs), whereas private domestic banks have seen a slight reversal in recent years. Table 14.8 also highlights the persistence of the relative inefficiency of the government-owned and government-influenced banks. As noted above, from 2000 to 2005, spreads declined for private banks, but after that, the paths of the foreign and private domestic banks diverged, with foreign banks continuing the decline through 2007 and private domestic banks showing an increase. This is partly due to the lending rate that we calculate for private banks, which increased substantially from 2005 to 2007 because of jumps in interest in suspense for some banks. Because the private domestic banks tend to be smaller than the foreign banks, one could view this as additional support for fostering consolidation among some of those banks.

The increase in spreads for private domestic banks from 2005 to 2007 is accounted for by interest in suspense and the slight increase in overhead costs during that period. The government-owned banks also saw steep declines in overhead costs from 2005 to 2007, consistent with some improvement in their efficiency, although their levels remained well above those for the foreign and private domestic banks. For the government-influenced banks, overhead costs remained stable and high relative to the private banks. Charges for loan loss provisions declined for all banks, although the declines for the foreign and government-influenced banks were steeper than for the government-owned and private domestic banks (Table 14.8).

Lurking in the background of this simple analysis of spreads are issues of market segmentation. Clearly, higher spreads, margins, and interest rates charged on loans for the private domestic banks could be consistent with the notion that those banks serve a market niche of relatively riskier borrowers. The stratification by bank size also indicates that smaller banks, many of which have private domestic ownership, occupy a market niche where interest rates and spreads tend to be higher. In contrast, the profit margins and spreads of the largest banks, many of which are foreign owned, are substantially lower, indicating that they operate in a more competitive niche. This type of segmentation has implications for the discussion of sector consolidation below. To the extent that the smaller private banks and larger foreign banks operate in different market niches, the consolidation of the private domestic banks could lead to oversaturation of the market for top-end borrowers and reductions in services for the less-than-blue-chip customers of the private domestic banks.

Regressions enable us to assess the relationship between spreads and a number of additional bank characteristics that could affect interest spreads and to better pinpoint the banks and their activities that were responsible for the decline in spreads. The regression model is based on that in Martinez Peria and Mody (2004) for developing countries in Latin America and in Beck and Hesse (2009) for Uganda:[11]

$$\begin{aligned} Spread_{it} = \alpha &+ \beta_1 overheads_{it} + \beta_2 liquidity_{it} + \beta_3 equity_{it} \\ &+ \beta_4 provisions_{it} + \beta_5 market\ share_{it} \\ &+ \beta_6 interest\ income_{it} + \beta_7 loan\ share_{it} \\ &+ \beta_8 Herfindahl_t + \beta_9 T\ bill\ rate_t + \beta_{10} inflation_t \\ &+ \beta_{11} RealGrowth_t + \beta_{12} PrivateDomestic_{it} \\ &+ \beta_{13} Government_{it} + \varepsilon_{it} \end{aligned} \tag{14.1}$$

where the interest spread is calculated as described above for bank *i* at time *t*. *Overheads* are the ratio of overhead costs to total assets. As in the simple decomposition, we expect that higher overhead costs are passed on to borrowers in the form of higher spreads. *Liquidity* is the ratio of liquid assets (cash and deposits with other banks) to deposits, whereas *equity* is bank capital plus reserves over total assets, both of which we can expect to be positively associated with spreads, given the opportunity costs.[12] *Provisions* are the ratio of loan loss provisions to total loans, our measure of portfolio quality. As described above, we expect that higher loan provisions reflect riskier borrowers, which raises *ex ante* interest rates charged on loans, resulting in higher calculated spreads. *Market share* is the bank's share of total banking sector deposits, our measure of bank size. To the extent that larger banks can take advantage of economies of scale, we would expect market share to be negatively related to spreads.[13]

We control for bank orientation using *interest income*, the ratio of total interest income to operating income, and *intermediation*, the ratio of net loans and advances to total liabilities. Using bank-level data across countries, Laeven and Levine (2007) demonstrate that specialized loan-making banks have different performance characteristics from specialized investment banks, and that loan-making banks tend to have a higher share of interest income. We expect competitive pressure in the lending market to be better reflected in the banks specialized in that area, and thus we expect a negative association between *interest income* and spreads. Similarly, we expect those banks that lend a relatively high share of their available liabilities to be most responsive to the same competitive pressures, and thus a negative relation between *intermediation* and spreads.

Following the literature, in some specifications, we include a control for banking sector structure and three macroeconomic control variables. *Herfindahl* is a standard index of sector concentration, which we calculated based on bank shares of total deposits.[14] If deposits are concentrated in the hands of a few banks, those banks might be able to drive up lending rates, as they control the supply of funds. We would therefore expect a positive relation between concentration and spreads. The macroeconomic controls are the *T-bill rate, inflation,* and *real growth.* The *T-bill rate* is the rate of interest on short-term treasury bills, which is included as a proxy for the marginal cost of funds faced by banks. *Inflation* is included because price shocks might not be passed through equally to the nominal lending and borrowing rates, and thus these differential effects would be reflected in the spread. *Real growth* is included to capture business cycle effects that are reflected in spreads. As an economy slumps and growth slows, borrowers become less creditworthy, and thus banks must charge higher lending rates, which are then reflected in higher spreads (all else being equal).

Finally, we control for ownership type. *Private domestic* is a dummy variable equal to 1 if a bank is owned by private Kenyan interests, whereas *Government* is a dummy equal to 1 if a bank is owned by the Kenyan government. In some models, we further differentiate between banks that are majority owned by the government and those in which the government owns only a minority stake (which we call 'government-influenced' banks). The coefficients on these ownership variables are therefore intended to capture any differences in spreads relative to banks owned by foreign interests (our omitted ownership category) that are not accounted for by the other explanatory variables.

The base results in Table 14.9 suggest that overhead costs are the driving factor of interest rate spreads. Both models are estimated via ordinary least squares (OLS), and model 2 includes bank-specific fixed effects.[15] In model 2, the estimated coefficients therefore reflect departures from each bank's average spread for the period. The main results from the base models are that spreads are highly sensitive to overhead costs: the estimated coefficient indicates that a 1 percentage point increase in the ratio of overheads to total assets is associated with a 1.8 percentage point increase in interest spreads. The fixed effects models also indicate that increases in equity and provisions for loan losses were associated with higher spreads during this period, whereas an increase in the intermediation ratio was associated with lower spreads. All of these results are in line with our hypotheses.

The results in Table 14.10 show that the significant results from our base models are not a reflection of the banking sector as a whole, but are rather driven by specific subsets of banks. To see this, we re-run the base models in Table 14.9 with interaction terms for each of the three ownership categories that appeared in the original regression (private domestic, government-owned,

Table 14.9 Base interest spreads regressions

	OLS	Fixed effects
Explanatory variable	(1)	(2)
Overheads	1.7680***	1.7510***
	(0.6352)	(0.3350)
Equity	–0.0061	0.2065**
	(0.0198)	(0.0876)
Liquidity	0.0301	–0.0080
	(0.0416)	(0.0367)
Loan loss provisions	–0.0910	0.3761**
	(0.2540)	(0.1740)
Market share	–0.1577	0.4170
	(0.1439)	(0.5112)
Interest income	–0.1314	–0.0121
	(0.1255)	(0.0867)
Intermediation	–0.0499	–0.1363**
	(0.0475)	(0.0598)
Herfindahl index	–0.0425	0.0657
	(1.0109)	(1.1181)
Real T-bills rate	0.1362	0.0611
	(0.1529)	(0.1206)
Inflation	0.1676	–0.0294
	(0.2909)	(0.2532)
Real growth	–0.0058	0.1482
	(0.2583)	(0.3309)
Private domestic	0.0211*	
	(0.0120)	
Government-owned	0.0126	
	(0.1057)	
Government-influenced	0.0525	
	(0.0362)	
Constant	0.2064	0.1274
	(0.1348)	(0.1541)
Observations	327	327
Number of banks	45	45
Adjusted R^2	0.5634	0.7295

*, **, and *** mean significance at the 10%, 5%, and 1% levels respectively.
Source: Own calculations, based on CBK data.

and government-influenced). In this way, the association between each explanatory variable and the interest spread is allowed to differ by ownership type. The coefficients on the non-interacted variables therefore summarize the effects for foreign banks, our omitted ownership category. Rather than present the full specification, we present the effect of each variable on the spreads of each bank ownership type. What appears in Table 14.10 is the coefficient for

Table 14.10 Determinants of interest spreads, by bank ownership type

	Foreign	Private domestic	Government-owned	Government-influenced
A. OLS				
Overheads	3.6074***	1.7806*	1.0115**	2.8742***
	(0.7355)	(0.0924]	(0.0420)	(0.0000)
Equity	–0.1384	–0.0237	0.7840***	–1.6306***
	(0.0952)	(0.3454)	(0.0000)	(0.0083)
Liquidity	0.0434*	0.0343	–0.0322	0.1203
	(0.0239)	(0.5188)	(0.6371)	(0.4475)
Loan loss provisions	–0.3046	–0.1359	–0.0541	0.4891
	(0.2189)	(0.5621)	(0.9405)	(0.1792)
Market share	0.0818	–0.8175	2.4479***	–0.9582**
	(0.0706)	(0.2280)	(0.0000)	(0.0328)
Interest income	0.0728*	–0.2983	–0.4491***	–0.0508
	(0.0379)	(0.2033)	(0.0001)	(0.7614)
Intermediation	–0.1043**	–0.0193	0.0284	–0.0967
	(0.0447)	(0.7574)	(0.7369)	(0.5984)
Herfindahl index	0.4067	0.8696	–1.8256	0.1929
	(0.9961)	(0.3934)	(0.7554)	(0.9615)
Real T-bills rate	0.1527**	0.1368	–0.2494	0.0280
	(0.0588)	(0.3853)	(0.8504)	(0.9000)
Inflation	0.2958**	0.2637	–1.9958	0.3035
	(0.1438)	(0.2640)	(0.4841)	(0.6907)
Real growth	–0.1566	0.4587	0.2042	0.1894
	(0.2041)	(0.3661)	(0.8282)	(0.7451)
B. Fixed effects				
Overheads	3.3104***	2.0472***	1.1984***	2.6637***
	(0.7093)	(0.0017)	(0.0016)	(0.0000)
Equity	0.0317	0.2325*	0.9098**	–2.2986**
	(0.1131)	(0.0535)	(0.0115)	(0.0229)
Liquidity	0.0048	–0.0233	–0.0171	0.5983*
	(0.0239)	(0.7940)	(0.8802)	(0.0869)
Loan loss provisions	–0.2050	0.4047*	0.1487	0.7378
	(0.2746)	(0.0794)	(0.9216)	(0.2785)
Market share	0.1116	1.6164	–6.4134	0.2384
	(0.3982)	(0.1383)	(0.2800)	(0.7720)
Interest income	–0.0099	0.0575	–0.3730	–0.1859
	(0.0692)	(0.7782)	(0.3980)	(0.4070)

Table 14.10 (cont.)

	Foreign	Private domestic	Government-owned	Government-influenced
Intermediation	–0.1191**	–0.1326	0.0568	0.4690
	(0.0496)	(0.1410)	(0.7807)	(0.2786)
Herfindahl index	0.1924	0.9183	2.1135	0.6619
	(0.8472)	(0.5494)	(0.8070)	(0.8218)
Real T-bills rate	0.2200**	0.0907	0.3199	–0.1687
	(0.1060)	(0.5866)	(0.7339)	(0.6623)
Inflation	0.3849*	0.0639	–0.7747	–0.1773
	(0.1988)	(0.8500)	(0.6889)	(0.8185)
Real growth	–0.2113	0.4306	0.8667	–0.1336
	(0.2435)	(0.3537)	(0.6850)	(0.9085)

*, **, and *** mean significance at the 10%, 5%, and 1% levels respectively.
Source: Own calculations, based on CBK data.

each variable for each ownership category and a test of whether the coefficient is different from zero. P-values appear in parentheses below the coefficients.

The results in Table 14.10 enable us to further pinpoint the type of banks that are responsible for the significant relationships in our base regressions. In Table 14.10A, which summarizes the results from the OLS model, the positive relationship between overhead costs and interest spreads is much stronger for foreign banks. The relationship for all bank types is significant, but the coefficients are smaller, especially for the government-owned and private domestic banks. Similarly, only the interest spreads of the foreign banks are significantly associated with the intermediation ratio, the real T-bills rate, and inflation, and this holds for both the OLS and fixed effects regressions.

The determinants of the interest spreads of the foreign banks are much closer to what would be expected based on the existing empirical literature from other countries than are those of the other bank types. For example, aside from the overhead costs variable, none of the other variables is strongly associated with the interest spreads of the private domestic banks. There is some weak evidence from the fixed effects models that higher equity ratios and loan loss provisions were associated with higher spreads for private domestic banks, but those variables are only significant at the 10 per cent level. Similarly, in the fixed effects models, which are our best tool for assessing the changes in spreads, none of the variables is significant for the government-owned and government-influenced banks except for the aforementioned overhead costs and the equity variable. The significant equity coefficients most likely reflect spurious correlation rather than a causal link, a reflection of the government's recapitalization strategy for these banks. For example, the positive coefficient on *equity* for government-owned banks in the fixed effects regressions is because of the large capital infusion into the NBK, a bank that happens to have high interest spreads. The infusion of equity did not cause the NBK's spreads to increase. Lacklustre performance and a high share of non-performing assets were already reflected in high spreads. The capital infusion occurred as a result of those factors.

The general conclusion from the interest spread regressions is that reductions in overheads led to lower spreads for all banks during this period, but the results were especially pronounced for the foreign-owned banks. Other factors such as the reduction in the T-bill rate and lower inflation also contributed to lower spreads during this period, but those reductions were only significant for the foreign banks. The regressions therefore indicate that the lion's share of the sectoral reduction in interest spreads with which we began this analysis (Figure 14.1) is attributable to the foreign banks. Moreover, the lack of significant results for the other ownership types suggests either that they are competing in a separate market niche (as seems likely for many of the private domestic banks) or that they are pursuing some of the same clients as foreign banks but pricing loans in a less rationale way (as seems likely for the government-influenced banks).

14.5 Access to financial services

FinAccess 2006 and FinAccess 2009, two household surveys conducted by the Financial Sector Development Trust Kenya jointly with the Central Bank of Kenya, confirm three previously assumed conclusions about access to financial services: (i) a large proportion of the Kenyan population has no access to financial services, whether formal or informal; (ii) there is a general tendency for access to services from formal and semi-formal providers (banks, savings and credit co-operatives (SACCOs), and monetary financial institutions (MFIs)) to decline as one goes from urban to rural, from high income to low income, and from better educated to not educated; and (iii) although the percentage of the population that is served is similar in urban and rural districts, the mix of those services is different.[16] In urban areas, respondents rely more heavily on services from banks and semi-formal sources (SACCOs and MFIs), whereas in rural districts, there is greater reliance on services provided via informal groups.

Table 14.11 shows that the use of formal financial services in Kenya is at similar levels to other East African countries, but below that in several countries in Southern Africa. As the surveys are not completely consistent across countries, we follow Porteous (2007) in his definition of formal bank and bank-like financial services, which varies from the definition to be used in the remainder of this section.[17] Here, we show the share of population that (i) uses formal bank services, (ii) uses other formal financial but not bank services,

Table 14.11 Use of financial services across Africa

	Formal	Formal, other	Informal	Excluded
Kenya	21.5	15	29.5	34
Tanzania	15	2	7	75
Uganda	18	0	29	52
Zambia	14	12	11	62
Botswana	44	5	5	48
South Africa	54	6	9	31
Namibia	53	3	1	42

Source: Porteous (2007) and Beck (2009).

(iii) uses only informal financial services, and (iv) does not use any financial services. Kenya has a higher share of population using formal financial services (21.5 per cent) than Tanzania and Uganda, and also Zambia, where this proportion is below 20 per cent, but a lower share than in Botswana, Namibia, and South Africa, where this share is above 40 per cent. The share of the population that uses non-bank formal but not bank services is relatively high (with 15 per cent) – mostly driven by M-Pesa – and higher than in the other African countries for which we have such data. The share of the population that is completely excluded from any formal or informal financial service is lower in Kenya (34 per cent) than in any other country except for South Africa, suggesting the strong role that informal and other formal arrangements play in Kenya.

Table 14.12 shows that the access frontier has been pushed out between 2006 and 2009, especially as a result of an increase in the users of other formal financial services. Whereas in 2006, 18.5 per cent of the population used formal financial services – banks, PostBank, and insurance companies – 22.6 per cent do so in 2009. The share of the population that uses only other formal financial services – MFIs, SACCOs, M-Pesa, and other formal money transfer operators – increased from 8.1 per cent in 2006 to 17.9 per cent in 2009. On the other hand, the proportion of the population with access to only informal financial services decreased from 35 per cent to 26.8 per cent, and the share of the population excluded from any financial service decreased from 38.3 per cent to 32.7 per cent.

Table 14.12 also confirms significant differences in the use of financial services across different subgroups. Men are more likely to use formal banking services, whereas women are more likely to be restricted to informal financial services. Financial exclusion, on the other hand, is at similar levels for men and women. Urban Kenyans are more than twice as likely to use formal financial services as rural Kenyans, while the share of Kenyans restricted to informal financial services or completely excluded is almost twice as high in rural as in urban areas. Finally, we note a strong positive correlation of the use of formal

Table 14.12 Use of financial services in Kenya, over time and across different groups

	2006	2009	2009							
	Overall	Overall	Female	Male	Urban	Rural	None	Primary	Secondary	Tertiary
Bank	18.5	22.6	17.8	27.8	40.9	17.6	4.9	13.4	34.7	70.2
Formal, other	8.1	17.9	15.9	20.2	21.5	17	7.2	16.6	25	19.5
Informal	35	26.8	33.3	19.5	16.4	29.6	32	35.8	15.2	2.2
Excluded	38.3	32.7	33	32.4	21.1	35.8	55.9	34.2	25.1	8

For definitions, see text.
Source: Beck (2009).

Table 14.13 Use of different financial services in Kenya

	2006 Overall	2009 Overall	2009 Female	Male	Urban	Rural
Transaction	15	45.2	40.7	50.2	71.6	38.1
Savings	25.6	27	21.2	33.4	40.7	23.2
Insurance	5.9	6.8	6	8.2	14.1	4.8
Credit	6.7	7.3	4.7	9.1	10.3	6.2

For detailed definitions, see Beck (2009).
Source: Beck (2009).

financial services with the level of education. The gap between groups at different levels of educational attainment is starkest for Kenyans with tertiary education compared with all other groups. Only 10 per cent of this segment is either limited to informal finance or excluded from any financial service.

Savings and transaction services are the most prevalent financial services, whereas there is very limited use of credit and insurance services. Table 14.13 reports the use of different financial services provided by banks and other formal financial institutions (SACCOs, MFIs, and money transfer operators, including M-Pesa) in 2006 and 2009, as well as for different subgroups of the population in 2009. We see that less than 10 per cent of the population uses credit or insurance services, whereas one in four Kenyans uses savings services. The share of Kenyans using transaction services has increased dramatically over the past three years, mostly due to M-Pesa, a cellphone-based transaction service offered by Safaricom, a telecom and thus non-financial corporation. Comparing male and female Kenyans, we see that men are more likely to use all financial services than women. The differences are even starker between rural and urban Kenya, with the use of transaction, savings, and credit services almost twice as high in urban as in rural areas and the use of insurance services almost three times as high.

The entry of M-Pesa into the remittance market has been powerful and has been behind the increase in the use of transaction services. Some 39.9 per cent of those surveyed claim to have used M-Pesa, more than the users of any other financial institution or product in Kenya. The popularity of M-Pesa is also reflected in Kenyans' perceptions. Whereas in 2006, a relative (weighted) majority of those surveyed named 'specialist money transfer operator' as the least risky and fastest channel to send remittances and friends and family as the least expensive and easiest to obtain, in 2009, it was M-Pesa that was rated the least risky, the fastest, and the easiest to obtain, while it came in as second under the category least expensive (friends and family continue to be rated as the least expensive channel).

Although many individual characteristics are associated with the use of financial services, many of these characteristics are also correlated with each other. For example, inhabitants of rural areas are typically poorer and less likely to work in formal jobs – which of these characteristics is the decisive one explaining whether an individual has access to financial services or not? In order to determine the decisive factors, we utilize multivariate regression analysis. Specifically, we regress dummy variables that indicate whether an individual has (i) access to banking services, (ii) other formal financial services, (iii) informal financial services, or (iv) is excluded.[18]

The regression results in Table 14.14 suggest that, controlling for other characteristics, women are not less likely to use formal or other formal financial services, but they are more likely to use informal services than men and are less likely to be excluded. Rural Kenyans, on the other hand, are less likely to use formal and other formal financial services, but not informal services. Income is one of the strongest predictors of usage of both formal and informal financial services. To illustrate the economic size of this effect, consider Kenyans with a monthly income of less than 10,000 Ksh, Kenyans with a monthly income between 10,000 and 50,000 Ksh, Kenyans with an income between 50,000 and 100,000 Ksh, and Kenyans with a monthly income above 100,000 Ksh. The predicted probability of being formally banked – controlling for the other individual characteristics – increases from 11.9 per cent to 40.8 per cent to 73.7 per cent to 82.7 per cent as we move across the income brackets.

We also find that education is a strong predictor of the use of formal banking and other formal financial services. Kenyans with tertiary education are more likely to use formal and other formal financial services (any of the four service types) than Kenyans with secondary education, who in turn are more likely to use these services than Kenyans with only a primary education, who in turn are more likely to use these services than Kenyans without any formal education. Older Kenyans are more likely to use financial services. Salaried employees are more likely to use formal financial services and are less likely to be excluded. Compared with Kenyans dependent on pensions or remittances, employed, self-employed, and agricultural workers are more likely to use bank and other formal financial services and are less likely to be excluded. They are also more likely to use informal financial services. Although cellphone users typically have higher incomes, the ownership of a cellphone has an additional positive effect on the likelihood of using financial services, whereas it is negatively associated with the likelihood of being excluded.

Numeracy is associated with greater use of formal bank services, but is not significantly associated with the use of other formal or informal financial services or with being excluded. The survey included several questions on basic calculus problems and on risk diversification. We find that people who correctly respond to these questions are more likely to use formal banking services, whereas there is no significant association with the other dependent variables. Finally, more risk-averse people are more likely to use informal financial services and are less likely to be excluded.[19]

Table 14.14 Who uses financial services in Kenya?

	Formal	Formal, other	Informal	Excluded
Own cellphone	0.166	0.422	0.084	–0.270
	(0.000)***	(0.000)***	(0.000)***	(0.000)***
Female	–0.018	–0.025	0.191	–0.097
	(0.115)	(0.132)	(0.000)***	(0.000)***
Log (age)	0.180	0.144	0.088	–0.159
	(0.000)***	(0.000)***	(0.001)***	(0.000)***
Employed	0.140	0.160	0.118	–0.144
	(0.000)***	(0.000)***	(0.000)***	(0.000)***
Self-employed	0.126	0.100	0.210	–0.164
	(0.000)***	(0.001)***	(0.000)***	(0.000)***
Agriculture	0.079	0.122	0.164	–0.156
	(0.000)***	(0.000)***	(0.000)***	(0.000)***
Risk aversion	0.015	0.027	0.057	–0.047
	(1.26)	(0.092)*	(0.004)***	(0.009)***
Rural	–0.081	–0.112	–0.015	0.062
	(0.000)***	(0.000)***	(0.624)	(0.023)**
Log of total expenditures	0.078	0.064	0.074	–0.090
	(0.000)***	(0.000)***	(0.000)***	(0.000)***
Primary education	0.085	0.105	0.118	–0.123
	(0.000)***	(0.000)***	(0.000)***	(0.000)***
Secondary education	0.214	0.278	0.077	–0.141
	(0.000)***	(0.000)***	(0.034)**	(0.000)***
Tertiary education	0.422	0.422	0.017	–0.202
	(0.000)***	(0.000)***	(0.696)	(0.000)***
Numeracy	0.023	0.015	–0.006	–0.006
	(0.000)***	(0.117)	(0.460)	(0.489)
Observations	6326	6323	6328	6328

The dependent variable is whether a respondent uses (i) bank, (ii) other formal, (iii) informal services, or (iv) is excluded. Marginal effects are reported. Regressions are weighted and stratified.
*, **, and *** mean significance at the 10%, 5%, and 1% levels respectively.
Source: Beck (2009).

Over 90 per cent of Kenya's bank branches are in urban and rural districts (Figure 14.2). Branches in semi-arid districts account for 4.7 per cent of the national total; those in arid districts account for 2.8 per cent. Even if the definition of a branch is expanded to include all types of access points – agencies, pay points, mobile units, satellite branches, and subbranches – this picture is essentially unchanged (93 per cent in urban and rural areas, 7 per cent in arid and semi-arid areas). The distribution also reflects a difference in geographical emphasis between private and government-owned or -influenced banks.

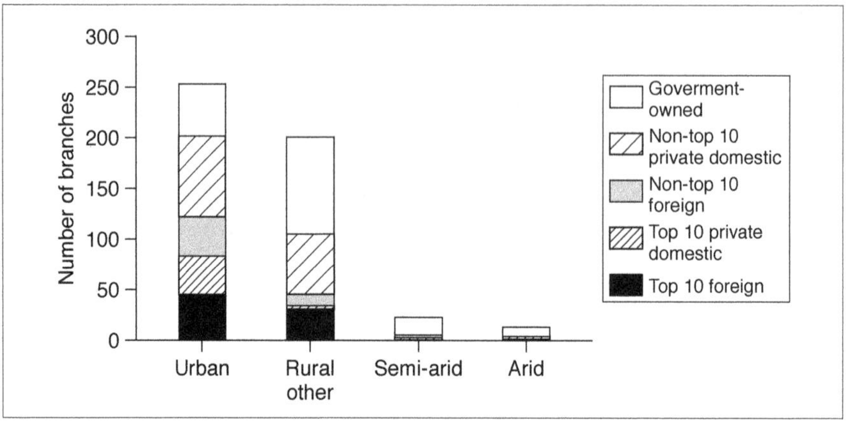

Figure 14.2 Number of bank branches by location.[20]
Source: CBK.

The government-owned and government-influenced banks represent about a fifth of total branches in urban districts, over half in rural districts, three-quarters in semi-arid districts, and almost 90 per cent in arid districts. This suggests that government influence has a positive impact in promoting access to financial services but, in the absence of an analysis to assess the costs of government-influenced banks' poor lending practices, it should not be concluded that government ownership is either the best or the cheapest way in which to maintain rural access to the banking system.

In 2006, a member of the Top 10 was the main bank for 75 per cent of the banked respondents in urban areas, 67 per cent in rural and semi-arid areas, and 55 per cent in arid areas. The PostBank provides most of the remaining access, playing an increasingly important role as one goes from urban to arid districts. Banks that are not in the Top 10 play a much more marginal role, and then only in urban and rural districts. Although the branching figures in Figure 14.2 indicate that non-Top 10 banks account for 45 per cent of urban branches and 35 per cent of rural branches, those branches provide services to far fewer people than do the branches of the Top 10 banks.

The analysis of interest spreads in the previous section and the discussion in the next section suggest that consolidation of the private banking sector might yield benefits in terms of both improved stability and efficiency (lower interest spreads, wider range of service offerings). Given the geographical segmentation of bank branches described in this section, such private sector consolidation would not have a major negative impact on the depth of outreach of the banking sector.

At the same time, the figures in this section also show that depth of outreach remains a serious problem for the Kenyan financial sector. The banks best positioned to maintain or extend outreach are government-owned banks, which are also most in need of efficiency improvement. Ownership restructuring could be a solution, but efforts to privatize these banks would need to balance competing objectives so that profitability and efficiency improvement do not come at the expense of reduced outreach. Such tensions have been successfully balanced in bank privatizations in both Uganda and Tanzania, which offers some hope (see Cull and Spreng, 2008; Clarke *et al.*, 2009). A more effective – and cheaper – approach to foster outreach may be to provide subsidies to private sector banks to increase their rural presence using lower cost mechanisms (such as mobile offices and new technologies such as mobile payments) and reinforce this by promoting the development and regulation of non-banking institutions such as SACCOs and MFIs.

14.6 Consolidation as an instrument for more efficiency and stability

Kenya's *Vision 2030* seeks to facilitate the transformation of the banking sector to bring in fewer stronger and larger banks. The higher capital levels in banks are expected to create a vibrant and globally competitive financial sector that will create jobs and also promote high levels of savings to finance Kenya's overall investment needs. What does theory and international experience tell us about the relationship between market structure, stability, and efficiency?

Theoretical models have made contrasting predictions on the relationship between bank concentration, competition, and stability.[21] On the one hand, bank concentration may enhance profits and therefore lower bank fragility. High profits provide a buffer against adverse shocks and increase the franchise value of the bank, reducing incentives for bankers to take excessive risk. In addition, proponents of this 'concentration–stability' view argue that larger banks can diversify better so that banking systems characterized by a few large banks will tend to be less fragile than banking systems with many small banks (Allen and Gale, 2004). Further, few large banks might be easier to monitor than many small banks. On the other hand, proponents of the concentration–fragility view argue that market power might result in higher interest rates, which in turn provides incentives to borrowers to take higher risks (Boyd and de Nicoló, 2005). Second, advocates of the concentration–fragility view argue that (i) relative to diffuse banking systems, concentrated banking systems generally have fewer banks, and (ii) policy-makers are more concerned about bank failures when there are only a few banks. Based on these assumptions, banks in concentrated systems will tend to receive larger subsidies through implicit 'too big' or 'too important to fail' policies that intensify risk-taking incentives and hence increase banking system fragility (e.g. Mishkin, 1999). Further, having larger banks in a concentrated banking system could also increase the contagion risk, resulting in a positive link between concentration and systemic fragility.

Cross-country evidence shows that more concentrated banking systems are less likely to suffer systemic fragility; at the same time, competition also contributes to greater stability (Beck *et al.*, 2006a; Schaeck *et al.*, 2009). When analysing the channels through which concentration might be positively associated with banking system stability, Beck *et al.* (2006b) find tentative evidence that more concentrated banking systems allow better possibilities for banks to diversify risk. On the other hand, they do not find any evidence that it is easier for bank supervisors to monitor more concentrated banking systems or that stability results from market power and the consequent increase in the franchise values of banks in more concentrated banking systems. In summary, higher concentration levels do not necessarily imply less competition, but might affect bank stability through other channels. Considering bank-level data, researchers have arrived at different conclusions. On the one hand, Boyd *et al.* (2006) find that banks are closer to insolvency, i.e. more likely to fail, in countries with more concentrated banking systems. On the other hand, Schaeck *et al.* (2009) and Schaeck and Cihak (2010) show that banks have higher capital ratios in more competitive environments.

Summarizing, there is no clear indication that competition is detrimental *per se* for bank stability nor that a more concentrated banking system necessarily implies less competition. Similarly, cross-country studies have shown little effect of market structure on net interest margins, but rather highlighted the importance of a contestable and open banking market without restrictive regulatory policies (Demirgüç-Kunt *et al.*, 2004). Evidence from Uganda has shown that macroeconomic policies and deficiencies in the contractual framework are the most important factors explaining high spreads and margins (Beck and Hesse, 2009). While small scale can also explain high spreads, market structure indicators are not significantly associated with bank efficiency. Overall, although larger banks might result in greater overall efficiency, the resulting higher concentration is not necessarily associated with increased or reduced efficiency. The effect of market structure on access to financial services, on the other hand, points to a potentially negative effect of a more concentrated banking system on access to loans by small firms (Beck *et al.*, 2004) and lower geographical outreach (Beck *et al.*, 2008).

Although the Kenyan banking sector is often seen as highly oligopolistic with remarkable features of market concentration and leadership, it is also characterized by small fringe banks with very high overhead costs and weak capital bases. The capital levels of most of the banks are below US$25m, which is lower than that of the smallest banks in Nigeria. The Government of Kenya, through the Finance Act, 2008, has therefore begun increasing minimum capital requirements for banks from Ksh 250m (US$3.1m) to Ksh 1bn (US$12.5m) by 2012.

Cross-country evidence and the evidence across Kenyan banks presented above point to potential gains from such a consolidation on both the efficiency and the stability of the financial system. On the other hand, there might be a negative impact on access, especially on customers of small niche banks. Critically, however, the impact of consolidation on efficiency, stability, and access will depend on the implications of a more concentrated banking system for competition. Beyond the effect of changes in the size distribution on stability, efficiency, and access, one should not forget the repercussions of ownership structures for these three dimensions of financial development.

14.7 Conclusion

From this overview of recent developments in the Kenyan banking sector, a number of themes emerge. First, the government reform strategy has produced a number of benefits, especially with regard to soundness and stability. Reducing government borrowing and creating a stable macroeconomic environment did much to ease lending rates and reduce spreads during this period. Increasing banks' capital requirements, introducing a limited deposit insurance scheme, and provisioning aggressively against non-performing loans also contributed to greater banking sector stability. There was also improvement in the efficiency of intermediation beyond that attributable to improved government finances and a stable macroeconomic environment. In particular, banks' overhead costs declined through competition, although the results were more evident for foreign-owned banks than for others. Indeed, private domestic banks saw their interest spreads increase from 2005 to 2007, and plans to force the consolidation of some of these smaller banks are being considered. Access to financial services is limited to a relatively small subset of the Kenyan population, although this is true in much of the developing world. The banks with the physical infrastructure (branches) to expand access beyond the urban areas, mostly banks in which the government has an ownership interest, tend also to be among the least efficient. Obvious tensions therefore emerge in pursuing improvements in access, efficiency, and stability at the same time. Although much has been accomplished with regard to banking reform in Kenya, there remains much left to do. Beyond maintaining macroeconomic stability and significant improvement in the contractual and informational frameworks (including the credit registry), regulatory and competition policies will play an important role. A priori, however, it is not clear that the push towards larger banks will allow Kenya to reap benefits in terms of outreach. It will be more important to focus on the ownership structure and a competitive environment for all banks to achieve the goals of *Vision 2030*. This would imply privatization of the remaining government-owned banks and a level regulatory playing field for all deposit-taking institutions. The latter includes effective, but not overly burdensome, regulation and supervision of MFIs and SACCOs. It also implies maintaining an openness to new, even non-bank, providers of financial services, which has enabled the success of M-Pesa.

Notes

1 We are grateful for useful comments from the editor, Christopher Adam, and Yira Mascaro. This chapter's findings, interpretations, and conclusions are entirely those of the authors and do not necessarily represent the views of the Central Bank of Kenya, the World Bank, its Executive Directors, or the countries they represent.
2 The figure for sub-Saharan Africa is taken from Allen *et al.* (2009).
3 We note, however, that Kenya's net interest margins are on a par with the rest of sub-Saharan Africa (Table 14.1). While there are some countries in Latin America that have higher interest margins and spreads than Kenya, a recent comparison shows that Kenya ranked eighth of 37 countries in interest spreads in 2008 and twelfth of 66 countries in net interest margins from 2001 to 2009. Also, Uganda's spreads and margins, which are higher than those in Kenya, rank in the top five on both dimensions. In all, the evidence points to Kenya's margins and spreads as being relatively high. See Jorgensen *et al.* (2010) for the international comparisons of interest spreads and net interest margins.
4 NPLs to gross loans for Nigeria, Kenya, and Malaysia. NPLs to total loans for all others.
5 Capital adequacy ratio (CAR), NPL for 2005, ROA and ROE for March 2006.
6 CAR, September 2006; NPLs include compromised assets ratio, restructured loans, and foreclosed assets for the largest sixteen banks. ROE is based on the twelve largest banks.
7 ROA is before tax.
8 All entries are for March 2007.
9 Interest accrued but not collected from the date an account is classified as non-performing is included as interest in suspense.
10 The formula we use is:

Profit margin = (1–tax rate) × (weighted average lending rate–weighted average deposit rate/(1– reserve requirement)–operating costs/loans–loan loss provisions/loans).

The tax rate is calculated from actual tax payments. The reserve requirement is 10 per cent. Operating costs are those attributable to lending, and thus are equal to the share of income from lending multiplied by total costs.

11 That model is motivated by the dealership model of bank spreads developed by Ho and Saunders (1981), in which banks are risk-averse dealers trying to balance loan and deposit markets. Because loan requests and deposit flows can be asynchronous, spreads are seen as fees charged by banks for the provision of liquidity under un-

certainty. See Martinez Peria and Mody (2004) for further description of the model and extensions by other authors.

12 In the Latin American context, high liquidity was thought to inflict a cost on banks, as a bank must forgo the opportunity to hold a higher yielding instrument. Thus, Martinez Peria and Mody (2004) hypothesize that banks will try to transfer this cost to borrowers, resulting in a positive association between liquidity and spreads. Similarly, those authors hypothesize that there is an opportunity cost associated with holding excessive capital, and thus they expect a positive relation between capital and spreads.

13 This is consistent with some of the regression results in Beck and Hesse (2009) for Uganda from 2000 to 2004. Martinez Peria and Mody (2004) note, however, that market share could also be equated with market power, and thus the ability to charge higher rates on the loans. The coefficient on this variable will therefore indicate which of these two hypotheses is better supported by the data.

14 The index is calculated by summing the squared market shares of all banks.

15 In model 1, standard errors are clustered at the bank level.

16 The discussion of the findings of FinAccess 2006 and 2009 is based on Beck (2009).

17 Porteous (2007) classifies banks and PostBank as formal, and insurance companies and formal money transfer operators, such as M-Pesa, as non-bank formal. SACCOs and MFIs, on the other hand, are classified as informal financial institutions. In the FinAccess definitions for Kenya, as reported in Table 14.12, on the other hand, SACCOs and MFIs are classified as other formal providers.

18 Unlike in Tables 14.10–14.13, individuals can therefore belong to several categories.

19 Risk aversion is a dummy variable that takes on a value of 1 if the individual responds yes to the following question: do you avoid taking risks with your money or resources?

20 Foreign banks in the Top 10 include Barclays, Standard Chartered, and Stanbic. The domestic banks in the Top 10 are Equity, K-Rep, Baroda, and Commercial Bank of Africa. Cooperative, KCB, and NBK are the government-owned banks that round out the Top 10.

21 See Carletti and Hartmann (2003) for an in-depth literature survey, and Allen and Gale (2004) for an excellent exposition on the different theoretical mechanisms that can lead to contrasting relationships between competition and stability. See Beck (2008) for an overview of the recent empirical literature.

References

Allen, F. and D. Gale, 2000, *Comparing Financial Systems*. Cambridge, MA: MIT Press.

Allen, F. and D. Gale, 2004, 'Competition and Financial Stability', *Journal of Money, Credit, and Banking*, 36 (3 Pt 2), 433–480.

Allen, F., E. Carletti, R. Cull, J. Qian and L. Senbert, 2009, 'The African Financial Development Gap'. Mimeo.

Beck, T., 2008, 'Competition and Financial Stability: Friends or Foes?' in Bank Indonesia and Banco de Mexico (eds) *Competition in the Financial Sector*. Central Banks.

Beck, T, 2009, 'FinAccess 2009: Trends, Analysis and Policy Conclusions'. Consultant report for FSD Trust Kenya.

Beck, T. and M. Fuchs., 2004, 'Structural Issues in the Kenyan Financial System: Improving Competition and Access'. World Bank Policy Research Working Paper 3363.

Beck, T. and H. Hesse, 2009, 'Why Are Interest Spreads So High in Uganda?' *Journal of Development Economics*, 88 (2), 192–204.

Beck, T, and L. Laeven, 2008, 'Resolution of Failed Banks by Deposit Insurers: Cross-Country Evidence', in Demirgüç-Kunt, A., E. Kane and L. Laeven (eds) *Deposit Insurance around the World, Issues of Design and Implementation*. Cambridge, MA: MIT Press.

Beck, T., A. Demirgüç-Kunt and V. Maksimovic, 2004, 'Bank Competition and Access to Finance: International Evidence', *Journal of Money, Credit and Banking*, 36, 627–648.

Beck, T., A. Demirgüç-Kunt and R. Levine, 2006a, 'Bank Concentration, Competition, and Crises: First Results', *Journal of Banking and Finance*, 30, 1581–1603.

Beck, T., A. Demirgüç-Kunt and R. Levine, 2006b, 'Bank Concentration and Fragility: Impact and Mechanics', in Stulz, R. and M. Carey (eds) *The Risks of Financial Institutions*. Cambridge, MA: National Bureau of Economic Research.

Beck, T., A. Demirgüç-Kunt and M. S. Martinez Peria, 2008, 'Banking Services for Everyone? Barriers to Bank Access and Use around the World', *World Bank Economic Review*, 22, 397–430.

Beck, T., M. Fuchs and M. Uy, 2009, 'Finance in Africa: Achievements and Challenges', in World Bank, African Development Bank and World Economic Forum (eds) *African Competitiveness Report 2009*. Washington, DC: World Bank.

Beck, T., A. Demirgüç-Kunt and R. Levine, 2010, 'Financial Institutions and Markets across Countries and over Time: Data and Analysis', *World Bank Economic Review*, 24, 77–92.

Boyd, J. H. and G. De Nicoló, 2005, 'The Theory of Bank Risk-taking and Competition Revisited', *Journal of Finance*, 60, 1329–1343.

Boyd, J. H., G. De Nicoló and A. Jalal, 2006, 'Bank Risk Taking and Competition: New Theory, New Empirics'. IMF Working Paper 06/297.

Carletti, E. and P. Hartmann, 2003, 'Competition and Stability: What's Special about Banking?', in Mizen, P. (ed.) *Monetary History, Exchange Rates and Financial Markets: Essays in Honor of Charles Goodhart*. Cheltenham, UK: Edward Elgar.

Clarke, G. R. G., R. Cull and M. Fuchs, 2009, 'Bank Privatization in Sub-Saharan Africa: The Case of Uganda Commercial Bank', *World Development*, 37, 1506–1521.

Cull, R. and C. P. Spreng, 2008, 'Pursuing Efficiency while Maintaining Outreach: Bank Privatization in Tanzania'. World Bank Policy Research Working Paper 4804.

Demirgüç-Kunt, A. and E. Detragiache, 2002, 'Does Deposit Insurance Increase Banking System Stability? An Empirical Investigation', *Journal of Monetary Economics*, 49 (7), 1373–1406.

Demirgüç-Kunt, A. and E. Kane, 2002, 'Deposit Insurance around the Globe: Where does it Work?' *Journal of Economic Literature*, 60, 175–195.

Demirgüç-Kunt, A., L. Laeven and R. Levine, 2004, 'Regulations, Market Structure, Institutions, and the Cost of Financial Intermediation', *Journal of Money, Credit, and Banking*, 36 (3 Pt 2), 593–622.

Ho, T. and A. Saunders, 1981, 'The Determinants of Bank Interest Margins: Theory and Empirical Evidence', *Journal of Financial and Quantitative Analysis*, 4, 581–600.

Honohan, P. and L. Laeven, 2005, *Systemic Financial Crises: Containment and Resolution*. Cambridge, UK: Cambridge University Press.

Jorgensen, O. H., A. Apostolou, A. Lagerborg, Y. S. Sakho and B. Cunha, 2010, 'Brazil's Bank Spread in International Context', *World Bank*, mimeo.

Laeven, L. and R. Levine, 2007, 'Is There a Diversification Discount in Financial Conglomerates?' *Journal of Financial Economics*, 85, 331–367.

Martinez Peria, M. S. and A. Mody, 2004, 'How Foreign Participation and Market Concentration Impact Bank Spreads: Evidence from Latin America', *Journal of Money, Credit, and Banking*, 36 (3), 511–537.

Mishkin, F. S., 1999, 'Financial Consolidation: Dangers and Opportunities', *Journal of Banking and Finance*, 23, 675–691.

Porteous, D., 2007, 'Finance Service Access and Usage in Southern and East Africa: What do Finscope Surveys Tell Us?' Finmark Trust South Africa.

Schaeck, K. and M. Cihak, 2010, 'Banking Competition and Capital Ratios'. *European Financial Management*, forthcoming..

Schaeck, K., M. Cihak and S. Wolfe, 2009, 'Are Competitive Banking Systems More Stable?', *Journal of Money, Credit, and Banking*, 41, 711–734.

15

The Capital Market and Economic Growth in Kenya

Rose W. Ngugi, Daniel Amanja, and Isaya Maana

15.1 Introduction

Kenya's development plan, the *Vision 2030*, envisages long-term annual economic growth of 10 per cent, which will be achieved by increasing the savings rate from 17 per cent to 30 per cent of gross domestic product (GDP), of which about 20 per cent will be raised from the domestic market. The *Vision* anticipates an increase in bank deposits from 44 per cent to 80 per cent of GDP and the growth of stock market capitalization from around 50 per cent to 90 per cent of GDP. These projections reflect a view that sees the capital market playing an important role in the growth process by providing firms with the opportunity to raise capital and savers with the ability to diversify and increase their return on their savings. Capital market development is an important component of broader financial sector development, supplementing the role that the banking system plays in economic development (Demirguc-Kunt and Levine, 1996). Specifically, well-functioning capital markets can assist in price discovery, through the generation and dissemination of information on firms' performance; they provide liquidity to the market, which gives savers valuable exit strategies allowing for efficient mobilization and allocation of savings, and they reduce transaction costs and allow for efficient pricing and diversification of risk (Garcia and Liu, 1999; Yartey and Adjasi, 2007).

Thus, countries with efficient and well-functioning financial systems and liquid and vibrant stock markets tend, on average, to enjoy faster and more stable economic growth by efficiently mobilizing and pooling savings into productive investment (Demirguc-Kunt and Levine, 1996). Capital market development does, of course, bring with it risks: markets may be vulnerable to speculative bubbles, which can negate the efficient signalling role of prices, and they may be prone to market crises that put at risk the broader financial sector. At the microeconomic level, concerns have been expressed that poorly functioning or poorly regulated pricing and takeover mechanisms tend to encourage short-termism, rendering prices volatile, excessively sensitive to short-term sentiments and, ultimately, threatening efficient corporate governance (Yartey and Adjasi, 2007; Yartey, 2008).

The economics literature is replete with studies designed to explore the magnitude and direction of the relationship between capital market deepening and economic growth. A simple framework for this analysis and a short review of some of the empirical evidence from around the world is contained in the Appendix. In this chapter, however, we focus principally on the development of the capital market in Kenya and the constraints that the authorities face in ensuring that it can play a key role in supporting the growth process laid out in *Vision 2030.*

We highlight three principal messages. First, like elsewhere in Africa, the Kenyan capital market remains small in size with a limited number of listings, relatively low liquidity, and significant structural and regulatory weaknesses. There is, however, significant scope for improvement. Second, we note important disincentives for firms to seek to finance their investment needs through the capital markets. Low liquidity and other market weaknesses mean that the market does not always price the cost of capital appropriately, leading to potential misallocation problems. Third, there remain important institutional weaknesses, and gaps in the market infrastructure risk undermining confidence and efficiency in the market. In particular, legal and regulatory factors that enhance investor confidence and develop the culture of participating in the capital market need to be developed and tax incentives appropriately aligned.

The rest of the chapter is organized as follows. Section 15.2 looks at recent capital market performance in Kenya. Section 15.3 discusses capital markets as a source of financing, and Section 15.4 looks at the microeconomic and structural factors that are central to capital market development. Section 15.5 concludes and makes some recommendations.

15.2 Capital market performance

The ambitious projections for the capital market laid out in *Vision 2030* assume a strong positive relationship between market capitalization/market size and economic growth. These ambitious targets are not out of line with recent experience: the Kenyan stock market has experienced considerable growth since 2003, as shown in Table 15.1. Before 2003, market capitalization was less than 20 per cent of GDP. During the boom period from 2003 to 2007, there was a significant growth in the number of shares listed through initial public offers (IPOs) with almost 1 billion new shares being listed, compared with only half this amount in the previous five years. The share price index (1966=100) increased from 1,935 to 5,146 between 2003 and 2007, which represents a 97 per cent increase compared with the decline from 2,962 to 1,087 in 1998–2002. By comparison, the consumer prices index (CPI) increased by 19 per cent between 2003 and 2007: as a result, market capitalization increased from 27.9 per cent of GDP to 46.6 per cent in the recovery period compared with a decline from 15.2 to 10.8 per cent between 1998 and 2002. Liquidity, as measured by either the value of shares traded as a percentage of GDP or the turnover ratio – the ratio of traded shares to the outstanding shares – has also seen significant growth since 2003, rising in the first case from around 1 per cent of GDP in 2003 to over 6 per cent in 2006.

Nonetheless, as Table 15.1 also shows, although the Kenyan market is performing well relative to those in Ghana and Nigeria, it remains relatively small and illiquid compared with other emerging market economies, including some in Africa. The market in Mauritius, for example, is almost twice as large (as a share of GDP) and South Africa is six times as big.

The Kenyan market is also small in the number of listed firms. By 2007, Kenya had fifty-one listed companies, whereas South Africa, Nigeria, and Malaysia had 422, 212, and 1036 respectively. Before independence, the stock market experienced tremendous growth in the number of firms listed. For example, by 1954, the Nairobi Stock Exchange (NSE) had forty-six listed companies increasing to fifty in 1956. By 1959, the market had a total of thirteen new listings and four de-listings, but no listing of firms from the financial sector. In the 1960s, the number of new listings increased to nineteen while the number of de-listings rose to eleven so that the total number of listed companies increased from fifty-six in 1960 to sixty-three in 1969. By 1998, the market had fifty-eight companies. Currently, the market has fifty-one listed companies, almost exactly the same number as at independence.

With the exception of South Africa, few African countries have anything other than fledgling markets in bonds, either public or private bonds, and none have markets in derivatives or futures. But there is some progress. In Mauritius, government treasury bills were introduced to the exchange in December 2003 with series of different maturity dates. The Kenyan bonds market saw the entry of the first corporate bond in 1996. With the efforts to develop the treasury bonds market, this has seen extended maturities of treasury bonds to twenty years and the introduction of infrastructure bonds. The corporate bonds market, however, remains very small with fewer than ten firms participating after more than a decade and offering short- to medium-term paper.

Table 15.1 Comparative market performance

	Kenya	Mauritius	Nigeria	Ghana	South Africa	Egypt	Morocco	Malaysia	Singapore	Brazil	Peru	Israel
Market capitalization (% of GDP)												
1997	14	40	10	17	156	27	36	93	111	29	30	42
2000	10	29	9	10	154	29	29	125	165	35	20	51
2003	28	35	14	19	161	33	26	153	246	42	26	64
2007	49	75	52	16	294	107	100	174	212	103	99	142
1997	58	40	182	21	642	654	49	708.0	303	536	248	640
2000	57	40	195	22	616	1076	53	736.0	418	459	230	654
2003	51	40	200	25	426	967	53	757.0	551	367	197	576
2007	51	90	212	32	422	435	74	795.0	472	442	190	654
Stock traded, turnover ratio (%)												
1997	0.0	4.0	5.0	6.0	29.0	53.0	10.0	73.0	50.0	77.0	26.0	26.0
2000	4.0	5.0	7.0	1.0	34.0	35.0	9.0	45.0	52.0	43.0	13.0	36.0
2003	7.0	6.0	11.0	4.0	45.0	14.0	6.0	34.0	71.0	32.0	6.0	68.0
2007	11.0	8.0	28.0	4.0	55.0	46.0	42.0	54.0	122.0	56.0	9.0	55.0
Stock traded, total value (% of GDP)												
1997	1	3	0	1	30	7	3	153	67	23	7	10
2000	0	2	1	0	58	11	3	62	99	16	3	19
2003	1	2	1	1	62	4	1	45	94	11	1	35
2007	5	5	10	1	150	41	35	80	230	44	7	68

Source: World Development Indicators (World Bank).

15.3 The capital market as a source of finance

Firms can finance investment through a variety of means. They can use internal funding such as retained earnings or borrow externally by raising either external equity or debt. The choice of alternative channels depends on the cost factors including the interest rate and agency costs, access and availability, and the ability to service the loan or debt. Firms often seek external funding when they face liquidity constraints, but when the capital market is shallow and thin with few instruments and low liquidity, this not only leaves the firms with minimal financing options, but has also exposed them to high bank lending rates; the private sector has had to rely mainly on the banking sector to finance both their operations and their investments. At the same time, savers have been left with a thin basket of financial assets, which has seen them with little or no bargaining power for expected returns even on their deposits. This can then be a constraint on the mobilization of adequate and appropriate resources. Further, with an illiquid and immature capital market, the cost of financing increases while the channelling of resources from savers to good investment opportunities tends to be poor.

Table 15.2 reports the financing strategies for new investments among manufacturing firms in Kenya in 2003. These results are drawn from a sample of 282 manufacturing firms ranging from small to large firms. New investment was mainly financed through internal funding and, to some extent, through bank loans. Overdraft facilities were also a major source of finance, whereas the contribution of foreign loans and development financial institutions (DFIs) was minimal. For firms that opted to use internal funds, they financed an average of 77 per cent of the total investment. External equity was not a popular alternative, possibly because of the level of development of the capital market. The situation may also reflect a constraint to accessing appropriate finance. For example, in the mid-1990s with the government policy to consolidate the banking sector, most non-bank financial institutions (NBFIs), some of which were offering specialized asset financing products, converted to commercial banks, and this reduced the provision of such products in the market. Those hardest hit by these developments were the small to medium-sized enterprises (SMEs), which face collateral issues with banking institutions. Ngugi (2002, 2008), studying listed firms in the NSE, shows that capital market imperfections had a direct impact on capital financing behaviour through their effect on the ease of access to and availability of capital. Such uncertainty in the market created by market imperfections adversely affects investment expenditure.

Have things changed in the market since then? Only three additional IPOs came to the market by the end of 2008 and only five additional firms listed bonds – some making more than one listing (Table 15.3). The number of listed firms still remains less than existed in the market at independence. Compared

Table 15.2 Investment financing

	Proportional no. of firms using the service (%)	Average percentages of new investment financed (%)
Internal funds or retained earnings	51.9	77
Local commercial bank loans	17.3	74
Overdraft facility	11.7	74
Trade credit (supplier or customer credit)	4.8	56
Parent company	3.0	33
Lease arrangement	2.6	47
Foreign bank loans	2.2	77
Equity, sale of stocks	2.2	37
Family, friends	2.2	52
Development financial institutions, NBFIs, NGOs	1.3	40
Credit card	0.9	20

Source: Computations based on World Bank/KIPPRA (2003).

with other markets, South Africa has more than ten times the number of listed firms in Kenya, whereas Nigeria has about four times the number listed in the Kenyan market. Further, Kenyan listings are intermittent and, in the recent period, with the important exception of Safaricom, the participation of the general public in Kenya has been minimal.

Equity markets are most useful when allowing new firms and existing listed firms to raise capital. Ritter and Welch (2002) argue that the primary reason for going public is the desire to raise equity capital for the firm and to create a public market in which the founders and other shareholders can convert some of their wealth into cash at a future date. By going public, firms relax their financial constraints, especially those that have large current and future investments, high leverage, and high growth. Following the listing, we would expect that investment financing constraints are relaxed and investment growth is accelerated as, in addition to raising equity, firms going public reduce their costs of credit with reduced information asymmetry problems associated with the disclosure of information. It is also possible that firms go public to rebalance their capital structure after implementing substantial investment plans so that IPO activities follow high investment and growth and not vice versa (Pagano *et al.*, 1998).

Two indicators for this function of an equity market are the number or value of IPOs and the ratio of new capital raised to market capitalization and GDP. Table 15.3 shows that the stock market contribution to GDP has been less than 1 per cent. These figures are comparable to other stock markets. For example, in South Africa, the figure is about 0.34 per cent, Malaysia 0.16 per cent, India 0.52 per cent, and Nigeria 0.37 per cent. However, there are significant differences in terms of the number of listed firms and thus the number

Table 15.3 Trends in issuance of ordinary shares and corporate bonds

	IPOs			Issuance of corporate bonds		
Period	Amounts raised (% of GDP)	Number	Ksh (millions)	Amount (Ksh million)	Share of GDP (%)	Number
1986	0.07	1	80.0			
1988	0.10	3	228.0			
1989	0.18	1	304.0			
1991	0.02	1	40.8			
1992	0.17	3	496.0			
1994	0.45	3	1,260.0			
1996	0.52	4	3,908.0	800	0.12	1
1997	0.07	2	449.4			
1999				1,200	0.13	1
2000	0.05	1	378.0	150	0.02	1
2001	0.13	1	1,456.2	6,200	0.61	3
2002				1,000	0.09	1
2004				800	0.06	1
2005				2,100	0.15	3
2006	0.56	3	9,077.9			
2007	0.17	2	3,080.0	3,100	0.17	3
2008	2.64	2	55,358.8	4,000	0.19	3

Source: NSE information desk, NSE Annual Reports and monthly reviews and CMA Annual Reports.

of firms raising funds using the capital market. Table 15.3 shows that no IPOs came to the market in the period 2002–05. It was only in 2006 that the market had three new listings, which raised about Ksh 9.1 billion (0.6 per cent of GDP). However, the momentum slackened in 2007 with only two IPOs and capital raised dropping to Ksh 3 billion. This contrasts with other countries where listing activity has been high and rising. This was so for the major emerging market economies of China and India, but also for South Africa where the stock exchanges experienced a listing boom that saw twenty-two IPOs, with US$675 million of capital raised during the fourth quarter of 2007 alone. Importantly, most IPOs were on the Johannesburg Stock Exchange's Alternative Exchange Board, the AltX (catering for small, medium, and growing companies). Although these stock exchanges with higher listings are much more developed, IPOs in Kenya are extremely few compared with the existing potential. The recent listing of Safaricom provided an important example of the potential of the Kenyan market to raise capital, but also of the challenges faced in doing so (see Box 15.1).

Box 15.1 Safaricom initial public offer (IPO)

Safaricom Limited is a mobile telephone company jointly owned by the government of Kenya (60 per cent) and Vodafone plc of the United Kingdom (40 per cent). It is the leading telephone service provider and one of the most profitable companies in Kenya. The government of Kenya, in consultation with Vodafone plc, agreed in early 2008 to sell 25 per cent of the issued ordinary shares in the company to the public. It therefore floated 10 billion shares on the stock market at a price of Ksh 5 per share. The government aimed to raise Ksh 52 billion to support its development programmes. The offer was split into two categories: (1) domestic investors who were allocated 65 per cent of the shares; and (2) international investors who were allocated 35 per cent of the shares. For the domestic investors, the minimum number of shares was 2,000 shares, whereas the international investors' category was open only to institutional investors. The transaction was handled by Dyer & Blair and Morgan Stanley plc as the transaction advisers and Equity Bank, National Bank, Post Office Savings Bank, and Citibank as receiving banks. The share distribution of 10 billion shares on offer was as indicated below:

Performance of Safaricom IPO

Category of investors	Shares offered	Shares applied	Subscription rate (%)	Allocation rate (%)
Retail	3,380,000,000	22,637,470,460	464	21.2
Institutional	2,730,000,000	8,758,740,000	321	31.1
Authorized dealers	130,000,000	422,158,200	325	30.7
Safaricom employees	260,000,000	307,549,800	118	84.5
International investors	3,500,000,000	14,220,000,000	711	14

Source: CMA and NSE.

The Safaricom IPO was one of the largest in sub-Saharan Africa and attracted Ksh 236 billion against a target of Ksh 52 billion, giving an oversubscription of over 350 per cent. This allotment resulted in public holdings of 25 per cent, leaving the government with 35 per cent and Vodafone Kenya Ltd with 40 per cent. The Safaricom IPO was eagerly anticipated by the financial markets as it provided most players with an excellent opportunity to make money. The biggest winners would be the Nairobi Stock Exchange (NSE) and the banks. The impact of the Safaricom transformation into a public company was huge. It represented approximately 17 per cent of the total capitalized value of the NSE. As a result of the activity surrounding the IPO, turnover at the exchange grew to an average of over Ksh 1 billion per day. The number of Central Depository System (CDS) accounts grew by over 700,000. The number of investors in the stock market increased from 800,000 to 1.5 million after the IPO

Successful development of a primary market requires institutional developments such as an effective legal and regulatory framework, listing procedures and requirements, effective market-makers, and competitive listing costs. These institutional factors are required to establish a competitive enabling environment to facilitate the listing of firms on the stock exchange. They define the procedures for listing, the listing requirements, and allow for the negotiation of effective public policy towards the market. In a number of countries, privatization of public assets through IPOs has been an important catalyst for this kind of market development. Privatization, it is argued, generates positive externalities in terms of placing demand on the markets themselves to develop their infrastructure, by improving investors' diversification opportunities and by increasing market participation, admittedly through heavy discounting of shares to new retail investors (Pagano, 1989; Dewenter and Malatesta, 1997; Subrahmanyam and Titman, 1999). The slow pace of the privatization process in Kenya has also meant that the market has yet to benefit from the divestiture process through the stock market, although the Safaricom divestiture demonstrated not just that the market could absorb large issues but that, in doing so, key market developments were stimulated.

The bond market is no different. Table 15.3 reports the trends in amounts raised through the corporate bonds, which is minimal, less than 1 per cent of GDP, compared with such countries as South Africa (12.94 per cent), Malaysia (52.36 per cent), and Singapore (18.85 per cent). The bonds market in Kenya saw the introduction of corporate bonds in 1996. However, the market has not been very active with fewer than ten companies having made listings and fewer than twenty issues made in more than a decade later. A major challenge with the bonds market is that the liquidity level is low, which makes it difficult for investors to adopt alternative exit strategies in the market. Pricing is also difficult but, recently, the government has started using its own borrowing to develop a benchmark yield curve to provide a basis for the pricing of bonds and other longer term products in the market. The government now issues benchmark bonds and has extended the maximum bond maturity to twenty years. In 2009, it introduced its first infrastructure bonds, which are expected to encourage the development of more asset-backed bonds in the market, from both public and private sectors.

The other source of long-term finance in Kenya is the development finance sector. However, as Table 15.2 shows, firms appear to make very little use of this market. DFIs were created in a deliberate effort to fill a development financing gap in the belief that the private capital market would not do so. Before independence, only two public institutions provided development finance, the Land and Agricultural Bank and the Industrial Development Corporation These were joined, after independence, by a raft of new DFIs including the Agricultural Development Corporation, the Industrial and Commercial Development Corporation, the Development Finance Company of Kenya, and the Kenya Tourist Development Corporation, all designed to boost the provision of long-term credit, and all with considerable donor support in the 1960s and 1970s.

In practice, although DFIs were created to alleviate perceived market failures in the provision of long-term capital investment, by providing equity and loans to industrial enterprises as well as agricultural business, they tended to concentrate on funding state enterprises and failed to promote the growth of private enterprises. Ultimately, the DFIs essentially failed to meet their objectives, both in their role of providing long-term capital and as a means to catalyse the local capital market in Kenya. They lacked effective statutory powers to raise funds independently, they were unable to resist political pressures and, ultimately, became vehicles of political patronage and abuse, preventing them from developing into viable developmental and commercial entities (Nasibi, 1992), and ending up as a drain on budgetary resources

Despite their track record, *Vision 2030* persists in seeing the DFIs as playing a role in the provision of long-term finance for growth, principally by acting as venture capital organizations providing start-up capital to nurture firms in anticipation of raising long-term equity or bond capital on the stock market.

15.4 Factors determining capital market development

For the capital market to play a decisive role in mobilizing and allocating resources for long-term investments, there has to be a critical mass of products and services, issuers of securities, market players, market infrastructure, and an enabling environment. Investor protection creates confidence in the market, enhancing liquidity. Investors need assurance that they are engaging in a fair game and that they have the ability to take advantage of market opportunities in good time. Firms, who are issuers of securities, consider ease of entry and continued control of the ownership of their companies as key considerations in participating in the market. On the other side, diversification of products gives an opportunity to investors to diversify their portfolio while the availability of professionals in the market reduces information asymmetries and smoothes investors' participation. As such, the institutional and policy environments become major determinants in the growth of the market, creating an enabling environment for the participation of the firms/issuers, investors, and professionals. This section looks at these factors.

15.4.1 Infrastructure requirements for capital market development

A well-functioning market infrastructure reduces obstacles to trading flows, provides secure custody of claims, and safeguards against systemic risk. These factors allow for low-cost settlement of financial transactions and raise investor confidence. On the firm side, such developments also encourage greater market liquidity, which in turn enhances efficiency in the price discovery process (Amihud *et al.*, 1990; Bessembinder and Kaufman, 1997) and hence ensures that efficient stock prices act as benchmarks for evaluating the costs of capital and investment returns for investment projects (Green *et al.*, 2000).

For investors, improved investor protection encourages participation in share trading, which improves liquidity. It has been shown that countries that protect shareholders have more valuable stock markets, a large number of listed securities per capita, and a high rate of IPOs, and, moreover, that this protects markets against excess volatility (La Porta *et al.*, 2000). By ensuring investors' confidence, this enhances investors' participation in market activities, encouraging saving and channelling these savings into productive real investment, thus fostering capital accumulation and efficiency in investment and real sector development. It is, however, debatable whether investors' protection promotes market efficiency.

On the other hand, systems of information disclosure are more likely to promote market efficiency by providing informed traders with low-cost information (Georgakopoulos, 1996). For example, it is observed that securities may deviate from their fundamental values because of irrationalities in the market including uninformed trading or noise trading. As this type of trading interferes with the optimality of market allocation of capital among competing firms, there may be a strong argument for tightening disclosure rules. However, Yartey (2008) observes that, when exchanges are demutualized, there is a conflict of interest as exchanges tend to shy away from enforcing actions against their customers who are sources of income, and there is also commercialization of services including data and trade information, which would retract any gains in reducing information asymmetry. Similarly, listing standards and oversight can be lax.

In addition to the market-specific regulations, Yartey (2008) finds that the quality of overall institutional structures such as law and order, democratic accountability, and bureaucratic quality are also important determinants in the development of stock markets. These factors reduce the political risk that external investors would be factoring in to their expected earnings and enhance the viability of external finance. This finding is consistent with La Porta *et al.* (1997, 1998), who show that countries with lower quality of legal rules and law enforcement have smaller and narrower capital markets and that listed firms have more concentrated ownership. Similar links between the general level of political governance and capital market development are found by Demirguc-Kunt and Maksimovic (1998) and Bekaert (1995).

Two final factors that appear to be important for market development are the presence of foreign investors and overall macroeconomic stability. The latter is rather obvious. As Gertler and Rose (1996) argue, growth and macroeconomic stability enhance the pool of net-worth borrowers, whereas high and volatile inflation, a volatile and fast depreciating exchange rate, and high interest rates destroy this pool. On the other hand, the role of foreign investors is less straightforward. On the one hand, foreign investors may catalyse small emerging markets by bringing capital and skills to the market and, as a result, may provide depth and liquidity in the early stages of market development, thereby dampening latent volatility. But equally, large-scale foreign participation in (small) emerging markets may be de-stabilizing if they raise the risk that capital inflows are quickly reversed (the so-called 'sudden stop' problem) as a result of small changes in the domestic or, indeed, international risk environment (see, for example, Sellin (1996) on the risks associated with large foreign participation in domestic markets).

15.4.2 Kenyan market structures: achievements and challenges

The capital market in Kenya has taken a number of significant steps towards developing a mature and efficient market environment. In this final section of the chapter, we review what has been done and where further progress is required.

MARKET INFRASTRUCTURE

The trading system

The NSE is currently implementing trading system reforms, starting with the introduction of a central depository system (CDS) in November 2004 and an automated trading system (ATS) in September 2006, all aimed at reducing the trading cycle of equities from within seven days of the transaction date (T+7) to within five days of the transaction date (T+5). This has also seen the Capital Markets Authority (CMA) implement an electronic surveillance of ATS in order to review securities trends, authenticity of price movement, and trade volumes. The installed CDS has become a platform for electronic clearing, delivery, and settlement of securities traded. The CDS system will, it is hoped, reduce risk in the settlement process and also streamline the trading process while reducing the transaction period, delivering quicker and safer trading to the investor and delivering faster and larger earnings to brokers. For the market regulator, surveillance is now easier, whereas for all participants, the cost of doing business and ease of entry and exit have reduced. The CDS is in its early stages, and it is difficult to yet discern its impact. However, Ngugi *et al.* (2003), surveying a wider range of exchanges, found that, as a stock market adopts trading system reforms, there is a marked increase in liquidity and lower transaction costs. For example, the stock exchange of Mauritius (SEM), which is a newer stock market having been established in 1989, saw the implementation of a CDS in January 1997, then SEM's automated trading system (SEMATS) was launched in June 2001, marking the move from open outcry system. This constitutes a state-of-the-art electronic trading system built on third-generation technology. SEMATS put an end to traditional trading patterns, which had typified the SEM since its inception. Trading in securities is conducted through dedicated trading workstations located at intermediate dealers and linked by communication lines to the SEM trading engine. Further, in April 2008, SEM introduced 'turn-around trading', which enables an investor to buy and sell shares within the same trading session and to take advantage of intraday price movement, and is expected to improve trading volumes and liquidity.

Market segments

In many developing country environments, including Kenya, fiduciary concerns combined with informational requirements and high minimum capital requirement have raised the cost of listing on the local stock exchange. As a result, listed firms are large, old, and frequently have significant foreign ownership. Prohibitive listing requirements drive medium-scale, young, and locally owned firms from the market. In Kenya, as elsewhere, deliberate efforts are made to accommodate the SMEs in the market by introducing a second-tier market so as to formalize the current informal over-the-counter (OTC) equity market. Formal OTC markets for SMEs have been shown to be successful in other countries, for example in Malaysia, Japan, and Mauritius. In Mauritius, the SEM set up the Development and Enterprise Market (DEM) in 2005, specifically targeted at SMEs and newly set up companies that possess a sound business plan and demonstrate good growth potential. This market tier is meant for companies wishing to avail themselves of the advantages and facilities provided by an organized and regulated market to raise capital to fund their future growth, improve liquidity in their shares, obtain an objective market valuation of their shares, and enhance their overall corporate image. Establishment of a formal OTC market in Kenya will be important in enabling SMEs to raise capital; providing a breeding ground for small companies to list in the main securities exchange; enhancing efficient transfer of securities; facilitating unlocking of investments in closely held companies such as family businesses; availing investors of additional investment avenues; enhancing market discipline in financial reporting, disclosure, and corporate governance in SMEs (CMA Annual Reports). In principle, this accommodation of emerging small companies exists in Kenya: in 2001, the NSE trading board was divided into three segments, including the main investment market segment (MIMs); the alternative investment market segment (AIMs), which is aimed at SMEs with potential to grow; and the fixed income securities markets segments (FISMs). To date, however, there has been no significant growth in the AIMs sector.

Networking

The CMA recognizes that international co-operation is critical for growth of the market. In March 1997, the East Africa Member State Securities Regulatory Authorities (EASRA) was formed between securities regulators in Kenya, Uganda, and Tanzania. Although initially the EASRA comprised the regulatory authorities, the opening of stock markets in Tanzania and Uganda implied that membership was extended to the stock exchanges. This was followed in 2000 by the creation of the Capital Market Development Committee (CMDC), the objective of which was to harmonize capital market policies in the East African Community. These market initiatives were supported by a commitment to enable investors to operate freely within the East African capital markets. The CMA was admitted as a full signatory of the International Organization of Securities Commissions Multilateral Memorandum of Understanding (IOSCO MMOU). Thus, the CMA is a full signatory to the IOSCO concerning consultation, co-operation, and exchange of information. For a regulatory body to qualify to sign the IOSCO MMOU, it must have demonstrated capacity, legally and practically, to meet the specific MMOU provisions for mutual assistance and exchange of information in order to successfully enforce securities laws. Thus, it means that the CMA is making a significant step towards meeting international standards in its operations.

LEGAL AND REGULATORY FRAMEWORK

Market regulation is geared towards protecting the integrity of the marketplace, member firms, and the customer, with more emphasis put on investors' protection, fairness, market integrity, and minimization of systematic risk. Thus, statutory bodies generally set up during the reform process have two core responsibilities in the emerging markets: surveillance and market development. The Kenyan CMA was set up in 1989 charged with a broad responsibility of promoting and facilitating the development of an efficient capital market in Kenya. The CMA aimed to develop all aspects of the capital market with particular emphasis on the removal of impediments and the creation of incentives for long-term investment in productive enterprises. It also aims to protect investors' interests by operating an insurance fund to protect investors from financial loss arising from the failure of a licensed broker or dealer to meet his contractual obligations. The regulatory structure enables the building of an effective system of market oversight, including a mechanism for monitoring compliance with specific regulatory requirements. Market surveillance enhances the level of intelligence information on market operations, hence acting as an early warning system. Since its establishment, we have seen a steady stream of legislation aimed at strengthening market governance.

BROADENING THE INVESTOR BASE AND PROFESSIONALIZING THE MARKET

African capital markets are often characterized by a narrow investor base dominated by a small number of institutional investors (the pension funds, mutual funds, unit trusts, endowment and provident funds). In recent years, retirement benefit schemes have become increasingly important. Such funds provide long-term savings that can be used to finance large-scale infrastructure projects. Such funds have been important applicants for new financial instruments such as long-term (fifteen-year) government bonds that were non-existent prior to 1999. More recently, collective investments have been established and foreign financial institutions have been set up in Kenya to provide much needed services by the retirement benefits industry. Involving the retirement benefits industry in infrastructure investment might go a long way to overcoming the current shortcomings in the infrastructure network, and in particular the road transport network.

Participation of foreign investors in the stock market is also being encouraged. With the Capital Markets (Foreign Investors) Regulations 2002, every listed company is now required to reserve 25 per cent of its share capital for investment by domestic investors, but any shareholding in excess of 25 per cent can be defined as a 'free float' and is available for investment by East Africans and foreign investors as well as domestic investors without any limitation whatsoever. Similarly, issues of shares through IPOs are required to reserve 25 per cent of the value of the shares for domestic investors. Foreign investors are allowed to take ownership of stock brokerage firms up to 49 per cent. Further, in the recent period, there are proposals to demutualize the NSE, aiming to enhance good corporate governance and open up ownership to public investors. Demutualization is a key initiative being implemented to restore investor confidence and facilitate the capital market to effectively perform its role of mobilizing long-term resources. Demutualization entails changing the legal status from a mutual association with one vote per member into a company limited by shares with one vote per share. Considerable progress has been made, and a draft demutualization bill is ready for submission to parliament.

In parallel, the regulatory authorities have also sought to encourage the development of securities intermediaries such as stockbrokers and underwriters/merchant banks. Since 2000, the capital market has seen the arrival of new intermediaries including collective schemes, investment banks, stock dealers, fund managers, and investment advisers. However, there are still very few individual investors, for example using the collective schemes, as evidenced by the huge number of central depository accounts being opened. Similarly, the presence of the global rating agencies in Kenya has yet to be felt with only a few firms having been rated. In principle, investment banks should emerge as key underwriters of IPOs – as they do elsewhere – but in Kenya, these institutions have yet to develop strong enough balance sheets to play this role.

TAX INCENTIVES

The final area where public policy has sought to develop the capital market is through changes to the tax regime. As reported in Table 15.4, tax incentives are aimed at encouraging market participation by lowering the marginal

Table 15.4 Tax incentives in the stock market

Area focused	Policy incentive	Objective
Product development	Transfer of assets involved in the issuance of asset-backed securities exempt from stamp duty 2000/01	To support the development of asset-backed securities
Institution development	Registered venture capital funds tax holiday of 10 years on the funds income (1997/98) Licensed dealers tax benefit as long as they turn their portfolios within 24 hours (1999) Income accruing to registered collective schemes tax free (1999) Collective schemes set up by employers for employees to invest in listed shares to be exempted from income tax (2002) Exempt investment income of special purpose vehicles from income tax (2005)	Encourage setting up of institutional structures
Investor earnings	35 per cent capital gains tax introduced in 1975, suspended 1985 Reduction in withholding tax applicable to dividend income arising from investment on listed securities for both local and foreign investors: foreign, 10 per cent; local 10 per cent to 7.5 per cent to 5 per cent (1995/96/97) Investments by insurance companies in listed securities exempt from tax arising out of capital gains on sale of shares (1996/97) Investment ceiling for retirement benefit schemes in fixed securities raised from 15 per cent to 30 per cent (2002)	To encourage savers to use this as a channel for their savings
Foreign investors	Participation of foreign investors in listed securities to a maximum of 40 per cent of share capital in aggregate and 5 per cent for individual investors Foreign investors allowed to acquire up to 49 per cent of brokerage firms and 70 per cent of local fund management companies (1999) Foreign investors to acquire shares freely in the stock market subject to minimum reserved ratio of 25 per cent for domestic investors in each listed company (2002)	Expand the investor horizon
Listing of firms	Exemption from stamp duty and value added tax on transfer of listed securities (1995) Expenses incurred by companies in having their financial instruments rated by an independent rating agency are tax deductible (1997/98) Firms that apply and are listed to get a tax amnesty on past omitted income provided they make full disclosure of their assets and liabilities and undertake to pay all their future taxes due (2001) Newly listed companies taxed at 27 per cent compared with 30 per cent for a period of three years following the date of listing but offer 20 per cent of shares listed (2001) New and expanded share capital of listed firms or those seeking listing exempt from stamp duty (2000/01) Newly listed companies to pay 25 per cent corporation tax for 5 years when floating 30 per cent of shares listed (2002) Newly listed companies to pay 20 per cent corporate tax for 5 years with at least 40 per cent of their shares listed (2005)	To encourage participation of firms in using the stock market to raise funds and also to increase the volume of shares in the market

Source: CMA Annual Reports.

tax rate on dividends from listed companies; supporting the creation of new investment institutions and vehicles such as registered collective investment schemes; and lowering the barriers to entry for listing firms. For example, listed firms enjoy a range of tax breaks, including lower corporate tax rates, lower withholding taxes, deductible issuing costs, and tax holidays for newly listed firms. These are significant concessions, making the NSE an attractive listing environment. The challenge for all tax incentive schemes, however, is that these alone cannot overcome other structural barriers to market expansion, such as the dearth of medium-to-large firms, and the risk is always that the tax regime becomes too generous in the belief that an additional marginal tax benefit will 'do the trick'. The cost of such actions are that, if listings and general market participation improves, the authorities are left with a tax regime that fails to raise sufficient revenue from listed firms (who are often the biggest and most profitable) and must make up the revenue shortfall through other, less attractive means.

15.5 Conclusions and policy recommendations

This chapter addresses the question of whether the Kenyan capital market can play a key role in supporting the growth process laid out in *Vision 2030*. We have argued that this can only happen if the market grows in size with more firms utilizing the various products to finance their investment; attracts investors to save using the long-term products and to use the market to develop more diversified financial asset portfolios; and has the right institutional structure to support a vibrant market. Progress in recent years has been encouraging. Regulatory and tax reforms, along with microstructural developments and an open policy towards foreign investors, have put the market on a reasonable institutional footing. The successful Safaricom listing has provided an important demonstration to market participants, regulators, and the general public that the capital market can manage a large public offering. And finally, the growth and macroeconomic stability from 2003 to 2007 saw the market deepen, turnover and liquidity surge, and pricing performance improve. All three factors have combined to build confidence in the long end of the capital market in Kenya and, although there is still a long way to go before it matches other regional markets' performance, these developments augur well for capital market development in the future.

Appendix: Does capital market development matter for economic growth?

This appendix examines the links between capital market development and economic growth process. There is a large literature on this question. Recently,

Rao *et al.* (2008), using a panel of five Asian countries over the period 1970–2007, found that financial developments have a significant positive correlation with economic growth in all but one country where the relationship was weak. Similar results were found by Apergis *et al.* (2007), who investigated the causal linkage between financial development and economic growth using panel co-integration and panel estimation on sixty-five countries over the period 1975–2000 and found a significant positive impact of financial development on growth. In the case of a single country, Kularatne (2001) used Johansen's VECM to investigate the finance–growth link in South Africa over the period 1954–1992 and found a strong feedback relationship between the two.

Here, we develop a simple framework underpinning these results. We start with a general AK-type growth model, which brings out the relationship between savings and economic growth.

$$Y_t = A_t k_t \tag{15.A1}$$

where k is the capital labour ratio, A is technology, and Y is per capita output. The model assumes that investment is defined by change in capital stock overnight and that all savings are invested.

Technology grows at a constant rate (g_a). The rate of growth of per capita is defined as:

$$\frac{1}{y}\frac{dy}{dt} = g_a + \alpha s \tag{15.A2}$$

Thus, the model assumes that per capita growth rate is defined by the savings rate, the rate of change in technology, and the productivity of labour. Assuming an imperfect financial market, not all of the savings may be channelled to investment. Thus, following Pagano (1993), we assume that a proportion of savings (δ) leaks out of the financial system; if δ is equal to zero, it means that nothing leaks out of the system, whereas δ=1 means that all savings leak out; 0<δ<1. Thus, the rate of per capita growth is defined as:

$$\frac{1}{y}\frac{dy}{dt} = g_a + (1-\delta)s\alpha \tag{15.A3}$$

Financial sector development is assumed to affect growth through the amount of savings put into investment ($(1-\delta)s$) and the technological development (g_a). It is also important to note that enhanced financial development reduces the transaction cost of external finance to firms, which results in increased investment and promotes growth (Rajan and Zingales, 1998). This affects the proportional share leaking out of the financial system (δ). Further, Wurgler (2000) shows that, even if financial development does not lead to higher levels of investment, it allocates existing investment better and therefore promotes economic growth through production processes. This can be summarized in the linear, reduced form relationship:

$$g_y = f(FD_t) = \lambda_0 + \lambda_1(FD_t) + \varepsilon_t \qquad (15.A4)$$

where g_y is growth in per capita income, *FD* is financial sector development, and ε_t is the error term with the usual properties. We estimate variants of Equation (15.A4) to investigate the relationship between financial development and growth in Kenya.

In the empirical model, financial development is defined by various indicators including market capitalization/GDP ratio, stock traded value/GDP ratio, and stock turnover ratio (value traded/market capitalization). The model also incorporates control variables: investment measured by gross capital formation/GDP ratio and trade openness measured by trade/GDP ratio. An investment variable is used to capture other factors that influence investment including other sources of investment financing. The model is estimated using a generalized method of moments approach. A total of thirty developing countries are included in the sample; these countries were selected on the basis of the availability of data. The data cover the period 1996–2007.

Table 15.A1 summarizes the results, showing a positive correlation between the various measures of capital market development as well as between these measures and economic growth, saving, and investment. Kenya is not an

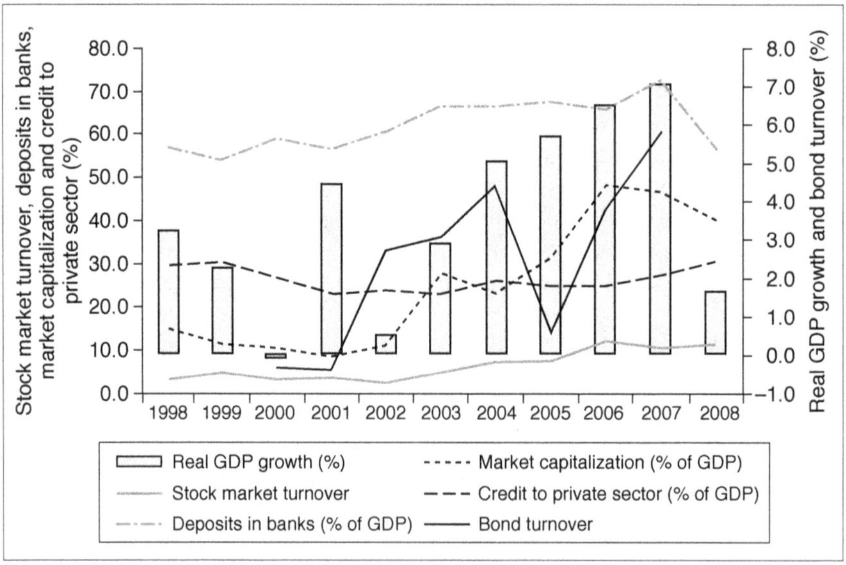

Figure 15.A1 Relationship between measures of financial development and growth in Kenya.
Source: Central Bank of Kenya (CBK), Kenya National Bureau of Statistics (KNBS), and NSE.

Table 15.A1 Correlation analysis among the key variables: 1996–2007

	Market capitalization of listed companies (% of GDP)	Stocks traded, turnover ratio (%)	Stocks traded, total value (% of GDP)	GDP per capita growth (annual %)	Gross savings (% of GDP)	Trade (% of GDP)
Market capitalization of listed companies (% of GDP)	1.0000					
Stocks traded, turnover ratio (%)	0.1359 (0.0132)	1.0000				
Stocks traded, total value (% of GDP)	0.5941 (0.0000)	0.6486 (0.0000)	1.0000			
GDP per capita growth (annual %)	0.1103 (0.0447)	0.0788 (0.1517)	0.1381 (0.0118)	1.0000		
Gross savings (% of GDP)	0.2435 (0.0000)	0.2360 (0.0000)	0.3955 (0.0000)	0.2596 (0.0000)	1.0000	
Trade (% of GDP)	0.5217 (0.0000)	–0.0247 (0.0000)	0.3153 (0.0000)	0.0846 (0.0000)	0.4931 (0.0000)	1.0000 (0.0000)

P-values are in parenthesis.
Countries included: Bangladesh, Indonesia, Republic of Korea, Malaysia, Pakistan, Philippines, Singapore, Sri Lanka, Thailand, Kenya, Israel, Saudi Arabia, Argentina, Brazil, Chile, Colombia, Ecuador, Jamaica, Mexico, Peru, Botswana, Egypt, Mauritius, Morocco, Namibia, South Africa, Tunisia, Cote d'Ivoire, Ghana, and Nigeria.
Source: World Development Indicators (World Bank).

Table 15.A2 Regression results of the growth model (per capita growth)

	Model 1	Model 2	Model 3	Model 4
Per capita growth rate (–1)	–0.051 (0.000)	–0.053 (0.000)	–0.074 (0.000)	–0.126 (0.000)
Gross capital formation/ GDP	0.465 (0.000)	0.528 (0.000)	0.453 (0.000)	0.485 (0.000)
Stocks traded/GDP	0.030 (0.000)		0.034 (0.000)	
Market capitalization/GDP	0.028 (0.000)	0.035 (0.000)	0.007 (0.136)	–0.001 (0.823)
International trade/GDP			0.086 (0.000)	0.0144 (0.000)
Stock turnover ratio		0.041 (0.000)		0.050 (0.000)

P-values are in parenthesis.
Countries included: Bangladesh, Indonesia, Republic of Korea, Malaysia, Pakistan, Philippines, Singapore, Sri Lanka, Thailand, Kenya, Israel, Saudi Arabia, Argentina, Brazil, Chile, Colombia, Ecuador, Jamaica, Mexico, Peru, Botswana, Egypt, Mauritius, Morocco, Namibia, South Africa, Tunisia, Cote d'Ivoire, Ghana, and Nigeria.
Source: World Development Indicators (World Bank).

outlier in these data, but rather lies close to the regression line described by Equation (15.A4). Deep and liquid markets tend to be associated with higher growth. Granger causality tests indicate a unidirectional causality from market capitalization to savings and investment rates, although we cannot accept that market capitalization granger causes GDP growth. Figure 15.A1 illustrates these positive correlations for Kenya.

The results in Table 15.A2 reinforce these simple pairwise correlations, showing that, conditional on investment and measures of openness, all measures of capital market development are strongly and positively correlated with growth. This is the case whichever measure of liquidity is used in the estimation; the coefficient sizes are not significantly different. The size of the market also has a positive and significant relationship with economic growth.

References

Amihud, Y., H. Mendelson and M. Murgia, 1990, 'Stock Market Microstructure and Return Volatility: Evidence from Italy', *Journal of Finance*, 14, 423–440.

Apergis, N., I. Filippidis and C. Economidou, 2007, 'Financial Deepening and Economic Growth Linkages: A Panel Data Analysis'. Kiel Institute, Paper No. 06/05. University of Cambridge: Centre for Economic and Public Policy.

Bekaert, G., 1995, 'Market Integration and Investment Behavior in Emerging Stock Markets', *World Bank Economic Review*, 9, 75–107.

Bessembinder, H. and H. M. Kaufman, 1997, 'A Cross Exchange Comparison of Execution Costs and Information Flow for NYSE Listed Stock', *Journal of Financial Economics*, 46 (3), 293–320.

CMA, Annual Reports, various issues.

Demirguc-Kunt, A. and R. Levine, 1996, 'Finance, Financial Sector Policies, and Long-Run Growth', Policy Research Working Paper No. 4469. Washington, DC: World Bank.

Demirguc-Kunt, A. and V. Maksimovic, 1998, 'Law, Finance and Firm Growth', *Journal of Finance*, 53, 2107–2137.

Dewenter, K. L. and P. H. Malatesta, 1997, 'Public Offerings of State Owned and Privately Owned Enterprises. An International Comparison', *Journal of Finance*, 52, 1669–1679.

Garcia, V. F. and L. Liu, 1999, 'Macroeconomic Determinants of Stock Market Development', *Journal of Applied Economics*, 2, 29–59.

Georgakopoulos, N. L., 1996, 'Why should Disclosure Rules Subsidize Informed Traders?' *International Review of Law and Economics*, 16, 417–431.

Gertler, M. and A. Rose, 1996, 'Finance, Public Policy and Growth', in Caprio, G. Jr, I. Atiyas and J. Hanson (eds) *Financial Reform: Theory and Practice*. New York: Cambridge University Press.

Green, C. J., P. Maggioni and V. Murinde, 2000, 'Regulatory Lessons for Emerging Stock Markets from a Century of Evidence on Transactions Costs and Share Price Volatility in the London Stock Exchange', *Journal of Banking and Finance*, 24, 577–601.

Kularatne, C., 2001, 'An Examination of the Impact of Financial Deepening on Long-run Economic Growth: An Application of a VECM Structure to a Middle-Income Country Context'. Trade and Industry Policy Strategies (TPIS), 2001 Annual Forum.

La Porta, R., F. Lopez-de-Silanes, A. Shleifer and R. W. Vishny, 1997, 'Legal Determinants of External Finance', *Journal of Finance*, 52, 1131–1150.

La Porta, R., F. Lopez-de-Silanes, A. Shleifer and R. W. Vishny, 1998, 'Law and Finance', *Journal of Political Economy*, 106, 1113–1155.

La Porta R., F. Lopez-de-Silanes, A. Shleifer and R. Vishny, 2000, 'Investor Protection and Corporate Governance', *Journal of Financial Economics*, 58, 3–27.

Nasibi, R. I., 1992, 'Financial Institutions and Monetary Policy in Post-Independent Kenya', in Ochieng, W. R. and R. M. Maxon (eds) *An Economic History of Kenya*. Nairobi: East African Educational Publishers Ltd.

Ngugi, R. W., 2002, 'Four Essays in Capital Market', Unpublished PhD Thesis, Birmingham University, UK.

Ngugi, R. W., 2008, 'Capital Financing Behaviour: Evidence from Firms listed on the Nairobi Stock Exchange', *European Journal of Finance*, 14, 609–624.

Ngugi, R. W., V. Murinde and C. Green, 2003, 'How have Emerging Stock Exchanges in Africa responded to Market Reforms? ' *Journal of African Business*, 2 (2), 89–127.

NSE, Annual Report, various issues. Nairobi: NSE.

Pagano, M., 1989, 'Endogenous Market Thinness and Stock Price Volatility', *Review of Economic Studies*, 56, 269–287.

Pagano, M., 1993, 'The Flotation of Companies and Stock Market: a Coordination Failure Model', *European Economic Review*, 37, 1101–1125.

Pagano, M., F. Panetta and L. Zingales, 1998, 'Why do Companies go Public? An Empirical Analysis', *Journal of Finance*, LIII (1), 27–64.

Rajan R. and L. Zingales, 1998, 'Financial Dependence and Growth', *American Economic Review*, 88, 559–586.

Rao, B. B., A. Tamazian, R. Sungh and K. C. Vadlamannati, 2008, 'Financial Developments and the Rate of Growth of Output: An Alternative Approach'. MPRA Paper No. 8605. University Library of Munich, Germany.

Republic of Kenya, various dates, *Economic Survey*, various issues. Nairobi: Government Press.

Republic of Kenya, 2007, *Kenya Vision 2030*. Nairobi: Government Press.

Ritter, J. R. and I. Welch, 2002, 'A Review of IPO Activity, Pricing and Allocations', *Journal of Finance*, LVII (4), 1795–1828.

Sellin, P., 1996, "Inviting Excess Volatility? Opening up a Small Stock Market to International Investors', *Scandinavian Journal of Economics*, 98, 603–612.

Subrahmanyam S. and S. Titman, 1999, 'The Going Public Decision and the Development of Financial Markets', *Journal of Finance*, 54, 1045–1082.

World Bank, World Development Indicators. Available from http://data.worldbank.org/data-catalog.

World Bank and Kenya Institute for Public Policy Research and Analysis (KIPPRA), 2003, 'Kenya Investment Climate Assessment'. Study conducted through the Regional Program for Enterprise Development (RPED), Kenya.

Wurgler, J., 2000, 'Financial Markets and the Allocation of Capital', *Journal of Financial Economics*, 58, 187–214.

Yartey, C. A., 2008, 'The Determinants of Stock Market Development in Emerging Economies. Is South Africa Different?' IMF Working Paper 32. Washington, DC: International Monetary Fund.

Yartey, C. A. and C. K. Adjasi, 2007, 'Stock Market Development in Sub-Saharan Africa: Critical Issues and Challenges'. IMF Working Paper 209. Washington, DC: International Monetary Fund.

16

Policies for Prosperity, Innovation, and Financial Access: The Role of M-Pesa

Rosemary Atieno, Dulacha Barako, and Crispin Bokea

16.1 Introduction

Access to financial services is viewed as one of the main constraints to development in Kenya. Kenya's *Vision 2030* recognizes the critical role of financial services in the country's development, through intermediation between borrowing and investment and mobilizing funds for the implementation of the vision projects. The 2030 vision for financial services is to have a vibrant and globally competitive sector driving savings and investments in the country. However, the vision acknowledges that access to financial services still remains low, as demonstrated by the low number of people owning bank accounts and the limited access to financial services outside major cities. Addressing the problem of access to financial services therefore requires, among other things, strengthening the alternative financial service providers such as microfinance institutions (Republic of Kenya, 2007). This position is echoed in the Economic Recovery Strategies Paper (Republic of Kenya, 2004). The Sessional Paper Number Two of 2005 on Small and Micro Enterprise Development (Republic of Kenya, 2005), while recognizing the importance of the Micro and Small Scale Enterprises (MSEs), identifies lack of finance as one of the constraints to the sector's development.

Lack of access to finance has been seen as one of the reasons for the slow growth of firms (Nkurunziza, 2005), and the main reason for the closure of many MSEs (CBS, ICEG, and K-REP, 1999). Bigsten *et al.* (2000) observe that, although small firms have less financial market involvement, large firms receive more loans, have higher indebtedness, rely less on informal loans, and have more access to credit compared with small firms, the majority of which get their loans from informal sources of finance.

In response to the limited access to financial services, a number of institutions have emerged offering financial services to small firms and poor households excluded by the formal institutions from their services. This is demonstrated by the emergence of alternative sources of finance as a means of reducing the access problem for the poor and small firms. Although most small firms have relied on informal sources of finance, microfinance has emerged as an important source focusing on small businesses and low-income households (Morduch, 1999; Khandker, 2005).

The emergence of microfinance was expected to improve access to finance for small firms by operating programmes targeting specific activities of MSEs. It has been argued that the emergence of microfinance has offered the hope of addressing the problem of access to finance by small-scale firms, as they serve mainly clients excluded from the formal banking system. The programmes have used innovative approaches to reach their clientele, who use the borrowed funds to finance self-employment activities. The number of microfinance institutions has therefore grown rapidly in the last decades, giving hope for addressing the problem of poverty.

Various discussions have emerged regarding the success of these programmes in addressing the financial access problems (Morduch, 1999; Khandker, 2005). In Kenya, microfinance institutions have faced problems that have limited their outreach. These include little co-ordination within the sector, resulting in duplication of resources and activities, high credit costs, and high dependence on donor financing. Since 2001, the Central Bank of Kenya (CBK) has taken keen interest in the activities of the microfinance institutions (MFI) sector as an alternative source of financial services for households and MSEs. With the enactment of the Microfinance Act in 2006, the CBK is expected to play a crucial role in supporting the performance of this sector by putting in place the regulatory framework for the establishment, licensing, and supervision of deposit-taking MFIs.

Although there is overwhelming evidence on the problem of financial access faced by small firms and the development of microfinance as an alternative source of finance, the emerging policy challenge is how to harness new options of financial service delivery to increase access, especially for those excluded from the formal financial system. Innovative financial services, especially m-banking such as the M-Pesa, have been viewed as a major channel for increasing access to financial services in the country. The challenge is how to support this concept to increase both the breadth and the depth of financial access and its adoption by MFIs. This chapter discusses the development of microfinance, its relationship to financial access, especially for small firms in

Kenya, and the question of the extent to which microfinance has addressed the problem of access to financial services, especially among small-scale firms. The chapter addresses the role of technological innovations in the form of mobile banking in improving access to financial services. It focuses on the role of the M-Pesa technology in transforming access to finance and the policy options for using mobile banking technology to improve access to finance in the country. The chapter is organized as follows. Section 16.2 gives an overview of the financial sector in Kenya, and presents the theoretical explanation for financial access, while Section 16.3 discusses microfinance in Kenya. Section 16.4 concludes.

16.2 Overview of the financial sector in Kenya

16.2.1 The nature and performance of the financial sector in Kenya

The financial sector in Kenya is diverse, comprising banking, insurance, capital markets, pension funds, the quasi banking institutions, the savings and credit co-operatives (SACCOs), microfinance institutions, development finance institutions, and a number of informal financial institutions (Republic of Kenya, 2007). However, it has been argued that, despite the relative development of Kenya's financial sector, it is characterized by limited penetration, and hence lack of access for a majority of the population. Although progress in the sector has been fast, by international standards, the percentage of the population owning bank accounts remains low, with access to financial services outside the main cities still limited (Beck and Fuchs, 2004; Republic of Kenya, 2007).

Limited access to finance in the country has been attributed to a number of factors, among which are market, institutional, and political barriers to competition. A number of structural features of the financial sector, such as the lack of information sharing, weak legal and institutional frameworks, and limited branch network that can enhance competition and uncertainty, contribute to the limited access to financial services. Lack of information on debtors increases banks' credit risk and reduces their competitiveness. Deficiencies in the legal and institutional frameworks also increase the credit costs whereas, for borrowers, these limit access to unsecured loans. The limited number of large and strong banks has constrained the competitiveness of the banking system, leading to market segmentation (Beck and Fuchs, 2004). All these have combined to limit access to financial services.

COMMERCIAL BANKS

The Kenyan banking sector is dominated by a few commercial banks, with four banks accounting for the bulk of the deposits. The remaining banks are small and limited in their outreach. This has reduced competition, resulting in high credit costs. However, this also presents significant opportunities for the expansion of banking services to parts of the population without banking services such as rural areas. Expansion will, however, require addressing a number of challenges: establishing the branch network in rural areas to reach the large section of the population lacking banking services and introducing a more rapid adoption of banking technology (Republic of Kenya, 2007).

QUASI BANKING INSTITUTIONS

The quasi financial institutions in the country include the microfinance institutions, rotating savings and credit associations (ROSCAs), SACCOs, and other informal financial institutions. Given the low penetration of formal financial services, these institutions have enormous potential to mobilize additional savings and provide credit to income groups excluded by the banking services.

The performance of formal financial institutions in Kenya in terms of alleviating financial constraints, especially of the smallholder sector, has been the subject of much discussion. The criteria of creditworthiness, delays in loan processing and disbursement, and the government approach to preferential interest rates resulting in non-price credit rationing, have limited the amount of credit available to smallholders. With the inability of the formal financial sector to satisfy the demand for financial services, a number of informal and semi-formal institutions such as microfinance institutions have developed to fill the gap. The most notable innovation on the supply side towards filling this gap is the M-Pesa electronic money transfer solution that is currently offered under the Safaricom mobile telephone platform. The M-Pesa business model is based on high volumes of simple electronic transactions, structured around multiple access points at a significantly reduced cost.

A look at Kenya's financial landscape shows that users of financial services have access to formal, semi-formal, or informal sources. The Central Bank of Kenya Finaccess survey of 2006 shows that only about 19 per cent of those aged 18 years and above use formal financial institutions, whereas 35 per cent are served by informal institutions (Figure 16.1). These results conform to earlier studies, which show that the majority of the population relies on informal sources of finance (CBS, ICEG and KREP, 1999; Atieno, 2001). On the other hand, only 8 per cent are served by other formal financial institutions such as SACCOs and MFIs. The unbanked, defined as those without a bank account, constitute 38 per cent (CBK, 2007).

When considered by gender and regions, the use of financial services is twice as high in urban areas as it is in rural areas (Figure 16.2). Although only about 11 per cent of the rural population use banking services, 25 per cent of those in urban areas use banking services. Although the use of microfinance is below 5 per cent in both rural and urban areas, it is lower in rural than in urban areas. The use of informal sources of finance is however higher

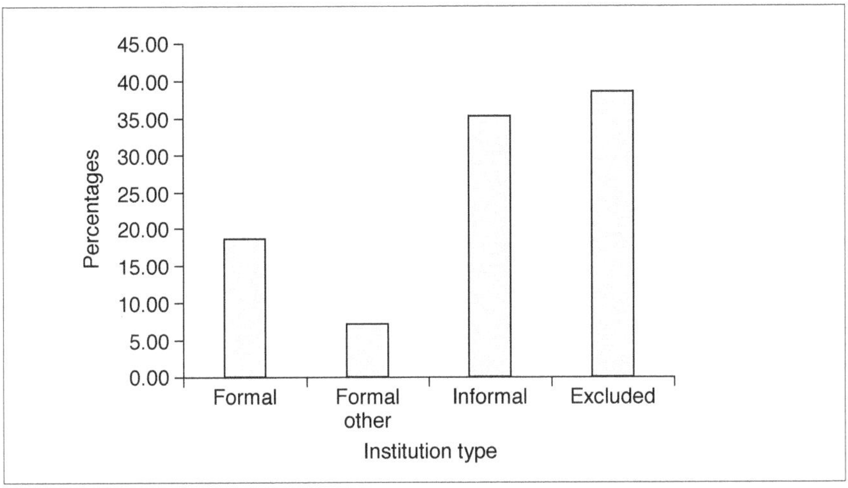

Figure 16.1 Distribution of financial access by institution type.
Source: CBK.

(53.4 per cent) in rural areas than in urban areas (42.1 per cent). By gender, more males appear to be using financial services than females. The exception is in the informal sources category where more females (54.6 per cent) use informal sources compared with males (46.3 per cent). This may suggest that informal sources of finance appear to serve those categories of the population who are likely to be excluded by the formal financial system such as those in rural areas and women. It is also likely to be a reflection of the concentration of financial institutions in urban areas and exclusion of certain categories of the population such as women. The policy challenge for financial access is to

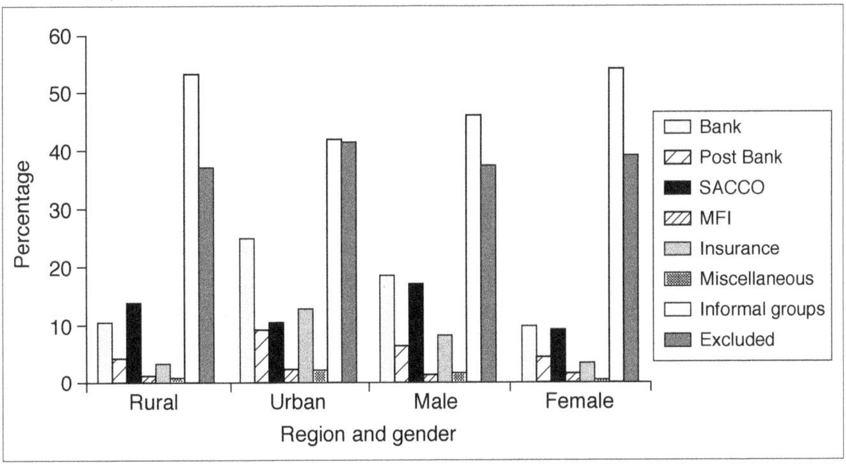

Figure 16.2 Use of financial services by region and gender.
Source: Central Bank of Kenya Finaccess survey, 2007.

develop financial service delivery options such as the MFIs that address the needs of those excluded by the formal financial system. Such options should address the factors that make access difficult for the excluded categories.

16.2.2 Microfinance and financial access

Microfinance refers to the practice of providing financial services such as microcredit, microsavings, or microinsurance to poor people, to help them to accumulate larger sums of money, thus expanding their choices and reducing their risks. Institutions providing these services are referred to as MFIs. Microfinance involves small-scale transactions in credit and savings designed to meet the needs of small and medium-scale producers and businesses. In most cases, microfinance operations mainly support the poor and women engaged in informal activities.

Microfinance institutions serve mainly clients who have been excluded by the formal financial services, such as those in self-employment activities, most of whom do not require collateral. In most cases, borrowers from such institutions do so to finance self-employment activities, and many start by taking loans as small as $75, repaid over several months or a year. Most programmes do not require borrowers to put up collateral, enabling would-be entrepreneurs with few assets to participate. Although some programmes serve just a handful of borrowers, others serve a larger number. It has helped to overcome some of the stereotypes and constraints that restricted the majority from accessing financial services, mainly through innovative lending approaches such as regular repayment methods and collateral substitutes among others. Group lending, by making borrowers co-sign the loan, mitigates problems created by information asymmetry between borrowers and lenders (Morduch, 1999).

Another innovation has been the dynamic incentives. Programmes typically begin by lending just small amounts and then increasing the loan size upon satisfactory repayment. The repeated nature of the interactions together with the credible threat to cut off any future lending when loans are not repaid can be exploited to overcome information problems and improve efficiency (Morduch, 1999).

Microfinance is documented to have made great progress in delivering financial services (Khandker, 2005). But, despite the promise of microfinance, concerns still remain regarding its effectiveness in expanding access to financial services. High repayment rates have not translated into profits, and the programmes continue to be subsidised while some of the best programmes have not benefitted the poorest.

16.2.3 Policy scenario

Kenya currently has no national microfinance policy. The only regulation covering the sector has come with the enactment of the Microfinance Act of

2006, which gives the Central Bank of Kenya the power to regulate and supervise deposit-taking MFIs. The Act is expected to play an important role in deepening the financial market and expanding access to financial services for a majority of Kenyans. The relevant question, however, is how this legislation helps to expand access to financial services. The existing microfinance institutions operate under diverse forms of legislation, ranging from grassroots organizations registered as self-help groups with the Ministry of Social Services to banks registered under the Banking Act. Others are registered under the Companies Act, NGO Co-ordination Act, Kenya Post Office Savings Bank Act, and the Kenya Industrial Estates Act (Aleke Dondo, 1999).

The main policy objectives of the strategy for the financial sector in *Vision 2030* include improved access and deepening of financial services for a larger number of the Kenyan households and small businesses, mobilizing additional savings to support higher investment rates, and greater efficiency in the delivery of financial services to reduce the cost to affordable levels (Republic of Kenya, 2007).

The enactment of the Microfinance Act in 2006 marks a significant step in the development of the microfinance industry in Kenya. The Central Bank of Kenya has in response developed the prudential microfinance regulations meant to enhance efficiency and promote broader and deeper access to financial services and products. The Act is viewed as providing an opportunity for the growth of the microfinance sector, thereby enhancing access to financial services. As a result of the Act, some commercial banks such as Barclays Bank of Kenya, have registered Barclays Deposit Taking Microfinance Ltd to provide services and products suitable to this market. On the other hand, some deposit-taking microfinance institutions such as *Jamii Bora* have bought an existing small local bank (City Finance) as a going concern to further broaden its scope of services delivery.

Although regulation and compliance are viewed as necessary for the safety and soundness of MFIs, regulation has the potential to significantly impact on an institution's resources and result in more expensive financial products and lower economic growth. However, on the other hand, reduction in the cost of regulation and compliance would support additional lending, which would have a significant positive impact on the economy. In developing the regulations, therefore, the Central Bank of Kenya has ensured that the cost of compliance is significantly reduced through producing positive externalities. One such area is the expectation that microfinance institutions will achieve a reduction in the high fixed costs associated with running branches, especially in rural areas, through a recommendation in the Place of Business Regulation, allowing microfinance institutions to expand outreach through agencies. Experience from other countries has shown that agency arrangements result in lower operating costs for microfinance institutions through sharing point of service interfaces with commercial retailers. The proposed microfinance prudential regulations therefore provide a window for MFIs to establish agency agreements with non-bank entities, typically comprising retail commercial outlets including post offices, retail shops in rural market centres, supermarkets, pharmacies, and fuel stations as their outlets for financial services. The application of significantly lower levels of annual licence fees and the removal of fees for the opening of a branch/outlet for community-based microfinance institutions is also intended to address the issue of the cost of compliance.

16.3 Microfinance in Kenya

16.3.1 Development of microfinance in Kenya

Microfinance institutions in Kenya have emerged as a major source of credit to MSEs over the last two decades. This has mainly been in response to the limited access to formal sources of finance. The major organizations providing microfinance services include commercial banks, microfinance non-governmental organizations, limited companies, SACCOs, Post Office Savings Bank (POSB), ROSCAs, and Accumulating Savings and Credit Societies (ASCAs) as well as grassroots groups.

The microfinance industry in Kenya has experienced major transformations over the past 20 years, growing from a fledgling concern dominated by a few donor- and church-based organizations to a vibrant industry increasingly driven by commercial sustainability. The providers of microfinance services in Kenya can be classified into three broad categories of formal, semi-formal, and informal institutions, with the level of formality defined by the degree of regulation applied in each sector. Under the formal category are commercial banks and the Post Office Savings Bank. The semi-formal category includes SACCOs and microfinance institutions, while ASCAs, ROSCAs, and money lenders dominate the informal category. The main focus of microfinance in Kenya over the past 20 years has been microcredit, which is provided by many institutions with diverse institutional forms. In the recent past, a number of commercial banks have become involved in microfinance lending in the country. The main advantage of commercial banks is their wide branch network, which is accessible to most MSEs.

Despite their proliferation, MFIs in Kenya have experienced a number of challenges in their activities. The lack of access to local deposits has constrained the growth of these institutions, whereas high client dropout rates have also contributed to the lack of growth among the MFIs. There are also a number of gaps in the provision of financial services through MFIs. These include the development of microinsurance, micropensions, and microleasing products. It is also argued that there has been little innovation in delivery methodologies among the MFIs, with most MFIs offering only a single credit product to specific sections of the population, mainly operators of MSEs. The restrictions of the Banking Act meant that most MFIs have developed as credit-led programmes, limiting the extent to which they can mobilize resources for investment (Aleke Dondo, 1999). This means that they are able to reach only a limited proportion of the potential market. The implication is that, despite the huge investment and rapid growth in the microfinance sector in Kenya, the delivery methodologies and products do not allow the sector to have as extensive an outreach as it demands. The 1999 survey of MSEs in the country found that only 10 per cent of the MSEs had used financial services from any source, including MFIs (CBS, ICEG, and KREP, 1999). The 2006 financial access survey also shows that only about 8 per cent of the adult population use MFI financial products. There is therefore still a large gap in the demand for financial services not yet met even by the microfinance institutions. It can therefore be argued that financial access still remains a challenge to the majority, especially among the low-income activities.

A significant innovation in improving access to financial services has been the M-Pesa. M-Pesa's main value is the reduction of transaction costs in person-to-person money transfers. It also increases the liquidity of those previously excluded from financial services. Although M-Pesa customers are not mutually exclusive, it is instructive to note that, with a growing clientele of 5 million as of December 2008, there is a real possibility that the 12 million Kenyans with mobile phones can now have access to a financial service.

Regionally, the rural areas have very few formal financial institutions, and these are selective about their clientele through their terms and conditions. Most of the MFIs are also located in urban areas, with most concentrated in the Nairobi, Mt Kenya, and Western Kenya regions. There are even fewer programmes in the arid and semi-arid lands. The microfinance systems focusing on MSEs also exclude a large section of the poor such as smallholder agriculture, which supports a majority of the population. The inadequacy of the services is evident from the fact that not only do businesses need credit, at the same time, people also need financial services other than credit.

16.3.2 Microfinance and financial access in Kenya

Microfinance in Kenya has experienced rapid growth in the last decade. A relevant question, however, is whether this growth has translated into increased access to financial services and what policy options it leads to. Surveys on access to financial services show that only a small proportion of the population still have access to financial services (CBS, ICEG, and KREP, 1999; Bigsten *et al.*, 2000; CBK, 2007). A survey of the use of financial services shows that only about 3 per cent save with microfinance institutions. The main reasons for the low use of microfinance savings are the low interest rates and many elaborate procedures. The same pattern is true for credit use, with only 3 per cent having used credit from MFIs. The reasons include high loan processing costs, high interest rates, difficult requirements to qualify for the loans, and the fear of loss of assets or property.

Microfinance was expected to address the access problem through the lending terms and conditions. However, research has shown that MFIs employ lending terms and conditions that restrict access. Akoten *et al.* (2006) argue that microfinance borrowing has been relatively uncommon in Kenya because of stringent borrowing conditions. Hence, although MFIs are potentially an effective source of credit, their lending terms have become increasingly constraining to the majority of potential borrowers. In order to maintain a revolving fund pool and to reduce the risk of default, most MFIs in Kenya require their customers to save regularly with the institutions and make compulsory weekly repayments. Although interest rates are lower for MFIs compared with commercial banks, interest rates represent only one aspect of the terms and conditions of these loans. Other terms employed by MFIs significantly increase the cost of borrowing.

Loan conditions such as loan size, minimum and maximum loan period are important in determining whether potential borrowers use services from a provider. Microfinance offers loans with repayment periods as short as one month. Together with smaller loan amounts, this gives the flexibility that allows MSEs and the poor to access loans that fit their needs. The diversity of the products offered is also important for access. Although microfinance has grown as a credit-led industry, it has diversified over time into other financial services such as credit for human capital development, agricultural loans, and social welfare loans such as housing, insurance, working capital, and cheque cashing. Some microfinance institutions have also initiated measures aimed at expanding access to financial services. An example is Equity Bank, which has expanded its branch network and initiated credit services to women with specific loan products for women. The bank has experienced growth in its branch network from five in 2004 to 107 branches in 2007. By 2007, women constituted 54 per cent of equity borrowers, and there is a specific loan product targeting women in small and medium enterprises.

Branch network, outreach in terms of loans, mobilization of funds through deposits, and clients served are also important in access to finance. The category of clients served is also important in expanding access. Looking at the outreach in terms of the people served, informal financial providers, ASCAs and ROSCAs serve over half the population (Table 16.1). This is followed by commercial banks at 14 per cent and SACCOs at 13 per cent. The MFIs serve less than 2 per cent of the population. This may conform to the argument that, despite the proliferation of MFIs, their impact in terms of expanding the access frontier is not yet clear. MFIs have been operating in Kenya for over 10 years but have not reached 5 per cent of the population.

Existing evidence shows that, among the MFIs operating in Kenya, the majority have less than five branches countrywide. It is the banks offering

Table 16.1 Level of outreach by type of financial institution

Level of formalization	Type of financial service provider	Number of people reached (millions)	Percentage of population
Formal	Banks	2.5	14.2
	Postbank	1.0	5.6
	Insurance	1.0	5.9
Formal (other)	SACCOs	2.3	13.1
	MFIs	0.3	1.7
	Miscellaneous providers (government)	0.2	1.1
Informal	ASCAs, ROSCAs, other informal group	8.8	50.6
None	Excluded (no formal or informal product used)	6.7	38.3

ASCA, accumulating savings and credit society; MFI, microfinance institution; ROSCA, rotating savings and credit association; SACCO, savings and credit co-operative.
Source: Central Bank of Kenya, Finaccess survey.

microfinance services that have the largest branch network in the country. Among the MFIs, the highest number of branch networks is fifty-seven, while the minimum is one branch. Among the microfinance-giving commercial banks, the highest branch network is 107, with the lowest being thirty-one. The branch network of banks that are classified as providing microfinance services comprise 28 per cent of the total 887 bank branch network as of December 2008 (Central Bank of Kenya, 2009). This proportional representation indicates that, although fewer in number (four out of forty-three), the commercial banks providing microfinance services have a relatively strong physical presence.

Although SACCOs control an estimated Ksh 150 billion and commercial bank assets stand at Ksh 795 billion, it is still not clear what the asset base of the MFIs is. This presents major challenges in addressing the issue of microfinance and financial access. There is therefore a need to establish a mechanism for providing information on MFIs.

The issue of access brings to light the role of technology in financial services, with the question of whether new technology in financial transactions addresses demand for financial services not covered by microfinance and other financial institutions. In the next section, we discuss the case of M-Pesa, a major innovation in financial transactions.

16.3.3 Improving access through technology: the case of M-Pesa

This section discusses the development of M-Pesa[1] technology in the country as a way of improving financial access. It presents the structure and development, as well as advantages and challenges facing the technology.

STRUCTURE

M-Pesa is a mobile phone-based money transfer service for sending and storing money offered by Safaricom, one of the major mobile service providers in Kenya. The M-Pesa business model is based on high volumes of simple person-to-person transactions structured around multiple access points around the country. A critical component of the transaction is time, as it allows for real-time settlement unlike similar financial transactions with other financial institutions. Through the service, Safaricom customers can register for M-Pesa by visiting one of more than 10,000 merchants who act as 'agents' for account opening, handling of deposits and withdrawals to and from the customer's virtual 'wallet', and customer support. Customers can then use an application on their mobile phone to check their balance, send money to other people, pay bills, and purchase mobile phone airtime. Customer funds are held in a special trust account with a commercial bank, the Commercial Bank of Africa (Morawczynski and Pickens, 2009).

The key feature behind the M-Pesa technology is that it has brought the unbanked into the financial system. The service targeted mainly the unbanked, although it also serves the banked. This is significant in expanding the access frontier, as available evidence shows that, although only 23 per cent of Kenyans hold bank accounts, 80 per cent have access to mobile phones (Central Bank of Kenya, 2009). The main factors behind the success of the M-Pesa service are the convenience, safety, and low cost with which it allows the unbanked to engage in financial transactions. The main value of M-Pesa is the reach achieved through the distribution network and the increased efficiencies gained from using the network. This, it is argued, has contributed to the significant uptake in the its services. Since its launch in March 2007, M-Pesa has experienced significant growth in its customer base, agents, and the volume of transactions. As of November 2009, about 9 million customers had registered with the service, and it has about 14,000 M-Pesa agents countrywide. The monthly value of person-to-person money transfers through the service is estimated at Ksh 23.96 billion (www.Safaricom.co.ke).

The agents offer substantially more points of service than the number of formal bank branches and automated teller machines (ATMs) in the country combined, which are currently estimated at 887 and 1,435 respectively. This significantly increases the access to those previously unable to access financial services. It is estimated that an average of Ksh 150 million is transferred through M-Pesa per day, mostly based on small amounts averaging Ksh 1,500 per transaction (Liu and Mithika, 2009; Morawczynski and Pickens, 2009). The M-Pesa success with agents is also attributed to some features such as partnership with quality agents such as banks and financial institutions, having agents in diverse sectors such as petrol stations and supermarkets, strong operational support from the service provider Safaricom, and increased settlement efficiency through agent-to-agent transactions. There are also stringent penalties for agents who fail to comply with Safaricom policy. Although the MFIs have the greatest outreach to the unbanked, they have not yet adopted mobile banking as a service delivery channel, hence the challenge of making them adopt the service (Liu and Mithika, 2009).

THE DEVELOPMENT OF M-PESA

M-Pesa was conceptualized and developed by Sagentia, a technology firm based in Cambridge. It was initially started as a tool for the repayment of MFI loans. As the M-Pesa service targeted the unbanked, and had to operate in the absence of bank accounts, this meant that it had to partner with a commercial bank, the Commercial Bank of Africa, to provide the necessary conventional banking requirements. In order to find customers with real market needs, M-Pesa had to partner with a local MFI, Faulu Kenya, with a significant number of borrowers in urban areas for loan repayment. The Commercial Bank of Africa therefore provided banking services while Faulu Kenya provided local expertise to test a microfinance payment platform through M-Pesa. The initial concept of M-Pesa was to create a service that would allow microfinance borrowers to receive and repay loans using the Safaricom network. This would in turn enable microfinance institutions to offer more competitive loans due to the reduced cost of dealing with cash.

M-Pesa was first piloted in 2005 with an MFI group identified by Faulu in Nairobi. Apart from loan management, there were also deposit and withdrawal services for the users. The M-Pesa service was launched in March 2007 after a successful pilot. Within the first month, it had registered 20,000 customers, well over the targeted business plan. This was viewed as a clear indication that the service filled a clear gap in the market (Hughes and Lonie, 2007). Within the first year, it had registered 2 million customers compared with the initial target of 250,000 customers in the first year. The monthly value of person-to-person money transfers is estimated as Ksh 14.5 billion, with a customer base of 6 million (Liu and Mithika, 2009). This compares with the total value of bank accounts of about Ksh 6 million, showing the extent of access that it has facilitated.

ADVANTAGES OF THE SERVICE

The concept of the product is such that an M-Pesa customer can use his/her mobile phone to send money quickly, safely, and over a large distance to another mobile phone user without the use of a bank account. Users are able to turn cash into e-money and carry out transactions through their M-Pesa accounts, which are secure and PIN protected. As the service targets the unbanked, operations are wholly outside commercial bank accounts. Real money in the system therefore needed to be held in a bank on behalf of the customers.

The M-Pesa service is fast, secure, and cost-effective, and is opening up new opportunities for businesses. At the end of the pilot, the service was launched with three features of deposit and withdrawal of money, person-to-person transfer, and purchase of airtime. The quick adoption of M-Pesa in Kenya strongly suggested that the service met an existing market need. The high number of Kenyans excluded from financial services together with the sparse branch network meant that there was low penetration of the banking system in the country. The M-Pesa features such as speed, convenience, and low transaction fees attract a large number of those already using banks.

The initial design of the M-Pesa product was to facilitate loan repayment. Since its launch, other uses of the service have emerged. These include people paying loans for others in return for services, and businesses using M-Pesa as an overnight safe because banks closed before the agents close their shops, thus providing security over time. The service has also been used to provide security over distance with people depositing cash at one point to withdraw it hours later at another point. Other new ways of using the service are hinged on the existing demand for faster, cheaper, and more efficient ways of moving money. Currently, M-Pesa offers services in the form of cash deposit to client accounts, money transfer, withdrawal of money through agents, payment of bills, buying of Safaricom airtime, and management of the client's M-Pesa account.

It is important to underline that M-Pesa has a monopoly of the delivery channel, handling more than 80 per cent of electronic money transactions in Kenya. But competition is responding, with new mobile money transfers already in the market. However, the situation is peculiar in Kenya as Safaricom controls more than 80 per cent of the mobile market and hence the delivery channel, and has the ability to block access by imposing an interchange fee. This means that new electronic financial solutions may not be able to find competitive linkages, that is, whether and how they will integrate with Safaricom customers.

The initial partnership involved the network provider, Safaricom, an MFI, and a commercial bank as a way of improving access to finance for the unbanked. The network operator brings connectivity and wide reach through the airtime distribution network, the MFI brings an understanding of the market need for financial services, whereas a commercial bank brings the discipline and compliance aspects of financial management (Hughes and Lonie, 2007). The MFI Faulu provided clients that could participate in the trial, mainly in Nairobi. After initial identification of agents and training of customers, the pilot started in 2005 with eight agents and 500 clients. In addition to the standard loan repayment, the system grew to include other services such as payment for business transactions and exchanging money between individuals.

The M-Pesa technology is simple, quick, and reliable, which has significantly reduced the transaction costs. It thus offers very competitive services with attractive transaction costs, cheaper than using a bank account. As the service has developed, users are integrating the M-Pesa into their savings portfolio, leading to changing savings patterns. M-Pesa is being used in conjunction with popular savings mechanisms such as bank savings accounts and informal savings clubs. This is intended to spread risks and ensure users have money all the time (Morawczynski and Pickens, 2009). The M-Pesa technology offers more settlement points through agent-to-agent transactions, thus reducing the liquidity problems likely to be faced by agents. The integration with ATMs has also expanded its usage.

CHALLENGES

The service has faced challenges in its activities. Major among these is the operational risks. Rapid expansion is already causing incredible stress in the system. Although measures to upgrade the system have considerably reduced outages, the risk of system failure remains an important one. There is also the question of consumer protection. The major areas of concern relate to protection of customers' e-balances and incomplete transactions. Accordingly, the provider has put in place mechanisms that allow for incomplete transactions to revert within seven days, and enhancing customer complaint management by outsourcing the call centres. Agents in rural areas have run into problems, suffering from lack of adequate cash floats where banks are far away, causing delays in service deliveries.

Among the initial challenges faced by the project were political will and the need to train and support the needs of customers who were unbanked, illiterate, and with no financial security. Security challenges also included the need to include an insurance package as well as training on security tips. The need to guard against fraud through the use of the service and continuous training for agents is important.

In terms of regulation, the rapid growth of M-Pesa presents a challenge to policy-makers. The lack of regulatory policy and laws regarding e-money in Kenya to some extent attributed to the fact that this is a unique dynamic innovation, with no clear expertise on how to regulate it. The innovation is growing and changing so rapidly that regulations might not keep pace with the changes.

Some observations can be made regarding the M-Pesa service. The M-Pesa case shows that efforts to expand financial access need to focus on cost-cutting innovations, in addition to expanding the outreach of existing services. Information technology, and especially cellular telephony, seems to hold great potential for reducing the costs of delivering basic financial services. If the current rate of diffusion is maintained (about an additional million phones a year), universal access could be achieved in five years, with the implication that nearly all the 15 million mobile phone subscribers will access financial services. The low cost of cellular phone services and the small size of transactions that can be handled are major contributors to the rapid penetration of cellular phone services. These magnitudes are far below the financial transactions that any financial institution would be able to handle cost-effectively. Cellular banking – such as the M-Pesa initiative – offers future prospects for providing basic transactions and savings services for the unbanked.

Another important observation is that the rapid adoption and frequent use of M-Pesa has led to a variety of positive and unintended outcomes resulting from the design of the service. Allowing money to be electronically transferred, M-Pesa lessens and even eliminates both spatial and temporal barriers to money transfer. This, it is argued, facilitates the flow of money to rural areas where access to finance is difficult, and also increases income inflows to rural areas.

There is therefore a need to support the mobile platform to increase the breadth and depth of financial access as well as the services offered. Of more significance is the need to encourage adoption of the services by MFIs. The mobile platform's main value is the reach achieved by the distribution network and the increased efficiency gained from the use of the network. Although MFIs have the greatest outreach to the unbanked and provide credit to those excluded mainly by formal financial institutions, they are relatively weaker institutions, and have not embraced the use of m-payments as a delivery and service channel as fast as would be expected. M-Pesa on the other hand, addresses other financial needs without credit services. It is therefore necessary to support MFIs to adopt m-banking and payments for loan disbursements, loan repayments, and other financial transactions. Despite this growth, Safaricom is not yet authorized to operate as a bank, with the money circulating deposited in a physical bank account with a commercial bank, which services the daily transactions of the M-Pesa service.

16.4 Conclusions

This chapter has addressed the development of microfinance and financial access in Kenya. The critical role of finance in the country's development is recognized at policy level. However, despite the development of the financial sector, access to financial services remains a challenge. The failure by the formal financial institutions to address the demand for financial services by a majority of the population has largely contributed to the growth of microfinance institutions as a major source of financial services, especially to small firms and poor households. Despite this growth, the sector has faced problems that have limited its growth and outreach. The challenge in improving financial access is therefore to identify policies to alleviate such barriers and streamline the activities of microfinance-providing institutions to enhance their efficiency. This will bring them in line with the goals of *Vision 2030* for the financial sector. The enactment of the Microfinance Act is an important step in this effort.

Increasing access to financial services for a wider section of the population also requires strengthening the stability of the financial sector and creating an enabling environment for different players in the financial system. This is important for realizing the *Vision 2030* goal of reducing the share of the population without financial access. This calls for, among other things, the need to review the legal, regulatory, and supervisory frameworks for the financial system. Given the lack of sustainability for MFI funding, the establishment of a Microfinance Trust Fund from which MFIs can borrow for onward lending is also important. Microfinance growth has also been dominated by a single product of credit targeting a specific clientele. MFIs therefore need to diversify their products to be able to satisfy more credit needs.

An emerging policy question with respect to the role of microfinance is the role of technology in increasing access to financial services. The emergence of the M-Pesa service has illustrated the potential for increasing financial access to those previously excluded from the financial system. The key question is how the M-Pesa service can complement MFIs to increase access to finance. There is therefore a need to support the mobile platform to increase financial access. The complementarity requires that MFIs adopt the mobile platform and use it in transacting their businesses. The main advantage of M-Pesa is its wide distribution network and cost reduction. This provides great potential for MFIs to expand their coverage at minimum cost and to be able to diversify their services. Policies for increasing financial access therefore need to address how to link microfinance to the mobile platform, to reduce the transaction costs that have been one of the major factors in creating access barriers.

Note

1 M-Pesa is a combination of two words: M stands for mobile while *pesa* is a Kiswahili word for money. M-Pesa can therefore be translated roughly to mean mobile money.

References

Akoten J., Y. Sawada and K. Otsuka, 2006, 'The Determinants of Credit Access and Its Impacts on Micro and Small Enterprises: The Case of Garment Producers in Kenya', *Economic Development and Cultural Change*, 54 (4), 927–944.

Aleke Dondo, 1999, 'The Status of Microfinance in Kenya'. K-REP, mimeo.

Aryeetey, E., H. Hettige, M. Nissanke and W. Steele, 1997, 'Financial Market Integration and Reforms in Ghana, Malawi, Nigeria and Tanzania', *World Bank Economic Review*, II (2), 195–218.

Atieno R., 2001, 'Formal and Informal Institutions' Lending Policies and Access to Credit by Small Scale Enterprises in Kenya'. African Economic Research Consortium Research Paper No. 111.

Atieno, R., 2004, 'Small Scale Enterprises in Kenya. How Important is Access to Credit?' in Wohlmuth, K., A. Gutowski, T. Knedlik, M. Meine and S. Pitamber (eds) *African Entrepreneurship and Private Sector Development*. Africa Development Perspectives Yearbook 2002/2003. Munster: LIT Verlag.

Beck T. and M. Fuchs, 2004, 'Structural Issues in the Kenyan Financial System: Improving Competition and Access'. World Bank Policy Research Working Paper 3363.

Beck T., A. Demirguc-Kunt and M. S. M. Peria, 2006, 'Banking Services for Everyone? Barriers to Bank Access and Use around the World'. World Bank Policy Research Working Paper 4079.

Bigsten A., P. Collier, S. Dercon, M. Fafchamps, B. Guthier, W. Gunning, M. Söderbom, A. Oduro, Oostendorp, C. Patillo, F. Teal and A. Zeufack, 2000, 'Credit Constraints in Manufacturing Enterprises in Africa'. CSAE Working Paper, WPS/2000.24.

CBS, ICEG, and KREP, 1999, *A National Survey of Small and Micro Enterprises in Kenya*. Nairobi: CBS, ICEG, and KREP.

Central Bank of Kenya, 2007, *Financial Access in Kenya. Results of the 2006 National Survey*. Nairobi: CBK.

Central Bank of Kenya, 2009. *Finaccess National Survey 2009, Dynamics of Kenya's Changing Financial Landscape*. Nairobi: CBK.

Claessens, S., 2006, 'Access to Financial Services: A Review of the Issues and Public Policy Objectives', *The World Bank Research Observer*, 21 (2).

Hossain, M., 1988, 'Credit for the Alleviation of Rural Poverty: The Grameen Bank in Bangladesh'. IFPRI Research Report No. 65.

Hughes N. and S. Lonie 2007, 'M-PESA: Mobile Money for the Unbanked Turning Cell phones into 24-Hour Tellers in Kenya', *Innovation*, Winter/Spring.

Isaksson A., 2004, 'Access to Formal Finance in Kenyan Manufacturing', in Wohlmuth K., A. Gutowski, T. Knedlik, M. Meine and S. Pitamber (eds) *African Entrepreneurship and Private Sector Development*. Africa Development Perspectives Yearbook 2002/2003. Munster: LIT Verlag.

Khandker, S. R., 2005, 'Microfinance and Poverty: Evidence Using Panel Data from Bangladesh', *The World Bank Economic Review*, Oxford University Press.

Liu, A. T. and M. K. Mithika, 2009, 'Mobile Banking – the Key to Building Credit History for the Poor? Kenya Case Study: Linking Mobile Banking and Mobile Payment Platforms to Credit Bureaus'. Report of the Kenya Credit Bureau and M-banking Research Study. USAID.

Morawczynski, O. and M. Pickens, 2009, 'Poor People Using Mobile Financial Services: Observations on Customer Usage and Impact from M-PESA'. CGAP Brief, Washington, DC.

Morduch, J., 1999, 'The Microfinance Promise', *Journal of Economic Literature*, XXXVII, 1569–1614.

Mosley P., D. Olejarova and E. Alexeeva, 2004, 'Microfinance, Social Capital Formation and Political Development in Russia, Slovakia and Romania', *Journal of International Development*, 16, 407–427.

Ngugi, R. W., 2001, 'An Empirical Analysis of Interest Rate Spread in Kenya'. AERC Research Paper No. 106. Nairobi: African Economic Research Consortium.

Nkurunziza, J., 2005, 'The Effect of Credit on Growth and Convergence of Firms in Kenyan Manufacturing'. CSAE WPS/2005-01.

Okten, C. and U. O. Osili, 2004, 'Social Networks and Credit Access in Indonesia', *World Development*, 32 (7), 1225–1246.

Republic of Kenya, 2004, 'Economic Recovery Strategy for Wealth and Employment Creation'. Nairobi: Government Printer.

Republic of Kenya, 2005, *Sessional Paper Number 2 of 2005 on the Development of Micro and Small Scale Enterprises for Wealth and Employment Creation for Poverty Reduction.* Nairobi: Government Printer.

Republic of Kenya, 2007, *The Vision 2030*. Nairobi: Government Printer.

17

Democracy and Prosperity[1]

Paul Collier, Roxana Gutiérrez-Romero, and Mwangi S. Kimenyi

17.1 The issue: has ethnic violence shown that Kenya is unsuited to electoral democracy?

Since 1991, Kenya has, at least nominally, been a multiparty democracy. The 2002 election ushered in genuine competition between parties and resulted in a peaceful change of government. The 2007 elections were expected to be concluded equally smoothly but, in the event, the election triggered a serious outbreak of violence, largely ethnic. A post-election coalition government was formed only after the conciliating intervention of Kofi Annan. What are the likely economic implications of democracy in Kenya, and what are the lessons from the 2007 election? We draw upon some evidence from other developing countries and upon surveys of citizen attitudes conducted in Kenya just before and soon after the 2007 election.

Democracy is certainly compatible with good economic performance. Comparing democracies and autocracies over the period since 1970, Collier and Hoeffler (2009) find that, with the exception of countries richly endowed with natural resources, democracies on average grow significantly more rapidly than autocracies. One reason for this is that elections tend to discipline governments into adopting better economic policies. Chauvet and Collier (2009) analyse the effect of elections on policy in developing countries. They use a global sample covering three decades, and measure policy annually using both ratings made by the World Bank (the Country Policy and Institutional Assessment) and those of the International Country Risk Guide. On both measures, they find that elections have cyclical and structural effects on policy.

Cyclically, policies tend to deteriorate with the approach of an election, perhaps because governments are tempted into policies that deliver short-term benefits at the expense of costs that are only realized after the election. But these adverse cyclical effects are more than offset by a structural improvement that frequent elections bring to the average level of policies. This is certainly consistent with the improved economic performance in Kenya following the election of 2002. Not only did growth accelerate but, as we show below, most citizens recognized that policies had improved.

However, Chauvet and Collier find an important caveat to these benign results. Elections only improve policies if they are well conducted. Badly conducted elections have at best no significant effect on policy. Hence, from the perspective of the economy, the contested results and the aftermath of the 2007 election may constitute a setback to what had until then appeared to be a beneficial process of democratization.

More fundamentally, the ethnic nature of much of the election-related violence potentially calls into question the viability of democracy in Kenya. If allegiance is based on ethnic identity, the normal beneficial consequences of elections may not hold: elections may fail to discipline governments into improved economic performance. Conversely, they may leave a dysfunctional legacy of violence and uncertainty.

Although prior to the era of democratic politics, ethnicity had been downplayed, in practice, it had been at the core of Kenyan politics, as evidenced by patterns of resource allocation and also cabinet and civil service appointments (Kimenyi and Shughart, 1989). The introduction of multiparty politics brought ethnic politics to the fore as opposition parties quickly splintered along, although not exclusively, ethnic groupings (Muigai, 1995; Kimenyi, 1997). As a result, the first multiparty election held in 1992 was a contest that largely rotated around ethnic alignments (Oyugi, 1997), a pattern that was repeated in the 1997 general elections. Both the 1992 and the 1997 elections were preceded by ethnic clashes, especially in the Coast and Rift Valley provinces. These clashes subsided after the elections. In 2002, a coalition of parties under the banner of the National Rainbow Coalition (NARC) defeated KANU in the presidential elections in what was a relatively peaceful election. Nevertheless, the ruling coalition splintered after only three years following disagreements over proposed constitutional reform.

Following the disputed 2007 election, violence spread to areas that hitherto had not experienced election-related violence, such as the city of Kisumu. Most of the violence and displacements occurred in the Rift Valley, much as in 1992 and 1997 (Apollos, 2001). Other affected areas included the cities of Nairobi (especially in the slums) and Mombassa. To a large extent, the violence was between members of different ethnic groups. In the cities, violence was primarily, but not exclusively, between the Kikuyus and the Luos, the two groups that had produced the leading presidential contenders (Kibaki and Odinga). In the Rift Valley, the violence involved members of the larger Kalejin ethnic groups and those considered migrants to the Rift Valley. Also affected were communities bordering the Rift Valley in Western and Nyanza provinces. Violence in Kisumu does not appear to have been directed to any specific group, was generally more of a protest against the election result, and took the character of looting and destruction of businesses and government property.[2]

These cycles of ethnic violence around election periods appear to support the views expressed by the first generation of independent African leaders, who argued that Africa was best suited to single-party systems of governance because multipartyism would result in increased ethnic fractionalization with adverse consequences such as exacerbating conflicts and tribalism.[3] Thus, for the most part, recent post-election violence appears to be largely ethnic and, as in past episodes, seems to give credence to the conventional wisdom that electoral choices in Africa are primarily driven by ethnicity.

Our survey data can help to inform these fundamental questions. They show to what extent political preferences in Kenya are defined by ethnicity.

17.2 Voter attitudes in the 2007 elections

The discussion that follows is based on two nationally representative surveys that were conducted before and after the 2007 Kenyan elections. The first survey was conducted just two weeks ahead of the General Election of 27 December 2007 and focused on voter intentions, attitudes towards violence, and the socio-economic characteristics of Kenyans. The sample includes 1,207 Kenyans aged 18 years and over from all eight provinces, and covering 76 out of 210 electoral constituencies. The sample captures the rural/urban split consistent with the most recent Kenyan census, which shows that 65 per cent of respondents live in rural areas and the remainder in urban areas. The ethnic distribution of the sample respondents also matches that of the national population.[4] Whenever possible, interviews were conducted in the respondents' mother tongue. In total, interviews were conducted in ten of the most widely spoken languages in Kenya. The second survey, conducted in August 2008, revisited previous respondents to find out about their experiences in the aftermath of the election, their expectations from the new coalition government, and whether their views had changed regarding trust among Kenyans, democracy, land conflict, and decentralization, among other issues. As the surveys were conducted immediately before the elections and some time after the formation of the coalition government, they provide a good picture of the factors that influenced voting intentions and how economic/political perceptions changed in the aftermath of the elections.

17.2.1 Voting and ethnic identity

According to the pre-election survey, most respondents (96 per cent) claimed they would cast their vote in the presidential elections. The voting intentions were divided, showing a virtual statistical tie between the leading candidates, Kibaki and Odinga. The headline numbers show an electorate clearly divided along ethnic lines. The three main presidential candidates, Kibaki (of Kikuyu origin), Odinga (of Luo origin), and Kalonzo (of Kamba origin), were overwhelmingly supported by the people from their own ethnic group.

Are Kenyans primarily identity voters, and what else appears to motivate their voting behaviour? We asked respondents why they intended to vote as they did. Evidently, the answers to such a question need to be discounted: in all such surveys, people are inclined to give answers that put them in a good light with the interviewer. With this important caveat, the self-described motivations are shown in Figure 17.1.

As the results show, over 90 per cent of the respondents stated that they would select a candidate based on the candidate's track record in terms of honesty, experience in handling funds, and care for the community. Less than 1 per cent of survey respondents stated that the ethnicity/tribe of the candidate was the most important factor in shaping their voting motivations. The denial of ethnicity as an influence lacks credibility in view of the fact that the three main presidential candidates were overwhelmingly supported by the people from their own ethnic groups (as shown in Figure 17.2). Indeed, even those ethnic groups that did not have a major presidential candidate voted as ethnic bloc votes: the Luhyas and Kalenjins primarily supported Odinga, whereas the Merus and Embus supported Kibaki.

The contrasting evidence in our survey between voting intentions by ethnicity and the self-described voting motivations suggests either that preferences over policy vary massively between ethnic groups, or that people are

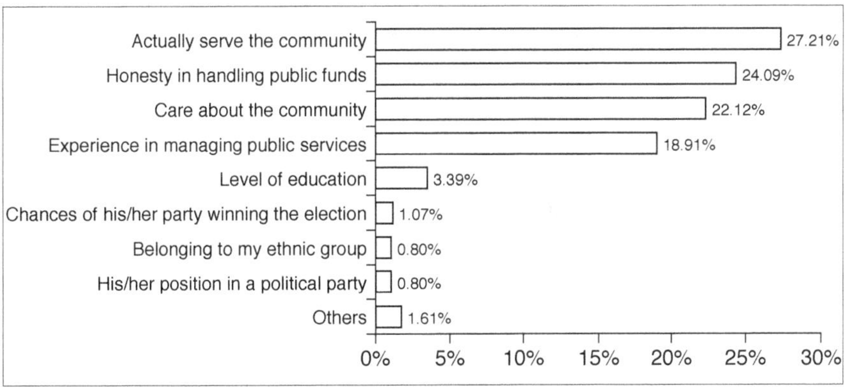

Figure 17.1 Self-described voting motivations.

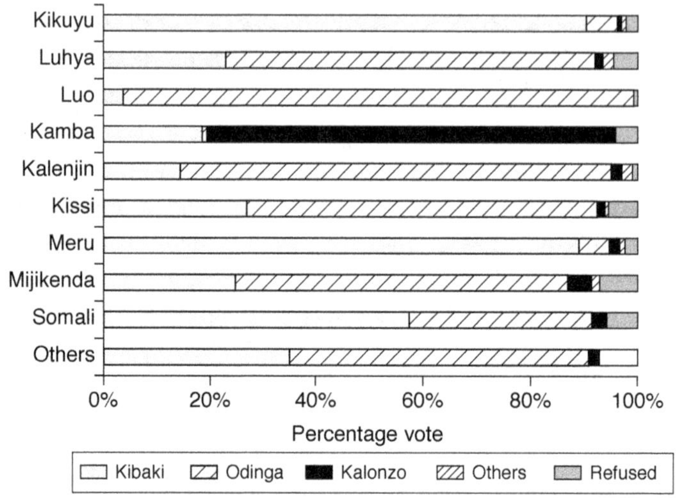

Figure 17.2 Voting intentions by people's ethnicity.

embarrassed by the reality of ethnic voting. The latter might arise if people do not trust those from other ethnic groups. Lack of trust might motivate voters to select a candidate from their own ethnic group over an otherwise better quality candidate from another group. People might expect those from other groups to vote along ethnic lines, and feel that unless they also vote ethnically they will be at a disadvantage. The belief that others would vote on the basis of ethnicity could be reinforced by the fact that much of the political campaigning played on ethnic sensitivities and loyalties.

One of the survey questions sought to investigate the expressed trust for members of other ethnic groups. As Table 17.1 shows, Kenyans mistrust members of other ethnic groups, a phenomenon particularly strong among those of Kikuyu and Luo origin. For these two groups, up to 60 per cent of the respondents trust those from other groups either 'not at all' or 'only a little'.[5]

17.2.2 Voting and perceptions of policy performance

Recall that, in a well-functioning democracy, voters succeed in disciplining government to improve economic policy. Voter assessments of the economic performance of the government are therefore particularly pertinent. Ideally, those who judge that the government has performed well would mostly vote for it, whereas those who judge that it has performed badly would vote against it. The survey finds that the performance of the Kibaki administration was judged favourably by most respondents, with 60 per cent of respondents perceiving that economic conditions were better than during the previous

Table 17.1 Ethnicity and trust

	How much do you trust Kenyans from other ethnic groups?			
Respondent's ethnic group	Not at all	Just a little	Somewhat	A lot
Kikuyu	20.8	42.0	28.8	7.5
Luo	20.3	41.9	30.4	4.7
Kamba	6.2	43.8	44.6	4.5
Luhya	16.3	42.6	28.9	5.8
Kalejin	13.6	45.6	30.1	9.7
Mijikenda	2.7	36.0	41.3	13.3
All	14.3	42.6	31.9	7.8

regime, as against only 25 per cent who perceived it to be worse. There was indeed a large difference in the voting intentions of people with these contrasting assessments: those with favourable assessments were much more likely to vote for the government (Figure 17.3).

The match becomes even stronger when the question is changed from an overall assessment to a personal judgement of how the respondent's own economic situation has changed (Figure 17.4). Some 29 per cent perceived that their own living conditions were better during Kibaki's rule, 26 per cent thought them unchanged, and 45 per cent thought that their living conditions had worsened. These opinions mapped fairly closely into voting intentions.

However, the encouraging correlation between assessments of the economy (whether overall or the consequences for the individual) and voting preferences results not from ethnicity being dominated by judgement of the economy, but because judgement of the economy is dominated by ethnicity (see Figure 17.5). Further, even where assessments of economic performance ran counter to ethnic identity, this did not substantially weaken the grip of ethnicity on voting. Among those Kikuyu voters who judged economic per-

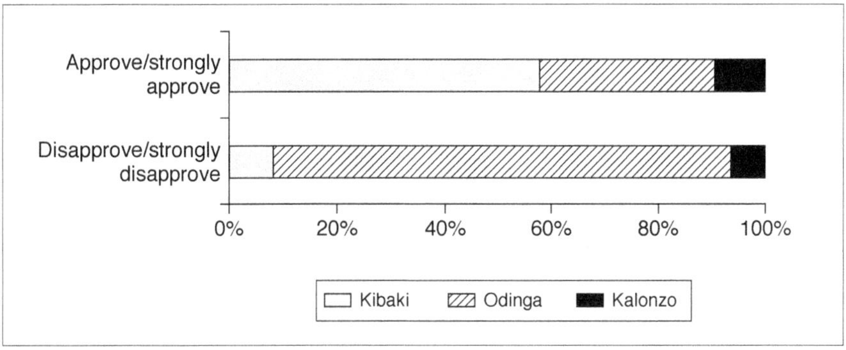

Figure 17.3 Voting intentions by Kibaki's approval rating.

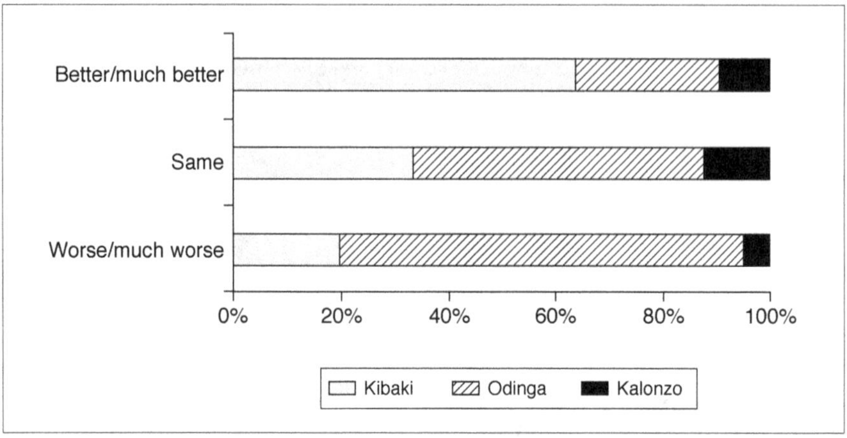

Figure 17.4 Voting intentions by how people perceive their living conditions.

formance to have worsened during the Kibaki government, a large majority (88 per cent) still supported Kibaki. Conversely, among those Luo voters who judged economic performance to have improved during the Kibaki government, only a tiny minority (5 per cent) supported Kibaki.

During the election campaigns, the opposition candidates raised issues of ethnic favouritism and discrimination by the incumbent government. One question asked about respondents' perceptions of how their ethnic group was treated by the government relative to other ethnic groups. Table 17.2 reports

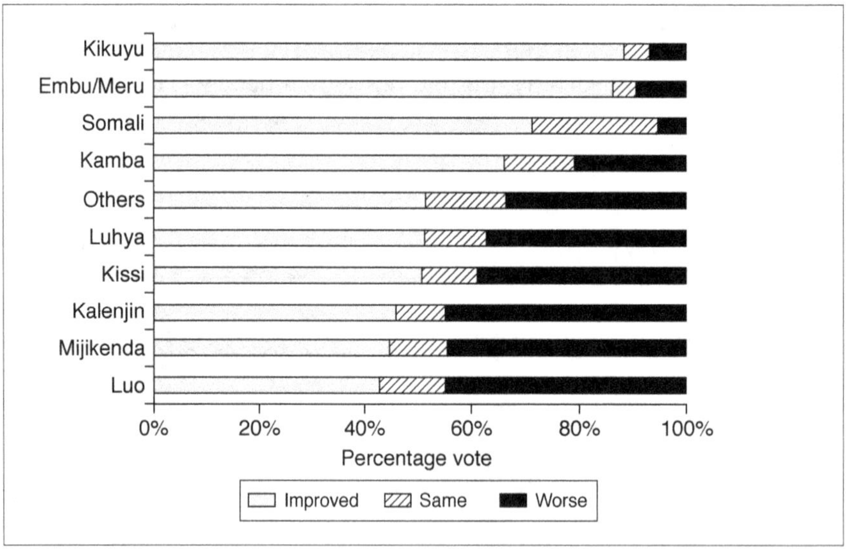

Figure 17.5 Judged the economy to have improved by ethnic group.

Table 17.2 Opinions about group treatment by government

	Is your group's treatment by government, worse, the same, or better?					
Respondent's ethnic group	Much worse	Worse	Same	Better	Much better	Not available
Kikuyu	0	3.1	31.4	16.8	4.9	43.8
Luo	10.1	31.8	17.6	2.7	1.4	36.5
Kamba	0.9	10.7	31.2	3.6	0.9	52.7
Luhya	1.1	7.4	21.6	10	1.1	56.8
Kalejin	4.9	7.8	34.0	1.9	0.0	50.5
Mijikenda	2.7	28.0	13.3	5.3	0.0	50.7
All	2.6	13.5	25.8	9.1	1.9	46.4

the summary of the responses by ethnicity. Whereas only 3 per cent of Kikuyus felt that their group was treated worse or much worse than others, 42 per cent of Luos felt so. Likewise, although over 20 per cent of Kikuyus considered that their group was treated better than other groups, only 4 per cent of Luos did so. Irrespective of the reality, the government was widely perceived as favouring its own group.

17.2.3 Voting and decentralization

In addition to Kibaki's record, the future governance structure of the country was another major issue that divided Kenyans ahead of the election. In particular, the electorate was deeply divided on how the constitution should be reformed and whether to adopt a *Majimbo* system (a federal type of arrangement). The pre-election survey reveals a strong correlation between how people voted in the 2005 referendum on the issue and people's intention to vote in the 2007 presidential elections. Among those who supported the referendum, a large majority (83 per cent) intended to vote for Kibaki. In contrast, 82 per cent of those who voted against the draft constitution stated that they would vote for Odinga or Kalonzo (Figure 17.6).

The pre-election survey also reveals that there was some confusion among voters as to what *Majimbo* actually means. Among those who intended to vote for Odinga, the majority (75 per cent) understood *Majimbo* as a policy whereby regions would take control of their own resources. In contrast, among those who supported Kibaki, only 18 per cent defined it in this way. A further 16 per cent believed that *Majimbo* meant that each tribe would have its own government, whereas fully 37 per cent thought that *Majimbo* would expropriate the land of those people living outside their homeland and force them to return to where they came from. In other words, Kibaki supporters tended to see the issue directly in ethnic terms.

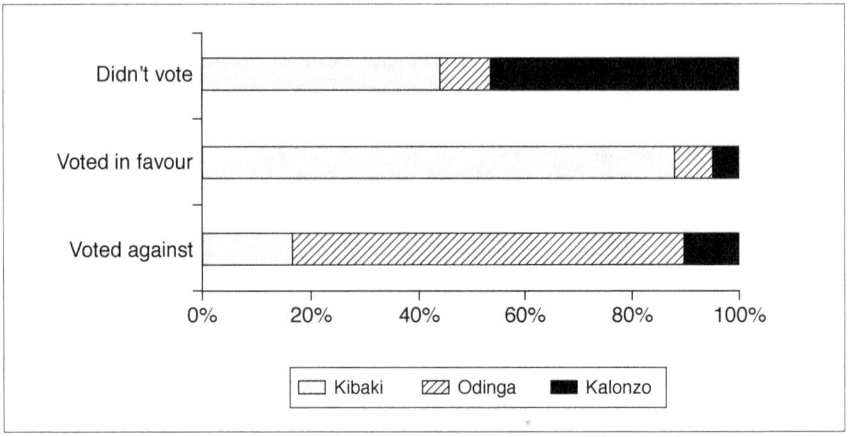

Figure 17.6 Voting intentions by how people voted in the 2005 referendum.

17.2.4 Ethnic voting by generation and income

Although ethic identity was clearly predominant in shaping voting intentions, the power of ethnicity varied somewhat according to age. The voting intentions of the young were driven to a lesser extent by their ethnicity than those of the older generations. Similarly, ethnicity played a more important role in shaping voting intentions among the higher income groups than among the poor. In other words, the older and wealthier Kenyans are, the more likely it is that their voting intentions are shaped along ethnic lines. Over time, the two effects may be working in opposite directions. Unless younger voters acquire stronger ethnic allegiances as they age, generational change will tend to weaken voting according to ethnic identity. On the other hand, however, unless the effect of economic success changes, economic growth may accentuate identity voting.

17.3 The impact of the 2007 elections

Since the 2007 elections ended in dispute that culminated in widespread violence, they may actually have weakened political institutions. We now turn to perceptions of this issue.

17.3.1 Extent and causes of violence

The data show that there was widespread violence before and after the election. Electoral violence was reported in 80 per cent of the surveyed constituencies. Roughly 50 per cent of respondents were afraid that electoral violence would spread into their constituency before the election, and this figure went up to

58 per cent after the election. Roughly 30 per cent of respondents claimed that politicians in their areas had been openly advocating violence before the election. These figures remained practically unchanged after the election. Twenty-eight per cent of respondents report a specific personal impact after the election, whether through personal injury, being displaced from home, destruction of property, loss of employment or earnings, or having friends or relatives who died in the violence.

Many respondents (43 per cent) blamed election irregularities and a weak electoral commission as triggers for the electoral violence. Presumably, the violence erupted through a combination of the trigger event and more structural causes of division. However, only 10 per cent of respondents believed that electoral violence was due to tribal conflict.

17.3.2 Long-term consequences of violence

The post-election survey gives an indication of the legacy that violence has left. The outbreaks of violence significantly contributed to the deterioration of trust and of confidence in the rule of law. One in four Kenyans judged that violence is justified. Those who were affected by violence were 20 per cent more likely to favour actions outside the law and 40 per cent more likely to resort to violence. People were evenly divided on whether amnesty should be given to those who were involved in the outbreaks of violence, with victims of violence being less likely to support amnesty.

17.3.3 Democracy and elections

The events that followed the disputed general election of 2007 do not appear to have reduced support for democracy. As prior to the election, around 70 per cent of respondents viewed democracy as the most preferable type of government. However, the perception that Kenya is a full democracy has changed. In December 2007, 20 per cent of respondents described Kenya as a fully democratic country. By August 2008, the proportion had dropped to only 6 per cent. There was a sharp increase, from 10 to 30 per cent, in the proportion preferring some method other than an election for choosing leaders. Presumably related to the decline of faith in elections, the Kenyan Electoral Commission (ECK) suffered a severe loss of credibility, this being regardless of which candidate the respondent had supported for president. The president also suffered a decline in trust, both among those who had voted for him and among the supporters of the main opposition party, the Orange Democratic Movement (ODM). However, some political institutions were actually trusted more as a result of the election: trust in parliament increased by 10 percentage points. Indeed, overall, Kenyans still had a high regard for their institutions. For instance, the majority of people (70 per cent) trusted the president, the vice-president, the prime minister, the parliament, and the coalition government either 'a lot' or 'to some extent'.

17.3.4 Trust among individuals

Although the decline in trust in institutions was thus patchy, a more damaging legacy was the impact on trust between ordinary Kenyans of different ethnic groups. Even prior to the election, intergroup trust was rather limited, so that the decline resulting from the election left the society with disturbingly limited interethnic confidence. It is well established that trust enhances the scope for economic transactions. Hence, a loss of trust can be expected to have detrimental economic effects. Consistent with this expectation, a third of respondents claim that, since the elections, they do less business with people from other ethnic groups.

17.3.5 What identity do people give themselves?

The strength of ethnic identity evidently played an important part in voting. Potentially, the potency of ethnic identity can be weakened by strong national identity. Other subnational identities, defined in terms of ethnicity, religion, or economic class, are, of course, compatible with a national identity, but arguably, if the national identity dominates, it is easier for democratic politics to function well. People would be more likely to place the good of the nation ahead of the good of their own ethnic group. Hence, the relative importance of the two sources of identity is of potential significance.

In both pre- and post-election surveys, the respondents were asked: 'We have spoken to many Kenyans and they have all described themselves in different ways. Some people describe themselves in terms of their language, ethnic group, race, religion, or gender, and others describe themselves in economic terms, such as working class, middle class, or a farmer. Besides being Kenyan, which specific group do you feel you belong to first and foremost?'.

In December 2007, a few respondents (20 per cent) answered that they identify in terms of their ethnicity, and 37 per cent of respondents insisted on identifying themselves first and foremost in nationalistic terms, that is as Kenyans. Most others (43 per cent) identified themselves on neither basis, choosing instead occupation (18 per cent), social class (7 per cent), gender (4 per cent), or religion (3 per cent).

The survey conducted in August 2008 shows that, far from having undermined national identity, the violence had strengthened it. The proportion identifying first and foremost as Kenyans increased from 37 per cent to 47 per cent (a statistically significant increase). Perhaps many Kenyans learnt from the brief episode of violence that national unity was more important than they had realized.

17.3.6 Expectations from the coalition government

The great majority of Kenyans (70 per cent) were hopeful of the coalition government. For instance, most people (regardless of whom they claimed to have voted for) thought that the coalition government would perform the same, or better, than the past administration of President Kibaki in terms of reforming the constitution, distributing resources, solving land conflicts, and tackling government corruption. Sixty per cent of respondents thought that both national and their personal economic conditions would be the same or better than under the previous government.

17.3.7 Tribalism/ethnic violence in the future?

Opinions were divided as to whether the coalition government would combat tribalism in politics better than the previous Kibaki administration. On average, 43 per cent believed that tribalism in politics would be worse than under the previous administration, against 33 per cent who thought that it would be reduced. Perceptions differed widely across ethnic groups. Those groups that felt they had suffered discrimination during the previous administration, notably the Luos and Luhyas, expected tribalism to be reduced. In contrast, the Kikuyus expected it to get worse.

17.4 A tentative assessment

The survey revealed a degree of confidence in Kenyan democracy on the part of ordinary citizens. Ihis confidence is not necessarily misplaced: as we have noted, as long as elections are properly conducted, they do succeed in disciplining governments into improved economic policies.

However, the events that followed the general election of 2007 revealed prior weaknesses and have left a difficult legacy.

The key weakness concerns interethnic trust, which even prior to the election was very limited. A realistic approach to the lack of trust is to build robust supervisory institutions in which all citizens can have confidence. A key such institution is the electoral commission. A potential model is Ghana, where the commission is structurally independent of candidates and has built considerable credibility with citizens.

One legacy of the violence is a collapse in interethnic trust from already low levels. However, a more encouraging legacy is a strengthening in national, as opposed to ethnic, identity. Perhaps many Kenyans 'looked over the brink' and did not like what they saw might happen if identity conflicts continued unabated. This response is potentially important for fundamental political choices. International experience suggests that two quite different models of society could be appropriate for social peace. These models can be referred as the 'hotel' and 'building a house together'.

The hotel model is where people can do what they like as long as they do not disturb the other guests and they pay their bills. That is the Rawlsian liberal model. In this case, politics is not run by a vision of the common good. All politicians should do is to offer the best public services for the least cost in taxation. This vision is economically efficient, but with the problem that it does not generate loyalties or a sense of belonging. It does not develop a national identity, a sense of common good or social solidarity. Examples of this type of model are Switzerland and Canada. Like Canada, Switzerland is a rich paradise, yet what many people do not realize is that it is actually composed of three very distinct ethno-linguistic groups: German, Italian, and French. At the risk of offending Swiss sensibilities, it often appears to outsiders that the main thing that these groups really agree on is that they do not trust each other. The Swiss designed their public sector to take into account this lack of trust across the ethno-linguistic groups. In this type of model, the solution is to shape the public sector to achieve ethnic equity. For instance, the Swiss public sector has quotas and a rotation of jobs, which are based strictly on each group's proportion in the population. Under the Swiss model, therefore, the allocation of posts cannot favour a particular ethnic group. So if Kenya is to live with the current ethnic identities and lack of trust across ethnic groups, then the adoption of the Swiss model could help to facilitate the achievement of peaceful co-existence and prosperity. This could be done by redesigning the public sector and by implementing policies that promote ethnic equity.

The second model is not understood as a hotel. Instead, society is understood as a home that we build together. It is the home where we belong. It is a shared project. It is a society where the different subcommunities can strive and pursue a collective good. In this model, all share the responsibility of building the nation. Each person and family has the responsibility of pursuing the well-being of the nation. This task should be enhanced by the institutions, government public discourse and actions, placing the common goal of the nation above anything else.

An example of this second model is Tanzania. If we compare the policies pursued by Tanzania and Kenya right after their independence, in terms of economic policies, Tanzania's President Nyerere made serious mistakes. For instance, Nyerere's economic policy of *'ujama'*, community-based farming collectives, proved disastrous. If we remember when the Tanzanians accused Kenyans of being of a 'money man' society, Kenyans laughed back and said Tanzanians are a 'money nothing' society. However, in political terms, Nyerere got things right. He emphasized the sense of a national identity over 'subnational' identities. He was very careful in how the education system was run. The public school curriculum was designed to stress common Tanzanian history, culture, and values, and inculcate a strong sense of national identity (Court, 1984). Nyerere also employed Kiswahili as a nation-building tool. After independence, Tanzania established Kiswahili as the national language, and its use was quickly transferred to government administration and all spheres of public life (Polome, 1980). A keystone in Tanzanian policies to build a sense of national unity has been the focus on an equitable regional distribution of public investment in education, health, and infrastructure (Court and Kinyanjui, 1980).

To date, Kenya has pursued neither of the above models. The state lacks the powerful independent checks-and-balances that the hotel model requires to ensure ethnic balance. In this model, although people do not trust each other, it does not matter because they trust the institutions. But nor has it pursued the other models. Kenya has not used the school curriculum to promote a coherent national identity. For instance, the school curriculum does not study Kenya as a nation until grade 5. The Kenyan focus on provincial geography and history in grades 1–4 perhaps deepens ethnic divisions, especially among the many who drop out of primary school before grade 5 (Miguel, 2004). Although Kiswahili has long been widely spoken in Kenya as a 'lingua franca', it competes with other languages such as English and local languages in political forums and schools. On top of that, the regional distribution of central government resources has favoured some groups over others, greatly politicizing ethnicity (Court and Kinyanjui, 1980). Our surveys show that Kenyans are not opposed to resources being equally shared across regions, but they do oppose policies such as *Majimbo* that have been used to mobilize partisans.

The evidence presented in this chapter confirms the finding by Miguel (2004), who compares similar areas in Kenya and Tanzania (Busia and Meatu) located near each other on opposite sides of Lake Victoria, which were similar along key dimensions in the 1960s when Tanzania gained independence and adopted its nation-building programme. Miguel finds that Tanzania has had more effective interethnic corporation and higher public good funding than Kenya. These are the contrasting legacies of 45 years of discourses of national unification from the top in Tanzania and of ethnic differentiation in Kenya.

Both the Swiss–Canadian 'hotel' model of the state and the Tanzanian model of building a common national identity look to offer viable routes to a peaceful and prosperous democracy. But the past Kenyan model of ethnic politics without the support of trusted institutions may expose the society to the risk of further violence without disciplining governments sufficiently into good economic performance.

Notes

1 The CSAE surveys presented in this chapter were funded by the UK Department for International Development (DFID) as part of the Improving Institutions for Pro-Poor Growth (iiG), a research consortium aimed at studying how to improve institutions in Africa and South Asia. The views expressed are not necessarily those of the DFID.

2 Nevertheless, non-Luo business owners in Kisumu were targeted, and most are reported to have left the area.
3 A common explanation for the 1992 and 1997 violence is that it was meant to weaken the voting strength of the opposition, especially in the Rift Valley. This idea is supported by the fact that such conflicts subsided after the elections (see Kimenyi and Ndung'u, 2005). Of note, however, is that, in the 1992 and 1997 general elections, most of the conflicts were before the elections, and furthermore there was no notable violence during the 2002 elections
4 In piloting and fieldwork, we found that the vast majority of Kenyans were welcoming and eager to talk freely about their voting intentions. The survey reached a response rate of 80 per cent, a high rate for studies of this kind in Kenya.
5 Nonetheless, it is important to note that we cannot infer from these responses which specific ethnic groups they mistrust.

References

Apollos, M., 2001, 'Ethnicity, Violence and Democracy', *Africa Development*, 26 (1 and 2), 99–144.

Chauvet, L. and P. Collier, 2009, 'Elections and Economic Policy in Developing Countries', *Economic Policy*, 24 (59), 509–550.

Collier, P. and A. Hoeffler, 2009, 'Testing the NeoCon Agenda: Democracy in Resource-rich Societies', *European Economic Review*, 53 (3), 293–308.

Court, D., 1984, 'The Education System as a Response to Inequality', in Barkan, J. D. (ed.) *Politics and Public Policy in Kenya and Tanzania*. New York: Praeger.

Court, D. and K. Kinyanjui, 1980, 'Development Policy and Educational Opportunity: The Experience of Kenya and Tanzania'. IDS Occasional Paper, no. 33. Nairobi: University of Nairobi.

Kimenyi, M. S., 1997, *Ethnic Diversity, Liberty and the State: The African Dilemma*. Cheltenham, UK: Edward Elgar.

Kimenyi, M. S. and W. Shughart, 1989, 'Political Succession and the Growth of Government', *Public Choice*, 6 (2), 173–179.

Kimenyi, M. S. and N. S. Ndung'u, 2005, 'Sporadic Ethnic Violence: Why Has Kenya Not Experienced a Full-blown Civil War? ' in Collier, P. and N. Sambanis (eds) *Understanding Civil War, Vol. 1, Africa*. Washington, DC: World Bank.

Miguel, E., 2004, 'Tribe or Nation? National Building and Public Goods in Kenya and Tanzania', *World Politics*, 56, 327–362.

Muigai, G., 1995, 'Ethnicity and the Renewal of Competitive Politics in Kenya', in Glickman, H. (ed.) *Ethnic Conflict and Democratization*. Atlanta, GA: The African Studies Association Press, 161–196.

Oyugi, W. O., 1997, 'Ethnicity in the Electoral Process: The 1992 General Elections in Kenya', *African Journal of Political Science*, 2 (1), 41–69.

Polome, E., 1980, 'Tanzania: A Socio-Linguistic Perspective', in Polome, E. C. and C. P. Hill (eds) *Language in Tanzania*. Oxford: Oxford University Press.

Index

Index

The manufacturer's authorised representative in the EU for product safety is Oxford University Press España S.A. of el Parque Empresarial San Fernando de Henares, Avenida de Castilla, 2 – 28830 Madrid (www.oup.es/en or product.safety@oup.com). OUP España S.A. also acts as importer into Spain of products made by the manufacturer.

www.ingramcontent.com/pod-product-compliance
Lightning Source LLC
LaVergne TN
LVHW011903200926
848484LV00002B/510

* 9 7 8 0 1 9 9 6 0 2 3 7 7 *